Medieval Market Moral[

Life, Law and Ethics in the En

This important new study examines the market trade of medieval England from a new perspective, by providing a wide-ranging critique of the moral and legal imperatives that underpinned retail trade. James Davis shows how market-goers were influenced not only by practical and economic considerations of price, quality, supply and demand, but also by the moral and cultural environment within which such deals were conducted. This book draws on a broad range of cross-disciplinary evidence, from the literary works of William Langland and the sermons of medieval preachers, to state, civic and guild laws. Davis scrutinises everyday market behaviour through case studies of small and large towns, using the evidence of manor and borough courts. From these varied sources, Davis teases out the complex relationship between morality, law and practice and demonstrates that even the influence of contemporary Christian ideology was not necessarily incompatible with efficient and profitable everyday commerce.

JAMES DAVIS is Lecturer in Medieval History in the School of History and Anthropology at Queen's University Belfast.

Medieval Market Morality

Life, Law and Ethics in the English Marketplace, 1200–1500

James Davis

CAMBRIDGE
UNIVERSITY PRESS

CAMBRIDGE
UNIVERSITY PRESS

The Edinburgh Building, Cambridge CB2 8RU, UK

Published in the United States of America by Cambridge University Press, New York

Cambridge University Press is part of the University of Cambridge.

It furthers the University's mission by disseminating knowledge in the pursuit of education, learning and research at the highest international levels of excellence.

www.cambridge.org
Information on this title: www.cambridge.org/9781107633124

First published 2012
First paperback edition 2013

A catalogue record for this publication is available from the British Library

Library of Congress Cataloguing in Publication data
Davis, James.
Medieval market morality : life, law and ethics in the English marketplace,
1200–1500 / James Davis.
   p.   cm.
Includes bibliographical references and index.
ISBN 978-1-107-00343-9 (hardback)
1. Markets – Great Britain – History.   2. Retail trade – Great
Britain – History.   3. Cities and towns, Medieval – Great Britain.
4. England – Social life and customs – 1066–1485.   5. Social
history – Medieval, 500–1500.   6. Ethics – Great Britain – History.
I. Title.
HF5474.G7D38   2011
381′.109420902 – dc23   2011033054

ISBN 978-1-107-00343-9 Hardback
ISBN 978-1-107-63312-4 Paperback

Contents

Contents   vii

Figures and tables

Figures

Tables

Acknowledgements

This book began life as my Ph.D. thesis at Jesus College, Cambridge, and has since gone through numerous revisions and amendments, particularly during a British Academy post-doctoral fellowship at Wolfson College, Cambridge. It was completed during research leave funded by the Arts and Humanities Research Council. During the long gestation of this book, I have been touched by the generosity of my colleagues and friends. There are several people to whom I owe a particular debt of gratitude. John Hatcher, my supervisor and mentor, has been unstinting with his encouragement, expertise and inspiration. The examiners of my thesis, Richard Britnell and Richard Smith, have given me exceptional support and guidance over the past years. Mark Bailey pointed me towards the excellent Newmarket sources, while Nicholas Amor generously allowed me to compare his work on the Ipswich leet courts to my own transcripts. I am very grateful for Steve Rigby's expert insights and challenging comments on Chapter 1. Helen Fulton similarly gave me advice on the literary evidence, while John Lee has aided me throughout the drafting process. Kaele Stokes valiantly read the whole manuscript several times, providing invaluable comments and an unparalleled eye for detail. Numerous other colleagues have been generous with their time and advice, challenging me to develop my research. Without them, this book would have been infinitely poorer: Robert Braid, Chris Briggs, Bruce Campbell, Catherine Casson, Marie Therese Flanagan, Steve Flanders, Martin Heale, Derek Keene, Stephen Kelly, Keith Lilley, Chris Marsh, Ed Meek, Sinead O'Sullivan, Phillipp Schofield, Peter Spufford, Ted Westervelt, Keith Wrightson and Margaret Yates.

I would like to thank the many librarians and archivists whom I have encountered during my research, particularly the staff of Cambridge University Library, the British Library, the Suffolk Record Offices of Bury St Edmunds and Ipswich, and the National Archives. In addition, the completion of this book would not have been possible without generous funding from the British Academy and the Arts and Humanities Research Council. I must also mention further support from the Economic

History Society, as well as from the Folger Institute, who funded a superb three-day seminar to discuss issues of market culture (under the expert guidance of Craig Muldrew). Queen's University Belfast kindly provided funds towards reproduction of images. This book was completed amidst the supportive environment of my colleagues at Queen's University who have all provided inspiration during my early career, with particular thanks to David Hayton, Katy Turton, Paul Corthorn, Andrew Holmes and Sean O'Connell. Thanks must also go to the staff at Cambridge University Press, especially Liz Friend-Smith, Michael Watson and the two anonymous readers.

Many other people have provided immeasurable friendship and encouragement during the writing of this book, and space permits me to mention just a few: Jane, Alex, Julia, Sinead, Kirsten, Nathan, Vicky, Yolanda, Dominic, David, Cass, Maria, Andrew, Leanne, Amy, Judith, Lynsey and Katherine. I must give special thanks to Carol Emerson, whose love and patience over the last two years have been extraordinary. I owe her a great deal. Finally, the strength of support and love from my mother and father, and my brother and sister, has always been unwavering. This book is for them.

JAMES DAVIS

Abbreviations

Alsford, *Towns*	*Medieval English Towns*, at: http://users.trytel.com/~tristan/towns/towns.html (accessed 11 October 2009)
Ayenbite of Inwyt	R. Morris (ed.), *Dan Michel's Ayenbite of Inwyt, or, Remorse of Conscience. In the Kentish Dialect, 1340 AD* (Early English Text Society, o.s. 23, London, 1866)
BBC, 1042–1216	A. Ballard (ed.), *British Borough Charters 1042–1216* (Cambridge, 1913)
BBC, 1216–1307	A. Ballard and J. Tait (eds.), *British Borough Charters 1216–1307* (Cambridge, 1923)
BBC, 1307–1660	M. Weinbaum (ed.), *British Borough Charters 1307–1660* (Cambridge, 1943)
Beverley	A. F. Leach (ed.), *Beverley Town Documents* (Selden Society, 14, London, 1900)
BL	London, British Library
Black Book	T. Twiss (ed.), *The Black Book of the Admiralty or Monumenta Juridica*, 2 vols. (Rolls Series, 55, London, 1873)
Bridgwater	T. B. Dilks (ed.), *Bridgwater Borough Archives, 1200–1485* (Somerset Record Society, 48, 53, 58, 60 and 70, 1933–71)
Bristol	F. B. Bickley (ed.), *The Little Red Book of Bristol*, 2 vols. (Bristol, 1900)
Britton	F. M. Nichols (ed.), *Britton*, 2 vols. (Oxford, 1865)
CChR	*Calendar of Charter Rolls*, 6 vols. (London, 1903–27)
CCR	*Calendar of Close Rolls*, 46 vols. (London, 1892–1963)
Chaucer	L. D. Benson (ed.), *The Riverside Chaucer* (Boston, Mass., 1987)

CIM	*Calendar of Inquisitions Miscellaneous*, 7 vols. (London, 1916–68)
CLB	R. R. Sharpe (ed.), *Calendar of Letter-Books of the City of London*, 12 vols. (London, 1899–1912)
Coventry	M. D. Harris (ed.), *The Coventry Leet Book* (EETS, o.s. 134, 135, 138, 146, London, 1907–13)
CPR	*Calendar of Patent Rolls*, 54 vols. (London, 1891–1916)
CUL	Cambridge University Library
DB	A. Rumble (ed.), *Domesday Book, 34: Suffolk* (Chichester, 1986)
Dives and Pauper	P. H. Barnum (ed.), *Dives and Pauper* (Early English Text Society, n.s. 275 and 280, Oxford, 1976–80)
Fasciculus Morum	S. Wenzel (ed.), *Fasciculus Morum: A Fourteenth-Century Preacher's Handbook* (London, 1989)
Fleta	H. G. Richardson and G. O. Sayles (eds.), *Fleta* (Seldon Society, 72, London, 1953)
Gower, *Mirour*	W. B. Wilson (ed.), *John Gower, Mirour de l'Omme (The Mirror of Mankind)* (East Lansing, Mich., 1992)
Great Red Book	E. W. W. Veale (ed.), *The Great Red Book of Bristol* (Bristol Record Society, 2, 4, 8 and 16, 1931–51)
Handlyng Synne	F. J. Furnivall (ed.), *Robert of Brunne's 'Handlyng Synne', AD1303* (Early English Text Society, o.s. 119, London, 1901)
Henley	P. M. Briers (ed.), *Henley Borough Records: Assembly Books i–iv, 1395–1543* (Oxfordshire Record Society, 41, Oxford, 1960)
HMC	Historical Manuscripts Commission, *Report on Manuscripts in Various Collections* (London, 1907)
Jacob's Well	A. Brandeis (ed.), *Jacob's Well: An English Treatise on the Cleansing of Man's Conscience* (Early English Text Society, o.s. 115, London, 1900)
King's Lynn	D. M. Owen (ed.), *The Making of King's Lynn: A Documentary Survey* (Records of Social and Economic History, new ser. 9, London, 1984)
Leicester	M. Bateson (ed.), *Records of the Borough of Leicester*, 3 vols. (London, 1899–1901)

Liber Albus	H. T. Riley (ed.), *Liber Albus: The White Book of the City of London* (London, 1861)
Memorials	H. T. Riley (ed.), *Memorials of London and London Life in the XIIIth, XIVth, and XVth Centuries, AD1276–1419* (London, 1868)
Northampton	C. A. Markham and J. C. Cox (eds.), *The Records of the Borough of Northampton*, 2 vols. (Northampton, 1898)
Norwich	W. Hudson and J. C. Tingey (eds.), *The Records of the City of Norwich*, 2 vols. (Norwich, 1906)
Nottingham	W. H. Stevenson (ed.), *Records of the Borough of Nottingham: 1155–1485*, 2 vols. (London, 1882–3)
Oak Book	P. Studer (ed.), *The Oak Book of Southampton*, 2 vols. (Southampton Record Society, 10–11, Southampton, 1910)
Parl. Rolls	C. Given-Wilson, P. Brand, A. Curry, R. Horrox, G. Martin, S. Philips and W. M. Ormrod (eds.), *The Parliament Rolls of Medieval England, 1275–1504* (PROME) (Scholarly Digital Editions, Leicester, 2005)
Piers Plowman, A	G. Kane (ed.), *Piers Plowman: The A Version – Will's Visions of Piers Plowman and Do-Well* (Berkeley, Calif., 1988)
Piers Plowman, B	G. Kane and E. T. Donaldson (eds.), *Piers Plowman: The B Version – Will's Visions of Piers Plowman, Do-Well, Do-Better and Do-Best* (Berkeley, Calif., 1988)
Piers Plowman, C	D. Pearsall (ed.), *William Langland, Piers Plowman: The C-Text* (Berkeley, 1978; repr. Exeter, 1994)
RCh	T. D. Hardy (ed.), *Rotuli Chartarum* (London, 1837)
Red Paper Book	W. G. Benham (ed.), *The Red Paper Book of Colchester* (Colchester, 1902)
RLC	T. D. Hardy (ed.), *Rotuli Litterarum Clausarum*, 2 vols. (London, 1833–44)
RP	*Rotuli Parliamentorum*, 6 vols. (London, 1783)
Salisbury	D. R. Carr (ed.), *The First General Entry Book of the City of Salisbury 1387–1452* (Wiltshire Record Society, 54, Trowbridge, 2001)
SRO (B)	Suffolk Record Office (Bury St Edmunds)

SRO (I)	Suffolk Record Office (Ipswich)
SRP, i	J. F. Larkin and P. L. Hughes (eds.), *Stuart Royal Proclamations. Volume I: Royal Proclamations of King James I, 1603–1625* (Oxford, 1973)
SRP, ii	J. F. Larkin (ed.), *Stuart Royal Proclamations. Volume II: Royal Proclamations of King Charles I, 1625–1646* (Oxford, 1983)
Statutes	*Statutes of the Realm (1101–1713)*, 11 vols. (ed. A. Luders, T. Edlyn Tomlins, J. France, W. E. Tauton and J. Raithby, London, 1810–28, repr. 1963)
STC	A. W. Pollard and G. R. Redgrave, *A Short-Title Catalogue of Books Printed in England, Scotland and Ireland and of English Books Printed Abroad, 1475–1640*, 3 vols. (rev. edn W. A. Jackson, F. S. Ferguson and K. F. Pantzer, London, 1986)
TNA	London, The National Archives
TRP	P. L. Hughes and J. F. Larkin (eds.), *Tudor Royal Proclamations*, 3 vols. (New Haven, Conn., 1964–9)
VCH	*Victoria County History*
Vices and Virtues	W. N. Francis (ed.), *The Book of Vices and Virtues* (Early English Text Society, n.s. 217, London, 1942)
Winchester	W. H. B. Bird (ed.), *The Black Book of Winchester* (Winchester, 1925)
York, i–ii	M. Sellers (ed.), *York Memorandum Book, volumes I–II* (Surtees Society, 120 and 125, Durham, 1912–15)
York, iii	J. W. Percy (ed.), *York Memorandum Book, volume III* (Surtees Society, 186, Durham, 1973)

Notes to the text

Currency and measures

A pound sterling (£) consisted of 20 shillings (s., 'solidus') and 240 pence (d., 'denarius'), with 12 pence to a shilling. A 'mark' was worth two-thirds of a pound (13s. 4d.) and a 'groat' was worth 4d.

A 'quarter' was a dry measure, equivalent to eight 'bushels'; a bushel was equivalent to eight gallons. Other measures included the 'peck', which was equivalent to two gallons or a quarter of a bushel, the pottle or potel ($\frac{1}{2}$ gallon) and the 'quart' ($\frac{1}{4}$ gallon). The ell was a measure of length, particularly for cloth, equivalent to 45 inches in England.

The troy pound was mostly used for money and bread and often delineated in pounds, shillings and pence: 20 pennies to an ounce, 12 ounces to a pound (lb.), 64 lb. to a bushel, and 512 lb. to a quarter. A tower pound consisted of 5,400 barley grains, a troy pound of 5,760 barley grains, and an avoirdupois pound (of 16 ounces) of 7,000 barley grains. Many other scales were also employed throughout the period covered by this book, with numerous local variations.

Extracts from contemporary texts

The original Middle English versions of vernacular texts are given where possible, and modern English translations are provided for certain difficult words or passages. Middle English includes the letters þ (thorn), generally pronounced 'th', and 3 (yogh), similar to 'gh'. Translations of Middle English, Latin and French texts are either the author's own or taken from published sources as referenced.

Introduction

The fifteenth-century poem *London Lickpenny* provides a vivid portrait of a town's streets, brimming with the vibrant noises and sights of market life. Within the marketplaces of medieval London swarmed a multitude of hawkers, pedlars, cooks and stallholders, all crying their wares and pestering potential customers:

> Then went I forth by London stone,
> Throughout all Canwyle streete;   *Candlewick Street*
> Drapers mutch cloth me offred anone.
> Then comes me one, cryed, 'Hot shepes feete!'
> One cryde, 'Makerell!'; 'Ryshes grene!' another
>   gan greete   *Rushes*
> One bad me by a hood to cover my head –
> But for want of mony I myght not be sped.[1]

The poem portrays a young man from the country who is bewildered by the cacophony of sounds, but is perhaps also seduced by the contrasting sights and smells of a commercial world in which money is the prime motivational force. The writer emphasises the variety of goods on sale, as well as the belligerent persistence of the vendors. However, a distasteful undercurrent is implied. A hood lost by the young man is later spotted by him on a stall, being sold amidst other stolen goods.

A similar touting for wares is seen in the Prologue of William Langland's *Piers Plowman* (*c.*1360–87) in the 'Fair Field Full of Folke', in which cries of 'hote pyes, hote!, Good goos and grys'[2] ring out. Bakers, brewers, butchers, cooks, taverners, weavers, tailors and other craftsmen are all represented in this 'Fair Field'.[3] Yet, Langland's commercial world, though brimming with opportunities and variety, belied another

---

[1] Gray (ed.), *Oxford Book*, pp. 18–19, ll. 50–98; BL, MS Harleian 367, fols. 126r–127v. Authorship is uncertain, but the poem is traditionally attributed to John Lydgate, a monk of Bury St Edmunds, writing in the early fifteenth century.

[2] (hot pies, hot! Good goose and young pig.)

[3] *Piers Plowman*, A.Prol.97–109; *Piers Plowman*, B.Prol.217–31; *Piers Plowman*, C.Prol.221–32.

more insidious, deceitful and harmful environment, where people and traders competed with each other for material goods, driven by their own venality, avarice and gluttony. An early fourteenth-century preacher's handbook, *Fasciculus Morum*, described this dualism: 'A marketplace or a fair is now filled with people, stocked with all sorts of goods, joyful and magnificent, and in a little while everyone goes back to his home, one with profit, another with loss, and the place at once becomes deserted, ugly, dirty, and contemptible'.[4] A thirteenth-century French Dominican, Humbert de Romans, similarly lamented the quarrels, drinking, fraud, perfidy and injustice that pervaded medieval marketplaces. He related the tale of a man who entered an abbey and found many demons in the cloister, but in the marketplace there was only one, alone on a high pillar. He was told that the abbey and cloister were arranged to help souls find God, so that many devils were needed to lead the monks astray. But in the marketplace, since each man was a devil to himself, just one other demon sufficed.[5]

In these examples, the dilemmas of medieval market morality are starkly evident. The opportunities of commerce and the vital needs it served were counterbalanced by the realisation that money and profit dominated trade, which in turn was driven by avarice and self-interest. It was this paradox that lay at the core of representations of market traders in the literary and religious works of medieval England. Moralists found it difficult to fit retail traders and middlemen into concepts of social harmony. Traders were considered to be the epitome of selfishness, greed and dishonesty, yet their activities were also recognised as essential to the sustenance of society. The marketplace was the setting where these paradoxes and attitudes were played out on a day-to-day basis. How did medieval people view the market and traders with whom they interacted; was it the problematic economic and social space that consternated medieval moralists? This book is an attempt to examine and evaluate the moral undercurrents and discourses that influenced everyday medieval market practices, but also to determine the extent to which the cultural and religious environment both informed and was shaped by wide-reaching commercial developments. Retail traders, small-scale artisans and middlemen dominated the transactions of internal trade in late medieval England (1200–1500). The following study explores how they were represented in literary and cultural artefacts, how they were regulated in their commercial affairs, and how they practised their occupations in the marketplace.

---

[4] *Fasciculus Morum*, pp. 558–9.
[5] Cf. Jarrett, *Social Theories*, p. 164; Murray, 'Religion'.

Market trade and traders

Exchange, commerce and credit have long permeated society, in a daily and often informal manner, wherever one person has something that another needs or desires. It is likely that medieval people regularly bought and sold items and services from each other in an informal manner, agreeing prices for a pound of apples, the hire of a plough, the rent of a room, or a day's wages.[6] However, when production and demand reached a significant level, many marketing practices became more formal and sophisticated. This does not mean that informal trade declined, merely that formal institutions developed to assist transactions and commercial growth. This included not just physical sites for the facilitation of marketing, but also processes for the movement, sale and purchase of goods. Regular market places and times, enforcement of contracts and debts, quality-controls, supervision of prices, and protection against stolen goods were just some of the devices that helped lower transaction costs and expedite trade. These marketing developments not only encouraged new patterns of consumption and expenditure, but may have also shifted contemporary attitudes towards trade and traders.

In late medieval England, the periodic rural or small-town market, usually held once a week, was predominant because of the localised structure of society and the pervasive agricultural economy. Periodicity allowed an efficient use of time for vendors, who would be ensured a maximum number of consumers gathered for a minimum time, while consumers could concentrate their efforts to a single day. In addition, periodicity facilitated itinerant traders who could not find enough custom in a single, permanent location and could thus travel around several markets. Annual fairs were also held when the surplus agricultural produce of an area was ready to market in bulk, or to cater for luxury imports or specialist goods. More frequent marketing, as seen in larger towns, required heavier and broader consumer demand.

The marketplace was the accepted physical location where regular economic, social, cultural and political interchanges took place and attitudes were readily formed. It facilitated a dynamic congregation of professional traders, marginal retailers, part-time hucksters, peasant producers and sundry consumers, who created a hive of haggling, shouting and gossip. The core of any medieval town was the marketplace, often symbolised by a market cross. These structures, varying from simple cruciform wooden

---

[6] Schofield, *Peasant and Community*, pp. 137–9; Britnell, 'Proliferation', 211; Britnell, 'Markets, shops, inns'; Dyer, 'Hidden trade', 153.

pillars to more elaborate stone shelters, were symbolic reminders to market users of a multiplicity of influences over their activities: the royal market charter, regulatory oversight by local officials, and the moral imperatives of divine authority.[7] The market cross was the economic, social and cultural heart of any market town or village. Markets were thus places where the forces of supply and demand converged, but also where such economic factors were circumscribed by contemporary regulations, morals, attitudes and prejudices.

There has been much academic interest in medieval market trade, particularly in the wake of growing research on commercialisation, internal marketing networks and small towns. Richard Britnell, Christopher Dyer, James Masschaele and others have reinforced the historical importance of smaller markets and towns to the commercial environment of medieval England. They recognised that small-scale trade was a vital lifeline for many in an increasingly market-oriented society, and that petty commodity production and exchange lay at the heart of numerous economic changes.[8] There has been less work on market traders specifically, but Judith Bennett and Heather Swanson have produced substantial research on brewers and artisans respectively, including the role of women who often supplemented household income by engaging in part-time retailing.[9] Many women would bake and brew, make butter and cheese, and raise poultry for meat and eggs, within the context of the household economy. They were common sights, sitting under the cross on market day, selling their victuals to raise extra income for the family, though their profits were often marginal.[10]

Rodney Hilton also highlighted the pervasiveness of hucksters and retailers in late medieval England, in both urban and rural settings, full-time and part-time, male and female.[11] In his investigations of Halesowen and Thornbury, he presented a medieval world dominated by petty production and petty retail trade. In particular, he drew attention to the prevalence of victuallers in court rolls and argued that this demonstrated both the volume of trade in foodstuffs and the earnestness of authorities to control such transactions. Hilton suggested that market traders and retailers were regarded with suspicion and closely controlled, though our historical perception of such people may have become distorted by the level of prosecutions evident in late medieval court rolls, as well as the

---

[7] Davis, 'The cross and the pillory'.
[8] Britnell, *Commercialisation*; Dyer, 'Market towns'; Masschaele, *Peasants*; Bailey, 'Historiographical'; Kowaleski, *Local Markets*.
[9] Bennett, *Ale*; Swanson, *Medieval Artisans*.
[10] Goldberg, 'Women in fifteenth-century town life'; Mate, *Women*, pp. 45–6.
[11] Hilton, 'Lords, burgesses and hucksters'; Hilton, 'Women traders'.

literary representations of cheating and corruption. David Farmer, in contrast, assumed that retailers and victuallers suffered daily harassment and opprobrium on the scale suggested by moralists such as John Gower and William Langland.[12] The relationship between the literary and legal representations of traders is still not clearly understood. Indeed, despite a number of studies on alewives, the role and behaviour of medieval market traders more generally has not been fully examined.

Medieval market traders encompassed a wide range of people, engaged in commerce for a variety of reasons and levels of gain. The following study concentrates on those that can be broadly defined as engaged in retail trade, petty wholesale transactions and small-scale commodity production, but such individuals ranged from lesser merchants and middlemen to urban shopkeepers and stallholders, and from itinerant hawkers and pedlars to marginal and part-time hucksters. Market traders did not form a contained, self-aware and homogeneous group, but were a broad and varied constituency. This book is concerned primarily with those retail traders who sold goods in the marketplaces on a regular or semi-regular basis, but it is recognised that any who were involved in vending were expected to abide by legal and moral injunctions. Indeed, retailers merely constituted the base of a commercial pyramid, at the apex of which resided the wholesaling, international merchants.

The label 'merchant' normally conjures up images of a wealthy Stapleman, exporting wool or cloth in exchange for various luxury goods, which he then distributed throughout the realm. Typically, he aspired to gentry life and perhaps retirement to a country estate, where he could enjoy the benefits of his commercial gains and a higher social status.[13] Rosemary Horrox argued that merchants wanted the best of both worlds, town and country.[14] The activities of such merchants have been widely investigated by historians, attracted by the abundance of customs records detailing the trade in international commodities.[15] There are also several studies of individual merchants and their families, as well as research into the merchant class as a whole.[16] However, merchants were a rank apart from the mass of small-scale traders and artisans in late medieval England. Swanson suggested that the fourteenth century saw the polarisation of wholesalers, retailers and artisans into more definitive sub-categories, whereas

---

[12] Farmer, 'Marketing', p. 377.

[13] Thrupp, *Merchant Class*, p. 234; O'Connor, 'Adam Fraunceys and John Pyel'.

[14] Horrox, 'Urban gentry', pp. 22–44.

[15] Power, *Wool Trade*; Thrupp, *Merchant Class*; Kermode, *Medieval Merchants*; Nightingale, *A Medieval Mercantile Community*; Spufford, *Power and Profit*.

[16] Hanham, *The Celys*; James, *Studies in the Medieval Wine Trade*; Power, *Medieval People*, pp. 123–57; Penn, 'A fourteenth-century Bristol merchant', 183–6.

previously 'merchant' had been a more generic term.[17] By the later Middle Ages, the designation of 'merchant' was confined to those engaged in wholesale trade, though this covered a range of people, from international dealers to lowly intra-regional traders.[18] Thirteenth-century London, for instance, was well served by cornmongers, with places like Henley-on-Thames operating as entrepôts for the collection of London grain supplies.[19] At the higher end of the marketing scale, usually in the bigger boroughs, there were the merchants and specialised traders who dealt in imports like dyes, spices and wine, or higher-quality manufactures like cloth and metalware.[20] All these required distribution networks and would have differentiated the regulatory and political structures in larger towns from those in small towns and markets. The merchant elite thus dominated international and regional trade and often governed larger towns, but they were partially detached from the day-to-day retail trade in basic, low-value commodities. It was the petty retailers and craftsmen who represented everyday marketing and who were the main, accessible link between the peasantry and market dealings.

Retailers were generally poorer and less influential than wholesaling merchants, and often processed their own goods, sold them from shop fronts, stalls or moveable carts, or hawked them in the streets. On market day, simple timber stalls were erected in the marketplace, though over time some became more permanent in style and structure, encroaching upon the public space. Those without a stall would carry goods in baskets, either wandering around the marketplace or standing in designated areas. More substantial retailers might have had permanent shops under arcades or within a ground-floor room. A typical urban shop was contained within the front of a house and opened onto the street by the lifting or removal of window boards. Professional craftsmen-retailers also had workshops in the yard behind, as well as living quarters above.[21] Very often, resident traders with shops might seek to enlarge their commercial space by renting a stall on market day. There is also evidence that some traders travelled to other markets to sell goods.[22] In particular, there were itinerant pedlars or chapmen who sold minor manufactured goods: cheap clothes, pottery, metalware, buckles, purses, combs and other knick-knacks. These were often low-quality, small-scale and

[17] Swanson, *Medieval Artisans*, pp. 20, 110–13.
[18] Thrupp, *Merchant Class*, p. 6; Britnell, *Growth and Decline*, p. 109.
[19] Campbell, Galloway, Keene and Murphy, *A Medieval Capital*, pp. 47–9. The operations of London cornmongers seem to have contracted significantly after the Black Death.
[20] Britnell, 'Town life', pp. 148–9.
[21] Morrison, *English Shops*, pp. 19–27; Keene, 'Shops and shopping'.
[22] Mate, *Trade and Economic Developments*, pp. 23–4.

second-hand items, and may have been distributed around regular circuits of periodic markets.[23] Minor middlemen similarly wandered the
countryside in search of raw materials to sell at local markets, particularly staple products such as grain, wool and fish.

There were certainly professional traders, such as brewers, bakers,
cooks, butchers and various artisans, who operated from fixed shops or
stalls as specialised retailers or petty commodity producers. They might
sell goods acquired from local producers or wholesalers, or process raw
materials themselves to retail. Indeed, the craftsmen-retailer or producer-
retailer was common in all market towns.[24] However, the level of specialisation should not be overemphasised.[25] Many retailers were general
dealers rather than specialists, seeking profit where they could find it:
taverners were often vintners; chandlers often sellers of wax or tallow
products; innkeepers were brewers and grain dealers. Other traders were
irregular, part-time and *ad hoc* in their marketing patterns, often as an
adjunct to another primary occupation or domestic activity. For instance,
brewing was a domestic industry which many women undertook on a
supplementary basis in order to earn extra household income.[26]

Victuallers constituted the most common trading group in late medieval markets, supplying sustenance to an increasing non-agricultural,
landless or smallholding population. Indeed, with fluctuating harvests,
poor transport and a lack of storage facilities (especially for perishables),
the supply of food was a prime consideration for officials. Consequently, the activities of bakers, brewers, fishmongers, butchers, poulterers
and other producers or sellers of foodstuffs were closely monitored
and intensely regulated. In larger market centres, victuallers were seen
throughout the streets, and probably throughout the week, alongside
cooks who sold the 'fast-food' of the Middle Ages – pies, pastries and
breads.[27] In a similar manner, inns, alehouses and taverns became an
increasingly dominant part of the everyday marketing landscape, providing food and drink to a variety of customers.

Many regular victuallers also sold a percentage of their products to
hucksters or regraters, who were purely retailers, buying goods directly
from producers in order to sell them onto consumers. The term 'huckster' was frequently applied to those who dealt in small batches of victuals on a casual basis. They were often women (hence the feminine form

---

[23] See Veale, *English Fur Trade*, pp. 13–14; Davis, 'Men as march with fote packes'; Davis,
    'Marketing secondhand goods'.
[24] Swanson, *Medieval Artisans*, p. 2; Hilton, *English and French Towns*, p. 78.
[25] Britnell, 'Specialization'; Kowaleski, *Local Markets*, pp. 131–2.
[26] Mate, *Women*, pp. 39–40.
[27] Carlin, 'Fast food'; Carlin, 'Provisions for the poor'.

'-ster'), dealing in a selection of low-priced vegetables, poultry and dairy products. These derived from either their own holdings or from local producers, and were then carried into the marketplace in baskets on their heads or in their arms. Some resided in the market settlement, while others travelled from the surrounding countryside. They paid the appropriate market tolls, and then sold their goods from under the market cross, in the streets, or occasionally from hired stalls, depending on the arrangements and costs of the particular marketplace. Many purchased and resold ale, bread and fish, or diversified into petty manufactures like coarse cloth, yarn and candles. Hucksters were usually at the bottom of the marketing hierarchy in both status and wealth, making only meagre gains through trade.[28] It appears that hucksters, hawkers and regraters were closely watched, and authorities were anxious that they should not usurp the privileges of more permanent retailers, sell substandard foodstuffs, or engage in unacceptable regrating, forestalling or other price-raising activities.[29]

At its most basic extent, trade involved manorial officials or peasants, selling surplus agricultural produce or by-products, such as ale and cheese, and entering the market on a transient basis. Several studies have emphasised the extent to which the medieval peasantry were producing goods to sell in nearby markets.[30] They sold either to producer-retailers or directly to consumers. In turn, they would purchase a diversity of manufactures and commodities, such as pottery, metalwork or cloth, which they could not find in their own communities. For smallholders and labourers, there was a great dependence on the market simply for obtaining basic foodstuffs. But most peasants, whether they held large or small holdings, also needed to raise cash to pay fines and rents to their lords.

Market trade thus supplied the small-scale needs of numerous consumers, whether resident or visitors, in foodstuffs and cheap manufactured goods. Traders were a mix of the regular and irregular, the well-off and the poor, all seeking to make a profit. Periodic markets would throng to the sound of traders hawking their wares, while a more steady retail business for victuals and manufactures undoubtedly continued throughout the week. These petty traders constituted the backbone of a growing

---

[28] McIntosh, *Working Women*, pp. 130–2.

[29] Regrating was the practice of buying goods simply in order to sell them again, without added value, in the same market at a higher price. The act of forestalling involved the interception of goods either before they reached the marketplace or before the scheduled market time. See below, pp. 253–63, for a fuller discussion of these offences.

[30] Smith, 'A periodic market', pp. 472–3; Schofield, *Peasant and Community*, pp. 147–8; Britnell, *Commercialisation*.

commercial system from the twelfth to fifteenth centuries, facilitating the exchange of goods and shaping local market ethics.

The commercialisation of English society

The history of retail trade is an important indicator of the sophistication of the English economy. Some historians argue that the expansion of market trade and production was a small, but important, stepping-stone towards a new form of economic organisation.[31] Consequently, the function and importance of market traders should be examined within a context of the wider economic and social environment of medieval England. Changing economic trends in the later Middle Ages ensured that petty traders did not remain peripheral or irregular figures. Indeed, it is important to recognise that there was a proliferation of market traders from the twelfth to fifteenth centuries and a general immersion of the English population in commercial endeavours.

Medieval economic history has turned full circle as scholars have revitalised the study of commercial institutions and practitioners. Late nineteenth- and early twentieth-century economic historians stressed the importance of markets and other commercial institutions to the economic growth of late medieval England. Ephraim Lipson and Norman Gras, for example, viewed the rise of monetarisation, merchant oligarchies and markets as part of an evolutionary progression towards a modern economy.[32] However, by the 1960s, the dominance of commercialism in economic histories was questioned by Munia Postan, who advocated a greater emphasis on agricultural and demographic factors, in the economic tradition of Ricardo and Malthus.[33] Postan moved the historical debate away from markets and monetarisation towards a more pessimistic model based upon the relationship between resources, population and income. He argued that the striking population growth of the twelfth and thirteenth centuries caused demand to outstrip available resources, leading to a decline in living standards. Postan saw agriculture as stagnant, reliant on poor marginal lands and lacking in technological innovation. As the population expanded, resources became scarce for the peasantry, particularly smallholders and the landless. Land was subdivided to such an extent that more units of production were unable to support a family group. Consequently, a growing number of peasants

---

[31] Hilton, 'Introduction', pp. 21–7. See below, pp. 19–22.
[32] Lipson, *Economic History*; Salzman, *English Trade*; Gras, *Evolution*.
[33] Postan, *Medieval Economy*; Postan, *Essays*.

were struggling to subsist on their own landholdings and had to find by-employment and labouring wages in order to buy their food from local markets. Postan's thesis has been criticised, especially in its application to less populated parts of the realm.[34] The model also downplays important agricultural and technological innovations, efficient and appropriate use of marginal lands, and questions about the relationship between demographic trends and economic indicators.[35] The complexities of change, especially considering the stagnant population after the Black Death, are not convincingly accommodated. Others, employing a Marxist perspective, argued that more account was needed regarding the lack of seigneurial investment and the lordly exploitation of dependent peasants. Hilton and Robert Brenner both suggested that excessive burdens precipitated a crisis in both peasant welfare and lord–tenant relations, though John Hatcher argued that such a model neglected the customary and economic restraints upon lordly action.[36]

Issues of internal trade thus became sidelined until work in the 1980s looked anew at the commercial sector, markets, money supply and agrarian innovation. Scholars proposed a model of commercialisation in which the English medieval economy was driven by an increasing demand for grain from an expanding population.[37] Richard Britnell redeveloped concepts of 'commercialisation' in his book *The Commercialisation of English Society 1000–1500*, in which he studied changes in the medieval economy and emphasised the formal institutional frameworks for those changes.[38] In particular, he noted that the facilities of commercial exchange grew in size and number in the twelfth and thirteenth centuries. This was part of a wider commercial transformation, which included: a denser, organised market structure; an increase in the value and volume of coinage in circulation; growing credit markets; urban expansion and new towns; a proliferation of non-agricultural occupations; and a more market-oriented peasant society. For instance, the urban population may have, on aggregate, doubled over the twelfth and thirteenth centuries, sustained by immigration from the burgeoning ranks of the rural population.[39] Some towns grew in their physical size and density of settlement, while others

---

[34] Britnell, *Britain and Ireland*, pp. 85–6.
[35] Bailey, *A Marginal Economy?*; Smith, 'Human resources', pp. 202–11; Dyer, *An Age*, pp. 30–2.
[36] Hilton, *Class Conflict*; Aston and Philipin (eds.), *Brenner Debate*; Hatcher, 'English serfdom'. For further delineation of these models, as well as additional theories such as Schumpeter's model of limits to investment opportunities and catastrophe models, see Britnell, *Britain and Ireland*, pp. 84–90.
[37] Britnell, 'Commercialisation'; Bailey, 'Historiographical'.
[38] Britnell, *Commercialisation*.
[39] Miller and Hatcher, *Medieval England: Rural Society*, pp. 70–1.

were new foundations established by lordly enterprise.[40] It is difficult to be exact about the proportion of the medieval population that lived in towns, especially given the problematic nature of defining an urban settlement, but most historians assert that some 15–20 per cent lived in towns by 1300 and that this remained buoyant despite the post-Black Death demographic decline.[41] By the late fourteenth century, London was still by far the largest city, with a population of over 50,000; this was followed by the provincial centres of York, Coventry, Bristol and Norwich (8,000–15,000); some 30–40 towns between 2,000 and 8,000 inhabitants; and over 500 small towns, where half of the aggregate urban population lived.[42]

Britnell estimated that by 1300 there was a substantial non-agrarian sector (perhaps 20 per cent of the population) dependent upon producing goods and services for sale. In addition, some 20 per cent of agricultural produce, as well as most wool, was sold through markets.[43] In this analysis, monetarisation, urbanisation and market facilities increased in proportion to demographic expansion. Indeed, in addition to the needs of the rural peasantry, urban expansion itself both fed and generated demand. Commercialisation thus enabled a growing population to subsist at the existing levels of welfare.[44] Ambitious landlords were drawn into producing for the market in order to profit from increasing levels of consumption, and their success was aided by buoyant prices, high rents and cheap labour. The peak of demesne agriculture consequently occurred during the thirteenth century.[45] The peasant tenants of medium to large holdings also put their surpluses into circulation. Kathleen Biddick showed that many higher-status peasants were using thirteenth-century Bedfordshire markets in a proactive manner for commercial gain.[46] William Lene of Walsham-le-Willows (Suffolk) was one such early fourteenth-century wealthy peasant, whose possessions unusually were listed in the court roll. He had surplus corn, dairy produce, wool and meat, all of which he could have sold in nearby markets, as well as russet cloth, linen sheets and brass pots that he had probably bought there.[47]

---

[40] Beresford, *New Towns*.
[41] Dyer, 'How urbanized'; Dyer, *An Age*, p. 24.
[42] Rigby, *English Society*, pp. 145–6; Holt and Rosser, 'Introduction', p. 6; Palliser, 'Urban society', p. 133.
[43] Palliser, 'Urban society', pp. 115, 120–3.
[44] Hilton, *English Peasantry*, p. 126; Britnell, *Commercialisation*, p. 164; Bailey, 'Historiographical', 308–9.
[45] Miller and Hatcher, *Medieval England: Rural Society*, p. 182; Dyer, *Lords and Peasants*, p. 67.
[46] Biddick, 'Medieval English peasants'; Biddick, 'Missing links'; Dyer, *An Age*, pp. 25–6.
[47] Lock (ed.), *Walsham le Willows 1303–1350*, pp. 133–5; Dyer, *An Age*, pp. 25–6.

A minority of the peasantry may have benefited from the market opportunities of the thirteenth century, but the majority were smallholders or landless who faced a period of acute poverty and heavy seigneurial burdens and needed the market for subsistence.[48] It has been argued that the increasing impoverishment of a significant sector of the peasantry meant that they were compelled to sell their produce in the market. Lords and the state demanded that certain rents, dues and taxes were met in cash.[49] Not all market involvement was thus liberating in the classical economic mode; it was a dependence on the market driven by necessity rather than opportunity.[50] Nevertheless, the market was instrumental in sustaining population and urban expansion, and demand came from all sectors of medieval society. Market exchange also facilitated agricultural and industrial specialisation and thus increased economic efficiency, though admittedly this was an uneven process.[51] There were limitations to commercial improvements, including an unequal distribution of gains both socially and regionally, and perhaps a glut of commercial expansion by the early fourteenth century.

The wider benefits of commercialisation were probably not felt until after the Black Death when, paradoxically, historians have noted a declining number of markets and fairs, a monetary slump, agrarian recession and a crisis in towns. Population decline was perhaps already evident in the early fourteenth century, but the Black Death of 1348–9 was a significant exogenous episode, with up to 40–50 per cent of the population lost, followed by more than a century of demographic non-recovery.[52] Postan did not regard the fifteenth century as conducive to market-oriented production, because the compulsion to grow cereals for cash weakened.[53] Instead, he viewed it as an 'age of recession, arrested economic development and declining national income'.[54] Postan also noted a depression in urban areas as well as a decline in corporate towns and marketing, demonstrated by changing overseas trade, monetary shortage and urban revenue crises.[55] In addition, Hatcher highlighted a general recession in the mid-fifteenth century, exacerbated by a shortage of coinage.[56]

---

[48] Dyer, *An Age*, pp. 107–12.   [49] Dyer, *Making a Living*, p. 168.

[50] Britnell, *Commercialisation*, pp. 121–3; Bolton, *Medieval English Economy*, p. 137. For a further discussion of peasantry and the market, see Schofield, *Peasant and Community*, pp. 131–56; Dyer, *Making a Living*, pp. 163–78.

[51] Campbell, *English Seigniorial Agriculture*, pp. 411–14, 424–30.

[52] England's population fell from a peak of 4.5–6 million in the early fourteenth century to 2–3 million during the late fourteenth and fifteenth centuries, with little sign of recovery during the latter period; Hatcher, *Plague*, pp. 25, 55–7, 68–9.

[53] Postan, *Medieval Economy*, pp. 201–4.   [54] Postan, 'The fifteenth century', p. 42.

[55] Postan, *Medieval Economy*, pp. 201–5.   [56] Hatcher, 'The great slump'.

Anthony Bridbury, in contrast, saw the fifteenth century as a period of widespread prosperity, 'resurgent vitality and enterprise', based mainly upon the growth of new industries and the resilience of the urban sector in comparison to rural England.[57] He used subsidy returns to argue that there was an increasing urban share of national wealth, as well as prosperity in areas of cloth production and rural industry. Indeed, although the corporate base of prosperity diminished, the individuals of many towns often benefited and some towns suffered only short-term fluctuations in their fortunes. Subsequent debates of the 1970s and 1980s on fifteenth- or sixteenth-century urban decline became embroiled in arguments over evidentiary reliability and inadequacy. Urban documentation was ambiguous and all too often historians seemed to forget that contraction was not necessarily commensurate with decline. Decline could be relative in comparison with other towns or absolute compared to previous levels. Indeed, a town could be smaller and less wealthy in aggregate, with decayed buildings, lower populations and falling rents, but its output, trade and income per person might be buoyant. In some respects the academic controversy floundered on the difficulty of quantifying 'decay' or 'growth' and on the wide regional and chronological variations which defied generalisation. Some towns, notably York, Boston, Yarmouth and Lincoln, suffered in the later Middle Ages, while others did well, particularly London, Southampton, Norwich, Ipswich and Exeter. Many places, like Colchester, experienced inconsistent fortunes during the post-Black Death period. The causes of decline were complex, since towns differed in their manufacturing specialities, regional networks, local circumstances and overseas markets.[58]

Many English towns certainly suffered decline due to the fall in total population and aggregate demand after the Black Death, but a few centres developed vibrant specialisms and prospered, particularly those towns which promoted the cloth industry. In the country as a whole, there was a movement of wealth towards the south-west and south-east, where textile industries predominated. However, one result of the growing rural cloth industry was that many erstwhile urban cloth centres struggled. For places like York and Coventry, the realignment, caused by cheaper rural manufacturing costs and the development of fulling mills, created a period of decline. By contrast, Colchester and Ipswich benefited from

---

[57] Postan, 'The fifteenth century', pp. 41–8; Bridbury, *Economic Growth*.

[58] The debate on medieval urban growth and decline is extensive. Some of the more notable contributions include: Dobson, 'Urban decline'; Phythian-Adams, 'Urban decay'; Rigby, 'Urban decline'; Reynolds, 'Decline and decay'; Saul, 'English towns'; Rigby, '"Sore decay" and "fair dwellings"'; Rigby, 'Late medieval urban prosperity'; Palliser, 'Urban decay revisited'; Dyer, *Decline and Growth*; Dyer, 'Urban decline'.

acting as distributors for their surrounding hinterlands of cloth manufacture, though Colchester also experienced short-term fluctuations in its fifteenth-century economy.[59]

In general, the late fourteenth and fifteenth centuries can best be characterised as incorporating factors of both decline and prosperity. There was a contraction in population, settlement and cultivation, as well as evident decline in production, wool exports, grain prices and rents.[60] However, Postan recognised that an aggregate decline in national wealth was compatible with increasing freedoms and standards of living for some groups. After the mid-1370s, as harvests became relatively plentiful for the existing population, grain and land prices fell and, consequently, demesne farming was less profitable than in times of demographic expansion. Lordly profits were hit hard by the general shortage of labour, land abundance, falling grain prices and rising real wages. Increasing amounts of demesne land were leased in response to these economic pressures and landlord–peasant struggles also became more commonplace.[61] The manorial system of serfdom subsequently declined and some peasants prospered by accumulating acres at lower rents and using their new-found bargaining power to obtain freer copyhold tenure in place of customary burdens.[62] By the mid-fifteenth century there were numerous substantial tenant farms producing for the market, while larger demesne production had declined.[63] The demographic plunge presented the peasant elite with new opportunities, creating a divergence between prosperous yeomen and labourers, but the market conditions still had to be judged very carefully in order to make a profit.

The economic upheavals had significant implications for the marketing networks of late medieval England. The demands for exchange facilities in the thirteenth century had fed a proliferation and formalisation of markets. But the Black Death and subsequent demographic stagnation meant that the total demand for grain fell significantly, lordly income decreased and many rural markets declined or disappeared. In general, retail trade also fell, but there was a rise *per capita* in demand for certain goods and changes in consumption patterns. The labouring classes benefited

---

[59] Britnell, *Growth and Decline.*   [60] Dyer, *An Age,* pp. 8–9.

[61] Dyer, *Lords and Peasants,* pp. 275–82. Neo-Marxist historians have stressed the social structure and conflicts between lord and tenant, and have downplayed the part of demographic changes. See below, pp. 19–22.

[62] Bailey, 'Historiographical', 300; Britnell, *Commercialisation,* p. 223. There was a general movement from customary to contractual tenures, though customary tenures still existed well into the sixteenth century.

[63] Britnell, *Commercialisation,* pp. 199–201; Dyer, 'A small landowner'; Dyer, *An Age,* p. 3. Postan called these farmers the English 'kulak' class; Postan, *Medieval Economy,* pp. 138–41.

from the population decline through higher wages and a choice of work, despite attempts by lords to limit their movements and payments. For an average basket of cereals and peas the spending power of the average wage-earner increased by 137 per cent from the 1330s to the 1470s, and for meat and fish twofold.[64] Ultimately, living standards increased, and although the aggregate demand for basic cereals remained slack, there was a heightened domestic, *per capita* demand for basic consumer and manufactured goods, such as meat, cheese, butter, ale, leather, cloth and pottery.[65] Surviving wills for wealthier peasants in Worcestershire show valuable landholdings and items such as pewterware, furred gowns and silver spoons.[66] Also, the diet of harvest workers developed to include more fresh meat and stronger ale, while cheaper legumes and grains were used for fodder rather than human consumption.[67]

With improved standards of living, consumerism spread slowly down the social ladder and had profound effects on the goods and services available and the variety or specialisation of occupations practised. Maryanne Kowaleski states: 'The appearance of such occupations as beer-brewer, butcher-grazier, pewterer and pinner, and increasing specialisation in the leather, cloth and clothing trades, reflect the impact of growing consumer demand'.[68] Demand for produce from occasional retailers and craftsmen decreased as consumers sought better-quality wares from professionals who operated in larger units of production. A wider range of products were offered and bought in the average market, including imported goods of cloth, glass, pewter and linen. There were also decreasing transaction costs and increasing specialisation and production by market traders. Agricultural producers responded to market conditions by switching to more commercial outputs like barley, wool and livestock.[69]

Judith Bennett has argued that the brewing industry was similarly transformed during the fifteenth and sixteenth centuries, from large numbers of casual, small-scale and domestic operations to fewer professionalised, regular and large-scale enterprises. This was partly driven by socio-economic changes and technical improvements, including the greater use of hops for beer-brewing, and also by the increased demand for ale and beer in alehouses. The introduction of beer from the Low

[64] Farmer, 'Prices and wages', pp. 491–3.
[65] Dyer, *Standards*; Dyer, *An Age*, pp. 126–57.
[66] Dyer, *Lords and Peasants*, pp. 352–4.
[67] Dyer, 'Changes in diet'. Bailey found that, in East Anglia, the rabbit altered from being a luxury commodity in the early fourteenth century to a high-output, medium-priced commercial concern in the fifteenth century. Bailey, 'The rabbit', 10–12.
[68] Kowaleski, 'A consumer economy', p. 258.
[69] Dyer, *Lords and Peasants*, p. 339; Britnell, *Growth and Decline*, pp. 144–6; Campbell, 'A fair field once full of folk', 68–9; Campbell, *English Seigniorial Agriculture*, pp. 430–40.

Countries and its increasing popularity during the fifteenth century was surely aided by heightened consumer spending. In towns, in particular, and in the south and east of England, the brewing industry became more capital-intensive and male-dominated. Women lacked both the capital and legal autonomy to compete in this growing industry and Bennett argues that the reputation of the corrupt alewife also contributed to their exclusion. Many women were forced out of the brewing process, while others had to rely solely on retailing in the streets as tapsters and hucksters.[70] Although there are still some examples of women setting up more permanent alehouses and brewing regularly, in both towns and villages, they were usually supported heavily by their husbands who were bakers, butchers, fishmongers or artisans. By the sixteenth century, women brewers were seemingly fewer in number and brewing for sale became a more full-time, male occupation.

Economic and social changes also precipitated an important realignment in the hierarchy of local marketing centres. Village markets frequently floundered in the new competitive environment, while many larger boroughs also struggled. It was often small towns that survived and prospered in this leaner marketing system, especially with the increased spending ability of the middling peasantry.[71] Many historians have turned their attention away from large provincial towns towards the smaller market towns that peppered the country. The importance of these places in the marketing networks of medieval England has generated a spurt of modern historical research.[72] Hilton highlighted the importance of England's numerous small towns, containing less than 2,000 inhabitants, to the medieval commercial environment.[73] He cited Thornbury as a typical example of a small town, with a population of about 500 and some thirty-five separate occupations.[74] He recognised that a significant number of petty transactions took place in this local market town and that

---

[70] Bennett, *Ale*; Dyer, *Lords and Peasants*, pp. 347–8; Postles, 'Brewing'; Clark, *Alehouse*, pp. 31–2; Mate, *Women*, pp. 38–45; Mate, *Daughters, Wives and Widows*, pp. 59–68; Mate, *Trade and Economic Developments*, pp. 60–80. McIntosh examined this transition in more detail across five market centres and concluded that the female-to-male shift was fairly abrupt in the late fifteenth century. McIntosh, *Working Women*, pp. 170–81.

[71] Bailey, 'A tale of two towns', 351–6; Hilton, 'Medieval market towns', 10; Dyer, 'Hidden trade'; Dyer, 'Consumer', 325; Britnell, *Commercialisation*, pp. 160–71; Dyer, *Making a Living*, pp. 298–313.

[72] For studies of small towns, see Bailey, 'A tale of two towns'; Dyer, *Bromsgrove*; Hilton, 'Small town and urbanization'; Postles, 'An English small town'; Dyer, 'Small towns 1270–1540'; Dyer, 'Small places'; Lee, 'The functions and fortunes of English small towns'.

[73] Hilton, 'Medieval market towns'; Hilton, 'Lords, burgesses and hucksters'.

[74] Hilton, 'Small town society'; Hilton, 'Low-level urbanization'.

the development of Thornbury and other such small towns was a good indication of the progress of commercialisation and urbanisation.

The distinction between a small town and a large village is sometimes uncertain, especially given that many inhabitants of the former were still engaged in agrarian-based activities. However, the definition of a small town depends mainly upon evidence of urban characteristics: a formal market, diverse occupational structure and a non-agricultural bias. Such urban characteristics have tended to displace the definitions of early urban historians, such as James Tait, who concentrated upon the constitutional definition of towns, highlighting their legal privileges and borough status.[75] A borough charter was granted by the Crown or lord ('mesne boroughs'), and gave burgesses certain privileges, such as burgage tenure, freedom from servile dues, structures of self-government and exemption from tolls.[76] Burgage tenure was granted for small plots of non-agricultural land, often of a standard long and narrow shape, facing onto a market or road. Such tenure freed burgesses from customary dues, allowed freedom of transfer and a fixed money rent.[77] Burgage tenements, and their associated privileges, were grasped eagerly by traders and artisans. Generally, larger boroughs gained a high degree of corporate autonomy, while smaller boroughs had less sophisticated structures of government and fewer rights. Significantly, however, many other settlements managed to acquire urban characteristics without being granted borough status, while some boroughs never developed recognised urban functions.[78]

Historians now define urban settlements primarily in terms of their function, particularly focusing on the idea that a majority of the concentrated population was engaged in a multiplicity of non-agricultural occupations.[79] While a small-town community contained non-trade professionals, such as lawyers and clerks, as well as vagrants, labourers and servants, the bulk of the residents were petty retail traders and artisans involved in small-commodity production that served local interests and small purses.[80] Additionally, the topography of a small town and its marketplace, including modest tenement rows and a dense concentration of buildings, were visible guides to urban status. Archaeological evidence supports the assertion that most small towns were directed towards processing low-cost agricultural surplus rather than large

---

[75] Tait, *Medieval English Borough*.   [76] Bailey, 'Trade and towns', 195.
[77] Britnell, 'Burghal characteristics', 147.
[78] Laughton and Dyer, 'Small towns in the East and West Midlands', 26.
[79] Dyer, 'Small places', 8–9; Holt and Rosser (eds.), 'Introduction', pp. 3–4; Hilton, 'Low-level urbanization', p. 482.
[80] Dyer, 'Consumer'.

industrial production.[81] Ultimately, there was an intimate interaction between a market town and its rural surroundings, and a movement of goods, people and skills that encouraged the commercialisation and monetisation of society.

Late fourteenth- and fifteenth-century England thus witnessed a realignment of marketing and consumer patterns. This included a greater consumption of manufactured and imported goods, which were distributed through regional mercantile networks. Numerous pedlars and chapmen supplied the country with goods and this brought them into direct competition with sedentary merchants. Itinerant traders had lower overheads, mobility and freedom from town restrictions, and took advantage of the contraction of urban trade and the rise of rural industry. Pamela Nightingale regarded them as entrepreneurial figures, working outside traditional and official commercial forums in order to bypass provincial wholesalers and deal with London dealers directly. This advanced the distributive position of London at the expense of many provincial centres. It also led to the greater use of inns as staging and meeting posts and the need for fewer commercial centres.[82]

It is possible that individuals were increasingly prepared to trade beyond the confines of official institutions during the fifteenth century, where they could evade tolls and tight controls.[83] In addition, there is evidence that alehouses, shops and inns in small towns and villages were becoming more prevalent. Wage-earners appear to have indulged in more leisure time, particularly in the alehouse and tavern, and these institutions grew in number and prominence.[84] Tottenham, for example, saw its first mention of common hucksters, inns and embryonic shops in the fifteenth-century court rolls.[85] However, informal trade activities had been going on for centuries, including in permanent shops, suburbs, inns and alehouses, and it is difficult to document any changing balance between formal and informal trade.[86] Britnell has argued that

[81] Astill, 'Archaeology and the smaller medieval town', 48.

[82] Nightingale, *A Medieval Mercantile Community*, pp. 364–9, 440–1.

[83] Bailey, 'Historiographical', 307; Benton, 'Archaeological notes'.

[84] Hatcher, 'Labour, leisure and economic thought'; Hatcher, 'England in the aftermath', 28–33; Mate, *Daughters, Wives and Widows*, p. 62; Kowaleski, 'A consumer economy', p. 243. Hatcher suggests that we should not dismiss the medieval criticisms of idle labourers as mere propaganda, but Dyer argues that the widening consumption possibilities would have motivated peasants to work more, not less. Dyer, 'Work ethics'.

[85] Moss, 'Economic development', 112–13. See also McIntosh, *Autonomy and Community*, ch. 6; McIntosh, 'Local change and community control', 222; Searle, *Lordship and Community*, p. 365; Dyer, *Lords and Peasants*, p. 349; Bailey, *Medieval Suffolk*, p. 268; Jeayes (ed.), *Court Rolls*, iii, p. 17 (1373); *Bristol*, ii, pp. 71–2.

[86] Dyer, 'Hidden trade'; Britnell, 'Markets, shops, inns'; Keene, 'Suburban growth'; Carlin, *Medieval Southwark*, pp. 201–4; Rosser, *Medieval Westminster*, pp. 121–9.

informal or 'hidden' trade may not have been superseded by formal practices during the twelfth and thirteenth centuries, and possibly even grew
in parallel with commercial developments at that time.[87] Indeed, landlords are known to have long sold their produce in bulk direct from their
demesnes to woolmongers or cornmongers, avoiding formal marketing
institutions.[88]

There were, nevertheless, some significant commercial developments
in the fourteenth and fifteenth centuries. Even though aggregate demand
had fallen and the number of retailers had declined, it appears that more
of the remaining market traders were becoming full-time, permanent and
professional. They specialised more in their occupation, though often
diversifying in the products they processed and offered.[89] The decline
in village markets was a natural consequence of population decrease,
but this local institution failed to recover because increasing demand and
incomes after the late fourteenth century meant that fixed traders in larger
settlements could be more profitable.[90] By the fifteenth century, more
commercial products, such as ale, meat, dairy produce, leather and cloth,
were consumed *per capita*, even if the overall market had understandably
lessened since the early fourteenth century.[91] A more substantial and
sustained consumer boom came in the seventeenth century, but its roots
were laid in the new prosperity for many of the post-plague peasantry.
This was a commercial demand that had to be matched by the marketing
strategies of traders.

The transition from feudalism to capitalism

The commercialisation of late medieval English society, including the
growth of petty trade and small-scale commodity production, is part of
a much wider discussion in economic history. In particular, commercial
developments and changes in attitudes towards the market are regarded
as aspects of the transition from feudalism to capitalism. For instance,
Rodney Hilton suggested that the transition from a feudal to a capitalist economy was helped as much by petty commercialisation in market
towns as by the growth of merchant capital in larger centres.[92] Simple commodity production, based on small-scale household units, began

---

[87] Britnell, 'Markets, shops, inns', pp. 109, 116–18, 121.
[88] Britnell, 'La commercializzazione', 646–8.
[89] Britnell, 'Specialization'; McIntosh, *Autonomy and Community*, pp. 208–9, 249–52;
Postles, 'An English small town', 13.
[90] Plattner, 'Markets and marketplaces', p. 190.
[91] Dyer, *Standards*, pp. 158–60, 197–202.
[92] Hilton, 'Medieval market towns', 22–3. See also Kowaleski, *Local Markets*, p. 1.

long before the thirteenth century, but it grew in size and specialisation as the demand for commodities extended. Hilton argued that feudal
restrictions on such production virtually disappeared by the fifteenth
century, giving free rein to larger-scale agricultural and industrial commodity producers. For example, yeomen farmers extensively employed
wage labour and craft production moved out of guild-dominated towns.
In this neo-Marxist argument, relatively unfettered commodity production in the fifteenth century was the necessary precondition for later
capitalist production.[93]

There has been a long-lived debate regarding the 'prime movers' for
economic change, including the transition from feudalism to capitalism. This has generated three main schools of thought, espoused by
the various adherents of Karl Marx, Thomas Malthus, David Ricardo
and Adam Smith.[94] The Marxist school stresses property relations and
social crisis. These historians view the pre-industrial economy as driven
and shaped by the nature of property relations and class conflict. The
population-resources school, based on the economic theories of Malthus
and Ricardo, emphasises the stagnancy of the feudal system, the balance of resources and the prime mover of population change. Lastly, the
'commercialisation' viewpoint draws partly on the classical eighteenth-
century economics of Adam Smith, but encompasses many other theories. It focuses on the development of markets, expanding trade and
urban growth as liberating, thus permitting the evolution of greater economic efficiency. The proponents of these three schools of thought all
agree that a change in economic organisation took place, but they differ
on how this came about, when the main shift occurred and the prime
causal mover. In many ways, there can be reconciliation between the
theories, as population decline realigned market forces and allowed the
peasantry the bargaining power to more effectively resist lordly exactions
and gain freer conditions of tenure and trade.[95]

Part of the problem in understanding the process of transition from
feudalism to capitalism is that the term 'capitalism' has been accorded a
variety of differing criteria by historians. An old definition saw 'capitalism' primarily as a system of exchange relations and profit-accumulation,
driven by entrepreneurs and the rise of the market ethic.[96] However,
the associated view that the late Middle Ages were fundamentally non-
commercial and dominated by a 'natural economy', to which markets and

[93] Hilton, 'Introduction', pp. 21–7.
[94] For a fuller discussion of these, and other, models, see Hatcher and Bailey, *Modelling*.
[95] Hatcher, 'England in the aftermath', 5–6.
[96] Dyer, 'Were there any capitalists', pp. 1–2.

money were alien, has long been discarded. Traditionally, towns and merchants were viewed by historians as catalysts in undermining the feudal system and bringing about a capitalist economy.[97] The town, in particular, was seen as the dynamic harbinger of a new market ethic and as inimical to feudalism. Postan viewed towns as 'non-feudal islands in a feudal sea'.[98] Conversely, the countryside was static, inert and subsistence-based, with the feudal system lacking the ability to be innovative and flexible. However, historians now negate this stark opposition between town and country and have argued that the two had a symbiotic relationship. Money and credit were both widespread in the rural world and lords and the peasantry understood market mechanisms very clearly.[99] Equally, the town was embedded in the feudal hierarchy through the structure of its society, government and local trading networks.[100] It is clear, then, that there was not a straightforward dichotomy between a backward, stagnant feudal countryside and an innovative, free and mobile urban economy.[101] Many marketing transformations took place in the twelfth and thirteenth centuries, in both urban and rural society.[102] Feudal forces encouraged trade as much as they were inimical to it.

According to Marxist theory, commerce itself did not transform feudal society and the transition from a largely subsistence economy to a profit-based commercial economy was only one aspect of capitalism.[103] Change was instead dependent on internal contradictions within society.[104] In Marx's view, feudalism involved small-scale production for the use of the producer or lord. It was predominantly agrarian, with a low level of output and innovation, and the customary relationship between the lord and tenant was exploitative in appropriating surplus rent and labour services. In this model, craftsmen were small-scale, independent operators based upon the household unit. Mostly, they and petty traders lay outside the basic lord–peasant relationship and transactions between peasant and trader could not be viewed as directly exploitative.[105] In contrast, capitalism was an economic organisation where there was large-scale production for exchange, with higher levels of accumulation and innovation. The ownership of production and capital came to be concentrated in

[97] Pirenne, *Medieval Cities*, pp. 213–34; Sweezy, 'A critique', pp. 33–56.
[98] Postan, *Medieval Economy*, pp. 212–13, 239.
[99] Briggs, *Credit and Village Society*; Stone, *Decision-Making*.
[100] Hilton, 'Towns in English medieval society'; Hilton, *English and French Towns*; Merrington, 'Town and country'.
[101] For the traditional view, see Lopez, *Commercial Revolution*.
[102] Britnell, *Commercialisation*; Masschaele, *Peasants*.
[103] Kowaleski, *Local Markets*, pp. 1–2.
[104] Hilton, 'Capitalism – what's in a name?', pp. 268–71.
[105] Hilton, 'Introduction', p. 21.

the hands of a few entrepreneurs and separated the labour force from the means of production, as well as establishing contractual wage relations.[106] The growth of commerce and a market economy themselves do not necessarily lead to capitalist methods of production and relations. However, a capitalist economy did presuppose an effective marketing system, a money economy, private property and individualism. The commercialisation of the twelfth to fifteenth centuries was perhaps an intermediate stage in such a transition.[107] Increasing levels of market transactions, specialisation, petty trade and production could be viewed as solvents to feudal structures.

The movement to capitalist economic production was complex, multicausal and far from smooth. Many market systems were already in place in the twelfth and thirteenth centuries, while feudalism lingered well into the early modern period. Indeed, the development of agrarian capitalism was drawn out, continuing well into the sixteenth and seventeenth centuries, while a truly capitalist factory system of industrial production did not develop until the eighteenth or nineteenth centuries. Instead of arguing for a direct transition from one economic state to another, some economists and historians have suggested that there were intermediate, piecemeal stages. The higher levels of demand and production by the fifteenth century led to an increasing division of labour and technological process, yet only in the cloth industry was demand and capital extensive enough to support the putting-out system and then an embryonic proto-capitalist organisation based upon mercantile capital.[108] Mostly, there were *ad hoc* stages of economic organisation, as wage-labour, markets and mercantile capital developed, and as pre-industrial neo-capitalist modes formed.

Morality in the pre-industrial marketplace

The transition debate has also involved the issue of a wider mental transition, whereby collective feudalism was dissolved by the cash nexus, giving free rein to commodification, ambition, individualism and accumulation. Some have asserted that the increasing market consciousness of medieval and early modern society led to greater polarisation and a markedly possessive individualism which displaced 'common profit' or traditional 'community'.[109]

---

[106] Britnell, 'Commerce and capitalism', 360–1.   [107] *Ibid.*, 359–76.
[108] Glennie, 'A commercialising agrarian region', pp. 367–9.
[109] Aers, *Community*, pp. 15–16, 82–3; McIntosh, *Autonomy and Community*, pp. 136–8, 152–66; Kermode, 'Introduction', pp. ix–xiii; Muldrew, 'From a "light cloak"', pp. 156–7.

In Max Weber's opinion, writing at the beginning of the twentieth century, Protestantism (especially Calvinism) offered a rational mental climate to facilitate the growth of capitalism, with the idea that the accumulation of money was righteous and a sign of being predestined.[110] Christopher Hill similarly argued that since the Reformation 'the sordid sin of avarice has been transmuted into the religious and patriotic duty of thrift';[111] hard work was thus a religious duty and the accumulation of capital was good in itself. This Weberian theory of the 'Protestant work ethic' was linked to the notion that Catholicism was tightly bound to the distributive tradition and was unresponsive to external forces and the needs of commercial growth. Conversely, Protestantism was seen to be free to reject past doctrines and respond to secular needs, thus encouraging a capitalistic and individual ethic (in combination with structural changes). Yet, orthodox views of merchants frequently changed in medieval times and there is little evidence to suggest that victuallers and petty traders were any more or less vilified in the early seventeenth century than in the Middle Ages. It is also arguable that Calvinist writers responded to changes in the economy, rather than generating an innovative, ethical stance.

On similar grounds, Richard Tawney disagreed with Weber's causal emphasis, but he suggested that there was a noticeable change in economic ethics during the early modern period. Tawney argued that there was general anxiety about salvation because the traditional Church's attitudes towards trade and money did not seem to reflect the actual changes people were facing. The dominant contemporary ideology was based on production for consumption and not trade, and there was no room for the middle classes or market values.[112] Similarly, Lester Little suggested that commercial developments in the later Middle Ages raised problems of impersonalism, money and moral uncertainty.[113] We must certainly not underestimate how much late medieval society was infused with a sense of customary and fixed values, rather than negotiable, market rents. Many medieval writers did subordinate matters of the economy to issues of salvation and individual morality.[114] However, the arguments of many economic historians are overly seduced by medieval moral conventions, and they belie the fact that many moralists, legislators and traders understood market mechanisms and the need to balance ethical stringency with a sense of pragmatism.

[110] Weber, *Protestant Ethic*.
[111] Hill, *Puritanism and Revolution*, p. 218; Todd, *Christian Humanism*, pp. 118–19.
[112] Tawney, *Religion*, pp. 30–1; Bisson, *Chaucer*, pp. 171–2; Parry and Bloch, 'Introduction', pp. 2–3; Parry, 'On the moral perils of exchange'.
[113] Little, *Religious Poverty*, p. 19.   [114] Tawney, *Religion*, pp. 30–1.

Several historians have assumed that moral and religious idealism continually clashed with the practicalities of everyday life in late medieval
England. The Church, in particular, has been characterised as a constraint on economic forces due to its conservative stance on credit and
interest and its negative attitude towards trade in general. Postan argued
that Church doctrine and official intervention linked prices with the
divinely ordained structure of society, thus presuming a natural, customary price. This implied that any changes in prices at times of difficulty
or crisis were deemed unjust.[115] Aron Gurevich posited that the Church
stuck to traditional ethics and was slow to recognise any semblance of
market values.[116] Similarly, nineteenth- and early twentieth-century historians, such as William Ashley and William Cunningham, viewed the
attitudes of the medieval Church as restrictive and monopolistic. Christian ethics opposed market change and innovation, and consequently
there was a conflict between 'restrictionist' Church policies and the reality
of 'homo economicus'.[117] Based on this approach, many historians have
suggested that law and practice were so hampered by religious strictures
and social disapproval that economic growth was stifled. They argued
that the organisation of medieval trade was burdened by usury laws and
the ethical concept of the 'just price', which meant that traders had few
inducements for investment.[118]

To what extent was the development of market behaviour allied to
an increasing desire to accumulate; part of a supposed evolution from
communal cooperation to the 'modern' possessive and individualistic
attitudes of competitive capitalism?[119] This paradigm assumes the existence of 'organic', harmonious medieval communities. Yet studies have
demonstrated a more complex picture of a balance between conflict
and compromise, self-interest and community; all part of the long-term
'shifting boundaries between collective welfare and private property'.[120]
Another approach, based upon the 'commercialisation' model, argues
that there was little mental transition, merely a liberation of the forces
of economic maximisation, innovation and production from the fetters
of religious and social inhibition.[121] Indeed, the uniqueness of the 'modern' acquisitive urge and exchange mentality has been questioned. Alan
Macfarlane posited that individualistic and profit-oriented people were

[115] Postan, *Medieval Economy*, pp. 225–6.   [116] Gurevich, 'The merchant', pp. 275–7.
[117] Ashley, *Introduction*, i, ch. 3; Cunningham, *Growth*, pp. 9–10. See also Sombart,
Quintessence of Capitalism.
[118] North and Thomas, *Rise*, p. 92; Bridbury, 'Markets and freedom', pp. 85–6.
[119] Muldrew, 'From a "light cloak"', pp. 156–7.   [120] Dyer, *An Age*, ch. 2.
[121] Patterson, *Chaucer*, pp. 324–6; Aston and Philipin (eds.), *The Brenner Debate*; Hilton
(ed.), *Transition*.

already a significant part of English society in the thirteenth century.[122] He and others regarded the repetition of laws and religious condemnations as evidence of a society that ignored moral restrictions. Instead, individuals were driven by an inherent accumulative and self-interested streak, with little reference to moral strictures.

Classical economic theorists were proponents of the idea that self-interest was an innate human characteristic. Adam Smith remarked that 'human society has an innate propensity to truck, barter and exchange one thing for another'.[123] In the eighteenth century, Enlightenment thinkers emphasised the inherent individualistic pursuit of profit and gain, which in turn leads to a desire for greater efficiency in economic practice.[124] Smith was a champion of free-market competition, 'laissez-faire' and 'invisible hand' economics, and a disparager of interventionist regulation. He argued that economic forces and individuals, left to their own devices, lead naturally to an efficient form of organisation: 'It is not from the benevolence of the butcher, the brewer, or the baker, that we can expect our dinner, but from their regard to their own interest'.[125] The market itself will thus bring general material good and benevolence through the private pursuit of maximum profit: 'led by an invisible hand to promote an end which was no part of his intention'.[126] The 'moral economy' is superseded by a utilitarian ethic. In Smith's view, competitive forces should be freely allowed to set the agenda of exchange and all will benefit.

However, conversely, many historians have argued that classical economic theories, based upon free-market forces and the profit rationale, do not necessarily fit into an age when commercial developments were constricted by custom, privilege and theology. Cultural forces were certainly influential in medieval economic choices. For instance, customary or fixed rents for land could be based on traditional, non-market relationships in medieval England. Craig Muldrew has also highlighted how sixteenth-century ideas of debt, credit and trust were deeply bound up with moral notions of God, sin and salvation.[127] Medieval markets, especially, were embedded in social and cultural controls and thus not self-regulating and driven by maximising self-interest.[128]

---

[122] Macfarlane, *Origins*, p. 163.   [123] Smith, *An Inquiry*, i, p. 25.
[124] *Ibid.*, i, chs. 1–3, 9–10. For a short discussion about neoclassical economists who adopted Smith's notion of the self-interested, rational economic man, see Muldrew, 'Interpreting', 164–7.
[125] Smith, *An Inquiry*, i, pp. 25–7.   [126] *Ibid.*, i, p. 456.
[127] Muldrew, *Economy of Obligation*, pp. 130–4; Muldrew, 'Interpreting'.
[128] Polanyi, *Great Transformation*, pp. 55–76; Polanyi, 'Our obsolete market mentality'; cf. Muldrew, 'Interpreting', 167.

The extent to which individuals were always economically rational and driven by acquisitive impulses, or whether they were constrained by cultural and social forces, has thus been intensely debated. Were the market attitudes of medieval man somehow different due to the cultural, social and political conditions of their time? Similar arguments have been applied to the absence of free markets, which were allegedly distorted by 'a variety of non-economic forces, including custom, villeinage and religious teaching'.[129] Consequently, like Weber and Tawney, many historians have tried to pinpoint when self-interested market relations usurped traditional paternal and communal values;[130] though, in the Smithian model, this is regarded as a natural, teleological progression where man's acquisitive inclinations gradually facilitate the emergence of a true market society and modern 'capitalism'. Indeed, Smith's analysis has been highly influential and informed the way in which many view historical market behaviour. However, the assumptions of Smith's typology of a *homo economicus* have been questioned. Muldrew stated that studies of historical markets 'should take into account the cultural meaning which economic phenomena have for everyday people, and recognise that people do make ethical decisions within the market'.[131] In his study of early modern economic relations, he argued that most transactions below the level of wholesaling were undertaken on trust and credit, based on communal reputation and contractual morals, which both emphasised and reinforced reciprocal cooperation.[132]

The interaction between morals, culture, economic rationale, laws and commercial development is undoubtedly complex. A number of studies have looked further at this relationship, both in terms of how market institutions and attitudes were shaped over time and also the connection to success and prosperity. In particular, those who seek to explain economic growth often discuss the development of commercial facilities, behavioural constraints, legal rights, and the rules that make up the 'economic system'. Such systems are not static, nor are human motivations, despite the implications and assumptions of neoclassical theory. In the 1970s, Douglass North and Robert Thomas argued that the existence of efficient institutions was a necessary prerequisite for economic growth. Institutions are defined as sets of rules, procedures and norms designed to constrain conduct and allocate resources. They are deemed economically efficient if they serve to equate private costs and benefits with public costs and benefits. Capitalism has thus been viewed as more efficient for

---

[129] Hatcher and Bailey, *Modelling*, p. 10.
[130] Macfarlane, *Origins*, p. 163; Appleby, *Economic Thought*.
[131] Muldrew, 'Interpreting', 168.   [132] Muldrew, *Economy of Obligation*.

economic growth than feudalism and, indeed, North and Thomas conceptualised a steady transition from less to more efficient institutions.[133] Institutional arrangements can either restrain incentives for growth or else enhance economic activity. However, they are not static and may not always develop towards a more efficient form. An institution might be the most appropriate to facilitate the lowest transaction costs in a certain time and conditions, but require active adaptation or innovation as economic and social conditions change.[134]

Douglass North also outlined a 'transaction costs framework', whereby the output of goods and services of a society was a function of both the costs of production and the costs of transacting necessary to produce and exchange those goods and services.[135] The measurement of exchange efficiency was related to the transaction costs of search, negotiation and enforcement. The institution of the market itself presented a means of lowering these costs through the agglomeration of buyers and sellers: search costs derived from the finding of buyers and sellers with whom to trade; negotiation costs involved the agreement of quality, price and place; while enforcement costs accrued in ensuring a bargain was kept.[136] It is the variation in these costs which must be borne in mind when studying the efficiency of medieval market administration. To lower them, a successful market needed to encourage into its midst as many exchanges as possible, with a variety and quantity of goods. The market also needed to reduce risk and uncertainty, both in reality and perception, in order to encourage commercial interaction. To this end, administrative devices were put in place to ensure a regular time and place for exchanges, a secure environment, consistent trading guidelines, regulation of dishonest dealing, debt-recovery mechanisms, low enforcement costs and good access. The laws of the market were a fundamental aspect of its efficiency, in providing bodily and commercial protection to transactors.

However, market institutions are usually complementary to, or embedded in, more traditional institutions. Cultural beliefs are an integral part of the operation and effectiveness of institutions, such as collective norms and social networks that can act as a reinforcement for more formal contract enforcement. North recognised the importance of behavioural norms and culture in influencing the stability of institutional frameworks and lowering transaction costs.[137] Similarly, Avner

---

[133] North and Thomas, *Rise*; North, *Structure and Change*; Hatcher and Bailey, *Modelling*, pp. 192–3.

[134] Hatcher and Bailey, *Modelling*, p. 196.   [135] North, 'Transaction costs'.

[136] Kowaleski, *Local Markets*, pp. 179–80.

[137] North, 'Transaction costs', 559–60, 571–2; North, *Structure and Change*, p. 19; North, *Institutions*; Persson, *Pre-Industrial Economic Growth*, p. 36.

Grief has argued that culture plays an influential role in determining the nature of institutions.[138] Traditional cultural forms were not necessarily incompatible or less efficient than modern, formal market arrangements. Institutions could be stable because parties found it in their own interests to follow the rules, and this can refer to both economic logic and cultural imperatives. Moral norms could modify the degree to which participants maximised at the margins of production, especially when there was consensus as to accepted moral behaviour. In the absence of such moral convictions, the costs of economic organisation increased markedly, especially given the problem of the free rider.[139] In what has been termed 'free-rider theory', it was in the rational self-interest of a neoclassical economic actor to both agree to rules of constraint, but also to disobey those rules when a comparison of costs and benefits dictated as much. However, in reality, people probably obeyed the rules even when economic rationale suggested they should not. This was because of a wider context of social opprobrium and the moral constraints of the cultural milieu.[140] Anthropologists have long recognised that the 'invisible hand' of rational self-interest alone cannot ensure that individuals will not use fraud and illegal methods to make profit. Additional behavioural norms will modify the degree to which participants engage in fair exchange and hence the level of enforcement costs. These factors become even more important in increasingly impersonalised marketplaces, where traders are less open to informal, social constraints.

In the Middle Ages, the formation of ideological constraints was partially embodied by the Church and literature, particularly in their stereotypes of fraudulent and avaricious traders. Economic activity was viewed through a general ethical system, extolled by the Church and drawing on traditional assumptions of an agrarian society, a single Christian community and social order.[141] Profits were expected to be directed towards good causes and an individual's own salvation, while profit-making itself was discouraged as a temptation towards avarice. Assumptions of corruption underlaid the laws which provided the framework for stable marketing institutions. The problem of the free rider was thus diminished by communal institutions and ideological conditioning. Accepted moral

---

[138] Grief, 'Cultural beliefs'; Grief, *Institutions*.

[139] North, *Structure and Change*, pp. 45–65, 201–5.

[140] Dilley (ed.), *Contesting Markets*, p. 11. Social ideologies develop to understand behaviour and surroundings, while ethics (or morality) concern what is considered to be correct behaviour. Attitudes are more individualistic, empirical variations upon basic ideology and ethics. Ideologies are formed both top-down and bottom-up and thus there will be variations based on experience and particular perspectives, but there are certain consensual principles.

[141] Muldrew, 'From a "light cloak"', p. 157.

norms raised the margin at which it was beneficial for a trader to commit flagrant fraud. Consequently, systems of law, morality and sociability were often directed towards combating dishonesty and heightening the level of trust. Exchanges required mutual trust and confidence could be reinforced by both market laws and moral standards. These ideals go beyond mere economic rationalism and are an important consideration in discussing the regulation of petty traders. As Britnell suggested, it is possible that medieval philosophy had a larger impact upon everyday life than hitherto has been realised.[142]

The terminology of modern economics can therefore serve as a useful model, but we must be careful not to misunderstand the social and moral foundations of historic economic relationships and institutions. It is hazardous to apply modern economic standards to a medieval context. Farmer and Dyer have rightly pointed out that traders and consumers were not bound completely by economic theory and modern deterministic notions. They often made decisions based upon attitudes, perceptions and local knowledge.[143] Similarly, the distributive and communal aspects of market ethics reflected the contemporary economic conditions of unstable supplies and the widespread need for basic foodstuffs.[144] A fear of famine, dearth and social disorder meant that many town councils desired detailed supervision of the victual trades, a policy often referred to as 'paternalism'. There were both ethical and practical pressures for close regulation of the marketplace. It is therefore not self-evident that the medieval authorities saw their role as encouraging or facilitating economic exchanges to the exclusion of all other considerations. Civic harmony, social unrest, commercial privileges of burgesses and residents, as well as vested political interests: all were prominent influences. There was not a straightforward conflict between the Church and market forces. Instead, society was attempting to reconcile itself to new economic conditions.

Studies by Odd Langholm and Lianna Farber have stressed the sophistication of medieval economic thought, particularly in relation to usury and just price, which might even have anticipated more modern ideas.[145] Similarly, Joel Kaye and Diana Wood both argue that medieval scholars were prepared to adapt their economic ideas to the changing realities of the marketplace, providing complex justifications for trade.[146] At the

---

[142] Britnell, 'Price-setting', 15.
[143] Dyer, 'Market towns', 18; Farmer, 'Marketing'; Farmer, 'Two Wiltshire manors'.
[144] Muldrew, *Economy of Obligation*, pp. 47–8; Dilley (ed.), *Contesting Markets*, pp. 3–4.
[145] Langholm, *Legacy of Scholasticism*, pp. 1–11, 139–200; Langholm, *Economics*; Farber, *An Anatomy*, pp. 6–8; Baldwin, 'Medieval theories'.
[146] Kaye, *Economy and Nature*, pp. 16–40; Wood, *Medieval Economic Thought*, pp. 206–9.

same time, many medieval writers and moralists remained tied to traditional condemnations of trade. This was the bewildering context in which economic thought was shifting and contemporary writers tried to fit changes into conventional justifications. Legislators also shaped laws that could suit both moral assumptions and vested interests, and the enforcement of law could be flexibly interpreted and enacted.

This book will demonstrate the complexity and intimacy of the interrelationship between morals, law and reality. New economic realities were introduced into inherited values and behaviour patterns, while economic developments were undoubtedly influenced by cultural norms.[147] There was no direct conflict between morals, law and reality, but neither was there a cohesive harmony. Instead, there was a continual flux and realignment in ideology, laws and behaviour, with moral commentary and law often lagging behind the reality of economic circumstances.[148] The ideological apparatus of the state, in law and religion, tended to extenuate a particular viewpoint, perhaps to vindicate a particular social model. However, any ethical consensus was not just formed in the considered writings of moralists, preachers and poets, but also in the practices, rituals and actions of everyday society. The reception and acceptance of ideas was as important as their transmission.[149] We also need to beware the notion of a shared, dominant ideology common to all. Instead, we shall see that there were varied discourses regarding market ethics and commercial morality, which were sometimes contradictory and often involved compromises between conflicting interests.

Nevertheless, we should not underestimate the importance of the Church's standards of morality in influencing market practice and acting as a lubricant as much as a brake. Christian doctrines and beliefs permeated everyone's lives in the Middle Ages.[150] But this was no simple and single moral code, imposed from above, which was blindly accepted by all. The interactions between literary and legal texts from the late Middle Ages were much more complicated, with writers and compilers drawing upon a variety of experiences and assumptions. Church moralists, for instance, often drew directly upon statute law as an exemplar of practical order. There was a continual process of modification and filtration, as the practitioners, lawyers and moralists adapted to changing circumstances and to one another, deciding what could and should be legislated and enforced. The Church perhaps became more flexible as commercial practices developed from the thirteenth century onwards, particularly

---

[147] Chartier, *Cultural History*, pp. 12–40.   [148] Bourdieu, *Logic of Practice*.
[149] Rigby, *English Society*, pp. 305–6, 320–2.   [150] Lilley, *Urban Life*, pp. 11–12.

since, as landholders, they were intricately linked to the developing market practices.[151] However, there were also aspects of their strict ethics that aptly suited the circumstances of the medieval marketplace.

Summary

Too many historians and literary scholars have assumed either complete agreement or, conversely, opposition between medieval morals and practices. Yet, influences upon petty trade were complicated and often determined by vested interests and shared assumptions. By comparing different categories of sources, it may be possible to achieve a greater understanding of the experiences of medieval petty traders, as well as reveal how these sources can be utilised in social and economic history.[152] This book examines the ideological and legal representations of traders in late medieval England, providing a critical comparison to the practicalities of everyday trade. Three different types of evidence are used to reveal the attitudes and regulations that pervaded the medieval market and affected the lives of local traders.

Firstly, literary, artistic and didactic sources frequently touched upon the vices and figures of the marketplace. Chapter 1, in addition to consulting the well-known texts of John Gower, Geoffrey Chaucer and William Langland, examines a broad range of other cultural productions, such as sermons, plays, poems, liturgical handbooks and artists' images. From the scholarly debates of the thirteenth century through to the secular complaint poetry of the fifteenth century, the activities of the everyday marketplace and retail traders were intermittently touched upon as part of a rhetorical discourse that sought to address more fundamental issues of virtue and salvation. The writers were seeking to engage with ethical issues and moral concerns, and on occasion the marketplace and its users provided an expedient explanatory tool. Many of these sources have been under-used by historians even though they reveal a multiplicity of conceptual and pragmatic attitudes towards the market and trade. This is partly because the relationship between these cultural outputs and reception, attitudes and practice is complex. We cannot hope to reveal the mindset of medieval men in all its diffusion and idiosyncrasies, merely

---

[151] Gilchrist, *Church and Economic Activity*, pp. 23–47; Little, *Religious Poverty*, pp. 3–41; Wood, *Medieval Economic Thought*, pp. 2–6.

[152] The approach is analogous to that of the Annales School of historians in the 1950s and 1960s, such as Jacques le Goff and Georges Duby, who studied medieval social attitudes (or *mentalités*) by drawing on a wide range of sources, including literature, in order to write a history of popular attitudes and behaviour.

the cultural environment that helped shape their general principles and influenced their decision-making.

Some of these literary notions and perceptions are mirrored in the second category of sources, namely statutes, laws and ordinances at both a central and municipal level. Legislation was a means of expression for the primary concerns of certain social groups and as a basis for order and communal trust. In many ways, law itself generated concepts of a market ethic. Commercial law was constituted through a variety of forums, from national statutes and proclamations to civic and guild ordinances. Chapter 2 provides an overview of the main regulatory developments in late medieval England and attempts to draw out the prominent themes and concerns.

However, legislation cannot necessarily be regarded as evidence for everyday practice, reliant as it was on interpretation and enforcement. In this context, case studies from towns in Suffolk provide the third tier of evidence for this comparative study. The court rolls of the Suffolk towns of Newmarket, Clare and Ipswich form the basis of the empirical research in Chapter 3, investigating retailers, pedlars and middlemen in their everyday environment. These case studies concentrate on the late fourteenth and early fifteenth centuries, and on only one county, which inevitably compresses our viewpoint into a short chronological and regional span. However, this level of detail allows us to view the tangled links between morals, law and practice at a formative time of economic and social upheaval when many of the debates about a developing market economy were intense. A thorough reconstruction of small town and borough retail markets is required in order to understand the complex environment in which medieval buyers and sellers operated and interpreted moral discourses about their activities.

Finally, in Chapter 4, a brief examination of early modern market morality raises questions about longer-term commercial ethics, highlighting debates about the apparent continuities of a 'moral economy' in eighteenth-century food markets. Many aspects of medieval commercial legislation and morality appear to have persisted into the early modern period, but they represented a more market-oriented outlook than perhaps some historians have recognised.

The main focus of medieval market laws concerned such concepts as just price, dishonesty and fraud, middlemen practices and responsibilities towards the consumer. The retailers and middlemen of basic foodstuffs and small-scale manufactures undoubtedly bore the brunt of commercial regulation after the Black Death, as well as having their responsibilities outlined in great detail by religious commentators and secular moralists. Subsequently, the dominant debate in economic history has been whether medieval theory and practice were in complete alignment or else divergent and antagonistic. The relationship between morals and behaviour was certainly complex, with a continual interplay between the ideas expressed in different forums of religion, literature and law. This was to lead to flexibility in when and how regulations were implemented in the marketplace. A greater understanding of how moral perceptions shaped law and practice is needed, as well as a better sense of whether the changing social and economic environment forced moralists and legislators to adapt their preconceived ideas to create a distinctive medieval market morality.

1 Images of market trade

The conduct of market traders, customers and officials was informed by shared moral concerns, which were reinforced and reflected by the educated elite of Church and state. Ethical and economic issues relating to the marketplace were addressed in a variety of sources, by theologians, friars, canonists, moralists and secular complaint poets. They discussed money, justice, value, profit, contracts, usury and other commercial activity, primarily with moral issues in mind and a focus on the spiritual salvation of the individual.[1] To this end, certain moral principles were recurrent throughout the late medieval period, and traders were reminded continually of their communal responsibilities, especially towards the poor and vulnerable. In particular, petty victuallers who supplied the necessities of life were expected to adhere to a consensus regarding the 'common good' and social justice.

Most medieval writers viewed economic practices in terms of morality, ethics and the values of the Christian Church. However, this should not lead us to assume that they were ignorant of market forces and the economic processes that determined the circulation of goods. Indeed, there was an underlying economic dilemma in many medieval writings about how to achieve equity and benefit in markets. How were moral concerns and justice to be met while not inhibiting or undermining market prosperity and the livelihood of traders? Medieval moralists also grappled with the seeming contradictions of commercial life. Trade was often regarded as counter to the Christian ideal of an agrarian subsistence lifestyle, as well as providing unavoidable temptations to sin. Yet, many medieval writers also recognised that commerce was economically necessary and even beneficial for the common good. In the context of growing commercialisation and a developing market society, some

---

[1] For an in-depth discussion of scholarly works, see Langholm, *Economics*; Langholm, *Legacy of Scholasticism*; Langholm, *The Merchant*; Baldwin, 'Medieval theories'; Baldwin, *Masters*; Gilchrist, *Church and Economic Activity*; Wood, *Medieval Economic Thought*; Kaye, *Economy and Nature*.

writers demonstrated certain anxieties as they discussed the role of market trade within medieval society. They often reacted to the contemporary economic environment by emphasising the potential sinfulness of commercial pursuits and the constant clash between private motivations and public duty, between personal interest and the common good. Not all writers agreed on the relationship of trade to society, or what market activities were justified; nor did they approach the subject in the same manner, particularly those writing within different genres.[2]

This chapter examines prevailing moralistic attitudes towards petty traders through a range of cultural sources, such as poems, sermons, pastoral works, drama and art. These texts and images cannot be divorced from the social and economic worlds in which they were created and are therefore valuable residues of contemporary beliefs and assumptions. This chapter concentrates mostly on texts and images that circulated in late medieval England, but examples will be drawn from further afield where appropriate, such as the formative scholastic debates concerning just price. In studying literary, religious, scholarly and artistic sources, which have a moralistic content or function, we can uncover some of the mentalities and cultural attitudes that pervaded late medieval England and examine how these views influenced both the regulation and activities of commerce. However, using literary and religious sources to determine 'popular' attitudes can undoubtedly be problematic and the methodological pitfalls of such an approach need to be firstly explored before the substance of the texts can be discussed.

History and literature

The use of literary sources has provoked intense debate in the field of social history. At the centre of the discussion lies the problem of how to distinguish conventions of literature from the conditions of real life, as well as how the differing roles of literary criticism and history should interact. Literary critics were traditionally interested in explaining the meaning of a text on the basis of its own content, language and structure, as exemplified by the 'new criticism' of the 1960s and 1970s. This methodology rendered history superfluous to literature and the meaning of a text was seen to transcend its historical context. However, the orthodoxy of literary critics over the past forty years has been to discuss medieval literature more in terms of its broader social context, in an

---

[2] Farber, *An Anatomy*, p. 5.

attempt to discern contemporary reception.[3] Modern critics now increasingly accept the need to establish a writer's perception of moral values and social principles within a specific historical context. This approach has been termed by some as 'new historicism' and involves a careful textual reading of literary and historical sources, as well as an understanding of the semiotics, symbolism and other influences which contributed to a text's construction.[4]

By contrast, many historians traditionally considered literature to be redundant as historical evidence or else concentrated on looking for allusions to real people or events.[5] Peter Laslett warned that literary evidence and conventions can be a trap for the unwary social historian, especially those who intend to use literary sources as an illustrative and mimetic adjunct to empirical evidence.[6] Such texts are not passive mirrors of reality, but active and distorting interpretations of society and morality, embedded in ideological aims and vested interests.[7] Historians have now moved away from purely mimetic schemes and more towards the use of literature as an historical source which should be interpreted within the limitations of rhetorical and semiotic conventions.[8] Literary texts are used to reveal a general understanding of social, cultural and political attitudes.[9] The theoretical approaches of literary critics and historians have become partly reconciled, based upon recognition of the interrelationship and textual qualities of all sources.[10]

Literary and didactic moral texts do not provide historians with a straightforward, realistic depiction of society or political events, but such texts can be used as a gauge for past mentalities and concerns.[11] At the very least, they provide us with a refracted sense of the most prominent social and moral questions of the day.[12] After all, these writers were attempting to make sense of the world around them, even if traditional concepts, paradigms and assumptions shaped their way of thinking.[13]

---

[3] Rigby, 'English society', p. 25.
[4] Hanawalt, 'Introduction', p. xi; Spiegel, 'History, historicism'; Simpson, 'Literary criticism'; Sponsler, 'Society's image'. Green suggested that this 'new historicism', and the recognition of social context in re-creating the meanings of texts, was an exercise in reinventing the wheel for historians; Green, 'John Ball's letters', pp. 178–9.
[5] Rigby, 'England: literature and society', p. 497.
[6] Laslett, 'The wrong way through the telescope'; Mann, Chaucer, pp. 8–9.
[7] Rigby, Chaucer in Context, p. 2; Rigby, 'England: literature and society', pp. 497–8.
[8] See also Davis, Fiction in the Archives, pp. 3–4; White, Content of the Form.
[9] Thomas, History and Literature; Fleming, 'Historians'.
[10] Patterson, 'Critical historicism'; Patterson, Negotiating the Past, p. 44; Aers (ed.), Medieval Literature, p. 3.
[11] Rigby, 'England: literature and society'; Aers (ed.), Medieval Literature, p. 3.
[12] Rigby, Chaucer in Context, pp. 15–16.   [13] Stevenson, Praise and Paradox, pp. 3–5.

Some historians have argued that such texts were often the unrepresentative products of a ruling elite, who were attempting to impose their doctrines on the majority in order to force conformity and order.[14] The Church and the landholding classes of late medieval England relied upon the labour and services of the majority and their self-interests were thus served by legitimising the social model upon which their wealth and status depended. However, it is not self-evident that the moralistic ideology and literature of the clergy was continually divergent from the practice and beliefs of the people. Some texts partially represent a transmission of culture from a popular to intellectual level, as in the stories and exempla of the preachers and the articles of the confessional.[15]

The extent to which the ideology and ethics of the elite were shared by all is difficult to ascertain. However, we should remember that the representations in many cultural artefacts were themselves important generators of ideologies and daily attitudes, which were bolstered by regulation and prejudice.[16] As a result, we can look at the books, poems and sermons of the late Middle Ages, which both created and drew upon contemporary and traditional beliefs, in order to understand shared habits of ideology, thought and behaviour.[17] Although the thoughts and beliefs of the average 'popular' medieval man cannot be necessarily reproduced, there are remnants of the formal cultural context within which society operated. Ultimately, in the absence of letters, diaries and other self-written texts by market traders from late medieval England, historians are reliant upon the opinions and cultural productions of the literate elite. This chapter will therefore draw upon sermons, compilations, treatises, plays, poems, satire and pastoral works to understand how they presented the moral 'mentality' that underlay medieval trade and the inherent paradoxes of commercial activity.

There has been a long tradition of academic work on the 'merchant class' and their social ambitions, pious anxieties and literary portrayals. Sylvia Thrupp, Jenny Kermode, John Thomson and others have examined the mercantile class and religious justifications for trade based upon criteria of national prosperity, risk and charitable offerings.[18] The medieval merchant was thus portrayed as courageous and enterprising,

---

[14] Strohm, *Social Chaucer*, pp. 2–9; Duby, *The Three Orders*, pp. 76–109, 271–92.

[15] Gurevich, *Medieval Popular Culture*, p. 2; Karras, *Common Women*, p. 105.

[16] Spiegel, 'History, historicism', 77; Bennett, *Ale*, p. 123; Mann, *Chaucer*, p. 8.

[17] Platts, 'South Lincolnshire', pp. 18–20; Chartier, *Cultural History*, pp. 27–9, 47–8.

[18] Thrupp, *Merchant Class*; Kermode, 'The merchants'; Kermode, *Medieval Merchants*; Gurevich, 'The merchant'; le Goff, *Time, Work and Culture*, pp. 29–42; Thomson, 'Wealth, poverty'. For a discussion of justifications provided for merchant endeavours, see pp. 90–5.

undertaking long, risky journeys and reconciling their apparent acquisitive urge with a moral and social conscience. Mercantile endeavours were appreciated in terms of financial benefits accrued to the kingdom as a whole. This was linked to actual developments within the mercantile community, as many had become owners of landed property, married into knightly families and acted as moneylenders to the princes and nobles of Europe. These wealthy businessmen and burgesses aspired to the position and trappings of the gentry, as well as to traditional indicators of social status.[19]

The lives and images of these prosperous wholesale merchants were a far cry from the portraits of petty traders, often characterised as grotesques or figures of ridicule or shame. These ranged from lecherous alewives and faux-friendly innkeepers, to flirtatious peddlers and stinking tanners. There has been an increasing interest in the literary portrayals of petty traders and in their importance for social historians. Rodney Hilton's work on small towns is a case in point. He compared William Langland's 'Rose the Regrator' (from *Piers Plowman*, written *c*.1360–87) with court cases in the borough of Thornbury and decided that 'Langland's world was not a world of low life, but of normality'.[20] Another significant study was Bennett's examination of alewives, in which she highlighted the often virulent fifteenth- and early sixteenth-century depictions of female traders.[21] Yet, representations of retailers, hawkers, peddlers, stallholders and minor middlemen as a group merit further attention, particularly as a means to uncovering prevalent attitudes towards market trade.

Several scholars have examined the portrayal of brewers and bakers in *Piers Plowman* from a literary perspective. David Aers, in keeping with 'new historicism', realised the need for a greater awareness of the real commercial environment in studying the emotional responses of Langland and other moralists to petty traders.[22] Aers has argued that the changing social and economic circumstances of medieval England influenced writers of moral texts. In this viewpoint, society became increasingly steeped in market values and this was reflected in the increasing

---

[19] Horrox, 'Urban gentry'; Kermode, *Medieval Merchants*, pp. 110–18; Thrupp, *Merchant Class*, pp. 290–3; Rigby, *English Society*, p. 193.

[20] Hilton, 'Women traders'; Hilton, 'Lords, burgesses and hucksters'; Hilton, 'Small town society'.

[21] Bennett, *Ale*, pp. 122–44; Bennett, 'Misogyny'. Hanna argued that Judith Bennett had succumbed to mimetic tendencies in her views on the representations of alewives. Hanna, 'Brewing trouble'. For Bennett's response, see Bennett, *Ale*, p. 226. Also, for a brief comparison of the ale trade in literature, law and court rolls, see Britnell, 'Morals'.

[22] Aers, *Chaucer*, pp. 1–37; Aers, *Community*, pp. 1–20.

representations of money, avarice and merchants in clerical and literary texts.[23] Patricia Eberle has similarly argued that such commercial language and values infiltrated all social groups, rather than simply merchants, by the late fourteenth century.[24] Other literary critics have commented on Geoffrey Chaucer's seemingly conflicting attitude in accepting the ambiguities of the post-Black Death market while he also condemned the supposedly rampant cash nexus.[25] New historicists often stress the interaction between texts and contemporary power relations, and whether authors sought to challenge or reinforce the existing social hierarchy.[26] They have, however, tended to overstate the context of commercial changes after the plague, which in turn informs their reading of Chaucer and Langland. Historians now tend to agree that such commercial changes occurred long before, with the main expansions in urban society, money and trade taking place during the twelfth and thirteenth centuries.

Nevertheless, the Church and moralists were not as at variance with contemporary economic practice to the extent that some historians and literary critics have previously suggested. It must be remembered that the Church in England was a prominent landowner and the clergy were actively involved in commercial matters, selling agricultural produce and buying a variety of commodities.[27] They knew well enough the changes that were taking place in the market between 1200 and 1500, at least from the perspective of a landlord, producer or consumer. It is clear that conventional stereotypes and imagery dominate many texts. Ecclesiastical writers and moralists were certainly presenting ideals of behaviour within traditional ideological models and were not seeking to directly reflect reality, but the market and traders were useful rhetorical devices to pinpoint areas of contemporary concern. Commercial developments from the twelfth to the fifteenth centuries were a vibrant context. The petty trader was also a strong presence in society throughout these centuries and presented challenges to theological thought and conventions. Such traders were a class apart from the gentrified aspirations of the provincial and city merchants, and much more relevant to the majority of the population. There are references to market traders and victuallers

[23] Aers, *Community*, pp. 171–3, 176; Yunck, *Lineage*, pp. 185–6, 235–6, 273; Shoaf, *Dante*; Murray, *Reason and Society*; Coleman, *English Literature*, p. 64. The personification of money was an increasingly common theme in medieval compositions, such as 'Sir Penny' (fifteenth century). Greene (ed.), *Early English Carols*, p. 261, no. 392; Sisam and Sisam (eds.), *Medieval English Verse*, pp. 441–2, no. 196; BL, MS Sloane 2593, fol. 26v.

[24] Eberle, 'Commercial language'.

[25] Knight, *Geoffrey Chaucer*; Patterson, 'No man his reson herde', pp. 114–15.

[26] Rigby, 'England: literature and society', p. 498; Rigby, 'English society', pp. 25, 30.

[27] Gilchrist, *Church and Economic Activity*.

in a host of medieval works, such as William Langland's *Piers Plowman* and John Gower's *Mirour de l'Omme*.

This chapter concentrates primarily on sources of English provenance, though this includes a broad sweep of secular, religious, elite and popular material. From the sermons, devotional handbooks and exempla of clerics and friars to the literature of Langland and Chaucer, via the misericords and wall-paintings of parish churches and the satirical poems of John Lydgate and John Skelton, we can begin to piece together the moral framework that influenced and reflected the thoughts of all medieval market users.

Sources of morality

The Church was the dominant cultural force in medieval English society, forming opinions and shaping attitudes. From the scholars who passed through the monastic, cathedral and university doors to the priests preaching from the pulpit and taking confessional, Christian doctrine permeated all sectors of life. In everyday life, the Christian calendar and church bell marked time, while the Church courts had jurisdiction over a host of daily sins, from oaths to Sabbath-breaking.[28] Within the Church, the apparatus of liturgy, sermons, pastoral texts, wall-paintings and sculptures was a continual reminder of God's ultimate jurisdiction over men's souls. Images of the Last Judgement and damnation in Hell were evocative reminders of the eternal pains of secular sin and the need for spiritual salvation. For medieval people bombarded with such concepts, it is likely that religious and moral undercurrents could not be easily separated from their everyday material concerns.

One of the foundations for many didactic and pastoral texts, as well as the categorisation of trading abuses, lay in the Church reforms of the twelfth and thirteenth centuries, which sought to reinvigorate the interest of congregations. Such motivations were abundantly clear in the proclamations of the Fourth Lateran Council, convened in 1215. The prime aim of the Council was for a clearer and more effective transmission of Church doctrine to the general laity. The delegates feared that congregations misunderstood basic doctrines. The Council thus demanded competent preaching, regular confession and better-educated clergymen.[29] For instance, the Lambeth Council of 1281, summoned by John Peckham, Archbishop of Canterbury, commanded parish priests to teach their flock the main doctrines of Christianity: articles of the creed, Ten

---

[28] Wood, *Medieval Economic Thought*, pp. 2–3.
[29] Wenzel, *Latin Sermon Collections*, pp. 229–30.

Commandments, two angelic precepts, seven works of mercy, seven chief virtues, seven deadly sins and seven sacraments.[30] Various manuals were written for the clergy to aid them in their pastoral duties, as illustrated by the *Summa Confessorum* by Thomas de Chobham (*c*.1216), William of Pagula's early fourteenth-century *Oculus Sacerdotis* and a popular catechism by Archbishop Thoresby of York in 1357.[31] These works provided guidance for priests in how to communicate with their unlearned congregations, adapting the dogma of Christian morality to the practicalities of daily life.

Many of these works were conventional, basic and derivative in their formulation. However, simultaneously, the growing mendicant movement of Franciscans, Dominicans and others developed popular rhetorical ideals within the framework of the vernacular sermon.[32] To aid this purpose, many mendicants produced devotional manuals (for example, *Somme des Vices et des Vertues* (*c*.1279) by Dominican friar, Lorens d'Orléans) to forge a link between theology and secular morality, and to integrate pastoral doctrines with popular proverbs and humorous anecdotes.[33] These friars provided a new impetus for preaching in English, with their emphasis upon clear, entertaining sermons that could both interest and educate. Anxious to engage with their listeners, preachers increasingly drew upon popular oral culture,[34] while their attempts to empathise with their lay audience left a legacy of socially relevant stories, exempla and admonitions of supposedly real abuses.[35] Preachers launched direct attacks upon everyday life when tackling the sins of human conduct, which mixed together conventional tales with popular observations that appealed to the layman. As Stephen Langton said in the early thirteenth century, 'very often a popular story is more effective than a polished subtle phrase'.[36]

---

[30] Powicke and Cheney (eds.), *Councils and Synods*, ii, pp. 886–918 (see also, i, p. 268); Wilkins (ed.), *Concilia*, ii, p. 54.

[31] Broomfield (ed.), *Thomae de Chobham*; Simmons and Nolloth (eds.), *Lay Folks' Catechism*. See also Newhauser, *Treatise*, pp. 142–7; Wenzel, *Latin Sermon Collections*, pp. 232–4; Langholm, *The Merchant*.

[32] Pfander, *Popular Sermon*, pp. 1–14; Spencer, *English Preaching*; d'Avray, *Preaching*.

[33] Dan Michel's *Ayenbite of Inwyt* (*c*.1340) and *The Book of Vices and Virtues* (*c*.1400) were later English translations of *Somme des Vices et des Vertues*.

[34] Thompson, 'Popular reading tastes', pp. 83–9; Smalley, *English Friars*, pp. 41–4; Spencer, *English Preaching*, pp. 80–1; Withington, 'Braggart', 124–5.

[35] Tubach, *Index Exemplorum*; Grisdale (ed.), *Three Middle English Sermons*, pp. x–xxviii; Wenzel, *Latin Sermon Collections*, pp. 288–96. An exempla collection was compiled by John Bromyard (d. 1352), an English Dominican, and was widely used by preachers. Bromyard, *Summa Predicantium*. See also Crane (ed.), *Exempla of Jacques de Vitry*; Little (ed.), *Liber Exemplorum*; Swan (ed.), *Gesta Romanorum*; Wenzel, *Latin Sermon Collections*, pp. 322–5.

[36] Roberts, *Studies*, p. 47.

Numerous English sermons survive from the fourteenth and fifteenth centuries, such as the *Festial* sermon collection (*c*.1400) of John Mirk, an Augustinian canon from Shropshire.[37] *Festial* was produced to aid clergy in their own preaching: 'so that whoever wishes to study in it shall find readily for all the principal feasts of the year a short sermon that is necessary for him to teach and for others to learn'.[38] By including simplified examples from daily life, clerics perpetuated popular stereotypes and reinforced them by continual exposure. Emphasis on the penitential process reinforced categorisation and was responsible for a clerical approach that was preoccupied with outlining sin and repentance. Works for private moral instruction included *Handlyng Synne*, *Somme le Roi* and the *Book of Vices and Virtues*, all of which classified sins and virtues so that laymen could examine their own consciences regarding transgressions committed in their everyday lives. *Ayenbite of Inwyt*, written in *c*.1340 by a monk named Dan Michel, was specifically intended for popular consumption, stating:

> þis boc is ywrite
> uor englisshe men þet hi wyte
> hou hi ssolle ham-zelue ssriue
> and maki ham klene ine þise lieu[39]

The laity was therefore continually bombarded from the pulpit and the confessional with an 'authorised' view of conduct, sin and morality, which they absorbed into their thinking and basic assumptions. Because most people were illiterate, the images that adorned church walls, pews and stonework were equally effective devices in transmitting summarised cultural messages. 'Psychomachia' (Battle of the Vices and Virtues), the 'Seven Deadly Sins', the 'Wheel of Fortune' and the 'Dance of Death' were all popular images in the churches of medieval England, and acted as visual aids for preachers.[40] *Dives and Pauper* (*c*.1405–10), an English didactic treatise, stated, 'for often man is more steryd be syghte þan be heryng or redyngge'.[41] For many people, the iconography of church painting and sculpture, alongside sermons, was the only formalised

---

[37] Erbe (ed.), *Mirk's Festial*.   [38] Wenzel, *Latin Sermon Collections*, pp. 58–9.

[39] (This book is written / for English men that they know / how they shall themselves confess / and make them pure in this life), *Ayenbite of Inwyt*, p. 5. See also *Handlyng Synne*, pp. 2–3, ll. 43–4, 54–6 – 'For lewde men y vndyr-toke / On englyssh tunge to make þys boke' (For unlearned men I undertook / In English tongue to make this book').

[40] Katzenellenbogen, *Allegories*; Anderson, *History and Imagery*, pp. 83, 145–53, fig. 90; Anderson, *Imagery of British Churches*, pp. 164–71.

[41] (for often man is more stirred by sight than by hearing or reading.) *Dives and Pauper*, I, i, p. 82, ll. 41–2.

education they received. They were certainly the only explicit moral codes they were expected to follow.

Many images were simply aesthetic or humorous in purpose, and it is all too easy to over-interpret their relationship to morality lessons or everyday life. Certain works, such as illuminated manuscripts, were also aimed at more prosperous levels of society, including the upper commercial class, and their broader appeal may be questioned. However, the wider influence of many religious images and moral messages can be discerned. For instance, a varied audience attended the mystery plays and morality plays that flourished in the fifteenth century. These plays often highlighted the struggle for man's soul between good and evil, using allegorical figures of particular vices to emphasise the message. *The Castle of Perseverance*, a morality play written in *c.*1425, illustrates the struggle between the seven deadly sins and the seven moral virtues, and each vice or virtue appears as an allegorical figure.[42] The influence of the local environment and contemporary social debates in such plays is also notable, and the use of the alewife in the early sixteenth-century *Chester Mystery Play* demonstrates how everyday life could be incorporated as a didactic and humorous device.[43]

Other works, often more secular in nature or author, also reinforced medieval moral codes. It is in the complaint poetry, debate prose and satirical literature, which blossomed in the fourteenth and fifteenth centuries, that we find explorations of numerous social issues, including the problems of trade. Examples include *The Simonie*, *Wynnere and Wastoure* and *Song of the Husbandman*. These poems highlighted the evils of society and made topical allusions within conventional paradigms. Often, they called for the correction of sins in vitriolic and bitter terms.[44] Although the writers presented themselves as espousing the common will, they were usually intellectuals or clerics who had the technical skills to produce verse and reflect the stock phrases and methods of the pulpit.

William Langland's *Piers Plowman* is an exceptional example of complaint verse combined with theological allegory, and in his work can be found all the emotions of anger, lamentation, bitterness and despair that were so resonant of the genre. The author, about whom we know little, was concerned with the condition of society and the redemption of men's souls. He and many complaint poets argued for reforms of Church and

---

[42] Bevington (ed.), *Medieval Drama*, pp. 227–35, 637, 791–2, 822–9.
[43] See below, pp. 106–7.
[44] Maddicott, 'Poems of social protest'; Kinney, 'Temper of fourteenth-century English verse'.

society, advocating a nostalgic return to a traditional social order which was based on tripartite or estates ideology.[45] They wanted people to turn away from excessive material desires, for such actions had apparently corrupted social relations and spiritual salvation. Each estate or profession was criticised for falling short of the required standards for social harmony, from fraudulent traders to cheating lawyers, vain nobles and bribable officials.

English literary texts may have regurgitated clerical concerns about sin, confession and penance, but there was also a more subtle recognition of social and economic realities that conflicted with Christian ideals. Traditional ideology and stereotypes could be adapted to changing circumstances and writers could disagree on their significance.[46] Complaint poems are saturated with references to civil law, political events and everyday activities. The audiences for written texts, both secular and clerical, were also both widening and deepening. Increasing lay literacy, especially among the merchant class, meant that many writers sought to appeal to the sensibilities of their audience. They proffered contemporary social commentary while also plundering the resources of traditional rhetoric.[47] However, the extent to which well-known writers like Geoffrey Chaucer and John Gower found audiences among middling merchants and urban burgesses is difficult to ascertain.[48] Gower addressed his works to Richard II, the Archbishop of Canterbury and courtly nobility, and the use of French in *Mirour de l'Omme* (c.1376–9) certainly limited its audience. Copies of *Confessio Amantis* (c.1386–93) were seemingly disseminated via stationers and the use of the vernacular in this text suggests that Gower intended it to be read aloud to knightly and gentry audiences.[49] However, the issues of strict morality, law and order, religious piety and conservative reform that dominated his texts showed no affinity for the common people, and were intended to appeal mainly to the concerns of the nobility and aspirant local worthies. Even 'lesser' writers of complaint poems, and other cultural outputs that reached a wider audience, were rarely themselves merchants and certainly not petty traders. Authors, therefore, viewed the local markets from the

---

[45] See below, pp. 46–9.   [46] Rigby, 'England: literature and society', p. 507.

[47] Justice, *Writing and Rebellion*, pp. 31–3; Middleton, 'Audience and public of *Piers Plowman*', pp. 101–3; Edwards, 'Manuscripts and readers'; Thrupp, *Merchant Class*, pp. 162, 248–9. For the commonplace books of Richard Hill, a grocer, and John Colyn, a mercer of London, containing a variety of poems, romances, petitions and other texts, see Gray (ed.), *Oxford Book*, p. xviii; BL, MS Harleian 2252.

[48] Strohm, 'Social and literary scene'.

[49] Yeager, 'Gower's French audience'; Edwards and Pearsall, 'Manuscripts'; Coleman, 'Lay readers'.

vantage point of the consumer, producer or landlord, supporting their needs above all others, and were perhaps suspicious of certain market mechanisms.

Sources that reveal contemporary attitudes towards traders were therefore wide-ranging in their form, audience and style, leading to divergent conceptions of the market. Some texts made great use of satirical humour in order to contrast social realities with traditional ideals of morality and spirituality. Geoffrey Chaucer was impressive in his subtle use of irony, satire and individualistic traits to highlight estate stereotypes in *The Canterbury Tales* (*c.*1388–1400). He concentrated on the pomposity and self-importance of figures such as the Merchant, Sergeant of Law, Physician and Guildsmen, as well as the ways in which their occupations shaped their character and implied dubious practices. John Gower was more didactic and verbose in his approach. He sought to explore the moral and religious failings of all degrees of society and couched his traditional rhetoric within the schema of a world turned upside-down and the loss of a golden past. Vernacular literature, in general, demonstrated an increasing tendency to incarnate traditional 'types' as realistic personifications located in contemporary settings, which appealed to the audience's own sense of propriety and ideological assumptions.

However, the broader social rhetoric and moral goals of all these works tended to be similar.[50] Ultimately, the Church provided the official religious and social framework that medieval writers drew upon. We must therefore avoid falling into the trap of believing that English society was deteriorating and that commercial fraud was omnipotent. Many of the exempla and doctrines were merely copied from older manuals, while vernacular works rarely strayed beyond generalisations and conventions. Additionally, although parishioners were confronted with Church doctrines on a regular basis and probably accepted many of the basic principles, we cannot know how they actually interpreted the details. One preacher suggested that the laity viewed the world through practical eyes: 'If a preacher speaks about the contempt of the world, a host of worldly thoughts cries out in opposition: "How is that so? The more goods you will have, the more good you will be able to do". And so they do not allow the voice of God's counsel to be heard.'[51] The set formulae and idealistic aspirations of moral writings are not an open window into men's thoughts, and merely provide us with the contexts and teachings that helped to shape medieval mentalities.

---

[50] Rigby, 'England: literature and society', pp. 499–500, 508.
[51] Oxford, Bodleian Library, MS Laudian Misc. 511, fol. 61v; translated by Spencer, *English Preaching*, p. 95.

Medieval social theory

Basic, long-held tenets of faith and structures of thought were integral to the moralists' view of trade. Medieval notions of justice, work ethics and social order were thus important elements in any discussion of trading behaviour. The main model of social organisation was the three estates theory. In this model, society was divided into three orders: the clergy (*oratores*: those who prayed), the nobility (*bellatores*: those who fought) and the labourers (*laboratores*: those who worked). This tripartite social theory was based on assumptions of stability, order, privilege and conformity, rather than individualism and social mobility. The ideal was for harmonious, stable interrelationships within a strict social hierarchy, based more upon feudal concepts of the insolubility of land and rent than the fluidity of money and commerce. This was not intended to be a straightforward reflection of reality but rather an ideological abstraction. The rhetoric of the three estates was primarily a tool to consolidate the powers and vested interests of the ruling orders, and Georges Duby and Maurice Keen have argued that the concepts of the model were largely accepted and internalised.[52] Differences in rank were regularly defined, whether in lists of precedence or taxation.[53] Medieval people were encouraged to accept their given role in society and perform according to their degree. Inequality was an integral part of the model and those who questioned the hierarchical structure were seen as committing the sin of pride.

However, in reality, society was much more fluid than medieval social theories implied, with retailers and artisans aspiring to the mercantile life and peasants ambitious for improvements in their status.[54] Such ambition was evident before the Black Death, but the plague provided new opportunities for social mobility. As Stephen Rigby has argued, people's actual behaviour did not suggest a society that deferred to traditional social models.[55] Later legislation, in the form of the Statute of Labourers of 1351 and sumptuary laws of 1363, 1463 and 1483, as well as the Peasants' Revolt of 1381, show both raised tensions and attempts to

[52] Duby, *The Three Orders*, pp. 76–109, 271–92; Keen, *English Society*, pp. 1–15. For examples of such rhetoric in the late fourteenth century, see Bromyard, *Summa Predicantium*, 'Civitas'; Stockton (ed.), *Major Latin Works*, 'Vox Clamantis', bk. III, ch. 1, p. 114, bk. V, ch. 15, p. 215.

[53] Furnivall (ed.), *Babees Book*, pp. 186–95, 381. This placed merchants as being above gentlemen and equal with squires, preachers, masters of chancery, franklins, and serjeants of law. Mann, *Chaucer*, appx A, pp. 203–6.

[54] Rigby, 'English society', pp. 26–30; Du Boulay, *An Age*, pp. 61–79; Keen, *English Society*, pp. 22–3, 40–1.

[55] Rigby, 'English society', p. 34.

preserve an idealised social and feudal hierarchy.[56] The sumptuary laws defined what clothes and apparel could be worn, and conceptualised the social strata as being based on detailed criteria of either landed income or urban wealth. The precedence and security of landed wealth remained paramount, with merchants needing five times the value of goods that an equivalent gentleman had in annual rents from land in order to dress to the same standard. The sumptuary laws, however, were difficult to enforce and the 1363 statute was actually repealed the following year.[57] Such legislation illustrates that recurrent attempts were made, some-times unsuccessfully, to defend the established hierarchy from upstarts and social upheaval. Social mobility and tension was also consistently highlighted in literature. Peter Idley, in a mid-fifteenth-century moral treatise, complained that it was hard to tell 'a tapester, a cookesse, or a hostellers wyffe [wife] ffro [from] a gentilwoman', while Chaucer por-trayed the guildsmen pilgrims being adorned with daggers and clothes that presumed to a higher status than they deserved according to sump-tuary legislation.[58]

Some medieval models of traditional estates theory were modified to include finer gradations of other classes and occupations, notably mer-chants and craftsmen.[59] In the late fourteenth century, Thomas Brinton (c.1330–89), Bishop of Rochester, included merchants and artisans as the left hand of the social body, while citizens and burgesses formed the heart.[60] Each part of the body was assigned a particular task necessary for the health and common good of the whole. This organic metaphor

[56] *Statutes*, i, pp. 311–13, 25 Edw III st.2 cc.1–7, 'Statute of Labourers' (1350–1); i, pp. 379–81, 37 Edw III c.5–11 (1363); ii, pp. 399–402, 3 Edw IV c.5 (1463); ii, pp. 468–9, 22 Edw IV c.1 (1482–3).

[57] Rigby, 'English society', p. 34.

[58] Scattergood, 'Fashion and morality'; Hodges, *Chaucer and Costume*, pp. 135–6; Chaucer, *Canterbury Tales*, 'General Prologue', p. 29, ll. 361–78; d'Evelyn (ed.), *Peter Idley's Instructions*, p. 163, Liber Secundus, ll. 267–9; Lisca, 'Chaucer's guildsmen', 321–4. The statute of 1363 stated that artisans and yeomen should not wear cloth of a higher price than 40s., nor stone, silk, silver, girdle, knife, ring, garter, riband, chains, gold or embroidered. Merchants, artisans and burgesses, with goods worth more than £500, could wear clothing akin to esquires, but with no gold, embroidered, ring, and buttons, nor silk, silver, riband, girdle or fur, unless they had goods over £1,000. *Statutes*, i, pp. 380–1, 37 Edw III cc.9–11 (1363).

[59] Hilton, 'Status and class'.

[60] Devlin (ed.), *Sermons of Thomas Brinton*, pp. 109–17, sermon 28. The head was formed by the king, princes and prelates, the eyes by judges and councillors, the ears by the religious, the tongue by doctors, the right hand by soldiers, and the feet by farmers and labourers. This drew upon John of Salisbury's social model in *Policraticus* (c.1159) that failed to include merchants, whom he regarded as involved in a sordid, selfish occupation and unable to contribute to the public good. See also Rigby, *English Society*, pp. 306–9; Mohl, *Three Estates*; Dickinson (ed.), *Policraticus*; Nederman, 'Virtues of necessity'; Brodie (ed.), *Tree of Commonwealth*, pp. 46–7; Nottingham University Library, MS 50

was intended to stress the reciprocal and complementary structure of hierarchical society, where all have to work justly and assiduously in their role in order for the body to function properly. Thomas Wimbledon's sermon at Paul's Cross in 1388 declared: 'And so eueri man trauayle [labour] in his degre, for whanne þe euen is come þat is þe ende of þe world, þanne euery man shal take reward, good oþer euyl, after þat he haþ trauayled here'.[61] Sin was the disruptive force that disrupted the unity of the 'body'. Individuals were directed to reform and turn away from sin in order to return society to a golden age of justice and harmony;[62] this was considered to be as important for merchants and traders as for any other class. In the 1320s, the writer of *The Simonie* stated:

> Fore somtyme were chepmen þat trewly boȝt and solde;
> Now is þe sise ybroke, and was noȝt ȝore yholde.
> Cheffare was woneþ to be ymaynteneþ al with trewþe;
> And now is al torneþ to trecherie; and þat is moche rewþe.[63]

Similarly, John Gower declared: 'In olden days everyone acted well, without deceit and without envy. Their buying and selling was honest, without trickery. But now everything is changed; if one speaks the truth, another lies. Very few are good companions. Therefore, one sees nowadays that everything is getting worse – both trades and merchandise.'[64] This convention of lamenting a lost 'Golden Age' not only emphasised the sins and corruption supposedly current in late medieval England, but also the possibility of reform with divine help, providing people performed their pre-ordained duties. Such accusations against merchants and traders were therefore part of a wider discourse that blamed social disruption on evils that were palpable within every part of society, even if their sins were manifest in differing ways.[65] The remedy was not institutional change but individual redemption.

The theory of social interdependence was also transposed onto the image of the town as a body corporate. This was emphasised in civic ceremonies and myths, particularly Corpus Christi processions in which the

---

(previously Lincoln Cathedral Library, MS A.6.2), fols. 68v–69v; Kail (ed.), *Twenty-Six Political and Other Poems*, pp. 64–8, 'The Descryvyng of Mannes Membres'.

[61] Owen, 'Thomas Wimbledon's sermon', 180, ll. 74–6.

[62] Rigby, 'England: literature and society', pp. 505–9.

[63] [Before a certain time were traders that truly bought and sold; / Now is the assize broken, and was not long held. / Trade was accustomed to be maintained with truth; / And now is all turned to treachery; and that is much lamented]. Embree and Urquhart (eds.), *The Simonie*, p. 99, B469–72.

[64] Gower, *Mirour*, p. 339, ll. 25801–12.

[65] For a similar discourse (*c*.1419–20), see Heyworth (ed.), *Jack Upland*, pp. 55–6, ll. 40–4, p. 65, ll. 251–4.

structure and unity of the town hierarchy was stressed. In Coventry, the order of the procession reflected the precedence of certain crafts in the town polity, with humble fishmongers and victuallers leading the way and wealthy drapers occupying the prestigious rear ranks.[66] Guild regulations often required all members to attend such festivities and pageants, to reaffirm their solidarity and craft status. Social theories were therefore subsumed and accepted by the urban authorities, and this was to influence the way in which such communities were governed.

Avarice and trade

The sins of the individual were therefore decried in estates theory as a cause of dissension in society, and traders and craftsmen came to be associated with particular vices.[67] Traders were particularly apt figures to exemplify the deadly sin of avarice (or covetousness), which encouraged acquisitiveness and selfishness to the destruction of others.[68] Covetousness was interpreted as an inordinate and selfish love of worldly goods, leading the avaricious man to use deceits, usury, theft, violence, false claims, sacrilege, simony, treachery, wicked crafts (such as prostitution or professional fighting) and gambling to gather riches. The avaricious did not think about God, their soul, the poor or the unfortunate in their pursuit of excessive gain.[69] It was a vice that could never be satisfied and knew no bounds: 'þe see drinkiþ al þe watres of þe world; so þe couetous mannes wille swoleweþ [swallow] alle þe richessis of þe world, þerfore he is þus vnsaciable (þat is, vnable to be fulfilled)'.[70] Another fifteenth-century

---

[66] Hilton, 'Status and class', pp. 14–15; James, 'Ritual'; Rubin, *Corpus Christi*, ch. 4; Phythian-Adams, 'Ceremony'; Justice, 'Trade symbolism'.

[67] Nottingham University Library, MS 50, fol. 80r; Gallagher (ed.), *Doctrinal*, pp. 147–8; *Jacob's Well*, p. 137, ll. 19–23.

[68] Little suggested that the rising importance of money and the commercial economy by the twelfth and thirteenth centuries promoted avarice as the primary vice above pride, which had been the traditional vice of the feudal nobility. However, Newhauser argues that this overlooks precedents for the importance of avarice in earlier moral writings, particularly in the fourth and fifth centuries. Little, 'Pride'; Newhauser, *Early History of Greed*. See also Bloomfield, *Seven Deadly Sins*, p. 95; Yunck, *Lineage*, pp. 185–6, 235–6, 273; Wood, *Medieval Economic Thought*, p. 54.

[69] *Ayenbite of Inwyt*, pp. 34–5, 44–5; *Vices and Virtues*, p. 30, ll. 5–23, p. 40, l. 14 – p. 41, l. 9; BL, MS Harleian 2398 ('Memoriale Credencium'), fols. 3v, 21v, 22r, 100v. Ross (ed.), *Middle English Sermons*, p. 264, l. 34 – p. 265, l. 25; Blake (ed.), *Quattuor Sermons*, p. 54, ll. 6–14; *Jacob's Well*, p. 117, ll. 12–25, p. 119, l. 32 – p. 120, l. 2; *Fasciculus Morum*, pp. 336–7; *Dives and Pauper*, I, ii, p. 254, ll. 26–31; Nelson (ed.), *Myrour*, p. 131, ll. 30–4 (BL, MS Harleian 45, fol. 63v); Power (ed.), *Goodman of Paris*, pp. 82–3, 89.

[70] Cigman (ed.), *Lollard Sermons*, p. 144, ll. 476–82.

Lollard sermon viewed the temptations of covetousness in typically rustic fashion, likening the vice to a dunghill. When gathered together a dunghill is stinking and rotten, but when the dung is spread on the fields it can bear fruit. Similarly, accumulation of wealth leads to a rotten soul, but remission can be gained by distributing riches to the poor.[71]

Most moral texts used avarice and covetousness as interchangeable terms.[72] *The Book of Vices and Virtues* (*c*.1400) declared, 'þe synne of couetise and auarice, þat is roote of alle yueles [evils], as seiþ seynt Poule'.[73] However, Robert of Brunne's *Handlyng Synne* (1303) distinguished subtly between covetousness and avarice, regarding avarice as an overarching, insatiable and consuming appetite, while covetousness was specific to an individual's love of the things of the world.[74] In a similar manner, Gower described Covetousness as the first of five daughters of Avarice (the others being Rapine, Usury, Simony and Stinginess), who selfishly desires worldly riches, subverts justice and neglects her soul in that pursuit.[75] Generally, however, avarice and covetousness were both vices that usurped both moderation and self-control.[76] Avarice was therefore regarded as a common motivation for the abuses of all estates, for it overcame Truth and seduced men from their traditional obligations.

John Trevisa, in his late fourteenth-century Middle English translation of Giles of Rome's *De Regimine Principum* (*c*.1270–85), declared: 'a man is to[o] coueitous of money ȝif al his workes bygynnen [begin] at money and endeþ at money'.[77] Avarice and covetousness were often personified as money-grubbing merchants or usurers. *The Romance of the Rose* (*c*.1230) declared:

> I say no merchant ever lives at ease.
> He has for life enlisted in the war
> Of gain, and never will acquire enough
> Though what he has he fears to lose, he runs
> After the remnant which he'll never possess.
> His only thought's to get his neighbour's goods.[78]

[71] *Ibid.*, p. 146, ll. 525–32. See also Morris (ed.), *Old English Homilies and Homiletic Treatises*, pp. 102–3; *Fasciculus Morum*, pp. 314–15.

[72] Peacock (ed.), *Instructions*, p. 39, ll. 1281–2; BL, MS Harleian 2398 ('Memoriale Credencium'), fol. 22r.

[73] *Vices and Virtues*, p. 30, ll. 5–6; I Timothy 6:10: 'For the love of money is the root of all evil'. See also *Ayenbite of Inwyt*, pp. 34–5; Chaucer, *Canterbury Tales*, 'Parson's Tale', p. 313, ll. 739–47.

[74] *Handlyng Synne*, pp. 174–5, ll. 5325–42; Furnivall (ed.), *Pilgrimage*, pp. 461–89.

[75] Gower, *Mirour*, p. 86, ll. 6181–216.   [76] Wood, *Medieval Economic Thought*, pp. 53–6.

[77] Fowler, Briggs and Remley (eds.), *Governance*, bk. II, pt. III, p. 269, ll. 10–12.

[78] Lorris and Meun, *Romance of the Rose*, pp. 108–11, ll. 4975–5182.

Sculptures and other images of avarice depicted rich men surrounded by chests and sacks of money, or with full moneybags hanging from their necks. Indeed, a purse or a pile of money was often the illustrative accoutrement for richly attired merchants, such as in an accompanying picture for a 1427 manuscript of *Piers Plowman*.[79] A fifteenth-century mural of the 'Seven Deadly Sins' at Hesset Church (Suffolk) appears to show the sin of Avarice represented by a humble retailer or baker grasping a bag of money. Avarice might also be depicted sitting at a counting table or before a money chest covered with coins.[80] This image was easily construed as a merchant, as implied by Chaucer's description of the merchant at his counting table in the 'Shipman's Tale'.[81]

The Castle of Perseverance outlined the intimate association of merchandise, avarice and sin:

And whanne thou vsyste marchaundyse,	*merchandise*
Loke that thou be sotel of sleytys;	*subtle; sleights*
And also swere al be deseytys;	*deceits*
Bye and sell be fals weytys;	*false weights*
For that is kyndë coueytyse.[82]	*natural*

The play suggested that traders readily used deceits, oaths, cunning and false measures, because they were close attributes to the sin of covetousness and the selfish desire for gain. Mankind in the play becomes beguiled by Covetousness's knowledge of money and the world:

Thi purs schal be thi beste frende	*purse; friend*
. . .	
If thou have a peny to pey,	*penny; pay*
Men schul to thee thanne lystyn and lende.[83]	*listen; lend*

It is only on his deathbed that Mankind finally realises that Covetousness has led him astray and that he will pay a bitter price.[84] Similarly,

---

[79] Pearsall and Scott (eds.), *Piers Plowman*, pp. lxxv–lxxvi, 'Merchant', fol. 102v; Scott, 'Illustrations', 69–70. Purses could also be depicted on noblemen.

[80] BL, Additional MS 28162, fol. 9v, 'La Somme le Roy (Paris, c.1290–1300); Oxford, Bodleian Library, MS Bodley 283, fol. 59r ('The Mirrore of the Worlde', c.1470–80); Grössinger, *World Upside-Down*, p. 132.

[81] Little, 'Pride', 26, 37–8; Gardner, *Minor English Wood Sculpture*, p. 25; Anderson, *Drama and Imagery*, plate 4a (Avarice at his counting table, Ingatestone, Essex); Chaucer, *Canterbury Tales*, 'Shipman's Tale', p. 204, ll. 75–88; Katzenellenbogen, *Allegories*, p. 58.

[82] Adams (ed.), *Chief Pre-Shakespearean Dramas*, 'The Castle of Perseverance', p. 273, ll. 851–5.

[83] *Ibid.*, 'The Castle of Perseverance', p. 279, ll. 2522, 2525–6.

[84] *Ibid.*, 'The Castle of Perseverance', p. 282, ll. 3018–20.

a fifteenth-century Lollard sermon stated: 'þe þridde synne is couetise... þere lernen also in þis cursid scole marchauntis and artificeres to be perfite in þis lore, wiþ wilis and wiþ falsede, for to gete good'.[85] Influenced by the same convention, William Langland personified Covetousness as a shabby miser who confessed to all the traditional sins of the trader ('wikke chaffare').[86]

Ultimately, theologians had long warned traders that it was difficult not to incur the sin of avarice through the buying and selling of goods, and this in turn led to fraud, deceit and lying. They cited biblical texts such as Ecclesiasticus 26:29, 'A merchant shall hardly keep himself from doing wrong'.[87] Many medieval scholars viewed merchants as invariably sinful, who could not desist from dishonesty and greed and who also undertook an occupation lacking any transformative skill or extensive labour. Instead, they made shameful profit ('turpe lucrum') through watching the market in order to buy and sell articles unaltered.[88] Even ascetic guides for anchorites in the twelfth and thirteenth centuries warned female recluses that involvement in commerce incited avarice and fraud.[89] Similarly, in the late fourteenth century, John Wyclif denounced clerics who acted as merchants and conducted themselves like crafty and false men of the world.[90]

Coin and money became supplementary symbols of materialistic greed and any process that made money was considered by moralists to be inherently grubby and sordid. This was aptly illustrated in the many depictions of misers counting money, while apes, the personification of debased man, were sometimes depicted as defecating or vomiting coins.[91]

---

[85] (the third sin is covetousness... there are taught also in this cursed school merchants and artisans to be perfect in this learning, with wiles and with falsehood, for to gain well.) Cigman (ed.), *Lollard Sermons*, p. 142, ll. 382, 409–11. See also Gallagher (ed.), *Doctrinal*, pp. 147–8; Royster, 'Middle English treatise', 22.

[86] *Piers Plowman*, A.V.107–30, B.V.188–212, C.VI.196–219.

[87] Wood, *Medieval Economic Thought*, p. 112 (also Ecclesiasticus 27:2: 'As a nail sticketh fast between the joinings of the stones; so doth sin stick close between buying and selling'); Lefébure (ed.), *St Thomas Aquinas*, II–II, q.58, a.11; Broomfield (ed.), *Thomae de Chobham*, pp. 290, 301; le Bras, 'Conceptions', iii, pp. 554–75; Haren, *Sin and Society*, p. 163; Bisson, *Chaucer*, pp. 172–3; Melitz and Winch (eds.), *Religious Thought*, pp. 15–38; Gilchrist, *Church and Economic Activity*, pp. 50–1.

[88] Wood, *Medieval Economic Thought*, pp. 112–13; Langholm, *Economics*, pp. 128–9, 573–4; Langholm, *The Merchant*, pp. 23, 29, 38, 44, 70, 113, 124, 234–5.

[89] Ayto and Barratt (eds.), *Aelred of Rievaulx's De Institutione Inclusarum*, p. 2, ll. 54–5, 66–70; Millett and Wogan-Browne (eds.), *Medieval English Prose*, pp. 134–5; Shepherd (ed.), *Ancrene Wisse*, pp. x, xxxv; Bozire and Colledge (eds.), *Chastising*, p. 207, ll. 11–20. See also *Piers Plowman*, A.Prol.58–63, C.Prol.59–64.

[90] Matthew (ed.), *English Works of Wyclif*, p. 172.

[91] Little, 'Pride'; BL, MS Additional 29253, fol. 410v; Murray, *Reason and Society*, pp. 27–30, 59–107.

Theologians argued that money enabled the acquisitive urge. However, they also recognised that money was an important tool for traders, as an artificial measure of value by which to compare very different commodities and equalise their exchange. Money facilitated the exchange of necessities, particularly those transported over great distances, as well as permitting commodities to be divided into smaller lots for different buyers. In the late fourteenth century, following Aristotelian commentators such as Giles of Rome, the French scholar Nicholas Oresme remarked: 'It was necessary, therefore, to find some medium, small in quantity, so that it may be transferred readily from place to place, and its depreciation or diminution easily weighed'.[92] Money was considered merely a human convention for balancing exchange and could not itself be bought and sold.[93] This conventional scholastic approach was tempered during the fourteenth century, as bullion shortages forced the debasement of coinage. Such debasement led theorists, such as Oresme and Giles of Rome, to recognise that coins had a precious metal content that was in demand and thus had an inherent value. Money was itself a commodity.[94]

Nevertheless, scholarly debates encouraged the idea that money was an added temptation towards avarice and venality. Moralists decried the development that all things were seemingly for sale, from property to salvation.[95] The power of money to submerge virtues was dramatised in Langland's depiction in *Piers Plowman* of 'Lady Mede', who tempered justice and oppressed the poor. She was the enemy of Truth and the Holy Church, and embodied the use of money for inordinate gain. However, she also represented the dual function of money in the economy and a recognition that money could be used for just reward for labour or service.[96] Church writers attempted formally to delineate the boundaries of trading behaviour, but this was complicated by their paradoxical view of trade as an embodiment of necessary endeavour as well as the accumulative urge. Most moralists increasingly argued that money-making could

---

[92] Burke (ed.), *Treatise*, pp. 19–21; Fowler, Briggs and Remley (eds.), *Governance*, bk. II, pt. III, pp. 266–7; Farber, *An Anatomy*, pp. 32–7; Lefébure (ed.), *St Thomas Aquinas*, pp. 232–53, vol. 38: Injustice, II–II, q.78.

[93] This notion was important for the theory of usury. See below, pp. 65–8.

[94] For a fuller discussion of medieval theories about money, see Wood, *Medieval Economic Thought*, pp. 69–88 (esp. 80–1).

[95] Greene (ed.), *Early English Carols*, pp. 261–3, no. 393; Robbins (ed.), *Historical Poems*, pp. 134–7, no. 51; BL, MS Royal 17.B.xlvii, fols. 160v–162r; Cambridge, Gonville and Caius College, MS 261, fol. 234r; Bromyard, *Summa Predicantium*, 'Avaritia'; Yunck, 'Medieval French money satire'; Camille, *The Gothic Idol*, pp. 258–63.

[96] Yunck, *Lineage*, pp. 5–10; Mitchell, 'Lady Meed'; Baldwin, *Theme of Government*, pp. 24–31.

be legitimised by justifiable intent, just as Mede might be controlled by Conscience and Reason. However, if the principal object of a merchant was cupidity then his trading activities were sinful.

Medieval portraits of merchants, and commerce in general, almost inevitably had connotations of avarice, selfishness and corruption. Although trade could be ostensibly undertaken without sin and for the common good, medieval moralists suggested that men of business in their pursuit of profit were disposed towards covetousness and thus, in turn, fraud, deceit and theft.[97] John Gower stated: 'I will not except a single one as not attending on Fraud – neither merchant nor victualler, nor retail shopkeeper. Everyone who knows how to beguile, beguiles others in his trade.'[98] Merchants and traders had become literary emblems of certain vices and through such images moralists sought to reinforce the message that everyone ought to be more aware of their social and spiritual responsibilities.

Medieval writers generally considered the sinful temptations associated with market trade to be rampant and rarely avoidable by a fallible mankind. The marketplace itself was depicted as a highly competitive forum in which exaggeration and fraud were expected on a daily basis: 'It is in the nature of a marketplace that everything is sold and bought there and that the sellers and buyers cheat each other'.[99] A Lollard sermon of the fifteenth century similarly described the market 'in whiche is miche [much] byinge and sellynge and deceite of hire breþeren as custummabli falleþ in such place'.[100] Several writers also suspected that apprentices were being indoctrinated in the secrets of fraudulent practices. Gower remarked: 'Just as an old whore trains and starts her young girls in the trade, I notice that Fraud likewise first teaches his young apprentice trickery and fraud, and then trains him to bargain and sell too'.[101] Wyclif deplored the situation where any apprentice or servant who was honest and truthful was held to be 'but a fool and vnþrifty'.[102] Bishop Brinton (late fourteenth century) summarised the standard moral view of traders in the medieval world:

---

[97] BL, MS Harleian 2398, fols. 3v, 100v; BL, MS Harleian 4894, fols. 68v, 180v; *Piers Plowman*, B. v.201–27; Gower, *Mirour*, p. 90, ll. 6505–13; *Handlyng Synne*, p. 193, ll. 5945–50; du Méril (ed.), *Poésies Populaires*, p. 131 ('Frequenter cogitans'); Mozley and Raymo (eds.), *Nigel de Longchamps*, p. 48, ll. 785–90; Ross (ed.), *Middle English Sermons*, p. 124, l. 24 – p. 125, l. 21 (BL, MS Royal 18.B.xxiii, fol. 94r); Oxford, Bodleian Library, MS Bodley 95, fol. 6r.

[98] Gower, *Mirour*, p. 346, ll. 26341–52. See also Stockton (ed.), *Major Latin Works*, 'Vox Clamantis', bk. v, ch. 14, pp. 214–15.

[99] *Fasciculus Morum*, pp. 558–9.   [100] Cigman (ed.), *Lollard Sermons*, p. 81, ll. 41–5.

[101] Gower, *Mirour*, p. 335, ll. 25741–7.

[102] Matthew (ed.), *English Works of Wyclif*, pp. 185–6, 238.

false traders, in these days, infringe the rule of justice. In every craft so much trickery is employed – in measures, in usury, in weight, in the balance, in mendacious mixtures and false oaths – that each man strives to deceive his neighbour, whom he should rather serve in mutual charity . . . Therefore let traders beware![103]

Such a stark image of deceit and falsity reinforced the message that common justice was being undermined. Fraud in trade was deliberately depriving one party of pertinent information that both buyer and seller had a moral and legal duty to disclose. This could include the intentional use of improper weights and measures, spoken deceptions, selling adulterated goods, counterfeiting and substituting good commodities for bad.[104] *The Simonie* and *Fasciculus Morum* suggested that there was scarcely any man in trade and crafts who was not dishonest.[105]

In several manuals concerning faith and penance, the sins of trade were categorised as the eighth branch (of ten) within the overall vice of avarice (alongside usury, theft, rapine, false claims, sacrilege, simony, treachery, wicked crafts and gambling).[106] The sins of buying and selling, as outlined by medieval moralists, can be summarised as:

- Unjust Prices – selling as dear as possible, but buying as cheaply as possible;
- Usury – giving usurious credit;
- False Oaths – swearing and lying in order to sell goods;
- False Wares – selling a different and inferior article from that first bargained for;
- Concealment – hiding the faults of an article;
- Misrepresentation – making merchandise look better than it was;
- False Weights and Measures;
- Lyther Bargaining – profiting by a purchaser's need.

We will examine these specific condemnations in turn.

Price and profit

The problem of what constituted a 'just price' or 'reasonable profit' was discussed by some of the most eminent medieval scholars. At a basic level, profit-making was considered a short step away from avarice and all the

---

[103] Devlin (ed.), *Sermons of Thomas Brinton*, pp. 214–15, sermon 48; cf. Owst, *Literature and Pulpit*, p. 353.

[104] Langholm, *The Merchant*, pp. 238–9.

[105] Embree and Urquhart (eds.), *The Simonie*, p. 100, B475–80, A361–6, C439–44; *Fasciculus Morum*, pp. 344–7. See also Jamieson (ed.), *Ship of Fools*, ii, pp. 222–3; Zeydel (ed.), *Ship of Fools*, pp. 327–30.

[106] See *Ayenbite of Inwyt*, pp. 44–5; *Vices and Virtues*, p. 40, l. 14 – p. 41, l. 9; *Jacob's Well*, p. 133, l. 17 – p. 134, l. 7; BL, MS Harleian 45, fol. 71r–v.

accompanying vices this entailed. Such sinful pursuit of gain might be particularly detrimental to the more vulnerable sectors of society. Indeed, for petty traders who served the poor with the necessities of life, excessive profits were deemed to be akin to theft and even homicide. Yet, the service provided by retailers to lowly consumers was often vital. In order to have a healthy marketplace and encourage a level of competition, traders needed to be allowed to make a fair living and maintain their households: thus profit-making was an integral part of their work.

Some of the contradictions of this commercial world were starkly laid out in Langland's personification of 'Lady Mede', through which he tackled the issues of just price and measurable reward.[107] Mede represented payments and rewards, the accepted glue of a materialistic world; yet she was also the destroyer of just price and the creator of venality and bribes.[108] In *Piers Plowman*, Holy Church feared that all corruptions stemmed from a union of False with Mede. Conversely, Theology argued that Mede was a potentially good force in society, representing the hire of labour, the medium of commerce and reward for good service. Instead of being intrinsically evil, she was, according to Theology, an innocent led astray by False. Thus, Mede's own personality is ambivalent;[109] she epitomises the ambiguous nature of a money economy, with its inordinate rewards, bribes and acquisitiveness of wealth ('mesurles'), but also its proportionate payments for service and simple exchanges in trade ('mesurable hire'; 'a penyworth for anoþer').[110] Ultimately, Conscience rejects the role of money and materialism in 'good' society arguing that the only true mede was heavenly reward. Langland perhaps yearned for an idealistic, simpler society which drove out the corrupting power of wealth, but his works also suggest that he recognised the futility of such idealism.[111] Consequently, it could be argued that his own strict ideology seems to have 'fragmented' as he attempted to reconcile the role of money and exchange with his sense of justice and community. Langland refined part of his argument in the C-Text of *Piers Plowman*, regarding

---

[107] *Piers Plowman*, C.III; Mitchell, 'Lady Meed'; Griffiths, *Personification*, pp. 26–35; Yunck, *Lineage*; Stokes, *Justice*, pp. 165–9.

[108] This is very similar to Gower's description of Covetousness. Gower, *Mirour*, pp. 86–7, ll. 6181–240.

[109] Godden, *Making*, pp. 34–7; Griffiths, *Personification*, p. 29; Murtaugh, *Piers Plowman*, pp. 40–3.

[110] 'In marchaundise is no Mede, I may it wel auowe; It is a permutacion apertly [open exchange], a penyworth for anoþer'; *Piers Plowman*, B.III.257–8. This does not necessarily imply 'mutual exchange for use' based on pre-market subsistence ideology, as suggested by Aers, *Chaucer*, p. 10. Instead it was a reiteration of the scholarly theory of commutative justice, see p. 58.

[111] Aers, *Chaucer*, pp. 1–37.

'mede' as unjust and declaring that there should be merely an exchange of one thing for another, directly proportionate in value. However, he also stated that traders should receive rightful 'mercede' for their services, and mercede was measurable according to the needs of their social degree. In this way, Langland appears to have accepted a compromise for the conduct of trade, constructed upon traditional social and religious theories, but disassociated from the corrupting power of Mede.

Langland's arguments relating to the nature of reward and justice are largely based upon traditional medieval theories of the 'just price' and commutative justice in exchanges. The just price was a guiding principle of economic ethics in the late medieval world and was one of the few ostensibly commercial topics which preoccupied theologians (together with usury). The commonplace deceits of traders were more often tackled in clerical manuals and secular satire than in the writings of Church academics. Nevertheless, medieval scholars discussed the just price not only in the context of theological preoccupations but also as a practical concern in applying ethical principles to the affairs of men. The basic principles of just price and equality in exchange were drawn from theologians, canonists and scholars of the twelfth and thirteenth centuries, such as Thomas Aquinas (1226–74) and Albertus Magnus (1193–1280), and continued to underlay the works of later centuries, even if there was still much debate. These scholars drew upon various influences, including the scriptures, classical theory, law and metaphysical theories of reason and justice. For instance, Roman law regarded free bargaining as the determinant of price, as long as there was no force or fraud, and extolled the maxim 'res tantum valet quantum vendi potest' (a thing is worth the amount for which it can be sold).[112] Aristotle's theory of exchange in *Nicomachean Ethics* (*c*.350BC) played down market forces and instead emphasised need or demand as the criterion of value. He was suspicious of business, acquisition and money, and saw only trade for necessities as natural. He was, nevertheless, interested in how the exchange of different, necessary articles could be achieved in 'commensurate' or just fashion and how money could be a useful intermediate in such exchanges.[113] Additionally, early medieval theologians, such as Augustine of Hippo (354–430), posited the ontological theory that objects had an inherent, constant value distinct from exogenous influences. This did not necessarily preclude fluctuating valuation for the purposes of human utility, but these theologians regarded unfettered market forces as incapable of determining a just price. There were moral standards and

[112] Langholm, *Legacy of Scholasticism*, pp. 20–42, 77–82.
[113] Wood, *Medieval Economic Thought*, pp. 133–5; Kaye, *Economy and Nature*, pp. 54–5.

estimations, external to the market, against which just exchanges ought to be judged.[114]

Thomas Aquinas attempted to reconcile these different sources of inspiration. In *Summa Theologiae*, he discussed whether something could be legitimately sold for more than its cost of production and identified two types of business exchange. The first was natural, necessary and virtuous, and involved the direct exchange of one commodity for another in order to allow the necessities of life to circulate. The second largely concerned traders and was the exchange of money for goods. This had the potential to be unnecessary and sinful since it fed the acquisitive urge. For such dealings, Aquinas stressed the connection between trade and justice: 'justice is first of all and more commonly exercised in voluntary interchanges of things, such as buying and selling'.[115] Drawing on the theories of Aristotle, Aquinas wanted commercial exchanges to be ruled by a twofold system of justice: commutative and distributive justice. Commutative justice was the achievement of arithmetic equivalence in exchanges, whereas distributive justice was geometric and related to the medieval theory of a hierarchical society in which everyone was accorded wealth according to their status.[116]

Aquinas recognised that the idea of an item with an absolute natural value was irreconcilable with the needs of everyday life: 'sometimes the just price cannot be determined absolutely, but consists rather in a common estimation, in such a way that a slight addition or diminution of price cannot be thought to destroy justice'.[117] Thus, he took into consideration the practical mechanisms of the marketplace and suggested that the just price was an estimation relating to the overt criteria of the market. Need, utility, labour, scarcity, risk, supply and demand were all recognised as legitimate comparative tools in calculating the extrinsic value of a commodity in the marketplace.[118] Aquinas did not give an exact formula

---

[114] Nederman, 'The monarch and the marketplace', 54–6; Langholm, *The Merchant*, pp. 235–7.

[115] Lefébure (ed.), *St Thomas Aquinas*, pp. 212–31, vol. 38: Injustice, II–II, q.77.

[116] Justice itself was the cardinal virtue of theology, divided into 'jus naturale' (natural justice) and 'jus positivum' (human or social justice). Every man was guaranteed a share in justice provided he ensured that others also received their particular share within the social structure (i.e. the common good). Lilley, 'Moral and spiritual factors', pp. 46–52; Langholm, *The Merchant*, p. 235.

[117] Lefébure (ed.), *St Thomas Aquinas*, II–II, q.77.

[118] Baldwin, 'Medieval theories', 74; Wood, *Medieval Economic Thought*, pp. 137–8; Lefébure (ed.), *St Thomas Aquinas*, pp. 216–21, vol. 38: Injustice, II–II, q.77, a.2. Albertus Magnus also reached this conclusion, eventually combining cost, supply and demand in his theory of value. Farber, *An Anatomy*, pp. 43–4; Langholm, *Economics*, p. 187; Kaye, *Economy and Nature*, pp. 68–9. For a further discussion of the theological debates concerning how an object might be valued (e.g. usefulness, work in making

for calculating the just price, arguing simply that both parties should find it acceptable and mutually advantageous. This meant expenses and a livelihood for the seller and a utility cost-benefit for the buyer. Both sides should benefit from an exchange while still maintaining justice.[119] According to Aquinas's theory, the just price effectively oscillated within a range determined by market forces. This accorded with the standards of commutative justice; equality of value between goods exchanged could be achieved by common estimation ('communis aestimatio'). Alexander of Hales (c.1186–1245) similarly stated that trade should be conducted 'by a just estimation of the thing, and by commerce, according to the way it is commonly sold in that city or place where trade occurs'.[120] Aquinas effectively argued that the market price could answer communal needs and social justice if reached without fraud or collusion.

Despite Aquinas's writings, some early twentieth-century historians argued that medieval theologians espoused a rigid just price based upon a labour and production theory of value alone, with no reference to market mechanisms of supply and demand. In this context, the just price supposedly protected producers from losses by establishing a price which stemmed from their costs and sustenance needs but also protected the poor from being overcharged.[121] William Ashley, Richard Tawney, George O'Brien and others viewed the just price as having been firmly entrenched in the feudal world and argued that it encumbered market development by protecting the inefficient producer and preventing the free flow of market forces.[122] In response, John Baldwin and Raymond de Roover instead asserted that the majority of medieval theologians had advocated a just price based upon free-market criteria of utility, scarcity and demand. Indeed, in their opinions, far from being a restriction upon

---

it, transportation, individual or communal need), see Farber, *An Anatomy*, pp. 50–65; Langholm, *The Merchant*, pp. 244–55.

[119] A stance supported by scholars such as Richard of Middleton (late thirteenth century). See Farber, *An Anatomy*, pp. 26–30.

[120] Wood, *Medieval Economic Thought*, p. 135. See also Langholm, *The Merchant*, pp. 245–6.

[121] Their theory was based largely upon a misreading of Henry de Langenstein (1325–97), who actually stated that the producer should charge enough to maintain his status and expenses. He did not suggest that the producer should expect to get this price, above the market estimation, nor did he contradict the workings of the market in formulating price. Indeed, Langenstein, like other medieval scholars, held that the just price should be determined by human needs and scarcity or abundance. De Roover, 'Concept', 418–20; Langholm, *Economics*, p. 583.

[122] For these early views see Ashley, *Introduction*, i, pp. 391–3; O'Brien, *An Essay*, pp. 111–12; Kaulla, *Theory*, pp. 37–44; Tawney, *Religion*, p. 40. Max Weber and Werner Sombart viewed guilds as the upholders of this ideal, protecting customers, preventing unfair competition, and providing the buyer with an assured standard of living. For a discussion about Weber and Sombart, see de Roover, 'Concept', 418–19.

practice, just price theory largely reflected the reality of competitive price-making in a free market.[123] The just price did not protect inefficient craftsmen or merchants or penalise the efficient and there was always competition and consumer resistance.[124] However, de Roover and Baldwin did accept that non-economic and institutional forces still played a part in price formation, and that the conditions of medieval marketing encouraged restrictions and intervention to ensure supplies of necessities at the lowest possible price. Medieval scholars may have accepted market practices and the forces of supply and demand in basic price formation, but their uncompromising views of commercial justice did not allow them to accept absolute competitive freedom for individual traders. Prices within the same market for the same commodity were still expected to be equivalent.

Ultimately, the ideal espoused by Aquinas was that of an open market, where participants were aware of their social and moral obligations and dealt without collusion and deception. However, the teachings of scholars and moralists emphasised human fallibility and avaricious tendencies, and they knew that a real marketplace could not be entirely free from sin and fraud. Individual morals would not be enough to maintain a just price for essential foodstuffs, but neither would competitive forces. Bernardino of Siena (1380–1444) and John Buridan (1300–58) suggested that there should be a general estimation of usefulness and supply for the whole market by a panel of prudent and knowledgeable men. Such men would base their statement of the just price upon a common estimation, probably established by the activities of wholesale bargaining. This theory may well have drawn upon actual urban practices.[125] There was thus an increasing acceptance of governmental intervention in the marketplace, plus an assumption by some moralists that governments would support Christian principles of social justice. When the free market failed to function properly, particularly during times of crisis, moralists began to argue that public authorities had the right to step in with price regulation and that a legal price would supersede the market price. This was, however, usually only applicable to necessities, for which the aim was to secure abundant supplies as cheaply as possible and eliminate middlemen or other price-raisers. Scholars like Alexander of Hales condemned monopolists as 'abominable', while Wyclif cursed combinations of merchants or victuallers who 'conspired wickedly together'

---

[123] Baldwin, 'Medieval theories'; Gilchrist, *Church and Economic Activity*, pp. 58–9; Barath, 'Just price', 413–30; de Roover, 'Concept'; de Roover, 'Scholastic economics', 163–5.
[124] Gilchrist, *Church and Economic Activity*, pp. 58–61.
[125] Langholm, *Economics*, pp. 261–2; Farber, *An Anatomy*, pp. 26–7. See below, pp. 222–31, for the actual workings of price-fixing in the market.

that none of them 'schal bie over a certeyn pris'.[126] The poor and honest consumers had to be protected in purchasing the necessities of life. By comparison, luxury and manufactured goods had a lower ceiling of demand and wider price variation was allowed, often dependent upon individual, free bargaining.[127]

The process of bargaining was expected to take into account the level of personal need and use appropriate to each party. The price estimated through free bargaining was therefore not strictly arithmetical; thirteenth-century scholars also took into account distributive (geometrical) justice for individually negotiated bargains, as long as both parties felt that they had gained from the deal and neither had taken advantage of the other's need ('lyther bargaining'). If the buyer valued an article more highly than the seller, the seller was still to abide by the principles of justice and thus sell at the lower valuation. However, this scheme of valuation also meant that a seller could charge above the normal market price if he would otherwise suffer loss through selling at a lower price.[128]

Indeed, although the theory of the just price was allied to market forces, not all medieval writers rejected every element of production costs and reasonable livelihood in their calculations. 'Distributive justice' was important in Aquinas's arguments and a distinction must be made between just price and just profit. Acceptable profits were based upon the level of improvements made to a commodity, either by skill, transportation or labour, as well as the means of subsistence required for a man of certain status. Aquinas understood riches to be either natural or artificial. Natural riches were those that supplied the natural needs of sustenance, housing and family. Artificial riches were sought for no purpose but the accumulation of riches themselves and these he classed as avaricious and unnecessary. Consequently, Aquinas considered unjust any intention to trade for self-gain or to profit beyond the maintenance of natural household needs.[129] Those who merely bought at a lower price and sold at a higher one, either during the same day or by hoarding goods and waiting for a price rise, were not deemed to have made any noticeable improvements on goods. Thus, regraters, forestallers and

---

[126] Wood, *Medieval Economic Thought*, pp. 138–43; Arnold (ed.), *Select English Works*, p. 333, ch. 28 ('The Grete Sentence of Curs Expounded').

[127] De Roover, 'Concept', 425–8.

[128] Kaye, *Economy and Nature*, pp. 79–115; Wood, *Medieval Economic Thought*, pp. 149–52; Langholm, *Economics*, pp. 232–3. See below, pp. 63–4.

[129] Sigmund (ed.), *St Thomas Aquinas*, pp. 73–4; Baldwin, *Masters*, i, pp. 263–4; Lefébure (ed.), *St Thomas Aquinas*, pp. 225–31, vol. 38: Injustice, II–II, q.77, a.4. The theory that traders should only gain what is necessary to their livelihood is reiterated in fifteenth-century sermons. Blake (ed.), *Quattuor Sermons*, p. 32, ll. 17–34.

engrossers were disparaged because their services were not recognised within the traditional schema of identifiable labour or improvement, and because of suspicions that they caused unreasonable price hikes to the deception of their customers.[130]

Medieval theories on just profit can be partially regarded as economically sound by modern standards. Nevertheless, writers of the late Middle Ages considered most production costs, expenses and living costs to be fairly static, even as levels of supply fluctuated; only variations in supply and demand should produce proportionate changes in the market price.[131] In other words, the just price was the market price because other additional elements in price formation were expected to be constant, particularly for foodstuffs and necessities. Medieval theologians thus supposed that there were measurable criteria upon which moderate profits could be calculated. This notion was even more important for the petty retailer than for the producer, since officials in the market had less control over the base price of wholesale goods (determined by bargaining and supply) than they did over the activities of local retailers and artisans. Retailers' profits could be strictly controlled according to the level of market prices.[132]

Medieval theories of the just price need to be understood in the context of actual economic practices. Market prices were a major part of the 'just price', which could vary with time and place, while aspects of production costs and expenses were also applied to medieval justifications of profit.[133] However, in essence, the just price was accepted as the market price that both vendor and purchaser were willing to accept, provided that any deceit, manipulation or coercion had been excised

---

[130] See below, pp. 117–20.

[131] See below, pp. 231–48. The assizes operated on this theory of stable costs and living expenses.

[132] Secular lawyers draw upon Roman law in suggesting that market traders made a gross error ('leasio enormis') if they sold goods in excess of 50 per cent above the market (just) price. Wood, *Medieval Economic Thought*, pp. 148–9; Langholm, *Economics*, p. 55; Baldwin, 'Medieval theories', 67–8. However, there is little indication that English market officials applied this specific margin in their assessment of 'excessive price', while moralists were often more stringent in their admonitions. Thomas de Chobham (c.1158–1235) stated: 'the secular law says that no seller is allowed to receive above half the just price for the goods he sells, but it is a sin if he has received anything above the just price'. Broomfield (ed.), *Thomae de Chobham*, p. 302 (cf. Wood, *Medieval Economic Thought*, p. 149).

[133] Langholm sees this as part of the 'double rule' elucidated by medieval scholars, whereby a seller may increase the normal market price in order to cover a loss. In other words, the seller can justly claim indemnity if it is rightly associated with legitimate labour and costs, though this may be to their own disadvantage in a competitive marketplace. In contrast, a seller should not raise the price above the market estimation if the buyer gains advantage from the bargain, nor exploit the buyer if they are in great need. Langholm, *The Merchant*, pp. 253–5; Langholm, *Economics*, pp. 579, 583.

from the deal.[134] William of Pagula, in his *Speculum Regis Edwardi III* (c.1331), also advanced principles of market liberty, free contract and a 'true price', as the best means to protect producers from economic exploitation and to aid the common good.[135] For William, the true price was that achieved when both buyer and seller had reached amicable agreement; an unregulated market price that depended on locality, supply and demand. In a similar vein, Alain de Lille, in the late twelfth century, had stated: 'A thing bought by the laws of the market place is not dearly bought for there the buyer and seller are equal in the deal'; though he also warned against those who might knowingly use flattery and guile to influence a bargain: 'there is nothing under heaven more dearly bought than what long wheedling buys with a blushing face'.[136] Medieval moralists thus attempted to impose an ethical rationalisation and moral framework upon normal market activity, rather than taking a proactive interventionist stance.

There was also discussion regarding the flow of information and attempts to take advantage of the necessity or weakness of the seller or buyer. Aquinas asked whether a merchant with a load of grain to sell in a famine-stricken area, where prices were high, was obliged to tell customers that ample supplies were on their way and thus lower the price and his profits. Aquinas's solution was that the merchant was not obliged to tell according to strict justice, though a virtuous merchant probably would.[137] This was an explicit acceptance of the competitive and impersonal urges of the marketplace as a practical means to ascertain the 'just' price, but also involved an additional appeal to individual morals. As long as trade was conducted within certain moral parameters, theologians approved of buying in cheap markets and selling in dear markets at prevailing prices.

Pragmatic theological attitudes towards pricing and marketing filtered down to confessional manuals and sermons in a simpler, more concise form. The *Dispute between a Good Man and the Devil* (c.1400) discussed the issues of justifiable profit, particularly focusing on the concept that a trader should provide first for his own needs and, beyond that, for church offerings and for the poor.[138] A late fourteenth-century text, *Memoriale*

[134] Baldwin, 'Medieval theories', 43; Bolton, *Medieval English Economy*, p. 335; Kaye, *Economy and Nature*, p. 98; Langholm, *The Merchant*, pp. 246–7.
[135] Nederman, 'The monarch and the marketplace', 56–8.
[136] Thomson and Perraud (eds.), *Ten Latin Schooltexts*, 'Parabolae' of Alain de Lille, p. 301, 2.13.
[137] Lefébure (ed.), *St Thomas Aquinas*, pp. 222–5, vol. 38: Injustice, II–II, q.77, a.3; de Roover, 'Concept', 422; Gilchrist, *Church and Economic Activity*, p. 60.
[138] Horstmann (ed.), *Minor Poems*, p. 342, esp. ll. 521–7.

Credencium, similarly justified profits provided they are made without covetousness and fraud.[139] Pastoral guides also reiterated the need for just prices and equal exchange. Some works, such as the prose dialogue *Dives and Pauper*, understood Aquinas's reasoning that traders needed to sell goods for more than they bought them or else they would not be able to make a living or give alms.[140] In fact, it appears that the writer of *Dives and Pauper* had access to Aquinas's work, since he drew almost directly upon Aquinas's arguments and effectively summarised some of his main conclusions. Pauper castigates Dives for pursuing worldly gain at the risk of 'heuene blysse', but reassures him that God does not hate the rich, only those who are niggardly and fail to dispense alms and keep the Ten Commandments. Selling goods for more than they are worth is necessary for a trader to sustain himself and for him to help the poor: 'Sent Powyl [St Paul] seith þat no man is holdyn to trauaylyn [labour] on hys owyn costys [own costs] for þe comounte [community], neyþer in knyȝthod ne in chapmanhod ne in warcmanchepe'.[141] Dives personifies the newly literate, worldly, yet pious layman, striving to understand theological injunctions. Indeed, the text of *Dives and Pauper* appears to question the conventional understanding of market mechanisms. Dives complains that it is hard to know the 'ryte value of a thing'. The reply is that a just price can be obtained by 'comoun estymacion', with 'a thing is as mychil worth as it may ben sold to be comoun merket' at the time ('tanti valet quanti vendi potest'), reflecting the Roman maxim that was also incorporated in *Corpus Iuris Civilis* (529–34).[142] This was also the concept adopted and adapted by Aquinas.

Dives and Pauper asked whether a commodity could be sold for more than it was worth 'be comoun estimacion' and the answer is a mixture of pragmatism and moral stricture. As long as no fraud was involved, a trader might sell a commodity to one man for more than he might to another, if the man needed it greatly and the seller could not sell it for less because it would cause loss. However, if no loss occurred to the seller then he should sell it by common estimation and not for greater profit. The author also suggested that the buyer should recompense the seller if the former made a great gain while the latter made a loss, but recognised that the law as it stood could not compel such an act; only conscience could do so.[143] *Dives and Pauper* thus reflects very similar teachings to those espoused by Aquinas, indicating that certain ethical principles remained significant throughout the late Middle Ages.

---

[139] BL, MS Harleian 2398, fol. 100v.   [140] *Dives and Pauper*, I, ii, pp. 149–56.
[141] *Ibid.*, I, ii, pp. 155–6.   [142] Farber, *An Anatomy*, p. 44.
[143] *Dives and Pauper*, I, ii, pp. 153–5.

Usury

Theories of justice, or more precisely injustice, were also applied to arguments about usury in the late Middle Ages, which was a sin often associated with merchants and traders.[144] Usury was strictly defined as any gain beyond the principal in a loan or sale, and was prohibited by the Second Lateran Council (1139).[145] It was considered to be a sin against natural justice because the lender was seeking profit without any requisite input or labour and money itself cannot reproduce.[146] Money was merely a medium for exchange, not a commodity in itself. Any money borrowed should be therefore returned in the same amount to the lender.[147] No charge was to be levied upon the use of money, because money could only perform one service for its owner and its ownership was transferred when borrowed.[148] As John Trevisa stated, 'in vsura þe vse is raveysched and wrongfullich itake'.[149]

Usury was therefore attacked vigorously in early canon law as an immoral means of gaining something from nothing.[150] Manifest usurers were seen as having made money from money without labour or service and at the expense of the poor and needy. *Fasciculus Morum* stated that a

[144] E.g. *Fasciculus Morum*, pp. 348–53; BL, MS Harleian 2398, fol. 21v ('Memoriale Credencium' – for a different version of the same text, see Kengen (ed.), *Memoriale Credencium*, p. 100, ll. 5–17); Royster, 'Middle English treatise', 29–30; *Handlyng Synne*, p. 181, ll. 5539–52.

[145] The main categories of usury were: (1) lending against collateral, (2) lending without collateral, but expecting and receiving interest, (3) using inherited money originally acquired by usury, (4) lending at interest through agents or servants, (5) lending another's goods supposedly kept in safety, (6) speculation by buying cheap and selling dear, (7) taking advantage of urgent needs of the poor, (8) buying on speculation before the proper time for selling, (9) retention of profit on money originally taken for surety, (10) retaining the deposit even after the full sum had been paid, (11) demanding full security with half the profits that may accrue to the borrower, (12) accepting excessive work in the payment of a bad debt. See Lefébure (ed.), *St Thomas Aquinas*, pp. 232–53, vol. 38: Injustice, II–II, q.78; *Dives and Pauper*, I, ii, p. 200, ll. 59–83; *Fasciculus Morum*, pp. 348–53; *Vices and Virtues*, pp. 30–1; *Jacob's Well*, p. 122, l. 26 – p. 124, l. 28; Peacock (ed.), *Instructions*, p. 12, ll. 372–83.

[146] Fowler, Briggs and Remley (eds.), *Governance*, bk. II, pt. III, p. 268, l. 36 – p. 269, l. 37.

[147] Wood, *Medieval Economic Thought*, pp. 69–88.

[148] This was based upon the Roman law notion of money as a fungible (i.e. consumed during use). See Wood, *Medieval Economic Thought*, pp. 75–6; Lefébure (ed.), *St Thomas Aquinas*, pp. 232–53, vol. 38: Injustice, II–II, q.78; *Dives and Pauper*, I, ii, p. 197, ll. 42–8.

[149] (in usury the use is ravished/rapined and wrongfully taken.) Fowler, Briggs and Remley (eds.), *Governance*, p. 269, ll. 40–1.

[150] Baldwin, 'Medieval theories', 36; Haren, *Sin and Society*, pp. 164–5. For a discussion of the theories behind the prohibition of usury, see Langholm, *Economics*; McLaughlin, 'Teaching', i, 81–147, and ii, 1–22; Baldwin, *Masters*, chs. xiv and xv; Gilchrist, *Church and Economic Activity*, pp. 62–70; Wood, *Medieval Economic Thought*, ch. 7.

usurer was sinful, 'because he sells to his poor neighbour what he owes him freely by the law of nature, namely help in his need'.[151] Usury was, in effect, theft. The intention to make a profit was the deciding factor in determining the usurious nature of certain transactions: 'what is freely given and freely accepted does not lead to usury, as long as there is no corrupt intention, for usury always rests upon such expectation or intention. Thus, whoever loans money with such expectation, whatever profit he makes is usury.'[152] As regards trade and exchange, those who sold something for more than it was worth at the time, or bought it for much less than its value, were accused of usury. These usurious traders, as much as the moneylenders, were seen as taking advantage of the needs of the poor.[153] Through such compulsion, usurers were ignoring their duty to the common good.

Memoriale Presbiterorum, dating from the mid-fourteenth century, discussed the selling of merchandise on credit, as well as the idea that delayed payment should be higher than the price at the time of sale because the merchant could otherwise gain goods from the money in the meantime. However, the author rejected this approach as unjustifiable profit.[154] Usurers were, in effect, selling time, which was a violation of natural and divine law. As Thomas de Chobham stated: 'The usurer does not sell the debtor something which is his own, but time, which belongs to God'.[155] However, Diana Wood and Odd Langholm have posited that the Roman maxim that time could be owned by individual sellers was revived and debated by scholars in the fourteenth century.[156] In this view, time could alter an article's value or quality and this therefore allowed merchants to speculate on future prices in credit sales without incurring the accusation of usury. Seasonal variations, natural reproduction and changes in supply and demand could all mean a natural increase or decrease in the price

---

[151] *Fasciculus Morum*, pp. 346–7. See also Bromyard, *Summa Predicantium*, 'Usura'.

[152] *Fasciculus Morum*, pp. 350–3. 'It is vsure for to lene for wynnynge' [It is usury to lend for gain], from Gallagher (ed.), *Doctrinal*, pp. 146–7; 'usurie is qwan a man lenyth for wynning be couenaunt preuy or opyn' ['usury is when a man lends for gain by private or open agreement'], from BL, MS Sloane 3160, fol. 20r. See also *Ayenbite of Inwyt*, pp. 35–7; van Zutphen (ed.), *A Litil Tretys*, p. 8, ll. 29–34 (BL, MS Royal 8.c.i, fol. 148r); *Dives and Pauper*, I, ii, pp. 195–8.

[153] *Ayenbite of Inwyt*, pp. 35–7; *Vices and Virtues*, p. 31, ll. 23–32, p. 32, ll. 2–17; *Fasciculus Morum*, pp. 348–51; Zeydel (ed.), *Ship of Fools*, pp. 302–3; Bowers, 'A Middle English mnemonic poem', 226–32; *Dives and Pauper*, I, ii, pp. 202–3, ll. 58–67.

[154] Haren, *Sin and Society*, p. 166.

[155] Broomfield (ed.), *Thomae de Chobham*, p. 504, cf. Wood, *Medieval Economic Thought*, p. 174. For 'selling time', see Furnivall (ed.), *Pilgrimage*, pp. 473–7, ll. 17689–822; Wood, 'Lesyng of tyme', pp. 107–16.

[156] Wood, *Medieval Economic Thought*, pp. 174–7; Langholm, *Economics*, pp. 311–15, 369–70.

of goods borrowed. This was not, it should be noted, the same as asking for a higher repayment simply because time had passed, which was still regarded as unjust and usurious.

The main concern of medieval moralists was intention. Transactions escaped accusations of usury if a fair risk and doubt was involved in ascertaining the value of the goods at a future date.[157] For instance, usury was not involved if the creditor bore his fair share of the risks as well as the profits in a similar way to partners in a business contract or a merchant on his voyage. Consequently, upon the basis of intention, justifications were developed for 'interest'. It could be legitimised as: a penalty for the late payment of a loan; a charge to compensate another investment lost; a fee for labour (such as travel and accounting); and compensation for the risk of possible loss and the uncertainty of enterprise.[158] In essence, interest was legitimate where it was a means to avoid loss.[159] There were thus increasing numbers of loopholes in canonical sanctions, especially for traders rather than manifest moneylenders.[160] *Fasciculus Morum* allowed claims for damages in contracts, provided this was used to enforce the payment of a debt or to punish an illegal creditor rather than to increase the debt. Also, damages could be claimed if a loan had not been repaid on a requested date, thus causing loss to the creditor in their own business dealings.[161] As with trade, usurers could justify their profits upon the basis of risk or losses. Such accommodation was widespread by the fourteenth and fifteenth centuries as a means of allowing trading credit to exist within the fundamental prohibition of usury.[162] Consequently, at an international level, many devices were employed to hide interest.[163] Even at a local level, it appears that commercial creditors found ways around prohibitions, which were often enforced only in exorbitant cases.[164] By the fifteenth century, *Dives and Pauper* recognised that the sin of usury, while still evil and unlawful, was suffered in practice in order to encourage rich men to lend to the needy and poor.[165]

---

[157] McLaughlin, 'Teaching', 117; Haren, *Sin and Society*, p. 167.

[158] Gilchrist, *Church and Economic Activity*, p. 67, McLaughlin, 'Teaching', 125 (from Hostiensis); *Fasciculus Morum*, pp. 348–53.

[159] This included a developing concept of 'opportunity costs', which relates to the value of the next-best alternative use for a resource that is passed up when making a (business) decision. Epstein, *An Economic and Social History*, p. 136.

[160] Thomson, 'Wealth, poverty', pp. 271–8; le Goff, *Your Money*, p. 92.

[161] *Fasciculus Morum*, pp. 348–51.

[162] Gilchrist, *Church and Economic Activity*, pp. 65–7. For canonical law on usury, see *ibid.*, pp. 165, 173, 182–3, 189–92, 194–6, 206. See also Friedberg (ed.), *Corpus Iuris Canonici*, ii, cols. 812–15, 1081–2 (Decretal Gregor. ix, Lib. v, Tit. xix, De Usuris; Sexti Decretal, Lib. v, Tit. v, De Usuris).

[163] Gilchrist, *Church and Economic Activity*, pp. 64–5.   [164] See below, pp. 213–15.

[165] *Dives and Pauper*, I, ii, p. 202, ll. 58–65.

Many modern historians have claimed that the Church misunderstood the mechanisms of interest and thus hampered the flow of credit that was so vital for economic growth.[166] In fact, it is likely that the Church was attempting to protect the consumer credit for the more vulnerable sectors of society. Early incarnations of usury law were therefore related more to the need for consumption loans for poorer sectors rather than to the transactional requirements of traders.[167] Indeed, the economic theories of Church scholars were not entrenched in traditional feudal notions to the exclusion of the expanding market economy. Theologians give every indication that they took account of the mechanisms of the market and continued to do so, addressing such issues as flexible prices, competition, middlemen, capital accumulation, speculation and functioning credit systems. The Church modified its attitudes significantly to commercial matters, such as usury, throughout the medieval period. However, this does not mean that writers could escape the need to espouse traditional Christian ethics.

Bargaining and oaths

The theory of the just price and honest profit was based upon the operation of market forces without avarice, fraud, usury and other vices. Hence, many moralists devoted their energies towards the elimination of fraudulent and dishonest practices. As already discussed, William Langland highlighted the need for justice in transactions, both in proportionate gain and honest dealing. One particular passage from *Piers Plowman*, involving Gluttony's expedition to the tavern, parodies commercial exchange, price-setting and the principle of one pennyworth for another. It is a burlesque and humorous episode, but the passage can be also interpreted as an indictment of wasteful and petty sectors of society.[168] In one section, the customers take part in a game of 'newe feire'.[169] This consists of evaluating the values of a cloak and a hood, belonging respectively to Clement the cobbler and Hikke the hosteler. The unequal value of the goods that are to be exchanged has to be made 'feire' by the man

---

[166] Melitz and Winch (eds.), *Religious Thought*, pp. 85–91.

[167] Gurevich, *Categories*, pp. 271–3; Tawney, *Religion*, pp. 37–9.

[168] See below, pp. 112–13 for a further discussion of the Gluttony passage and of Langland's preoccupation with petty traders and other lowly sectors of society.

[169] A so-called 'Newe Feire' developed informally as a market in the Cheapside area of London. This informal market had attracted disreputable elements of society and led to numerous fights, thefts and murders, before being abolished by the City authorities in 1297. It is possible that the reputation of this 'Newe Feire' still resided in the common memory. Riley (ed.), *Munimenta Gildhallae*, ii, 'Liber Custumarum', pp. 96–7.

who gains the more valuable object. The two protagonists choose two chapmen to appraise the items, but they find that they cannot agree on their valuations so they ask Robin the rope-maker to adjudicate. When agreement is reached, the receiver of the greater priced item is required by the mediator ('noumpere') to make up the debt by standing a round of drinks.[170] Anyone who wants his property back, and thus defaults on the game, has to pay for a gallon of ale for everyone. In this parody of a commercial transaction, there is exchange, common bargaining, evaluation by independent witnesses, adjudication of a dispute, the idea of just price and a distribution of excess profit to the common 'good'. Marketplace morality was a commonplace for these characters. However, by staging this scene in an alehouse, Langland highlighted the potential corruptibility of scholarly ethics in exchange, as well as the conflict between moral ideals and practical behaviour.[171]

Medieval clerics and moralists found actual market mechanisms disquieting, especially the process of exchange and bargaining which lay at the heart of many commercial transactions. In marketplace haggling, sellers often extol their goods while buyers denigrate them; both parties have to be on their guard.[172] Bargaining is described in a very realistic style in various medieval 'dialogues'.[173] These texts were used to teach languages and consisted of lines of conversation, much as can be found in modern language textbooks. The two-handed cut and thrust of a commercial transaction was obviously an ideal format for practising a language and, consequently, aspects of the dialogue appear to be based in realism. In 1483, William Caxton reprinted a fourteenth-century dialogue and suggested that merchants would find it of great use in their dealings: 'And to knowe many wares / which to hym shalbe good to be bouȝt [bought] / Or solde for riche to become. / Lerne [learn] this book diligently; / Great prouffyt [profit] lieth therin truly'.[174] The text included repartee in a cloth shop, with the buyer and seller haggling over the price, cut and measuring of the cloth, as well as delivery costs and the type of money to be exchanged. A typical extract includes an exaggeration of the price, an appeal to the need to make a profit, a declaration of a better market price elsewhere and the tying of the price to the quality of the cloth:

---

[170] *Piers Plowman*, A.V.166–82, B.V.318–44, C.VI.372–99; see Stokes, *Justice*, pp. 170–1.
[171] See pp. 112–13 for a discussion of literary portrayals of alehouses and inns.
[172] Langholm, *The Merchant*, p. 239.
[173] See Bradley (ed.), *Dialogues*; CUL, MS ii.vi.17, fols. 100v–106v; Kristol (ed.), *Manières de Langage*.
[174] Bradley (ed.), *Dialogues*, p. 4, ll. 3–7.

'Dame, what hold ye the elle of this cloth? Or what is worth the cloth hole? In shorte to speke, how miche thelle?'

'Syre, resone; I shall doo to you resone; Ye shall haue it good cheep.'

'Ye, truly, for catell, Dame, me must wynne [gain]. Take hede what I shall paye.'

'Four shelynges [shillings] for the elle, Yf it plese you.'

'Hit ne were no wysedom. For so moche wold I haue Good scarlete!'

'Ye haue right yf ye maye. But I haue yet somme whiche is not of the beste, which I wold not yeue [give] for seuen shelynges.'

'I you bileue [believe] well; But this is no suche cloth of so moche money, that knowe ye well! This that ye shall leue shall be solde.'

'Syre, what is it worth?'

'Dame, it were worth to me well thre shellyngs.'

'That is euyll boden [evil offer], or to moche axed [too much asked]; yet had I leuer [given] that it were gold in your cheste.'

'Damoyselle, ye shold not lese theron neuer a crosse [i.e. penny]; but saye certainly how shall I haue it withoute thynge to leue [give].'

'I shall gyue it you at one worde: certaynly, if ye haue it, ye shall paye fyue [five] shellyngs for so many elles which ye shall take; for I wyll abate no thyng.'[175]

The deal is concluded by a process of haggling, exaggeration and possibly downright lying. The parties continue to discuss measurements and the type of coinage, but Caxton eventually describes them as content with the bargain. They even trust one another enough not to call on the services of the official measurer, though this potential recourse is mentioned at one point and the seller calls the bluff. Although bargaining is an informal process, such dialogues hint that it was informed both by knowledge of etiquette and the potential support of official enforcement when required. Caxton argued that the text could provide guidance to traders and customers on how to bargain for any sort of merchandise and, presumably, how to reach an amicable agreement.[176]

Similarly, other late fourteenth- and fifteenth-century dialogues provide an elementary guide to how a conversation in an inn might proceed, including the ordering of rooms and meals. There is little moral guidance involved here since it is intended more as a practical guide to language. Consequently, in one dialogue the female innkeeper is presented in a

---

[175] *Ibid.*, pp. 14–18.
[176] For a brief discussion of how early modern bargaining was viewed in a similar fashion, see Muldrew, *Economy of Obligation*, p. 43.

fairly straightforward light. She haggles over certain prices, but her inn provides a range of services (looking after the horses, washing clothes), her ale is declared worthy of the payment and she provides numerous types of food (meat, bread, cheese, fruit).[177] The male hosteler in another script is more discourteous at first, thus livening up the dialogue, but soon reverts to the innkeeper's traditional flattery.[178] He describes his accommodation as 'good and honest, fit for the king if he should please to lodge here', and the rooms prove to be clean and well-kept. He also provides a fire and a variety of poultry, which is freshly purchased from the market, though again the dialogue provides an opportunity for haggling over the price. In this instance, the traveller openly accuses the innkeeper of charging much more than he originally paid for the poultry. This is not the clean-cut hosteler of the previous dialogue. Indeed, the ostensibly clean room hides a multitude of rats and mice that the innkeeper claims will be caught, while the implication that the traveller will find at the inn 'two beautiful girls, as you usually have' perhaps draws upon accusations that many inns doubled as brothels.

Such matter-of-fact representations of the usefulness of the bargaining procedure are far removed from traditional depictions in religious works. A homily of the twelfth century saw market processes as inherently fraudulent and evil:

The seller priceth his goods dear and saith they are well worth it or better worth it. The buyer biddeth little for them and saith they are not worth it, and they both lie; the seller bateth somewhat of his price, and sweareth that he will not sell it for less; the buyer increaseth his bid and sweareth he will not give more. Then cometh the devil and communeth with the thoughts of each, and causes the seller to take less than he swore and then the buyer to give less than he swore.[179]

Here, haggling is presented in a different way; the practical trading processes are condemned as deceitful and 'hindering'. They are even akin to perjury because often the parties involved have sworn the truth of their assertions: 'and with this snare catcheth the devil all who thus buyeth and selleth'.[180] In the late fourteenth century, John Gower similarly lamented the bargaining techniques of traders:

As for the selling, the price will be doubled or trebled more than the article is worth. To accomplish this, he swears by his God and by all His names, until he is able to deceive the customer by vain words. Thus the young apprentice, taught

---

[177] CUL, MS ii.vi.17, fols. 100v–106v. See also Bradley (ed.), *Dialogues*, pp. 49–50.
[178] Kristol (ed.), *Manières de Langage*; Myers (ed.), *English Historical Documents*, pp. 1212–13.
[179] Morris (ed.), *Old English Homilies of the Twelfth Century*, pp. 212–15.
[180] *Ibid.*, pp. 214–15.

by his master Fraud, defrauds others in selling; that which costs him five or six he offers to you at ten or twelve, swearing and saying that lower he cannot go without losing a great deal. So he leads you on until he has confused you so much that you believe him.[181]

The bargaining process, with its integral deceptions and oaths, eluded the moralists' sense of what was right. John Gower was not prepared to accept the methods involved in comparing the measures of quality, supply, quantity and added value in order to reach a just price. Instead, he wondered why a fair price could not just be estimated and accepted between the parties, based on known criteria.

The spiritual quandary remained that, in practice, bargaining involved a number of aspects that were vilified by the Church. In the eyes of moralists, traders were renowned for tricks of flattery, false oaths and 'tongis dowble'.[182] In particular, oath-breaking and false swearing were vilified as frequently used elements of the traders' verbal armoury in assuaging the doubts of customers. A mid-fifteenth-century Lollard sermon described how traders might use oaths in the bargaining process in order to support their claims about original prices.[183] However, such use of oaths took God's name in vain through their frequent application, and also endangered traders' souls when they pushed the margins of truth. The persistent image was of chapmen who cared not what they swore provided they made a profit. Wyclif decried those who beguiled their customers through swearing by Christ and God that their commodities cost so much and were true and wholesome. Yet, those that deceived the people by tricks and subtleties were also seemingly praised for their skill in using these tactics.[184] In such writings there was recognition that lying and concealment of the truth were essential facets of the traders' make-up even though they were also morally deplorable.

Jacob's Well (c.1440) explained the trader's own situation starkly: 'I muste swere nedys and forswere me in chaffaryng and in other wyse;

---

[181] Gower, *Mirour*, p. 338, ll. 25741–64 (also p. 332, ll. 25333–44). For guile becoming the apprentice of the shopkeeper, see *Piers Plowman*, A.II.173–6, B.II.214–17, C.II.221–4.

[182] 'Tongis dowble' [tongues double] is from a late fourteenth-century moral stanza: Kane, 'Middle English verse', 60, l. 14. For false oaths, see also Royster, 'Middle English treatise', 22, 30; BL, MS Harleian 4894, fols. 180v–181r (Robert Rypon); BL, MS Harleian 2398, fol. 100v ('Memoriale Credencium'); *Ayenbite of Inwyt*, p. 44; Stockton (ed.), *Major Latin Works*, 'Vox Clamantis', bk. v, ch. 13, pp. 213–14; *Piers Plowman*, B.XIII.379–82.

[183] Cigman (ed.), *Lollard Sermons*, p. 47. See also Morris (ed.), *An Old English Miscellany*, p. 76, ll. 139–44; *Fasciculus Morum*, pp. 370–3; BL, MS Harleian 2398, fol. 100v ('Memoriale Credencium').

[184] Matthew (ed.), *English Works of Wyclif*, p. 238. See also Haren, *Sin and Society*, p. 170 (for 'Memoriale Presbiterorum'); Owst, *Literature and Pulpit*, pp. 414–25.

ellys no man wyll beleuyn me'.[185] In other words, traders argued that they were not able to sell anything without swearing oaths and exaggerating. An early thirteenth-century exemplum from a Dominican friar, Jacques de Vitry, repeated in *Jacob's Well* some 200 years later, highlighted the dilemma faced by traders. In the story, a knight became a monk and, because of his secular past, was considered the perfect candidate to send to a fair to sell some old horses and asses and buy young ones in their place. However, at the fair he proceeded to tell intending purchasers the truth about their age and condition and subsequently failed to sell any: 'In the feyre [fair] men askyed hum yif the horse and the assys were yunge and clene of lymmes [young and fine of limbs]. The munke seyde, "nay, it arn olde and feble, and crokyd [crooked], wel more ye wyten [know], yyf they haddyn be yunge gode with-outyn defawte [without default], we wolde not haue brougt hem hyder to selle, for oure hows [house] hath noȝt so gret nede"'. Upon his return to the monastery he was upbraided, even though he declared he was unwilling to lie and injure his soul by deceiving his neighbours. He was never sent out of the monastery on secular business again.[186] Similarly, Caesarius of Heisterbach in *The Dialogue on Miracles* (*c*.1220–35) related how two merchants felt 'we can scarcely buy or sell anything without being compelled to lie and swear, and often to swear falsely'.[187] The personified Covetousness in *Piers Plowman* also learnt guile, fraud and lying while an apprentice under 'Symme at þe nok'. These deceits were deemed to be the only means to sell their wares at the fairs of Winchester and Weyhill or else they would remain unsold.[188] The implication was that ethics were being usurped by the competitive demands of the marketplace.

False words and false wares

Some moralists recognised the utility of advertising for vendors. Reginald Pecock, Bishop of Chichester (from 1450 to 1460), revealed an awareness of the need for traders to promote and display their wares when he compared mercantile endorsements with his own extolling of spiritual 'goods'. He compared his position to a merchant who had brought precious and important goods from across the sea, but would not be

---

[185] [I must swear of necessity and forswear myself in selling/trading and in other manner; else no man will believe me]. *Jacob's Well*, p. 261, ll. 15–16.

[186] Crane (ed.), *Exempla of Jacques de Vitry*, pp. 21, 156, no. liii; *Jacob's Well*, p. 311, l. 24 – p. 312, l. 28.

[187] Scott and Bland (eds.), *Dialogue*, i, pp. 177–8, ch. xxxvii; Banks (ed.), *An Alphabet*, no. 485; Tubach, *Index Exemplorum*, no. 3267.

[188] *Piers Plowman*, A.V.115–22, B.V.199–206, C.VI.204–11.

able to sell them unless 'he wolde denounce and proclame that he had such chaffre [merchandise]'. Should he not therefore 'holde a proude avaunter [boaster] of him silf or of his chaffare' without blame?[189] However, most writers were suspicious of traders who lavishly praised their own wares, particularly if such words emanated from humble stallholders and hawkers in the marketplace. Even the basic advertising of wares was considered to be a trick of flattery and lying, upheld by blasphemous oaths. Gower stated:

Standing outside before the door the youthful Fraud shouts her different wares, whatever you might wish to have. She will say the names of this and that, of as many things as there are stars in the sky, as she calls and allures you ... Indeed, when old Fraud utters her tricky words, no one can go away uncheated. If a smart man enters, she is smarter than he; and if a fool goes in, he goes away a bigger fool.[190]

Gower's mercer was even more aggressive in hawking his wares: 'he shrieks more than a sparrowhawk. When he sees unknown folk, he pushes and pulls, calls and cries out, saying, "Step up and come in! Beds, kerchiefs, ostrich feathers, silks, satins, imported cloths".'[191] Once the customer was in his shop the merchant was then portrayed as polite, entertaining and subtle in his talk 'to make vain people foolish, so that he can get their money'.

Flattery and bluster were considered tools of the trade. John Mirk warned against using 'fals countenans and glosynge' when bargaining.[192] Peter Idley compared his flattering counsellor to the village chapman who advertised his goods with fine words, but 'vndir hony he hideth galle'.[193] The taverner in the late fifteenth-century religious play *Mary Magdalene* boasted loudly of his wit and wisdom as well as his unrivalled selection of wines: 'ther be no bettyr as ferre [far] as ȝe can goo!'; which was probably regarded as a commonplace example of commercial exaggeration. He goes on to extol the restorative powers of his wines: 'To man and woman a good restoratyff, ȝe xall [shall] nat thynk your mony spent in wast[e] – From stodyys [firmness?] and hevynes [heaviness] it woll yow relyff!'[194] Such exalting of their own virtues and abilities was a common style for

[189] Hitchcock (ed.), *Donet*, p. 83, ll. 16–27.
[190] Stockton (ed.), *Major Latin Works*, 'Vox Clamantis', bk. v, ch. 13, pp. 213–14.
[191] Gower, *Mirour*, p. 332, ll. 25285–96. See also Gray (ed.), *Oxford Book*, 'London Lickpenny', pp. 18–19, ll. 50–98 (BL, MS Harleian 367, fols. 126r–127v).
[192] Peacock (ed.), *Instructions*, p. 40, ll. 1299–306. See also Bornstein (ed.), *Middle English Translation*; Nelson (ed.), *Fifteenth Century School Book*, p. 54, no. 232.
[193] D'Evelyn (ed.), *Peter Idley's Instructions*, Liber Primus, p. 87, ll. 400–6.
[194] Baker, Murphy and Hall Jr (eds.), *Late Medieval Religious Plays*, pp. 39–40, ll. 470–88.

certain characters in plays, but the audience would have readily associated traders with such characteristics.

Traders were regarded as unscrupulous in what they did in order to make a deal. For instance, moralists warned against traders' use of drink to lubricate a deal.[195] *Handlyng Synne* stated:

Or þou ledyst any man to þe ale	*leads*
And madest hym drunk with troteuale	*idle talk*
And he solde hys þyng to þe	*thing*
More þan he wulde yn soberte[196]	*sobriety*

Similarly, scorn was directed at the false friendship of hostelers and innkeepers, who fêted approaching customers but cared nothing for them once they had paid their bill or if it became clear that they had lost all their money.[197] In the minds of preachers, such actions were ultimately linked to the insatiable nature of covetousness and to how this sin could lead men to ignore honesty, courtesy and charity.

Moralists often emphasised the trivial, frivolous and unnecessary nature of the pedlar's trade, for their wares could seemingly only be sold by the use of deceit or lies. William Lichfield, a preacher in the early fifteenth century, wrote that 'a pore peddelere makiþ oftmore noise to sel his sope [soap] and his nedyll [needle] þan doiþ þe rych marchaunte with al þis dere worþi [dear worthy] ware þus þay þat do but lityl gode spekyn mych more þerof þen men of gret vertue don of hir god dedis [good deeds]'.[198] The 'chapmen lyght of fote' were thus seen as dishonest, and as John Heywood's pedlar, in the play 'The Foure PP' (*c.*1521–5), tells his companions, the apothecary, palmer and pardoner:

And all ye thre can lye as well	*lie*
As can the falsest deuyll in hell	
And, though afore ye harde me grudge	
In greater maters to be your iudge,	
Yet in lyeng I can some skyll	*lying*
And, yf I shall be iudge, I wyll[199]	

The pedlar thus declares himself the archetypal liar among others who have some knowledge in the matter. He has no luck in selling goods to

[195] *Fasciculus Morum*, pp. 436–7; Mozley and Raymo (eds.), *Nigel de Longchamps*, p. 47, l. 743 – p. 48, l. 790, esp. p. 48, ll. 781–8.

[196] *Handlyng Synne*, p. 194, ll. 5969–72.

[197] Ross (ed.), *Middle English Sermons*, p. 85, ll. 26–37 (BL, MS Royal 18.B.xxiii, fol. 80r); Bromyard, *Summa Predicantium*, 'Amor'.

[198] BL, MS Royal 8.C.i, fol. 124v.

[199] Adams (ed.), *Chief Pre-Shakespearean Dramas*, 'The Play called the Foure PP', p. 373, ll. 442–7.

these fellows, even though they all enjoy each other's company, because they can apparently discern his peddling deceits by drawing on their own experience of lying.

Flattery, subtle words and lies were thus considered part of the duplicitous armoury of all avaricious traders. Such deception was closely allied to selling a good despite prior knowledge that it was essentially flawed and yet still not openly declaring this fault.[200] *Dives and Pauper* stated: 'if man or woman sell a þing [thing] for good and he knowe defaute þerynne be whyche defaute þe byere is deceyuyd he doþ gyle and þefte [guile and theft]. And also if þe byere begyle so þe sellere . . . For ȝif he selle an halt [lame] hors for a swyft hors and a ruynous hous [ruinous house] for a strong hous it is perylous and harm to þe byere and he is holdyn to restitucioun.'[201] Horse-sellers, or 'coursors', were portrayed as especially corrupt for they were supposedly inclined to hide the faults of the goods they sold.[202] Jacques de Vitry's early thirteenth-century exempla portrayed horse-sellers as unscrupulous and liable to give buyers equivocal advice: 'If the horse turned out badly, he said: "I warned you not to buy it." If the horse turned out a good one, he said: "I advised you to buy it."'[203] Another exemplum described how a trader praised a horse he was selling by claiming that the horse ate everything and would not climb trees; the buyer found that the horse bit everything and would not cross wooden bridges.[204]

Jacques the Grete, in his fifteenth-century *The Book of Goode Maners*, implored traders not to hide the faults of their merchandise and asked them to declare openly any blemishes. He recognised the paradox in that it was a 'gret foly a marchaunt to dyspreyse hys owne marchaundyse', but concluded that truth should remain the most significant factor. No trader should seek to deceive their neighbours and they 'shuld suche wyse dresse her marchaundyse that yt mygth sownde treuly to euery party'.[205]

---

[200] Lefébure (ed.), *St Thomas Aquinas*, pp. 216–21, vol. 38: Injustice, ii–ii, q.77, a.2. Aquinas recognised that sellers might be ignorant of faults and sell their wares honestly. In such cases, the trader committed no sin, though he was still bound to make restitution once the true facts were uncovered.

[201] *Dives and Pauper*, i, ii, pp. 154–5, taken from Lefébure (ed.), *St Thomas Aquinas*, pp. 222–5, vol. 38: Injustice, ii–ii, q.77, a.3. See also Power (ed.), *Goodman of Paris*, p. 82. For a court roll entry that mirrored this moral indictment, see p. 344.

[202] Furnivall (ed.), *Pilgrimage*, p. 484, ll. 18100–2; Nelson (ed.), *Myrour*, p. 140 (BL, MS Harleian 45, fol. 71v); *Jacob's Well*, p. 134, ll. 2–7; Crane (ed.), *Exempla of Jacques de Vitry*, pp. 80–1, 211, no. cxciii; Zeydel (ed.), *Ship of Fools*, p. 328; Bromyard, *Summa Predicantium*, 'Falsitas'; *Ayenbite of Inwyt*, p. 44; *Vices and Virtues*, p. 41, ll. 2–3.

[203] Crane (ed.), *Exempla of Jacques de Vitry*, pp. 129, 268, no. cccix.

[204] Tubach (ed.), *Index Exemplorum*, no. 2616.

[205] BL, MS Harleian 149, fol. 239r–v. See also *Dives and Pauper*, i, ii, pp. 154–5; Bromyard, *Summa Predicantium*, 'Mercatio'; Furnivall (ed.), *Minor Poems*, 'Truth ever is best',

Verbal misrepresentation went hand in hand with the alleged alacrity of
traders in deceiving customers through physical sleights. Moralists gave
examples of trickery that made wares look better than they actually were.
For instance, drapers were often accused of using tricks of the light and
darkened rooms to make their cloth seem of higher quality than it was:
'false schewynge [showing], as when a marchant can sotelliche [subtly]
adresse his ware to make hit seme better than it is, and scheweth it in
derke place, to hyde the defaute therof, or to make seme the better, as
doth drapers, mercers, and many other suche'.[206] They might also stretch
cloth using needles and a press.[207] Tawyers might sell old, rotten skins as
new by cleansing and adorning them in a superficial manner and by using
sly words.[208] A fifteenth-century treatise on the Ten Commandments
(c.1420–35) summarised the deceitful activities of such artisans: 'þat
maketh euel werke and selleth it for good þinge and good werke, knoinge
wel þat he dooth defraude and begylynge to his euyncristen and so he
selleth with oothes his good falsly and be gilith his broþer untruly'.[209]
According to the preachers and moralists, these traders were not merely
negligent but deliberately fraudulent. By engaging in such activities they
were disregarding their Christian duty towards their fellows.

False weights and measures

Most trading fraud was related to lying, perjury, false-witness and
guile.[210] Traders were often accused of trying to bulk out or falsify the
quantity of their goods. John Gower wrote about butchers who used
wooden skewers to add fat to lean meat, so that there was more wood
than flesh in the sold victual.[211] In the mid-fourteenth century, John

---

pt. 2, p. 699; Nelson (ed.), *Myrour*, p. 139, l. 30 – p. 140, l. 11 (BL, MS Harleian 45,
fol. 71r–v); Harrison (ed.), *Examples*, pp. 97–8; Larson (ed.), *King's Mirror*, pp. 80–1.
[206] BL, MS Harleian 45, fol. 71v, cf. Owst, *Literature and Pulpit*, pp. 354–5. See also
Ayenbite of Inwyt, p. 45; *Vices and Virtues*, p. 41; Gower, *Mirour*, p. 332, ll. 25321–
32; Stockton (ed.), *Major Latin Works*, 'Vox Clamantis', bk. v, ch. 13, pp. 213–14;
Furnivall (ed.), *Pilgrimage*, pp. 483–4, ll. 18088–99; Nelson (ed.), *Myrour*, p. 140, ll.
4–7; Bromyard, *Summa Predicantium*, 'Mercatio'; Zeydel (ed.), *Ship of Fools*, p. 328;
Furnivall (ed.), *Jyl of Breyntford's Testament*, pp. 21–2.
[207] *Piers Plowman*, A.v.123–8, B.v.207–12, C.vi.212–17.
[208] Bromyard, *Summa Predicantium*, 'Luxuria'.
[209] (that make evil work and sell it for a good thing and good work, knowing well that
he does defraud and beguile his fellow Christian, and so he sells with oaths his goods
falsely and beguiles his brother untruly.) Royster, 'Middle English treatise', 30.
[210] One late medieval poem stated that 'gyle is chapman'. Cambridge, St John's College,
MS 37 / B15, fol. 56v.
[211] Gower, *Mirour*, p. 345, ll. 26233–44.

Bromyard (d. 1352) claimed that traders would 'mingle bad and extraneous matter with the stuff that is to be weighed in sly fashion, like those who mix sand with wool, or wet the wool to make it weigh heavier, or else blend old and bad stuff with new and good samples'.[212] If they could not alter their weights and measures directly then it was assumed that they had other means to deceive the scales.

Numerous biblical references mention good and just measurement, which is equated with God's justice and also the scales that weighed men's souls on the Day of Judgement.[213] A proper use of weights and measures was considered to be divinely ordained. Aquinas stated: 'if somebody knowingly uses a defective measure in a contract of sale, he is committing fraud and the sale is illicit' and this was considered 'an abomination to the Lord your God'.[214] The denunciation of false weights and measures was thus a commonplace in texts railing against medieval traders.[215] John Wyclif charged: 'for þei lyuen comynly [live commonly] bi falsnesse as bi false swerynge [swearing], false mesure and false weitis [weights]'.[216] *Jacob's Well* enunciated the main deception 'in bying be the more, and selling be the lesse; and thowgh thi mesure or weyghte be trewe, git thou takest it large inward and gevyst it scarse outward, agens trewthe [against truth]'.[217] In other words, traders deceitfully used a large measure to buy with and a small measure to sell with, even though

---

[212] Bromyard, *Summa Predicantium*, 'Mercatio'. There is a case in the Lincolnshire Sessions of the Peace, in 1373–5, where John Borde of Spalding mixed his wool with sand to increase the weight. Sillem (ed.), *Records*, p. 220 (Roll H), no. 1. See also *Leicester*, i, pp. 202–3 (1287).

[213] Wood, *Medieval Economic Thought*, pp. 91, 98 (who quotes Isaiah 40:12; Proverbs 16:11; Matthew 7:2; Leviticus 19:35–6).

[214] Lefébure (ed.), *St Thomas Aquinas*, pp. 216–21, vol. 38: Injustice, II–II, q.77, a.2.

[215] In the twelfth century, priests were instructed to warn their congregations against the use of false measures, Peacock (ed.), *Instructions*, p. 22, ll. 704–14, p. 32, ll. 1051–8. Such warnings can be seen through the following centuries. See Simmons and Nolloth (eds.), *Lay Folks' Catechism*, p. 51, ll. 796–801; Ross (ed.), *Middle English Sermons*, p. 24, ll. 17–21 (BL, MS Royal 18.B.xxiii, fol. 94r); Royster, 'Middle English treatise', 29; *Ayenbite of Inwyt*, pp. 44–5; *Vices and Virtues*, pp. 40–1; Bromyard, *Summa Predicantium*, 'Falsitas' and 'Mercatio'; BL, MS Harleian 4894, fol. 68v (Robert Rypon); BL, MS Harleian 2398, fols. 3v, 21v, 100v ('Memoriale Credencium'); Devlin (ed.), *Sermons of Thomas Brinton*, p. 77, sermon 19, pp. 147–8, sermon 35, p. 259, sermon 56, p. 289, sermon 63; Swinburn (ed.), *Lanterne*, p. 107, l. 18 – p. 108, l. 9; Gower, *Mirour*, p. 88, ll. 6301–12, p. 331, ll. 25261–72; Macaulay (ed.), *Complete Works of John Gower*, iii, 'Confessio Amantis', Lib. v, ll. 4396–9; *Piers Plowman*, A.v.131–2, B.v.208–9, C.vi.213–14; Furnivall (ed.), *Pilgrimage*, p. 483, ll. 18073–9; BL, MS Harleian 149, fol. 239r–v; Zeydel (ed.), *Ship of Fools*, pp. 328–9.

[216] Matthew (ed.), *English Works of Wyclif*, pp. 185–6, also p. 25.

[217] *Jacob's Well*, p. 133, ll. 28–31, also p. 19, ll. 8–13, p. 60, ll. 2–5. This drew on a biblical injunction against having both small and great weights: Deuteronomy 25:13–15. Wood, *Medieval Economic Thought*, p. 98. See also *Dives and Pauper*, I, ii, p. 154, ll. 43–9; Nelson (ed.), *Myrour*, p. 139, l. 40 – p. 140, l. 3 (BL, MS Harleian 45, fol. 71r–v); Jamieson (ed.), *Ship of Fools*, ii, p. 222; Morris (ed.), *Old English Homilies*

they might ostensibly look the same. In the late thirteenth century, Walter of Henley advised stewards and estate managers to buy and sell in the presence of witnesses because 'theare is much fraude to such as cannot espie it'. Walter also warned traders and consumers to 'beware off hym that holdithe the balaunce for he may do you grete fraude'.[218]

The scales and beams used by traders might be balanced in their own favour, or could be easily controlled by a sleight of the hand. Bromyard expressed the fear that traders (such as spicers) misused the auncel balance: 'with a certain trick they manipulate the balance and thus put weight on it, to press it down without good and true weight', and Jacques the Grete complained of the 'balaunce that ys falcely guyded'.[219] In the late fifteenth century, a merchant handbook, *The Noumbre of Weyghtes*, outlined the ban on the use of the auncel: 'Aunsell weyght is for boden [forbidden] be the parlement and also holy cherche [church] hath cursyd all theym þat by or sell by þat weyghtes ffor itt is a dysseyvabyll [deceivable] weyghtes and a ffalse'.[220] Sebastian Brant's *The Ship of Fools* (1494) summarised these anxieties about the users of scales:

> The seller gives the scale a shove,
> That toward the ground it lunge and move
> And asks: 'How much of this, I pray?'
> And with the meat his thumb does weigh.[221]

Ultimately, traders were expected to keep good measure according to parliamentary statutes and the king's standard and not to use deceitful weighing practices.[222] Depictions of good merchants and traders thus often included a balance or yardstick in their hand, emphasising their commitment to true weights and measures (see Figure 1, below).

Customers and 'lyther bargaining'

Market traders who took direct advantage of a customer, particularly those in need, were charged with 'lyther bargaining'. This accusation

---

of the Twelfth Century, pp. 212–15; Bromyard, *Summa Predicantium*, 'Mercatio'; *Vices and Virtues*, p. 40, ll. 19–27.

[218] Oschinsky (ed.), *Walter of Henley*, pp. 340–1, c. 108 and p. 384.

[219] Bromyard, *Summa Predicantium*, 'Mercatio'; BL, MS Harleian 149, fol. 239r. See also Nelson (ed.), *Fifteenth Century School Book*, p. 54, no. 230. See below, pp. 195–6, for a discussion of the auncel. Simplified images of a balance can be seen in Figures 1, 12, 18.

[220] BL, MS Cotton Vespasian e.ix, fol. 86v.

[221] Zeydel (ed.), *Ship of Fools*, pp. 328–9. In 1509, this work was translated into English by Alexander Barclay and printed by Richard Pynson.

[222] *Jacob's Well*, p. 60, ll. 2–5; MacCracken (ed.), *Minor Poems*, 'Mesure is Tresour', pp. 776–9, no. 62.

was part of broader anxieties regarding how vendors and customers inter-acted. Traders were frequently held in suspicion and medieval allegories depicted them as foxes, full of cunning and sly deceits, as seen in *Jacob's Well*:

the coueytous man is as a fox, for he, wyth dysseygtys [deceits], wyth false othys [oaths] and auncerys [auncels], and false weygtys and mesurys, harmyth and hynderyth more symple folk, that arn his neyghbourys and kan no wyles [know no wiles], þan he doth straungerys, þat arn slye and as wyly as he.[223]

Such imagery was even used in legislative sources. In the London Letter-Book for 1335, inquiries were made against 'fraudulent bakers who carry on their business secretly, hiding themselves like foxes'.[224] Traders were generally associated with worldly knowledge and a pragmatic realism that allowed them to advance their aims, usually at the expense of others. Bromyard described the subtle deceptions of shopkeepers who counted out change so fast that the customer lost count and took less than they should.[225] Customers were thus portrayed as 'simple men', unknowing in the ways of commerce and in need of protection from traders who were cunning and sly and more than prepared to beguile their neighbours.

The purpose of medieval clerical and literary texts was thus as much didactic as condemnatory. They informed consumers about the pitfalls and deceptions of the marketplace and outlined the moral codes to which traders and purchasers should adhere. Such advice and warn-ings, whether elucidated through the media of the pulpit, poems, plays, sculpture, or wall-paintings, shaped the medieval moral environment. Customers were frequently warned about their own need for prudence against deceptions. John Gower delivered the advice: 'you should remem-ber one thing: if you enter the shop, you should be very prudent about buying; for Fraud never reveals himself fully; rather, by his sly flattery he

---

[223] *Jacob's Well*, p. 118, ll. 21–33. See also BL, MS Royal 8.c.i, fol. 130r (theological tract by William Lichfield, rector of Allhallows the Great, early fifteenth century); Wilson (ed.), *English Text*, pp. 57–8; Morris (ed.), *An Old English Miscellany*, p. 14, ll. 444–51; Randall, *Images in the Margins*, pp. 8–19; Thomson and Perraud (eds.), *Ten Latin Schooltexts*, pp. 334–5; Rendell (ed.), *Physiologus*, pp. 22–4; Furnivall (ed.), *Pilgrimage*, pp. 385–6. Foxes were traditionally associated with flattery, cunning and deceit. Chaucer, *Canterbury Tales*, 'Nun's Priest's Tale', pp. 252–61; Sisam and Sisam (eds.), *Medieval English Verse*, pp. 24–35, no. 16, pp. 509–11, no. 239, pp. 511–12, no. 240; Robbins (ed.), *Secular Lyrics*, p. 43, no. 48, pp. 44–5, no. 49; BL, MS Royal 19.B.iv, fol. 97v; Sands (ed.), *History of Reynard the Fox*, p. 45; Varty, 'Reynard the Fox'; Varty, *Reynard the Fox*, p. 21; Blake, 'Reynard the Fox'; Fox (ed.), *Robert Henryson*, pp. 76–84.
[224] *CLB*, E, pp. 6–7 (1335); *Liber Albus*, p. 314.
[225] Bromyard, *Summa Predicantium*, 'Mercatio'. See also Harrison (ed.), *Examples*, pp. 128–9.

will give you chalk for cheese. You will think by his language that this wild nettle is a precious rose – so courteous a face he will put on for you – but if you will escape unhurt, do not trust yourself to his paperwork.'[226] In the prologue to his printed edition of *Reynard the Foxe* in 1481, Caxton hoped that the text would help lords, prelates, merchants and common people to understand some of the subtle deceits that were daily used in the world, to 'kepe hym from the subtyl false shrewis that they be not deceyuyd'.[227]

John Bromyard provided a subtle slant on the traders' traditional bargaining skills and their excuses for deceiving their customers: 'The buyers have their own senses and intellect...they can buy the things or leave them!' Bromyard's traders even argue that they often purchase goods that turn out false, so why should they not put the same wares up for sale and hide the defects.[228] Aquinas advanced the theory that all faults in a seller's goods should be announced, otherwise the contract could be declared null and void and the seller forced to make restitution. In particular, they should declare any faulty goods that might lead to harm or loss for the purchaser, 'as where one sells another a lame horse instead of a good runner, a tumble-down house instead of a solid one, or mouldy or even poisonous food instead of food in good condition'. Pragmatically, however, Aquinas suggested that, if a flaw was obvious and open, 'as where a horse has only one eye', and if the seller had already reduced the price fairly, he was justified in keeping quiet about the flaw in case the buyer tried to lower the price even further than was warranted.[229] In this way, traders were seen as relocating some of the responsibility for the conduct of the deal onto the consumer. Aquinas did, however, suggest that although a seller was not bound by strict justice to disclose anything further (if the commodity was not harmful and set at a fair market price), it was still virtuous to do so. Most moralists were not so ambivalent and traditionally dismissed any notion of *caveat emptor*. They declared that it was the duty of traders to reveal all and thus help and not deceive their neighbours. Sellers were expected to trade according to ideals of communal justice, whereas such 'lyther bargaining' took advantage of the buyer's ignorance or lack of bargaining skills as well as the urgency of their needs. Some customers had to buy or sell goods in order to obtain necessary victuals or money for dues, and moralists berated any trader

---

[226] Gower, *Mirour*, p. 332, ll. 25297–308.
[227] Crotch (ed.), *Prologues and Epilogues*, p. 60.
[228] Bromyard, *Summa Predicantium*, 'Mercatio', cf. Owst, *Literature and Pulpit*, p. 357.
[229] Lefébure (ed.), *St Thomas Aquinas*, pp. 222–5, vol. 38: Injustice, II–II, q.77, a.3; *Dives and Pauper*, I, ii, pp. 154–5, ll. 52–68.

who tried to benefit from such desperation by charging undue prices.[230]
The Noumbre of Weyghtes remarked: 'euery merchaunt to make hys barg-
ynnes trewly, sadly and wysly so þat he may haue resonabyll wynnynges
[gain] and dysseyve [deceive] noone Innoceyntes with noone vntreue
chaffyre [untrue selling] for þer dyspleasauns [displeasure] of god'.[231]
The poor and innocent should be protected not exploited. *Fasciculus
Morum* likened 'simulating the truth' or dissembling during commercial deals to the poison of an asp which enters the body imperceptibly,
spreads secretly, but then kills openly.[232] Ultimately, such practices led
to 'hidden and deceitful traps for the innocent' and could have profound
consequences.

Yet, deception was not only a sin of which sellers were guilty. Late
medieval writers also warned traders that they might too fall victim to
the frauds of their customers. For instance, a buyer might know that
a certain commodity was worth more than the seller realised. Keeping
silent about this was considered sinful and the purchaser was bound to
make restitution.[233] Other customers might be very slow to pay their
debts, as suggested by John Lydgate: 'A shrewed payer maþe muche
longe delaye / With fals byhestis [behests] and fals flatterye'.[234] Bromyard
similarly lamented deceitful debtors who failed to repay despite having
the requisite funds.[235] Traders were advised to keep careful records of
their transactions and debtors so that recompense in the courts would
be easier. A sermon from the fifteenth century warned wasters and the
untrustworthy that craftsmen and traders made tallies of their sales or
wrote them in their account books, and emphasised that if the waster
tried to evade his debt the trader would 'takyþe an accion [action] a
ȝenste [against] þe vntrew man and so puttiþe hym in preson [prison]
schewyng un to hym teyle [tally] or els his proper writyng'.[236]

The Noumbre of Weyghtes provides some brief guidance to those engaged
in commerce. Most of the discourse concerns weights, measures, various
sorts of merchandise and other technical matters. There is, however, a

[230] *Jacob's Well*, p. 133, ll. 17–21, and p. 211, l. 28 – p. 212, l. 5; Nelson (ed.), *Myrour*,
p. 139, ll. 36–40 (BL, MS Harleian 45, fol. 71r); Bowers, 'A Middle English mnemonic
poem', 230–2. See also Langholm, *The Merchant*, pp. 39–40, 65, 109–10, 117–18,
153–4, 160–2, 177, 192.
[231] BL, MS Cotton Vespasian E.ix, fol. 96r.
[232] *Fasciculus Morum*, pp. 346–7. For deceiving the simple and innocent through the devices
of false cheer and exaggerating a ware's quality and price, see also Furnivall (ed.),
Pilgrimage, pp. 483–4, ll. 18061–99; Jamieson (ed.), *Ship of Fools*, ii, pp. 167–8.
[233] Lefébure (ed.), *St Thomas Aquinas*, pp. 216–21, vol. 38: Injustice, ii–ii, q.77, a.2.
[234] MacCracken (ed.), *Minor Poems*, 'Every Thing to His Semblable', pp. 801–7,
esp. ll. 137–8.
[235] Bromyard, *Summa Predicantium*, 'Usura'.
[236] Nottingham University Library, MS 50, fol. 73r–v.

short section that advises traders on how to undertake their dealings and what to beware.[237] Firstly, the trader should look to where he can buy and sell wares to make a reasonable gain, making sure that he is not targeting places that already have adequate supplies, like sending stockfish to Norway. They should also carefully inspect what they buy to prove that it is good and whether the wares can be stored or need to be hastily sold. All traders should beware what they buy, when, where and from whom: 'yf a man by [buy] chaffor [merchandise] in suche a place as he may haue no delyuerauns [delivery] þeroff and he pay for ytt afore [before] and haue ytt nott he is dyseyved [deceived] or els yf he bye goodes of hym þat hath no power to sell ytt he ys dysseyved and þerfore euery man be ware howe he bye and sell and in whatt place and of whom'. The writer thus appears to reinforce the importance of franchised, open markets, where formal mechanisms are in place to redeem debts and to check for stolen or adulterated goods. Lastly, traders must inquire about the prices of all merchandise that they see or hear about, because such information was the source to better goods and prices. Within such guidance, traders are not only warned about possible deceptions by their fellow traders, but also about the importance of the transaction costs of search, negotiation and enforcement, and how these might be lessened by the use of formal markets. Some texts thus recognised that traders needed to be careful and knowledgeable in order to succeed in their profession. Even William Langland accepted that merchants and traders were given skills and a keen eye by God so that they could earn a living through buying and selling.[238]

The merchant

The wealthy merchant was the stock figure employed in most medieval writings that discussed trade, and he encapsulated the sins of avarice and fraud. Representations of such dealers thus provided the foundation for any discussions of more humble retailers. In contemporary literature, merchants were regularly grouped together with their petty trade counterparts, as well as with the artisanal classes.[239] However, despite an overlap in general accusations of avarice and types of fraud, leading merchants were also increasingly represented as a world apart from

---

[237] BL, MS Cotton Vespasian E.ix, fols. 96r–97r.   [238] *Piers Plowman*, B.XIX.234–5.

[239] Artisans were often grouped together with retailers in texts, particularly when they were selling their own products direct to the consumer. However, they were also praised for their hard work, sobriety and craftsmanship, and their labours were easier to justify than those of retailers. *Piers Plowman*, B.XIX.234–5; Bornstein (ed.), *Middle English Translation*, pp. 186–9; Gower, *Mirour*, p. 335, ll. 25501–12.

Figure 1: Merchant.

Notes: The woodcut shows a merchant, or money-changer, wearing a money-pouch and holding a balance (a rigid beam suspended at the centre and with identical weighing pans) and weight. This was an illustration for the fourth pawn in *The Game of Chess* (1483), which ordered society according to the layout of a chessboard.

Source: Cessolis, *De Ludo Scachorum*, bk. 3, ch. 4 (Cambridge, Trinity College Library, VI.18.3, fol. 47v).

retailers in their wealth, status and international endeavours. Images that depict their clothes and demeanour certainly imply that these men were above the normal ranks of traders, perhaps even more akin to the gentry. William Caxton's edition of *The Game of Chess* (late fifteenth century), presents a merchant or money-changer in very fine attire, possibly fur-lined, holding a balance and weight, and bearing a dignified expression (see Figure 1). The accompanying text describes 'at his gurdell [girdle] a purse fulle of monoye [money] redy for to gyue to them that requyre hit'.[240]

The most well-known literary representation of a merchant is the solemn, dignified and well-dressed figure in the General Prologue to

---

[240] Cessolis, *De Ludo Scachorum*, bk. 3, ch. 4. The text was originally written by Jacob de Cessolis, a Dominican friar, in the early fourteenth century.

Geoffrey Chaucer's *The Canterbury Tales*.[241] In his portrayal of the 'Marchant', Chaucer subtly drew upon tensions between the commercial world and conventional social ideology.[242] With his usual sense of irony, he presented justifications for the prosperous mercantile community yet also encapsulated many of the negative mercantile stereotypes that pervaded medieval literature. The Merchant is explicitly presented in a fairly positive light, but this portrayal is leavened by Chaucer's stylistic ability to provide a variety of implicit, unresolved discourses.[243] His choice of phrases and words implies that the Merchant's' façade of virtuous respectability might actually be hiding dishonesty and fraud.[244] Medieval audiences would have surely grasped the underlying questions of morality that accorded with the accepted ideology of the day, which in turn would have informed their understanding of the text.[245]

The Merchant of the General Prologue was involved in the international wool and cloth trade, as implied by his concerns for the sea route between Orwell and Middleburg.[246] The decorated and colourful apparel of Chaucer's Merchant in the early fifteenth-century Ellesmere manuscript presents an image of a man made rich by the proceeds of international commerce (see Figure 2). However, as Laura Hodges noted, the clothes described by Chaucer were perhaps not as publicly ostentatious or sumptuous as suggested by the Ellesmere illustration:

A Marchant was ther with a forked berd,	*beard*
In mottelee, and hye on horse he sat;	*motley (type of cloth)*
Upon his heed a Flaundryssh bever hat,	*head; beaver*
His bootes clasped faire and fetisly.	*neat/well-made*
His resons he spak ful solempnely,	
Sownynge alwey th'encrees of his wynnyng.[247]	*increase; gain*

According to Hodges, the Merchant's footwear and hat were conservative and respectable, while the choice of a 'mottelee' patterned fabric reflected developments in the domestic cloth trade. This all matched his bearing, which was described as 'solempne' and 'estatly', indicating a discrete and prudent character.[248] Hodges argued that funeral brasses of merchants often depicted them with forked beards, buckled shoes and fine clothes, intended to demonstrate well-being and elicit respect.

---

[241] Chaucer, *Canterbury Tales*, 'General Prologue', pp. 27–8, ll. 270–84; Bowden, *Commentary*, pp. 146–53.
[242] Mann, *Chaucer*, pp. 99–103.   [243] Rigby, *Chaucer in Context*, pp. 40–53.
[244] Woolf, 'Chaucer as a satirist'; Ladd, 'Mercantile mis(reader)'.
[245] Rigby, *Chaucer in Context*, pp. 168–71.
[246] Chaucer, *Canterbury Tales*, 'General Prologue', p. 27, ll. 276–7.
[247] *Ibid.*, p. 27, ll. 270–5.   [248] Hodges, *Chaucer and Costume*, pp. 75–89.

Figure 2: Chaucer's Merchant.

Notes: This marginal manuscript illustration is next to a passage relating to the Merchant in the General Prologue to Chaucer's *Canterbury Tales*. *Source:* San Marino, Calif., Huntington Library, EL 26 C9, fol. 102v (Ellesmere manuscript, early fifteenth century).

However, these same brasses show money-pouches as a standard mercantile emblem; this did not make purses immune from symbolic connections with avarice. A number of literary critics have argued that Chaucer was implying self-importance in his portrait of the Merchant, interpreting 'ful solempnely' as pomposity. Kenneth Cahn, Muriel Bowden and John Manly all viewed the Merchant's garb as expensive and designed to impress onlookers with a sense of wealth ('wynnyng') and status.[249] For them, a 'Flaundryssh' beaver hat and boots 'clasped faire and fetisly' suggested a sense of finery and international fashion. Beyond notions of well-being and respectability, such dress could be construed as Chaucerian hints at prosperity, vanity and ambition, as also indicated by the Merchant sitting 'hye on horse'. Indeed, pride was a characteristic traditionally associated with merchants in French fabliaux.[250] Admittedly,

[249] Cahn, 'Chaucer's merchants', 118; Bowden, *Commentary*, pp. 150–1; Manly, *Some New Light*, p. 513.
[250] Stillwell, 'Chaucer's "sad" merchant'; Hellman and O'Gorman (eds.), *Fabliaux*, pp. 17–21, 182–93; Eichmann and DuVal (eds.), *Cuckolds*, pp. 77–9. Fabliaux were humorous, often bawdy, verse tales.

Chaucer may have been merely portraying what he regarded as typical attire for such men, as seen in surviving funeral brasses. However, this medieval writer seldom wrote lines without purpose and often saturated his verse with sharp satire.

In another passage from the General Prologue, the Merchant's serious and dignified manner was seemingly undercut by Chaucer's use of language:

Wel koude he in eschaunge sheeldes selle.	*exchange; currency units*
This worthy man ful wel his wit bisette:	*mind is set/arranged*
Ther wiste no wight that he was in dette,	*knew; person; debt*
So estatly was he of his governaunce	*stately/dignified; conduct*
With his bargaynes and with his chevyssaunce.	*profit/agreement*
For sothe he was a worthy man with alle,	*truth*
But, sooth to seyn, I noot how men hym calle.[251]	*true to say; know not*

In this verse, Chaucer emphasises the ambiguous nature of outward appearance and raises the possibility that the Merchant might still be in debt beneath the façade of respectability. There has been much debate over the meaning that the above lines were intended to convey. Some have argued that the merchant was greatly in debt, just as Gower complained of debt-ridden merchants in *Mirour de l'Omme*.[252] A more subtle reading would suggest that if the Merchant was in debt, no one explicitly knew it as his respectable dress and dignified bearing presented a confident and prosperous man who could attract credit (but also hide misdemeanours).[253] Chaucer was tempting his audience to reappraise the Merchant's own view of himself. The use of the word 'wight' can be interpreted as a signpost to Chaucer's habitual use of ironical double meaning. His phraseology here would have raised questions in the audience's mind, based upon their traditional assumptions about traders regarding fraud and avarice. Also, by the late fourteenth century at the latest, the word 'debt' in medieval texts had both commercial and religious connotations. The latter were based upon notions of penance and restitution, whereby sinners were expected to repay their debts to God and others and uphold notions of natural justice. Usurers and fraudulent merchants were particularly upbraided for failing to provide restitution

---

[251] Chaucer, *Canterbury Tales*, 'General Prologue', p. 28, ll. 278–84.
[252] Gower, *Mirour*, p. 339, ll. 25813–72.
[253] Literary scholars have rightly pointed to the prevalence of credit in medieval commerce. Knott, 'Chaucer's anonymous merchant'; Stillwell, 'Chaucer's merchant'; Mann, *Chaucer*, p. 102. Johnson noted the ambiguity of line 280 on debt. Johnson, 'Was Chaucer's merchant in debt?'.

for wrongs committed during their trading lives.[254] Chaucer was alluding to both a profound spiritual debt as well as to monetary transactions.

The Merchant is depicted not only as concealing debts, but also engaging in shady dealings. Again, Chaucer makes no direct slurs, but uses weighted terminology to imply a darker side. He does not give the Merchant a name ('I noot how men hym calle') and this in itself could imply secrecy and dishonesty.[255] The references to money and commerce in the *Canterbury Tales* can be construed as an unspoken attack on avarice.[256] His dealings in 'sheeldes', which were currency units employed in money-changing, and his 'chevyssaunce' (profit/agreement) also suggest he was a trader who engaged in overtly legal transactions that were nevertheless morally suspect. The use of the word 'chevyssaunce' as a euphemism for usury or dishonesty was widespread in medieval texts.[257] This has led many scholars to view the merchant as deceitful in line with traditional estates satire.[258] Indeed, the implied transgressions and references to ambiguous legitimacy would have been readily picked up by audiences who were already immersed in stereotyped images of mercantile abuses.

In the 'Shipman's Tale', Chaucer identified other conflicts between the mercantile world and traditional social institutions. This story concerns another merchant, who is presented as hardworking, prudent and trusting. Indeed, his main crime appears to be his complete ignorance of his wife's adultery. The story revolves around the movement of a loan that the merchant makes to a young clerk, Daun John, who uses the loan to pay the merchant's wife to sleep with him. Upon the merchant's return from a business trip the clerk informs him that he has repaid the loan to his wife, thus tricking them both. In turn, the merchant's wife tells him she has already spent the money, but then suggests an implicit deal by which she will be more readily acquiescent in bed. The 'Shipman's Tale'

---

[254] Adams, 'The concept of debt'. See also below, pp. 125–9.

[255] There has been much debate about whether Chaucer based his pilgrims upon real people. Reale, 'A marchant', pp. 97–8; Crane, 'An honest debtor?', 85; Rickert, 'Extracts', 111–19, 249–56; Bowden, *Commentary*, pp. 151–3. Geoffrey Chaucer was a controller of wool customs from 1374 to 1386, as well as the son of a wealthy Ipswich vintner. He thus had dealings with merchants. Brown Jr, 'Chaucer', 252–3. Nevertheless, the most reasonable conclusion is that his portraits were not based on any one individual but were formed from a conglomeration of fiction, experience, estates ideology and literary convention.

[256] Nevo, 'Chaucer: motive and mask'; Eberle, 'Commercial language'; Bisson, *Chaucer*, pp. 181–2. Paul Olson similarly regarded Chaucer's Merchant as a critique upon commercial values and unabashed materialism. Olson, *The Canterbury Tales*, p. 39.

[257] Gower, *Mirour*, p. 100, ll. 7225–48; *Piers Plowman*, c.vi.249–50. Conversely, Park and Cahn defended the legitimacy of the Merchant's 'eschaunges' of 'sheeldes' as neither moneylending nor usury. Cahn, 'Chaucer's merchants'; Park, 'The character of Chaucer's merchant'.

[258] Mann, *Chaucer*, p. 100; Knott, 'Chaucer's anonymous merchant'.

is both an enjoyable fabliaux, where a supposedly respectable member of society is cuckolded, and a critique of the commodification of human relations. The language of commerce permeates the tale, especially in the puns that reduce marital sexuality to a commercial contract:

> For I wol paye you wel and redily
> Fro day to day, and if so be I faille,
> I am youre wyf; score it upon my taille[259]

The 'Shipman's Tale' is full of *double entendres*; 'taille' or tally related to the rendering of accounts, but it also had an explicit sexual meaning.[260] A similar image of marriage and sex, immersed in the world of commerce, was presented in the 'Merchant's Tale', where the costs of a wife are quantified.[261] Social and marital relations were apparently determined by market forces. Helen Fulton remarks how the merchant's use of a bill of exchange in order to finance his dealings is analogous to the type of sexual bargain between his wife and Daun John.[262] Lee Patterson argues that each of the three parties in the 'Shipman's Tale' profited from the tale: the wife repays her creditors, the clerk enjoys the merchant's wife and the merchant gets an eager sexual partner. There is thus a sense of an equilibrium achieved in the exchange. However, the commodification of sexual relations undermines any theory of absolute, inviolable values. Everything can be subject to exchange value, a notion that had long concerned theologians.[263] Several scholars, such as Janette Richardson, Robert Adams and Albert Silverman, have regarded the tale as a conventional attack on market materialism, profit-making and the corrupting effects of money. Natural law, justice and spiritual truth

---

[259] Chaucer, *Canterbury Tales*, 'Shipman's Tale', pp. 203–8, esp. p. 208, ll. 414–16.

[260] King, 'A shipman ther was', p. 216; Silverman, 'Sex and money'; Richardson, 'Façade of bawdry', 307–9; Woods, 'A professional thyng'; Fichte, 'Chaucer's "Shipman's Tale"'; Hahn, 'Money, sexuality'; Hamaguchi, '"Debt" and the wife'; Abraham, 'Cosyn and cosynage'; Scattergood, 'Originality', 212–13; Schneider, 'Taillynge ynough'. For a discussion of the tally, see below pp. 200–1.

[261] Chaucer, *Canterbury Tales*, 'The Merchant's Tale', pp. 154–68. The Wife of Bath also uses sex as an instrument to acquire money out of rich old husbands, cynically declaring, 'Wynne whoso may, for al is for to selle'. Chaucer, *Canterbury Tales*, 'Wife of Bath's Prologue', p. 110, l. 414. Shoaf described the Wife of Bath as a 'figure of the commercial idiom and the commercial imagination'. This is encapsulated in the Wife's basic understanding of forces at work in the marketplace: 'With daunger oute we al oure chaffare [trading]; Greet prees [Great crowds] at market maketh deere ware [dear goods], And to greet cheep [plenty] is holde at litel prys [low price]: This knoweth every womman that is wys [wise].' *Ibid.*, p. 112, ll. 521–4; Shoaf, *Dante*, p. 175; Brown Jr, 'Chaucer', 251; Amsler, 'The Wife of Bath', 67–8, 75.

[262] Fulton, 'Mercantile ideology', 318.

[263] Patterson, *Chaucer*, pp. 349–58; Farber, *An Anatomy*, pp. 69–77.

were usurped.[264] However, Chaucer is a subtle writer and he interweaves well-known condemnations and justifications of merchants in order to highlight the moral ambiguities of commercial endeavours. The 'Shipman's Tale' is not a straightforward and unrelenting attack on either the merchant or the market.

The merchant in the 'Shipman's Tale' is presented as a man of probity and honesty, who represents a justification of mercantile values. He is not jealous and trusts his wife, believing that he has given his wife sufficient income for a 'thrifty' household. He is also open and honest with Daun John, as well as keeping his oath to honour his financial contract.[265] But his serious and hard-working lifestyle is disparaged by his wife, who complains that the merchant spends too much time at his account books and not enough with her.[266] This elicits the merchant's reply that he must be careful because of so many uncertainties in his business life. Stillwell identified these careful and hard-working characteristics as a bourgeois 'sadnesse' determined by Fortune's Wheel.[267] Thus, in business matters the conduct of the 'Shipman's Tale' merchant appears exemplary. The merchant seemed to understand the risks of trade ('hap and fortune in owe chapmanhede') and how profits needed to be accrued to make up for possible losses in the next deal: 'Ye knowe it wel ynogh [enough] / Of chapmen, that hir moneye is hir plogh [plough] . . . / But goldlees for to be, it is no game'.[268] His skill was in avoiding and tempering such misfortunes.

John Gower similarly had an intrinsic respect for merchants and the risky overseas exchanges that brought wealth to England:

he who conducts himself well and trades honestly is blessed by God and man. The law allows, and it is only right, that he who can lose in a venture should also be allowed to gain from it when his fortune brings it about. Therefore I say to you that he who wants to become a merchant and risk his money is not to be blamed if he earns a profit, provided he can earn it in moderation and without fraud.[269]

Similar distinctions were made by earlier moralists between the sins of excessive profit and making a justifiable livelihood. Generally, a merchant's ability to supply (mostly luxury) goods for the realm provided

[264] Richardson, 'Façade of bawdry'; Silverman, 'Sex and money'; Adams, 'The concept of debt'; Finlayson, 'Chaucer's *Shipman's Tale*'.
[265] Chaucer, *Canterbury Tales*, 'Shipman's Tale', p. 206, ll. 245–8.
[266] *Ibid.*, p. 205, ll. 215–23; Copland, 'The Shipman's Tale', 18–19; Joseph, 'Chaucer's coinage'.
[267] Stillwell, 'Chaucer's "sad" merchant', 3.
[268] Chaucer, *Canterbury Tales*, 'Shipman's Tale', p. 206, ll. 287–90.
[269] Gower, *Mirour*, p. 330, ll. 25192–212.

some level of vindication for their profession. Examples of this are found
in Aelfric's *Colloquy* (late tenth century) and Thomas de Chobham's
Summa Confessorum (early thirteenth century), where it is maintained
that the merchant is useful to the king and nobility in supplying luxuries
not found in England.[270] Fifteenth-century poems, such as *The Libelle of
Englyshe Polycye*, praised the role of wool and cloth merchants in bringing
prosperity and rare commodities to the realm.[271] The early sixteenth-
century *The Play of the Wether* also stated how merchants transferred
commodities from one country where they were abundant to another
where they were scarce:

> We fraught from home thynges wherof there is
> plente,   *freighted; plenty*
> And home we brynge such thynges as there be
> scant.
> Who sholde afore us marchauntes accompted be?   *accounted*
> For were not we, the worlde shuld wyshe and want
> In many thynges, whych now shall lack rehersall.[272]

The play goes on to stress how such trade presented 'dayly daunger of
our goodes and lyfe', as well as the 'great care and stryfe' needed to bring
these endeavours to fruition.[273] Both Aelfric's *Colloquy* and a fifteenth-
century school-book similarly emphasised the likelihood of shipwreck
and piracy faced by merchants on long sea voyages.[274] Such extensive
labour and risks were an added justification for mercantile activities and
their gains. Indeed, Chaucer's 'Parson's Tale' was to provide a relatively
straightforward contrast between a merchant who is honest and lawful,
moving goods that are abundant in one country to another where they
are scarce, and a merchant who is dishonest and unlawful, filled with
fraud, deceit and false oaths.[275]

---

[270] Gem (ed.), *An Anglo-Saxon Abbot*, p. 189; Swanton (ed.), *Anglo-Saxon Prose*, pp. 107–15; Broomfield (ed.), *Thomae de Chobham*, p. 301.
[271] Furnivall (ed.), *Political, Religious, and Love Poems*, 'The Hors, the Shepe, and the Gosse', by John Lydgate (*c.*1421), pp. 15–22, esp. p. 16, ll. 36–42; Warner (ed.), *Libelle*; Gower, *Mirour*, p. 333, ll. 25369–92. Christine de Pizan valued merchants for providing the foundation for learning and culture; Bornstein (ed.), *Middle English Translation*, pp. 8–14, 184–9.
[272] Adams (ed.), *Chief Pre-Shakespearean Dramas*, 'The Play of the Wether' (*c.*1533), pp. 403–4, ll. 357–61. See also Bevington (ed.), *Medieval Drama*, pp. 1003–4; Roberts, *Studies*, p. 115.
[273] Adams (ed.), *Chief Pre-Shakespearean Dramas*, 'The Play of the Wether' (*c.*1533), p. 403, ll. 349, 351.
[274] Swanton (ed.), *Anglo-Saxon Prose*, pp. 107–15; Nelson (ed.), *Fifteenth Century School Book*, pp. 54–5, no. 233, p. 90, no. 377. See also Scattergood (ed.), *John Skelton*, 'The Bowge of Courte' (1498), p. 49, ll. 120–4.
[275] Chaucer, *Canterbury Tales*, 'Parson's Tale', pp. 314–15, ll. 775–80.

The merchant and his licit activities had become accepted by the majority of medieval religious commentators. The fickle nature of Lady Fortune loomed large in such portrayals, as with the merchant in the 'Shipman's Tale', but also provided a partial exoneration for their endeavours.[276] Martindale, Patterson, Cahn, Scattergood and McGalliard have all argued that there were few hints of dishonesty or immorality in the practices of the merchant in the 'Shipman's Tale'.[277] This businessman was diligent, prosperous and honest, in contrast to his own wife and Daun John, and Chaucer's portrayal could be interpreted as a justification for the commercial life.

However, literary depictions of merchants are typically steeped in ambiguity and uncertainty, perhaps reflecting the moral dilemmas of merchants themselves. For instance, the 'Shipman's Tale' merchant's notion of money as a plough which could be used for making more money lay at the heart of scholarly prohibitions of usury, even if his financial deals were strictly within the parameters of secular law.[278] There is also consternation regarding the notion of equity in exchange and whether sufficient repayment or restitution has been made.[279] There is a complexity and plurality in Chaucer's constructs that ambiguously both valorises and criticises commercialism.[280] This is not necessarily at variance with conventional approaches. In a similar manner, in many moral texts, the basic mercantile virtues of care in profit-making, thrift in spending and tenacity in the face of hardships were also interpreted as the signs of an avaricious man. *Fasciculus Morum* noted that the avaricious were eager to grasp riches and slow to give them. Avarice led to three qualities: 'hard work in acquiring, fear in possessing, and pain in losing . . . so that he [an avaricious man] never ceases by day or night, early or late, to satisfy the disorderly, indeed wretched lust of his eyes, whether by journeying about or riding or sailing, whereby he places himself in the greatest physical

---

[276] For the 'Wheel of Fortune', see Silverstein (ed.), *Medieval English Lyrics*, p. 58.

[277] Martindale Jr, 'Chaucer's merchants', 315; Patterson, *Chaucer*, p. 352; Cahn, 'Chaucer's merchants'; Scattergood, 'Originality', 225–6; McGalliard, 'Characterization', 10–17.

[278] In this analogy, money could not reproduce itself, like seeds in a field, except through a perversion of its true nature (e.g. usury). Burke (ed.), *Treatise*, pp. 7–10. Wood argues that this was a medieval misreading of Aristotle's theory, who nevertheless argued that making profit from money was an unnatural abuse of its role as a medium of exchange. Wood, *Medieval Economic Theory*, pp. 84–7. Bills of exchange avoided charges of usury because of the level of risk involved. Hunt and Murray, *History of Business*, p. 72.

[279] Mair, 'Merchants and mercantile culture', pp. 192–4.

[280] Fulton, 'Mercantile ideology', 313.

as well as spiritual dangers'.[281] The character of 'Medill Elde' in *The Parlement of the Thre Ages* (late fourteenth century) avidly accumulated worldly possessions even while dressed in grey and serious attire.[282]

The criticisms of late medieval moralists were thus balanced against portrayals of merchants as sober, responsible, reliable and hardworking. This was part of their attempt to reconcile the mercantile way of life with the values asserted by the Church. Several justifications were advanced in favour of the mercantile way of life: honest intent, the risk and labour involved in making a profit and the contribution of the merchant to the prosperity of the realm.[283] Trade was no longer condemned as inherently sinful and instead it was the individual who erred, tempted by commercial opportunities to make gain. Jacques le Goff, Aaron Gurevich and Diana Wood have argued that, by the thirteenth century, trade had been 'morally rehabilitated', and that, although there were still fears of damnation, merchants had also developed an ideological view of their worth based upon pragmatism and social prestige.[284] Many of these commercial men were powerful and wealthy, as well as consumers of urban culture, and were thus seemingly able to influence a reworking of the traditional stereotype of the avaricious merchant. From the thirteenth century, writers certainly developed a number of justifications for merchant activity, which demonstrate attempts to incorporate elements of the mercantile world into their ethical framework. Yet, the justifications formed were also based upon those very elements of the merchant's life – risk, instability, prudence – that bred cynicism, secrecy and sly tactics on the borders of legality. In *The Canterbury Tales* even the virtues of hard work and good reputation had the potential to be interpreted as instruments of avarice, which, in turn, gave way to an ignorance of the perilous state of the soul or else pride and vanity which disguised debts and dishonesty. A religious poem from the thirteenth century similarly described the extensive travels of a chapman, who neglected sleep, risked

---

[281] *Fasciculus Morum*, pp. 312–15. See also *Vices and Virtues*, p. 30, ll. 5–23; Nelson (ed.), *Myrour*, p. 131, ll. 19–34 (BL, MS Harleian 45, fol. 63r–v); Trigg (ed.), *Wynnere and Wastoure*; Warren (ed.), *Dance of Death*, p. 44, ll. 337–44, p. 45, ll. 489–96.

[282] Conlee (ed.), *Middle English Debate Poetry*, pp. 110–11, ll. 136–51.

[283] Thomson, 'Wealth, poverty'. See also Larson (ed.), *King's Mirror*, pp. 79–86. The *King's Mirror* was a thirteenth-century Norwegian dialogue and included passages intended as a code of conduct for aspiring merchants. They were expected to be courageous on their travels, pious, careful, hardworking, honest, studious and even-tempered.

[284] Le Goff, *Your Money*; Gurevich, 'The merchant', pp. 243–83; Wood, *Medieval Economic Thought*, pp. 115–20. This was in contrast to the unequivocal denunciations of merchants by John of Salisbury in the twelfth century. Nederman, 'Virtues of necessity', 62.

great perils and often lost his goods. One of the implications of the poem is that he took these risks for 'catel' (i.e. gain), with little care for his wife and children if he were lost.[285] A fifteenth-century sermon similarly placed a negative slant on the privations and hard work of traders:

so þese covetyse pepyll [people] for the grete love of worldly ryches some men put theyre bodyes to grete labor and grete travell bothe on londe [land] and on water / and many men sufferythe some tyme grete hynger and thurste and all is for þe riches of þis worlde.[286]

In this interpretation, the virtues of hard work, solemnity and risk were the by-products of a selfish and unscrupulous desire for profit. From as early as the thirteenth century, writers were beginning to depict a more competitive and individualistic environment in which hard work was not always a virtue but sometimes a vice leading to personal, excessive gain.[287]

Wynnere and Wastoure (c.1352–70) was a complaint poem that directly criticised acquisitive, selfish, miserly and sober accumulators ('Wynnere'), akin to merchants, who might be building up financial capital but were derided as hoarders. They were diverted from their duty to the community and their own salvation. On the other hand, however, there were the idle, gluttonous and profligate wasters ('Wastoure'), who were equally detrimental to the common good and social order. The text was thus condemning both avarice and prodigality.[288] However, as Lois Roney argued, the poet was also advocating moderation and the need for a state of equilibrium in the flow and exchange of commodities.[289] Merchants were expected to perform an honest communal service (in line with estates theory) which would reasonably sustain their family. Any excess profit was not to be accumulated but rather redistributed for the common good, particularly through charitable acts.

Service to the community and fair distribution of gains provided a central justification for mercantile activity. In *Piers Plowman*, Truth would not grant merchants a pardon 'a poena et a culpa', because they worked on Sundays and Holy Days and swore by God's name in order to sell goods and make extra profits. Nevertheless Truth recognised the necessity of the merchant in providing essential foodstuffs, goods and

[285] Horstmann (ed.), *Minor Poems*, p. 344, ll. 576–83. See also Owst, *Literature and Pulpit*, p. 352; Oxford, Bodleian Library, MS Bodley 649, fol. 44r; BL, MS Harleian 2398, fol. 22v.
[286] Nottingham University Library, MS 50, fol. 60v.   [287] Baldwin, *Masters*, i, p. 264.
[288] Bestul, *Satire*; Jacobs, 'Typology of debate'.
[289] Roney, '*Winner and Waster*'s "wyse wordes"'; Trigg (ed.), *Wynnere and Wastoure*, p. 13, l. 390.

services and thus allowed them a dispensation based on utility. As long as they dealt according to justice and distributed their profits (beyond their own sustenance) to charity, then they could continue to trade.[290] The exoneration of sins by giving was based upon traditional clerical moralism, whereby the vices of avarice and covetousness were opposed by the virtues of mercy and charity. In William Caxton's *Dialogues* (1483), for example, Fraunseys the draper represents an ideal trader who gave gladly 'for goddes sake' to the ill, prisoners, widows and orphans.[291] Similarly, in *Piers Plowman* merchants were expected to use some of their profits for hospitals, roads, bridges, prisons, religious institutions and in alms for the poor.[292] Truth promised them heaven 'vnder his secret seal' (an equivalent to a papal dispensation) and would overlook minor offences against spiritual honesty as long as they benefited the community. Myra Stokes has suggested that merchants were therefore offered a practical solution to excessive profit.[293] *Piers Plowman* implied that there were margins of acceptability in commercial practice provided traders accepted certain responsibilities. If they contributed to social justice they could further the cause of Truth and be included in the list of honest livings.

A number of positive and virtuous characteristics were associated with merchants in late medieval literature, but these same portrayals were also frequently tinged with ironic or suspicious overtones. Gower suggested that the merchants of his time not only tried to justify their 'faults', but dealt in large sums which were well beyond a sufficient and honest living.[294] Similarly, in the late fourteenth century, Christine de Pizan warned merchants against 'pompe or pryde' and told them to turn their earnings towards God and the poor rather than social ambitions and fashion.[295] Church scholars and moralists defended merchant profits on the basis of distribution, service and risk, and attempted to disentangle the sinfulness of trade and the fragility of man from the conduct of commerce itself. Mercantile endeavours could be thus legitimised, but merchants themselves were still presented as inclined towards sin.

---

[290] *Piers Plowman*, C.VII.24–33.
[291] Bradley (ed.), *Dialogues*, p. 34. Many works also exhorted merchants to pay tithes they owed, e.g. *Jacob's Well*, p. 40, l. 28 – p. 41, l. 3.
[292] See below, pp. 377–80, for a discussion of traders making bequests to such beneficiaries.
[293] Stokes, *Justice*, pp. 216–18.
[294] Gower, *Mirour*, p. 339, ll. 25811–24. A hankering for richly adorned possessions and dress was an allegation often made against the socially mobile, such as merchants, knights and lawyers.
[295] Bornstein (ed.), *Middle English Translation*, pp. 185–6. Christine de Pizan wrote *Livre du Corps de Policie* in late fourteenth-century France, and it was translated into English in 1521.

Market traders, hawkers and victuallers

Mercantile sins and suspicions were readily applied to petty market traders, but there was seemingly more reticence when it came to justifications. This was perhaps partly due to the difference in wealth accrued from their professions, but there was also something more fundamental in the divergent depiction of their aspirations and demeanour. John Gower, in particular, regarded retailers as utterly fraudulent in seeking profit:

They are the ones who mostly sell to poor people, and they are called retail shopkeepers. Fraud is their chief; this is seen often when they make a penny out of a farthing. The retail shopkeeper is very villainous.[296]

Images of market traders drew heavily upon contemporary notions of the common good, justice and their essential service to poorer sectors of society. Compared to merchants, there are perhaps fewer specific literary references to retailers, hawkers, brewers, bakers, pedlars and other humbler mainstays of the medieval marketplace. However, there is enough material to allow us to draw out both comparisons and contrasts with images of the wholesale, international dealer.

Early medieval depictions of petty traders are hard to find. The baker and cook in Aelfric's late tenth-century *Colloquy* were concerned mostly with the production of good quality food for the nobleman's table and the writer says little about the selling of such foodstuffs.[297] Fitzstephen's 'Description of London' in the late twelfth century provides a mouthwatering sample of the victuals on offer by the bank of the Thames: 'a public eating-house: there every day, according to the season, may be found viands of all kinds, roast, fried, and boiled, fish large and small, coarser meat for the poor, and more delicate for the rich, such as venison, fowls, and small birds'.[298] Other early representations of petty traders, dating from the twelfth century, describe petty trade as either a sideline or a stepping-stone to better things. These depictions often adhered to the literary conventions used for 'merchants', before this term became synonymous with international wholesalers. Consequently, petty traders were also initially portrayed as hardworking, honest and successful. One of the earliest images of petty trade can be found in the *Lay of Havelok the Dane*, translated into English in the thirteenth century. In this tale, Grim fished off the coast of east England, in the community that was to become

---

[296] Gower, *Mirour*, p. 345, ll. 26305–20.
[297] Gem (ed.), *An Anglo-Saxon Abbot*, pp. 190–1; Swanton (ed.), *Anglo-Saxon Prose*, pp. 107–15.
[298] Wheatley (ed.), *Stow's Survey*, p. 504.

Grimsby, while he and his foster-son, the prince Havelok, sold the catch. The poem describes them travelling door-to-door in town and country, eventually returning home with bread, corn and beans. If they managed to catch a lamprey, Havelok would go to Lincoln market, and with the proceeds from the sale he could return with simnel bread, meal, meat, hemp and rope.[299] Further tales from the twelfth and thirteenth centuries suggest that men could make their fortunes through hard work as traders, rising up from humble hawkers to wealthy wholesalers. Walter Map's *De Nugis Curialium* (late twelfth century) described the advancement of Ollo and Sceva from hawkers to packmen and, lastly, to partners in a successful merchant business. Similarly, St Godric of Finchale (*c.*1070–1170) famously rose from selling small wares around villages and farms to become a city merchant, before giving all his goods away to become a hermit.[300]

In twelfth- and thirteenth-century mentalities, then, medieval retailers and wholesalers were expected to be honest and hardworking and this would be rewarded by success. In later texts, these characteristics were most often associated with the merchant. Written sources of the fourteenth and fifteenth centuries rarely ascribed such qualities to petty traders, but instead disparaged them for having turned away from virtuous behaviour in preference for a life of venality, dishonesty and selfishness. There was an increasing separation in how wholesale merchants and petty traders were viewed. Compared to the wholesale merchants, one could argue that there was a deterioration, or at least a lack of rehabilitation, in the petty traders' reputation since the twelfth century. Petty traders were a ubiquitous presence in English towns and villages, particularly given the commercial developments during the twelfth and thirteenth centuries. The very prevalence of retailers could provoke abuse, especially against victuallers, who were hampered by inelastic demand and variable supplies, but also by expectations of low prices. For moralists, there appeared to be little inherent risk in petty trade. If small-scale traders became wealthy, it was assumed by moralists that this could only have been achieved by fraudulent means. Equally, if petty traders were not contributing to the communal need for essential items, then they were considered to be peripheral and fraudulent. Many retailers appeared to provide only negligible improvement to products.

---

[299] Skeat (ed.), *Lay of Havelok*, pp. 28–9, ll. 760–84, pp. 30–1, ll. 811–25. See also Smithers (ed.), *Havelok*, pp. 25–7.

[300] James, Brooke and Mynors (eds.), *Walter Map*, pp. 392–403, Dist.iv, c.16; Stevenson (ed.), *De Vita*. The Life of St Godric was written in the mid-eleventh century by Reginald, a monk of Durham.

The petty trader was a generalised figure in literary texts, with little in the way of characterisation or individuality. Even when they were ascribed personal names, such as Rose the Regrator, Beton the Brewstere or Haukyn in *Piers Plowman*, they remained sin-laden stereotypes. While Gower appeared to respect the honest merchant, his attitudes towards petty traders barely concealed his disgust for them and he charged all victuallers with fraud.[301] The fraudulent vices of petty traders become unified and personified in *Piers Plowman* and Langland's portrait of 'Rose the Regrator', who was the wife of Covetousness ('Coveitise'). She cheated in cloth-making and brewing, with poor quality, over-pricing, false measures, loosely spun yarn and favouritism in her vending. Covetousness is similarly represented as a trader with a beetled brow, puffy lips, baggy cheeks and bleary eyes, wearing dirty clothes which are torn and covered with lice. This image incorporated characteristics from carved figures of avarice and misers, as well as from contemporary depictions of Jews.[302] A 1427 manuscript of the C-Text of *Piers Plowman* provides a vivid marginal illustration of Covetousness and draws heavily on the accompanying passage (see Figure 3), though the clothes are not as threadbare and torn as the text exerts. Nevertheless, the eyes, lips and stubble are emphasised with red pigment, while the figure grasps a hanging purse that is redolent of both money-making and pendulous cheeks: 'And as a letherne pors lollede his chekes'.[303] According to Langland, Covetousness had been an apprentice and learned to lie, weigh falsely and use fraud in stretching cloths in order to make a profit.[304]

Another trader in *Piers Plowman* is 'Haukyn', the hawker cum minstrel, who personifies the whole body of the sinning, penitent laity in the 'Fair Field'. His form of 'Activa Vita' (Active Life) was far removed from Langland's vision of the honest toil of the saintly Piers Plowman. However hardworking and industrious Haukyn is, his coat is still stained with the seven deadly sins; he ultimately resorted to false measures, false oaths and cheating.[305] Stella Maguire sees Haukyn as being central to Langland's resignation that a good practical life would never be sufficient for salvation, because of man's ultimate inability to refrain from sin when material temptations are present.[306] Haukyn could not help but cast his

---

[301] Gower, *Mirour*, p. 345, ll. 26305–28.

[302] Covetousness refers to lessons from the Jews and Lombards later in the C-Text passage; *Piers Plowman*, c.vi.243–4. For depictions of the wandering Jew, see Wolfthal, 'The wandering Jew'; Camille, *The Gothic Idol*, ch. 4.

[303] *Piers Plowman*, c.vi.199. See Pearsall and Scott (eds.), *Piers Plowman*, pp. xlviii–xlix; Scott, 'The illustrations', 34.

[304] *Piers Plowman*, a.v.107–45, b.v.188–229, c.vi.196–233.

[305] *Ibid.*, b.xiii (esp. 355–61, 379–98), c.xvi.

[306] Maguire, 'The significance of Haukyn'; *Piers Plowman*, b.xiii.355–61, 383–98. The name 'Haukyn' might be a pun on 'hawking'.

Figure 3: 'Coveitise' in *Piers Plowman*.

Notes: This marginal manuscript illustration of Covetousness is part of a 1427 version of William Langland's *Piers Plowman*.
Source: Oxford, Bodleian Library, MS Douce 104, fol. 27r.

love 'moore to good[s] þan to god'.[307] Malcolm Godden claimed that Haukyn should be seen as a trifling pedlar considered wholly peripheral to society's needs, unlike the industrious Piers in the fields.[308] If the personification of Haukyn incorporates temptations and superficiality, it is possible that Langland wished for an idealistic return to what he perceived as old-fashioned, simple self-sufficiency. For moralists like Langland, the practice of trade was probably difficult to reconcile with spiritual redemption, and therefore the only solution was to turn to spiritual guidance and voluntary poverty.

[307] *Piers Plowman*, B.XIV.325–6.   [308] Godden, *Making*, pp. 111–12.

Figure 4: Sleeping pedlar robbed by apes.

Notes: This English marginal illumination is part of the 'Smithfield Decretals', produced *c*.1325–50.

Source: BL, MS Royal 10.E.IV, fol. 149v.

At the most humble end of the marketing scale were pedlars and itinerant chapmen, who were portrayed in a uniformly negative way. These mobile tradesmen were presented as exterior to the social body, potentially disorderly, fraudulent and frivolous. Many pedlars are represented in late medieval literature as habitual liars pandering to the vanities and fashions of women in order to sell them trifling, unnecessary knick-knacks. Several poems commented on the feminine goods and lecherous intentions of chapmen 'lyght of fote'.[309] In a sermon from *c*.1390, John Wyclif complained of friars who became pedlars, carrying purses, pins, girdles, spices, furs and silks to give to women in order to foster more amorous ambitions.[310] The friar in Chaucer's *Canterbury Tales* also had a hood 'ful of knyves [knives] and pynnes [pins], for to yeven [give] faire wyves'.[311]

A bestiary illustration of the fable of the 'Pedlar and the Apes', from the early fourteenth-century Smithfield Decretals, shows apes ransacking the goods of a sleeping pedlar and a miscellany of goods are strewn upon the ground, such as gloves, caps, mirrors and small musical instruments (see Figure 4). Against the backdrop of humorous vignettes, the moral

---

[309] Greene (ed.), *Early English Carols*, p. 279, no. 416; BL, MS Sloane 2593, fols. 26v–27r; Robbins (ed.), *Secular Lyrics*, p. 6, no. 7.

[310] Matthew (ed.), *English Works of Wyclif*, p. 12. See also Wright (ed.), *Political Poems*, i, pp. 264–5; *Piers Plowman*, A.Prol.58–63, C.Prol.59–64.

[311] Chaucer, *Canterbury Tales*, 'General Prologue', p. 27, ll. 233–4. See also Adams (ed.), *Chief Pre-Shakespearean Dramas*, 'The Play called the Foure PP', p. 370, ll. 214–15, 235–42; Randall, *Images in the Margins*, p. 555, plate cxv, fig. 551 (pedlar with silver beakers); Gardner (ed.), *New Oxford Book of English Verse*, p. 167, no. 169.

Figure 5: An ape as pedlar.

Notes: This marginal manuscript illustration from an English Book of Hours (early fourteenth century) depicts an ape carrying a board full of trinkets to sell.

Source: BL, MS Harleian 6563, fol. 100r.

messages are the sloth of the pedlar and the pride of the apes.[312] This image, drawing upon an episode in *Roman de Renart*, can be seen in numerous contexts, from marginal illustrations to misericords.[313] In a different marginal image, one of the roles is inverted as an ape is represented as the pedlar (see Figure 5). The use of apes for humorous effect again serves to emphasise the debased nature of these activities, since

[312] Janson, *Apes*, pp. 216–22; Grössinger, *World Upside-Down*, pp. 100–2.
[313] Randall, *Images in the Margins*, plates VI–VII, figs. 20–4. Misericords depicting apes robbing the pedlar can be found at Manchester Cathedral (early sixteenth century); St George's Chapel, Windsor (*c.*1477–83); Bristol Cathedral (*c.*1520); Beverley Minster (*c.*1520). Remnant, *Catalogue*, p. 7, no. 4, p. 46, no. 4, p. 82, no. 8 (plate 9b), p. 173, no. 6; Varty, 'Reynard the Fox', 350–1; Varty, *Reynard the Fox*, pp. 72–3.

Figure 6: Pedlar or tinker.

Notes: This marginal image from the Luttrell Psalter (*c.*1320–40) shows a pedlar or tinker carrying his wares and bellows on his back, while a dog seemingly bites his ankle.

Source: BL, MS Additional 42130, fol. 70v.

they were identified with fraud and deceit.[314] The association of pedlars with apes and thieves only served to reinforce their own suspect activities on the very boundaries of acceptability. The Luttrell Psalter (*c.*1320–40) includes a marginal illustration of a wandering pedlar or tinker (see Figure 6); the latter is implied by the bellows on his back, which was used when making repairs to pots and pans, although humble pedlars and tinkers were often engaged in similar trading activities. In this image, the dog biting at his ankle is symbolic of both marginality and slander, with the pedlar's own lowly status emphasised by the dog apparently chasing him away. In addition, the movement towards another marginal image of a mermaid holding a mirror and comb is perhaps related to the pedlar's frivolous and flirtatious wares. It was assumed that only through fraud and lying could such wares be sold.[315]

---

[314] For the ape as a baker, see Randall, *Images in the Margins*, plate xv, fig. 69.
[315] Davis, 'Men as march with fote packes'.

Figure 7: Bakers.

Notes: This is a marginal manuscript image from the 'Smithfield Decre-tals' (*c.*1325–50) and shows two bakers loading balls of dough into an oven.

Source: BL, MS Royal 10.E.IV, fol. 145v.

Another itinerant trader was the 'tynker' or 'sprongbolle' who wan-dered the countryside and towns offering his services as a repairer of household vessels, and 'when he sees a jar, cooking pot, bowl, cup, or plate that is cracked or in pieces, he is at once joyful and expects to make some money from it'.[316] In the mid-fourteenth century, John Bromyard highlighted the humble nature of these tinkers and pedlars by claim-ing that it was their own clothes and pots that often needed mending most of all.[317] Hawkers, hucksters, pedlars and tinkers were regarded as marginals in society, prone to dishonesty, frauds and lies.

However, trade itself, of course, served a useful communal purpose and could not be regarded as inherently dishonest, whether it was mer-chants involved or more humble retailers. Trade was an important part of everyday life and local market ethics needed to be reconciled with traditional morality. Indeed, William Langland recognised the utility of trade and included business abilities in the list of talents bestowed on men by Grace to facilitate honest living.[318] A few images show orderly and uncontroversial retail trading practices, particularly when linked to regulation. There are illustrations of hard-working, clean bakers with uniform ranks of loaves and no sign of deception (Figure 7), or butchers and fishmongers working from bloodless stalls.[319] There are also depic-tions of tapsters and victuallers serving contented customers, such as in

---

[316] *Fasciculus Morum*, pp. 158–9.   [317] Bromyard, *Summa Predicantium*, 'Correctio'.
[318] *Piers Plowman*, B.XIX.234–5.
[319] E.g. Oxford, Bodleian Library, MS Douce 5, fol. 8r; BL, MS Additional 18852, fol. 13r (Book of Hours, Bruges, late fifteenth century), cf. Basing, *Trades and Crafts*, p. 88; Hammond, *Food and Feast*, plate 5.

Figure 8: Victualler or taverner.

Notes: The woodcut shows a victualler, hosteler or taverner on the left, with keys at his waist, holding out a piece of bread and a cup of wine to a customer. The victualler represented the sixth pawn in Caxton's translation of *The Game of Chess* (1483).

Source: Cessolis, *De Ludo Scachorum*, bk. 3, ch. 6 (Cambridge, Trinity College Library, VI.18.3, fol. 57r).

Caxton's *The Game of Chess*, or even customers helping themselves from the barrel (Figures 8 and 9).[320] Robert Wyer's early sixteenth-century book about the assize of bread included woodcuts that showed a well-organised bakery with uniform loaves and prominent scales.[321] Similarly, Caxton's dialogues intermingled honest, hard-working traders among the corrupt; the former included Eustace the tailor ('good diligence that he doth to the peple'), Fraunseys the draper ('he gyueth gladly for goddes sake'), Forcker the cordwainer ('put more lether to werke than thre othir') and Gombert the baker ('He selleth so well his flessh').[322]

Nevertheless, in the majority of literary depictions, petty traders were regarded as sinful and degenerate members of the community, holding

[320] See also BL, Additional MS 27695, fol. 7v (fifteenth century).
[321] Wyer, *Assyse of Breade*, VII. The assizes of bread and ale were standardised laws for price, quality and quantity, based on agreed custom. See below, pp. 231–48.
[322] Bradley (ed.), *Dialogues*, pp. 34–46.

Figure 9: 'Tapster'.

Notes: This wood carving is part of a mid-fifteenth-century misericord (a small shelf on the underside of a hinged seat in the choir stalls). The style of dress suggests that this is a man filling a tankard of ale or wine from a barrel, though it is traditionally called 'The Tapster'.
Source: St Laurence's Church, Ludlow.

little regard for their neighbours or clientele. Victuallers, in particular, were traditionally disparaged by medieval commentators. John Gower, for example, accused bakers, brewers, taverners, butchers and poulterers of regularly selling at excessive prices, and of failing to fulfil their divinely ordained station of providing the community with food and drink at a reasonable price.[323] Bakers, brewers and other victuallers were especially prone to accusations that they harmed the community through poor-quality and adulterated foodstuffs. The late thirteenth-century *Lutel Soth Sermun* denounced false chapmen, bakers and brewers for caring only about money. They would end up in Hell for their sins of false measures and poor quality.[324] Gower similarly accused the brewer of often making bad ale from rotten grain, so that even 'God himself hates him', and of

---

[323] Gower, *Mirour*, p. 345, ll. 26305–20.
[324] Morris (ed.), *An Old English Miscellany*, p. 189, ll. 33–48; Sisam and Sisam (eds.), *Medieval English Verse*, pp. 11–12, no. 7, ll. 5–12.

supplying good ale to gain customers, but then mixing good and bad ale thereafter to regulars without lowering his price. Even with good ale, the combination of both false measures and high prices meant that it was almost as expensive as wine.[325]

Langland's Rose the Regrator was an archetypal alewife who was depicted as adulterating ale:

I bouȝte hire barly; heo breuȝ it to selle.	bought; she brewed
Penyale and pilewhey heo pouride togidere.	Penny-ale; spring water?; poured
For laboureris and louȝ folk þat lay be hymselue;	humble folk
þe beste in my bedchaumbre lay be þe wouȝ.	wall
And whoso bummide þerof, bouȝte it þeraftir,	tasted thereof
A galoun for a grote, god wot no lasse,	gallon; groat; knows no less
Whanne it com in cuppemel; þat craft my wyf vside.	cupfuls
Rose þe regratour was hire riȝte name;	
Sheo haþ yholde huxterie elleuene wynter.[326]	huckstery [for] eleven winters

She is thus depicted as watering down her cheaper ale ('penyale'), which is sold to labourers and the poor. Rose kept her best ale hidden in her bedchamber so that it could be served to favoured customers by unstandardised cups, at the excessive price of a groat (4d.) for a gallon. These were violations of trading regulations. The cheating alewife, who adulterated her ale and sold by irregular measures, became a commonplace stereotype by the fifteenth century and can be seen in drama and the visual arts. In a surviving early sixteenth-century text of the *Chester Mystery Play*, an alewife or tapster was included in the pageant of cooks and innkeepers as an optional comic interlude.[327] Such mystery plays were usually staged by guilds during the fifteenth century, combining a major religious feast (such as Corpus Christi) with civic pageantry. The realities of trade were never far from the presentations of each guild and the scenes might include figures, such as the alewife, with which the audience could readily associate. Left behind in Hell after all the other souls

[325] Gower, *Mirour*, p. 343, ll. 26137–72.
[326] *Piers Plowman*, A.V.133–41, B.V.217–25, C.VI.221–9.
[327] Lumiansky and Mills (eds.), *Chester Mystery Cycle*, i, pp. 337–9, play xvii, 'Harrowing of Hell', ll. 277–336; Lumiansky, 'Comedy and theme'; Axton, *European Drama*, pp. 183–4; Bennett, *Ale*, p. 125.

had been delivered, and about to be wedded to a demon, the alewife laments her several misdemeanours, including the use of short measures ('of kannes I kept no trewe measure'), excessive pricing for poor ale ('My cuppes I sould at my pleasure, deceavinge many a creature, thoe my ale were nought'), brewing watery ale ('bruynge so thinne'),[328] and the use of prohibited additives to hide the ale's weakness ('esshes [ashes] and hearbes I blend amonge and marred so good malt'). She warns her audience that others will face cruel torments in Hell because of their fraudulent activities, for offending against the statutes of the realm and for 'hurtinge the commonwealth'. The dramatists were thus drawing upon actual regulations and laws, such as the assize of ale:[329]

> Tavernes, tapsters of this cittye
> shalbe promoted here with mee
> for breakinge statutes of this contrye,
> hurtinge the commonwealth,
> with all typpers-tappers that are cunninge,
> mispendinge much malt, bruynge so thinne,
> sellinge smale cuppes money to wynne,
> agaynst all trueth to deale.[330]

It might appear to be counter-productive advertising for cooks and innkeepers to highlight the corrupt alewife since they themselves were associated with similar trading abuses, while the innkeepers probably employed tapsters. Indeed, the sins of the tavern are mentioned repeatedly in this scene, referring to both sellers of ale and wine within permanent premises. However, the damned alewife was a stereotype by the late fifteenth century.[331] The image seemingly amused audiences, and by recognising this character the cooks and innkeepers were actually emphasising their own watchfulness over such misdemeanours, particularly those committed by humbler retailers, and the need to uphold the law for the common good.

There is a significant number of surviving depictions of alewives that highlight the reinforced image of these female traders. A fifteenth-century misericord from St Laurence's Church, Ludlow, depicts a dishonest alewife holding her measuring cup and being cast into the mouth of Hell by demons, while a third demon reads from a scroll of misdemeanours

---

[328] For poetic complaints about 'small ale' (weak or watered-down), see Chambers and Sidgwick (eds.), *Early English Lyrics*, pp. 229–31, no. cxxxiii.

[329] Market laws, including the assize of ale, are discussed further in Chapter 2.

[330] Lumiansky and Mills (eds.), *Chester Mystery Cycle*, i, p. 338, play xvii, 'Harrowing of Hell', ll. 301–8.

[331] Robert Reynes, a local official in Acle (Norfolk), included in his commonplace book a satirical verse: 'A fryer [friar], an heyward, a fox, and a fulmer [polecat] sittyng on a rewe [row], / A tapster hym sytting by to fylle þ cumpany, þ best is a screwe [wretch]'. Louis (ed.), *Commonplace Book*, p. 299, no. 96.

Figure 10: A dishonest alewife being cast into Hell.

Notes: This mid-fifteenth-century misericord shows an alewife, with a horned headdress and tankard, being carried over the shoulder of a demon, while another demon plays the bagpipes. Flanking this central wood carving are a demon reading a list of the alewife's offences and a depiction of the alewife disappearing into the mouth of Hell. The carver's mark is just visible above the alewife's mug.

Source: St Laurence's Church, Ludlow.

(see Figure 10). Carvers of misericords had a great deal of freedom in the subjects and designs they chose and many carvings were taken from bestiaries, satires and fables. They were often intended to be amusing vignettes of society, and carvers drew on their own experiences of daily life as well as the exempla of preachers.[332] The whole tableau in the Ludlow misericord reflects the admonitions and ridicule of the pulpit and stage. The alewife wears a fashionably 'horned' headdress, but is almost completely naked, perhaps highlighting her female vanity or drawing on images of lechery that commonly accompanied portrayals of alewives.[333]

---

[332] Anderson, 'Iconography', pp. xxiii–xxxix; Grössinger, *World Upside-Down*, p. 13.

[333] Anderson, *History and Imagery*, no. 65; Mullaney, 'Fashion and morality', pp. 81–2. For horned headdresses, see Stevens and Cawley (eds.), *Towneley Plays*, i, p. 412, ll. 391–2, where Tutivillus the demon reads out a list of offenders, including one who 'is hornyed like a kowe [cow] – a new-fon syn'.

Images of the Last Judgement were widespread in the parish churches of late medieval England, reminding people of their eternal fate for sins committed in this world.[334] Many were located above the chancel arch as part of Doom paintings, emphasising that the souls of the good would enter Paradise but that the sinful would burn in the flames of Hell. The early fifteenth-century mural at Holy Trinity Church, Coventry, vividly depicts the fate of sinners. This includes three alewives, again adorned with horned headdresses and tankards, who are in chains and being led by a demon to their fate (see Figure 11). The earlier *Holkham Bible Picture Book* (*c*.1325–30), in its illustration of the Last Judgement, similarly includes a baker (with a paddle and scales) and alewife (with a jug of ale) being carried by devils to a boiling cauldron fuelled by the mouth of Hell (see Figure 12). Below them is a barrow full of lost souls, perhaps symbolic of the tumbrel or dung-cart in which alewives were often punished.[335] A similar use of a demon and cart to carry such sinners to the mouth of Hell is seen on a fifteenth-century roof boss at Norwich Cathedral.[336] The link between spiritual and temporal punishment for sinful behaviour was thus being reinforced in the minds of both congregations and readers.

Such negative portrayals of alewives were widespread in early sixteenth-century texts. In John Skelton's satirical poem, *The Tunnyng of Elynour Rummyng*, Elynour is an alewife who serves a multitude of drunken and lecherous female customers. Like the *Chester Mystery Play* alewife, Skelton says of Elynour 'The devyll and she be syb'. She serves anyone who can provide payment and a variety of goods are offered in exchange for a mug of ale: ragged clothes, brass pans, wedding rings and even a cradle.

> She breweth noppy ale,   *rough ale*
> And maketh thereof port-sale   *sale at the door?*
> To travellars, to tynkers,
> To sweters, to swynkers,   *toilers; labourers*
> And all good ale drynkers,
> That wyll nothynge spare,
> But drynke tyll they stare
> And brynge them selfe bare.[337]

---

[334] Images of alewives in Doom paintings can be found at: Bacton (Suffolk), Barking (Essex), Brooke (Norfolk), Croughton (Northamptonshire), Mears Ashby (Northamptonshire), St Thomas's Church, Salisbury (Wiltshire), St Michael's Church, St Albans (Hertfordshire), Stoke-by-Clare (Suffolk), Wymington (Bedfordshire). See Ashby, 'English Medieval Murals of the Doom'. Diana Wood has noted how some depictions of the Last Judgement also included St Michael weighing souls in the balance, akin to a commercial transaction. Wood, *Medieval Economic Thought*, p. 3.

[335] See below, pp. 263–4.   [336] Rose and Hedgecoe, *Stories in Stone*, pp. 113–14, 137.

[337] Scattergood (ed.), *John Skelton*, p. 217, ll. 102–9; Wyrick, 'Withinne that develes temple'. The existence of a real 'Alianora Romyng' in Leatherhead in 1525 lends

Figure 11: Alewives in a medieval Doom painting.

Notes: These three alewives, with their horned headdresses and tankards, are being led by devils on the Day of Judgement. They are part of a larger Doom wall-painting (*c.*1430s).

Source: Holy Trinity Church, Coventry.

Her customers are represented as being so obsessed about acquiring ale that they will frequent a dirty establishment which is run by an

a veneer of authenticity to Skelton's misogynistic satire. Alianora was a 'common tippellar of ale' who was fined 2d. for selling ale in small measures for an excessive price. Scattergood (ed.), *John Skelton*, p. 450.

Figure 12: The Last Judgement: the blessed and the damned.

Notes: This is an illustration from the Holkham Bible (1325–30). In contrast to the peaceful entrance to Heaven on the left, the devil is taking a chained group to Hell's mouth (centre), including a baker with his paddle and scales, and an alewife with her drinking jug.
Source: BL, MS Additional 47682, fol. 42v.

unscrupulous dealer. The grotesque humour of Skelton's poem is intended to highlight the absurdity of drunkenness, but it also touches upon familiar criticisms of the alewife.[338] For example, John Lydgate emphasised the womanly wiles and wantonness of the alewife in his *Ballade on an Ale-Seller*. Through flirtatious laughter, kissing and 'counterfett cheer, medlid withe dowbilnesse', Lydgate's alewife used guile to lure men to pay more money for their ale.[339] The *Chester Mystery Play* alewife is described as a 'gentle gossippe', implying that she was an affable companion, but also later as someone who used 'many false othes to sell thy ale'.[340] In a similar way, the tapster, Kitt, in *The Tale of Beryn*

---

[338] Bennett, 'Misogyny', 169–71. In her study of alewives, Bennett identified the threads of general antipathy towards victuallers, fears about drunkenness and gluttony (particularly in the alehouse), and misogyny. See also Bennett, *Ale*, pp. 122–44.

[339] MacCracken (ed.), *Minor Poems*, 'A Ballade on an Ale-Seller', pp. 429–32, no. 9, esp. ll. 46–52.

[340] Lumiansky and Mills (eds.), *Chester Mystery Cycle*, i, pp. 337–9, play xvii, 'Harrowing of Hell', ll. 286, 335.

(an anonymous fifteenth-century continuation to the *Canterbury Tales*), leads on the Pardoner with seductive talk in order to pry money out of him:

> As tapsters, and oþer such, þat hath wyly
> wittis   *wily wits*
> To pik mennys pursis, and eke to bler hir
> eye;   *pick; purses; blear his eye*
> So wele they make seme soth, when þey
> falssest ly.[341]   *true; lie*

The implication of all this was that women were universally duplicitous and that an alewife embodied female vices.

If those running alehouses were roundly criticised, the alehouse itself was also widely denigrated in literature of the fourteenth and fifteenth centuries where it was associated with the vices of gluttony, drunkenness, idleness and lechery.[342] It also drew people away from church, as *Dives and Pauper* claimed:

> þey han leuer gon to þe tauerne þan to holy chirche, leuer to heryn a tale or a song of Robyn Hood or of some rybaudye þan to heryn messe or matynys or onyþing of Goddis seruise.[343]

Indeed, an alehouse or a tavern was regarded as the devil's church. *The Book of Vices and Virtues* remarked:

> þe tauerne is þe deueles scole hous [devil's school house], for þere studieþ his disciples, and þere lerneþ his scolers [scholars], and þere is his owne chapel, þere men and wommen redeþ and syngeþ and serueþ hym [serve him], and þere he doþ his myracles as longeþe deuel to do.[344]

In the Gluttony passage from *Piers Plowman*, Beton the Brewster's alehouse is a hive of temptation, gaming and drinking. Many of the activities are in direct contrast to Church liturgy, as signified by the luring of Gluttony from his journey to Mass by promises of ale and food. During his time in the alehouse, the ale-cup is passed around like a holy chalice

[341] Furnivall and Stone (eds.), *Tale of Beryn*, p. 15, ll. 442–6, also p. 2, ll. 22–9, p. 21, ll. 652–5.
[342] There were also secular songs which celebrated the drinking of ale; Chambers and Sidgwick (eds.), *Early English Lyrics*, p. 226, no. cxxx, p. 230, no. cxxxiii; Sisam and Sisam (eds.), *Medieval English Verse*, p. 564, no. 319; see also Seymour (ed.), *Selections*, p. 15, ll. 121–52.
[343] (They rather go to the tavern than to holy church, rather hear a tale or a song of Robin Hood or of some ribald than to hear Mass or Matins or anything of God's service.) *Dives and Pauper*, I, i, p. 189, ll. 38–41 (also, I, i, p. 199, ll. 4–6).
[344] *Vices and Virtues*, p. 53, l. 29 – p. 54, l. 7. See also *Ayenbite of Inwyt*, pp. 56–7; *Jacob's Well*, p. 147, l. 25 – p. 148, l. 12; *Handlyng Synne*, p. 37, ll. 1017–34 ('Tauerne ys þe deuylys [devil's] knyfe'); Britnell, 'Morals', p. 21.

and the rowdy songs are sung like hymns.[345] If the alehouse was traditionally the antithesis of the Church, then the people who frequented
Beton's alehouse represented those groups that were seen as perverting
the traditional structures of society – petty traders, wasters, labourers,
cooks, cobblers, tinkers, butchers, millers, hostelers and clerics – with
their 'service' provided by the alewife. This was the commercial world
parodied and set against the values of the Church.

Judith Bennett has identified much fifteenth- and sixteenth-century
misogynistic literature against alewives and alehouses, perhaps reflecting
social anxieties in that period. She argued that male victuallers received
less virulent and personal criticism than alewives. Attacks upon male
victuallers centred on their business practices rather than their person,
physical appearance, establishments, piety, sexuality or likely salvation.[346]
Bennett also argued convincingly that there were few medieval depictions of male victuallers or petty retailers that matched the personalised
description of Elynour Rummyng. The closest were those personifications created by William Langland in the form of Haukyn and Covetousness. However, a lack of such literary images before the fifteenth
century was perhaps related more to the type of literary output at this time
than to any difference in treatment between male and female victuallers.
Medieval texts usually involved generalised stereotypes rather than individual portraits, which only began to appear with Chaucer. Bennett has
perhaps overstated her case for the different treatments of alewives and
victuallers, mostly based on evidence from sixteenth-century sources
since many portrayals of late medieval male victuallers appear no less
vitriolic than those for female alewives.[347] Indeed, John Lydgate's attack
on male bakers and millers is quite extreme. He suggested that these
traders should build their guild chapel under the pillory, since so many
were sent there to be punished, and he called for persistent offenders to
be hanged.[348] Literary texts, as we have seen, do not exactly bristle with
virtuous or positive representations of male petty traders.

---

[345] *Piers Plowman*, A.V.146–92, B.V.296–344, C.VI.350–406; Gray, 'The clemency of cobblers'; Aers, *Community*, p. 39; Owst, *Literature and Pulpit*, pp. 434–41. The passages
from *Ayenbite of Inwyt* and *The Book of Vices and Virtues* were simpler versions of Langland's later work, with Glutton entering a tavern upright but leaving without speech,
reason or the ability to walk. The writers described these as the devil's miracles and
the tavern as a den of thieves. *Ayenbite of Inwyt*, pp. 56–7; *Vices and Virtues*, p. 53,
l. 26 – p. 54, l. 19.

[346] Bennett, *Ale*, pp. 131–2; Bennett, 'Misogyny'.

[347] Bennett did note a gradual change in alewife depictions over the fifteenth and sixteenth
centuries. Bennett, *Ale*, pp. 136, 140.

[348] MacCracken (ed.), *Minor Poems*, 'Put Thieving Millers and Bakers in the Pillory',
pp. 448–9, no. 15 (BL, MS Harleian 2255, fol. 137r). Millers were often depicted as
having a 'golden thumb', which they used to take more toll than they were actually

This is not to disagree with Bennett that depictions of women drew on earlier male stereotypes, to which extra female-associated vices of gossip, lechery and unfaithfulness were appended. John Gower displayed an unconcealed misogyny in *Mirour de l'Omme*, arguing that women retailers connived more than men and had an inherent coldness and covetousness in their desire for profit.[349] Interestingly, Lydgate's depiction of a beautiful alewife who tempts male customers with 'counterfett cheer', but then discards them when they run out of money, has many parallels with an earlier tradition of male innkeepers who used flattery and false friendship to sell their foodstuffs.[350] Similarly, the alewife's bogus mugs are paralleled by Dan Michel's taverners who falsified their measures by filling the bottom of them with scum.[351] Gower accused male tavern-keepers of deceitfully mixing new wines with old, or even water, in order to gain more money. They, like the innkeepers, are faux-friendly and ingenious in the ways of deceit when they need to conceal the defects of their wines.[352]

The early fourteenth-century image of the innkeeper in the Holkham Bible is an unflattering portrayal, complete with a snout-like nose, broad chin and grasping hands (see Figure 13). This image, of course, has particular connotations due to the innkeeper that turned Mary and Joseph away (Luke 2:7). However, the taints of such a religious association may have been influential in other depictions, and the outward appearance is meant to suggest corruptness or trickery within.

In the same way, Skelton parodied these conventions by making the alewife, Elynour, an aged, drowsy and scurvy-ridden woman, with a hooked nose, bleary eyes, slavering lips and slack skin, wrinkled 'lyke a rost pygges eare, brystled with here'.[353] Her customers are all women, drawn to the alehouse not only by ale but an atmosphere of gossip and lechery. These developments thus drew upon a variety of conventions, not least the prominence of women in the ale trade and the association of the alehouse with prostitution.[354] The sexualised imagery was also intended to provoke humour, perhaps drawing upon the audience's own

---

allowed. Chaucer, *Canterbury Tales*, 'General Prologue', p. 32, ll. 562–3; Jones, 'Chaucer and the medieval miller'.

[349] Gower, *Mirour*, p. 345, ll. 26329–40.

[350] See above, p. 71. Chaucer's host or innkeeper, Harry Bailly, was tactful, sensible and genial, even perhaps overbearingly merry. Bowden, *Commentary*, p. 292; Page, 'Concerning the host'.

[351] *Ayenbite of Inwyt*, pp. 44–5.

[352] Gower, *Mirour*, pp. 341–3, ll. 25993–6124.

[353] (like a roast pig's ear, bristled with hair.) Scattergood (ed.), *John Skelton*, pp. 214–16, ll. 1–90. This has remarkable parallels to the description of Covetousness in *Piers Plowman*, see p. 98.

[354] For a preacher's discussion of taverners' wiles in attracting customers, compared to the use of clothes and kisses to stir someone to lechery, see Ross (ed.), *Middle English Sermons*, p. 234, ll. 22–31, p. 235, ll. 19–34, p. 236, ll. 1–9.

Figure 13: The innkeeper.

Notes: This illuminated illustration from the Holkham Bible (1325–30) shows Mary and Joseph approaching the innkeeper and his wife for a room.

Source: BL, MS Additional 47682, fol. 12v.

prejudices. However, Elynour was also subject to the same, traditional criticisms that many victuallers faced. For instance, she sold bad ale, made under the roosts of hens so that the subsequent brew was deliberately thickened by the 'donge [dung] of her hennes'.[355]

These images were partly an appeal to the sensibilities of an audience which expected its prejudices to be reinforced. Some texts went further and accused victuallers of potentially harmful, even homicidal, activities. The *Chester Mystery Play* complained of mixtures of wines and inadequate fermentation of ale that led to 'sycknes and disease'.[356] Such adulteration

---

[355] Scattergood (ed.), *John Skelton*, p. 219, ll. 190–215.
[356] Lumiansky and Mill (eds.), *Chester Mystery Cycle*, i, p. 339, play xvii, 'Harrowing of Hell', ll. 317–20.

caused concern in other sources. *The Ship of Fools* illustrated the anxieties felt about adulterated wine:

> Saltpeter, sulphur, bones of dead,
> Potash, milk, mustard, herbs ill-bred
> Through bungs are pushed into the kegs.
> The pregnant women drink these dregs,
> That they bear children premature,
> A wretched sight one can't endure.
> From out such drink diseases grow,
> Some people to the churchyard go.[357]

A tongue-in-cheek passage from Jacques de Vitry tells of a butcher who sold cooked meat and was asked by a customer to lower his price, on the grounds that he had bought meat from no one else for seven years. The butcher answered in great wonder, 'Have you done that for so long a time and yet live?'[358] In a similar vein, Bromyard complained about sellers of corrupt mutton who smeared and coloured sheep's eyes with blood to make the carcasses appear fresh.[359] Even Chaucer's Cook, whose culinary skills were praised, had a festering mormal (ulcer) on his shin in a recognisable Chaucerian juxtaposition that suggested a lack of personal hygiene behind his tempting dishes. This forewarns us of the Host's claims that the Cook had actually sold many twice-cooked pies, owned a fly-ridden shop and was cursed by pilgrims for selling food that made them sick.[360] In the early sixteenth-century *Wyll of the Deuyll*, the victualler is associated with thin, stale meat; rotten, stinking fish; and mouldy, maggoty pies, which all provide work and profit for the physician.[361] There was almost an expectation of unhygienic practices in victualling trades.[362]

Victuallers as a whole, whether male or female, were thus subject to negative depictions and suspicions of cheating, verbal duplicity and low

---

[357] Zeydel (ed.), *Ship of Fools*, p. 328. See also Gower, *Mirour*, pp. 341–2, ll. 25993–6016.

[358] Crane (ed.), *Exempla of Jacques de Vitry*, pp. 70, 201, no. clxii.

[359] Bromyard, *Summa Predicantium*, 'Ornatus'.

[360] Chaucer, *Canterbury Tales*, 'General Prologue', p. 29, ll. 379–87, and 'Cook's Prologue', p. 84, ll. 4336–52; Hieatt, 'A cook', pp. 203–4; Lisca, 'Chaucer's guildsmen', 322–4.

[361] Furnivall (ed.), *Jyl of Breyntford's Testament*, pp. 26–7. See also BL, MS Harleian 463, fol. 15r–v.

[362] Other practices were complained of as unwanted by-products of trade, such as butchers and fishmongers leaving stinking waste in the streets, the smells of the tanning and meat industries, and the noises of the blacksmiths. Baildon (ed.), *Poems of William Dunbar*, 'To the Merchantis of Edinburgh', pp. 34–6; Furnivall (ed.), *Early English Poems*, pp. 154–5; Wright and Halliwell (eds.), *Reliquiae Antiquae*, ii, pp. 174–7; BL, MS Harleian 913, fol. 7v; Davies (ed.), *Medieval English Lyrics*, p. 213, no. 115; Spearing and Spearing (eds.), *Poetry*, pp. 220–1; Robbins (ed.), *Secular Lyrics*, pp. 106–7, no. 118.

hygiene, while alewives faced supplementary accusations relating to traditional female vices. The very ubiquity and importance of such traders in supplying everyday staples meant that they were a readily identifiable and perhaps easy target for moral condemnation. All were warned of the potential fires of Hell as punishment for their deceptions. By adulterating and over-pricing their foodstuffs, victuallers were regarded as having disregarded their social responsibility at the expense of the common good.

Middlemen and hoarding

Cornmongers who stored grain in the hope of profiting during times of scarcity were similarly vilified for taking advantage of the necessities of their neighbours.[363] Robert Rypon (sub-prior of Durham) preached in the early fifteenth century about those who 'suspect that things will be very dear in the future, and, in hope of future gain, withhold corn from the market, which if sold would be a timely benefit to the whole country. Without doubt such men harm not one person only, but the whole countryside'.[364] *Wynnere and Wastoure*, *Jacob's Well* and *Handlyng Synne* also drew upon the same themes, universally condemning those who bought up needful things in times of plenty to sell at times of scarcity, damning them for theft, covetousness, usury and even murder.[365] *Jacob's Well* even implied that the merchants themselves could be the cause of dearth: they 'gadryst to-gedere corn or vytayles for to makyn a derthe, and that the poore peple schulde nedys bygge of the at thi prise be thi lust, thou synnest horrybely'.[366] Hoarders were seen as vile because they profited from the misery of their fellows and kept back the fruits of the earth while the poor went hungry.[367] Caxton, in his 1483 dialogues, alluded to the same practice of hoarding among bakers. Fierin the baker 'hath vpon his garner lieng an hondred quarters of corn. He byeth in tyme and at hour, so that he hath not of the dere chepe.'[368] Gower decried those who were even more devious in their manipulative activities, sending their

---

[363] Langholm, *The Merchant*, p. 241.

[364] BL, MS Harleian 4894, fol. 36r; cf. Owst, *Literature and Pulpit*, p. 356.

[365] Trigg (ed.), *Wynnere and Wastoure*, p. 13, ll. 368–78; *Handlyng Synne*, p. 176, ll. 5377–98. See also *Ayenbite of Inwyt*, pp. 35–7; Furnivall (ed.), *Pilgrimage*, pp. 472–3, ll. 17645–88; *Dives and Pauper*, I, ii, pp. 201–2, ll. 24–47.

[366] (gather together corn or victuals to make a dearth, and that the poor people should by necessity buy from thee at the price thy desires, thou sins horribly.) *Jacob's Well*, p. 212, ll. 22–6.

[367] Jordan, *Great Famine*, prologue.

[368] (has lying in his granary a hundred quarters of corn. He buys up in time and 'at hour', so that he has not a dear purchase.) Bradley (ed.), *Dialogues*, p. 35, ll. 28–34.

own wheat to be sold in the market and then offering more money to buy it themselves, thus increasing the price.[369]

Such disparagement of hoarding and market manipulation was, of course, a useful pulpit device to condemn miserly, avaricious behaviour and exhort generosity. Jacques the Grete went even further by asking of traders: 'why desyrest [desire] thou to desseyue [deceive] thy neyghbours, why desyrest thou famyne, or why desyrest thou the tyme of nede. Certeynly thou demest thy self subtyl, but yf thou do thus or desyrest thus, yt ys no subtylte, but ys very schrewdnes [shrewdness] and euelnes [evilness].'[370] He argued that many traders sought personal prosperity despite the poverty and adversity of others and that, through these actions, they ignored notions of truth and justice. This drew upon similar themes developed earlier in the fourteenth century and perhaps reflected memories of the Great Famine of 1315–18. In *Wynnere and Wastoure*, Wynnere also hopes for bad harvests so he can make a great profit from grain stored the previous year. But if the harvest is good he wants to hang himself in despair.[371] Several writers lamented that corn kept back from the poor often ended up merely as food for mice or rotting in the barns, thus meaning that grain merchants were both oppressors of the poor and profligate in their use of earth's bounty.[372]

The poor were commonly portrayed as victims of middlemen's guile, with the latter represented as cold-hearted about the plight of those in distress. A thirteenth-century poem saw hoarders of grain as pitiless and uncaring, ignoring the weeping, hungry, sick and unclothed poor. They sent the needy on their way with the words: 'Goþ or wey, corn is dere!' God's reply was to send the hoarders and usurers to Hell.[373] The poor, as one of the most vulnerable sectors of the community, proved ideal rhetorical victims for dishonest traders.[374] Langland described how those who grew rich on mercantile trickery were seen to have established their fortunes on 'that the poure puple shoulde putten in hure womben'.[375] *Memoriale Credencium* implied a responsibility for the poor that should be adhered to by all: 'man is iugged [judged] coueytous þat wiþholdeþ to him self more þan him nedeþ. eynge a pore man deye [die] for hungere

369   Gower, *Mirour*, p. 88, ll. 6289–300 (also p. 343, ll. 26197–208, for those who conceal their stocks of wheat in order to see the market price increase).
370   BL, MS Harleian 149, fols. 238v–239v.
371   Trigg (ed.), *Wynnere and Wastoure*, p. 13, ll. 368–78. See also Crane (ed.), *Exempla of Jacques de Vitry*, pp. 71, 202, no. clxiv.
372   *Handlyng Synne*, p. 176, ll. 5377–98; Jamieson (ed.), *Ship of Fools*, ii, pp. 166–9; *Jacob's Well*, p. 212.
373   Horstmann (ed.), *Minor Poems*, p. 171, ll. 47–62, p. 172, ll. 75–86.
374   Langholm, *Economics*, pp. 578–9; Langholm, *The Merchant*, p. 241.
375   *Piers Plowman*, C.IV.83.

oþer for defaute þat he my3te helpe him'.[376] Any harm that came to them was seen as a slight on the whole community.

Overall, conventional criticisms were laid at the door of cornmongers concerning hoarding, speculation and failure to heed their communal responsibilities. Britnell has suggested that such fears about the activities of middlemen might have caused problems for traders, since they made the enterprise to seek out scarce supplies morally dubious.[377] The storing of grain was also potentially immoral, even though manorial accounts show that landlords, both lay and ecclesiastical, often sold late in the agricultural year when prices were higher.[378] However, not all literary portrayals were wholly negative about the functioning of the grain trade. The author of *Dives and Pauper* (drawing on Aquinas) recognised the potentially beneficial purpose of cornmongers, declaring: 'but 3if it be don pryncipaly for comoun profyt and for saluacion of þe contre it is medful'.[379] The writer drew a pertinent biblical parallel with Joseph feeding the people of Egypt at a time of hunger (Genesis 47): 'þou he selle forth in tyme of nede to helpe of oþere as þe merket [market] goth he doth no synne [sin] in þat'. In this line there is an implicit understanding of the power of market forces ('as þe merket goth') and thus a recognition that a trader had a right to make a living: 'Also it may be don be comoun rygt [common right] of merchandye, thei to wynnyn [gain] therby her lyuynge [living], so that thei causyn no derthe [dearth] be her byyne [buying]'. As long as their prime intention was not avaricious in seeking to worsen the market conditions by manipulation, then there were conditions whereby merchants could trade legitimately in grain. The writer understood the unreliability of grain supplies when harvests were bad and that generally middlemen did have an important role to play in supply and distribution at times of dearth, as long as they adhered to notions of social responsibility.

However, the only means of supply for the average consumer, especially in towns, was through the petty retailers and middlemen, and they subsequently received the brunt of criticism.[380] *The Simonie* particularly complained of brewers and bakers who, through their deceptions, stole the hard-earned wages of simple labourers. Gower similarly accused butchers of refusing to sell their meat in amounts of less than a penny, thus disadvantaging poor people.[381] He also disparaged those traders

---

[376] BL, MS Harleian 2398, fol. 22r.   [377] Britnell, *Commercialisation*, p. 174.
[378] See Stone, *Decision-Making*.   [379] *Dives and Pauper*, I, ii, pp. 201–2, ll. 24–47.
[380] Bennett suggested that such depictions served as a safety valve for the release of social tensions; Bennett, *Ale*, pp. 136–7.
[381] Embree and Urquhart (eds.), *The Simonie*, p. 98, B439–44; Gower, *Mirour*, p. 344, ll. 26221–32. See also King (ed.), *Life of Marie D'Oignies*, p. 83, no. 52.

who sought to buy large quantities of goods at a low price from people in distress, or who sold small quantities at a high price to the poor on credit, since such practices damaged the commonalty.[382] Any profits so accrued were considered to be against justice, reason and truth, since it seemed that any petty trader who became rich must have been avaricious and fraudulent. Indeed, William Langland berated urban traders for their pretences, luxuries and large houses, which he claimed had been acquired at the expense of others.[383] Petty traders were expected to live as moderately as their customers, otherwise the principles of both commutative and distributive justice had been usurped.

Readers were encouraged to identify with or imagine themselves as a victim of trading abuses, while the writer highlighted the responsibilities of petty victuallers and middlemen in the increasingly commercial environment of late medieval England. The trader's denial of responsibility for customers, especially the poor, was regarded as a rejection of the common weal and traditional hierarchies. Only an acceptance of their communal and 'natural' duty would lead to Christian salvation.[384] Consequently those who personally prospered were seen to have done so illegally or at the expense of others, for all excess gains should have been distributed for charitable uses: to restore the debt that someone else must have lost in the trader's dealings. The poor were therefore viewed in medieval literature as the beneficiaries of restitution and redistribution as well as the victims of fraud and avarice.

Livelihood and credit

Unusually, *Jacob's Well* provided a justification for a trader's deceit on the basis of the needs of subsistence:

I muste nedys weyin falsly chese and wolle, spyserye and othere thinges, and selle be false mesurys as othere don; ellys schulde I loose ther-on . . . I muste nedys be wyles, defraude and falsnesse dysseyven my neygboure. For yif I dede truthe, I shulde nevere thryve, but ben a beggere. And nedys I and my wyif and my chylderyn and my meyne muste lyve![385]

---

[382] Gower, *Mirour*, p. 91, ll. 6553–64.
[383] *Piers Plowman*, A.III.65–84, B.III.76–94, C.III.77–122.
[384] Yunck, 'Satire', pp. 151–2.
[385] (I must by necessity weigh falsely cheese and wool, spices and other things, and sell by false measures as others do; else should I lose therein . . . I must by necessity by wiles, fraud and falseness deceive my neighbour. For if I was true, I should never thrive, but be a beggar. And by necessity I and my wife and my children and my household must live!) *Jacob's Well*, p. 261, ll. 13–20.

This is one of the few instances where the poverty of the petty traders themselves was espoused and it drew attention to their need to operate on the margins of acceptability just in order to survive. Another rare example was proffered in a late medieval Norfolk sermon regarding a lender of money: 'according to his view of things, he lays all the blame on God, saying, "There's nothing else we can do. Times are hard. Unless we cheat like this, and extort interest when we lend money, we wouldn't be able to live."'[386] Some moralists therefore addressed the idea that honest traders might be spiritually saved but, because of their virtue, might well go out of business. Caxton alluded to this in his 1483 *Dialogues*, where his character, Gombert the butcher, is honest yet poor: 'He selleth so well his flessh that to hym it appereth [harms/impairs]; For I sawe hym so poure [poor] that he knewe not what to put in his mouth'. By comparison, Guy the fishmonger sells all manner of fish (perhaps implying rotten as well as wholesome) and owns a prosperous property.[387] Successful traders were implicated as corrupt and dishonest people, while poor, hard-working dealers were struggling to survive. This was perhaps why Langland was unusually pragmatic in his acceptance of minor offences like oath-giving and Sunday trading, as long as trade was otherwise undertaken according to social justice.[388] There was also a realisation that traders might be tricked by fellow traders, especially through the unwitting purchase of stolen goods. However, as soon as a trader discovered that a ware was stolen they were expected to return it to the rightful owner and bear the cost (though they could track down the seller), or else they too would be branded a thief. Profits made while the buyer held the commodity in good faith could be kept, but restitution should be made to the true owner for any other profits.[389] Ultimately, intention and reputation determined the validity of a trader's actions.

In Caxton's *Dialogues*, the hosier made clothes so badly shaped that the writer counselled that no man should buy from him; while the brewer had large quantities of ale unsold because he was renowned for 'euyll drykne'.[390] Medieval writers realised that a seller's good reputation was an increasingly important attribute that determined the success of his business and the extent of his credit.[391] For Caxton, word of mouth and

---

[386] Oxford, Bodleian Library, MS Laudian Misc. 77, fol. 37r–v, cf. and trans. Spencer, *English Preaching*, p. 96.

[387] Bradley (ed.), *Dialogues*, pp. 37, l. 31 – p. 38, l. 8.   [388] See pp. 94–5.

[389] *Dives and Pauper*, I, ii, pp. 149–50, ll. 70–100.

[390] Bradley (ed.), *Dialogues*, pp. 34–46.

[391] Chaucer, *Canterbury Tales*, 'General Prologue', p. 28, ll. 280–1; Knott, 'Chaucer's anonymous merchant'; Reale, 'A marchant', pp. 95–6. Christine de Pizan advised that 'marchauntes ought to be true of their woorde and soueraynly of their promysses',

reputation were influential factors in deciding quality and vendors. Some of his stereotyped traders did maintain a solid reputation. Eustace the tailor worked diligently throughout the night to deliver clothes at the promised time, while Forcker the cordwainer worked more leather than any other because his good shoes sold well. This need to maintain a trustworthy reputation was also alluded to in the Christian precept of acting towards your neighbour as you would expect them to act towards you: 'And yf thou wold he shold be trewe to the and pay his dettis [debts] and begyle the not wyth subtiltees [subtleties] and sleyghtis [sleights] in byyng and sellyng, do the same thyself to hym'.[392] Those who failed to heed this advice were likely to find their reputation difficult to redeem. In Caxton's translation of Aesop's fable of the wolf, fox and ape, the fox's past deceptions and sleights mean that even when he offers to undertake a deed profitable to all, he is derided as a thief and knave: 'For they that ben customed to doo ony frawde or falshede / shall euer lyue ryȝte heuyly [heavily] and in suspycion'.[393] Within the broad moral conceptions of medieval England, traders continually operated on the cusp of acceptability. They were viewed as treading a fine line between honest profit and covetous deceit, so it is unsurprising if actual reputations were fragile and easily lost.

Repentance and punishment

Market trade was often depicted as inordinately dominated by worldly matters to the neglect of salvation. Religious texts commonly upbraided markets and fairs that were held on a Sunday or in a church, criticising traders who worked through religious festivals.[394] They not only missed divine services for the sake of material profit but encouraged others to do so. *Dives and Pauper* was, however, more circumspect in its approach and exempted victuallers from the prohibition of working on Sunday, provided they were serving those attending Christian services.[395] Nonetheless, there were vibrant biblical pretexts for the suspicion of trading activities on Sundays and in churches.[396] *The Book of Vices and Virtues*, for example, quoted the passage from the Bible in which Jesus drove buyers

as this led to the establishment of trust. Bornstein (ed.), *Middle English Translation*, pp. 184–9.

[392] Blake (ed.), *Quattuor Sermons*, p. 47, ll. 15–21.

[393] Lenaghan (ed.), *Caxton's Aesop*, p. 101.

[394] Swinburn (ed.), *Lanterne*, p. 91, ll. 1–6, p. 92, ll. 18–25; Matthew (ed.), *English Works of Wyclif*, p. 280; *Fasciculus Morum*, pp. 370–1; Stockton (ed.), *Major Latin Works*, 'Vox Clamantis', bk. v, ch. 11, pp. 210–11.

[395] *Dives and Pauper*, i, i, p. 10, l. 31, and p. 291, ll. 24–34.

[396] Langholm, *Economics*, pp. 102–3; Wood, *Medieval Economic Thought*, pp. 112–13.

Figure 14: The cleansing of the Temple.

Notes: The manuscript illustration from the Holkham Bible (1325–30) shows Jesus driving traders from Jerusalem's Temple.

Source: BL, Additional MS 47682, fol. 26r.

and sellers out of the Temple.[397] This image of retailers being driven from the Temple by Christ can be seen twice in the early fourteenth-century Holkham Bible, including a butcher, a stock-dealer, a money-changer and an unusual illustration of a female poulterer selling doves (based on Matthew 21:12; Mark 11:15; John 2:14) (see Figure 14).[398] The context of their trading indiscretions and the physical berating of Jesus are only too clear in the scriptures: 'but you have made it a den of thieves' (Luke 19:46; Matthew 21:13). 'He told those who were selling the doves. "Take these things out of here! Stop making my Father's house a marketplace!"' (John 2:16).

Traders' disdain for God and salvation was also highlighted in discussions of those who dealt in sacred relics. Sacrilege and simony were placed alongside trading fraud and theft in moral texts that discussed avarice. John Lydgate asserted that many sellers of relics had stolen them from churches and repainted them, as well as making holes for blood and

---

[397] *Vices and Virtues*, p. 237, l. 26 – p. 238, l. 5; Matthew 21:12, Mark 11:15–17, Luke 19:45–6, John 2:14–16. See also Erbe (ed.), *Mirk's Festial*, pp. 115–16; Lefébure (ed.), *St Thomas Aquinas*, pp. 225–31, vol. 38: Injustice, ii–ii, q.77, a.4.

[398] BL, Additional MS 47682, fols. 20r, 26r; Hassall (ed.), *Holkham Bible Picture Book*.

milk to run out as if by a miracle and using sham cripples to demonstrate their efficacy.[399] In a late fifteenth-century Suffolk play, *The Play of the Sacrament*, Aristory, a Christian merchant of Aragon, steals the Eucharist to sell to the Jews.[400] They proceed to desecrate the sacrament; a common accusation against Jews. However, it is the wealthy, well-travelled merchant who is deemed to err more. The play initially emphasises how much he has to thank God for the riches he has accrued during his life. His outwardly pious nature is noted: 'I wyll atteyn to wourshyppe my God that dyed on þe roode [cross]'. The sacrilegious nature of his deal with the Jonathas the Jew is thus put into stark contrast. Aristory succumbs to the deal after a lengthy bargaining process that persuades him to take and sell the Eucharist for a hundred pounds. Avarice has outweighed the spiritual risks:[401] 'To fullfyll my bargayn haue I ment, / For þat mony wyll amend my fare'. However, Aristory's conscience is not allayed by the money and he eventually confesses his crime. As punishment, the merchant is forbidden to ever sell or buy again and has to undertake a strict penance of fasting and praying. His action, partly reluctant, partly avaricious, parallels that of Judas, who was sometimes compared to merchants: 'for he made marchauntyse by false menys [means] when he solde cristes [Christ's] owne persone and so solde himselffe to þe devyll bothe body and sowle [soul]'.[402] It also drew on a popular image of the traders' own predilections, whereby avarice and material gain took primacy over spiritual salvation.[403]

Late medieval moralists commonly portrayed traders who ignored the plight of their souls. Langland's 'Fair Field Full of Folke', with its many petty traders, was located between the tower of Truth and the Deep Dale, essentially metaphors for salvation and damnation. Yet, the people of the 'Fair Field' seemed unaware of either destination and continued busily in their material activities.[404] The inclination of traders to ignore the instructions of the Church and so commit sacrilege and sins in the pursuit of profit was a common theme. Devotional literature often pinpointed the temptations of covetousness to the neglect of salvation. Gower even suggested that some merchants were ambivalent towards the fate of their

---

[399] Furnivall (ed.), *Pilgrimage*, pp. 484–5, ll. 18104–165; Ross (ed.), *Middle English Sermons*, p. 125, ll. 1–21 (BL, MS Royal 18.B.xxiii, fol. 94r); *Fasciculus Morum*, pp. 336–7; Royster, 'Middle English treatise', 29–30.

[400] Davis (ed.), *Non-Cycle Plays*, pp. 58–89.

[401] Similar accusations were made by preachers against covetous men who profess virtue, but whose actions are ultimately dictated by greed. Ross (ed.), *Middle English Sermons*, p. 264, l. 34 – p. 265, l. 25.

[402] Nottingham University Library, MS 50, fol. 198v.

[403] Ross (ed.), *Middle English Sermons*, pp. 98–9.

[404] *Piers Plowman*, A.Prol.97–109, B.Prol.217–31, C.Prol.221–32.

soul compared to material pleasures: 'one of them said to me the other day that he who can have the sweetness of this life and turns it away would, in his opinion, commit folly, for afterwards no one knows truly where we go nor by what way'.[405] John Wyclif accused traders of hypocrisy for, despite their busy and hard-working lives, their efforts went towards worldly gain, using subtleties and false oaths, and nothing was spared for spiritual salvation.[406] One sermon disparaged the way in which some traders falsely believed they could pacify God: 'I wil gyffe [give] a boke or a chalys [chalice] to the chyrche, or a bell or a vestment, and so schall I be prayed for every sonday, or ells I wyll do some other good deede lyke to the same'.[407] However, moralists insisted that giving ill-gotten gains as alms and church offerings would not necessarily save a man's soul or be pleasing to God. Ultimately, their lies and frauds would be revealed on the Day of Judgement and they would go to Hell.[408] The bakers and brewers of the *Lutel Soth Sermun* cared only for silver and were warned that, unless they relinquished their sinful practices and covetousness, they would never enjoy the kingdom of heaven.[409] In the *Chester Mystery Play*, when everyone else had left Hell, the alewife, with her false weights and measures, remained.[410]

Traders were expected to relinquish any unreasonable profits during their lifetime through alms or gifts to the Church. *Jacob's Well* provides a list of abuses for which traders needed to make immediate restitution under the pain of eternal damnation. This included the selling of adulterated or defective goods, the use of false weights and measures, the artificial inflation of corn prices to the harm of the poor, the hiding of faults through false words and oaths, and the myriad sins of usury.[411] A merchant's last opportunity for repentance and restitution was on his

---

[405] Gower, *Mirour*, p. 340, ll. 25915–20; *Piers Plowman*, B.XIII.383–98, C.VI.258–77. See also Nelson (ed.), *Fifteenth Century School Book*, p. 54, no. 230.

[406] Matthew (ed.), *English Works of Wyclif*, pp. 24–5. Paradoxically, Italian merchants often wrote 'In the name of God and of profit' at the head of their ledgers. Origo, *Merchant of Prato*, p. 9.

[407] Nottingham University Library, MS 50, fol. 198r.

[408] Ross (ed.), *Middle English Sermons*, pp. 125, 182; *Dives and Pauper*, I, i, pp. 17–18, ll. 14–20; *Fasciculus Morum*, pp. 344–7; Cigman (ed.), *Lollard Sermons*, p. 228, ll. 746–53; Warren (ed.), *Dance of Death*, p. 44, ll. 329–44, p. 45, ll. 481–96, p. 47, ll. 497–512, pp. 51–2, ll. 393–416; Zeydel (ed.), *Ship of Fools*, p. 67; Gower, *Mirour*, pp. 90–1, ll. 6517–64, p. 340, ll. 25933–44; BL, MS Harleian 149, fol. 239r–v; *Handlyng Synne*, p. 176, ll. 5377–98 ('To þe deuyl, body and bone').

[409] Morris (ed.), *An Old English Miscellany*, p. 189, ll. 33–48; Sisam and Sisam (eds.), *Medieval English Verse*, pp. 11–12, no. 7, ll. 5–12.

[410] Lumiansky and Mills (eds.), *Chester Mystery Cycle*, i, pp. 337–9, play xvii, 'Harrowing of Hell', ll. 277–336.

[411] *Jacob's Well*, p. 212, ll. 6–29 (also p. 66, ll. 3–27; p. 138, ll. 6–11; p. 208, l. 14 – p. 209, l. 4).

deathbed.[412] However, some did not recognise their peril until it was too late. The *Chester Mystery Play* alewife despaired that she had dealt so deceitfully in life: 'Sorrowfull maye I syke [sigh] and singe that ever I so dalt [dealt]'.[413] Another scene in the play cycle lists the damned souls' laments, including that of a merchant who finally understood that his worldly actions of false 'winning' brought him nothing but torment in Hell:

> Alas, alas, now woe is me!
> My foul body, that rotten hath be,
> and soul together now I see.
> All stinketh, full of sin.
> Alas! Merchandise maketh me –
> and purchasing of land and fee –
> in Hell-pain evermore to be,
> and bale that never shall blin.[414]   *sorrow; cease*

The lament continues by highlighting the misery he had caused to the poor during his dealings in merchandise and land and as a court official. He had also failed to pay his tithes to the Church because he felt this was a waste of his gains.[415] Such neglect of social duties and spiritual salvation reflected many of the concerns expressed in the wills of medieval people.[416] Indeed, the seven corporal works of mercy were prominent in the teachings of the medieval Church, and all were expected to show mercy and relieve the poor, sick and vulnerable before they faced the ultimate judgement.[417] It was hoped, in sermons, devotional literature and plays, that stressing the fate of sinners in the afterlife would encourage immediate repentance because death could come at any time. In the *Chester Mystery Play*, the warning to the merchant was stark:

> To work in world so wickedly
> and now burn in the Devil's belly?
> Alas, that ever I was born![418]

Illustrating the fate of the body and soul after death was a widely used device against those who worried about their worldly wealth. There were

---

[412] Borgström, 'The Complaint of God', 519, ll. 345–52; *Vices and Virtues*, p. 42, l. 14 – p. 43, l. 2; Gallagher (ed.), *Doctrinal*, pp. 146–7.

[413] Lumiansky and Mills (eds.), *Chester Mystery Cycle*, i, p. 338, play xvii, 'Harrowing of Hell', ll. 299–300.

[414] Mills (ed.), *Chester Mystery Cycle*, pp. 425–6, ll. 325–32.

[415] *Ibid.*, pp. 425–6, ll. 333–52.   [416] See below, p. 379.

[417] Duffy, *Stripping of the Altars*, pp. 357–9. The seven corporal works of mercy are: feeding the hungry; giving drink to the thirsty; clothing the naked; visiting the sick; visiting the prisoner; sheltering the stranger; and burying the dead.

[418] Mills (ed.), *Chester Mystery Cycle*, p. 426, ll. 354–6.

many vivid descriptions of the torment of merchants and usurers after death and in Hell.[419] A conventional scene was the unrepentant usurer who was buried with his money; he was later uncovered to reveal demons filling the dead man's mouth with red-hot coins.[420] Many exempla contain tales of usurers who refused to repent or to provide restitution for their usurious gains and who subsequently went to Hell, with their corpses stinking, full of burning coins and fed on by toads. Preachers told traders and usurers that temporal goods were transient and that to make a god of them was sin. They should care more for their soul or else it would exist in pain after death, while 'wormes schul eten [eat] þe, and sone schalte þou be for-ȝeten [forgotten]'.[421] Wyclif recognised that those who practised usury did it so subtly that few would be able to prove it, but this merely meant that the usurer would not be amended 'bi-fore þe day of do[o]m' and would be condemned to eternal damnation.[422]

The figure of Covetousness in *Piers Plowman* confesses his sinful ways and claims he will no longer use short measures or beguile his customers. Instead, he offers to go on pilgrimage to Walsingham, so that his spiritual debt might be cleared.[423] However, in the C-Text, pardon or absolution is only offered if he makes full restitution to all those that he has deceived and stolen from.[424] All debts must be paid and proportionate exchange given.[425] In Langland's writings, Fraud and Avarice were the main corrupters of 'iustitia' and just price, and anyone who succumbed to these vices was expected to make full restitution if they wanted salvation for their souls. At one point, Covetousness misunderstands a question about

---

[419] 'The XI Pains of Hell' (thirteenth century), in Morris (ed.), *An Old English Miscellany*, p. 214, ll. 105–17 (usurers suffered here with those who gave false measures); Sinclair (ed.), *Divine Comedy*, i, 'Inferno', pp. 19, 147.

[420] Crane (ed.), *Exempla of Jacques de Vitry*, pp. 71–2, 203, nos. clxvii and clxviii. See also Scott and Bland (eds.), *Dialogue*, ii, pp. 270–3, chs. xxxix, xlii; Barnicle, 'Exemplum'; Crane (ed.), *Exempla of Jacques de Vitry*, pp. 49, 178, no. cvi; *Fasciculus Morum*, pp. 352–5; Bromyard, *Summa Predicantium*, 'Gloria'; Tubach, *Index Exemplorum*, no. 1143; Moffat (ed.), *Complaint of Nature*, p. 67, ll. 36–43. For an image of heated coins being poured down the throat of Avarice, see Green, 'Virtues and vices', 151.

[421] Horstmann (ed.), *Minor Poems*, p. 343, ll. 540–51, especially ll. 550–1.

[422] Matthew (ed.), *English Works of Wyclif*, p. 238. See also *Fasciculus Morum*, pp. 350–3; Gallagher (ed.), *Doctrinal*, pp. 146–7; BL, MS Additional 37677, fol. 100v; *Dives and Pauper*, I, ii, pp. 203–4, ll. 2–13; Crane (ed.), *Exempla of Jacques de Vitry*, pp. 75, 206, no. clxxvii, pp. 90, 221, no. ccxvi; *Handlyng Synne*, pp. 92–4; *Jacob's Well*, p. 197, l. 9 – p. 199, l. 13; BL, MS Additional 11284, fol. 91r; Tubach, *Index Exemplorum*, no. 375. A long verse of the fifteenth century concerned a usurer who would not give anything to the poor or needy and thus died without repentance or restitution. It was left to the son to reconcile the wrongs of the father before the latter's soul could rest in happiness. Hopper (ed.), *Childe of Bristow*. See also Ross (ed.), *Middle English Sermons*, p. 210, l. 21 – p. 211, l. 5.

[423] *Piers Plowman*, A.V.142–5, B.V.226–9, C.VI.230–3.   [424] *Ibid.*, C.VI.234–57, 331–49.

[425] Stokes, *Justice*, pp. 165–6.

restitution and instead tells of a time he robbed a merchant while he slept, rifling through his bags.[426] This was obviously not the kind of restitution to which Repentance referred; rather, Covetousness was expected to repay his debts of sin in satisfaction of justice ('redde quod debes'). This formed part of a system of obligations to God, the poor, neighbours and the self, rooted in divine and natural law. The lack of care for the poor and needy in the pursuit of material gain needed to be redressed. Covetousness states: 'I haue as muche pite of pouere [poor] men as pedlere haþ of cattes [cats], / That wolde kille hem if he cacche [catch] hem my3te for coueitise of hir skynnes [skins]'.[427] He fails to comprehend the extent of his sins. However, without restitution and justice, penance and repentance could not take place, nor could Covetousness use any of his ill-gained capital for future deals. *Jacob's Well* similarly declared that sellers of defective goods should provide restitution to their victims:

3yf þou selle copyr [copper] for gold, wyne medlyd [mixed] wyth watyr for wyn, or makyst ony oþer suche fals dyssey3tys [deceits], þe muste restore. 3if þou dysseyue oþere with aunserys [auncels], wey3tis, or mesurys, þou art boundyn to restore in peyne [pain] of dampnacyoun.[428]

Merchants were sometimes depicted as recognising the perilous spiritual dilemmas of undertaking commerce. Langland's merchants, for example, expressed tearful relief ('many wepe for ioye [joy]') when they received a conditional pardon for their deeds.[429] But the most infamous medieval example of a commercial life confronting spirituality was that of Margery Kempe. She was born in Lynn in *c*.1373, of middle-class parents. Her father, John Brunham, was a burgess, alderman and mayor, while she herself was married to a merchant whom she seemingly regarded as beneath her social status. She was nevertheless immersed in the ways of the market, even as a female, and was able to become economically autonomous and exercise commercial authority.[430] *The Book of Margery Kempe* (dated to 1436), which may have been dictated by Margery herself, briefly summarises her life before her spiritual transformation, pilgrimages and hysterical devotion. The text describes Margery as full of pomp, pride and covetousness, which inspired her to start a brewing business. However, she found her ale went flat, her brewings were lost and her

---

[426] *Piers Plowman*, c.vi.234–57. This scene recalled the fable of the 'Apes and the Sleeping Pedlar', see pp. 100–1 and Figure 4.

[427] *Piers Plowman*, b.v.255–6.

[428] *Jacob's Well*, p. 212, ll. 6–11. See also *Fasciculus Morum*, pp. 338–9; Simmons and Nolloth (eds.), *Lay Folks' Catechism*, p. 51, ll. 800–1; Morris (ed.), *Old English Homilies and Homiletic Treatises*, pp. 30–1.

[429] *Piers Plowman*, a.viii.10–44, b.vii.10–42, c.ix.12–42.

[430] Ashley, 'Historicizing Margery'; Aers, *Community*, pp. 77–8; Jewell, *Women*, pp. 98–9.

servants left. A second enterprise of a horse-mill to grind corn also failed because the horses would not pull and another servant left her. This was all interpreted by the author as God's punishment for her pride and sin, and it was implied that she should forsake her secular desires.[431] This might at first appear to be an entirely negative appraisal of the mercantile endeavour, reflecting the difficulties in reconciling trade with religious norms. Yet, her commercial values were not completely excised, for she bargained with God for forgiveness in return for works and prayers. This was the same 'economy of salvation' which was implicit in chantries and Masses.[432]

Salvation was often described in commercial language, as demonstrated by a fifteenth-century sermon: 'þan it is necessarie to men þat shall make a bargayn for to acorde [agree] of couenauntes [covenants], þan what will ȝe ȝeue [give] to God oþer to me in [h]is name, and I shall take hym to you?'[433] The Church became imbued with commercial values, despite condemning many aspects of the marketplace, bargaining and mercantile 'urges'. This paradox mirrored the traditional spiritual unease of the trading classes about their way of life, but also how moralists were subtly transforming traditional clerical assertions.[434] Many writers sought to validate the mercantile and commercial life in light of both market developments and emerging, wealthy merchants. There was an accommodation between the need to emphasise traditional moral concerns and Church doctrines and the changing requirements of the marketplace. However, this was not a blanket acceptance of market values and there was still a firm sense that market conduct, like all earthly activities, should be subsidiary to the salvation of the soul. In the medieval mindset, the realities of Hell appeared as lucid as the realities of the market.

There was a pragmatic recognition by moralists that the fears of spiritual punishment had to be matched by everyday enforcement of law. The perceptions of the marketplace as a den of iniquity, of traders as inherently corrupt and untrustworthy, and of poor customers needing protection, were natural precursors to the moralists' demand for strict and close intervention in the marketplace and an end to leniency. *The Simonie* highlighted the sins of victuallers, and feared that the authorities were lax in their punishments: 'þe pilory and þe cukkyng-stole beþ

---

[431] Windeatt (ed.), *Book of Margery Kempe*, pp. 38, 44–5.

[432] Atkinson, *Mystic and Pilgrim*, pp. 16, 59–60, 80; Ellis, 'Merchant's wife's tale', 609–12; Fienberg, 'Thematics of value', 136; Aers, *Community*, pp. 79–82.

[433] Ross (ed.), *Middle English Sermons*, p. 33, ll. 30–4; also 'By þre maner of wyze men is delyvered from dette', *ibid.*, p. 43, ll. 11–20.

[434] Thrupp, *Merchant Class*, pp. 169–81.

moche mad[e] fore no[u]ght'.[435] The writer also complained that brewers and bakers seemed only to receive minor amercements and could do 40s. worth of shame and pain upon the poor for only a 12d. penalty imposed by the court.[436] William Langland similarly suggested that officials were often bribed to allow corrupt traders to continue unhindered. He urged officials to punish all fraudulent traders in the pillory or cucking-stool:

As to punisshen on pillories – on pynyng-stolis	*cucking-stools*
Breweris – bakers, bocheris – cokes,	*butchers; cooks*
For þise arn men of þise molde þat most harm werchiþ	*this earth; harm do*
To þe pore peple þat parcelmel biggen.[437]	*poor people; buy piecemeal*

This was an allusion to mid-thirteenth-century regulations that governed the victual trades, with Langland almost quoting verbatim the statute *Judicium Pillorie*.[438] Similarly, the Chester alewife accepted the 'statutes of this contrye [country]' as the upholders of moral law.[439]

Other poets and moralists were vehement in their demands for harsh punishments. A satirical verse on Kildare (*c*.1308) warned both bakers and brewers to avoid fraud or else be sent to the pillory or cucking-stool where 'þe lak is dep and hori'.[440] In 1509, Alexander Barclay was adamant that the covetous and fraudulent should be judged by the law 'with extreme rygour and mortall punysshement'.[441] John Lydgate hoped that all false bakers would be placed in the pillory and be pelted with eggs, 'body, bak, and syde'.[442] John Gower was equally vitriolic about taverners who sold spoilt wine, as well as fraudulent brewers and bakers, and demanded that they all be hanged, especially bakers 'for bread is man's sustenance, and he who offends against bread contrary to the common laws takes people's lives away'.[443] The moralists expressed stark views on

---

[435] Embree and Urquhart (eds.), *The Simonie*, p. 98, B428. For a discussion of the pillory and cucking-stool, see below, pp. 263–70.

[436] *Ibid.*, p. 99, B445–450. An 'amercement' was a financial penalty levied by a court. For the relevance of these figures to real amercements, see Chapter 3.

[437] *Piers Plowman*, A.III.67–70, B.III.78–81, C.III.79–82.

[438] *Statutes*, i, p. 201, *Judicium Pillorie*.

[439] Lumiansky and Mills (eds.), *Chester Mystery Cycle*, i, p. 338, play xvii, 'Harrowing of Hell', l. 303.

[440] (the lake is deep and dirty.) Furnivall (ed.), *Early English Poems*, pp. 154–5; Wright and Halliwell (eds.), *Reliquae*, ii, pp. 174–7; BL, MS Harleian 913, fol. 7v.

[441] Jamieson (ed.), *Ship of Fools*, ii, p. 167.

[442] MacCracken (ed.), *Minor Poems*, 'Put Thieving Millers and Bakers in the Pillory', pp. 448–9, no. 15 (BL, MS Harleian 2255, fol. 137r).

[443] Gower, *Mirour*, pp. 341–6, ll. 25981–6353; Stockton (ed.), *Major Latin Works*, 'Vox Clamantis', bk. v, ch. 14, pp. 214–15.

Figure 15: The market official.

Notes: This woodcut depicts the seventh pawn in *The Game of Chess* (1483), the town or market official. He is holding keys and an ell (a stick for measuring cloth), as well as carrying a pot on his back for measurements and an open purse for collecting tolls and customs.
Source: Cessolis, *De Ludo Scachorum*, bk. 3, ch. 7 (Cambridge, Trinity College Library, VI.18.3, fol. 62r).

the application of secular law as well as spiritual ethics, and expected town authorities to support their own ardent admonitions of market abuses. Whether officials did so in practice is another matter, and the extent to which market laws and enforcement were actually influenced by shared moral assumptions will be explored in Chapters 2 and 3.

William Caxton's *Game and Playe of the Chesse* (1483), which describes society in terms of the pieces on a chessboard, placed victuallers and hostelers in front of judges and law-enforcers, because they 'ofte tymes amonge hem contencion noyse and stryf whiche behoueth to be determyned and trayted [treated] by the alphyn, whiche is Iuge [judge] of the kynge'. The accompanying woodcut depicted a town official holding an ell and carrying a pot on his back to measure with, and a purse to collect fines and tolls (see Figure 15). They were expected to watch the victuallers and traders diligently, wisely and as 'louers of the comyn prouffit and wele'.[444] There was, however, recognition that the authorities were fallible and negligent. In *Piers Plowman*, Lady Mede bribed the mayor to allow dishonest craftsmen and traders to take advantage of the law, 'to sulle sumdel aȝeyn resoun' (to sell something against reason). She was patently unaware that she was doing anything wrong and suggested that punishments should be lightened or the law strained to help traders make a bit more profit.[445] Lady Mede was irredeemable because she could not accept her own sin in transactions, nor that her actions made the law ineffective and left the poor unprotected. Mede corrupted government and prevented impartial justice. Yet, Langland implied that such indiscriminate help made Mede popular in the world and that consequently everything was for sale, including government and the law.

Although the confessional and penitential emphasis of moral works meant that they demanded personal repentance and legal reforms, there was nevertheless a resignation that little would actually change. Langland clearly despaired of petty traders ever achieving salvation, abandoning their vices or accepting traditional moral values:

> Thauh thei take hem vntydy thyng. thei hold hit no treson,
> And thauh thei fulle nat ful. that for lawe is seled,
> He gripeth ther-for as greet. as for the gete treuthe.[446]

In the B-Text of Langland's *Piers Plowman*, Haukyn the Active Man, who is presented as a wayfarer or pedlar, tried to work for salvation, but his coat remained stained with sin and could not be cleaned by way of penance alone. This suggests a rejection of the active life or work ethic and a realisation that working in the world inevitably led to sin. Later in the text, 'Conscience' suggests a new way of life of voluntary poverty, but the common people, represented by the brewer, reject such spiritualism.

---

[444] (lovers of the common profit and weal.) *Caxton's Game and Playe of Chess*, pp. 128–9, 138–9, 143: 'for as moche as the byars and sellars haue somtyme moche langage, they ought to haue with them these vertues, that is to wete pacience and good corage with honeste'.

[445] *Piers Plowman*, A.III.65–84, B.III.76–94, C.III.77–122; Mitchell, 'Lady Meed', p. 23; Baldwin, *Theme of Government*, pp. 27–30. The C-Text includes an additional section that has the victims of profiteering calling for God's vengeance, which is sent in the form of a fire in which both good and bad men suffer. The implication is that the community is indivisible and that all will suffer if the law is not upheld.

[446] (Though they deliver to them a dishonest quantity. they consider it no craft, and though they fill it not full. that by law is sealed, they grasp there for as much. as for the true gain.) *Piers Plowman*, C.IV.87–9.

Langland pessimistically bowed to the realistic nature of the marketplace through the words of a brewer:

> 'Ye? baw!' quod a Brewere, I wol noȝt be ruled,
> By Iesu! for al your Ianglynge, with Spiritus
>   Iusticie,   *chatter*
> Ne after Conscience, by crist! while I kan selle
> Boþe dregges and raf and drawe at oon hole   *dregs; waste*
> Thikke ale and þynne ale; þat is my kynde   *thick; thin*
> And noȝt hakke after holynesse; hold þi tonge,
>   Conscience![447]   *struggle*

Conscience had appealed to the trader's own responsibilities to his customers, especially the poor and labourers who depended upon his supplies, as well as to the traditional boundaries of moral integrity. But the brewer, representing those imbued with commercial values, reverted to 'kynde' or nature, and so perhaps justified the suspicions of customers about professional practices and mores. The brewer argued that he would lose more in earnings than he would gain in absolution. He thus rejected the principle of justice ('Spiritus Iusticie') in his measures, quality and dealings; he would go on mixing dregs with good ale to make money as long as no one stopped him.[448] Spiritual salvation was thus ignored in favour of economic self-interest and profit at the margins of acceptability. He placed personal gain above the common weal and rejected the social and penitential principle of 'redde quod debes'.[449] In effect, moralists regarded the market and commerce as blinding forces that prevented traders from seeing that their actions were morally wrong and spiritually hazardous.[450] Conscience and clerical teachings were often ignored and only hunger or imminent death might compel them to obey the law.

The despair and resignation of fourteenth- and fifteenth-century complaint poets forms part of conventional rhetoric, but other writers also expressed the futility of their criticisms. Bishop Thomas Brinton of Rochester upbraided traders and merchants in several of his late fourteenth-century sermons, but in a sermon of July 1382–3 he despaired that anyone heeded his messages:

---

[447] *Ibid.*, B.XIX, 396–400, C.XXI.396–400.   [448] Stokes, *Justice*, pp. 274–6.

[449] Yunck, 'Satire', pp. 150–2; Aers, 'Justice and wage-labor'; *Piers Plowman*, B.XIX.396–408, C.XXI.396–408.

[450] Pearsall referred to this as the 'remorseless ethic' of money; Pearsall (ed.), *William Langland*, p. 14.

I say for my part with tears that for these past ten year I have preached against the sins prevalent in my diocese, nor, however, have I seen anyone rise effectually from sin . . . For what adulterer having given up his mistress is faithful to his lawful wife? What usurer restores what he has unjustly taken? What unjust maintainer or false witness refrains from his sins? What user of fraudulent weights and measures through which he has deceived his neighbours and poor wayfarers has broken or burned them?[451]

Conclusion

Richard Britnell has argued that many literary texts and sermons were uncomplicated in their content, misrepresenting everyday moral values and overstressing the seriousness of offences.[452] Certainly, the images presented were not intended as a passive reflection of reality. They were steeped in traditional values and stereotypes, either idealistic or derogatory, and were grounded in broader questions of morality and social theory – what should or should not take place, rather than what actually did.[453] According to medieval moralists, avarice, fraud and an inordinate desire for money were the bedfellows of the average trader. Vendors were reminded of sin involved in even the simplest trading malpractices, while customers were continually alerted to the potential deceits they might face in market transactions.

It is possible that traders and customers identified with the traditional condemnations and theories of moralists, viewing some of their fellow traders and consumers as dishonest and selfish, to the detriment of the whole community. Indeed, many of the comments of the moralists appear intended to pander to the concerns and practical experiences of their audience. They also reinforced negative and moral perceptions, which may have influenced everyday market interactions and how society construed their marketplaces. What is striking is that there are virtually no positive references in the literary and religious sources to capital accumulation, middlemen and retailers, entrepreneurship, product development or even economic growth. Instead, texts and images are remarkably consistent in their adherence to familiar principles. Many writers continued to denounce petty traders and middlemen as irredeemably fraudulent and dishonest, and criticised them for being scornful of the requirements for salvation. They indicated that petty traders were reluctant to disrupt

---

[451] Devlin (ed.), *Sermons of Thomas Brinton*, p. 465, sermon 101 (trans. p. xxiv).
[452] Britnell, 'Town life', pp. 164–5; Britnell, 'Urban economic regulation', ch. xix, pp. 1–2.
[453] Rigby, 'England: literature and society', p. 502.

their personal profit margins and market practices for any abstract ideologies of social justice and communal welfare. Those writers who did try to understand the dilemmas of traders at the bottom of the commercial ladder found it difficult to accommodate elements of petty trade with the greater needs of social order, and thus demanded extensive intervention by the authorities.

It is significant that Langland chose petty traders, alongside wasters, labourers and friars, as targets of his indignation. These figures were a pervasive presence in medieval towns and villages and thus useful examples through which to explore broader issues of society and salvation:

> And somme chosen chaffare [trade], they cheueden [succeed] the
>   bettere,
> As it semeth to owre sy3t [sight] that suche men thryueth [thrive][454]

For Langland, social disorder was caused by the traders' rejection of their personal and communal obligations, in favour of more selfish and acquisitive needs. It does appear that there was a vibrant debate amongst medieval moralists about the developing market economy throughout the twelfth to fifteenth centuries. David Aers was, however, wrong in suggesting that Langland dismissed the market and commercial economy as peripheral to a feudal, fixed social order.[455] Langland in fact accepted 'mercedem' as a reward for trade undertaken honestly and reasonably. He both acknowledged that commerce was of ever-growing importance in providing necessities and services yet he despaired that it might never truly be reconciled to traditional Christian ethics.

Generally, moralists recognised that society was often dependent upon market mechanisms for the basic necessities of life, but that trade had operations and intrinsic values that potentially ran counter to the ethics and doctrines of the Church. One compromise was the view that trade in itself could be utilitarian and beneficial, but it was the individual who was sinful and whose intentions should be fully examined.[456] Consequently, some texts began to examine the possibility of an ideological reconciliation between the two institutions of Church and market, within the parameters of heavenly salvation. Theologians of the twelfth and thirteenth centuries attempted this for merchants, price formation and usury, accommodating secular social and economic changes within their divine conceptions.[457] Moralists found ways to accommodate the market within their teachings, as long as the intention was not avaricious and gain was

---

[454] *Piers Plowman*, A.PROL.31–2, B.PROL.31–2, C.I.33–4.

[455] Aers, *Chaucer*, p. 8. Aers quoted Hilton on this subject (Hilton, *English Peasantry*, pp. 43–57, 82–94, 196–214).

[456] Farber, *An Anatomy*, pp. 15–18.   [457] Wood, *Medieval Economic Thought*.

matched by charity.[458] By the fourteenth and fifteenth centuries, there was a continuing process of adaptation and modification in literary attitudes and an acceptance that traders could make reasonable profits and that the realities of market forces were unavoidable. However, there was still a reluctance to allow petty market traders much leeway in comparison to wholesaling merchants. Although representations of traders were increasingly allied to the realities of market values, flexible law enforcement, competition and self-interest, they ultimately remained negative and pessimistic because the acquisitive urge compromised the basis of traditional Christian ethics. Petty traders were on the cusp of moral acceptability, but simultaneously remained in the margins of suspicion.

If unremitting suspicion reflected the opinion of all medieval market users then exchange would have been very difficult, lacking in mutual trust and requiring constant (and costly) surveillance. However, the reception of these images and their influence upon attitudes and action was much more complex. Literary portrayals attempted to influence attitudes in society but were also influenced by the social context in which they were written. The very condemnations of moralists constantly reminded market-goers of the need for both self-regulation and communal responsibility, and these accepted ethical conceptions may have bolstered confidence in market transactions. Even if the edicts of the Church and moralists were not followed to the letter, they informed and reflected an accepted cultural context for behaviour in the marketplace.

By the later Middle Ages, writers were demanding greater self-regulation by traders, more self-awareness by consumers and effective deterrents by the authorities in support of the admonitions of the Church. If two principal themes have emerged from the literary sources it is those of social justice and communal responsibility. Members of society at all levels were acutely aware of religious and literary condemnations of market misdemeanours and the means by which moralists wished to redress them. Late medieval society was also intensely concerned with matters of law and order and it is likely that legislation was formulated with religious ideals in mind.

[458] Langholm, *The Merchant*, pp. 234–5.

2   Regulation of the market

Medieval attitudes towards market traders can be discerned further through an analysis of the legal pronouncements and jurisdictions that sought to regulate their behaviour. The enactment of medieval law was intimately connected to the predominant moral assumptions of the age, and notions of social justice and the common good figure prominently. Legislation represented the most covert means by which society could control the behaviour of its members and codify common expectations. While moral and religious strictures defined the wider context of human behaviour, often within a spiritual context, the creators of trading legislation established more exact and tangible guidelines for secular offences and implemented a number of administrative mechanisms to enforce conformity.

The growth of markets and petty trade in the late Middle Ages was accompanied by a multitude of laws. From the thirteenth century onwards, traders were confronted by a proliferation of statutes, town ordinances and manorial by-laws, which sought to outline the standards of commercial practice. Such laws and ordinances were also a reminder of the authority vested in the king, lord or corporation, but commercial law was shaped as much by the needs and morals of market-goers as by the state. As Richard Britnell has stated, 'urban commercial regulations has complex origins in early English royal traditions, in canon law, in the privileges of chartered boroughs and in *ad hoc* pragmatism'.[1]

The use of legislative texts requires a similarly cautious approach to that used for literary evidence. The enactment of an ordinance or statute did not necessarily elicit compliance nor directly mirror the practice of traders in the market. David Farmer rightly stated: 'Royal proclamations, statutes both parliamentary and informal, and even Magna Carta, usually exemplify the aims of those in power, rather than the practicalities of the market place'.[2] Some historians have gone further and suggested that

---

[1] Britnell, 'Town life', p. 164.   [2] Farmer, 'Marketing', p. 326.

the continual reiteration of particular laws merely indicated their ineffectiveness and the lack of stigma attached to offences. In a similar manner to medieval moralists, historians like Eric Hirshler, Joel Rosenthal and Louis Salzman have described medieval trading communities as rife with dishonesty, fraud and moral indifference, which the authorities could do little about except increase punishments, repeat regulations and reiterate theological condemnations.[3] In essence, many of the commercial laws were ineffectual and ignored, with inadequate legal and moral barriers to dissuade the free rider. Other historians, such as Anthony Bridbury, viewed medieval trading regulations as very narrow-minded and disadvantageous to traders because of the dominant Christian ideology that underpinned them.[4] According to this theory, the law was intrusive and obstructive; medieval man was encumbered by the moralistic intransigence of officialdom. Customary restraints thus worked in conflict with the developing complexities of market forces.

The argument that medieval authorities were highly restrictive and exclusive in their commercial outlook has been a dominant theme, particularly in studies of institutions like boroughs and guilds. Charles Gross regarded the Merchant Guild as a body that hampered free commercial intercourse, diminished the spirit of mercantile enterprise, and was utterly hostile to merchant strangers.[5] Vested interests were paramount and consumer interests were only met when they coincided with merchant interests.[6] Munia Postan regarded local monopoly as the mainstay of urban policy; townsfolk dominated the local commercial hinterland and were supported by elaborate rules limiting the activities of outsiders.[7] Rodney Hilton argued that the mercantile elites of large towns were also uneasy about retail traders more generally and that they were closely controlled.[8]

Thus, a number of historians have viewed the regulations of medieval trade as either defunct and ineffectual, or restrictive and exclusionary. However, just because medieval commercial laws and morality did not

---

[3] Hirshler, 'Medieval economic competition', 52; Rosenthal, 'Assizes', 418–19, 422; Salzman, *English Life*, pp. 75, 83, 241; Postan, *Medieval Economy*, p. 255; Bolton, *Medieval English Economy*, p. 329; Farber, *An Anatomy*, pp. 170–1, 178, 184; Mate, *Trade and Economic Developments*, pp. 26, 35–6.

[4] Bridbury, *Economic Growth*, pp. 56, 73–4; Bridbury, 'Markets'; Bridbury, 'English provincial towns', 2; Lipson, *Economic History*, pp. 616–18; Dyer, *Standards*, p. 198; Langholm, *Economics*, pp. 38–9, 64–5.

[5] Gross, *Gild Merchant*, i, pp. 50–1. See also Pirenne, *Economic and Social History*, pp. 179–86; Unwin, *Gilds and Companies*, pp. 38–46.

[6] Hibbert, 'Economic policies', pp. 201–6.

[7] Postan, *Medieval Economy*, pp. 214–17. See also Thrupp, 'Gilds'.

[8] Hilton, 'Women traders', p. 208.

coincide with classical economic theory regarding the efficacy of free markets, we should not assume that they were impotent, useless or damaging.[9] There was certainly a degree of dishonesty and fraud in the medieval commercial world, but the evidence can be somewhat deceptive when evaluating the effectiveness of the law. Indeed, a long list of offenders may imply that the law was being enforced strictly and well; equally, many cases might simply involve legal rhetoric or local interpretations that hid much more mundane administration. Even complaints in literature and royal mandates that the law was being inadequately administered need to be considered carefully as regards particular interest groups and their priorities. As Gwen Seabourne has suggested, the 'success' of market laws cannot be determined purely by the number of prosecutions or a failure to impose the strictest sanctions, since their enforcement and effect may have been influential beyond the formal courts. Similarly, a reiteration of law does not necessarily imply that it is ineffective, since it may have been repeated for purposes of permanency or refinement.[10]

Several studies of medieval commercialism have provoked a reappraisal of the regulatory standards of marketing. Maryanne Kowaleski contended that an efficient market needed effective law and enforcement to engender the confidence of its buyers and sellers.[11] Both she and Richard Britnell agreed that the prime object of the medieval market was to operate for the benefit of the burgesses and to the disadvantage of other participants.[12] However, such beneficial treatment was not incompatible with regulations for consumer protection, especially since the burgesses were consumers as well as traders. Heather Swanson went further and stated that the 'principle behind much of the regulation was consumer protection'.[13] For some historians, then, trade regulations were implemented in the interests of the consumer, by ensuring adequate supply, honest measures, reasonable prices and minimum standards, and by circumscribing the practices of middlemen and monopolists.[14] Such regulations were motivated by fears of scarcity and instability within the economy, but were also steeped in contemporary moral ideology and in themselves effectively constituted a commercial ethic.

Britnell has argued that the internalisation of 'moral' factors in town regulations should not be easily dismissed.[15] In studying the regulations of medieval trade, it is too simplistic to suggest that they were implemented purely for self-interest or communal benefit. Instead, we need to

---

[9] Seabourne, *Royal Regulation*, p. 15.   [10] *Ibid.*, pp. 15–16.
[11] Kowaleski, *Local Markets*, pp. 179–221.   [12] Britnell, 'Price-setting'.
[13] Swanson, *British Towns*, p. 78.   [14] Thrupp, *Merchant Class*, pp. 92–4.
[15] Britnell, 'Urban economic regulation'.

consider the ideological context in which the laws were created and, in turn, the economic theories that the legislators applied to them. When drawing up commercial regulations, officials were undoubtedly influenced by not only the social, economic and political conditions that faced them, but also by the prevailing medieval market morality. However, this was a morality shaped by many more influences than simply the teachings of the Church and scholastics.[16]

The laws of medieval England were constructed in several forums, from Parliament and the royal courts of central government, through to borough courts, craft guilds and even manorial courts. These different legislating bodies did not necessarily produce distinct codifications, and mutual influences are starkly evident. The customs and ordinances of London, in particular, were a strong influence upon both royal government and other towns.[17] The following examination of market laws draws upon five principal groups of sources: statute law and royal ordinances, borough charters, town custumals and ordinances, guild ordinances, and law manuals. Much of the detailed evidence derives from borough and guild ordinances and it is likely that not all of their regulations were applicable to smaller market towns and village markets. The particular circumstances and requirements of larger towns do not always overlap with each other, let alone with more humble rural marketplaces. In addition, many of the laws were directed more towards wholesaling merchants than petty retailers. Generally, this book is not concerned with delving into the complexities of overseas trade, manufacturing and industry, and these specific regulations will not be considered in depth.

A study of medieval market regulation is extremely instructive since law encapsulated the authorities' notions of ideal practices. In turn, their official commercial outlook can be viewed as the culmination of an amalgam of interests. Medieval law was not a static entity, but a flexible body of rules that were continually modified and redefined in official forums in response to the changing needs and mores of society. However, legislation was also a formalised code. This very formality meant that laws could, and did, lag behind more dynamic social and economic changes. Redefinition did not always lead to innovation. Instead, laws reflected the assumptions and wishes of the ruling classes to a greater extent than the remainder of society, and once established they were easier to modify than to usurp.

[16] Seabourne, *Royal Regulation*, pp. 21–2.
[17] R. Braid, 'Laying the foundations for royal policy: economic regulation and market control in London before the Black Death' (unpubl. paper, 2010), with thanks to Robert Braid; Casson, 'A comparative study', pp. 69–72, 89–98.

PART I: THE FORUMS OF REGULATION

National legislation

The Crown was increasingly involved in matters of commercial regulation during the twelfth to fifteenth centuries. Kings expressed an early interest in the maintenance of weights, measures and the coinage, which were regarded as symbols of strong and secure royal government. There was an associated desire for social order, leavened by financial interests, which meant that the Crown also intervened increasingly in primary victual trades, particularly bread, ale and wine. In addition, fiscal needs drove royal interference in export trades like wool (and later cloth) from the thirteenth century onwards. Consideration towards other prices and wages was put on the agenda in the fourteenth century, motivated partly by the pervading crises of that century but also by local petitions. All these royal legal interventions were invariably more reactive than proactive, driven by the king's vague duty to uphold justice, morality and the common good, but more specifically by the need to maintain social order, royal rights and authority, crown revenue and the economic well-being of the realm.[18]

However, the motivations behind state commercial regulations are not easily generalised, and we should not be overly eager to dismiss appeals to morality and justice as mere trappings to conceal aspirations to self-interest, revenue and political power. Indeed, different motivations could often work together in concert, and the proclamations of statute law and royal ordinances were tempered by the realities of local customs. Nevertheless, there was a general recognition that the authority of local courts in manors and towns ultimately derived from the Crown and common law, even if borough custom and Merchant Law gave a different texture to some aspects.

The statutes created by the authority of king and Parliament thus formed a body of national legislation to which the towns and markets of England were expected to adhere. One of the most fundamental and ancient national customs relating to commerce was the freedom and security to travel and trade throughout the kingdom. *Magna Carta* stated:

All merchants are to be safe and secure in leaving and entering England, and in staying and travelling in England, both by land and by water, to buy and sell free from all maletotes [unjust taxes] by the ancient and rightful customs, except in time of war, such as come from an enemy country.[19]

[18] Seabourne, *Royal Regulation*, pp. 19–23.
[19] Holt, *Magna Carta*, pp. 326–7, c.41; *Statutes*, i, p. 11.

This freedom was extended and reconfirmed by a number of statutes throughout the later Middle Ages.[20] A statute of 1335 stated that all traders 'of whatever estate or condition' could 'freely and without disturbance sell to whomsoever they please'.[21] Any customs or grants contrary to this, and thus to the 'common detriment' of the people, were to be overturned, and no market official was to interfere with the open and honest sale of victuals.[22] Borough charters often stated that there should be liberty of access to the market for whoever wished to buy, reasserting the provision of *Magna Carta*. A charter for the borough of Dunwich (Suffolk), in 1285, stated that all the merchandise of burgesses coming to Dunwich by sea or land should be sold and bought openly by those merchants and that there should be no brokers ('abrocatores'), who impeded buyers and sellers to the damage of the town.[23] However, foreign traders were still expected to pay any due customs and there were occasionally restrictions regarding what they could buy.[24] Merchants from overseas were also restricted in some of their marketing practices. According to a statute of 1378, alien and foreign traders were free to 'buy and sell, in gross and by retail, provisions and small wares', but aliens could sell great wares by gross only and the retailing of such goods had to be left to the inhabitants of the towns. Similarly, a statute of Richard II stated that no merchant aliens were to trade wholesale with other aliens, nor to retail any merchandise except victuals (but not wine).[25] Freedom to move between markets, and to buy and sell in general terms, did not mean that traders were free of restrictions. The statutes merely confirmed privileges granted to Merchant Guilds and burgesses in royal charters during the previous two centuries.

From the thirteenth century, statutory legislation regarding market traders noticeably increased and expanded, beginning with the assizes of bread and ale and then extending into other areas of price regulation, forestalling, the cloth industry, the herring industry and market days. Such legislation was supported by numerous royal commissions that sought to maintain regulations regarding reasonable prices and standards

---

[20] *Statutes*, i, p. 117, 25 Edw I c.30 (1297); i, pp. 314–15, 25 Edw III St.3 c.2 (1350–1); ii, pp. 6–8, 2 Ric II St.1 c.1 (1378); ii, pp. 23–4, 5 Ric II St.2 c.1 (1382); ii, p. 28, 6 Ric II St.1 c.10 (1382); ii, p. 83, 16 Ric II c.1 (1392–3); ii, p. 118, 1 Hen IV c.19 (1399); ii, p. 197, 4 Hen V St.2 c.5 (1416).

[21] *Statutes*, i, pp. 267–71, 9 Edw III St.1 (1335).

[22] *Parl. Rolls*, c.43, February 1351; *RP*, ii, p. 249 (1351).

[23] *CChR*, ii, p. 315 (Dunwich, 1285).

[24] *BBC, 1042–1216*, pp. 197–216; *BBC, 1216–1307*, pp. 289–90; Maitland and Bateson (eds.), *Charters*, pp. 6–7; *Liber Albus*, pp. 249–50 (1284–5).

[25] *Statutes*, ii, pp. 6–8, 2 Ric II St.1 c.1 (1378); ii, p. 83, 16 Ric II c.1 (1392–3); *Parl. Rolls*, c.33, January 1393.

of weights and measures.[26] For instance, in December 1307 the sheriffs were ordered to appoint two men in every borough and market town ('villa mercatoria') to proclaim and enforce such commercial legislation and detain offenders.[27] There was a developing central concern for local affairs, spurred on by petitioners, the expanding economy and, later, the changing labour resources of post-Black Death England.[28] After 1349, the central government sought to restore the socio-economic status quo to its pre-plague condition. The control of wages and prices was an important element of these efforts, particularly through the 'Ordinance of Labourers' (1349) and 'Statute of Labourers' (1351). Subsequently, royal justices were given wide powers of enforcement which augmented local supervision and they often used local men for investigation and enforcement. For instance, in 1353, justices of the peace and of labourers were appointed from worthy men in the counties 'to punish innkeepers for their outrageous prices, and the regraters of victuals. And that they shall inspect the measures, ells and weights in each county.'[29]

Consequently, by the fourteenth century, there were increasing attempts to nationalise trading regulation and intervene in everyday life, either by standardising old customs or enforcing new laws.[30] Statute law was particularly important in providing an overarching context upon which local authorities could draw, even though it was perhaps interpreted in a variety of ways in the local marketplace. Nonetheless, in larger towns, these regulations spurred the creation of more detailed laws concerning traders and many parliamentary statutes were entered into town custumals. In smaller towns, the effect was less obviously intrusive, but a certain increase in trading regulation can be discerned in the later fourteenth century and most courts referred to the requirements of statute law. These were related to new economic circumstances, such as the rising cost of labour and new patterns of consumption and demand.

General trading principles were thus promulgated by the state and town authorities drew regularly upon familiar sources such as royal charters and statutes. However, the statutes themselves rarely advanced drastic innovation, but rather summarised existing customs, responded to local

---

[26] Rosenthal, 'Assizes', 414–15.

[27] *CPR, 1307–13*, pp. 29–31. See also *CPR, 1313–17*, pp. 688–9.

[28] Britnell, *Growth and Decline*, pp. 134–5; Seabourne, *Royal Regulation*, p. 120.

[29] Palmer, *English Law*, pp. 14–22, 139–41; *Parl. Rolls*, c.36, September 1353; *Statutes*, i, pp. 312–13, 25 Edw III st.2 cc.5–7, 'Statute of Labourers' (1350–1); ii, p. 63, 13 Ric II st.1 c.7 (1389–90); Kimball (ed.), *Rolls*, pp. lxiv–lxv.

[30] Seabourne, *Royal Regulation*, pp. 4, 6. Palmer has argued that the Black Death had a significant and new impact for the intervention of government regulation upon the activities of the lower orders. Conversely, Musson suggests that there was merely a quickening of pre-existing trends. Palmer, *English Law*; Musson, 'New labour laws'.

petitions, or exemplified vague ideals.[31] In addition, while local legislative bodies rarely contradicted statute law, they were mostly concerned with the non-statutory minutiae of everyday trade, such as the details of time, place and administration of a market, as well as the privileges of the burgesses and townsfolk. Enforcement remained in local hands and the interpretation of the law reflected local concerns. Many retailing rules were not intended to account for trade beyond the region, the hinterland or the town itself. Trading regulations thus became increasingly uniform in their general approach, driven by pressure from central government, but borough and market ordinances could show variation in the detail, based upon the degree of autonomy granted to them in royal and seigneurial charters.[32]

Seigneurial markets

One of the most basic commercial institutions that demonstrated manifest royal authority was the market franchise itself. The markets of medieval England varied in their size, role and authority, from small village markets controlled by a lord up to large urban boroughs under the auspices of self-governing corporations. Nevertheless, they were all maintained by general principles of governance emanating from their market charters, statute law and leet or frankpledge jurisdiction. Periodic markets, whether in boroughs, towns or villages, were legalised entities and were granted by the crown (or occasionally a lord) upon the condition that beneficiaries maintained certain trading regulations. A market charter gave a lord or corporation the right to organise, control and profit from trade at a specific place and time. By the reign of King John (1199–1216), the grant of a market or a fair was treated as a royal franchise with commensurate customs and liberties. Such grants stated the day of the week for a market, or the time of year and duration of a fair. Any markets held without licence could be shut down, though the *Quo Warranto* proceedings of Edward I also confirmed those markets that claimed prescriptive rights, meaning that the market had existed pre-1199.[33] Equally, any market or fair overstepping the remits of its charter, such as a fair overrunning its prescribed length, was liable to have its franchise seized back into the king's hands.[34]

---

[31] Kiralfy, 'Custom', 27–8.   [32] Bateson (ed.), *Borough Customs*, i, pp. ix–xvii.

[33] Britnell, 'King John's early grants'; Salzman, 'Legal status', 205; Sutherland, *Quo Warranto*.

[34] *Statutes*, i, p. 260, 2 Edw III c.15 (1328); i, p. 266, 5 Edw III c.5 (1331).

This was all part of continuing efforts by the Crown to draw trading (and other) activities into the regal pot. The assertion of franchisal conditions was as much a means of justifying royal claims to these lucrative rights as a serious attempt to enforce minimum standards. Nevertheless, by the later Middle Ages, the royal Clerk of the Market was a prevalent force in many small towns, making irregular visits to uphold the national standards of weights, measures and commercial practices within marketplaces. When John Sibill was appointed in 1484 he had 'supervision of all artificers, labourers, victuallers, bakers and brewers with power to imprison those... found guilty of fraud in the exercise of their crafts'.[35] Although his jurisdiction stretched only as far as the verge of the royal household (twelve-mile radius), this was a moveable jurisdiction and the Clerk of the Market could still act as a potential check upon the activities of local markets and lords, ensuring that they were operating their franchises correctly and following statute law in matters of commerce.[36]

Yet, although the institution of the market was designed to reduce transaction costs, set competitive prices and eliminate fraud and manipulation, we should be wary of seeing the market as policed solely for the public good of traders and consumers.[37] Most seigneurial market franchises were regulated in such a way that they protected the rights of a lord and maximised his revenue. A condition for the grant of markets and fairs was that new foundations should not be a nuisance to neighbouring establishments ('nisi sit ad nocumentum').[38] This was intended to protect a lord's toll revenue for an existing chartered market from the vagaries of economic competition. Seigneurial markets could also offer singular opportunities to lords. The charter for Dunster in 1254–7 allowed the lord to have first access to market wares before the burgesses and they in turn had primacy over outsiders.[39] The costs of running a medieval market or fair were far from negligible, with regulation, hygiene, stalls and maintenance of the marketplace typically encroaching upon a lord's purse. However, a market could also benefit the lord, providing an

---

[35] *CPR, 1476–85*, p. 436, cf. Williams, 'Sessions', 78.

[36] *Britton*, i, p. 4, ch. 1, c.6, pp. 189–93, ch. 31, cc.5–10 (1291–2); *Fleta*, ii, pp. 117–22, bk. II, cc.8–12 (late thirteenth century); Willard and Morris (eds.), *English Government at Work*, pp. 245–8; *Parl. Rolls*, c.87 [37], April 1376 and c.35, January 1390; Seabourne, *Royal Regulation*, pp. 92–3. The Clerk of the Market mostly visited small towns, since many larger boroughs were exempted from his authority; e.g. *CChR*, iii, pp. 487–8 (Bury St Edmunds, 1326); *Bristol*, i, pp. xvi, 122–3 (*c.*1373); Maitland and Bateson (eds.), *Charters*, pp. 32–9 (Cambridge, 1385).

[37] Britnell, 'Price-setting', 2–3.

[38] Masschaele, 'Market rights'; Britnell, 'King John's early grants'.

[39] *BBC, 1216–1307*, pp. 265, 299 (Dunster, 1254–7).

outlet for demesne produce as well as income from tolls, rents, stallage and the profits of jurisdiction.

Charters, however, required market franchise holders to administer trade closely, according to statutes and specified rules, and implied the right to hold a market court in which to enforce regulations and resolve trading disputes.[40] For instance, although not strictly part of the market franchise but rather of the view of frankpledge, markets needed the *judicialia* of a pillory and tumbrel in order to punish breaches of the assize of bread and ale.[41] Additionally, lords were not allowed to exploit market traders to excessive levels by imposing unreasonably high toll and stallage. A statute of 1275 threatened the seizure by the king of any market franchise where excessive toll had been taken.[42] The provision of a market also included the duty of providing safe and unencumbered access, provided traders upheld the peace and paid the customs of the market. The charter for Woodbridge in 1447 stated 'that all persons coming to the said markets and fairs shall be in the king's protection'.[43]

The broad base of the medieval marketing system consisted of small town and village markets, usually still under the control of a lord. These markets proliferated dramatically during the twelfth and thirteenth centuries as lords sought out market charters, partly to profit from the commercial opportunities at this time.[44] These markets included seigneurial boroughs, where residents might have privileges of burgage tenure or freedom from toll in their market. A few small towns gained extra privileges, such as the right to farm market tolls.[45] Otherwise they were little different to rural settlements in their structures of control and administration; indeed, tenants in village markets might expect the same right to trade without paying toll.[46] Other small towns never attained even the nominal status of borough, especially in the east of England. Many of these places were still controlled mostly or entirely by a lord and their appointed nominee. The landlord had rights to rents from landholdings, tenement plots and market stalls, as well as the profits of tolls and petty jurisdiction. Many towns were effectively unchartered or received minimal privileges, and had developed an urban economy without the active patronage of a lord. These included relatively large towns

---

[40] Britnell, 'English markets'; Britnell, *Commercialisation*, pp. 10–19, 81–5; Bailey, 'Trade and towns', 199; Kowaleski, *Local Markets*, pp. 41–2.

[41] Sutherland, *Quo Warranto*, pp. 75, 135, 137, 155, 217, 248, 298, 370, 372, 380, 410, 414; Coates, 'Origin and distribution of markets', 93–4; Seabourne, *Royal Regulation*, pp. 94–5.

[42] *Statutes*, i, p. 34, 3 Edw I c.31 (1275).

[43] *CChR*, vi, p. 81 (Woodbridge, 1447), see also, p. 59 (Lowestoft, 1445).

[44] Britnell, 'Proliferation'.   [45] Dyer, *Making a Living*, p. 219.

[46] Britnell, 'Town life', p. 156.

like Bury St Edmunds, St Albans and Durham, all of which were controlled by powerful ecclesiastical institutions and resisted townsmen's demands for more extensive liberties.

Seigneurial boroughs and markets still needed established administrative systems to ensure that urban administration and trade regulations were enforced. These systems differed from place to place, depending upon urban size and occupational profiles. Small-town and village market activities tended to be controlled through manorial courts and presided over by the lord's steward, in which juries and officials were chosen from local, leading men.[47] The leading townspeople, usually independent craftsmen and petty traders rather than the substantial merchants seen in larger boroughs, thus served as bailiffs, constables and jurors. Indeed, they often constituted a local elite who effectively ran everyday affairs, though the degree of freedom and compromise varied between communities.

Leet courts were perhaps the most significant official bodies that dealt with various trading offences and public nuisances in small towns and market villages. These courts were royal franchises, usually held in conjunction with the view of frankpledge which inquired into tithing groups. In the shires, jurisdiction of the view of frankpledge generally lay with sheriff's tourns. However, in most boroughs and many manors, enforcement had been franchised out to corporate bodies or lords and they were responsible for holding the view in their annual or biannual leet courts. For lords, the leet court provided both revenue and a means to maintain order. Indeed, in smaller towns and manors, the tithing system was an important means of local control throughout the medieval period since it was inexpensive and reliant on communal enforcement.

The view was a collective system of policing, whereby all males over the age of twelve were placed in a 'tithing' (*decenna*) for mutual security and control. Within each tithing it was the duty of a 'capital pledge' to present the offences of his fellow members, usually once or twice a year, and to ensure that alleged offenders appeared in the leet court. Capital pledges and their tithings could be fined for concealment. The most significant body in these courts was the jury of presentment, which was chosen from the most 'sufficient men' of the town or village. They had a significant say in how the court dealt with offences, no doubt influenced by their own morals and attitudes. Indeed, there was no necessity to provide witnesses in presentments of offences to the court, which were considered conclusive testimony if the leet jury accepted them. In private leet courts,

---

[47] Holt, *Early History of the Town of Birmingham*, pp. 12–13.

the jury was often not formally empanelled and simply comprised of the capital pledges, so that the two bodies of men were interchangeable.[48]

Thirteenth-century compilations of precedents, such as *La Court de Baron*, provided stewards with information on how to proceed in enforcing jurisdiction and answering pleas.[49] The potential articles that fell under the jurisdiction of the view of frankpledge and the leet court covered a multitude of public offences against the peace: petty misdeeds, nuisances, minor assaults, the hue and cry, and market regulations. These included trading offences such as counterfeiting, clippers of money, usury, selling stolen meat, bleaching or selling skins of stolen animals, buying stolen clothes and recutting them, breaches of the assizes of bread and ale, unwholesome victuals, excessive price, faulty workmanship, use of double measures and false or unsealed weights and measures. These phrases were the standard formulae used by local courts and their clerks and officials, and were also included in many law manuals and statutes.[50] Thus, court proceedings were increasingly formalised and standardised, driven by the professionalism of the clerks and the competition of common law practice.[51]

Any statutory requirements were interpreted at manorial level by both the lord's steward and court jurors, and in the town by senior town officials, probably in association with articles of inquiry.[52] Since local officials drew upon the same formulaic statutes and articles, leet court rolls usually recorded the offences of traders in a generalised and rhetorical fashion. For instance, tourns for Nottingham in October 1395 and 1396 listed market offences as:[53]

- Bakers and brewers taking excessive profit from the common people.
- Butchers keeping meat too long and selling corrupt meat.
- Fishers selling long-dead fish and forestalling.
- Taverners selling against the assize.
- Poulterers and hucksters selling garlic, flour, salt, tallow, candles, butter, cheeses and other goods against statute, as well as making candles without wicks and being common forestallers at street ends.

---

[48] Schofield, 'Late medieval view of frankpledge'. See also DeWindt and DeWindt, *Ramsey*, ch. 5.

[49] Maitland and Baildon (eds.), *Court Baron*, pp. 23–7, 50–1 (thirteenth century); Maitland (ed.), *Select Pleas in Manorial*, pp. xxxii–xxxiii; Hearnshaw, *Leet Jurisdiction*, p. 115.

[50] *Britton*, i, pp. 179–80, ch. 30, c.3 (1291–2); Maitland and Baildon (eds.), *Court Baron*, pp. 71–106; Hilton (ed.), *Stoneleigh*, pp. 98–100 (fourteenth century); Myers (ed.), *English Historical Documents*, pp. 548–53 [BL, MS Harleian 773, fol. 39r] (c.1440); Beckerman, 'Articles of presentment'.

[51] Smith and Razi, 'Origins of the English manorial court rolls'.

[52] *Statutes*, i, pp. 246–7. See also Hilton, *English Peasantry*, p. 45.

[53] *Nottingham*, i, pp. 268–73 (1395), 316–19 (1396).

- Tanners selling leather badly tanned and in secret.
- Shoe-makers charging too much and mixing leathers and cloths.
- Cooks selling badly prepared and reheated meat and fish, harmful to man's body.
- Hostelers receiving guests against the assize and selling hay and victuals against the assize.
- Weavers and fullers charging too much.
- Dyers and tanners causing pollution and blocking highways.
- Spicers selling by unfaithful weights and mixing old and new spices.
- Common forestallers.

This borough leet court was dominated by concern for victuallers, and it is likely that similar concerns were predominant in small markets where food-sellers and producers were the majority of traders, though some occupations might not have been as common.

The conventional condemnations of moralists can be clearly seen in these regulatory formulae. However, an even more stark expression of the intersection between law and literature is provided in the treatises that sought to illustrate the proceedings in a manor or leet court. One particular version was written in dialogue form, in French, in the late thirteenth or early fourteenth century. Although partly humorous, and almost certainly creative in its text and characters, it was intended to provide precedents for the conduct of a court.[54] One case concerns William le Peister, the baker, who admits to breaking the assize of bread. In passing judgement, the court extract quotes from the New Testament: 'thou wicked servant, out of thine own mouth I judge thee' (Luke 19:22). Another passage condemns Thomas le Folour for selling stinking and putrid fish in the market because he had kept it so long 'whereby folk may receive damage or hurt or bodily ill'. The defendant is keen to clear his name through a jury rather than see his reputation tarnished.[55] Although such cases were probably artificial, they do highlight the moral opprobrium heaped upon certain offences, particularly foodstuffs that might cause bodily harm.

In addition to the basic articles covered by all leet courts, there are examples of by-laws for small market towns and villages, framed either through the mechanism of the manor or leet court.[56] As long as they did not contravene common law, such by-laws were a useful local supplement to statutory legislation. They were proclaimed in order to meet

---

[54] Briggs (ed.), *'Here may a young man see'*.
[55] *Ibid.*, pp. 1–2, 9, 10. See also Maitland and Baildon (eds.), *Court Baron*, 'La Court de Baron', pp. 26–7, 50–1.
[56] Briggs, *Credit and Village Society*, pp. 55–6.

local needs, such as gleaning or pasture rights, and often had communal or moral undertones. They could also be applied to market matters. For instance, a by-law 'per commune consilium' (suggesting common consent, at least from the capital pledges) was passed in the leet of Walsoken (a manor of the abbey of Ramsey) in 1299. It followed the amercement of six fishmongers and stated that no fishmongers should take fish out of the vill to sell if anyone of the parish still wanted to buy their fish, under penalty of half a mark.[57] The court of Petworth (Sussex) drew up some basic trading regulations in 1440, related to commercial activities both at market and fair time. Tolls were summarised for cattle-dealers ($\frac{1}{2}$d. for every horse, cow and ox, $\frac{1}{4}$d. for each pig and sheep), corn merchants, butchers and fishmongers, and also for buyers of animals, brassware, pewterware and saddles. Cartloads of victuals and salt, being brought into the market or fair to sell, had to pay a toll of 4d. In addition, butchers were warned about the condition of their meat, while bakers, brewers and tapsters were to be presented by the tasters during the fair and amerced.[58]

These by-laws were often formulated by local juries in either the leet or manorial court, acting on behalf of the tenants as a whole. Jurors thus did not merely present offences, but took an active role in decision-making, local policy and enforcement.[59] Through the empanelment of inquisition juries, usually from the same sub-set of respected local men, they also arbitrated on disputes between their neighbours stemming from various types of plea. This generated both prestige and antagonism for jurors and officials within their small town or village, and even slander or bodily harm from irate tenants.[60] Consequently, there were mechanisms to assuage the anxieties of residents, such as a fairly regular turnover of jurors (amongst the upper echelons of the town) and the use of special inquest juries. Above all, jurors and local officials had to act within the bounds of common consensus and accepted moral principles in order to maintain their legitimate authority. Although heavy fines were promulgated upon those who attacked or insulted officials, effective enforcement was ultimately reliant on cooperation and social order.

Indeed, conflict occurred in small towns for a variety of reasons, over tenure, rents, services, commerce or social relations.[61] The authority of

---

[57] Ault (ed.), *Ramsey*, p. 179.
[58] West Sussex Record Office (Chichester), 6/1/18 HVI Petworth (with thanks to Maria Osowiecki for this reference).
[59] DeWindt, 'Local government', 628–35; Olson, 'Jurors of the village court'; Yates, *Town and Countryside*, p. 80.
[60] DeWindt, 'Local government', 635–7.
[61] Dyer, 'Small-town conflict', 183–4; Dimmock, 'English small towns'.

lordship and the courts, and the influence of religious ideology, only went so far in creating cohesion. Religious or social guilds were one source of solidarity, trust and mutual support and even the basis of a surrogate government in some small towns, beyond the auspices of the lord.[62] In Stratford-upon-Avon, the Holy Cross Guild played an important political role in town affairs, discussing by-laws, promoting harmony amongst its members by resolving disputes at 'lovedays', and developing wider links by recruiting from outside Stratford.[63] As communities arguably became less cohesive in the fifteenth century, with greater immigration and more strangers, the ties of personal credit became stretched and social guilds were even more important in overcoming any diminution in trust. Such guilds and fraternities certainly became more numerous and prestigious in the century after the Black Death and were heavily involved in organising social events and the upkeep of local facilities such as schools, chapels, bridges and roads. Indeed, in Henley-on-Thames, the religious fraternity that maintained the important bridge over the Thames had already become a *de facto* town government by the 1290s.[64] However, it is uncertain whether such direct involvement by socio-religious guilds in trading regulation was common. Manorial court rolls usually show that it was designated court officials who supervised commercial matters, such as aletasters, surveyors of leather, meat-tasters, or bailiffs.

The lords of small towns and seigneurial boroughs thus included tenants in local government as bailiffs, constables, jurors, aletasters and affeerers.[65] It is likely that they had their own interpretations of the law, influenced by broader concepts of morality. However, to conduct their duties correctly, officials needed to know the extant regulations both at a national and local level. There were many detailed regulations for the protection of consumers and limitation of outsiders, and these could differ slightly from market to market in the times, places and procedures they had in place. Larger towns usually had custumals where ordinances were recorded and could be referred to. However, even in smaller towns, individual officials might copy extracts from statutes and ordinances for their own use. For instance, the commonplace book of Robert Reynes of Acle (Norfolk) was a fifteenth-century compilation of various texts,

---

[62] Holt and Rosser, 'Introduction', pp. 12–13; Rosser, 'Essence of medieval urban communities'; Palliser, 'Urban society', p. 143; Dyer, 'Urbanizing of Staffordshire', pp. 25–6. Bailey suggested that such a local religious fraternity probably controlled affairs in late medieval Buntingford (Herts.). Bailey, 'A tale of two towns', 362–3. See also McRee, 'Religious gilds'; Bainbridge, *Gilds*, p. 17; Britnell, 'England: towns', p. 56.

[63] Dyer, 'Medieval Stratford'; Carpenter, 'Town and "country"'; Hilton, *English Peasantry*, pp. 93–4.

[64] Dyer, *Making a Living*, pp. 220, 316–17.

[65] An affeerer was a court-appointed suitor who advised on the level of amercements.

including taxes and trading assizes, which were probably used by him in his official capacities.[66] He was clearly an active man in his local community and both involved and concerned about the day-to-day running of the marketplace.

Chartered boroughs

In comparison to seigneurial markets and boroughs, by the beginning of the thirteenth century larger royal towns had been commonly granted more extensive autonomy to manage their increasingly complex affairs. Leading inhabitants thus took control of revenues, litigation and the supervision of the market, in return for paying an annual fee to the Crown. Gradually, urban constitutions became more elaborate, with elected councils, independence from royal officials and improved rights of self-government.[67] A defined group of burgesses or freemen, distinct from the main body of urban dwellers, received privileges that gave them and their household advantages in the borough's marketplace. Given that the majority of such freemen were craftsmen and traders, these privileges were highly sought after and defended. The right to a formal Merchant Guild reinforced the ability to control commerce and enforce trading regulations. There were thus many commercial and political advantages to be gained from greater urban self-government.

There was a proliferation of borough charters in the twelfth and thirteenth centuries, partly due to increasing bureaucratisation and documentation and also due to urban growth, both of existing towns and new foundations.[68] Urban expansion and the ambitions of the growing mercantile class were also brought under greater royal control. Borough charters were granted by the king, and sometimes by lords, and bestowed certain rights and privileges upon town communities for the conduct of their own jurisdiction, including the policing of markets and trade. Often these charters were only a royal recognition of customary legal privileges already gained or established, but the importance of charters to municipal autonomy was shown in their continual confirmations (such as at the succession of a new king) and in the grants of new liberties.[69] Although

[66] Louis (ed.), *Commonplace Book*, pp. 121–5, 136–8.
[67] In the early twentieth century, Tait, Bateson and Stephenson studied the borough as a privileged legal entity, with their research based primarily upon royal charters and town customs. Tait, *Medieval English Borough*; Bateson (ed.), *Borough Customs*; Stephenson, *Borough and Town*.
[68] Lilley, *Urban Life*, pp. 111–22; Beresford, *New Towns*; Beresford and Finberg, *English Medieval Boroughs*.
[69] *BBC, 1307–1660*, pp. xviii–xxvii.

charters were essentially similar in content, the balance and size of privileges did vary according to the size and position of the town, the date of
the charter and whether it was a royal or mesne borough.[70] The grants
usually protected the interests of the recipient burgesses and allowed
them control of supplies which entered their town.[71] This burgess class
mostly consisted of merchants or wealthy artisans, who had obtained
their burgess status and privileges through birth, purchase or appren-
ticeship. They were jealously determined to express their commercial
exclusiveness against the rights of 'outsiders'; though sometimes 'foreigners' themselves could pay for the right to share urban privileges. For
instance, foreigners in Maldon could buy and sell by retail as long as they
had purchased a 40s. licence for the privilege.[72]

A burgess normally had the benefits of burgage tenure, jurisdictional
rights and trading privileges, though this differed from borough to borough. In smaller seigneurial ('mesne') boroughs, there might be only a
few nominal rights that accorded a town the title of 'borough', such as
burgage tenure or exemption from paying tolls in the town's market. The
further up the burghal scale, particularly in royal boroughs, the greater
the liberties and autonomy that burgesses enjoyed. The basic privileges
within a royal chartered borough contained some, or all, of the following: burgage tenure; the right to farm taxes and tolls;[73] the right to their
own jurisdiction in their own borough court; a Merchant Guild; the
right to retail freely; exemption from tolls, both within the borough and
elsewhere; and the right to share in bargains.

In many royal charters, the borough was granted the right to form a
Merchant Guild. This was the institution that collected commercial revenues and had the right to make trade regulations.[74] Although merchant
guildsmen and burgesses were not necessarily an identical body of men,
the membership of the two groups increasingly overlapped and merged
as time went on. These were, after all, the wealthiest and most powerful men in a town. At Leicester, the alderman of the guild was mayor
of the borough, by-laws passed in the guild were described as acts of
the commonalty, and property transfers were recorded in the Merchant
Guild roll.[75] The organisation of such guilds was attuned to commercial

---

[70] For studies of burgess privileges, see Britnell, *Growth and Decline*, pp. 35–7; Kermode,
   'The merchants', 8; Rigby, *Medieval Grimsby*, pp. 11–12, 37–47.
[71] Britnell, *Commercialisation*, p. 27.
[72] Alsford, *Towns* (Maldon, fifteenth century); *Leicester*, i, p. 92 (1260); Masschaele, 'Urban
   trade'.
[73] *BBC, 1042–1216*, p. 176 (Bridgwater, 1200).
[74] Gross, *Gild Merchant*; *BBC, 1042–1216*, pp. 202–3; *Leicester*, i, pp. 1, 3.
[75] *Leicester*, i, pp. 183, 241. In other towns, the relationship was perhaps not quite so close.

interests, including officers and a court to adjudicate disputes between guildsmen. The Merchant Guild might also foster a sense of civic and convivial unity among privileged townsfolk through its meetings and festivities.

However, not all townsfolk enjoyed such borough privileges. Below the ranks of freemen were a broad range of people without legal privileges and trading rights, who constituted the dependent urban labouring class and poor. Indeed, burgesses, guildsmen or freemen might comprise only 20–40 per cent of a town's population.[76] Even within the privileged ranks of burgesses another elite group, often with mercantile interests, commonly dominated the high offices and levers of urban power. This urban mercantile elite had a vested interest in regulating crafts, trades and the tools of exchange and credit, whether directly through the borough court, ordinances and by-laws, or through close supervision of the craft guilds. These craft guilds emerged in the thirteenth and fourteenth centuries as compositions of specialised groupings of craftsmen and traders, often burgesses themselves, who were seeking to bolster their occupation. Increasingly, such craft guilds issued ordinances that touched upon marketing matters, particularly the retailing activities of their members and the quality of their products.

Borough customs and ordinances were a legacy of the urban and commercial expansions of the twelfth and thirteenth centuries, in the wake of assertions of city autonomy. They reveal much about the priorities and attitudes of burgesses, influenced not only by the need to protect and enhance their privileges but also broader matters of the common good and consumer welfare. The *Domesday Book* of Ipswich, *Liber Rubeus* of Bristol, *Liber Albus* of London, the *Oak Book* of Southampton and many others were all compiled by medieval officials as compendiums of their local customs of government and trade. These custumals aided day-to-day administration and codified their acquired privileges. Some also claimed the spurious stamp of antiquity, when, in fact, the customs were usually established or adapted to suit changing conditions. Although many of these regulations date from the thirteenth century, their application as a basis of law remained largely intact at a later date; copies of several custumals, such as at Ipswich, were made into the thirteenth, fourteenth and fifteenth centuries with only slight modifications.[77] The large number of trade ordinances in borough custumals is a testimony both to the interest in trading matters and the requirement to address local circumstances and privileges.

[76] Kowaleski, 'Commercial dominance'.
[77] Allen, *Ipswich Borough Archives*, pp. 413–21.

Boroughs, as with manors, also passed by-laws that accorded with common law and often drew on parliamentary legislation or royal ordinances which suited local needs or addressed grievances. Sarah Rees Jones has argued that the actual exercise of authority at grass-roots level in York was largely left to the discretion of town and court officials, and they made many compromises between royal law, civic policy and common custom, usually based on local experience.[78] In Coventry, leet by-laws were based on petitions presented by aggrieved individuals or groups to the mayor four days before the court assembled.[79] The trading privileges of burgesses and guildsmen thus derived not only from borough charters and statute law, but also from subsequent formulations of town ordinances. Chartered privileges also became entangled within the conflicts of various parties: between trades, greater and lesser burgesses, town and country and, not least, between king and locality. Varied interest groups created a complex interplay of influences in the enforcement of regulations. However, in general, the basic burgess privileges discussed below demonstrated a self-interested concern for the equity of the enfranchised at the expense of the unenfranchised.

Lot and scot

The phrase 'lot and scot' encompassed basic rights that were claimed by burgesses or guildsmen. 'Lot' was the right to share and have an equal opportunity in bargains, while 'scot' represented the payment of common charges to the grantor of their charter, usually the king. Together burgesses paid a yearly lump sum ('firma burgi') that acquitted them of all tolls and charges in their town.[80] Borough status thus not only brought privileges and benefits, but also costs and burdens, in the form of the fee-farm, the charter itself, offices and the town's infrastructure.[81] Burgesses jealously guarded their trading rights in order to obtain recompense for their 'scot' expenditures. This attitude was reflected in the customs of Ipswich, where no foreign merchant could be accorded the status of burgess without holding a tenement in the town.[82]

The ownership of a tenement was deemed vital as both a distrainable asset during procedures of justice and as a contributor to the taxes of a town. Those who no longer had property or were not paying taxes were

[78] Rees Jones, 'York's civic administration', pp. 125–7.
[79] *Coventry*, pp. xx–xxii, xxvii–xxviii. See also Wood, *Medieval Tamworth*, pp. 74–87.
[80] Reynolds, *Introduction*; Bailey, 'Trade and towns', 195.
[81] Bailey, 'Trade and towns', 203.
[82] *Black Book*, ii, pp. 152–5, c.63 [61] (c.1309); *Liber Albus*, p. 235 (1273–1307); Britnell, *Growth and Decline*, p. 36.

to have their franchise revoked and were subsequently liable to tolls. In other boroughs, foreign burgesses and the gentry could purchase a franchise for life in order to obtain the right to buy and sell in a town without paying tolls.[83] However, this still accorded with the general principle that communal payments gave burgesses the right to certain privileges in trade and jurisdiction. Burgesses had to contribute to the costs to maintaining the market, running the borough courts, collecting levies, upkeeping public buildings and paying the annual 'fee-farm' to the Crown.[84] Borough law was based on the premise that outsiders who did not contribute directly to the common purse should pay for their use of the market.

The other trading privilege of 'lot' concerned the right to a share in wholesale bargains, provided the burgess was present at the deal. The thirteenth-century Berwick ordinances made provision for large purchases of herring whereby those present could demand a share at cost price, but anyone not present could also claim a share by paying an extra 12d. to the original buyer.[85] The regulations of fifteenth-century Sandwich stated: 'freemen of our community are wont to be sharers of all trade when they are present at a purchase or sale, whether the buyer or the seller be a fellow-freeman or a stranger'.[86] Occasionally, the first to strike a bargain was given a larger share as compensation for their efforts. However, in general, entrepreneurial behaviour was perhaps discouraged by the principle that all full members of the community had an equal right to a reasonable livelihood. The penalties for refusing to allow bargain-sharing were severe: guildsmen or burgesses could be excluded from buying or selling in the town for a year (except for necessary victuals).[87]

Non-guildsmen or non-burgesses were excluded from such 'lot' rights, though they might have to allow burgesses to share in their purchases of merchandise.[88] It was only those privileged sections of the trading classes who were given prior bargaining rights (before any strangers or

[83] Dyer, *Making a Living*, p. 193.
[84] *Memorials*, pp. 166–7 (1327); *CLB*, E, pp. 220–2 (1327).
[85] Toulmin Smith (ed.), *English Gilds*, p. 345 (Berwick, 1283–4).
[86] Bateson (ed.), *Borough Customs*, ii, p. 178 (Sandwich, fifteenth century).
[87] *Ibid.*, i, pp. 38–9, c.25 (c.1300). See also *Coventry*, p. 193 (1440). For cases of refusing 'lot', see *Leicester*, i, pp. 78, 83–4, 180, 182–3, 271. For instance, in 1258, William Sturdy accused John Folebarbe of refusing him lot in a stock of fish 'to his damage and dishonour' and to the contempt of the community, and Folebarbe had to pay 5s. and a cask of ale.
[88] *Oak Book*, i, pp. 38–9, 64–5 cc.24, 61 (c.1300). For right to 'lot', see also *BBC, 1216–1307*, pp. 299–300 (Grimsby, 1258); Bateson (ed.), *Borough Customs*, ii, p. 168 (Preston, twelfth century; Grimsby, 1259), ii, p. 171 (Berwick, thirteenth century; Chesterfield, 1294), ii, p. 177 (Torksey, c.1345), ii, pp. 178–9 (Sandwich, fifteenth century); *Black Book*, ii, pp. 128–31, c.44 (c.1309); *Bristol*, ii, pp. 22–5 (1339); Myers (ed.), *English Historical Documents*, p. 570 (Canterbury, c.1430); *Coventry*, p. 338 (1468).

non-burgesses) to wholesale merchandise entering the town.[89] 'Lot' thus gave all franchised dealers an equal opportunity to buy from foreign merchants, but also ensured that they were able to monitor communally all wholesale bargains made in a borough. Indeed, the system could only work effectively if all bargains were conducted publicly, though customs varied in the extent to which deals were openly declared or implicitly witnessed in the marketplace.

The rules for bargain-sharing were primarily intended for wholesale transactions of raw materials and manufactures, rather than goods for household consumption.[90] Indeed, victuals were a staple commodity that all residents expected a share in, provided they were purchasing them for sustenance and not resale. In thirteenth-century Berwick, anyone who bought victuals was expected to provide a cost-priced share to neighbours who wanted it for their own household's consumption, with the original purchaser left with at least a quarter of his initial acquisition. Those who took such a share and sold it again were to be punished.[91] Town authorities presumably did not want unnecessary price rises in victuals, or a lack of supply. But neither did they wish to restrict the incoming movement and sale of victuals. In Coventry, bakers, fishers and butchers from the surrounding countryside were freely allowed to enter the city and sell retail, in order to safeguard supplies. However, they all had to first show their victuals to officials to check they were 'abull for manns meite'.[92]

Burgesses or guildsmen who attempted to circumvent borough regulations, such as by forming partnerships with outsiders or non-guildsmen, were liable to forfeit their goods and even their own guild or burgess status.[93] In Southampton, such partnerships were regarded as a 'manner of coverture, art, contrivance, collusion'.[94] Similarly, any burgess who disclosed Ipswich affairs or provided trading information to outsiders was to be disenfranchised.[95] This penalty was also imposed upon those burgesses who tried to help strangers to avoid tolls by acting as intermediaries and masquerading the merchandise of an outsider as their

[89] *Oak Book*, i, pp. 36–9, c.23 (c.1300).   [90] Bateson (ed.), *Borough Customs*, ii, p. lxix.
[91] *Ibid.*, ii, p. 172 (Berwick, thirteenth century). See also *BBC, 1216–1307*, p. 300 (Grimsby, 1258); *Norwich*, i, pp. 184–5 (early fourteenth century).
[92] *Coventry*, pp. 24, 26, 29 (1421), 386–7 (1473).
[93] Schopp and Easterling (eds.), *Anglo-Norman Custumal*, pp. 26, 29, 37, nos. 20, 31, 66 (mid-thirteenth century); Toulmin Smith (ed.), *English Gilds*, p. 342 (Berwick, 1283–4); *Liber Albus*, p. 231 (1272–1307); Hill, *Medieval Lincoln*, appx VII (c.1300); *Leicester*, i, pp. 88–93, 102, 115, 167, 169, 202, 205; *Norwich*, i, p. 187 (early fourteenth century?); *Northampton*, i, pp. 230–1 (c.1460); Arnold, *Customs of London*, p. 84 (c.1519).
[94] *Oak Book*, i, pp. 36–7, 42–3, cc.21, 30 (c.1300). See also *York*, ii, pp. 204–6 (1460).
[95] *Black Book*, ii, pp. 154–7, c.65 [63] (c.1309). See also *York*, ii, p. 209 (1463–4).

own.[96] In general, avoidance of toll was considered a grave matter which was heavily punishable.[97]

The heavy penalties directed at those who colluded to avoid toll were founded on the fact that exemption from tolls within their own town was another lucrative privilege for burgesses. Some borough charters additionally provided royal exemptions from tolls either throughout the kingdom or in partial areas or concerning particular commodities.[98] In these cases, traders from chartered boroughs were expected to carry proof of their exemption when travelling.[99] Otherwise, tolls were paid by anyone bringing and displaying goods for sale in a town, whether or not a sale was made. Different commodities and different types of transport paid varying dues, usually from a farthing to a few pennies, though very low-value goods (under 3d.) were quit of toll. Lists of tolls give a useful indication of the types of commodities that commonly entered markets, large and small. For instance, the thirteenth-century tolls payable at Egremont market included horses, cattle, sheep, pigs, woollen cloth, linen cloth, herrings, leather and iron, while those for Newark mentioned horses, oxen, cows, pigs, sheep, carts, ploughs, roofing materials, timber, bows, millstones, wool, leather, skins, wine and corn.[100] Willard noted that there are instances in which tolls were levied weekly upon carts carrying victuals into a market, suggesting a regular trade with men of the countryside.[101] The overall effect was that the main burden of customs and tolls fell on outside traders, as well as unenfranchised retailers who needed to buy supplies.

[96] *Black Book*, ii, pp. 156–7, c.66 [64] (*c*.1309). See also *Leicester*, i, p. 92 (1260); *CLB*, E, pp. 56–7 (1316); *Liber Albus*, p. 328 (1334); Alsford, *Towns* (Maldon, fifteenth century). For some cases where burgesses and strangers colluded to circumvent tolls, see *Norwich*, i, pp. 362 (1288), 369 (1290); *Leicester*, i, pp. 102, 169, 179, 190, 202, 203–4, 205, ii, p. 31.

[97] *BBC, 1042–1216*, p. 179 (Pontefract, 1194; Okehampton, 1199–1242). See also Johnson (ed.), *Hereford*, p. 25; *BBC, 1042–1216*, p. 179 (Chichester, 1155); *BBC, 1216–1307*, p. 253 (Manchester, 1301); *Bridgwater*, p. 81 (1380).

[98] *BBC, 1042–1216*, pp. 176–90, 190–4; *BBC, 1216–1307*, pp. 254–68; *CChR*, iii, p. 482 (Orford, 1326), iv, p. 122 (Lavenham, 1329).

[99] There were some controversies when traders claimed exemption from toll. *Parl. Rolls*, c.212, October 1318; *Leicester*, ii, p. 230 (1420).

[100] *Winchester, Landscape and Society*, p. 127; Barley (ed.), *Documents*, pp. 19, 33–4. See also *BBC, 1042–1216*, pp. 177–8 (Okehampton, 1194–1242, Chesterfield, 1213); Schopp and Easterling (eds.), *Anglo-Norman Custumal*, pp. 31–3, 36, nos. 40, 47, 61 (mid-thirteenth century); Furley (ed.), *Ancient Usages*, pp. 32–3, 36–41 (late thirteenth century); *Liber Albus*, pp. 196–217 (1284–5), 324–5 (thirteenth century); *York*, ii, p. 13 (1393); *Black Book*, ii, pp. 178–207 (*c*.1309); *Norwich*, ii, pp. 199–204 (fourteenth century).

[101] Willard, 'Inland transportation', 365–9. Tolls would often be charged by the animal, pack, horseload or cartload.

Strangers and foreigners

Urban attitudes towards outsiders and strangers were prominent influences in the creation of trading regulations. Local town ordinances
provided safeguards and opportunities for resident traders, but many
obstacles for the itinerant and those outside the burgess community. For
example, those who unloaded merchandise brought by sea to Ipswich
and sold part of them ('broken bulk') were not allowed to remove the
remaining goods without the permission of the bailiff. They were not only
forced to sell against their wishes, but were expected to stay in Ipswich
for eight days to sell their goods at a 'reasonable price'. This may have
effectively forced outsiders to sell at a lower price. They could attempt
to gain permission from the bailiffs to leave, but had to pay the appropriate export customs.[102] In a similar manner, fishermen who had already
entered the market at Beverley were not allowed to take their fish elsewhere until all inhabitants of the town had been 'duly served'.[103] Such
restrictive policies may have forced outside traders to lower their prices
if they could not sell at their original rates.

Many boroughs might also curb how long a foreign merchant could
stay within their walls.[104] No stranger was to remain in Bristol for more
than three days without acquiring pledges for their good conduct.[105] A
similar bias against unknown traders is expressed starkly in one Norwich
Custumal, whereby strangers could be arrested for 'behaving themselves
in a suspicious and foolish manner whereby evil suspicion from men
of credit towards them deservedly arises'. They were required to find
someone to pledge them for their good behaviour. Foreign and alien
traders could also be limited in the places they could stay, as was shown
by the development of 'hosting' in international ports. This system forced
alien merchants, and even some foreign traders, to lodge with a burgess
and conduct all their business through their host.[106] The rules for hosting
as laid out in the Ipswich ordinances mentioned that only burgesses or
men of high renown could host foreign merchants. Such hosts were
expected to provide advice on when, and to whom, they could sell their
goods, while each host was allowed to buy a quarter of the merchant's
goods (except wine) at market price.[107] The precise details of hosting

---

[102] *Black Book*, ii, pp. 156–9, c.67 [65] (*c*.1309).   [103] *Beverley*, p. 58 (1467).
[104] *BBC, 1042–1216*, p. lxxi; *BBC, 1216–1307*, p. 287.
[105] *Bristol*, ii, pp. 225–6 (late fourteenth century); *Great Red Book*, i, p. 141 (1451–2).
[106] Ruddock, 'Alien hosting'. See *Great Red Book*, ii, p. 50 (1455?); *Norwich*, ii, p. 101
        (1473); Arnold, *Customs of London*, p. 7 (*c*.1519).
[107] *Black Book*, ii, pp. 146–9, c.60 [59] (*c*.1309). In fifteenth-century Dover, hosts were
        allowed to purchase up to half of a stranger's merchandise, Bateson (ed.), *Borough
        Customs*, ii, p. 179.

and the share they could claim differed from borough to borough, but
the main principles were the same. Hosts effectively acted as brokers for
visiting traders and also as official witnesses for their deals; they were the
appointed, local go-betweens for potential foreign buyers and sellers and
reduced such traders' search costs. However, they also circumscribed the
freedom of outsiders. There were additional concerns, expressed in both
civic and parliamentary sources, that hosts might actually undermine
the privileges of other burgesses through their priority access to foreign
traders.[108] At Coventry in 1421, fishers from outside the town were to be
hosted at inns, but not at the homes of native fishers, in order to prevent
forestalling and ensure all fish reached the market without pre-emptive
collusion.[109]

Merchant burgesses certainly influenced the development of certain
borough regulations in an attempt to secure control of particular commodities and temper competition from outsiders. Foreigners were often
limited to operating in the marketplace, excluded from selling certain
goods by retail and not allowed to deal with other foreigners. Such exclusion not only applied to foreigners and strangers but also to residents who
were non-burgesses or not members of the guild. In several boroughs,
anyone who wished to buy and sell in particular goods had to be a guild
member or a burgess.

Many borough charters granted certain retail monopolies to franchised
or guild members of the town, particularly those in cloth, hide or wool
trades. For instance, in twelfth-century Bristol no foreign merchant could
sell cloth by retail (except at fairs) and could only buy hides, cloth or
wool from a burgess.[110] The weavers and fullers of London and Beverley
were only allowed to sell their cloth to merchants of the city and not to
foreigners.[111] Strangers in Exeter were allowed to buy and sell wholesale,

[108] There were problems associated with both hosts' and brokers' activities, such as broken
deals, debts, hoarding, forestalling, avoiding tolls and by-passing privileges of guildsmen or franchise-holders. See *BBC, 1216–1307*, p. 294 (Great Yarmouth, 1256); Alsford, *Towns* (Great Yarmouth, 1300); *CChR*, ii, p. 315 (Dunwich, 1285); Ingleby (ed.),
Red Register, ii, p. 216, fol. 142d (1363); *Oak Book*, i, pp. 62–5, cc.59–60 (*c*.1300);
Thomas (ed.), *Calendar*, pp. 7–9, 12–13 (Roll A, 1298); *CLB*, D, pp. 219–20 (early
fourteenth century); *Leicester*, i, p. 268 (1329); *Statutes*, ii, pp. 28–9, 6 Ric II st.1 c.11
(1382); *Liber Albus*, pp. 235 (1272–1307), 273–4 (early fifteenth century); Arnold,
Customs of London, p. 97 (*c*.1519).
[109] *Coventry*, p. 33 (1421).
[110] *BBC, 1042–1216*, pp. 209–14 (Newcastle-upon-Tyne, 1100–35; Lincoln, 1154–63;
Chichester, 1155; Wells, 1174–80; Bristol, 1188); *BBC, 1216–1307*, pp. 169, 284–9
(Hereford, 1227; Bridgnorth, 1227; Shrewsbury, 1227; Worcester, 1227; Liverpool,
1229; Oxford, 1229; Wigan, 1246).
[111] Riley (ed.), *Munimenta Gildhallae*, ii, 'Liber Custumarum', pp. 122–31 (1297–1300);
Beverley, pp. 134–5 (*c*.1209).

provided they paid their tolls, restricted themselves to non-monopoly commodities and sold only to guildsmen or burgesses.[112] Although the precise nature of privileges varied from borough to borough, outsiders were often limited in the trade they could conduct in chartered boroughs. They were frequently denied access to specific, usually non-victual, retail trades and were restricted to wholesale trade in those goods.[113] The charter for Bakewell in 1286 even specified that no foreign traders should sell meat or fish within the town as long as native traders could provide sufficient supplies, though such an extension of restrictions to trade in foodstuffs was unusual.[114] In Oxford in 1311, an ordinance stated 'that all who have food to sell may sell it freely in Oxford, even though they are not burgesses'.[115]

Residents of boroughs could be excluded from certain types of retail trade, particularly in wares such as wool, cloth, hides and skins, if they were not guildsmen, burgesses or freemen.[116] In a Chesterfield charter for 1294, only burgesses could be dyers, tanners, retailers of meat, fish, hides, linen or woollen cloth (described as 'cutters' of such goods) and buyers of cut cloth, hides or skins ('whether green, raw, fresh, or salted') within the market and town, except at the time of the fair.[117] Only Southampton guildsmen could buy goods such as honey, salted herring, oil, millstones and hides outside of the market or fair days, or keep a tavern or sell cloth by retail.[118] The regulations highlighted the importance of the market day as an opportunity for outsiders and the unenfranchised, for on other days the urban authorities were wary of much trading activity.

In reality, in order to be successful, boroughs had to allow foreigners (whether from another town or another country) to trade and operate within their markets.[119] An entry in the late fourteenth-century records of Leicester requested that merchant guildsmen should not exercise their customary right to shares in sales, as this might frighten foreign traders

---

[112] Schopp and Easterling (eds.), *Anglo-Norman Custumal*, pp. 28, 34, 37, nos. 23, 25, 26, 50, 66 (mid-thirteenth century). See also *Leicester*, i, pp. 252–3, 292.

[113] *Norwich*, i, pp. 29, 107 (1415); *BBC, 1042–1216*, p. 213 (Okehampton, 1194–1242); *BBC, 1216–1307*, pp. 284–9 (Berwick, 1302); Hill, *Medieval Lincoln*, appx VII (c.1300); Arnold, *Customs of London*, pp. 5, 25 (c.1519).

[114] *BBC, 1216–1307*, p. 288 (Bakewell, 1286).

[115] Salter (ed.), *Munimenta*, pp. 17–18, no. 20 (1311). See also Salter (ed.), *Medieval Archives*, i, pp. 160–1, no. 103 (1355).

[116] E.g. Toulmin Smith (ed.), *English Gilds*, p. 342 (Berwick, 1283–4); *Bristol*, ii, pp. 26–7 (1348); Alsford, *Towns* (Maldon, fifteenth century).

[117] *BBC, 1216–1307*, p. 288 (Chesterfield, 1294).

[118] *Oak Book*, i, pp. 34–7, c.20 (c.1300).

[119] Hilton, 'Medieval market towns', 20–1; Britnell, *Commercialisation*, pp. 171–8.

away. Nor were they to force any trader to sell fish and goods against their will; rather merchants were to be free to come and go provided that they paid their tolls. By 1361, traders visiting Leicester were even remitted of any toll charges in order to encourage more buying and selling in the town's market.[120] Similarly, in Lynn in 1309, the bailiffs sought to annul any existing ordinances of the guilds or town that were deemed detrimental to free commerce and therefore harmful to the community.[121] Other towns provided opportunities for outsiders to pay for longer-term rights in their market, such as in thirteenth-century Exeter where the unenfranchised could pay 'chepgavel', which freed them from tolls while they traded in the city.[122]

The borough style of trade management was intended to restrict outsiders and favour burgesses who possessed inside knowledge about local trading arrangements.[123] It could be argued that this was to the detriment of boroughs in the long-run and hampered their ability to be flexible at times of crisis or opportunity. However, the ostensible picture provided by charters and regulations perhaps conceals a tacit acceptance by medieval boroughs that they needed a more flexible and conducive everyday marketing environment. Many town authorities recognised that outsiders would continue to use a particular market only if the inducements of convenient facilities, demand, efficient regulation, security and legal redress outweighed the costs of tolls and restrictions. Britnell suggests that, in reality, there was not the level of burghal autarchy suggested by the charters and borough regulations. Boroughs could not control their hinterlands to the extent needed to control production, prices and competition. Even the largest English boroughs did not have extensive territorial authority in the mode of Italian cities, and they certainly could not demand that the agrarian produce of the hinterland be brought to their marketplace.[124] Much trade was conducted outside the borough, in smaller markets and informal outlets, beyond their reach. The influence of royal authority was also notable, in the privileges it offered to competing boroughs and also in its efforts to standardise weights, measures, coinage and the assizes, as well as stressing the need for free trade within markets.

---

[120] *Leicester*, ii, pp. 88 (1352), 116–22 (1361).   [121] Alsford, *Towns* (Lynn, 1309).
[122] Schopp and Easterling (eds.), *Anglo-Norman Custumal*, pp. 28, 34, 37, nos. 23, 25, 26, 50, 66 (mid-thirteenth century); Kowaleski, *Local Markets*, pp. 185–7.
[123] Britnell, *Commercialisation*, pp. 27–8, 35–7. Minorities, such as the Welsh or Scots in border towns and the Jews, might also face specific laws that restricted their trading opportunities. Epstein, *An Economic and Social History*, p. 106.
[124] Britnell, *Britain and Ireland*, p. 139; Dyer, *Making a Living*, p. 223.

Borough government

The aims of borough market regulation were heavily influenced by the style and form of a town's administration. Borough government often lay with the mayor, council and officials who were chosen from the ranks of the burgesses, and they were usually the wealthiest and most successful citizens, such as merchants, lawyers and substantial property owners. As overseas trade and commercial opportunities grew after the twelfth century, it was mercantile wealth that came to dominate the upper ranks of borough society and government.[125] In studying borough government, some historians have emphasised the increasing proportion of freemen and the enlargement of councils by the fifteenth century, which supposedly provided greater popular participation.[126] Conversely, other historians have suggested that late medieval town government shifted from popular democracy to a closed oligarchy.[127] Boroughs certainly set differing requirements for entry to the freedom and the proportion of freemen could also change over time. However, it appears that membership of parts of borough government, and entry to the freedom of towns, became increasingly concentrated in fewer hands by the fourteenth and fifteenth centuries.

In late medieval Exeter, there was a council of twelve burgesses, while in Colchester, Winchester and Dunwich, there were councils of twenty-four. Kowaleski estimated that the governing elite of late fourteenth-century Exeter comprised just 1 per cent of the male population, while freemen constituted about 21 per cent of householders.[128] The form of government and level of oligarchy differed in various towns, but in all cases, there was an elite group who ran town affairs, supposedly with the tacit consent of the 'community'. In reality, formal approval was rarely sought. Thus, in larger boroughs there was a distinct class of leading citizens ('probi homines') separate from the 'communitas' of middling and poor people.[129] However, in both the formulation and enforcement of regulation, especially in commercial matters, other factors need to be considered. In particular, it should be noted that leading figures of larger boroughs required an element of conformity and general acceptance if their administration was to be successful. They might otherwise face

---

[125] Britnell, 'Town life', p. 161.
[126] Bridbury, *Economic Growth*, pp. 59–64; Reynolds, *Introduction*, p. 176.
[127] Kowaleski, 'Commercial dominance'; Rigby, *Medieval Grimsby*, p. 49; Dobson, 'Admissions'.
[128] Kowaleski, *Local Markets*, p. 358; Britnell, *Growth and Decline*, p. 119; Furley (ed.), *Ancient Usages*, pp. 26–7; Bailey (ed.), *Bailiffs' Minute Book*, p. 6.
[129] Thrupp, *Merchant Class*, p. 15; *Norwich*, i, pp. xxxvi–xxxvii, liii–lv.

civic and social disorder. This suggests that, to a certain extent, power was shared by society at large; as Lilley states: 'self-regulation and self-government emerged through complex social relations because power was being forever shared and negotiated'.[130]

According to Susan Reynolds and Gervase Rosser, medieval townsmen viewed government by an elite as natural and virtuous, provided these officials and council-men worked for the good of the whole community and did not simply represent vested interests. The legitimacy of their rule depended on an ostensible adherence to the rhetoric of communal government and principles of justice, consensus and harmony.[131] Officials were bound by oaths to perform diligent, honest services and to treat rich and poor alike. Failure was blamed, not so much upon the system of government, but the venality and indiscretions of individuals in power. Stephen Rigby has conversely argued that oligarchical government was only grudgingly accepted by those outside the ruling elite, and he posited that there was no adequate accountability.[132] Certainly, the ideals of common profit did not mean that members of an oligarchy were acting without prejudice when regulating a town's trade and industry. However, many borough rulers were themselves prominently involved in trade and undoubtedly saw aspects of their own welfare as integral to the prosperity and stability of the town.[133] Equally, all residents were potential consumers and many of the elite were employers who paid wages in conjunction with the needs of sustenance and food prices. They did not want the price of foodstuffs to lead to demands for higher wages. Additionally, attitudes to victuallers could not be antagonistic, for these traders made up a large and vital component of town populations.[134] Overall, a favourable commercial environment was conducive to general prosperity and order, enhanced the reputation of a town and helped in raising corporate revenue. The interests of the general community were thus often addressed because the sectional interests of the mercantile elite might benefit.

This all tends to suggest that borough communities were harmonious and efficient communities. However, there was obviously a fair degree of conflict within boroughs, such as between the poor and the rich, the retailers and the wholesalers, the burgesses and the non-burgesses. Civic

---

[130] Lilley, *Urban Life*, p. 43.
[131] Reynolds, *Introduction*, pp. 171–7; Rosser, *Medieval Westminster*, pp. 243–8; Swanson, *British Towns*, pp. 89–96.
[132] Rigby, *English Society*, pp. 145–77; Rigby, 'Urban "oligarchy"'; Swanson, *British Towns*, pp. 90–1.
[133] Britnell, *Growth and Decline*, p. 118.   [134] *Ibid.*, p. 35.

tension could arise from the clash of sectional interests.[135] Swanson argued that the distinction between the interests of the victualling crafts and the mercantile class had not been fully established before the fourteenth century. However, the concentration of urban government decisions in merchant hands after the Black Death seemingly subordinated victuallers in provincial towns.[136] It was not until the late fifteenth century that the victuallers gained in status and wealth once again, strengthened by the increasing standards of living and consumption demands. Thus, beyond the privileges and the tension between the merchant elite and aliens or strangers, it was the small dealer who faced the biggest limitations and burdens in chartered boroughs.[137] Compared to small towns and seigneurial boroughs, where petty retailers had a much greater involvement in the levers of government and administration, they were largely excluded from privileges in larger boroughs and their profits were limited and monitored carefully.

Tension could therefore occur between burgesses and non-burgesses, or greater and lesser burgesses, particularly when those in power advanced personal interests which were at odds with the wider community consensus, or if they limited access to office.[138] However, many of these conflicts were concerned with the fair conduct of government, rather than the actual construction of town authority. For instance, records from Exeter illustrate an awareness that members of the town's oligarchy manipulated their public office to their own advantage, but there were no organised challenges to this oligarchy. Instead, there was a buffer zone of middling men who sometimes accused those in power of improper behaviour.[139] There was an expectation that the leading members of a town should serve the common good and that the authority of officials resided in popular consent.

The oaths of officers, community rhetoric, the growth of pageantry and consumer regulations were all part of efforts to reinforce communal solidarity and order, and to demonstrate official recognition of the policy of 'fair government'.[140] In 1382, Parliament ordained that every mayor should include in his oath of office 'that he shall enforce and protect the said ordinance of victuallers without yielding to any party'.[141] The

---

[135] Reynolds, *Intoduction*, pp. 136–8; Miller and Hatcher, *Medieval England: Towns*, p. 357.
[136] Swanson, *Medieval Artisans*, pp. 24–5.   [137] Swanson, *British Towns*, p. 27.
[138] Kermode, *Medieval Merchants*, pp. 53–60; Reynolds, *Introduction*, pp. 135–6, 171; Fraser, 'Medieval trading restrictions'; Fleming, 'Telling tales', pp. 178–80.
[139] Kowaleski, *Local Markets*, pp. 116–19.
[140] Rigby, *English Society*, pp. 169–77; Kermode, *Medieval Merchants*, p. 26; Kermode, 'The merchants', 21; Fulton, 'Mercantile ideology', 321.
[141] *Parl. Rolls*, c.60, October 1382.

oath of the Mayor of Leicester outlined how he would maintain the customs of the town, punish forestallers and regraters, assess the assizes and 'do even right as well to the pore as to the riche'. The aletasters were also enjoined that they should 'nott lett for fauour [or for] hatred, kyn [kin] or alyence [alliance], but we shall do evyn [right and pun]nyghe as oure myndis [minds] and consciences woll serve'.[142] Consumers were thus partially protected to ensure adequate, sound and relatively cheap supplies of necessities. For instance, retailers were ordered by civic authorities to sell certain commodities in small lots that the poor could afford.[143]

One of the most prominent urban officials was the bailiff, whose role was particularly extensive and included restraining and distraining people on the orders of the courts, as well as the collection of tolls and fines. In many larger boroughs, bailiffs were chosen from the leading members of the town council. Legislative evidence suggests that the nature of his work may have made the bailiff an unpopular figure, for there are several regulations protecting him and other officials from potential abuse. In Ipswich, anyone who maliciously assaulted the bailiffs or coroners of the town was to be sent to prison, 'for the sake of the community', until they had fully amended for any damages and provided surety for their good conduct.[144] In Leicester in 1363, Lambert the butcher was placed under a surety of 100s. that he would never again contradict and abuse the mayor in the marketplace with base language ('turpis loquiis'), after he had been charged for selling unbaited bull flesh.[145] A fifteenth-century ordinance for Maldon specified a similar fine for those who called a bailiff 'by any name such as thief, knave, backbiter, whoreson, false, foresworn, cuckold, or bawd'.[146]

If town ordinances protected the body and integrity of officials, they also regulated their behaviour. The 'Articles of the Eyre', as set out in legislation of Edward I, included provisions to inquire into the correct

---

[142] *Leicester*, ii, pp. 319–23 (1489?). See also *Norwich*, i, pp. 123–4 (fifteenth century), ii, pp. 317–18; *Liber Albus*, p. 274 (early fifteenth century).

[143] Cooks were ordered to make halfpenny pies. *Coventry*, p. 111 (1427); *Memorials*, p. 432 (1379). Sellers of fresh salmon in Bristol had to cut small portions for those that required it. *Great Red Book*, i, p. 141 (late fifteenth century). Butchers of Hull had to sell meat in halfpenny, penny and twopenny lots. Gillett and MacMahon, *History of Hull*, p. 72. Wood-sellers in Bristol, selling in the 'Bak', were to ensure that they 'leve resonable stuff upon the bak fro spryng to spryng, to serue the pouere people of penyworthes and halfpeny worthes in the neep sesons'. Toulmin Smith (ed.), *The Maire*, pp. 83–4 (late fifteenth century).

[144] *Black Book*, ii, pp. 96–9, cc.24–5 (*c*.1309). See also *Liber Albus*, p. 231 (1272–3); *Beverley*, p. 41 (1364); *Memorials*, pp. 522–3 (1390), 595–6 (1413), 663–4 (1418); *York*, iii, p. 180 (1475); Stanford (ed.), *Ordinances of Bristol*, p. 14 (1519–20).

[145] *Leicester*, ii, p. 133 (1363).   [146] Alsford, *Towns* (Maldon, fifteenth century).

conduct of officials and whether any had taken bribes.[147] There were opportunities for officials to abuse their position and they were sometimes accused of favouritism, bribery, concealing offences and neglecting their duties. Negligent bailiffs in Ipswich who caused delays in the proceedings of the courts faced suspension or expulsion from their office.[148] The 'Ordinance of Labourers' (1349) also warned urban officials to be diligent in their convictions of victuallers selling at excessive prices or else be compelled to pay the aggrieved party three times the value of the item sold.[149] These enactments all demonstrated the need to keep control of unpaid officials as much as traders, since administrative corruption could lead to resentment and favouritism.

Borough government was a complex, heterogeneous structure that varied from town to town. It was certainly not egalitarian, but we should also be wary of suggesting precise 'class' divisions and a readily defined mercantile elite. Although wealth and status were the main determinants in attaining a position of authority, the ranks of the elite were not static and some social movement did occur. Office-holding could be burdensome and the elite seemingly welcomed new members of sufficient wealth and standing.[150] In addition, many administrative duties were carried out by minor officers drawn from the ranks of independent craftsmen and traders, as well as menial posts undertaken by unfree townsmen. In the fifteenth century, the number of petty posts, such as searchers, aletasters, porters and constables, grew significantly, partly as a consequence of the elaboration of many regulations.[151] Indeed, this expansion in petty office-holding occurred despite statutes in 1318 and 1382 which attempted to prevent any active victualler from exercising a judicial function in towns (only exempting those places where no other sufficient men could be found).[152] These statutes were intended either to prevent the use of the office for personal profit or to protect the dignity of the office from the slurs associated with petty victualling. They were anticipated by an oath for officers in London that ordered officers to desist from

---

[147] *Statutes*, i, p. 233, Edw I?.

[148] *Black Book*, ii, pp. 168–9, cc.76 [73], 77 [74], 78 [75] (*c*.1309).

[149] *Statutes*, i, p. 308, 23 Edw III c.6, 'Ordinance of Labourers' (1349). This was therefore a system of compensation for the buyer and sought to encourage the prosecution of offenders via the evidence of injured parties. Seabourne, *Royal Regulation*, p. 104.

[150] Britnell, 'Town life', p. 158.

[151] Kowaleski, *Local Markets*, p. 117; Kermode, *Medieval Merchants*, pp. 30–1, 39–47.

[152] *Statutes*, i, p. 178, 12 Edw II c.6 (1318); ii, p. 28, 6 Ric II st.1 c.9 (1382); *Parl. Rolls*, c.56, October 1382. The 1382 statute expanded upon the earlier statute of 1318, which had sought to prevent victuallers or vintners from taking any office in boroughs that involved managing the assizes of wines and victuals. See also *CPR, 1317–21*, p. 605; *Northampton*, i, p. 377 (late fifteenth century); Hull (ed.), *Calendar*, pp. 45, 52 (1465).

profiting in the victuals trade whilst in post.[153] However, such legislation implies that prominent burgesses were involved in victualling or running a hostelry and that they were reluctant to suspend their business.[154] A late fourteenth-century ordinance from Colchester complained of officials abusing their position by selling wine or ale contrary to statute.[155] An Ipswich ordinance of 1429 similarly excluded bailiffs from running an inn or tavern, or engaging in any sort of victualling whilst in office, otherwise they would face an exceptional fine of £10.[156] Thus, for some petty traders and retailers, involvement in town government was possible, even if the law did not encourage it.

Participation in borough government was thus a more complicated affair than simply a division between the mercantile elite and the rest. Although we should not take at face value rhetorical statements about 'commonalty', the need for consensus from a wider body than the oligarchical elite cannot be discounted. 'Community' sometimes referred only to the burgesses, or else to a parish or a craft organisation, but at other times the term meant the whole resident body. Nevertheless, retailers and victuallers were generally less wealthy than merchants and consequently lacked extensive political power and status in larger boroughs, despite their ubiquity in local markets.[157] The most prominent were butchers, and perhaps fishmongers and taverners, who had higher earnings and were more specialised. However, a majority of petty traders had little influence in actual borough government decisions, at least in the greater provincial centres.[158]

This, then, was the background to the burgess advancement of self-interested protectionism. Regulation was used both as a means of maintaining order and providing communal benefits, and also as an instrument for the advancement of vested interests and exclusive practices. However, for town officials and councils, the regulatory process was a precarious balancing act between individual ambitions, group interests and collective needs. If they were seen to go too far in advancing their own interests at the expense of the whole town, then they might cause

---

[153] *CLB*, D, p. 11 (late thirteenth century?). See also *Bristol*, i, p. 36 (1344).

[154] The statute forbidding victuallers to be officials was repealed in 1512 as towns had 'few or none person of substance' who were not victuallers. It was expected that they would work closely with non-victuallers who could thus provide a check on their activities. *Statutes*, iii, p. 30, 3 Hen VIII c.8 (1512).

[155] *Red Paper Book*, pp. 13–14.

[156] Alsford, *Towns* (Ipswich, c.86, fifteenth century). See also *Liber Albus*, pp. 237–8 (1272–1307), 272–3 (early fifteenth century); *Leicester*, ii, p. 304 (1482); *Coventry*, p. 684 (1522); *Winchester*, pp. 157 (1535), 179 (1549).

[157] Kowaleski, *Local Markets*, pp. 127–9, 136–7.

[158] Kermode, *Medieval Merchants*, pp. 40–1.

tension and conflict.[159] If they went too far in promoting protectionism, they might force outside traders to travel elsewhere to the detriment of the town.

Craft guilds

A body that perhaps widened participation in borough government and was highly influential in the creation of commercial regulation was the craft guild. Guilds were frequently studied by nineteenth- and early twentieth-century historians, whose work was heavily influenced by the political and economic conditions of their own time. Unwin, Sombart and Brentano attempted to present craft guilds as forerunners to trade unions or depicted them as romantic, social democratic icons. This viewpoint largely misunderstood the structure and purpose of medieval craft guilds, which primarily served the interests of masters not journeymen.[160] Other historical theories developed in which guilds were described as monopolistic and restrictive bodies, which held back economic entrepreneurship and were in continual conflict with municipal government.[161] Heather Swanson, however, suggested a more complex relationship between craft guilds and municipal authorities. She ascertained that guilds were instruments of town councils and had little independent power. They have, therefore, been given too much historical importance in their supposed ability to run a closed shop.[162] Although Swanson rightly asserted the guilds' subordination to municipal authorities, she perhaps goes too far in completely negating their influence. As Gervase Rosser rejoined, Swanson was unwise to acknowledge the vital role of the craft guilds within broader municipal government and yet also denigrate their impact upon the practical operation of trades.[163] This underestimates the vitality of craft organisations for their members and the degree of semi-autonomous self-governance which they developed.

Craft and trade guilds emerged in the late thirteenth and fourteenth centuries as manufacturing, particularly in textiles, expanded in larger towns and gave traders reason to divide into separate organisations. Some

---

[159] Holt and Rosser, 'Introduction', pp. 10–11.

[160] For a summary, see Bainbridge, *Gilds*, pp. 1–18. See also Lipson, *Economic History*, ch. 8; Ashley, *Introduction*, i, ch. 2; Cunningham, *Growth*, p. 342; Unwin, *Gilds and Companies*.

[161] Gross, *Gild Merchant*, i, p. 112. See also Tawney, *Religion*, p. 26.

[162] Swanson, 'Illusion', 29–48; Swanson, *Medieval Artisans*, pp. 108–20. It has long been recognised by historians that the guilds were used as agencies of enforcement by town authorities; Ashley, *Introduction*, ii, pp. 87–95; Green, *Town Life*, ii, pp. 135–6.

[163] Rosser, 'Crafts, guilds and the negotiation of work', 6; Swanson, *Medieval Artisans*, p. 8; Holt and Rosser, 'Introduction', pp. 10–11.

Merchant Guilds survived as congregations of the more wealthy merchant wholesalers, but most other trades were organised into lesser guilds. The structure of craft and trade guilds had a common coherence in all English medieval towns, at least where they were constituted. Guilds were not formed in a number of medieval boroughs, such as Ipswich, as well as in most English small towns. Indeed, craft guild formation was a slow process in England, outside larger conurbations like London and York, partly because they required a sufficient number of craftsmen engaged in the same trade and partly due to the way authority was exerted by particular urban authorities.

Craft guilds consisted of confraternities of both employers and employees, masters and apprentices. However, 'masters' were firmly at the top of the hierarchy, followed by journeymen and apprentices. Surveyors or searchers were elected to oversee the conduct of a particular trade, to maintain good working practice, protect members from 'unfair' competition and ensure a high quality of workmanship.[164] They also had the power to search the houses of practitioners and often to inspect the wares of outsiders. Like other urban officials, guild ordinances sought to protect searchers by punishing any who abused or hindered them in their duties, but also threatened penalties for those who neglected their office.[165] Artisans were ordered to work openly and not in secret, so that the searchers could easily monitor their craft.[166] Additionally, each guild member had to swear an oath to keep good order and not to bring scandal to the craft; the Durham weavers swore, 'to be true, to use and occupy his craft truly to the profit of the common people, to use no deceit in his craft and to fulfill the ordinances'.[167]

Guild ordinances usually followed a certain format and their primary interests were consistent with one another. This is largely because many craft guilds copied London craft ordinances. Typical ordinances stated that an artisan or trader had to be paid-up members to work within the liberty, they could not sue a fellow member without licence, and no one was to entice away customers from fellow masters and workers. Most demanded a good level of workmanship or else practitioners could

[164] Reynolds, *Introduction*, p. 165; Furley (ed.), *Ancient Usages*, pp. 28–31, nos. 17, 22–3 (late thirteenth century); *Norwich*, i, pp. 192–4 (early fourteenth century), ii, pp. 278–96 (1449); *York*, i, pp. 183–4 (1417), iii, p. 157 (1433); *Northampton*, i, pp. 304–7 (1465); *King's Lynn*, pp. 266–8, no. 323 (1449); *Leicester*, ii, pp. 322–3 (1489?).
[165] *Norwich*, i, pp. 193–4 (early fourteenth century?); *Bristol*, ii, pp. 77, 79 (1406); *York*, i, pp. 63–4, 83–4, 222 (fifteenth century); *York*, iii, p. 217 (1498); *Beverley*, pp. 78, 116, 127 (late fifteenth to early sixteenth century); *Coventry*, pp. 660–1 (1518).
[166] *Bristol*, ii, pp. 96–7 (1408).
[167] Bonney, *Lordship*, pp. 185–8. See also *Leicester*, ii, pp. 32–3 (1336?); *Beverley*, pp. 76–80 (1494), 125–6 (1468).

face heavy fines or banishment from their trade. A consistent rhetorical complaint was that a lack of knowledge and bad management led to faults and that substandard products caused loss to buyers and brought shame to the town and craft.[168] This attitude was intertwined with attempts to restrict competition by preventing non-members from exercising the craft within the town and by controlling the movement of raw materials and finished products out of the town.[169] People could not set up in business until they had received the consent of the wardens and had paid their dues. Guilds thus governed entry to certain trades, as well as journeymen wages and the system of apprenticeship.[170]

The ordinances that emanated from craft guilds covered various aspects of commerce and conduct, and this included aspects of retail trade. They were drawn up by guild members themselves and, in that sense, guilds broadened access to the administrative strings of towns. However, most ordinances had to receive the sanction of town authorities and often guild masters themselves were compulsory members of the freedom of the town or the Merchant Guild. In most towns (except perhaps London), the authority of municipal governments over the guilds was not questioned. In Durham, Bristol, York, Coventry and Winchester, the municipal authorities controlled the registration of ordinances, checked that they conformed to the standards of the town, and that they did not conflict with the liberties of others.[171] The dyers of Coventry had certain ordinances quashed in 1475 because they were considered harmful to the 'comon weyle'.[172] Fines were also split between the town and guild and oaths often included pledging obedience to the municipality. Craft guilds subsequently operated as subordinate supervisory bodies to municipal authorities. Guilds could nevertheless impose fines, banish members from crafts, or limit the kind of business an individual could undertake.[173] It was an understandable development; as trades and industries became more specialised and complex, the formation of guilds allowed the traders themselves to take on the responsibility of regulation.

---

[168] *Bristol*, ii, pp. 2–4, 8, 75–7, 85–6, 93–4, 108, 111–14, 123–7, 141–2, 170–80; *York*, i, pp. 63, 167, 171, 182, 185; *Coventry*, pp. 554, 660–1; *Leicester*, i, pp. 68, 71, 84, 102; *Memorials*, pp. 216–17, 234, 242, 546–7; Toulmin Smith (ed.), *English Gilds*, p. 317.

[169] *Bristol*, ii, pp. 6–8, 15–16, 26–30, 78–9, 82, 96, 113–14; *York*, i, pp. 99–100, 170–1; *Beverley*, pp. 74–6, 125–7; *Memorials*, pp. 232, 244–7, 354.

[170] *Bristol*, ii, pp. 5–6, 9, 12, 84–5, 104–7, 142; *York*, i, pp. 63–4; *Beverley*, p. 116; *Coventry*, pp. 554, 574; *Memorials*, pp. 216–19, 234, 354.

[171] Bonney, *Lordship*, pp. 187–8; Swanson, *Medieval Artisans*; *York*, i, p. 186; *Bristol*, i, p. xxviii, ii, pp. 80, 100, 109, 118–19; *Coventry*, pp. xxxi–xxxii, 29, 111, 170, 188, 222, 277, 554, 624, 639, 654–7, 703; Toulmin Smith (ed.), *English Gilds*, pp. 304–9, 312–17; *Norwich*, i, pp. 16–18.

[172] *Coventry*, pp. 418–19 (1475).   [173] *Leicester*, i, pp. xxxiii, 68–9, 170, 205.

In a practical sense, traders were more experienced in manufacturing processes and selling methods, as well as more aware of the possibilities of fraud. In effect, then, guilds provided an unpaid, knowledgeable administrative staff for large towns that were otherwise not able to afford such a myriad of officials.

There is little evidence that medieval English guilds exerted consistent or sustainable monopoly policies in retailing their manufactures in the face of a competitive marketplace with often elastic demand. There were also many markets, formal and informal, beyond their control and influence, which meant that the guilds could not afford to be overly restrictive and sell at high prices. Their monopsony power was also limited.[174] Their main influence on prices came indirectly through minimum quality standards, control of those who set up in a craft within a town, and who was employed as apprentices and journeymen. They did not have absolute authority to set prices for their products, and crafts that attempted to fix a price contrary to the market price were upbraided, such as the Norwich chandlers in 1300.[175]

Although guild regulations had to conform to the demands of town councils and incorporate existing trade legislation, these were not necessarily incompatible with the vested interests of craft members, either individually or as an occupational group. It has often been assumed by historians that guild-backed quality controls aided the 'public interest' by lowering the level of fraud and maintaining high standards.[176] These motivations are ostensibly supported by statements in guild regulations. Ordinances for Bristol hoopers in 1439 were said to be 'for the honour of God, of the town abovesaid and of the common people of the same town, and of those resorting thereto, for the common profit'.[177] When proclamations and ordinances assert the notion of 'common profit' or 'common good' it is worth asking who comprised the commonalty.[178] There were, after all, disparate and overlapping communities within boroughs, market towns and villages, often with differing interests, and a guild was one of those groupings. The evoking of 'common profit' was characteristic rhetoric in guild ordinances, in order to demonstrate a respect for law and uphold the reputation of the guild and its members: 'no ordinances shall be made against the common law' and 'the liberties of the town

---

[174] A monopoly is a market with only one seller and many buyers, whereas in a monopsony there is one buyer and many sellers. Swanson, 'Illusion'; Epstein, 'Craft guilds, apprenticeships', 685–93; Richardson, 'Guilds, laws, and markets'.
[175] Hudson, *Leet*, p. 52 (1300).
[176] Salzman, *English Life*, pp. 240–1; Veale, *English Fur Trade*, p. 116.
[177] *Bristol*, ii, p. 161 (1439).   [178] Farber, *An Anatomy*, pp. 161–74.

shall be upheld'.[179] However, this rhetoric could also serve as a useful justification for quashing the output and sale of non-members. It was just as likely that guilds attempted to keep prices up, prevented competition from outside the guild structure and thus reduced choice for consumers. The repeated ordinances against bad workmanship and inferior or adulterated materials are also evidence of the residual demand for cheap goods and the desire of masters to undersell one another in competition. This reminds us that craft guilds were not always heterogeneous and harmonious bodies, but could be riven by conflict and disputes within the craft, between crafts, and between crafts and town government. As with the burgess elite, the need to conform with accepted practice and assumed moral norms was often counterbalanced by forces of sectional interests.

Guild ordinances demonstrate their attempts to maintain stability and order within the crafts, as well as to provide a veneer of respectability. Stillwell pointed out that guild ordinances often required members to correspond to merchant 'qualities' of trustworthiness, discretion, wisdom and sobriety, in order to bolster their reputation.[180] The Merchant Guild of Beverley required that no brethren should 'set up detractions or false scandal' nor 'say of any brother of the craft in absence anything whereby the brother so defamed shall lose his name or any of his goods'.[181] Craft guilds retained a social role of mutual self-help, helping fellow members when they suffered illness or financial losses, as well as providing for burial services.[182] There were also annual feasts for conviviality, to conduct business and read out ordinances.[183] Additionally, members performed a religious function: candles were to be kept alight at chantries and chapels before the altar of a saint, and prayers and Masses were said for the dead.[184] Such shows of solidarity attempted to raise the moral integrity of members, discouraged traders and masters from cheating each other, and established informal and spiritual ties that controlled their behaviour.[185]

Similarly, the processions, pageants and feasts of the guilds and town can be interpreted as methods of communal bonding. From the late fourteenth century, the Corpus Christi cycle of pageants and processions

---

[179] Toulmin Smith (ed.), *English Gilds*, pp. 23, 30, 39, 167, 337.
[180] Stillwell, 'Chaucer's "sad" merchant', 14–18; McRee, 'Religious gilds'.
[181] *Beverley*, pp. 76–80 (1494). See also *King's Lynn*, pp. 266–8, no. 323 (1449).
[182] Toulmin Smith (ed.), *English Gilds*, pp. 35, 122, 172–3, 176–9, 182–4, 229–30, 232, 234, 340–1.
[183] *Ibid.*, pp. 176–8, 183, 229, 231–2.
[184] *Ibid.*, pp. 36–7, 172, 176, 178, 181, 230; *York*, i, p. 221; *Beverley*, pp. 76, 114, 123.
[185] Richardson, 'Craft guilds and Christianity'. Richardson argued that guilds linked spiritual and occupational endeavours as a means to tackle free riders and encourage cooperation between members.

developed and allowed guilds to display both their commercial prowess and the hierarchical structure of their town, which highlighted their own honour, dignity and prestige. Several examples of English 'mystery cycles' survive, such as from York, Wakefield and Chester.[186] Each craft took an episode of the cycle and encapsulated the concept of the body representing social integration and unity. In communities otherwise striven by tension and competitiveness, rituals and ceremonies were stage-managed to reinforce town identity and social hierarchy. However, as both James and Dyer have suggested, it is possible that the communal ceremonies and rituals were attempts to paper over the cracks that existed in medieval urban society.[187] Town hierarchies and pageantry perhaps even accentuated a contemporary sense of division, between 'inferiores', 'mediocres' and 'probi hommes'.[188]

The growth of guild regulation in the fourteenth and fifteenth centuries reflected the harsh competitive environment. Like burgesses, town guilds sought to safeguard their interests, particularly in manufacturing industries, often by producing greater protectionist legislation.[189] Guilds supported full-time traders and artisans and tried to exclude those who practised a trade as a by-employment. Some fifteenth-century towns saw increasing levels of restriction, which were mirrored in the heightened protectionism of guild regulations.[190] Adverse economic conditions accentuated the desire to restrict outsiders. However, it is arguable that such protectionism could be counter-productive or ineffectual.

The main concern of guilds was the control of supply and distribution, because these were the factors that determined the prosperity of small-scale, household craftsmen (before the growth of entrepreneurs, larger-scale production and technology). Most craftsmen sold direct to their customers and were as interested in marketing networks as manufacturing processes. The medieval economy was still fragmented, while the success of practitioners in suburbs and rural areas demonstrated that craftsmen could practise beyond the reach of urban and guild regulations. Swanson was perhaps right to see the notion of a tightly regulated town and guild economy as largely 'illusory'. Not all craftsmen and artisans were governed by the guilds, and the urgency of their ordinances was

---

[186] Toulmin Smith (ed.), *York Plays*; Stevens and Cawley (eds.), *Towneley Plays*; Lumiansky and Mills (eds.), *Chester Mystery Cycle*.
[187] James, 'Ritual'; Dyer, 'Taxation and communities', p. 169; Holt and Rosser, 'Introduction', p. 14; Goldberg, 'Craft guilds'.
[188] Kermode, *Medieval Merchants*, p. 12; Phythian-Adams, *Desolation of a City*, pp. 170–9.
[189] Hatcher, 'The great slump', pp. 269–70; Lipson, *Economic History*, i, pp. 308–439; Swanson, 'Illusion'.
[190] Saul, 'Herring', 39–41.

largely intended to counter the impact of extramural competition and inter-craft strife. Craft guilds were also a much stronger presence among wholesale and artisan crafts than the victual trades, especially in their formative years. In London and many boroughs, victualling trades remained under the authority of the town council or mayor, at least until the fifteenth century.[191] Although butchers, fishmongers, bakers and brewers became increasingly organised, town elites were still suspicious of any self-regulation and organisation among such traders.[192]

Conclusion

In large boroughs and towns, there were small and dominant elites who sought avidly to protect their privileges, as well as a wide number of sectional interests reflecting a diverse occupational and wealth range. As we go down the urban hierarchy to smaller communities, petty traders were able to have a greater say in the governance of their business affairs. There was perhaps greater communal consensus and more shared interests in small towns and villages, particularly since those in the elite group had similar occupations to the majority of residents.[193] Some principles recurred in smaller seigneurial markets, such as the need to protect consumers, to create an orderly and prosperous market, to raise revenue, and to develop artificial constructs of solidarity in order to dampen conflict.[194] However, the interests of retailers were perhaps given more leeway than in larger towns where the vested interests of the mercantile distributors held sway. A developed merchant oligarchy existed perhaps only in the top twenty-five to thirty boroughs, ports or distributive centres. In smaller towns, there was no real mercantile presence and retailers and craftsmen occupied leading offices.[195] Also, whereas larger boroughs developed relatively sophisticated self-government, many small towns did not develop much beyond manorial and leet court systems, perhaps adapting them to commercial needs. Craft guilds were also rarely established in smaller towns, because of a relative lack of specialisation and insufficient artisans in a particular craft. For smaller market towns

---

[191] *Norwich*, ii, pp. 87–8 (1436); Kowaleski, *Local Markets*, p. 100; Toulmin Smith (ed.), *English Gilds*, pp. 334–7 (Exeter bakers, 1483); *Coventry*, pp. 27, 29, 32 (1421). Phillip Willcox refers to an informal bakers' company or fellowship in Coventry that had probably existed since the thirteenth century, but it is not documented before the fifteenth century. Willcox, *Bakers' Company*, pp. 1–9.

[192] Thrupp, *Merchant Class*, pp. 95–6.

[193] Swanson, *Medieval Artisans*, pp. 3–5; Reynolds, *Introduction*, pp. 173–7.

[194] Dyer, 'Small-town conflict'.

[195] Dyer, *Standards*, pp. 24–5; Hilton, 'Lords, burgesses and hucksters'.

with no borough charters or privileges, their regulatory reference resided instead in central legislation and the leet or seigneurial courts.

The often localised and parochial nature of law enforcement is evident. Whether in large or small towns, there were various interest groups, often overlapping, who contributed to the enactment and enforcement of trading regulation. Ordinances and charters indicate that town authorities wanted stability, order and income; traders wanted flexible and secure facilities; burgesses wanted protection and profit in their trade and operations; guilds wanted high standards and exclusivity; and consumers wanted cheap and plentiful goods. Medieval markets encompassed a complex interplay of forces, which created a compromise between restrictive and free-market policies. Laws, and their enforcement at a provincial and local level, were therefore a product of both national proclamations and local vested interests.

PART II: THE PUBLIC MARKETPLACE

Sectional and burgess-centred interests were undoubtedly prominent factors in the formulation of market law, but in tandem many commercial regulations appear to have avowed conventions of common justice and welfare. Indeed, there were general ethical and practical principles that were applicable to all markets, large and small. One fundamental principle was the concept of the open and public market as a means to guarantee honest transactions, and the physical marketplace was designed with this in mind. There was often a single, open space, designated by a market cross, that served as the main marketing area and in which stalls were set out. Small towns had a single market day each week when outsiders brought their goods for sale, and the market day would open and close with the ringing of a bell. However, in larger towns, the market arrangements could be more complex, with a wider dispersal of market activity into the streets surrounding a main market space. They might also have more than one marketplace, each specialising in particular commodities. Larger towns additionally had markets on several days during the week, with the largest boroughs operating markets every day except Sundays.

Trade must have taken place frequently outside of the market day and marketplace, but this was generally reserved for residents and those with privileges to deal from private premises, such as inns or shops.[196] Britnell has described medieval shops, which varied in size and type, as 'an intermediate space between the public world of the market and the private world of the family home, a space where craftsmen could both

[196] Britnell, 'Markets, shops, inns', pp. 113–15, 118, 121.

work and meet their customers'.[197] Food and drink were probably often sold during the whole week and even in the streets, meeting essential consumer demands. Waterfronts or quaysides could also be important places of exchange when a town lay by the coast or a main river, particularly for the import–export merchants. It was useful for these goods to be sold at or near the point of unloading, especially when wharfs were some distance from town centres. However, these 'bulk markets' were as carefully regulated as central retail markets.[198]

Nevertheless, the essential concept of an open marketplace remained a constant throughout all sizes of commercial settlements. A formal market was primarily intended for congregations of outsiders and local households to meet immediate consumption needs, such as food and fuel, and this was its public significance. On the surface, the public marketplace inferred honesty, witnesses and social cooperation, while secret and hidden trade implied fraud, price-raising and other crimes because such transactions occurred outside the remit of official sanction. As Bateson has remarked: 'publicity in trade was the corner-stone of medieval commercial arrangements for the inspection of goods, for securing foreigner's debt, and for guarantees of contract'.[199] Indeed, saleable goods were expected to be displayed in public for a variety of reasons: to ensure that all the correct tolls were paid, to provide witnesses to deals, to guard against the exchange of stolen goods, to regulate quality and quantity, and to demonstrate there was no perceived shortage of a certain commodity that might push prices up.

The principles of open and public trade were gradually established by customs and through a process of modification throughout the Middle Ages. The laws of Anglo-Saxon kings were frugal in their treatment of trade and commerce, but still codified their demand that all transactions between strangers should have witnesses and that trade should only take place in specific forums. This was intended foremost as a guard against criminality, such as the transference of stolen goods and cattle.[200] The first extant and coherent set of English laws relating to trade was ascribed to the reign of Edward the Elder (c.900–25).[201] These asserted that buying and selling should take place only in a market town, under threat

---

[197] Britnell, 'Town life', p. 139.   [198] Lilley, *Urban Life*, pp. 224–7.

[199] Bateson (ed.), *Borough Customs*, ii, p. lxxiv.

[200] Attenborough (ed.), *Laws*, pp. 44–5, c.25 (laws of Ine, c.688–93), pp. 132–5, cc.10, 12, 13 (laws of Aethelstan, c.925–39); *Report of the Royal Commission*, i, appx I, pp. 32–3, Laws of Eadmund, c.5 (c.940–46), Laws of Eadgar, cc.4–11 (c.959–75), Laws of Aethelred, c.3 (c.978–1016), Laws of Canute, cc.23, 24 (c.1017).

[201] Attenborough (ed.), *Laws*, pp. 114–17, c.1, nos. 1–5 (laws of Edward the Elder, c.899–925).

of forfeiture, in order to hinder the movement of stolen property and facilitate the collection of tolls.

Anglo-Saxon laws established important types of facilitators for open sales: the warrantor, who was usually the seller and guaranteed that the commodity was of the condition stated and not stolen; the witness, who (in the absence of the warrantor) provided evidence that a sale had taken place honestly; and the pledge, who was not present at the sale but could provide evidence of the purchaser's good character under oath. The use of witnesses, warrantors, or trustworthy men became a mainstay of early trading law and under Aethelstan (925–39) heavy fines of 35s. were threatened if trustworthy witnesses were not used in the cattle trade, or if someone bore false witness. Those found to be untrustworthy were not allowed to be witnesses again.[202] Those described as 'trustworthy men' included reeves, priests, landowners or treasurers, and the laws stated that any purchases of goods worth over 20d. should take place within towns using such witnesses.[203] The late twelfth-century common law treatise, *Glanvill*, also required either 'men of credit' as witnesses or oaths which the other party could accept.[204] The use of witnesses or oaths thus provided a safeguard for the purchaser if an itinerant warrantor failed to appear, or when a certain sale appeared suspect, in order to prove that a purchase was honestly and openly made.[205]

The principle of visible trading practices continued throughout the Middle Ages in the form of open bargaining in daylight hours, whereby the public market came to represent a communal witness. The use of witnesses for high-value contracts remained, but became less important in basic transactions where proof of purchase in the open market itself protected traders against accusations of possessing stolen goods. Proof of purchase could be explicated through compurgation or inquest.[206]

However, there remained a fear that stolen goods might be brought into the market and sold. Butchers were particularly prone to accusations that they were disposing of stolen beasts and hiding the evidence. This was perhaps the reason why they were sometimes excluded from dealing in hides and wool or operating as tanners.[207] Mistrust of strangers

---

[202] *Ibid.*, pp. 132–3, c.10 (laws of Aethelstan, *c*.925–39).
[203] *Ibid.*, pp. 134–5, c.12 (laws of Aethelstan, *c*.925–39).
[204] Hall (ed.), *Glanvill*, pp. 130–2, x, 15–17 (*c*.1187–9).
[205] *BBC, 1042–1216*, pp. 218–19 (Pembroke, 1154–89; Chester, 1190–1212; Haverford-west, 1189–1219); *Britton*, i, pp. 57–60, ch. 16, cc.3–5 (1291–2).
[206] For a discussion of compurgation, see below pp. 200 (n. 326), 356–7.
[207] Toulmin Smith (ed.), *English Gilds*, p. 343 (Berwick, 1283–4); *Britton*, i, pp. 83–4, ch. 21, c.11 (1291–2).

and their goods was a recurrent theme of medieval trading legislation, partly due to the ease with which they could flee a town's jurisdiction.[208] Foreign butchers arriving at Bristol in the fifteenth century had to produce the hides and skins of any flesh they wished to sell at market, as a guard against accusations of theft and to boost the supply of such commodities.[209] For similar reasons, sheepskins sold by York butchers to glovers and parchment-makers were to include the cheek and ears.[210] Anxieties concerning the provenance of commodities was thus an important motivation behind the promotion of transactions in the open marketplace.

Regulating the public marketplace

The regulations that restricted trade to the open and public market are mostly found in borough ordinances and reflected local needs and mechanisms of supervision. In late thirteenth-century London, even resident bakers were expected to sell their bread in the open marketplace and not in private 'before his oven', so that their bread could be more easily checked.[211] Similar, if more basic, rules probably operated in most chartered markets. Any who traded outside the public forum did so at their own risk, but few towns allowed trade to carry on within their liberty except in designated spaces. For instance, in 1379, the Lord of Bridgwater called William Brere to his court to demand to know why there was a market for cloth in an unaccustomed site.[212]

Towns or markets were often divided up into designated areas for different trading activities, facilitating the administration of both regulation and searches, but also easing congestion.[213] Victuallers bringing cheese, milk, grapes, plums, apples, pears and other fruit to early fifteenth-century Salisbury were ordered to sell their wares in a specified place opposite the house of John Gage.[214] The cobblers of

---

[208] Britnell, *Commercialisation*, p. 25.

[209] *Great Red Book*, i, p. 144 (1452). See also *Oak Book*, i, pp. 68–9, no. 67 (c.1300); *Black Book*, ii, pp. 142–5, c.57 [56] (c.1309); Greaves (ed.), *First Ledger Book*, pp. 5–6, no. 8 (1313); *Liber Albus*, pp. 239, 243 (1272–1307); Bailey (ed.), *Transcripts*, pp. 96–7 (Winchester, 1399); *Coventry*, pp. 279 (1454), 557–8 (1494), 665–6 (1519); *Northampton*, i, p. 227, c.34 (c.1460); *Leicester*, ii, pp. 288–9 (1467); *Beverley*, p. 129 (1510).

[210] *York*, iii, pp. 218–19 (1500).

[211] *CLB*, A, p. 215 (1276–8); *Liber Albus*, pp. 231, 308 (1272–1307).

[212] *Bridgwater*, p. 40.

[213] E.g. *Coventry*, pp. 59 (1423), 100 (1425); *Henley*, p. 214 (1535).

[214] HMC, iv, p. 193 (Salisbury, 1408–9).

fourteenth-century Beverley were expected to hold stalls for selling their shoes only in the 'Shoemarket' on market and fair days, though they could apparently trade from their own houses on other days.[215] The fishwives of fifteenth-century Bristol were ordered to 'stonde vpon the bakke and in noon other places', which was an important and recognised commercial site near the river.[216] Similarly, in Northampton, petty vendors of hay, straw, timber, wood or ash could not place goods onto the ground from their heads until they were sold, since this normally incurred stallage payments; in London, any 'birlester' selling 'oysters, mussels, salt fish and other victuals' was not allowed to stand still to retail but had to be continually on the move.[217] Markets were thus highly regulated spaces, though the court evidence for encroachments and selling in non-designated sites suggests that the regulations were not always adhered to.

For the same purpose of regulatory oversight, certain traders were expected to congregate around the market cross, particularly peasants who brought in a myriad of agricultural produce to sell in small lots (such as poultry).[218] In 1403–4, strangers that came to Bristol to sell iron pennyware ('yclepid smythware') were told to vend by the high cross where any faults of their goods could be openly surveyed by the town's officials.[219] The same restriction applied to those outsiders selling bows and arrows, who were ordered to utter their wares at the high cross rather than hawk their goods about the town 'to the derogacioun of the burgeisez of the same craffte'.[220] The main legislative concern of a town was thus to ensure that outside traders did not circumvent official channels of inspection and revenue-collection.

Outsiders were particularly limited in their movements, both spatially and temporally, and could not sell privately, except perhaps through official hosts or brokers. This stipulation applied particularly to foodstuffs. Ordinances for York and Bristol outlined that victuals and other goods brought into the town from outside should only be sold in the assigned marketplaces during daylight and not in any secret places or inns, as these places were hidden from the eyes of officials and tolls might be avoided. Those bringing fish to sell in fifteenth-century Beverley were to set out their goods 'for sale publicly in the market and not in their

---

[215] *Beverley*, pp. 30–1 (1364).
[216] *Great Red Book*, i, p. 143 (1452). See also *ibid.*, i, pp. 135, 142 (1452); *Bristol*, ii, pp. 54–5, 226–7 (late fourteenth century).
[217] *Northampton*, i, pp. 224–5, cc.27–8 (*c.*1460); *Memorials*, p. 508 (1388).
[218] *Beverley*, pp. 29–30 (1409). Davis, 'The cross and the pillory', pp. 248–50.
[219] *Bristol*, ii, pp. 181–4 (1403–4); *Great Red Book*, i, pp. 147–8 (late fifteenth century).
[220] *Great Red Book*, i, p. 153 (1479).

houses or other private places'.[221] The York ordinances expressed anxiety that such concealment of fish and victuals led to 'mykyll yvell chafer an on able ys keped and solde thurgh the yere at outrage value, in great hinderyng of the kynges people'.[222] Similarly, Britnell has noted a case in Colchester in 1429 when five foreign fishmongers held back fish from the open market and sold them privately to outsiders 'to the very great extortion of the burgesses'; the word 'extorsio' perhaps implying moral indignation.[223] Selling victuals privately was deemed to be counter to the social and paternal needs of the community.

Strangers selling merchandise were thus corralled into assigned places within a town so that officials could better watch over them and collect dues, as well as to allow residents a commercial advantage. Indeed, resident traders in many towns were physically separated from foreign dealers, particularly fishmongers and butchers.[224] The fourteenth-century resident and outside butchers in Beverley were separated on market days, placed at each end of the market with the fish stalls in-between, so that they did 'not intermeddle with each other'.[225] The authorities in Oxford even considered a second marketplace for strangers to sell in, as an aid towards preventing forestalling, ensuring public transactions and disseminating market regulations.[226] Such spatial division suggests a strong element of competition or even animosity, as well as a desire

---

[221] *Beverley*, p. 58 (1467). For similar restrictions and cases regarding the prevention of transactions in private houses and assigning public places of sale for certain commodities, see *BBC, 1216–1307*, p. 295 (Grimsby, 1258); Prestwich (ed.), *York*, p. 13 (1301); *Liber Albus*, pp. 228–9 (1272–1307), 239 (1272–1307), 329–30 (1278–9), 400 (1383–4); Riley (ed.), *Munimenta Gildhallae*, ii, 'Liber Custumarum', pp. 393–4, 404–5 (1320–1); *CLB*, D, p. 229 (1310), E, pp. 56 (1316), 131 (1320), 179–80 (1323), G, p. 330 (1374), K, pp. 45 (1437), 249 (1440); *Bridgwater*, p. 50 (1379); *York*, i, pp. 45–6 (1389), 197–9 (1418), ii, pp. 174–5 (1428); Bailey (ed.), *Transcripts* (Winchester, 1399); *Winchester*, pp. 7–8 (1403), 120 (1486), 120–1 (1488), 131 (1520); *Salisbury*, pp. 75, 128, nos. 167, 260 (1416, 1427); *Norwich*, i, pp. 74–5 (1414), ii, pp. 86–7 (1422), 90 (1440), 92 (1455), 316–17; *King's Lynn*, p. 264, no. 312 (1423), p. 266, no. 319 (1443); Hull (ed.), *Calendar*, p. 3 (1433); Wood, *Medieval Tamworth*, p. 77 (1438 and 1511); *Coventry*, pp. 223 (1445), 361 (1470), 389 (1474), 565 (1495), 569 (1495); *Leicester*, ii, p. 292 (1467); *Northampton*, i, pp. 224, 254–5, cc.26, 30 and 73 (*c.*1460), i, pp. 307–9 (1467), 376–7 (late fifteenth century); Toulmin Smith (ed.), *English Gilds*, pp. 381, 384 (Worcester, 1467); *Great Red Book*, i, p. 141 (late fifteenth century).

[222] (much evil and unable merchandise is kept and sold throughout the year at outrageous price, in great hindering of the king's people.) *York*, i, pp. 222–3 (fifteenth century?). See also *Bristol*, ii, pp. 71–2 (late fourteenth century).

[223] Britnell, 'Town life', p. 166; Britnell, 'Urban economic regulation', p. 4.

[224] HMC, iv, p. 193 (Salisbury, 1408–9); *Salisbury*, pp. 89, 128, 141, 145, 147, 213, 231, nos. 203, 260, 286, 295, 298, 413, 440 (1418–50); *Memorials*, pp. 300 (1357), 389 (1375); *CLB*, K, p. 249 (1440); *Liber Albus*, p. 400 (1383–4).

[225] *Beverley*, p. 29 (1365).

[226] Salter (ed.), *Munimenta*, pp. 31–4, no. 34 (1320).

to give residents an advantageous location. Burgesses or guildsmen were certainly given a little more leeway to sell certain goods privately from within their houses or shops, especially since they could already sell free of market tolls. The freemen of fifteenth-century Canterbury, for example, were allowed to open their windows to sell goods, and thus establish a shop, whereas non-freemen had to approach the town authorities for the same privilege.[227] Freemen of towns were generally able to sell most goods from their own shops and homes during the day, though a few trades were restricted, such as fish and hides, because these were usually brought in from outside and there were concerns about potential theft.

The length of the market day was also strictly defined. Most towns opened their market place soon after sunrise (prime) and closed by sunset, but some did not open until 'terce' (three hours after daybreak). The market in fourteenth-century York opened at 5am in summer and 7am in winter, while in fifteenth-century Winchester, selling began at 9am and traders were expected to remain in their places until 1pm.[228] The division of the market day was often marked by the ringing of church bells for the canonical hours; thus religious time punctuated the market day.[229]

Additionally, there were rules in all towns which allowed domestic customers time to buy goods for their own consumption before commercial wholesalers and traders could enter the market. Consumers were effectively given privileged initial access to grain and other foodstuffs. In the markets of Southampton, London, Leicester and elsewhere, regraters, cornmongers, bakers, brewers and cooks were simply forbidden from buying grain and victuals to sell again before prime or before the commons had had an initial chance to purchase goods for their own needs.[230]

---

[227] Myers (ed.), *English Historical Documents*, p. 569 (Canterbury, *c*.1430). See also Furley (ed.), *Ancient Usages*, pp. 36–7 (late thirteenth century); *Red Paper Book*, p. 9 (late fourteenth century); *Nottingham*, i, pp. 316–17 (1396); *Great Red Book*, ii, p. 58 (1459?), iii, p. 82 (1467); *Leicester*, ii, p. 294 (1467); Toulmin Smith (ed.), *English Gilds*, p. 333 (Exeter, 1481).

[228] *York*, i, p. 46 (1389); *Winchester*, pp. 120–1 (1488). See also Gross, *Gild Merchant*, ii, pp. 205, 263 (Reading and Winchester).

[229] Epstein, 'Business cycles'.

[230] *Leicester*, i, p. 181 (1279), ii, pp. 21 (1335–6), 106–7 (1357), 291 (1467), iii, p. 19 (1521); *Oak Book*, i, pp. 70–1, c.70 (*c*.1300); *Black Book*, ii, pp. 102–3, c.28 (*c*.1309); *Liber Albus*, pp. 229 (1272–1307), 236 (1272–1307), 251 (1284–5), 328 (1278–9), 400–1 (1383–4); Riley (ed.), *Munimenta Gildhallae*, ii, 'Liber Custumarum', pp. 118, 193 (1299–1300); *CLB*, A, p. 217 (1276–8); Furley (ed.), *Ancient Usages*, pp. 32–3, no. 26 (late thirteenth century); Salter (ed.), *Medieval Archives*, i, p. 20, no. 11 (Oxford, 1255); *CPR, 1266–72*, p. 195 (Cambridge, 1268); Coss (ed.), *Early Records of Medieval Coventry*, p. 41 (1278); Prestwich (ed.), *York*, p. 13 (1301); *Memorials*, pp. 221 (1345), 300 (1357), 389 (1375), 481–2 (1382); *York*, i, pp. 46 (1389), 172 (1479); Jeayes (ed.), *Court Rolls*, i, p. 144 (1336); *Coventry*, pp. 25, 29 (1421), 115 (1428), 666 (1519);

For instance, those who bought victuals to sell again before the first hour in thirteenth-century Grimsby had to pay a penalty of half a mark to the common good of the town.[231] Regraters, in particular, were watched carefully and faced forfeiture of any goods bought before the correct time. The reason given in the Chesterfield charter of 1294 was: 'that the magnates and the good men of the country and the burgesses may not be hindered [by regraters] in buying their own necessaries in the market before the hour of prime'.[232] Such regulations were maintained throughout the later Middle Ages, though the precise division of the market day varied from town to town. In fourteenth-century Bristol, no butchers, fishmongers or regraters (or their servants) were to purchase fresh fish to sell again before the third hour.[233] In Nottingham, the first part of the day was set aside for the sale of goods for personal or household consumption, while after the ninth hour ('none') goods could be bought for regrating.[234] Cooks in the fifteenth-century York market could buy only at specified times, and just to the value of 18d. between Evensong and Prime the next morning 'for dyners of travelyng men'.[235] The application of the law thus varied from market to market, but the main distinction in operation was between those purchasing for immediate consumption or domestic use and those purchasing for further resale.

In general, then, a market day was divided into temporal sections, delineated by the ringing of the market or church bell, so that different market patterns were created during the day.[236] The morning was dominated by domestic and small transactions, the afternoon by the purchases of hucksters, hostelers and cooks, and the evening, before dusk fell, by their sales to travellers and those who had missed the morning market. There were thus specific controls dictating the actions of consumers according to the use to which they intended to put their purchases. Yet, there also appear to have been many attempts to circumvent these rules.

Winchester, pp. 10 (1409), 131 (1520); *Beverley*, pp. 23 (1405), 29–30 (1409), 38 (1401); *Norwich*, i, pp. 123–4 (fifteenth century), 181 (early fourteenth century), ii, pp. 82 (1373), 91 (1455); *BBC, 1216–1307*, pp. 293–8 (Grimsby, 1258; Cambridge, 1268; Bakewell, 1286); Bailey (ed.), *Bailiffs' Minute Book*, p. 19 (Dunwich, 1427); *Great Red Book*, i, p. 143 (1452); *Northampton*, i, pp. 225–8, cc.30 and 40 (*c.*1460); Bateson (ed.), *Borough Customs*, ii, p. 179 (Dover, fifteenth century); Toulmin Smith (ed.), *English Gilds*, p. 381 (Worcester, 1467); *Henley*, pp. 185–6, 189 (1517 and 1519).

[231] *BBC, 1216–1307*, pp. 293–8 (Grimsby, 1258)

[232] *Ibid.*, p. 298 (Chesterfield, 1294). See also Maitland (ed.), *Select Pleas of the Crown*, i, pp. 88–9 (Worcester, 1221).

[233] *Bristol*, i, pp. 38–9 (1344), ii, pp. 22–5 (1339), 225–6 (late fourteenth century).

[234] Mastoris, 'Regulating the Nottingham markets'.

[235] *York*, i, pp. 223–4 (fifteenth century).

[236] *Bristol*, ii, p. 225 (late fourteenth century); Toulmin Smith (ed.), *English Gilds*, p. 343 (Berwick, 1283–4); *Henley*, pp. 178, 184–5 (1517).

A note in the York Memorandum Book reveals the frustration of town authorities in dealing with petty cooks and regraters: 'and that cukes and regrators kepe theyr tyme of byyng als[o] thayr constitucions and governaunce of thys citee wyll, upon payn that falles tharfor. They knawe it wele ynogh.'[237]

Sunday trading

There was also a moral element to temporal restrictions, with trade prohibited on Sundays or during religious festivals. This tradition had old antecedents and was primarily enforced due to religious concerns rather than because of economic considerations.[238] Ecclesiastical authorities and others desired to keep commercial activity separate from specifically assigned religious days, not only to maintain a peaceful, non-working day, but to ensure that the sordidness of trade did not taint holy days. A regularly cited instance is the mission of Eustace, Abbot of Flay, to England in 1201 to preach for Sunday observance. This led to several towns, such as Bury St Edmunds, transferring their Sunday market day to a weekday or moving their market place away from the churchyard.[239] However, soon after, Roger of Hoveden complained of reversions to former habits and a slackening of enthusiasm, and some Sunday institutions survived.[240] For instance, in 1305, the town of Cockermouth complained about a Sunday market at the nearby church of Crosthwaite, where people 'buy and sell there corn, flour, beans, peas, linen, cloth, meat and fish and other merchandise'; though their concern was more about a loss of tolls than the morality of Sabbath trade.[241]

The most striking legislation on the issue of Sunday trading came during the reign of Henry VI, who seems to have been actively involved in an enactment of 1448–9. This statute decried the scandal of any fairs and markets held on Sundays or high feast days and ordered that they should be moved to another day. Only the four Sundays during harvest and the buying and selling of necessary victuals were exempted from this prohibition; a concession that recognised the exigency of some sorts of

---

[237] *York*, i, pp. 223–4 (fifteenth century).
[238] Attenborough (ed.), *Laws*, pp. 106–7, c.7 (laws of Edward and Guthrum, *c.*921), pp. 140–1, c.24 (laws of Aethelstan, *c.*925–39); *Report of the Royal Commission*, i, appx I, p. 33, cc.13 and 17 (laws of Aethelred, *c.*978–1016).
[239] Cate, 'English mission'; Cate, 'The church and market reform'; Salzman, *English Trade*, pp. 124–6; Butler (ed.), *Chronicle of Jocelin of Brakelond*, p. 132; Maitland (ed.), *Select Pleas of the Crown*, i, p. 20.
[240] Stubbs (ed.), *Chronica*, iv, pp. 123–4, 167–72. On 26 May 1290, Edward I prohibited Sunday markets in a proclamation, CUL, MS Additional 3584, fol. 251r–v.
[241] *Parl. Rolls*, Vetus Codex, mem. 134 [55] (1305).

trade and mirrored the prudence of *Dives and Pauper*.[242] However, there was also a passage in the statute which pondered explicitly the spiritual dangers of the marketplace and the intimate connection of trade, avarice and lying:

for great earthly covetousness, the people is more willingly vexed, and in bodily labour foiled, than in other ferial days, as in fastening and making their booths and stalls, bearing and carrying, lifting and placing their wares outward and home-ward, as though they did nothing remember the horrible defiling of their souls in buying and selling, with many deceitful lies, and false perjury, with drunken-ness and strifes, and so specially withdrawing themselves and their servants from divine service.[243]

The English episcopacy similarly continued to warn against Sunday trading and Bishop Braybrooke, in 1392, and Archbishop Arundel, in 1413, both issued letters against working on Sundays and feast days.[244] The London barbers had already been denounced by the Archbishop of Canterbury in 1413 for opening on Sundays, stating that 'the Lord hath blessed the seventh day and made it holy, and hath commanded that it shall be observed by no abusive pursuit of any servile occupations'. He threatened excommunication but despaired that 'temporal punishment is held more in dread than clerical, and that which touches the body or the purse more than that which kills the soul', and thus petitioned the city authorities to impose a pecuniary penalty upon offenders.[245]

Sunday trading was obviously still an issue in many towns during the fifteenth century. In 1444, when the London authorities ordered that nothing should be bought or sold on Sundays nor any wares made or delivered, the chronicler, Robert Fabyan, lamented that 'the whiche orde-naunce helde but a whyle'.[246] Ordinances for Maldon targeted butchers and ale-sellers, ordering them not to sell meat and ale on Sundays until after the bell was rung at All Saints' Church. After 1428, the butchers of York were also allowed to sell their meat on Sundays outside the time of divine service.[247] The authorities at Lynn similarly prohibited Sunday trading by an ordinance of 1465, but drew on statute law in allowing taverners and common cooks to continue, and others at times of harvest and need.[248] Town authorities were seemingly content to follow moral

---

[242] See above, p. 122.   [243] *Statutes*, ii, pp. 351–2, 27 Hen VI c.5 (1448–9).

[244] Thomson, 'Wealth, poverty', pp. 276–7.   [245] *Memorials*, pp. 593–4 (1413).

[246] *CLB*, κ, p. 293 (1444); Ellis (ed.), *New Chronicles*, p. 617; Flenley (ed.), *Six Town Chronicles*, p. 103; Thomas and Thornley (eds.), *Great Chronicle*, p. 177.

[247] Alsford, *Towns* (Maldon, fifteenth century); *York*, ii, pp. 182–3 (1428). See also *Memorials*, p. 354 (1371); *CLB*, κ, p. 10 (1423); *Beverley*, pp. 123–5 (1416); *Coventry*, p. 547 (1493); *Winchester*, pp. 65–6 (1428), 142 (1525).

[248] *King's Lynn*, p. 268, no. 325 (1465); *York*, ii, p. 161 (1425); *Northampton*, i, pp. 311–12 (fifteenth century?); *Norwich*, ii, p. 87 (1422).

precepts, provided exemptions were made for important times of year or for necessary victuallers. There was an ultimate recognition that certain Sunday trading was unavoidable and the exemptions were perhaps as important as the rule.

Order and sanitation

Besides the direct activity of buying and selling, municipal ordinances were also established to tackle the harmful by-products of commercial and industrial activities. Keeping peace and order in a town market was one major concern for market bailiffs and constables. Heated arguments and fights could easily occur over a disputed bargain and the normal mechanisms of the borough and leet court were employed to punish offenders. In early fourteenth-century London, there was an inquiry into bakers, taverners and other traders found guilty of committing assaults with swords, bucklers and other arms during the night.[249] In late fifteenth-century Leicester, those that fought and drew blood within sight of the high cross and on market day were fined more than those who caused trouble at other times and places.[250] The regulations of several towns tried to limit the use of weapons by insisting that innkeepers warned guests to leave their swords and daggers within the inn, or ordering butchers not to bring 'bills, halberds or great staves' within the city limits.[251] However, in fifteenth-century Norwich, holders of shops were actually ordered to have staves at hand 'for preserving the peace in the city and for resisting rioters and rebels'.[252]

The medieval marketplace would have been a bustling hive of activity, with hawkers and stallholders competing loudly for the attention of customers. The fishmongers of Coventry were apparently keen to take up as much room as possible in displaying their wares and were ordered to make their boards smaller in order to facilitate passing traffic.[253] Advertising was fairly rudimentary: simple signs were hung outside shops and stalls, and there would have been a cacophony of loud cries by vendors

---

[249] *CLB*, E, p. 116 (1319–20). In a similar vein, in 1327, London officials were ordered to punish lax victuallers in the same writ that warned of 'armed evil-doers who roamed the streets'. Braid, 'Laying the foundations', 19; Thomas and Jones (eds.), *Calendar of Plea and Memorandum Rolls*, i, p. 45; *CPR (1327–30)*, pp. 184–5.

[250] *Leicester*, ii, p. 317 (1488).   [251] *Coventry*, p. 29 (1421); *Liber Albus*, p. 335 (1363).

[252] *Norwich*, ii, p. 95 (1461).

[253] *Coventry*, pp. 276 (1453), 306 (1459). See also *Liber Albus*, p. 237 (1272–1307); *York*, iii, p. 180 (1475). Such temporary stalls and boards were often ordered to be removed when the market day was over. *Coventry*, p. 28 (1421); *CLB*, A, p. 217 (1276–8); *Liber Albus*, p. 290 (1307–27); Jeayes (ed.), *Court Rolls*, i, pp. 96–8 (1330); Walker (ed.), *Court Rolls*, v, p. 12.

or their servants.[254] The use of basic advertising was encouraged by officials as this increased the publicity of a sale and thus aided inspection. Nevertheless, a London ordinance in 1475 complained of overly forceful tactics by cooks, in a way reminiscent of John Gower's complaints:

divers persones of the saide Craft [of cooks] with their hands embrowed [covered in broth] and fowled be accustomed to drawe and pluk other Folk as well gentilmen as other comon people by their slyves [sleeves] and clothes to bye of their vitailles whereby many debates and strives often tymes happen ayenst the peas [against the peace].[255]

This ordinance neatly encapsulated various concerns about hygiene, dirt, aggressive sales tactics and potential disputes in the marketplace.

All towns, small or large, also faced problems of sanitation and refuse, especially with the presence of butchers and tanners who produced unhygienic waste in large quantities. Indeed, a prime concern of town laws was that no butchers, tanners, cooks or other traders should throw their rubbish into the streets.[256] The cooks and fishmongers of Coventry were separately warned against throwing their filth 'vndur hur bordys [boards], ne in the hye [high] stret'. They and other traders were expected to carry away any entrails and rubbish at the end of the market day, as well as to wash the paving stones and clean the channels.[257] Regulations repeatedly addressed the issue of sanitation by demanding the upkeep of a clean marketplace, while traders were discouraged from unhygienic habits. For instance, the fishmongers of Coventry were prohibited from cutting stockfish and salt-fish upon the same boards where previously meat had been cut; while victuallers in York were not allowed to place bread in their windows with contaminating items like oil, butter and fat.[258] People feared filth and 'stench' as sources of disease and contagion, and the York ordinances stated: 'The people of each trade shall be placed and ordained to remain in a specific place, so that no degrading business or unsuitable trade is carried out among those who sell food for humans'.[259]

Designated areas were set aside for the disposal of rubbish, intended to maintain the cleanliness of public spaces. The butchers of Beverley had to dispose of blood, offal and bones only in assigned places and

---

[254] *Nottingham*, i, pp. 218–19 (1380–1); *Northampton*, i, p. 378 (late fifteenth century).
[255] *CLB*, L, p. 129 (1475).
[256] Carr, 'From pollution to prostitution', 28–9.
[257] *Coventry*, pp. 26 (1421), 382–3 (1472), 555 (1494), 624 (1509).
[258] *Ibid.*, p. 312 (1459); Prestwich (ed.), *York*, pp. 11–12 (1301).
[259] Prestwich (ed.), *York*, p. 17 (1301). See also Carr, 'Controlling the butchers', 450–1, 460–1.

not leave them in the streets.[260] The Southampton *Oak Book* threatened a fine of 12d. for making highways 'more dirty, filthy, or corrupt'. No one was to leave dung, offal, rubble or timber in the marketplace, roads, gutters and quays.[261] Those who threw urine or stinking water out of windows or doors into the street were fined.[262] Instead, in many towns, residents were expected to keep clean the area in front of their door, particularly in time for the start of market day.[263] Nor were traders or town residents allowed to let pigs, ducks or dogs wander in the streets. Offending owners were usually amerced, but pigs found wandering in Bristol also had their tail docked so that they could be identified if found loose again, when they would be slaughtered for use at the gaol.[264] The pigs in Maldon were all expected to have a ring through their noses, by which they could be tied up, and anyone that killed a wandering pig could not be prosecuted by its owner.[265] Loose pigs were obviously considered a significant nuisance.[266]

Butchers were especially subject to accusations of unsanitary conduct, endangering public health and causing a nuisance and stench, because of their slaughtering and scalding practices.[267] A late fourteenth-century

[260] *Beverley*, pp. 28–9 (1365), 129 (1510).
[261] *Oak Book*, i, pp. 52–3, c.42 (c.1300). See also *CLB*, A, pp. 216, 219–20 (1276–8), G, p. 300 (1372), H, p. 355 (1390); *Memorials*, pp. 389 (1375), 435–6 (1379); *Liber Albus*, pp. 228, 237 (1272–1307); *Beverley*, pp. 4–5 (1359); *Bristol*, ii, pp. 31, 227–8 (fourteenth century); *York*, i, pp. lxviii–lxix, 17 (1377); *Nottingham*, i, pp. 274–9 (1395), ii, pp. 38–43 (1407), 60–3 (1408); *Coventry*, p. 23 (1421); *Great Red Book*, i, p. 142 (1452); *Northampton*, i, p. 229, c.44 (c.1460); *Norwich*, ii, pp. 84 (1380), 97–8 (1467); *Leicester*, ii, p. 290 (1467); Toulmin Smith (ed.), *English Gilds*, p. 398 (Worcester, 1467).
[262] *Leicester*, ii, p. 21 (1335–6); *Liber Albus*, p. 238 (1272–1307); *Bristol*, ii, p. 228 (late fourteenth century); *CLB*, G, p. 300 (1372), H, p. 355 (1390); *Great Red Book*, i, p. 142 (1452).
[263] Alsford, *Towns* (Lynn, early fifteenth century); *Coventry*, pp. 23 (1421), 217 (1444), 273 (1452); *Great Red Book*, i, p. 143 (1452); *Leicester*, ii, pp. 290–1 (1467); Toulmin Smith (ed.), *English Gilds*, p. 384 (Worcester, 1467).
[264] *Bristol*, ii, pp. 31–2, 227 (fourteenth century).
[265] Alsford, *Towns* (Maldon, fifteenth century).
[266] *Oak Book*, i, pp. 52–3, c.43 (c.1300); Prestwich (ed.), *York*, p. 16 (1301); *CLB*, A, pp. 216–17, 220 (1276–8), H, pp. 311 (1387), 355 (1390); *Liber Albus*, pp. 235–6 (1272–1307), 388–9; Ingleby (ed.), *Red Register*, ii, p. 224, fol. 185 (1331); *Norwich*, i, p. 190 (early fourteenth century), ii, pp. 88 (1437), 205–7 (1354); *Leicester*, ii, pp. 21–2 (1335–6), 103 (1355), 292–3 (1467); *Nottingham*, i, pp. 268–9 (1351–2); *Beverley*, pp. 19 (1360s), 29 (1367); *York*, i, pp. lxix, 18 (1377); *Northampton*, i, pp. 247–8 (1381), 289–90 (1457); *Salisbury*, p. 89, no. 203 (1418); *Coventry*, pp. 27 (1421), 217 (1444), 361 (1470); *Great Red Book*, i, p. 144 (1452); *Henley*, pp. 57, 75 (1452–3); Toulmin Smith (ed.), *English Gilds*, p. 398 (Worcester, 1467); *Winchester*, pp. 136–7 (1380), 149 (1531).
[267] Sabine, 'Butchering'; Carr, 'Controlling the butchers'; Barron, *London*, pp. 263–4. See *Norwich*, i, p. 365 (1289); Salter (ed.), *Munimenta*, pp. 13–14, no. 16 (1310); Salter (ed.), *Medieval Archives*, i, pp. 136–7, no. 89 (1339); *Winchester*, p. 18 (1409);

York ordinance ordained that no butchers should throw refuse or unwanted offal in the river, or wash skins where water was also drawn for brewing or baking.[268] The maintenance of fresh water supplies was a particular concern for town authorities.[269] Certain trades required large amounts of water, such as butchers, brewers, bakers, tanners and dyers, and town authorities tried to control the use of water conduits by victuallers in order to preserve supplies for domestic use.[270] There were concerns about keeping the water supply clean and associated unsanitary practices by producers. In London, there were complaints that the slaughtering of animals had led to putrefied blood in the streets and entrails in the Thames, so that 'the air in the same city has been greatly corrupted and infected, and whereby the worst of abominations and stenches have been generated, and sicknesses and many other maladies have befallen persons'. Butchers were thus ordered to slaughter beasts outside the city, and livestock markets were often located on the outskirts of towns because of such space and hygiene concerns.[271]

The maintenance of medieval marketplaces was obviously an ongoing and unenviable task for officials, who had to balance the needs of traders with the requirement to guard against unsanitary and harmful practices. It was probably a thankless endeavour since markets inevitably generated dirt, waste, stench and conflict. The continual reiteration of ordinances suggests a concerned intent to temper the worst commercial by-products, but the level of success is difficult to discern.

Weights and measures

The public marketplace provided a physical, formal space for trade, but further structures, devices and procedures were needed to facilitate transactions. The actual tools of trade, whether visual instruments such as weights, measures or coinage, or the mechanisms of bargaining and contract, were largely founded upon consensual and long-established principles of trading efficiency and expediency. They were also increasingly

---

Salisbury, p. 117, no. 236 (1423); *Henley*, p. 48 (1441); *Great Red Book*, i, pp. 143–4 (1452); Toulmin Smith (ed.), *English Gilds*, pp. 385, 396 (Worcester, 1467); *York*, iii, pp. 58 (1421), 217–18 (1498).

[268] *York*, i, p. 15 (1371). See also *Red Paper Book*, pp. 48–9 (1425–6).

[269] Britnell, 'Town life', p. 136.

[270] *CLB*, D, pp. 236–7 (1310), F, pp. 29 (1337), 128 (1345); Salter (ed.), *Munimenta*, pp. 11–12, no. 13 (Oxford, 1305); *Coventry*, pp. 208 (1442–3), 232 (1448), 255 (1451), 584 (1497); *Memorials*, pp. 77–8 (1310), 225 (1345); *Bristol*, ii, pp. 229–30 (late fourteenth century).

[271] *Memorials*, pp. 356–8 (1371).

enshrined in national statutes, common law and Merchant Law, which impressed a legal standard upon local centres.

The Crown was persistent in its attempts to enforce a standardis-ation of weights and measures in England, perhaps driven on by the extensive provisioning needs of the royal court as well as the needs of the country in general.[272] Legislative standardisation was also another means of increasing the range of royal authority. Ultimately, however, for those dealing in the marketplace, reliable weights and measures were an important aspect of commercial confidence. The desire for uniform weights and measures went back a long way; the laws of Edgar (c.959–75) stated: 'let one measure and one weight pass'.[273] William I was also keen to disseminate uniform measurements throughout the realm and he adopted the Winchester standards introduced by Edgar, demand-ing authentication by his royal seal.[274] However, the continual reiter-ation of the need for uniformity in weights and measures throughout the later medieval period demonstrates that the process of standard-isation was gradual and difficult. Prevalent local customs, as well as matters of convenience for buyers and sellers, meant that local mea-sures were still in use in several areas and trades.[275] It was not until the late fourteenth century, when the focus began to switch from the units themselves to the practices employed, and when approved royal vessels were widely distributed, that substantial progress appears to have been made.

The development of weights and measures regulation was focused in national laws and began in earnest with the 'Assize of Measures' of 1197, recorded in Roger of Hoveden's chronicle. This demanded standardisa-tion and stated that all vessels should bear a mark 'lest by guile they can be falsified'.[276] It differed from the earlier promulgations by also insisting that each city or borough should have four to six lawful men, as well as the sheriff or reeve, to keep the assize in that town: 'that they see and be sure that all things are sold and bought by the same measure, and that all measures are of the same size according to the diversity of wares'.

---

[272] For more detailed surveys of the development of weights and measures in England, see Connor, *Weights and Measures*; Zupko, *British Weights and Measures*; Hall and Nicholas (eds.), *Select Tracts*.

[273] *Report of the Royal Commission*, i, appx I, p. 32, Laws of Eadgar, c.8 (c.959–75). There is little evidence that the Anglo-Saxon kings pursued this issue by legislating for effective enforcement.

[274] Zupko, *British Weights and Measures*, p. 15; Wood, *Medieval Economic Thought*, p. 93.

[275] There is evidence that some local forms of measurements were still extremely haphazard in the thirteenth and fourteenth centuries, being abitrarily based on bodily strength or dimensions. Wood, *Medieval Economic Thought*, pp. 94–5.

[276] Stubbs (ed.), *Chronica*, iv, pp. 33–4.

The penalties for offenders were severe; they were to be imprisoned and all their chattels seized. Official 'keepers' of weights and measures, if negligent, were also at the mercy of the king and possible forfeitures. Thus, central regulations provided the groundwork for the enforcement of uniformity, but it remained heavily reliant upon the cooperation of local officials.

Weights and measures were again addressed in John's reign, most significantly in *Magna Carta* (1215), which demanded standard measures of wine, ale and grain and confirmed the London quarter as pre-eminent:

let there be one measure of wine throughout our kingdom and one measure of ale and one measure of corn, namely the London quarter, and one width of cloth whether dyed, russet or halberjet, namely two ells within the selvedges [woven edgings]. Let it be the same with weights as with measures.[277]

However, the means of enforcement and correction were not defined again by central legislation until the mid-thirteenth century. *Judicium Pillorie* ordered that six men of a town were to gather all the bushels, half-bushels, quarter-bushels, gallons, pottles, quarts, pounds, half-pounds, and all the other weights and measures kept in the market, taverns and bakehouses. All the vessels and weights had to be marked with the name of the owner and checked for uniformity.[278] This was expanded upon by *Statutum de Pistoribus* in 1274–5, which explained how the royal Exchequer would provide a standard bushel, gallon, yard and stone to the bailiff, mayor and six lawful men of certain towns. Each standard was marked with an iron seal of the king and had to be kept safe under pain of a £100 penalty. Any who used unsealed measures were to be amerced by local officials, while 'if any be convict for a double measure, that is to wit, a greater for to buy with, and a smaller to sell with, he shall be imprisoned for his falsehood, and shall be grievously punished'.[279] The use of double measures was a commonly denounced vice in medieval clerical

---

[277] Holt, *Magna Carta*, pp. 326–7, c.35; *Statutes*, i, p. 11. The provisions of Magna Carta were restated in several later statutes; *Statutes*, i, p. 117, 25 Edw I c.25 (1297); i, p. 285, 14 Edw III st.1 c.12 (1340); i, pp. 321–2, 25 Edw III st.5 cc.9–10 (1351–2); ii, pp. 241–2, 8 Hen VI c.5 (1429). Also see *Britton*, i, pp. 185–6, ch. 31, c.1 (1291–2). *Assisa de Ponderibus et Mensuris*, issued during Edward I's reign, advanced even more information on the different weights and measures that could be used. *Statutes*, i, pp. 204–5, 31 Edw I?.

[278] *Statutes*, i, pp. 201–2, 'Judicium Pillorie'.

[279] *Ibid.*, i, pp. 202–4, 'Statutum de Pistoribus'. This is possibly related to several royal commissions sent into the counties from 1273 to 1276 to examine measures and hold pleas of the market. *CPR, 1272–81*, pp. 16, 31, 73, 136. Statutory provisions were copied into borough custumals, e.g. *Bristol*, ii, pp. 218–19; *Northampton*, i, pp. 321–4; *Norwich*, ii, p. 207. In 1430, the Coventry mayor sent for brass standard measures from the Exchequer; *Coventry*, pp. 133–4 (1430).

literature, and regulations were couched in very similar terminology.[280] It is possible that preachers drew upon such statutes for their sermons and moral manuals, copying the phrasing. The specification of severe punishment for double measures suggests that this was regarded as a greater and more flagrant fraud than the use of unsealed measures, which could be excused as negligence.

In 1340, a statute of Edward III repeated that there should be 'one measure and one weight' throughout the kingdom.[281] A duplication in 1351–2 of the weights and measures provision in *Magna Carta* was accompanied by a recognition that standards had not been well kept.[282] Similarly, a statute of 1357 complained that merchants used different weights than those ordained by law and the 'Ordinances of the Staple' declared that some bought wool by one weight and sold by another.[283] The frequent reiteration of statutes in itself illustrates that the problems associated with weights and measures were difficult to quash, with increasing numbers of standards being produced by the Treasury during the fourteenth century and distributed to the counties and towns. By 1429, all towns and boroughs were expected to have a common balance and weights, or else face fines of 40s. for towns, 100s. for boroughs and £10 for cities.[284] Throughout the fourteenth and fifteenth centuries, the sheriffs, Justices of the Peace and Clerk of the Market were all enjoined to punish those using false measures and burn the offending vessels.[285] The penalties prescribed in statute law remained harsh and included imprisonment, forfeiture of goods and recompense to the aggrieved party of perhaps double the original value. Even in 1495, Parliament highlighted the fact that 'one weight and measure' was still not standard in the kingdom 'to the great harm and trouble of many different subjects'. In response, they

---

[280] See above, pp. 78–9. For instance, in Norwich in 1288, Agnes Gossip was accused of buying by the greater and selling by the less ('emit per majorem et vendit per minorem'). *Norwich*, i, p. 361 (1288), also p. 367 (1289). The provision concerning double measures was also stated in *Statutes*, i, pp. 201–2, 'Judicium Pillorie'; i, p. 285, 14 Edw III st.1 c.12 (1340); ii, p. 337, 27 Edw III st.2 c.10 (1353). See also *Fleta*, ii, pp. 121–2, bk. ii, c.12 (late thirteenth century); *Britton*, i, pp. 192–3, ch. 31, c.9 (1291–2); *CPR, 1358–61*, pp. 220–1 (York, 1359); *Northampton*, i, p. 376 (late fifteenth century).

[281] *Statutes*, i, p. 285, 14 Edw III st.1 c.12 (1340).

[282] *Ibid.*, i, pp. 321–2, 25 Edw III st.5, c.10 (1351–2). It did not help that some central legislation allowed certain jurisdictions to be exempted from standardisation, *ibid.*, ii, pp. 63–4, 13 Ric II c.9 (1389–90).

[283] *Ibid.*, i, p. 350, 31 Edw III st.1 c.2 (1357); ii, p. 337, 27 Edw III st.2 c.10 (1353).

[284] *Ibid.*, ii, pp. 241–2, 8 Hen VI c.5 (1429).

[285] *Ibid.*, i, pp. 365–6, 34 Edw III cc.5–6 (1360–1); ii, p. 62, 13 Ric II st.1 c.4 (1389–90); ii, p. 83, 16 Ric II c.3 (1392–3); ii, pp. 241–2, 8 Hen VI c.5 (1429); *RP*, iii, p. 267; *Parl. Rolls*, Vetus Codex, mem. 120r (1302), cc.39–40 [36–37], April 1343, c.25, January 1393.

ordered that brass standards should be delivered to every county and city and then distributed to market towns. All conforming weights and measures were to be stamped (with a crowned letter H) and faulty ones burnt.[286]

Statutory regulations thus outlined the control of measuring standards, with central officials and institutions, such as the Clerk of the Market and the Exchequer, playing a primary role. However, royal officials and commissions could not hope to police weights and measures throughout the realm and the actual enforcement of standards primarily remained a local task.[287] As with the regulation of trading offences, the right to supervise weights and measures was granted to town and seigneurial authorities by franchise or charter. Borough charters often specifically stated that officials of a borough had the assize, assay, punishment and correction of bread, wine, ale, victuals, measures, weights and other matters within the said town and liberty, to the exclusion of the Clerk of the Market or other royal officials.[288] Such privileges were held by Oxford University since the early fourteenth century and partly explains why, in 1427, the Chancellor had three different measures for grain (modium, half-modium, quarter-modium), four for liquids (lagenam, potellam, quartam, pintam), two weights (Troy for bread and money, and 'lyggyng' weight for spices and candles), a large and small scale, a gilt measure for cloth and two iron seals in the shape of an ox-head (one for wooden measures and the other for earthenware).[289] The Ipswich ordinances outlined that, at any time, bailiffs could test a trader's measures for conformity, 'so that non falshed be doon in the forseyd toun of Gippeswich among such maner of mesurys in esclaundre [slander] of the toun, ne of damage to the pepele'.[290] Other towns and markets had set places and times, such as during the leet court, when weights and measures could be tried and sealed, with false items destroyed. Strangers entering fifteenth-century Bristol with merchandise sold by weight had to use the common beam, overseen by the

---

[286] *Parl. Rolls*, c.44, October 1495.   [287] Rosenthal, 'Assizes'.

[288] *Norwich*, i, pp. 26 (1345), 33 (1403–4), 121 (1447); *Northampton*, i, pp. 68–70 (1385); *CChR*, vi, pp. 54–5 (Ipswich, 1446), pp. 194–5 (Dunwich, 1463), pp. 197–9 (Ipswich, 1463).

[289] Anstey (ed.), *Munimenta Academica*, pp. 284–5.

[290] *Black Book*, ii, pp. 176–7, c.83 [80] (c.1309). The sealing of measures might incur a small fee. *Liber Albus*, p. 290 (1307–27). See also Jeayes (ed.), *Court Rolls*, i, p. 50 (1311); *Norwich*, i, pp. 175–7 (early fourteenth century), ii, p. 89 (1440); Alsford, *Towns* (Lynn, 1309; Maldon, fifteenth century); *Bristol*, i, p. 38 (1344); Salter (ed.), *Medieval Archives*, i, pp. 140–2, no. 93 (1346); *York*, i, pp. 15–16 (1371); *Coventry*, p. 192 (1439); *Great Red Book*, ii, p. 51 (1455?); *Leicester*, ii, pp. 294–5 (1467), iii, p. 17 (1520); *Winchester*, p. 126 (1515).

Chamberlain or his deputies, and pay for the privilege.[291] The costs of maintaining standard weights and measures could thus fall on outside traders.

There were many other local provisions to ensure that the standard of weights and measures was openly maintained. For example, the turners of London were ordered not to make any other measures than gallons, pottles and quarts, and not to make cups or other false measures.[292] Every innkeeper of Bristol had to keep a balance and a weight of 6lb. hanging openly in their hostelry so that all guests could check the weight of hay sold to them.[293] By the late fifteenth century, standard measures were set up in several places within Bristol, at the High Cross, Bridge Corner and Stallage Cross, so that sacks and vessels could be easily tested.[294] However, traders still flouted the law and the language in some court entries displays a degree of outrage. William Godfrey of Colchester was convicted in 1452 of deceptively using false weights and he was placed in prison 'for perjury and as an infringer and violator of the public weal and liberty of the town'.[295] In Ingoldmells (Lincolnshire) on 12 June 1420, Thomas Toppyng of Burgh was fined for unjustly defaming the officers of Skegness in claiming that they held a false measure to the deception of the people.[296] The reputation of a town franchise and the protection of consumers were prominent aspects of local legislative rhetoric. Social pressure was exerted upon town authorities to conform to national laws.

Regulations also highlighted the issue that local customs were not easy to overcome, as seen in the statutes against heaping. The heaping of grain in a bushel was a custom that created irksome inconsistency in the eyes of Parliament, yet was considered to be beneficial to many merchants.[297] *Statutum de Pistoribus* took such customs into account and allowed oats to be sold with heapings on every bushel, but declared that

---

[291] *Great Red Book*, ii, p. 50 (1455?); Stanford (ed.), *Ordinances of Bristol*, pp. 10–11 (*c*.1515). See also *Liber Albus*, p. 248 (1284–5); *Norwich*, i, pp. 177–8 (early fourteenth century).

[292] *Memorials*, pp. 78 (1310), 234–5 (1347); Riley (ed.), *Munimenta Gildhallae*, iii, appx II, p. 432 (1307–27).

[293] *Great Red Book*, i, p. 144 (1452). See also *York*, iii, pp. 242–3 (1528).

[294] Toulmin Smith (ed.), *The Maire*, p. 84 (late fifteenth century). See also *Coventry*, pp. 169 (1434), 267 (1451), 334 (1467).

[295] *Red Paper Book*, pp. 59–60 (1452).

[296] Massingberd (ed.), *Court Rolls*, p. 241 (1420).

[297] Britnell discussed this custom in Britnell, '*Advantagium Mercatoris*'. For measuring corn by level or heaped bushels, see Oschinsky (ed.), *Walter of Henley*, pp. 276–7, c.39, pp. 324–5, c.55; *Norwich*, i, pp. 360 (1288), 371 (1293).

all wheat measures should be struck level and not heaped.[298] In 1413, it was stated that in times past the measure of corn could be eight bushels to the quarter, plus one bushel which could be heaped, yet now this was forbidden. However, this very terminology implies that the use of heaping was still in vogue and central legislation was not always successful in combating customary practices.[299]

Another dominant concern of central government was the apparatus called the auncel, which was banned outright in 1351–2, in response to petitions of the past half-century demanding that traders should use the balance instead.[300] The auncel was a weighing device used for small merchandise, consisting of a rod fulcrumed near one end and a weight that moved along the graduated longer limb in order to weigh goods hung at the other end.[301] Traders favoured it because it was a complete and self-contained weighing mechanism. However, the auncel could be falsely manipulated and was more difficult for a customer to scrutinise than the balance. A fraudulent trader could easily alter the weight of the auncel counterpoise or keep the position of the counterpoise concealed. The alternative beam scales or balances were simple equal-arm fulcrums with weights in one pan and goods in the other. However, even the balance could be used incorrectly and the legislators ordered 'that the tongue of the balance be even, without bowing to the one side or to the other, or without putting hand or foot, or other touch making of the same'.[302] Anyone that falsely used the balance was to be imprisoned for a year and his weighed goods forfeited, while any party who sued against the offending trader was to receive four times the value of the goods falsely weighed.

The auncel, despite the misgivings of traders who petitioned Parliament, continued to be used well into the fifteenth century. A statute of 1429 complained about the auncel, 'for the great hurt and subtile deceits done by the same measure to the common people'.[303] By this time, the Church had joined forces with the state, and Henry Chicheley,

---

[298] *Statutes*, i, pp. 202–4, 'Statutum de Pistoribus'. See also *ibid.*, ii, p. 79, 15 Ric II c.4 (1391); *Parl. Rolls*, c.28, November 1390.

[299] *Statutes*, ii, p. 174, 1 Hen V c.10 (1413), ii, pp. 282–4, 11 Hen VI c.8 (1433).

[300] *Ibid.*, i, pp. 321–2, 25 Edw III st.5 cc.9–10 (1351–2); reiterated in 34 Edw III cc.5–6 (1360–1), i, pp. 365–6; see also *RP*, ii, p. 239.

[301] Connor, *Weights and Measures*, pp. 133–41. Cheese was often weighed on an auncel; *Statutes*, ii, p. 267, 9 Hen VI c.8 (1430–1).

[302] *Statutes*, ii, p. 337, 27 Edw III st.2 c.10 (1353). In Leicester, no stranger or broker was to touch a balance in a merchant's house unless they were the buyer or seller; *Leicester*, i, pp. 112–13 (1273), 214–15 (1290), 225 (1299). See also Riley (ed.), *Chronicles*, pp. 26–7; *CLB*, F, pp. 113–14 (1344).

[303] *Statutes*, ii, pp. 241–2, 8 Hen VI c.5 (1429); see also *RP*, v, p. 30.

Archbishop of Canterbury, pronounced excommunication in 1428 upon all who used weights contrary to the king's standard, especially 'le Auncel, Scheft or Pounder or any of them'. The archbishop drew upon traditional moral invective in making his condemnation: 'For there are, as the voice of the public proclaims and authoritative experience of these things manifests, in some cities, boroughs and other places of our province of Canterbury, numerous ruthless purchasers, who, unmindful of their salvation, are wont to buy fraudulently from the simple common folk and others, wool, honey, wax, and other things required for human uses'.[304] Soon after, an entry in the Northampton civic records declared that any who used the auncel would be 'cursed be the chirche'.[305] There was a close similarity between secular law and ecclesiastical edicts, with the Church able to promulgate its condemnation through the forums of the pulpit and the confessional.

Many historians have suggested that the continual reiteration of the same rules, regarding the standardisation of weights and measures, highlighted the confusing and varied mensural system that existed in medieval England.[306] There were certainly complaints against infringements in a statute of 1340 and the distribution of weights and measures to an increasing number of towns by the fifteenth century suggests growing efforts and expenditure to uphold the process of standardisation.[307] Nevertheless, national legislation was important in establishing a principle of uniformity and a royal standard in which all traders could place their trust. Despite the seemingly endless litany of local measures and the need to reinforce the message of uniformity at regular intervals, there was a gradual recognition at all levels of the importance of measurement controls for commercial growth.

Coinage

Another instrument of trade, which was also subject to uniform standards and controls, was the currency of the realm. Coin was increasingly important in the growing market economy of late medieval England and to ensure confidence in this medium of exchange the sovereign attempted to exert control.[308] Coinage became a symbol of royal prestige and authority. Offa of Mercia in the eighth century, and Alfred of Wessex

---

[304] Wilkins, *Concilia*, iii, pp. 516–17; cf. Connor, *Weights and Measures*, p. 139; Owst, *Literature and Pulpit*, p. 362. See also Arnold, *Customs of London*, p. 191 (*c.*1519).
[305] *Northampton*, i, p. 375 (late fifteenth century).
[306] Salzman, *English Trade*, pp. 42–5.
[307] *Statutes*, i, p. 285, 14 Edw III st.1 c.12 (1340).
[308] Wood, *Medieval Economic Thought*, pp. 100–9.

in the ninth century, both sought to establish a uniform coinage of silver pennies in their respective domains.[309] In the tenth century, Aethelstan (929–39) was the first to declare that there should be one coinage in his realm and that money should be minted only in the towns ascribed. The penalty for base moneyers who produced light coins was for them to have their hand cut off and displayed on the mint.[310]

There were continuous attempts throughout the later Middle Ages to preserve a centralised monetary standard in England, either in terms of its supply, quality or denomination. Later statute law imposed stark penalties for counterfeit coins, with the Statute of Westminster (1275) declaring that it was akin to forging the king's seal and was thus treason.[311] Money was stamped with the mark of the king as a guarantee of its size and weight. In 1248, Matthew Paris complained about the debasement of the English coinage due to the practice of clipping: 'The coins were clipped almost to the inner circle and the inscription round the border either completely deleted or very badly defaced'.[312] The clipping of coins appears to have been a widespread problem in the thirteenth century, exacerbating bullion shortages. It was thus decreed that no one should trade with pennies that were not of legal weight, or else they would be suspended from the gallows. Yet, by the end of the fifteenth century, clipped pennies were declared legal tender due to the 'manifold inconveniences that daily ensue among his subjects for refusing of his coin, that is to say, of small, thin, and old pence'.[313]

Many statutes conveyed concern about the use of false money or foreign coinage, such as pollards and crockards, which had dispersed widely in the country 'to the damage and oppression of our people'.[314] The 1301 York civic ordinances declared that the reason people complained about high costs was due to the dissemination of low-quality coins.[315] Certain

---

[309] Zupko, *British Weights and Measures*, p. 11; Wood, *Medieval Economic Thought*, pp. 92–3.

[310] Attenborough (ed.), *Laws*, pp. 134–5, c.14 (laws of Aethelstan, *c*.925–39).

[311] *Statutes*, i, pp. 26–39, 3 Edw I, 'Statute of Westminster' (1275); Wood, *Medieval Economic Thought*, p. 100.

[312] Vaughan (ed.), *Chronicles*, pp. 139–40. For a literary example, where Covetousness admits to learning from Jews and Lombards how to clip coins, see *Piers Plowman*, B.v.242–4.

[313] *TRP*, i, p. 47, no. 42 (1498), pp. 48–9, no. 44 (1499), pp. 60–1, no. 54 (1504), pp. 70–2, no. 57 (1505).

[314] *Statutes*, i, pp. 131–5, 27 Edw I (1299); i, pp. 273–4, 9 Edw III st.2 cc.1–11 (1335). For the use of pollards and crockards, see *CLB*, c, pp. 39–40, 53–6, 68 (1299–1300); Hudson (ed.), *Leet*, pp. 51–4.

[315] Prestwich (ed.), *York*, pp. 14–15 (1301). See also Thomas (ed.), *Calendar*, pp. 60–1 (Roll c, 1299–1300).

types of coinage were also declared illegal in 1415, such as the gally half-pence, suskin, dotkin and Scottish silver.[316] The recurrent legislation on this matter during the fourteenth and fifteenth centuries implies that the use of varied unofficial coins was a blight on the monetary standard of the country.[317] Yet, the use of such low-quality coinage was seemingly difficult to prevent. It appears that the minted English coinage was not sufficiently diverse for the developing economy and often pennies were cut to make smaller denominations. Perhaps the most important development for petty retail traders was the introduction of the round farthing coin during the reign of Edward I in 1279, which was of undoubted benefit in small transactions even if they were still not produced in extensive numbers. Previously it was the practice to cut pennies into halves and quarters.[318] Peasants needed small coin to pay dues and the increasing number of petty transactions in the growing market network put a strain on the money available.

Increasing the volume of currency aided commercialisation, but a decline in money supply might trigger recession. Nicholas Mayhew and Martin Allen have both tracked the increases and decreases in the coin in circulation. Allen argued that the scarcity of small change, caused by the shrinkage of the English silver coinage in the fifteenth century, must have inhibited various economic activities.[319] For all coins, a heightened level of mint output undoubtedly had an inflationary effect on prices, while a shortage of coins could generally prove deflationary, though the exact relationship between monetary supply and recession remains much debated. Nevertheless, the basic aim of national regulations remained the establishment of a uniform currency and the elimination of bad coinage. For traders, a trusted and common medium was the basis for any bargains beyond equivalent exchange.

Bargaining and sale

The visual tools of trade were vital to the processes of bargaining and sale. Whether or not a commodity had a fixed price, a purchaser needed to know that the quantification of the goods was according to recognised

---

[316] *Statutes*, ii, p. 191, 3 Hen V (1415). For convictions of traders using Scottish or false money 'maliciously', see Kimball (ed.), *Rolls*, pp. 64–5 (Roll cii), nos. 6, 9.

[317] *Statutes*, i, pp. 131–5, 27 Edw I (1299); i, p. 219, 20 Edw I, 'Statuta de Moneta'; i, pp. 273–4, 9 Edw III St.2 cc.1–11 (1335); i, p. 299, 17 Edw III (1343); i, p. 322, 25 Edw III St.5 c.13 (1351–2); ii, p. 87, 17 Ric II c.1 (1393–4); ii, p. 191, 3 Hen V (1415); ii, p. 195, 4 Hen V c.6 (1415–16); ii, pp. 209–10, 9 Hen V St.2 cc.1–5 (1421); *TRP*, i, pp. 26–7, no. 25 (1491), p. 42, no. 39 (1498), pp. 47–8, no. 43 (1499).

[318] Eaglen, 'Evolution of coinage'; Salzman, *English Trade*, pp. 1–24.

[319] Mayhew, 'Money and prices'; Allen, 'Volume'.

standards and the seller needed to acknowledge the value of the currency he received. These are first-base principles of sales transactions, alongside factors of quality, value, demand and supply. The subsequent processes of bargaining and concluding a deal were subject to several laws in the late Middle Ages, though many of the details of haggling were perhaps contained in unwritten social mores. The haggling process in Caxton's 'Dialogues' showed a refined formula of cultural and ideological constraints, whereas written regulations primarily concerned the legal contracting of a deal or the procedures to be undertaken when one party reneged on an obligation.[320] These laws were designed for enforceability and also reflected notions of fairness and responsibility which are still evident in consumer law today. Indeed, David Ibbetson has suggested that the twelfth- and thirteenth-century common law manuals illustrate the movement from ideas of mere exchange, to one of bargains as mutual contracts with defined obligations.[321]

For a contract to be formally established, several criteria had to be fulfilled. Firstly, the item sold had to be defined by type, quality, weight, capacity and number, and a definite price-fixed; an undefined item, or one without an agreed price, could not be sued for in a court of law. Once these bargaining requirements had been fulfilled, the agreement of reciprocal obligations between the two parties could be contracted. This was signified by various devices, such as the giving and receiving of the good, an oral stipulation of promise, a written bond or a symbolic gesture.[322] Two of the most basic devices were the handclasp, which was the reduction of an early ritual ceremony, or a shared drink. Both acts were expected to be visible and audible, and thus needed to take place in the open marketplace or privately before witnesses in order to be valid. 'God's penny' was similarly symbolic and involved the public giving of a single, undistinguished coin from the buyer to the seller as indicative of an agreed sale. This was recognised by law as binding and heavy penalties could be invoked for breaking the agreement. The payment of 'God's penny' perhaps also implied a religious sanction. 'Earnest money' was an evolved form of 'God's penny' and represented not only a symbol of contract, but also an actual percentage of the purchase money; in essence, it was a forfeitable down-payment given to the seller. Medieval common law stated that any purchaser who withdrew from such an agreement forfeited the earnest. However, sellers faced potentially stronger sanctions if they had taken earnest money and then reneged. Both *Fleta* and the

---

[320] See above, pp. 69–70.
[321] This was based upon Roman law. Ibbetson, 'From property to contract'.
[322] *Fleta*, ii, pp. 186–90, bk. II, c.56 and pp. 194–6, c.58 (late thirteenth century).

twelfth-century customs of Preston stated that if a seller wished to with-draw he had to give the buyer double the earnest, unless this conflicted with law merchant, whereby the seller was to either deliver the wares or pay 5s. for every farthing of earnest money.[323]

However, the use of these simplified devices left room for one party to avoid the enforcement of the covenant, because they provided no intrinsic proof or witness (beyond the public market itself). The hand-clasp and God's penny might, theoretically, impose a legal obligation, but they did not necessarily provide sufficient proof for a court. A charter for Grimsby in 1258 placed restrictions upon the use of the handclasp and did not allow it to be used for major trading items, such as fish and grain, when the transaction involved a stranger. A more secure and enforceable device, such as a deed or tally, had to be used instead.[324] Agreements involving just burgesses could use the handclasp and bor-ough law accepted *fides facta* as pleadable, illustrating again the distrust of strangers that permeated local trading law. Nevertheless, in an efficient market, procedures were put in place so parties not only knew when a contract had been finalised, but had the means to compel agreement. There were thus stronger devices upon which to seal more valuable bar-gains. The 'Statute of Acton Burnell', in 1283, formulated the provision of recognisances, which were formal written acknowledgements before witnesses. These were then recorded by officials in certain town rolls in the presence of both the creditor and debtor. Recognisances were virtu-ally unchallengeable in court.[325] Similarly, a bill of obligation or an entry in a sales book were strong written proofs against which a defendant could not use compurgation.[326]

There was also the tally, a notched stick which was broken in two and each half given to the transacting parties. The notches represented the amount owed, and the tally, like a bond of obligation or recognisance, signified a debt as well as a contract made. Any party who produced a tally, which the other party denied, could have his proof according to

---

[323] *Ibid.*, ii, pp. 194–6, bk. II, c.58; Hall (ed.), *Glanvill*, pp. 129–30, x, 14 (*c.*1187–9). For civic legislation referring to earnest money and 'God's penny', see Bateson (ed.), *Borough Customs*, i, pp. 217–19 (Preston, twelfth century; Berwick, 1249; Northamp-ton, *c.*1460; Romney, 1498). For the use of such devices, see Farmer, 'Marketing', pp. 421–3; Gross (ed.), *Select Cases*, p. 50 (1291).

[324] *BBC, 1216–1307*, p. 301 (Grimsby, 1258).

[325] *Statutes*, i, pp. 53–4, 11 Edw I, 'Statute of Merchants' (1283); *Black Book*, ii, pp. 134–7, c.50 (*c.*1309).

[326] Bateson (ed.), *Borough Customs*, i, p. 204 (Lincoln, 1481). Compurgation involved finding a certain number of respectable persons who could swear that their statement was true. The Ipswich ordinances describe the procedure for waging law between two burgesses. In part, this involved spinning a knife to choose between two potential groups of compurgators. *Black Book*, ii, pp. 170–3, c.79 [76] (*c.*1309).

Merchant Law, which required two witnesses of the tally. If the plaintiff did not plead by Merchant Law then the defendant could deny the tally by inquest or oath.[327] The tally might also have a personal seal attached, which was considered strong proof for a deal, even on par with a written bond, and the defendant might be only able to argue the details of the debt rather than the debt itself.[328] A tally with a seal still required witnesses, who were used by inquest juries both to establish the facts of a contract or debt and to prove the validity of a tally. It was obviously preferable to produce both a visual instrument, as well as a witness, as this was stronger than a mere verbal agreement.[329] However, it is likely that written or practical instruments of proof were only used in wholesale dealing and that many smaller credit or sale transactions relied purely on a symbolic gesture. This was workable only when a sufficient level of trust had been created between participants, and transactions involving strangers were more likely to employ stronger contractual devices than those between local residents. However, these may not have been easy to obtain in the hectic conditions of a marketplace.

For a contract to be fulfilled, payment and delivery had to take place since ownership was only transferred with delivery. In common law, *Glanvill* stated that neither contracting party could withdraw from a contract without reasonable cause once a price had been agreed and the item subsequently delivered, or if part or all of the price was paid before delivery. This contractual obligation could only be excepted when a prior agreement had been made that either party could withdraw at any time with impunity.[330] Other commentators seemingly regarded the contract itself as binding enough. *Fleta*, a manual of common law, stated: 'When a person sells to another something of his own, whether movable property or immovable, the buyer is liable to the seller for the price and conversely the seller is under obligation to the buyer to hand over the thing concerned'.[331] In Bristol, any who made covenant for the purchase of victuals, but subsequently failed to make payment 'to the great injury

---

[327] Riley (ed.), *Munimenta Gildhallae*, i, p. 294; Bateson (ed.), *Borough Customs*, i, pp. 202–3 (Winchester, *c*.1280).

[328] Riley (ed.), *Munimenta Gildhallae*, i, p. 214.

[329] Bateson (ed.), *Borough Customs*, i, pp. 203–5 (Hereford, 1348 and 1486); *Fleta*, ii, pp. 209–12, bk. II, c.63 (late thirteenth century); Oschinsky (ed.), *Walter of Henley*, 'The Husbandry', pp. 440–1, c.51; *Black Book*, ii, pp. 126–7, c.40 (*c*.1309); *Norwich*, i, pp. 165–6 (early fourteenth century?). The tally appears to have fallen into disuse by the fifteenth century, because it was viewed as insubstantive proof as regards the level of obligation. Arnold (ed.), *Year Books*, pp. xxii–xxv.

[330] Hall (ed.), *Glanvill*, pp. 129–30, x, 14 (*c*.1187–9).

[331] *Fleta*, ii, pp. 194–6, bk. II, c.58 (late thirteenth century).

of the vendors and to the reproach of the commonalty of the town', was to be fined 40d. or face imprisonment.[332]

The Ipswich *Domesday Book* recognised the problems caused by disputed agreements, especially when one party claimed that the conditions of a contract had not been met and they withdrew.[333] To alleviate such wrangling, the 'communalte' ordained that a contract of sales should be declared before a bailiff at the time of sale and set down in writing if requested by the seller. This included the day when payment was due and the surety offered. The bailiff and four knowledgeable men or surveyors could then view the merchandise and judge whether it accorded with the original contract. Surveyors were also warned not to collude in fraud and told that they and the hosts should advise outsider merchants honestly.[334] Any traders who wanted to work outside of the regulations and safeguards established by the town's authorities did so at their own risk.

Conditions of contract were thus established in law and imposed an almost national standard of bargaining conduct. There was no reason why town authorities would have wished to undermine the validity of standard contracting procedures, though a suspicion of strangers continued to permeate their more detailed ordinances. This is understandable given the greater difficulties in distraining an outsider rather than a local man with visible property and chattels. In a broader sense, the basic premise of contract law was to formalise trust between buyer and seller and this was intimately related to the moralists' demands for honesty in transactions and bargaining.

Consumer protection

Deceptions and disagreements occurred in all medieval markets and there were many attempts to shore up the rights of the buyer and seller, as well as their recourse to the law. As already discussed, a seller was bound to vouch for his goods as saleable and unstolen. Contract law also stated that warranty on the condition and quality of the goods resided with the seller, so that if he sold an item as sound and without fault, but the buyer could later prove this was not so at the time of the contract, the seller was bound to take back the article. A contract remained uncompleted

---

[332] *Bristol*, i, p. 43 (1344).
[333] The document refers to 'wolvard', which conjures images of wolves or foxes squabbling among themselves; Alsford, *Towns* (Ipswich, c.37).
[334] *Black Book*, ii, pp. 118–21, c.37 (*c*.1309). A similar arrangement existed in Great Yarmouth to ensure that agreed bargains were fulfilled. Alsford, *Towns* (Great Yarmouth, 1300).

until goods of the agreed quality and quantity were delivered.[335] The risks of a sales contract for moveables, before delivery and afterwards, resided with the possessor. Thus, if an item was damaged before delivery, responsibility lay with the seller.[336]

Warranty can be traced back to the laws attributed to Ine (*c*.688–94), which stated that if any beast sold was found to have a blemish within thirty days of purchase then it could be sent back to the former owner. The law did, however, allow the seller the opportunity of swearing that he knew of no such blemish when he sold the animal, which presumably led to an inquest and presentation of proof.[337] Such cases are presented throughout the medieval period, particularly for horses that had been expressly warranted as sound and healthy but were later found to be sick.[338] There was always the possibility that such beasts had been sold deceitfully rather than mistakenly. Cases of warranty thus often revolved around whether faults had been deliberately hidden or a substandard product falsely substituted, in the manner decried by moral literature. In the Berwick Guild Statutes of 1249, any buyer who discovered his purchase 'to be good above and worse below' could cause the seller to make amends according to the decisions of appointed honest men.[339] In Nottingham, in 1432, Thomas Abbot of Colwick bought malt from Thomas Sharp under the latter's warranty, but the malt proved to be 'rawe reket et cum wevelys spevelled'[340] and the purchaser claimed 20s. damages.[341]

The variable qualities inherent in many medieval commodities made any policy of returnable goods both hazardous and haphazard. A sixteenth-century ordinance aptly summed up the buyer's dilemma that the onus was on them to prove wrongdoing on the part of the vendor. The buyer thus had to 'let their eye be their chapman, for yf it prove nought, thei shall have no remedie for it afterwards except thei can prove the

---

[335] *Fleta*, ii, p. 196, bk. II, c.58 (late thirteenth century); Hall (ed.), *Glanvill*, pp. 129–30, x, 14 (*c*.1187–9); *Black Book*, ii, p. 119, c.37 (*c*.1309); *Leicester*, i, p. 86.

[336] *Fleta*, ii, p. 196, bk. II, c.58 (late thirteenth century).

[337] Attenborough (ed.), *Laws*, pp. 54–5, c.56 (laws of Ine, *c*.688–93). See also *ibid.*, pp. 100–1, c.4 (laws of Alfred and Guthrum, *c*.880–90), pp. 134–5, c.12 (laws of Aethelstan, *c*.925–39).

[338] Thomas (ed.), *Calendar*, p. 68 (Roll C, 1300); Holland (ed.), *Year Books*, pp. 30–2; Thornley (ed.), *Year Book*, pp. 4–5.

[339] Bateson (ed.), *Borough Customs*, ii, p. 182 (Berwick, 1249).

[340] (smoked raw and with weevils spoiled/sprinkled?)

[341] *Nottingham*, ii, pp. 130–3 (1432). For examples of court cases where other such accusations were made regarding the sale of ale, dyes, tiles, cloth, wool, cheese, fish and liquorice, see *Nottingham*, i, pp. 166–7 (1357), 346–9 (1397), ii, pp. 70–3 (1410), 118–21 (1420); *Memorials*, pp. 332–3 (1366), 464 (1382); Gross (ed.), *Select Cases*, pp. 50, 60–1, 91 (St Ives, 1291–3, 1312).

seller thereof dyd warrant the same to be good'.[342] This ordinance summarised a process that was implemented throughout the Middle Ages.
For the buyer to expect any recompense after a transaction, he had to
ensure the seller had warranted the condition of the goods at the time
of sale and attest that this had been witnessed or recorded. If there was
no written statement of obligations of quality, the buyer had to accede
to *caveat emptor*, for the seller was not bound to take back goods if there
was no proof of a breach of contract.[343]

Many of the problems in wholesale trading occurred because of the
increasing use of samples, which the purchaser might subsequently claim
differed qualitatively from the goods actually delivered.[344] The Berwick
ordinances of 1283–4 stated: 'If any one buys goods, misled by false top
samples, amends must be made'.[345] However, it could be difficult to
prove such deception. In Exeter, the seller might claim that any damage or defect that was found after delivery was caused while the goods
were in the buyer's possession. It was the buyer's responsibility to prove
otherwise:

If a man sells to another a beast with a guarantee that it is without a fault, and it
is not so; and if then he denies that he gave that guarantee, the buyer must prove
by his suit that he [the seller] did so; and the other [the seller] must take back
the beast; but the bailiff must have the beast examined to see whether it is true
or not; and the other [the buyer] must swear his sole oath on halidom that the
beast is no worse through him or his keeping nor any negligence of his.[346]

In Grimsby and Ipswich, such disagreements about the quality of goods
were settled by the valuations of 'worthy men' of the town.[347] It is likely
that such inquests favoured locals over strangers, unless strong contract
instruments or witnesses could be produced. These warranty conditions
changed little in the late Middle Ages, and were recited by moralists who
exhorted that traders should not conceal faults in their goods or exaggerate their virtues.[348] The basic constructs of fair dealing and consumer
rights were evident in both literature and legislation.

---

[342] Bateson (ed.), *Borough Customs*, ii, pp. lxxxiii–lxxxiv, 183 (Lancaster, 1562), regarding
the purchase of malt.

[343] *Memorials*, p. 341 (1369).   [344] Gemmill, 'Town and region', p. 63.

[345] Toulmin Smith (ed.), *English Gilds*, p. 342 (Berwick, 1283–4). The London authorities
banned the sale of corn by sample. *CLB*, E, p. 56 (1316); *Liber Albus*, p. 229 (1272–
1307).

[346] Schopp and Easterling (eds.), *Anglo-Norman Custumal*, p. 34, no. 51 (1237–57); Bateson (ed.), *Borough Customs*, ii, pp. 182–3.

[347] *BBC, 1216–1307*, p. 301 (Grimsby, 1258); *Black Book*, ii, pp. 118–21, c.37 (c.1309).

[348] See pp. 75–7.

Credit, debt and trust

Trust and reciprocity were the mainstay of all medieval transactions, as can be seen throughout the regulations and literature already discussed. Markets were important early forums for creating a conducive and orderly commercial environment where commercial confidences could evolve. The assurance of standard weights and measures, customary bargaining procedures, acceptable coinage, quality standards and enforcement procedures raised the level of trust to a workable level. Social ideology and personal networks then reinforced this establishment of trust. As seen in the literature, the bargaining process consisted of a myriad of customs and minute gestures that were often taken for granted by participants. Nevertheless, certain acts were performed to establish a level of good faith, from amicable greetings to a handclasp. By establishing a degree of trust, transaction costs were lowered and future alliances could be created. If the buyer lacked certain vital information about a product, it is likely that his focus then switched to the vendor and his reputation. The potential impact of a bad reputation can be seen in cases of slander. In Colchester, in 1310, Hugh de Stowe used 'litigious and opprobrious language against several persons in the market', thus costing them sales and purchases. Similarly, in Alverthorpe (Yorkshire) in 1307, William de Wakefeud recited how the slander of Thomas Brounsmyth and his wife, in calling him a false, faithless man and a thief, and then raising the hue and cry, had cost him credit and a wine deal with Walter Gowere. The 'scandal and infamy' had come to Walter's attention and he refused to have any more dealings with William.[349]

Medieval society had several formal instruments to establish levels of probity, such as taking office, oaths and guild or burgess membership. Also, the use of a mark as a means of supervision developed associations with reputation and identification.[350] Every tiler in Worcester had to set a proper mark upon their tiles, so 'yf it be defectif or smalle, that men may have remedy of the seid partie, as law and resonne requirith'.[351] Initially devised as a means of inspection and control, merchant marks became signs of quality assurance and trust.

The early fourteenth-century custumal of Ipswich provides evidence that authorities understood the crucial part reputation played in the marketplace. One of the ordinances actually outlined procedures for

---

[349] Jeayes (ed.), *Court Rolls*, i, p. 13 (1310); Baildon (ed.), *Court Rolls*, ii, p. 110 (1307). See also Gross (ed.), *Select Cases*, pp. 57, 71 (St Ives, 1293).

[350] *Coventry*, p. 338 (1468); *Memorials*, pp. 360 (1371), 361 (1372), 569–70 (1408); *CLB*, K, p. 114 (1429–30).

[351] Toulmin Smith (ed.), *English Gilds*, p. 399 (Worcester, 1467).

claiming damages if anyone was falsely or maliciously slandered by another in the public marketplace with accusations of theft, robbery, treason or deceit ('falshed').[352] The Ipswich authorities also recognised the need for confidence in their own regulations in order to enforce contracts and payments expeditiously. Another ordinance stressed that those who failed to make payments on time were regarded as 'of eyl feith' and motivated by covetousness. Their actions served not only to bring the individual into disrepute but were also to the slander of the whole community, to the disadvantage of all.[353] If the usual mechanisms of enforcement failed, Ipswich's authorities were prepared to distrain or disenfranchise the offending burgess until he provided recompense. The need for reputation, trust and prestige was therefore important for trading success, social standing and the extension of credit.[354] An ordinance for Northampton, c.1260, stated that anyone giving credit at a fair should first 'find out how the borrower left his last creditor'.[355] In *La Court de Baron*, a court precedent outlined how a buyer's bargain for wine had been undermined by the interference of a third party who spoke 'much ill and villany of him to the merchant'. Consequently, the merchant 'told him right out that he heard tell so much evil of him that he would give him no credit' and the potential buyer returned home empty-handed.[356]

The use of credit in medieval trade was widespread and usually existed in the form of a postponement in payment for merchandise already delivered. Traders often needed to complete other transactions before ready money was available or, alternatively, they might not have wanted to unnecessarily carry round large amounts of coinage. At a petty level, many transactions between locals were conducted on a credit system, whereby their credits and debts were accounted at periodic intervals. For instance, London bakers regularly advanced credit to female regraters, though a late thirteenth-century ordinance prohibited a baker from giving credit 'as long as he shall know such woman to be in debt unto his neighbour'.[357] Poor artisans might also offer goods in exchange for victuals, or as surety for later payment.[358] The system of trade credit, akin to contracts, employed various levels of 'recognition', from a written recognisance to the split tallystick, but witnesses remained an important form of proof when many smaller credit transactions employed no visible devices. The Ipswich ordinances stated that because many credit

---

[352] *Black Book*, ii, pp. 162–5, c.73 [70] (c.1309).   [353] *Ibid.*, pp. 114–19, c.36 (c.1309).
[354] McIntosh, *Controlling*, pp. 11–12.
[355] *Northampton*, i, p. 227 (c.1260); Bateson (ed.), *Borough Customs*, i, p. 209.
[356] Maitland and Baildon (eds.), *Court Baron*, 'La Court de Baron', pp. 40–1 (thirteenth century).
[357] *Liber Albus*, p. 309 (1272–1307).   [358] *Black Book*, ii, pp. 132–5, c.47 (c.1309).

transactions were only for the day, traders, for the sake of convenience, often did not employ tallies or written records. In these cases, proof was through examination of two sworn witnesses.[359]

Nevertheless, the effective enforcement of credit agreements was of utmost importance to a trading community, both in terms of realised payments and speedy proceedings. Capital could all too easily become locked up in unpaid debts and the reputation of a market damaged. Resident traders who purchased corn in Norwich market were ordered to make swift payment to satisfy the vendor, 'so that the countrymen may not be put off nor hindered in receiving their payment and doing their business'.[360] In London, it was petitioned that no butchers should sell their wares in the 'Stokkes', if they had previously failed in making payments 'to the bad repute of the trade', until they had fully paid up all arrears.[361] The concern of the regulations was that repayment to creditors should not be delayed, whatever the value of the debt. In hundred courts, as well as the courts of freemen, pleas of trespass and debt could be pleaded without a royal writ, provided the goods or debt did not exceed 40s. in value.[362] But the regulations of Hereford in 1486 demonstrated the concerns of creditors about speedy and inexpensive recoveries of debts, stating that they should not need to go out of the city to recover debts over 40s., 'for divers dangers and misfortunes which might happen to our wives and children; and if we ought to spend our goods and chattels in parts afar off, by impleading and labouring for that by that means and the like, we shall be impoverished; and being made poor, we shall not have wherewith to keep the city, and so disheritance by such ways would easily fall upon our children'.[363]

Merchant Law

Merchant Law ('Lex Mercatoria') was a varied body of mercantile procedures, principles and modes of proof that began to develop into a uniform

---

[359] *Ibid.*, ii, pp. 105–9, c.33 (*c.*1309).

[360] *Norwich*, i, pp. 186–7 (early fourteenth century). A similar ordinance was issued in London that resident cornmongers and butchers who delayed payment by deceptions were to pay double to the vendor or else face the pillory. *Liber Albus*, pp. 229–30 (1272–1307).

[361] *Memorials*, pp. 179–80 (1331). See also Johnson (ed.), *Hereford*, p. 27; *BBC, 1216–1307*, p. 292 (Grimsby, 1258).

[362] *Britton*, i, p. 155, ch. 29, c.1 (1291–2); Beckerman, 'Forty-shilling'. The 'hundred' was a unit of local government (between the vill and the county).

[363] Bateson (ed.), *Borough Customs*, i, p. 207 (Hereford, 1486). The regulations for Torksey also suggested that their piepowder court had cognisance of pleas 'both exceeding 40s. and of less amount'. *Ibid.*, ii, pp. 189–90 (Torksey, *c.*1345).

code across Europe by the twelfth and thirteenth centuries, especially regarding debt and contract.[364] This commercial law was important in defining sales, the procedures of debt litigation and the nature of contractual obligations. It was applicable in various commercial scenarios where the borough customs allowed it and in staple courts and piepowder courts (usually held in fairs or markets).[365] It also had an increasing influence on general legislation concerning conduct, contract and pleas, even where common law applied. In particular, Merchant Law defined a system of quick justice that aptly suited the itinerant lifestyle of most traders, offering advantages over common law in its speed and effective distraint for recovery of a debt. For instance, in a piepowder court, no writ was needed for proceedings, few 'essoins' (excuses) were permitted and the whole process was expected to be concluded within a day or two. The piepowder courts in Torksey, Ipswich and Rye were held twice a day 'and from day to day'.[366] In early fourteenth-century Ipswich, three essoins were allowed to each party, while in fifteenth-century Colchester a defendant might be summoned five times during a single day before they defaulted.[367] Distraint was a temporary confiscation of goods and could be taken from a debtor in order to compel him to appear. A defendant's goods ('attachment') could be appraised and sold in order to satisfy a creditor. Not only could a defendant be impleaded quickly, but, by declaring that a contract had been made 'in the market' and was thus subject to 'Merchant Law', a trader could prevent his adversary from using compurgation and could plead in a court other than the neighbourhood in which the deed was done.[368]

Supplementary to Merchant Law, parliamentary legislation of 1283 at Acton Burnell (*Statutum de Mercatoribus*) provided regulations to encourage the speedy recovery of debts, stimulated by the needs of an

---

[364] Mitchell, *An Essay*, pp. 104–5. A treatise on Merchant Law ('Lex Mercatoria') was included in Bristol's *Little Red Book*, suggesting it was applied regularly. *Bristol*, i, pp. 57–85 (fourteenth century).

[365] They were called 'piepowder courts' because they were supposedly frequented by itinerant chapmen with dusty feet ('pieds poudres'). Gross (ed.), *Select Cases*, pp. xiii–xiv; Bateson (ed.), *Borough Customs*, ii, p. 184. Piepowder courts were often held during fairs when a large congregation of visiting traders was expected. This was recognised by statute law. *Statutes*, ii, pp. 461–2, 17 Edw IV c.2 (1477–8); ii, pp. 482–3, 1 Ric III c.6 (1483–4).

[366] Bateson (ed.), *Borough Customs*, ii, pp. 189–90, 192 (Torksey, *c*.1345; Rye, fifteenth century); *Black Book*, ii, pp. 22–5, c.1 (*c*.1309).

[367] Gross (ed.), *Select Cases*, pp. xxvi, 122–5 (1458).

[368] Bateson (ed.), *Borough Customs*, ii, pp. 188–9 (Norwich, 1306–11); *Norwich*, i, pp. 169–70 (early fourteenth century); *Black Book*, ii, pp. 126–7, c.40 (*c*.1309).

expanding economy.[369] By this law, debts were to be entered as recognisances in town rolls and sealed by both the debtor and the king's seal, with a bill obligatory given to the creditor. Such a procedure provided surety for the debt and ensured unassailable proof for repayment. Goods could be seized from recalcitrant debtors to repay the debt, or they could be imprisoned until agreement was reached. Pledges could also be used as surety for the debtor and they were liable if the debt was not paid or if the defendant failed to appear.[370] Although this legislation was primarily intended for the use of wholesaling or foreign merchants in larger towns, similar procedures and methods of surety were adopted throughout the commercial community, largely based upon the principles of 'Merchant Law'.

Several town ordinances thus outlined the standard regulations and procedures for bringing a debtor to court and recovering the debt. Reasonable time was to be allowed to a trader if he was not in the town at the time of the suit, but only a certain number of excuses or 'essoins' were tolerated. An essoin could not be made after one of the parties had defaulted and false essoins led them to lose the plea. Distraint took place after he had been called the required number of times and failed to appear and the seized goods ('attachment') were appraised in value by the bailiffs or appointed assessors. Assessors were warned not to collude in appraising goods at a higher value than they were worth, or else they themselves might be obliged to buy the goods at the price they had set. Such attachments could be taken throughout the case to encourage the defendant's appearance.[371] Distraint or 'distress' thus provided the main element of enforcement. If a debtor defaulted in repayment or was attainted, the chattels could be sold and the proceeds given to the plaintiff to the value of the debt.[372] If the debt was impleaded under common law, then the defendant could clear his name by waging his law (compurgation) or an inquest by jury, but compurgation was not normally an option

---

[369] *Statutes*, i, pp. 53–4, 11 Edw I (1283). It was confirmed and re-elaborated in *Statutes*, i, pp. 98–100, 13 Edw I (1285); *Fleta*, ii, pp. 212–14, bk. II, c.64 (late thirteenth century). In 1311, it was ordered that the 'Statute of Acton Burnell' should only apply to debts between merchants and that recognisances should be witnessed by four men. The seal of the king was available only at London and the main provincial towns of Newcastle-upon-Tyne, Nottingham, York, Exeter, Bristol, Southampton, Lincoln, Northampton, Canterbury, Shrewsbury and Norwich. *Statutes*, i, p. 165, 5 Edw II c.33 (1311). For an in-depth study regarding these debt-repayment mechanisms in Coventry, see Goddard, *Lordship and Medieval Urbanisation*, pp. 256–76.

[370] See also Bateson (ed.), *Borough Customs*, ii, p. 191 (Torksey, *c*.1345); *Norwich*, i, pp. 169–70 (early fourteenth century?).

[371] *Britton*, i, pp. 155–77, ch. 29 (1291–2).

[372] *Black Book*, ii, pp. 104–13, cc.33–4 (*c*.1309); Bateson (ed.), *Borough Customs*, ii, pp. 189–92 (Norwich, *c*.1340; Torksey, *c*.1345; Hereford, 1486); *Bristol*, i, p. 35 (1344).

under Merchant Law when either witnesses, a valid credit instrument, or an inquest was used. If a plaintiff withdrew his plea then he usually incurred a fine. Also, both parties could obtain a 'licence of concord' for a small fee, which allowed them to withdraw from court and privately agree on a settlement.[373]

Although Merchant Law sometimes expedited the process, debt cases more generally could take several months, especially for residents of a town and the neighbouring countryside. Burgesses might be allowed more leeway within their borough regarding level of proof needed for a debt, taking distraint on their own initiative, their excuses for delay and the time allowed to repay a proved debt.[374] If the plaintiffs were outsiders (whether foreigners or travelling traders), then more rigorous and speedy efforts were usually applied, since they could not wait around for lengthy processes of distraint. In Ipswich, anyone who delayed the rightful execution of distraint, perhaps by locking up his goods in a house so that bailiffs could not get at them, was to have his house blockaded until satisfaction was made.[375] The authorities obviously took the enforcement of contracts and debts seriously.

The system of 'withernam' operated for much of the late medieval period. This privilege was often enshrined in borough charters and allowed officials to enforce the repayment of a debt from a recalcitrant foreign merchant who had left the town, by seizing goods from another merchant from the same town. If the debtor still did not appear to respond to the plaintiff, then the attached goods were given to the creditor. The distrained merchant was expected to take on the burden and seek repayment in his own courts against the original debtor.[376] In effect, one town was requesting the corporate distraint of a debtor in another town. The customs of Romney in 1352 outlined a fuller procedure whereby letters were firstly sent to the debtor's home town, then a fellow merchant was sworn to let his mayor and bailiffs know about the need to recover the debt. If this produced no result, then finally withernam was taken on

[373] See below, pp. 356–7, for a discussion of these devices in the courts of Newmarket and Clare.
[374] Bateson (ed.), *Borough Customs*, i, pp. 111–13 (Wearmouth, 1154–95; Pontefract, 1194; Egremont, 1200; Chester, 1181–1232; Salford, c.1230; Ipswich, 1291; Winchester, c.1280; Manchester, 1301; Bury, 1327); Furley (ed.), *Ancient Usages*, pp. 38–9, 44–5 (late thirteenth century); Hill, *Medieval Lincoln*, appx VII (c.1300); *Black Book*, ii, pp. 128–9, c.43 (c.1309); *Norwich*, i, pp. 166–7 (early fourteenth century?); Myers (ed.), *English Historical Documents*, pp. 569–70 (Canterbury, c.1430).
[375] *Black Book*, ii, pp. 108–13, c.34 (c.1309). See also Bateson (ed.), *Borough Customs*, i, pp. 187–91 (Bristol, 1344; Southampton, 1348; Norwich, c.1340; Hereford, 1486).
[376] *BBC, 1042–1216*, p. 196 (Bristol, 1188); Bateson (ed.), *Borough Customs*, i, pp. 117–18 (Exeter, 1237–57), 120 (Bristol, 1188; Colchester, 1189), 125 (Dover, fifteenth century); Hill, *Medieval Lincoln*, appx VII (c.1300).

the next merchant from the said town.[377] Foreign traders thus faced the possibility of distraint due to the actions of a fellow burgess for whom they might owe no personal allegiance. The ordinances for Leicester in 1273 made provision for such burgesses who travelled to other market towns and were distrained for the debt of their neighbour. The bailiffs would warn the debtor to make compensation or else their house would be closed up until satisfaction was made.[378] However, in late thirteenth-century statutes, law manuals and some municipal charters, there were concerns about strangers being distrained when they were neither the debtor nor pledge.[379] Although elements of withernam survived beyond the thirteenth century, there was a growing suggestion that it was not advantageous to commercial prosperity nor to the encouragement of credit.

Femme sole

One associated feature of Merchant Law, and its development at a local level, was that it meant women or children below age who traded or kept shops for the sale of goods were liable for actions of debt.[380] In certain boroughs, married women who traded publicly could plead and be impleaded alone, without the husband's involvement. According to common law, husbands were guardians of the family's land and possessions and their legal representative in court. A woman married to a freeman in London (*femme couverte*) was generally in legal thrall to her husband. However, from around the beginning of the fourteenth century, wives could also follow a trade and be responsible herself for all debts (*femme sole*).[381] She could make contracts without her husband's approval and represent herself in court. This status of *femme sole* proved beneficial for women who needed to obtain or advance credit in their business. However, there were cases where the potential ambiguities of this status and household economics could have repercussions. In 1305, Mabel le Heymogger tried to avoid a debt of 13s. 10d. for beer purchased by disavowing *femme sole* status and arguing that her husband should have been

---

[377] Bateson (ed.), *Borough Customs*, i, pp. 121–4 (Romney, 1352). For a similar letter, and cases where withernam was taken, see *CLB*, c, pp. 59, 64, 76 (1299–1300), e, p. 42 (1314–15).

[378] *Leicester*, i, p. 114 (1273).

[379] *Statutes*, i, pp. 26–34, 3 Edw I c.23, 'Statute of Westminster' (1275); *Fleta*, ii, pp. 209–12, bk. II, c.63 (late thirteenth century).

[380] Bateson (ed.), *Borough Customs*, i, pp. 222–8 (especially London, 1419, Worcester, 1467, Lincoln, 1480).

[381] Barron, 'The "golden age" of women', 37; McIntosh, 'The benefits and drawbacks of *femme sole*'.

named in the debt plea. The plaintiff, Gilbert le Brasour, argued that she kept an inn and traded 'sole' in hay and oats.[382] It does appear that Mabel was deliberately exploiting the confusion around her legal status, though the court eventually found against her.

However, the potential for women to have independent access to credit could be regarded as beneficial to production and investment in the medieval economy, and forms of *femme sole* were certainly adopted in other boroughs across England.[383] For example, married female traders in fourteenth-century Torksey could also answer, or be answered, in a case of debt or broken contract without the presence of their husband.[384] Women identified as regular traders could thus plead as *femme sole* and act in court independently, while the goods of her husband could not be attached. However, McIntosh has argued that *femme sole* status was perhaps less popular than might be expected, and women were making active choices about whether to declare themselves or not. The apparent benefits of legal separation from their husband had to be weighed against the disadvantages of cutting themselves off from their best source of support, paying a fee to declare their status, possibly undermining their husband's credit, and representing themselves in a male-dominated court. Indeed, *femme sole* might have been most desirable when the husband was financially insecure.[385]

In addition, opportunities for women to claim unpaid debts or to be impleaded could be still circumscribed by their legal status and were also dependent on local customs. The fifteenth-century customs for Fordwich recognised that many women acted as professional traders, particularly in victuals and cloth, and such active traders could act as a plaintiff in a plea of debt, unlike most married women. However, they had to be accompanied by their husbands. If a woman trader was the defendant in a debt case, then it was left to the discretion of the plaintiff whether the husband should be present as well.[386] The ability of a wife to have independent agency as a trader thus varied between borough customs. In pre-Black Death Norwich, a husband was liable for his wife's transactions, unless they were no longer cohabiting. However, in this situation, creditors were to take heed in lending to women 'save at their own peril

---

[382] Thomas (ed.), *Calendar*, pp. 214–15 (Roll G, 1305). See also Bateson (ed.), *Borough Customs*, i, p. 227 (London, 1419). For further discussion of this case, see McIntosh, 'The benefits and drawbacks of *femme sole*', 419–20.

[383] McIntosh, 'The benefits and drawbacks of *femme sole*', 413; Lacey, 'Women and work', pp. 41–5.

[384] Bateson (ed.), *Borough Customs*, i, pp. 227–8 (Torksey, *c*.1345; Hastings, 1461–83; Lincoln, 1480).

[385] McIntosh, 'The benefits and drawbacks of *femme sole*', 426–7, 430.

[386] Bateson (ed.), *Borough Customs*, i, p. 228 (Fordwich, fifteenth century).

only'.[387] The creditworthiness of women was thus questioned. Although it could be argued that *femme sole* reflected an easing of this perception in some towns by the fifteenth century, the fact that many women preferred to remain *femme couverte* suggests that little had changed in this patriarchal society, for better or worse.

Usury

Many debt settlements provided for extra payment of 'damages'. Such provision is perhaps understandable in a commercial environment where sellers needed to ensure that their ability to offer credit was not abused and so they could claim recompense when it was. Damages were brought into action when a borrower failed to repay by a stipulated date, and this was considered to be a legitimate gain due to the inconvenience caused to the lender.[388] The use of damages evaded direct accusations of usury, since creditors were being compensated for a loss; in effect, they were unable to put the unpaid money towards another business opportunity. It could be argued that damages were a tangled means to hide illicit interest and thus avoid accusations of usury, but they were only claimed upon defaulted debts and were assessed by the court, so they did not guarantee a financial return to the creditor.[389]

Laws against usury highlighted it as a disreputable vice and deception, committed by people who did not fear God or even worldly shame. When Edward I expelled the Jews from England in 1290, he justified the action by accusing them of having 'wickedly conspired and conceived a new species of usury more pernicious than the old', while usurers more generally were described as greedy, wicked and depraved.[390] Usurers were expected to make restitution for their sin and were to be compelled by Church and state to do so. It appears that medieval people did take the accusation seriously. For John de Miggeley in Wakefield, in 1274, simply being called a usurer was enough for him to take his accuser to court for slander.[391] From 1363–4, the London authorities decided that convicted usurers should perform a quasi-penitential humiliation: 'they shall forswear the said city for ever, and shall be led through the City, with their heads uncovered, unshod and without girdle, upon horses without saddles'.[392] A parliamentary petition in 1376 wanted similar punishments across England, arguing that usurious activities had caused the virtue of

---

[387] *Norwich*, i, pp. 167–8 (early fourteenth century?).
[388] A London ordinance of 1345 stipulated damages for debts at a rate of 4s. for every 20s. withheld for one year. *Liber Albus*, pp. 404–5 (1345); *CLB*, F, p. 127 (1345).
[389] See pp. 365–7.   [390] Seabourne, *Royal Regulation*, p. 60.
[391] Baildon (ed.), *Court Rolls*, i, p. 80.   [392] *Liber Albus*, pp. 318–21 (1364).

charity to perish and brought many to poverty, thus drawing upon literary condemnations of the sin.[393] However, Richard II was unprepared
to extend such heightened secular jurisdiction outside London and the
status quo was maintained.[394]

Usurers were prosecuted by both Church and state, and it is known that
cases were brought before Church courts, royal courts, manorial courts
and the view of frankpledge.[395] It should be noted that there are relatively
few mentions of usury in borough custumals and ordinances. There
were numerous disputes over jurisdiction between the clergy and royal
justices, but it appears that the Church maintained overall jurisdiction
over usurers through their ecclesiastical courts.[396] Indeed, a statute of
1341 ordained that the king should have cognisance of usurers who had
died and the Church the right to censure living usurers.[397] The Church
and king appear to have regarded suppression of usury as an important
part of their obligations.

The extent to which usury legislation affected the flow of credit is
debatable, especially in the commercial arena as opposed to consumption
loans.[398] Credit was essential for lubricating the late medieval economy
and some form of profit was presumably needed to encourage lenders.
Historians have argued that, during the thirteenth century, the definition
of usury was narrowed so that only exorbitant rates of interest were
deemed to be sinful.[399] It appears that the Church's stance on usury
was circumvented through exploiting a variety of technical loopholes.
However, Gwen Seabourne's study of usury cases in royal courts suggests
that there was no exemption for minor profits on money loans or in sales
on credit. The usury ban appears to have been absolute, at least in those
cases that went to court.[400] A caveat is needed in that relatively few cases
appear to have actually proceeded through Church and secular courts,
while many cases were settled informally. The Church mostly dealt with
manifest usurers and rarely prosecuted moderate usury. More emphasis

---

[393] *RP*, ii, p. 350; *Parl. Rolls*, c.59, October 1382; Thrupp, *Merchant Class*, p. 175. For
a detailed discussion of the secular laws and enforcement of usury, see Seabourne,
Royal Regulation, pp. 25–69, 169–81, 185–92; Seabourne, 'Controlling commercial
morality'.

[394] Seabourne, *Royal Regulation*, pp. 48–9.

[395] *Ibid.*, pp. 49–55, 185–9; Hilton, *English Peasantry*, pp. 46–7, 103–4; Wood, *Medieval
Economic Thought*, p. 184. For cases involving usury, see *ibid.*, pp. 339–45 (fourteenth
century); *Norwich*, i, p. 368 (1290); Baildon (ed.), *Court Rolls*, i, p. 174 (1277); Walker
(ed.), *Court Rolls*, v, p. 160; Jewell (ed.), *Court Rolls*, p. 115 (1349).

[396] Seabourne, *Royal Regulation*, pp. 44–9.

[397] *Statutes*, i, p. 296, 15 Edw III St.1 c.5 (1341).

[398] Wood, 'Lesyng of tyme', pp. 113–14; Noonan, *Scholastic Analysis*.

[399] Gilchrist, *Church and Economic Activity*, pp. 67–70.

[400] Seabourne, *Royal Regulation*, pp. 32–4.

was assigned to the role of the priests in the confessional, while it could be argued that communities wanted to protect certain sources of credit provided at moderate rates. Clerical texts thus emphasised the risks and potential losses involved in transactions as a means to justify claims for compensation in moneylending.[401] Nevertheless, it is difficult to discern through the extant sources whether there was a growing leniency towards moneylending in practice. Ultimately, lenders still had to hide interest charges to avoid potentially damaging accusations of usury.[402]

Quality and fraud

A vital element in the contract and bargaining process was the assessment of quality in a product. The quality of wholesale commodities like wool, grain and cloth was graded and priced by recognised criteria. These included thickness, colour, uniformity, aestheticism, size, feel and so on; some were measurable and others were dependent upon personal assessment and opinion. The arbitrary nature of some of these criteria was alleviated by implementing quality categories, for example, best, second-best and standard for grain. But, on the whole, it was traders themselves who judged the quality of many products and offered a price based on these considerations. For retail consumers, an awareness of quality-control was also important: the lack of standardised output in the late Middle Ages multiplied the types and grades of goods available, as well as the number of non-standard or defective goods in a batch. In staple products, particularly foodstuffs, a consumer's concerns about quality were protected to a certain extent by market authorities. Officials would survey samples as a means of quality-control, and regulations outlined punishments for those that strayed from minimum standards. Additionally, although customers were partially constrained by communal price-fixing, many goods were available in a range of qualities. The consumer sometimes had the option to purchase lower-quality goods for a lower price.

Those working in the main manufacturing industries, such as in cloth and leather, needed to maintain a minimum quality for their products in order to encourage purchasers. Even if weights and measures, coinage and prices were increasingly standardised, the variations in quality caused by irregular manufacturing processes still made the transaction process complex. Also, many consumers may have lacked the necessary knowledge to detect low quality or even fraud. In the fourteenth and fifteenth

[401] Helmholz, 'Usury'; Poos (ed.), *Lower Ecclesiastical Jurisdiction*, p. 102.
[402] Nightingale, 'Money and credit', pp. 51–2.

centuries, craft guilds were expected to maintain high standards of work-manship and purity of goods, as defined in their ordinances. For instance, the ordinances of the craft guilds of Bristol, in 1346, highlighted a great concern for quality, in both the production process and materials used.[403] One ordinance for cloth in Bristol was enacted 'to the intent that good and true cloth shall be made in the town, as well for the preservation of the good fame of the same as for the profit which they shall take on the sale of their cloth'.[404]

The cloth industry particularly evoked detailed ordinances regarding the density of thread and the consistency of cloth and any defective cloths or equipment were to be burned. Craftwork was not to be carried out at night, since this might mean shoddy workmanship and that they were less able to be supervised.[405] Roger Hoveden, in 1197, warned against merchants who hung black or red cloths in their windows 'whereby the buyers' eyes are often deceived in the choice of good cloth'.[406] Many municipal court cases highlighted the damage caused by manufacturing frauds, employing the language of moral anxiety. In fourteenth-century Leicester, two weavers, William Martin and Janin French, were placed in the pillory 'for the falsity which people talk of and speak of, which was used in the craft concerning long thrums and concerning bad yarn which was prejudicial to the craft'.[407] In early sixteenth-century Norwich, weavers were accused of selling defective worsted in secret, and their deceptions had caused 'unyuersall hurte of the comen peple and great hurt of the said crafte'.[408] The fullers of Coventry were warned against 'open ffalshed' that brought shame to the craft, particularly the 'draweng out of kerseys and brode cloth to the gret dyssete of the werers and the high displesure of God'.[409] Guilds equated a high level of workmanship and fineness of materials with quality, morality and reputation.

During the fifteenth century, craft guilds had established relatively rigid identities, complete with elaborate rules of membership, manu-facture and business. Their members were increasingly subject to strict disciplinary procedures, while the use of journeymen and apprentices was controlled. Swanson has downplayed the economic influence of guilds

---

[403] *Bristol*, ii, pp. 2–14 (fourteenth century).   [404] *Ibid.*, ii, p. 40 (fourteenth century).

[405] Furley (ed.), *Ancient Usages*, pp. 30–1, nos. 20–1 (late thirteenth century); *York*, i, pp. 105 (1538), 181 (1307); *Bristol*, ii, p. 3 (1346?); Riley (ed.), *Munimenta Gildhallae*, ii, 'Liber Custumarum', p. 101 (1269–70); *Memorials*, pp. 226–7 (1345), 239 (1347), 243 (1348), 538 (1394).

[406] 'Assize of Measures', Stubbs (ed.), *Chronica*, iv, p. 33.

[407] *Leicester*, ii, pp. 195–6 (1379–80). 'Thrums' were the waste ends of warp after the cloth was woven.

[408] *Norwich*, ii, pp. 378 (1511), 108–9 (1512).   [409] *Coventry*, pp. 660–1 (1518).

to establish monopolies and control prices for their own interests. How-ever, craft guilds did not operate to meet the concerns of consumers; they policed their members in order to uphold the reputation of their craft and protect their own prosperity. Guild members were the ones who drew up regulations for their trade and then petitioned the munici-pal government. These rules might appear to be public-minded, but they were mostly a protection of their own standards and reputation, often to the exclusion of lesser practitioners. Thrupp has suggested that guilds did not have the economic power to raise prices through cartel agreements or suppression of local competitors. Yet, statutes in 1437 and 1504 both expressed suspicion that guilds were using their ordinances to raise prices 'for their singular profit and common damage to the people'.[410] Addition-ally, guilds almost certainly fixed the wages of journeymen and enforced strict discipline within their ranks, which allowed a high level of con-trol over manufacturing processes and standards. They did not eliminate competition, particularly from rural areas, but they could limit its scope within their own jurisdiction and use indirect means to achieve price rises. The 1381 ordinances of the dyers and fullers in Bristol ordered that no woollen thread should be sent out of the town to be woven else-where, on pain of forfeiture of the cloth, showing official attempts to keep a monopoly of business within the town.[411] Equally, no Bristol fuller was to receive cloth that had been fulled outside the town.[412]

Guilds became tools of quality assurance, monitoring each stage of pro-duction and providing a mark of guaranteed quality. Increased demands for production quality during the adverse economic conditions of the fif-teenth century were allied with ordinances to restrict entry and appren-ticeship. In Winchester, the supervision of weaving was tightened in 1408 because of complaints against unskilled workmen who were considered to be harming the reputation of the city's cloth.[413] Through their ordi-nances, manufacturing guilds recognised the existence of low-quality goods and low-skilled substitutes within their towns and sought to stamp them out. It is possible that guild quality-controls meant that certain entrepreneurs could no longer compete in the larger towns and were thus driven towards smaller towns and villages. Certainly, both town and guild regulations firstly looked to protect burgesses and guild members against outsiders. Quality-controls could thus be seen an indirect means to oust competition.

---

[410] Thrupp, 'Gilds', pp. 231, 247–9; Lipson, *Economic History*, i, pp. 418–22; *Statutes*, ii, pp. 298–9, 15 Hen VI c.6 (1437); ii, pp. 652–3, 19 Hen VII c.7 (1504).
[411] *Bristol*, ii, pp. 7–8 (1381).   [412] *Ibid.*, ii, pp. 15–16 (1340s).
[413] Keene, *Survey*, i, p. 302.

The corollary of higher quality and standardisation was elevated prices. Controlling the level of output in certain crafts similarly kept prices up.[414] Those who produced low-quality goods (with low amounts of capital) for the poorer sections of society were pushed to the margins and this reduction in choice cannot be seen as beneficial to the poor. Those who gained most were the guildsmen and richer members of society, who were, in turn, their town's officials and legislators. Small towns, with more relaxed or non-existent guild controls, may have been able to offer lower-quality goods at commensurate lower prices and probably attracted local peasant consumers. Similarly, the well-attested movement of cloth industries into rural or smaller urban areas in the late fourteenth and fifteenth centuries might well have been linked to the avoidance of guild restrictions in large towns. Away from large boroughs, entrepreneurial clothiers could employ workers and manufacturing techniques of their own choosing and produce cloths which were perhaps more varied.[415]

Numerous statutes outlined the strict measurements and 'aulnage' procedures for the assize of cloth.[416] However, on occasions after the Black Death, compromises were made that allowed cloths of various measurements to be sold to poorer customers, even if the material did not conform to the precise stipulations of law.[417] Over time, the assize of cloth was considered mainly applicable to cloth of ray and colour, with other cloths like 'cogware' and 'kendal' being too low in standard to be aulnaged. There was recognition of the need to provide a choice of goods for those too poor to afford high-quality products.[418] Undoubtedly, a high standard of cloth was still demanded by the international market, but, in England, the home market required a greater balance of choice, quality and convenience.

It is possible that many medieval goods were shoddy and lightweight, particularly goods sold by pedlars and small-town traders for everyday use at the lower end of the market range. Few everyday artefacts have survived, perhaps distorting our view of medieval handicraft in favour

---

[414] See also Veale, *English Fur Trade*, pp. 123–5, 131–2.

[415] Carus-Wilson, 'Evidences of industrial growth', 203–4; Bolton, *Medieval English Economy*, pp. 252–3.

[416] *Statutes*, i, p. 233, Edw I?, 'Articles of the Eyre'; i, p. 260, 2 Edw III c.14, 'Statute of Northampton' (1328); i, p. 314, 25 Edw III st.3 c.1 (1350–1).

[417] *Ibid.*, i, pp. 330–1, 27 Edw III st.1 c.4 (1353); i, p. 395, 47 Edw III (1373); ii, p. 88, 17 Ric II c.2 (1393–4); ii, pp. 153–4, 7 Hen IV cc.9–10 (1405–6); ii, p. 159, 9 Hen IV c.2 (1407); ii, p. 160, 9 Hen IV c.5 (1407); ii, p. 163–5, 11 Hen IV c.6 (1409–10); ii, p. 168, 13 Hen IV c.4 (1411); ii, pp. 403–14, 4 Edw IV (1464–5); ii, pp. 418–22, 7 Edw IV (1467).

[418] *Ibid.*, ii, p. 64, 13 Ric II st.1 c.10 (1389–90); ii, p. 119, 1 Hen IV c.19 (1399).

of the high-quality, expensive goods which are extant. Central legislation itself was not excessively concerned with standards of production,
except where they concerned public welfare or basic foodstuffs. However,
cloth-makers, goldsmiths and shoe-makers all received statutory sanctions during the later Middle Ages based upon methods and deceits that
were considered to be damaging to the 'common people'. For instance,
cloth-makers were accused of subtly concealing the nature of substandard cloths through tacking and folding, and then bribing the aulnager
to put their seal upon them 'in great deceit of the people and mischief
to the said buyers'.[419] Similarly, the cordwainers of Bristol (1408) were
disparaged for using 'false leathers, disloyally tanned or curried, called
sole-leather or over-leather' in making their shoes and boots, and faced
fines of 6s. 8d. for such deceit.[420] In 1403–4, a statute of Henry IV warned
against fraudulent artificers 'imagining to deceive the common people',
who made locks, rings, beads, candlesticks, harnesses, powder-boxes and
covers of copper and latten, and then overgilted them to look like gold or
silver.[421] The spicers of Nottingham not only used unusual weights but
also mixed old spices with new; while those of London were also accused
of moistening their ginger and saffron in order to increase their weight.[422]
Unavoidable quality variations inherent in medieval goods were thus supplemented by worries of flagrant fraud. It is likely that the two overlapped,
especially when traders attempted to pass low-quality goods off as of a
higher standard.

   Guild ordinances frequently mention the harm caused by both substandard manufacturing techniques and those who tried to cheat customers. They were couched in terms of disgracing both the craft and the
community, with the implication that a damaged reputation was disastrous for business. The Bristol crafts often used moral rhetoric in substan-
tiating their ordinances. The 1408 ordinance for skinners, for example,
stated: 'whereas through evil persons knowing nothing of their craft the
good people of the town and country are badly served and aggrieved to

---

[419] *Ibid.*, ii, pp. 13–14, 3 Ric II c.2 (1379–80); ii, pp. 33–4, 7 Ric II c.9 (1383); ii, p. 64, 13 Ric II st.1 c.11 (1389–90).

[420] *Bristol*, ii, pp. 101–17 (1408 and 1415). See also Thomas (ed.), *Calendar*, pp. 5 (Roll A, 1298), 154 (Roll F, 1303–4); *Memorials*, pp. 135–6 (1320), 364–5 (1372), 391–2 (1375), 420–1 (1378), 571–4 (1409); BL, MS Lansdowne 796, fol. 7r (late fifteenth century); *Northampton*, i, p. 374 (late fifteenth century).

[421] *Statutes*, ii, pp. 146–7, 5 Hen IV c.13 (1403–4). See also *ibid.*, ii, p. 221, 2 Hen VI c.10 (1423); *Memorials*, pp. 118 (1316), 337–8 (1369), 363 (1372), 398–400 (1376), 405 (1377). *Britton* likened such cheating to theft. *Britton*, i, pp. 60–1, ch. 16, c.6 (1291–2).

[422] *Nottingham*, i, pp. 280–1 (1395); *Memorials*, pp. 120–1 (1316). See also BL, MS Lansdowne 796, fol. 6v (late fifteenth century).

the great scandal and shame of all the aforesaid craft'.[423] Only burgesses were allowed to exercise this craft of skinning and each was expected to be 'well learned in his art'.[424] The York glovers were warned against buying cheap and 'unabill' wares from foreign traders and selling them again 'to the comon people in grete hurt unto tham'.[425] Such commercial fraud among artisans was often handled within the regulatory structure of the craft guilds and did not reach the town courts.[426] But consumers were also encouraged to pursue claims against fraudulent traders. A statute concerning tanners in 1423 promised half of any forfeiture and fine to the people who sued tanners who sold badly tanned leather.[427]

Nevertheless, it was guilds and their searchers who were instrumental in protecting consumers in larger towns from dishonest manufacturers and also upholding the reputation of crafts. One of the mechanisms employed to deter fraudulent behaviour, and also to protect the integrity of distinct crafts, was to prevent artisans from participating in another, complementary activity. For instance, in 1375, the shoe-makers of Beverley were forbidden from practising the craft of tanner, and vice versa.[428] This was reinforced by statutory legislation in 1389–90, but the principle had been a part of legislation for much longer.[429] The sumptuary legislation of 1363 also stated that artisans should only practise one trade and merchants deal in one sort of merchandise.[430] There was an addendum to the 1363 parliamentary rolls stating: 'but the intention of our lord the king and his council is that women, that is to say brewers, bakers, websters, spinsters and workers of wool as well as of linen and silk, embroiderers, carders, combers of wool and all others who work and labour at manual tasks, may work and labour as freely as they have done before this time, without any impeachment or restriction arising from this ordinance'. The prohibitions were thus supposedly aimed at artisans and full-time, skilled workers, rather than those engaged in low-skill, low-paid labour.

[423] *Bristol*, ii, pp. 93–4 (1408).
[424] *Ibid.*, ii, p. 96 (1408). See also *ibid.*, ii, pp. 75–7 (1406); *Beverley*, p. 33 (1437); *Norwich*, ii, pp. 149–52 (1442); *Northampton*, i, pp. 304–7 (1465).
[425] *York*, iii, p. 181 (1475).   [426] Thrupp, *Merchant Class*, p. 24.
[427] *Statutes*, ii, p. 220, 2 Hen VI c.7 (1423).
[428] *Beverley*, p. 31 (1375). See also *Coventry*, pp. 180–4 (1435), 557–8 (1494); *Memorials*, pp. 555–6 (1402).
[429] *Statutes*, ii, p. 65, 13 Ric II st.1 c.12 (1389–90). This statute was repealed temporarily in 1402 after a petition by the shoe-makers, who complained that the division of crafts merely encouraged false tanning and confederacies among tanners to reduce the price of hides and increase the price of tanned leather. An initial petition in 1395 had failed. *Parl. Rolls*, c.10 [4], January 1395, c.34, September 1402; *Statutes*, ii, pp. 142–3, 4 Hen IV c.35 (1402). The delineation between tanners and shoe-makers had certainly been reimposed by 1423. *Ibid.*, p. 220, 2 Hen VI c.7 (1423).
[430] *Statutes*, i, pp. 379–80, 37 Edw III cc.5–6 (1363); *Parl. Rolls*, c.24, October 1363.

However, perhaps reflecting the changing commercial environment, certain towns extended the scope of their ordinances. When answering a petition from Northampton bakers, the mayor and bailiffs replied that it was 'suspicious and unreasonable that a butcher should be a cook, shoe-maker a tanner, or an innkeeper a baker', since this made it more difficult to oversee the assizes and prevent price-raising activities.[431] The responsibilities and standards of each trade and craft were becoming strictly defined as occupational specialisation increased.[432] Occupations were not only protective of their own commercial territory, but quality-controls by officials and searchers were easier when each kept to their own trade.

Beyond quality-control in manufacturing, there were also concerns about quality in the victualling trades, particularly regarding the sale of unwholesome and out-of-date foodstuffs. Such practices were regarded with abhorrence, for they were not only deceptive but could potentially damage public health. Cooks were often punished for selling pasties and pies which had been reheated two or three days after they had first been cooked, or else which contained sub-quality or putrid meat.[433] *Judicium Pillorie* ordered officials to inquire of cooks who baked any victuals 'not wholesome for man's body', baked or roasted meat twice, or who stored foodstuffs for so long that they became unhealthy.[434] Central and urban regulations regarding cooks and butchers were mostly concerned about healthy and wholesome meat. *Judicium Pillorie* and *Statutum de Pistoribus* both expressed condemnation of those who sold 'meazled swines flesh' or 'flesh dead of murrain', and this was reiterated in numerous urban ordinances.[435] In late fourteenth-century Beverley, any butcher selling out-of-date, maggot-infested meat or any flesh obtained from diseased

[431] *Northampton*, i, p. 249 (1384); *CIM*, iv (1377–88), p. 143, no. 258. See also *Norwich*, ii, p. 81 (1373); Toulmin Smith (ed.), *English Gilds*, p. 405 (Worcester, 1467).

[432] Britnell, 'Town life', pp. 166–7.

[433] *Memorials*, pp. 266–7, 328, 367, 438, 448–9, 464, 471–2; *Norwich*, i, pp. 361 (1288), 368 (1289).

[434] *Statutes*, i, pp. 201–2, 'Judicium Pillorie'. See also *Britton*, i, pp. 83–4, ch. 21, c.11 and pp. 192–3, ch. 31, c.9 (1291–2); Prestwich (ed.), *York*, pp. 15–16 (1301); *Black Book*, ii, pp. 104–5, 146–7, cc.32, 59 [58] (*c*.1309); *Coventry*, p. 26 (1421); BL, MS Lansdowne 796, fol. 5v (late fifteenth century); *Great Red Book*, i, p. 142 (1452); *Leicester*, ii, pp. 289–90 (1467), 321 (1489?); *Northampton*, i, p. 375 (late fifteenth century); *Norwich*, ii, pp. 316–17 (fifteenth century?).

[435] *Statutes*, i, pp. 201–3, 'Judicium Pillorie' and 'Statutum de Pistoribus'. See also *Fleta*, ii, pp. 121–2, bk. II, c.12 (late thirteenth century); *Black Book*, ii, pp. 144–7, c.58 [57] (*c*.1309); *Oak Book*, i, pp. 50–3, no. 41 (*c*.1300); Prestwich (ed.), *York*, pp. 12–13 (1301); *Bristol*, ii, p. 218 (fourteenth century); *Liber Albus*, p. 400 (1383–4); *Coventry*, pp. 25–6 (1421); BL, MS Lansdowne 796, fol. 5r (late fifteenth century); *Great Red Book*, i, pp. 143–4 (1452); *Northampton*, i, p. 373 (late fifteenth century); *Leicester*, ii, pp. 288–9 (1467), 321–2 (1489?).

beasts faced hefty penalties of 6s. 8d. each time. Animals had to be slaughtered by the butcher who vended them and then sold within four days or else salted.[436] In Nottingham in 1314, William, son of Matthew, was accused by Hugh de Claxton and his wife, Alice, for selling diseased meat 'by which he lost the sale of his meat, and the credence of his neighbours', as well as being fined 6s.[437]

Fishmongers were warned against selling unwholesome fish that might harm people. A set of late fifteenth-century assizes ordained that fishmongers should 'water no maner of ffisshe twyes [twice] nor that sell no fectyf [infected] ffyssh'; the former practice presumably intended to deceive buyers into thinking the fish was fresher than it actually was. London fish-sellers were also told not to 'dub their baskets', which was the practice of putting the best fish at the top of the basket to conceal less desirable fish below.[438] An unusual ordinance for Lynn in the early fifteenth century outlined the quality expected in dairy products: 'Milk-wives are to sell good milk and cream that is sweet, in the form that it comes out of the cow – not combined or thickened with flour, nor diluted with water, to the deceit of the people, upon pain, etc. And they are to sell good, sweet butter, freshly made.'[439] How quality was judged and standardised in foodstuffs is difficult to ascertain, but time restrictions were the most common stipulations. In York, any meat which had been on a stall in the sun had to be sold after a day, while Colchester butchers were to sell their meat within three days in summer and four days in winter.[440]

Price and profit

Price and its regulation lay at the core of most market controls and an agreed price represented the culmination of the bargaining process. The

[436] *Beverley*, pp. 28–9 (1365, 1370).
[437] *Nottingham*, i, p. 81 (1314). See also *Norwich*, i, pp. 8, 16, 32, 48, 359–60; *Bridgwater*, p. 49 (1379); Jeayes (ed.), *Court Rolls*, i, pp. 14–17, 62, 72, 100 (1310–12, 1330); Walker (ed.), *Court Rolls*, v, pp. 111, 139, 147, 154 (1327–9).
[438] *Liber Albus*, pp. 326–7, 329 (1279–80); Prestwich (ed.), *York*, p. 13 (1301); *Black Book*, ii, pp. 104–5, c.30 (*c*.1309); *Memorials*, pp. 516–18 (1390); *Coventry*, p. 25 (1421); BL, MS Lansdowne 796, fol. 5r (late fifteenth century); *Great Red Book*, i, p. 141 (late fifteenth century); Toulmin Smith (ed.), *English Gilds*, pp. 396–7 (Worcester, 1467); *Norwich*, ii, pp. 316–17 (fifteenth century?). For cases of unwholesome fish being sold and traders punished, see Jeayes (ed.), *Court Rolls*, i, pp. 28–9, 75 (1311–12); *Bridgwater*, p. 49 (1379).
[439] Alsford, *Towns* (Lynn, early fifteenth century).
[440] Prestwich (ed.), *York*, pp. 12–13 (1301); *Red Paper Book*, p. 152 (early fourteenth century). Butchers in Leicester, Tamworth, Coventry, London and Northampton had three days to sell unsalted meat. *Leicester*, i, pp. 180–1 (1279); Wood, *Medieval Tamworth*, p. 75 (1319 and 1326); *Coventry*, pp. 25–6 (1421); *CLB*, к, p. 10 (1423); *Northampton*, i, p. 373 (late fifteenth century).

means of conveying value through price was not a simplistic equation for medieval salesmen, but relied on similar criteria to those employed today. Weights and measures had to conform to an understood standard; quality had to be measurable by certain defined terms; added value, either through transport, process, labour or scarcity, had to be assessed; and the terms of credit accounted for. These issues have been discussed above and demonstrated the concerns of both town authorities and traders with conformity, uniformity, quality and security. The price regulations of medieval authorities were also based on a number of economic assumptions and social theories, not least the theological notions of just price and the social theories of the 'body politic' and the commonweal.

Postan has suggested that medieval authorities deemed all increases of price unjust, even when demand was high or supplies were short.[441] Others have stated that the medieval authorities fixed prices by arbitrary enactment, without giving thought to principles of demand and supply.[442] However, to assume that the medieval authorities were blinkered by notions of 'natural values', rigid prices and abstract theology overlooks the regulatory mechanisms they put in place. They did have a pragmatic notion of a 'common market price' and understood that they could not overcome the economic forces of supply and demand, merely mitigate them. But they also applied the principles of 'just price' as an equitable method of calculating a legal price in the marketplace. The authorities in particular towns tried to prevent the exploitation of extreme market conditions by sellers, to the detriment of consumers, by making the legal price binding. Medieval economic legislators did not accept a Smithian theory of freely allowing supply and demand to set the retail price and allowing self-interests to provide for the communal benefit. Indeed, it is arguable that such a free-market system would not have been effective because of the imbalances of supply and competition within medieval trade. The medieval economy was particularly susceptible to exogenous shocks and disturbances, and it was this instability which much of the trading regulation sought to temper.[443]

The most significant national regulations for price control were the assizes of bread and ale, tied to the market price and drawing heavily upon scholastic notions of the just price. Wine was also regulated by specific national stipulations. These assizes will be discussed further below.[444] As regards the direct regulation of prices by royal intervention, one of the earliest examples comes from the local ordinances of York in 1301, which attempted to keep prices at the same level as before the arrival of

[441] Postan, *Medieval Economy*, p. 226.   [442] Cf. de Roover, 'Concept', 429–30.
[443] Persson, *Pre-Industrial*, p. 53.   [444] See pp. 231–50.

the king's court.[445] In response to the relocation to York of the Exchequer and Court of Common Pleas since 1298, prices were set for certain meat products. For example, a goose or capon was to sell for 3d., a hen for 1½d., rabbit for 5d., ten herrings for 1d., sixteen eggs for 1d., candles at 1½d. a pound, onions at 1d. a pound, mustard at 4d. a gallon and shoes at 5d.–7d., depending on the type and quality of leather. Anyone could complain about excessive prices and as an incentive they would receive the goods for free. Tailors and innkeepers were also given instructions regarding the prices to charge for their clothes and services.[446] However, Michael Prestwich argues that this was an exceptional example of price-fixing and it was certainly not repeated in subsequent York regulations.

Such broad-ranging price controls were rarely seen in national legislation. Occasional early fourteenth-century royal commissions and writs sought to stipulate reasonable prices based on earlier precedents. However, all these examples appear to be related to specific problems, such as royal household provision, the perambulations of the eyre, or a sub-standard coinage, rather than a general policy to extend price regulation beyond bread, ale and wine. Cases in common law tended to be related to misrepresentation of quality rather than 'fair price'.[447]

Unless there were exceptional or emergency circumstances, royal government generally left initial and wholesale price formation to market forces.[448] When they did try to impose arbitrary prices they often faced major problems. For instance, in April 1315 the government made an abortive attempt to fix the prices of beasts in reaction to a long-term rise in livestock prices.[449] A petition was presented by members of Parliament to the king and his council in January 1315, asking for specified prices to be ordained for oxen, sheep, pigs, geese, hens, capons, young pigeons, young chickens and eggs. In response, the council set a price on these commodities, which was to be issued to the sheriffs of England.[450] This ordinance was to be proclaimed in all cities, boroughs, towns and markets in March 1315. However, a number of chronicles, such as the *Anonimalle Chronicle*, the *Vita Edwardi Secundi* and the Bridlington chronicle, were critical of the ordinance. The Bridlington chronicler stated that the price-fixing ordinance was 'against reason' because 'the price of everything will

[445] Prestwich (ed.), *York*.   [446] *Ibid.*, pp. 14–16 (1301).
[447] Seabourne, *Royal Regulation*, pp. 73–4, 78; *CPR, 1301–7*, p. 487 (1306); *CPR, 1307–13*, p. 29 (1307–8); Sutherland (ed.), *Eyre*, pp. 9, 14, 22, 29, 32–4 (1329–30); *CLB*, E, p. 219 (1331).
[448] De Roover, 'Concept', 421–9; Seabourne, *Royal Regulation*, pp. 78–9.
[449] There is a copy of the writ in the Oxford archives, Salter (ed.), *Medieval Archives*, i, pp. 344–5, appx II, no. 1 (Oxford, 1315).
[450] *Parl. Rolls*, cc.35, 36 and 37, January 1315.

be in accordance with the fruitfulness of the harvest, not the will of men'. Edward II and his council soon backed down on this ordinance, amidst the crisis of the Great Famine, and the chroniclers report that they merely stated that people 'should buy and sell as cheaply as they could' or at 'reasonable prices'.[451] This suggests that there was a general recognition that the government did not have the power to enforce arbitrary prices that attempted to buck market forces.

The next important corpus of central price legislation came in the aftermath of the Black Death and the government imposition of controls over labour and wages. In the 'Ordinance of Labourers' in 1349, artisans were ordered not to take more than they had been used to three years previously, while:

butchers, fishmongers, hostelers, brewers, bakers, poulterers, and all other sellers of all manner of victual, shall be bound to sell the same victual for a reasonable price, having respect to the price that such victual be sold at in the places adjoining, so that the same sellers have moderate gains, and not excessive, reasonably to be required according to the distance of the place from whence the said victuals be carried.[452]

The punishment for excessive prices was to pay double to the aggrieved party. The 'Statute of Labourers' in 1350–1 also demanded that artificers, such as shoe-makers, saddlers, tanners and tailors, should sell their products at the same price as they had in 1346, or else face punishment at the hands of the Justices of the Peace. The justices were continually given special powers to enforce this legislation.[453] In 1363, the 'Statute Concerning Diet and Apparel' responded to a 'dearth' of poultry in the country by setting precise maximum prices of 3d. for a young capon, 4d. for an old capon, 2d. for a hen, 1d. for a pullet and 4d. for a goose.[454] The notion of 'reasonable gains' for victuallers and artisans was then repeated in a statute for 1389–90, which sought to tighten the enforcement of this aspect of the 'Ordinance of Labourers'.[455] By the end of the fourteenth century, the items covered by royal price-fixing legislation had expanded, though it was still not all-embracing in its

---

[451] Childs and Taylor (eds.), *Anonimalle Chronicle*, pp. 38–9, 88–91; Denholm-Young (ed.), *Life of Edward the Second*, p. 69; Stubbs (ed.), *Chronicles*, ii, pp. 47–8, 232–3, 237–8.

[452] *Statutes*, i, pp. 307–8, 23 Edw III cc.5–6, 'Ordinance of Labourers' (1349).

[453] *Ibid.*, i, p. 312, 25 Edw III st.2 cc.3–4, 'Statute of Labourers' (1350–1). See also *ibid.*, i, p. 345, 28 Edw III c.5 (1354). Proceedings before the justices in Suffolk in 1361–4 included many economic offences of excessive price and forestalling. Putnam (ed.), *Proceedings*, pp. 342–83.

[454] *Statutes*, i, pp. 378–9, 37 Edw III c.3 (1363).

[455] *Ibid.*, ii, p. 63, 13 Ric II st.1 c.8 (1389–90). See also *ibid.*, ii, p. 140, 4 Hen IV c.25 (1402); ii, p. 225, 2 Hen VI c.18 (1423).

principles.[456] It was not only foodstuffs that were targeted by the new regulations, but also certain minor manufactures were expected to be sold at a customary and 'reasonable price'. It appears that the legislation was linked to post-Black Death attempts to keep wages down, and the longevity of the labour crisis meant that these price lists became more of a fixture in both royal and civic law.

The legislation was relatively vague concerning the exact 'reasonable' prices involved, beyond recognition that travel costs should be incorporated. In most cases, the stipulations merely provided a broad theoretical framework upon which town authorities could regulate.[457] The loose phrasing of some of the statutes meant that officials could enforce the law in a way that suited local practices and needs. In addition, not all municipal price regulations drew on royal regulation. The prices of fish, wine, poultry, rabbits and other animals had been set in London since at least the late thirteenth century, and after the Black Death they added meat and ready-cooked food like pies.[458] Many statutes, such as those of 1315, 1363 and 1389–90, thus appear to have followed London's example, though the city's ordinances themselves were sometimes also influenced by royal regulation. Seabourne refers to this process as a 'cross-fertilisation' or 'hybridisation' of local and national laws.[459] For example, in 1361, there were complaints about the excessive prices of victuals and London's officials were ordered to set prices so 'that the sellers may gain a reasonable but not excessive profit' and 'the city by their efforts and diligence may be brought again to its due estate'.[460] This statement related directly to notions of the natural social order and communal responsibility, and it also reflected the wording of the Ordinance and Statute of Labourers.

Maximum prices of meat were occasionally set in a number of individual boroughs, perhaps drawing on statutory precedent, and showed how local price-fixing was sometimes tolerated. In Coventry (1445), no cook was to sell a goose for more than 4d., a pig for 7d. and the head

---

456 Seabourne, *Royal Regulation*, p. 74. For a more detailed discussion regarding the regulation of prices in fourteenth-century England, see *ibid.*, ch. 3.

457 Britnell, *Growth and Decline*, pp. 237–8.

458 Riley (ed.), *Munimenta Gildhallae*, ii, 'Liber Custumarum', pp. 82–3, 117–20 (*c.*1274–6), 192–3 (1300), 302–8, 603–5 (1320–1), 678–81 (1314–15); Thomas (ed.), *Calendar*, pp. 60–1 (Roll A, 1299–1300); *Memorials*, pp. 312–13 (1363), 426 (1378), 438 (1380), 643 (1416), 666–7 (1418); *Liber Albus*, p. 401 (1383–4); *CLB*, C, p. 134 (1300), F, p. 123 (1345), G, pp. 139 (1360–1), 148 (1362–3), H, pp. 61 (1377), 110 (1378), 257 (1384–5), I, pp. 35, 42–3 (1403–4); Barron, *London*, pp. 320–4.

459 York's 1301 ordinances display similar characteristics. Seabourne, *Royal Regulation*, p. 81.

460 *CCR, 1360–4*, pp. 284–5 (1361).

of a pig for 1d.[461] Cooks in late fourteenth-century Bristol were to sell well-roasted geese for 4d. each and their innkeepers had to sell hay at 4d. a bushel.[462] Fuel, like charcoal, oil, tallow and wood, could also be subject to certain price restrictions.[463] There were thus certain commodities, such as meat and fuel, whereby local officials stipulated the 'reasonable prices' that pertained. Were these prices arbitrary or did they bear some relation to market prices? There were instances where towns implemented certain market-determined criteria. Berwick ordinances for 1283–4 set maximum prices for mutton carcasses that depended on the time of year and the agricultural cycle: 16d. from Easter to Whitsuntide, 12d. from Whitsuntide to 25 July, 10d. from then to Michaelmas, and 8d. back to Easter.[464] Several national regulations also made allowance for different prices between cities, market towns and rural villages.[465] This appeared to take into account the cost of transport and perhaps even labour, and some regulations made a direct reference to these elements of price formation.[466] In normal circumstances, authorities seemingly expected prices to fluctuate to a certain extent, but would also take some remedial action of fixing retail prices when there were severe shortages or particular concerns.

A differentiation must be made between the price-fixing of different wholesale and retail commodities. Price-fixing by the authorities mostly focused upon retail food markets, where the assizes of bread and ale, as well as the profits of the butchers, fishmongers and cooks, were closely regulated. There were also retail markets in manufactured goods, such as clothes, shoes, woodware and metalware. Although these manufactures were subject to quality-controls and declarations that 'reasonable prices' should be upheld, processes of individual bargaining were often allowed provided that dishonest practices had been excised.[467] This was because the medieval demand for manufactured goods was fairly elastic and could

---

[461] *York*, i, pp. xx–xxi, 223 (fifteenth century); *Coventry*, p. 223 (1445).

[462] *Bristol*, ii, p. 227 (late fourteenth century); *Great Red Book*, i, p. 144 (1452). Cooks in Coventry were also ordered to sell geese for 4d., *Coventry*, p. 26 (1421). In Leicester, geese were again set at 4d., while the best pigs were set at 6d. *Leicester*, ii, pp. 289–90 (1467).

[463] *Leicester*, ii, pp. 294–5 (1467), 318 (1488), iii, p. 12 (1520?); *Northampton*, i, pp. 231–2, c.53 (c.1460); *Memorials*, pp. 358–60 (1371), 458 (1382), 509 (1388), 560 (1405); *Coventry*, pp. 632 (1511), 646 (1515).

[464] Toulmin Smith (ed.), *English Gilds*, p. 342 (Berwick, 1283–4).

[465] *RP*, i, p. 295 (1315); *CCR, 1313–18*, pp. 160–1 (1317); *Statutes*, i, p. 378, 37 Edw III c.3 (1363). For similar provisions in the assize of ale, see below, pp. 241–2.

[466] Seabourne, *Royal Regulation*, p. 86, cf. Prestwich (ed.), *York*, p. 12; *Statutes*, ii, p. 263, 4 Edw III c.8 (1330).

[467] Anthropologists emphasised the process of haggling to reach a price agreement in periodic markets. Geertz, 'Suq', pp. 221–9; Shanin (ed.), *Peasants*, p. 170.

sustain greater price variations. By contrast, the demand for bread, ale and fish was generally inelastic and this could allow traders to exploit consumers when supplies were short. Britnell has suggested that there was no unmediated bargaining in the medieval food markets and retail prices were set by the authorities on the basis of wholesale prices. He also argued that public intervention, inspired by canon law, was more active than previously supposed and that there was a binding official market price set by officials in the interests of the consumer.[468]

Nevertheless, at the source of agricultural production (on lordly estates and peasant holdings), the wholesale price of goods was determined by considerations of supply and demand. Grain prices were originally decided by negotiations between producers and middlemen, often beyond the reach of market authorities.[469] The 'Ordinance of Labourers' (1349) stated that prices should be set with respect to the prices in the region and a mark-up according to transport.[470] Thus, when medieval officials came to set the retail prices of foodstuffs, they merely reaffirmed a public estimate of the wholesale price for basic commodities, based on current market conditions. 'Trusted' men were chosen in a town, who had informal discussions with local traders in order to reach a judgement on prices sustained by the market.[471] In fourteenth-century Bristol, the retail price of fish was ordained by six elected officials, after they had dealt with the wholesale vendors and duly agreed a reasonable price 'according to their joint discretions and good accord'. Fish were to be sold 'as well to the profit of the commons of the said town as to all the gentle folk and all other people of the country round about for the provisioning of their houses'.[472] In the York Ordinances of 1301, inspectors were to visit butchers when they had received livestock and assess the retail price based on the price at which they bought the beasts plus the labour involved in slaughtering.[473] In early fourteenth-century Oxford, appointed jurors, under oath, inquired into the common selling price of wheat, barley and oats and thus at what price the assizes should be set.[474] Even on the manor of Downham (Cambridgeshire) in 1326, the current market prices of three grades of wheat (*melioris, mediocris, simplicioris*) were agreed upon by court officials under oath.[475]

[468] Britnell, 'Price-setting', 1–15.   [469] *Ibid.*
[470] *Statutes*, i, pp. 311–13, 25 Edw III st.2, 'Statute of Labourers' (1350–1).
[471] Britnell, 'Price-setting', 4; Seabourne, *Royal Regulation*, p. 88.
[472] *Bristol*, ii, pp. 72–4 (fourteenth century).
[473] Prestwich (ed.), *York*, pp. 12–13 (1301).
[474] Salter (ed.), *Medieval Archives*, ii, pp. 142–3, 151–2 (1309–10).
[475] Coleman (ed.), *Court Roll*, p. 99 (1326).

How often these prices were set is difficult to ascertain; it may have related to the arrival of large shipments of fish or agricultural and droving patterns. The system of 'lot' in many boroughs may have provided a useful framework for bargaining and communal acceptance of a market price. We also know that in different towns, the assize of bread was set weekly, monthly, quarterly or biannually. This may have depended on the size and turnover of the market in question, as well as the resources available for oversight. The price of grain certainly changed during the year, but knowledge of that year's harvest did not in itself provide precise predictions. The seasonal and yearly fluctuations for wheat can be seen in the prices declared by the jurors in Oxford from 1309 to 1327, which ranged from 3s. to 9s. 6d. per quarter, but not usually more than 1s.–2s. within an agricultural year.[476]

There were restrictions on the wholesale bargaining process within markets. Elizabeth Gemmill has looked at price-setting for grain in fifteenth-century Aberdeen, which may have been broadly similar to practices in England. She noted that buyers were forbidden from offering a higher price ('overbuying') once a bargain had been agreed between two other parties.[477] The bargaining process in the wholesale food markets was intended to keep prices down. In London in 1347, John de Burstalle was convicted of deceitfully enhancing the common market price of wheat. He connived to have a confederate bring two of his own bushels into the cornmarket for which he offered a price 1½d.–2d. over the present common price, and such misinformation made corn more dear 'to the damage of the commonalty'. He was imprisoned for forty days.[478] The flow of information was integral to the process of price-setting; burgesses controlled information zealously so as to keep prices down.[479] If certain products were in short supply and outside traders discovered this, they could take advantage by holding back goods to raise the price. Equally, spreading false rumours of scarcity or expected deliveries was condemned as conspiratorial and compounded any other offence. Outsiders who arrived in Colchester and Dunwich had to offer a price while in ignorance of the present state of the town market; this was an offer-price system which might give burgesses a bargain below the clearing-price of that day.[480]

---

[476] Salter (ed.), *Medieval Archives*, ii, pp. 143–82. See also *Oak Book*, ii, p. xxii.

[477] Gemmill, 'Town and region', p. 62.

[478] *Memorials*, pp. 235–6 (1347); *CLB*, F, p. 165 (1347). See also *Memorials*, pp. 317–18 (1364); *CLB*, G, p. 171 (1364).

[479] Britnell, 'Price-setting', 8–9.

[480] Britnell, *Growth and Decline*, pp. 35–7; Bailey (ed.), *Bailiffs' Minute Book*, pp. 19, 132 (1427).

Auctioning was also prohibited as a system of price-maximisation.[481] A statute of 1360–1 displayed the same disdain as preachers and moralists for certain bargaining practices at Great Yarmouth, suggesting that prices for fish were raised when traders 'by malice and envy increase upon the other . . . and such proffers extend to more than the price of herring for which the fishers proffered it to sell at the beginning'.[482] The legislation proposed that all sales of herring should take place openly, not privately, and at a price agreed between the purchaser and vendor. No one could enter into a bargain until the first trader had already agreed his price with the fish-seller.

Restrictions upon bargaining practices allowed the fixing of market retail prices to remain viable for authorities, even though officials realised that they could not keep prices static when harvests fluctuated and supply networks were regionalised. Nevertheless, formally announced common and retail prices gave buyers vital, irrevocable information that overcame ignorance of the exact state of the market. Consumers had to place confidence in the authorities that changes were being monitored, and that prices were being kept to a 'reasonable' level in line with statutory law, market forces, and commutative and distributive justice.

Additionally, reasonable prices were related to a concept of reasonable profit or gain for traders. A case from London in 1382 demonstrates this process at work. A fishmonger, Thomas Welford, was cajoled and persuaded by the mayor and aldermen into selling his fish to hucksters at a wholesale rate of six herrings for a penny, so that the hucksters could retail them at five for a penny. Thomas claimed that this was the lowest price at which he could sell his fish 'without doing too great an injury to himself'. However, it was discovered that Thomas soon after sold a bulk consignment to a stranger at ten herrings for a penny, even though 'he and all other freemen were bound of right to sell to their neighbours at as low a rate as to strangers, or even cheaper'. In response to this evidence that herring could have been sold at a lower price, the price of herring for all fishmongers was reduced by the mayor to nine herrings for a penny.[483] In this example, officials sought to ensure that foodstuffs were sold at as low a price as possible, but based on the minimum margins that traders themselves generally dealt at in order to make a living.

What constituted a reasonable profit in retail trades is not well elucidated in the sources. Victuallers, cooks and fishmongers in fifteenth-century Leicester were ordered to 'selle their vitaill at resonable prise takyng resonable encres [profit]'.[484] Protecting citizens and visitors

---

481 *Leicester*, ii, p. 22 (1335–6).   482 *Statutes*, i, pp. 369–70, 35 Edw III (1360–1).
483 *Memorials*, pp. 467–8 (1382).   484 *Leicester*, ii, pp. 289–90 (1467).

against sudden and excessive price rises was concomitant upon urban officials, and ordinances were couched in accusatory terms against traders who sold for profit. Searches were made for provisions that were sold 'to excessyue lucre [gain]'. Forestallers in fourteenth-century Tendring (Essex) were accused of selling fish and other goods for five times what they paid, while some in Scarborough had sold herring and salt for twice its value 'in great extortion'.[485] An example from the peace rolls for Suffolk (1361–4) describes how Thomas the Smith of Combs made an excessive profit by paying 4s. 6d. for each of six barrels of tar and selling them at 6s.: a gross profit margin of 33 per cent.[486] The fifteenth-century oath for the Mayor of Northampton provides a more precise indication as to what was considered a reasonable profit, stating that butchers were allowed to gain no more than 1d. on every 12d. worth of meat sold (8 per cent gross profit margin).[487] Regraters were similarly allowed a profit of one penny in every shilling, but the assize of bread allowed a 14 per cent net profit margin for bakers.[488] Ultimately, the decision on what constituted a reasonable price or profit varied and was often left to local officials, who consulted with local experts and dealers. There were thus margins for flexibility in determining acceptable levels of gain.

The assizes of bread, ale and wine

The most constantly monitored retail traders were bakers and brewers. Bread and ale were two of the basic nutritional elements of the medieval diet and their supply and price were of utmost concern to local authorities, particularly in towns where a majority of the population depended upon bakers and brewers to sustain them. Officials were thus provided with processes and mechanisms by which to control the manufacture and sale of these foodstuffs, to judge the weight, measures, quality and price, and to ensure open supply.

The most significant and well-known laws were the assizes of bread, ale and wine, which were promulgated nationally in the thirteenth century.[489] Such assizes involved the regulation of price, quality and

---

[485] Seabourne, *Royal Regulation*, p. 134.

[486] Putnam (ed.), *Proceedings*, p. 365, no. 463 (1361–4), cf. Seabourne, *Royal Regulation*, p. 135.

[487] *Northampton*, i, p. 373 (late fifteenth century). This profit does not include deductions for expenses and overheads.

[488] Davis, 'Baking', 479. For regraters, see below, pp. 261–2.

[489] The main statutes were: *Assisa Panis et Cervisie*, *Judicium Pillorie*, and *Statutum de Pistoribus* (also known as *Composicio ad puniendum infringentes assisam panis et cervisie, forestallarios, cocos, etc*); *Statutes*, i, pp. 199–204. Bennett referred to them as quasi-statutes, but they came to have the force of statutes; Bennett, *Ale*, p. 99.

quantity. They drew upon previous governmental assizes, such as those of King John and Henry II, which were similar in both their format and general principles.[490] There had also been general regulations governing the sale of bread and ale as part of local administration, well before they were codified in national statutes. In the *Domesday Book*, those using false measures at Chester were to be fined 4s. and anyone making bad ale faced the cucking-stool.[491] The twelfth-century charters of Shrewsbury and Egremont authorised burgesses to fix the assize of bread, and at Tewkesbury fines were assessed by twelve burgesses.[492] London authorities enforced a municipal assize of bread as early as the reign of King John.[493] However, it was the thirteenth-century statute *Assisa Panis et Cervisie* which laid down the basic assize formula which shall be studied in detail here.[494] This quasi-statute highlighted the importance of basic foodstuffs for the people of medieval England, as well as the increasing need for stricter controls at a time of increasing population and grain prices. The assizes were also part of continuous attempts by central government to control certain trading practices. Their interests, before the thirteenth century, had been select, focusing on such issues as weights and measures and coinage, but subsequently, their involvement and legislation gained momentum and encompassed an increasing number of trading concerns. The correlated tables of grain and bread or ale prices provided in *Assisa* were often found verbatim in borough and local customs.[495] There is little doubt that the national assizes were a

---

[490] Connor, *Weights and Measures*, p. 194; Hall (ed.), *Red Book*, ii, p. 750; Brewer (ed.), *Registrum Malmesburiensie*, i, p. 134; Maitland (ed.), *Select Pleas of the Crown*, i, p. 27. Britnell argued that it is unlikely that the earlier royal promulgations had any national significance beyond the verge of the royal court. Britnell, *Commercialisation*, pp. 26, 94.

[491] *VCH* Chester, i, p. 343. For early cases of the assize of ale in the bishopric of Winchester, see Hall (ed.), *Pipe Roll*, pp. 45, 47, 49, 65.

[492] *BBC, 1042–1216*, pp. lxiv, 157–9. See also Britnell, 'Morals', p. 26.

[493] Braid, 'Laying the foundations', 6.

[494] The statutes *Assisa Panis et Cervisie*, *Judicium Pillorie* and *Statutum de Pistoribus* were all attributed as of uncertain date in *Statutes*, i, pp. 199–204, but *Assisa* and *Judicium* were nominally assigned to 51 Hen III (1266–7), while 1274–5 is possible for *Statutum de Pistoribus*. However, there is evidence that *Assisa Panis et Cervisie* was promulgated around 1256. See Davis, 'Baking', 468. *Assisa* could have been formulated as early as 1254, as Robert Braid suggests. However, it is difficult to distinguish in the sources between the reinforcement of local assizes and the actual proclamation of a national standard. Braid, 'Laying the foundations', 5; *CCR 1253–4*, p. 256; *CCR 1254–6*, pp. 94, 173.The national promulgation of the assizes of bread and ale was possibly related to events in London in 1254, when the city was taken into the king's hands for non-observance of their assizes. In 1258, a special assay of London's bakers was undertaken. Riley (ed.), *Chronicles*, pp. 22–3, 43; Barron, *London*, p. 32.

[495] The assizes were copied in *Oak Book*, ii, pp. 28–31; *Northampton*, i, pp. 314–21 ('Judicium Pillorie'), 325–7 ('Assisa Panis et Cervisie'); Salter (ed.), *Medieval Archives*, ii, pp. 131–4. Summaries can be also found in *Britton*, i, pp. xxi–xxix, 186–9, ch. 31

primary influence on local trading practices and that schedules of prices and weights were distributed to the localities as a proforma for local regulation.

Seabourne argued that there was little financial profit for the Crown in such legislation and that paternal concerns about supply and quality were more important.[496] However, this does not mean that the assizes were designed only for the benefit of poor consumers; the supply of the royal household was also being protected. The king's household was undoubtedly a significant consumer and its members did not want unreasonable prices or unstandard measures.[497] In addition, English kings of the thirteenth century were adamant that the assizes of bread and ale were franchises, usually granted by the Crown and associated with the right to view of frankpledge. Their enunciation of the assizes must be seen partly as an attempt to stamp a royal claim on their enforcement, with the possible pecuniary benefits seen in the *Quo Warranto* proceedings of Edward I.[498] Lords who received royal liberties, usually in return for substantial payment to the Exchequer, regarded the assizes as lucrative investments from which they expected a monetary return. Although the primary aim of the assizes must still be viewed as ensuring a staple supply and price for vital foodstuffs, the supplementary effect of the franchising system was to create increasing restrictions and amercements for the producers of bread and ale in order to establish a return for the lord.

Bread

The bakers of late medieval England produced a variety of breads for daily consumption and, traditionally, historians have regarded the assize of bread as a means of controlling production and sale in the interest of poorer customers. The basic construct of the assize gave the different weights of farthing loaves of wastel bread in inverse proportion to the price of a quarter of wheat. As the price of a quarter of wheat increased by increments of 6d., so the weight of a farthing loaf was decreased.[499] This

---

(1291–2); *Fleta*, ii, pp. 117–18, bk. ii, cc.9–11 (late thirteenth century); Louis (ed.), *Commonplace Book*, pp. 121–4.

[496] Seabourne, 'Laws, morals and money'.

[497] Bennett, *Ale*, p. 101; Cunningham, *Growth*, p. 263.

[498] A grant to the manor of Ratcliffe (near Nottingham) in 1307, included the view of frankpledge, the assizes of bread and ale, a pillory, tumbrel, 'infangenethef' (right to judge thieves) and associated gallows and a fixed annual rent to the Exchequer of 2s. Bland, Brown and Tawney (eds.), *English Economic History*, pp. 155–6.

[499] Davis, 'Baking', 470–1. Different types of bread could be baked: simnel, wastel, cocket (of two grades), wholewheat, treyt, bread of common wheat, and horsebread. Horsebread was a coarse bread made from peas and beans, intended for horses but also eaten

mechanism ensured that a loaf costing a farthing was always available to the poorest consumer, even though they received less bread for a farthing when grain prices increased.[500] It was impractical to enforce laws that drove the bakers into major losses and out of business, so the assize was regarded as an effective compromise. It was based on the market price of wheat, determined by supply and demand, combined with notions of both commutative and distributive justice.[501]

Bakers were supposed to be continually informed about the current level of the assize. *Judicium Pillorie* stated that twelve lawful men were to summon all the bakers and brewers of a town, together with their measures. They were then to inquire into the standard prices of the best wheat at the last market day, as well as the second-best and third-best.[502] Assays of bread in London followed this procedure in its principles, by appointing four men to buy corn, bake three types of bread, and have the loaves weighed; through this method, the assize of bread was set regularly.[503] Assizes had to be set locally since they were tied to the local market price of wheat, but also as a demonstration to local bakers that the assize level was sustainable. In Beverley, in the 1360s, the customs stated that six burgesses were appointed and sworn in to keep the assize of bread and ale for the year. They took samples of loaves and ale to be weighed and measured by the bailiff in their presence and the quality

---

by the very poor. Horsebread was not included in the assize of bread, but Coventry bakers in 1473 were ordered to sell three $5\frac{1}{2}$lb. loaves for 1d., while bakers in York were to sell three 3lb. loaves for 1d. when the price of beans was over 4s., and 4lb. loaves when under 4s. The ordinances for Henley-on-Thames decreed that bakers should sell fifteen loaves of horsebread for 12d. *Coventry*, pp. 23–4 (1421), 385 (1473), 682–3 (1522); *York*, i, p. 170 (1482); *Henley*, p. 108; Connor, *Weights and Measures*, p. 195. *Assisa* only recorded in full the figures for wastel bread, but provided proportions from which to calculate the weights of other breads. It is difficult to ascertain the popularity of various types of bread, but the Oxford assize records for 1309–38 might be indicative in that they distinguish between different loaves detected for defects: 14 for simnel (3%), 163 cases for wastel (30%), 200 for 1st cocket (36%), 78 for 2nd cocket or clermatyn (14%), 57 for wheaten (10%), 3 for treyt (1%) and 33 for bread of mixed grain (6%). Salter (ed.), *Medieval Archives*, ii, pp. 138–82. Wastel thus consituted a fair proportion of the bread trade, though the two types of cocket had half the market. This may have been reversed in the different economic climate after the Black Death.

[500] *Liber Albus*, pp. 308–9 (1272–1307); *Coventry*, pp. 23–4 (1421); *Leicester*, ii, pp. 106–7 (1357), 287 (1467).

[501] Davis, 'Baking'.

[502] *Statutes*, i, pp. 201–2, 'Judicium Pillorie'. According to Reynes, the middle price of wheat was used for assize calculations. Louis (ed.), *Commonplace Book*, p. 136. For the market prices of three qualities of grain, see Coleman (ed.), *Court Roll*, p. 99; Jeayes (ed.), *Court Rolls*, i, pp. 55–6 (1311); *Leicester*, ii, pp. 89, 93, 130, 131, 133, 147, 149, 156; *Nottingham*, i, pp. 289–91 (1395–6).

[503] *Liber Albus*, pp. 302–5 (1272–1307); Riley (ed.), *Munimenta Gildhallae*, iii, appx I, pp. 411–29. See Seabourne, 'Assize matters', esp. 33–4; Davis, 'Baking', 474–5.

of the loaves or ale was also judged. At their discretion defaults were adjudged, amercements assessed and offenders punished.[504] The extent to which the assize was updated, based on changing grain prices, seems to have varied between markets. In Norwich, two bakers and two 'lawful' men were chosen annually to uphold the assize twice a year 'for the common good of the city and country'.[505] In fifteenth-century Worcester, the assize of bread was set weekly by the bailiffs.[506]

The medieval baker was thus tightly restricted in the weights of loaves he could produce when the price of wheat was at a certain level. However, the statute *Assisa* also specified that bakers should make a profit of 4d. and accrue total expenses of 5¾d. These expenses included overheads for their servants, salt, yeast, fuel, candles and sieves.[507] The traditional notion that this total allowance was attributable to every quarter of wheat baked is actually a misreading of the statute *Assisa*, which states that when a quarter of wheat was sold for 18d. then the baker should receive the gain specified in every quarter. This was not, however, intended to be applicable to a quarter of wheat at every price. If the allowed profits were derived from the sale of a quarter of wheat's worth of bread, then a baker had to sell 418 pounds Troy of bread out of every quarter of wheat and everything above that amount was 'advantage bread' for himself.[508] This type of calculation has led historians to view the assize of bread as a variable instrument, which could either greatly restrict or advance a baker's profits, depending on the price of wheat.[509] However, this runs counter to the actual sales practice and methodology behind the medieval assize, where a more understandable rationale, based upon pragmatism and communal 'justice', can be identified.

The compilers of the assize of bread expected a baker to have a constant turnover in bread sales, but in terms of the number of loaves sold rather than wheat purchased.[510] The assize was designed to allow bakers to make a profit of 4d. for every 111 farthing loaves sold, whatever the cost

[504] *Beverley*, pp. 8–9 (1360s).
[505] *Norwich*, i, pp. 174–6 (early fourteenth century). See also *CPR, 1266–72*, p. 196 (Cambridge, 1268).
[506] Toulmin Smith (ed.), *English Gilds*, p. 381 (Worcester, 1467). See also *Liber Albus*, p. 231 (1272–1307).
[507] *Statutes*, i, pp. 199–200, 'Assisa Panis et Cervisie'; Davis, 'Baking', 473.
[508] See *Oak Book*, ii, pp. xxi–xxix; Webb and Webb, 'Assize', 196–7; Beveridge, 'A statistical crime', 505; Nicholas, 'Assize of bread', 324; Gemmill and Mayhew, *Changing Values*, pp. 34–41; Boulton, 'London's "dark ages"?', 484–90; Ross, 'Assize of bread', 332–42. Ross correctly stated that the arithmetical relationship between the price of a quarter of wheat (w) and the weight of bread (p) was: wp = 136 (where w and p are in shillings).
[509] Gemmill and Mayhew, *Changing Values*, p. 36; Thrupp, *A Short History*, pp. 13, 21–2; Connor, *Weights and Measures*, pp. 195, 203–5.
[510] For a fuller explication of this argument, see Davis, 'Baking'.

of wheat, in addition to keeping two further loaves and the residual bran. This meant a gross income of 27¾d., where the wheat had cost 18d. and expenses had totalled 5¾d. The net profit of 4d. was therefore a margin of about 14 per cent on a baker's turnover. The original creators of the assize of bread envisaged stability in demand, output and profits of bakers. In essence, the assize of bread was designed upon the assumption that the daily financial outlay of most consumers would be stable, and this would enable a baker to earn a constant rate of 4d. for a stipulated turnover. The authorities did not want to encourage wage inflation and 4d. (plus the bran and two loaves) was comparable, and perhaps slightly more, than the daily wage of a skilled artisan.[511]

Of course, in reality, bakers were competing to sell their bread and demand shifted according to general economic conditions. Additionally, the above calculations were predominately for bakers of wastel bread, whereas many were also expected to produce sufficient quantities of lower-quality breads for poorer residents. In Tamworth, in 1419, all bakers were expected to bake both white and black bread in order to feed the townspeople.[512] The fifteenth-century ordinances of Leicester required that the 'town lak no manner of breed, wyght [white] ne browne, ne non other kyndes of breed in payne of impresonment'.[513] The necessity for such stipulations resided in the way the assize was structured for brown or black breads. There was an inherent error in the assize tables in relation to the weights and sale of brown bread.[514] For instance, wholewheat bread was calculated from the assize table by adding 5s. to the weight of wastel bread and then multiplying by $1\frac{1}{2}$.[515] This simple calculation did not lead to the same constant relationship between turnover and profit as seen for wastel bread. Instead, bakers not only had to sell more loaves to make the same profit as for wastel, but their sales of wholewheat loaves had to rise as the price of wheat increased in order to maintain the same profit. The need for baking trials may have resided in disagreements over these proportions and the London authorities were particularly assiduous in using experimental bakings throughout this period.[516] On the whole, it was more profitable for a baker to sell wastel bread rather than wholewheat. This meant that civic authorities had to regulate the production

[511] Farmer, 'Prices and wages'.   [512] Gould, 'Medieval burgesses of Tamworth', 34.

[513] *Leicester*, ii, p. 287 (1467). A later ordinance stated that rye bread was 'for pore people'. *Ibid.*, iii, p. 16 (1520).

[514] Davis, 'Baking', 487–8.

[515] Bread weight was measured by the Troy pound, which was divided into 240 pennyweights (12 pence to a shilling). Davis, 'Baking', 496.

[516] Seabourne, *Royal Regulation*, p. 83; Thrupp, *A Short History*, p. 15; Seabourne, 'Assize matters', 34–5.

and sale of lower-quality breads in order to ensure enough was being made, especially when wheat prices rose. The Ipswich Custumal even ordered that certain bakers should only produce wholewheat and common bread and not wastel or cocket, while London regulations divided the trade between the white and brown bakers.[517]

Bakers with a small and poor customer base were thus still working within tight margins, which the idealistic model of the assizes did not take into account. Nevertheless, the assize of bread was generally structured around both economic and moral principles, founded upon paternalism, just price, social stability, distributive justice and a firm understanding of fluctuating grain supplies. The law showed concern for poor customers, but also protected the livelihood of bakers.

Other regulations for bakers focused not just on prices, weights and measures, but on the quality of materials and equipment used, especially in the more detailed town ordinances. In Ipswich, wastel, simnel and first cocket bread had to be made using a bolter (a type of sieve for sifting flour) from Rennes, probably from the good-quality linen produced there. Those caught using lower-quality bolters would have them burnt beside the pillory. Also, no baker was to mix corns or bran with corn and had to accord with the assize, though bakers selling rotten bread was a less common offence than underweight loaves.[518] What needs to be borne in mind is that the assizes were still enforced locally by appointed jurors. If the national statutes standardised practices and prices, the exercise of enforcement was still very much in local hands and aspects of the legislation were open to differing interpretations. Nevertheless, the statutory assize was the formula adopted by authorities, as seen in the information they copied into their custumals and by the fact that many entries in manorial court rolls, even into the fifteenth century, stated that the assizes should be kept according to statute law.

Assisa provided a margin of error for bakers, declaring that bakers would be amerced if the weight of a farthing loaf was deficient by up to 2s. in weight; any deficiency above 2s. and the offender would be sent to the pillory. This margin was increased to 2s. 6d. in *Statutum de Pistoribus*, which was followed in the regulations of York and London.[519] However,

[517] *Black Book*, ii, pp. 172–5, c.80 [77] (*c*.1309); *CLB*, A, p. 216 (1276–8), K, p. 258 (fifteenth century); *Liber Albus*, p. 231 (1272–1307); Riley (ed.), *Munimenta Gildhallae*, iii, appx I, pp. 414–15 (1307–27).

[518] *Black Book*, ii, pp. 172–5, c.80 [77] (*c*.1309). See also Prestwich (ed.), *York*, pp. 10–11 (1301); *Memorials*, pp. 90 (1311), 121 (1316).

[519] *Statutes*, i, pp. 199–204, 'Assisa' and 'Statutum de Pistoribus'; Prestwich (ed.), *York*, pp. 10–11, 18–22 (1301); Riley (ed.), *Munimenta Gildhallae*, i, pp. 264–5. See also *Britton*, i, pp. 187–8, ch. 31, c.3 (2s.) and *Fleta*, ii, p. 118, bk. II, c.10 (2s. 6d.).

this only applied to wastel bread, and if the margin was the same for brown bread then it was effectively tighter as a percentage of the overall weight. The same applied for all breads when the price of wheat decreased and the size of loaf increased. Nevertheless, there is evidence that local courts interpreted this statutory stipulation in a flexible manner. The regulations for thirteenth-century Winchester stated that 'if the farthing loaf is in default of aught beyond twelve pennyweights the baker is in mercy, and for every default within the weight of three ounces according to the amount of the trespass; and when the farthing loaf is in default by aught beyond three ounces the baker shall bear the sentence of the city [i.e. the pillory]'.[520] This suggests that the bakers of Winchester were given leeway of up to 1s. in weight before they were convicted of an offence, though this leniency may have been connected to the basic toll that all bakers had to pay in Winchester of 2s. 1d. a year. Nevertheless, this more flexible interpretation of assize legislation was outlined in the *Assyse of Breade*, printed by Robert Wyer in *c*.1540, where only bakers who were in default of the weight of a farthing loaf by more than 2s. 6d. were to go to the pillory. Any weight discrepancy under 15d. was considered minor and was not to be amerced. Repeated offenders (up to four times) should, however, face corporal punishment.[521] It is possible that local courts were prepared to allow bakers a margin of error in their production of loaves before they even incurred an amercement, but this has to be set alongside the apparent presentments of all bakers under assize regulations.[522]

Bakers were seemingly concerned by the slight margins of weight that they were working within, given the vagaries of medieval equipment and the potential for false accusations. These anxieties are shown in the regulations. The Leicester ordinances of 1352 stated that bread should be weighed on the same day as it was taken, or else it might dry up while in the keeping of the bailiffs.[523] The fifteenth-century commonplace book of Robert Reynes suggested that bakers be allowed a pennyweight extra allowance each day after the first night to account for weight loss after cooling.[524]

---

[520] Furley (ed.), *Ancient Usages*, pp. 34–5, no. 37 (late thirteenth century). 1s. was the equivalent of 0.6 Troy ounces.

[521] Wyer, *Assyse of Breade* (*c*.1540). See also Louis (ed.), *Commonplace Book*, pp. 125, 136–7, 350–2. Reynes stated that bakers whose bread weighed more than an ounce over the specified weight were to be amerced 20d., and over an ounce and a half, 24d. Any offences over 2s. (presumably a copying error and should read 2 ounces; 2s. equals 1.2 Troy ounces) would lead to the pillory.

[522] This is discussed further on pp. 298–300.

[523] *Leicester*, ii, p. 87 (1352). See also *Northampton*, i, p. 324; *Liber Albus*, p. 310 (1272–1307); *Memorials*, pp. 71–2 (1310).

[524] Louis (ed.), *Commonplace Book*, p. 136.

Connor argued that the 'baker's dozen', which entailed giving thirteen loaves to consumers when they purchased only twelve, was a means by which bakers could assuage the tight tolerances of the assize.[525] It is possible that officials connived in such evasions, but it does not fit easily with the common inspection procedures, which involved weighing just single samples, each marked with the baker's seal.[526] The 'baker's dozen' appeared to relate more to the practice of bakers selling thirteen loaves for twelve to regraters or hucksters.[527] It was a device whereby regraters could make a small profit, with bakers effectively paying them $\frac{1}{4}$d. for every twelve loaves they sold in the streets.[528] The bakers were using the regraters as mobile salesmen, reaching out to more customers and taking on the burden of surplus stock. The *Little Red Book* of Bristol stated it was the practice for bakers to sell bread through 'hokesteres' (often women), who were allowed a penny for every shilling's worth of bread they bought and no more. If she bought more than she needed for a day's supply and the bread subsequently went stale, she did so at her own peril and loss.[529] The Winchester ordinances noted that hucksters of bread should make sure that the bakers' stamp of warranty was on the loaves, or else the hucksters themselves were liable for any weight infringements.[530] Not all authorities or bakers acquiesced in the use of regraters. An ordinance for Coventry in 1431 ordered bakers, both from the town and from the country, to sell their bread themselves and not through hucksters.[531] In Leicester, in 1323–4, the bakers complained that the regraters were keeping back their bread for over a week, 'by reason of which keeping the said bakers have often incurred great damage'. This presumably related to the quality and staleness of the bread, which still bore the baker's

---

[525] Connor, *Weights and Measures*, pp. 198–9.

[526] *Statutes*, i, pp. 201–4, 'Judicium Pillorie' and 'Statutum de Pistoribus'; Louis (ed.), *Commonplace Book*, pp. 136–7. Many civic ordinances demanded that bakers marked their loaves so that they could be identified if found to be defective. These marks were usually simple in form: X, W, Ø, Θ. *Oak Book*, ii, p. xxvii, n. 1. See also Salter (ed.), *Medieval Archives*, i, p. 20, no. 11 (Oxford, 1255); *CChR*, ii, p. 15 (Grimsby, 1258); *CPR, 1266–72*, p. 195 (Cambridge, 1268); *CLB*, A, p. 216 (1276–8); *Liber Albus*, pp. 231, 308 (1272–1307); Coss (ed.), *Early Records of Medieval Coventry*, p. 41 (1278); Prestwich (ed.), *York*, pp. 10–11 (1301); *Bristol*, ii, p. 224 (late fourteenth century); *Great Red Book*, i, p. 138 (late fifteenth century); *Henley*, p. 186 (1518).

[527] *Liber Albus*, pp. 232, 308 (1272–1307); *Coventry*, p. 682 (1522). Innkeepers also appear to have bought bread in this manner, *ibid.*, pp. 24 (1421), 29 (1421).

[528] Davis, 'Baking', 491.

[529] *Bristol*, ii, pp. 32–3 (fourteenth century); *Great Red Book*, ii, p. 100, fol. 220 (fifteenth century); McIntosh, *Working Women*, p. 190.

[530] Furley (ed.), *Ancient Usages*, pp. 34–5 (late thirteenth century); Keene, *Survey*, p. 255. See also *Memorials*, pp. 119–22 (1316).

[531] *Coventry*, p. 139 (1431). See also *Liber Albus*, p. 310 (1272–1307); Thomas (ed.), *Calendar*, pp. 19–20 (Roll A, 1298).

mark and rebounded on their own reputation.[532] Attitudes to regraters and hucksters thus differed between town governments.

Similar tensions were evident between innkeepers and bakers. Innkeepers in many towns were ordered not to bake their own horsebread but were expected to obtain it from common bakers; it is usually stated that this prohibition extended to other breads as well.[533] A petition for Northampton in 1384 outlines the origin of this prohibition. The bakers of the town complained that innkeepers were hiding their horsebread from assize inspection 'in deceit of people passing through the town', but were much more worried that their own profits were being eroded. As a safeguard for supplies and the livelihood of bakers, the town authorities agreed that innkeepers should no longer bake bread for sale.[534] This prohibition was passed into statute law in 1389–90.[535]

In general, bakers were tightly controlled as regards their profit margins and prices because of their vital role in providing communal sustenance. The authorities' prime concern remained the adequate provisioning of their communities. This did not prevent entrepreneurial bakers from seeking to raise their turnover, which could generate greater profits within the structure of the assize. But they also had to contend with a basic flaw in the assize of bread regarding the formulae for poorer-quality loaves, and this did sometimes cause problems. By the end of the fifteenth century there are examples of unrest among the baking profession.[536] For instance, the authorities of Coventry faced difficulties in satisfying bakers and their demands for a satisfactory income. This culminated in a strike by the bakers in December 1484. The bakers had been allowed leeway of 2s. weight in the farthing cocket loaf when the price of wheat was below 6s. 6d. (and 2s. in the halfpenny loaf when the price was higher), as long as they did not purchase wheat in the market before 2pm. However, they were still struggling to make a reasonable living and in protest they left the city *en masse* 'levyng þe seid Cite destitute of bred'. The mayor and officials saw their own obligations, of ensuring a steady supply of victuals to the town and its visitors, as under reproach. Consequently, they reacted strongly by fining the bakers £10 and forcing them to submit to an oath that they would never again 'make eny such

---

[532] *Leicester*, i, pp. 347–8 (1323–4). In York, bread had to be sold within six days of baking. Prestwich (ed.), *York*, pp. 10–11 (1301).

[533] *Memorials*, pp. 323–4 (1365), 347–8 (1371); *Coventry*, pp. 24 (1421), 637–8 (1513); *Henley*, p. 108 (1438); *Great Red Book*, i, p. 144 (1452); *Beverley*, p. lvii (1458); Toulmin Smith (ed.), *English Gilds*, p. 406 (Worcester, 1467); *York*, iii, pp. 241–3 (1477 and 1528); *Winchester*, p. 125 (1514).

[534] *Northampton*, i, p. 249, c.67 (1383–4); *CIM*, iv (1377–88), p. 143, no. 258. See also *Northampton*, i, p. 374 (late fifteenth century).

[535] *Statutes*, ii, p. 63, 13 Ric II st.1 c.8 (1389–90); ii, p. 140, 4 Hen IV c.25 (1402).

[536] Kowaleski, *Local Markets*, pp. 140–1; Davis, 'Baking', 472.

vnlawefull assemble, riotte, confederacye, nor departer oute of the seid Citie to þe grife or reproch of eny Maire of þe same Cite, and þat they and euery of theym woll duely obserue and kepe be their willes such due and lawefull assise [under pain of 20s.]'.[537] Although the authorities were prepared to make concessions to the bakers, and understood that they needed to make a reasonable living, they were not prepared to accept a direct threat to urban food supplies and recoiled at such temerity. The withholding of necessary victuals was considered akin to rebellion.[538] Similarly, in Leicester, the authorities warned of forfeitures for bakers who kept back flour when the town had a short supply of bread and, in the fifteenth century, imprisonment for all victuallers who did the same.[539]

Ale

If bread was the omnipotent medieval food, then ale was the equivalent drink. The grain in it not only provided nutrition, but the brewing process meant it was a far healthier drink than water. Ale sold commercially was expected to be of sufficient quality and strength, made from good malt and well brewed and blended.[540] It was measured in leathern vessels, usually of three official sizes (gallon, pottle (half-gallon) and quart), each of which had to be stamped to show it had been checked by officials. Some measures were also in wood and could be subject to warping or shrinkage with age, thus entailing regular examination.[541]

Assisa Panis et Cervisie calculated the prices of ale as follows: when the price of a quarter of wheat was 36d.–40d., or the price of barley 20d.–24d., or the price of oats 16d., then two gallons were to be sold for a penny in towns and three gallons for a penny in the country. When three gallons were sold for a penny in towns, then four gallons should be sold for a penny in the country.[542] This meant that those selling ale in towns, before expenses, needed to sell forty to forty-eight gallons from every quarter of barley to meet their costs, and those in the country required a substantial sixty to seventy-two gallons. Evidence for brewing rates can be found from the household of Elizabeth de Burgh

[537] *Coventry*, pp. 385 (1473), 518–19 (1484).

[538] Carrel, 'Food, drink and public order', 186.

[539] *Leicester*, ii, pp. 106–7 (1357), 289 (1467). Similar regulations concerned the supply of charcoal. *Ibid.*, ii, p. 295 (1467).

[540] For an excellent, detailed study of the ale trade and its regulations, see Bennett, *Ale*.

[541] *Liber Albus*, p. 233 (1272–1307).

[542] *Statutes*, i, pp. 199–200, 'Assisa Panis et Cervisie'. See also *Britton*, i, pp. 188–9, ch. 31, c.4 (1291–2); *Fleta*, ii, p. 118, bk. II, c.11 (late thirteenth century). This formulation is partially reiterated in Reynes's fifteenth-century commonplace book, though with errors. Louis (ed.), *Commonplace Book*, pp. 137–8.

of Clare in 1333–4. Her accounts state that they brewed sixty gallons from a quarter of a barley and oats mix.[543] It is possible that this was stronger than a commercial brew and the inclusion of oats might affect the quantity produced. However, if it is comparable to the assize figures for urban brewers, then it means they could earn 6d.–10d. per quarter of barley brewed. Other expenses, such as for fuel, malting, equipment and amercements, might account for perhaps another 3d.–4d. of that profit, though these are not specifically provided for by the law. Even so, it is possible that regular urban brewers had the potential to earn a similar percentage profit as bakers. Their final profit obviously depended on the level of demand and turnover, and country brewers were discriminated against regarding their profit margins. Why the prices were differentiated between town and country is not entirely clear given that any transport costs were effectively covered by the local wholesale price of grain. Possibly the legislators either considered that brewers in towns had higher costs and overheads besides the cost of grain itself, or that they were generally expected to make stronger and better ale than their rural counterparts.[544]

The vagueness of these regulations may indicate why the ensuing legislation of *Judicium Pillorie* was a little more precise, if no less simplistic. *Judicium Pillorie* differed from *Assisa* in that the prices for town and country were not differentiated, smaller capacities were used and ale was twice the price. *Judicium Pillorie* also provided a similar simplified price correlation between the price of a quarter of barley and the price of a quart of ale, whereby when the price of barley increased by 6d., the number of quarts that could be purchased for 2d. decreased by one.[545] In essence, in this formula, a brewer needed to sell between twenty-four and twenty-seven gallons from a quarter of barley to break even (before expenses), depending on the price of barley. If this had been enforced, profit margins for brewers would have been fairly comfortable.

Price of barley (per quarter)	Price of ale (per quart)
24d.	1/4d. (eight quarts for 2d.)
30d.	2/7d. (seven quarts for 2d.)
36d.	1/3d. (six quarts for 2d.)
42d.	2/5d. (five quarts for 2d.)
48d.	1/2d. (four quarts for 2d.)

[543] Bennett, *Ale*, p. 18.   [544] *Ibid.*, p. 21.
[545] *Statutes*, i, pp. 201–2, 'Judicium Pillorie'.

Thus, the sophisticated calculations seen above in the assize of bread were not evident in the assize of ale, which resorted to a more simplistic formula that was readily understandable. This is perhaps unsurprising given the different basis upon which the ale trade was conducted.

Brewing was usually undertaken as a supplementary occupation, often by women on an *ad hoc* basis, compared to the more permanent and sedentary baking profession. The ordinances at Ipswich refer to 'brewsteres' and in *Modus Tenendi Curias*, *c*.1342, the articles of the view of frankpledge included a specific reference to alewives or regratresses ('braceresses ou regrateressez') rather than any male brewers.[546] Such references illustrate the contemporary impression that women dominated the medieval brewing trade. The ability to make ale commercially was more widespread than baking, which required a comparatively expensive oven for large-scale production, and the selling of ale reflected the convenience of buying ale ready-made and the short lifespan of the liquid.

Like bread, jurors set the recommended costs of ale based on the common wholesale market rate for grain. In Berwick (1283–4), they recognised that there was a regular increase in barley prices during the agricultural cycle and stated that 'no woman shall sell ale, from Easter till Michaelmas, at dearer than twopence a gallon; nor, from Michaelmas till Easter, at dearer than a penny'.[547] At Ipswich, the assize of ale was to be announced at Michaelmas, when new barley became readily available.[548] Officials also had to take into account the malting process and the various strengths of ale, which depended not only on the amount and quality of grain but also the number of infusions during brewing. The brewers of Bristol were expected to make both 'gode ale' and 'small ale', wherein the small ale was sold at half the price and if a householder could prove that 'the secunde ale is nat halfe so gode as the gode ale that thei so grevid shall haue ther money a yen'.[549] The application of the assize of ale within local markets thus deviated from the particular figures provided in *Assisa* and *Judicium Pillorie*, though they appear to be much more akin to the stricter limits for brewers encapsulated in *Assisa*. In Leicester, brewers were to sell a gallon of the best ale for 1d. and other ale for ½d., when the quarter of the barley cost 4s.; while in Beverley, in 1371,

---

[546] Maitland and Baildon (eds.), *Court Baron*, p. 94. See also *Bristol*, i, pp. 43–4 (1344).

[547] Toulmin Smith (ed.), *English Gilds*, p. 343 (Berwick, 1283–4).

[548] *Black Book*, ii, pp. 174–5, c.81 [78] (*c*.1309). See also Prestwich (ed.), *York*, p. 11 (1301).

[549] *Great Red Book*, i, p. 139 (late fifteenth century). See also Stanford (ed.), *Ordinances of Bristol*, p. 5 (1505).

a gallon of ale was to be sold for $1\frac{1}{2}$d. when malt sold at between 5s. and 6s. 8d.[550]

Robert Reynes's transcription of the figures for the assize of ale drew mostly on *Assisa* rather than *Judicium Pillorie*, though his fifteenth-century English transcription has several scribal errors and additions. One passage, not found elsewhere, states: 'alle costages [expenses] and repryses of brewars acounted and alowed well and largely, þei may in a quarter of malt bruyng [brewing] gete iiiid and all the ȝyst [yeast], dreggys and draff as is prouyd in the brewhous of our lord þe Kyng'.[551] This suggests an allowance similar to the bakers, but based entirely on sales from a quarter of malt. According to Reynes's version, the price of a gallon of ale would increase or decrease only by a farthing as the price of a quarter of malt altered by 12d. This is a different formulation to *Judicium Pillorie* and gives the brewer a much a lower price for their ale. Somewhat vaguely, *Statutum de Pistoribus* provided two options for a farthing increase in the price of a gallon, when a quarter of malt increased by either 12d. or 6d.[552] Given the figures for ale prices shown above, it does appear that *Assisa*, and to a lesser extent *Statutum de Pistoribus*, were the basis for ale prices in England throughout the thirteenth to fifteenth centuries and not *Judicium Pillorie*, which was perhaps too generous towards brewers in its pricing schedule. It also appears that revised, amalgamated and simplified versions of *Assisa* and *Statutum de Pistoribus* were in circulation during the fifteenth century and even reached lowly village officials like Robert Reynes. The basis of the assize of ale, as much as the assize of bread, was intended to provide a reasonable livelihood to brewers similar to their counterparts in the baking trade. This does not seem to support the notion that the assize of ale was especially difficult for medieval brewers to obey.

Inspecting officials, known as aletasters, were specifically appointed to monitor the day-to-day activities of brewers and ale-sellers. They inspected batches of ale for offences against the assize, particularly regarding price, quality and measures. In Worcester, in 1467, these

---

[550] *Leicester*, ii, p. 21 (1335–6); *Beverley*, p. 41 (1371). Other ale prices are listed in *Bristol*, ii, p. 222 (1283); *CLB*, E, pp. 71, 73 (1316), F, pp. 27–8, 189 (1337), 178 (1347–8); *Liber Albus*, p. 233 (1272–1307); *Coventry*, p. 25 (1421); *Red Paper Book*, p. 18 (fifteenth century).

[551] Louis (ed.), *Commonplace Book*, pp. 137–8. The brewers of fifteenth-century Norwich were warned against trying to gain more for their by-product of barm or yeast ('god-disgood') than was customary – a farthing's worth of bread, eggs or grain in return for sufficient barm to brew a quarter of malt. 'Goddisgood' was seen as coming from the grace of God and its distribution as charitable, so those who sought to make excessive profit were committing 'fraude or subtilte' and causing 'great hurte and slander' to the city. *Norwich*, ii, pp. 98–9 (1468).

[552] *Statutes*, i, pp. 201–4, 'Judicium Pillorie' and 'Statutum de Pistoribus'.

Figure 16: Alewife and alestake

Notes: This marginal image from the Smithfield Decretals (*c.*1325–50) show an alewife holding a tankard and serving ale to an old man. She is standing outside her home, or alehouse, as denoted by the broom that is displayed to announce her brewing to the aletasters.
Source: BL, MS Royal 10.E.IV, fol. 114r.

aletasters (or aleconners) were to be 'sadd and discrete persons, to se that the ale be good and sete'.[553] Colchester aletasters were expected to 'make good, due and diligent serche' to ensure that the ale and beer was of 'good odour' and made from 'good, suffisaunt, and holsum corne . . . not over-moche dried, not stynkyng nor full of vermyn callid wevelis'.[554] Brewers who were about to sell their product were supposed to put out a sign, usually a brush or broom, as a public indication for customers and ale-tasters that ale was for sale.[555] Figure 16 clearly shows a broom-sign outside a modest dwelling where an alewife is serving an elderly man. Amercements were stipulated for those who did not put their sign above the door and for those who failed to remove it once their ale was gone.[556] The aletasters would then sample the ale before it was sold in order to

---

[553] Toulmin Smith (ed.), *English Gilds*, pp. 381–2 (Worcester, 1467). See also *CLB*, D, pp. 201–2 (late thirteenth century?); *Liber Albus*, pp. 311–12 (1272–1307); *Coventry*, pp. 191 (1439), 677–8 (1521); *Norwich*, ii, p. 100 (1471); *Leicester*, ii, p. 304 (1482); Stanford (ed.), *Ordinances of Bristol*, p. 14 (1519–20).

[554] *Red Paper Book*, pp. 20–1 (fifteenth century). See also *Leicester*, ii, pp. 288 (1467), 322 (1489?), iii, p. 16 (1520). Beer begins to appear in town regulations in the mid-fifteenth century.

[555] *BBC, 1216–1307*, p. 293 (Oxford, 1255); Salter (ed.), *Medieval Archives*, i, p. 20, no. 11 (Oxford, 1255); *CPR, 1266–72*, p. 195 (Cambridge, 1268); *Bristol*, ii, p. 30 (1346?); Hilton (ed.), *Stoneleigh*, p. 99 (fourteenth century); *Great Red Book*, i, pp. 139–140 (1452); Toulmin Smith (ed.), *English Gilds*, p. 405 (Worcester, 1467). In a similar manner, the innkeepers of Coventry had to keep a lamp hanging outside their doors until 9pm, and the inns of Worcester and York had to have a sign at the door. *Coventry*, p. 234 (1448); Toulmin Smith (ed.), *English Gilds*, p. 406 (Worcester, 1467); *York*, iii, pp. 241–3 (1477, 1528).

[556] E.g. Massingberd (ed.), *Court Rolls*, pp. 116, 240. These signs or alestakes appear to have become increasingly permanent and caused obstructions to passers-by. *Memorials*, pp. 386–7 (1375); *CLB*, H, p. 12 (1375); *Liber Albus*, p. 389.

check that it was brewed well and to set the price as required by the assize. Any infringements were presented at court, such as brewers refusing to sell ale at the correct price, not calling for aletasters upon the production of a new batch of ale, or using unsealed measures.

All brewers were expected to have correct measures sealed with a validating mark by the authorities. A recurrent concern was the use of leather or wooden cups and bowls that had no seal.[557] The fifteenth-century Bristol authorities were so concerned to ensure the use of standard measures that every brewer was required to have a level place at their door where anyone fetching ale could put vessels when checking for true measure. In addition, any that stood witness against a brewer using false measures received 4d. for their trouble.[558] There were also regulations against brewers who favoured in-house customers over those who wished to take away their ale.[559] This was presumably a guard against alewives who sought to cajole customers into buying more ale and those who used cups that were not standard measures.

As with bread, more regular brewers seemingly sold their remaining stocks to regraters and hucksters rather than make a loss.[560] To prevent this from causing unnecessary price rises the authorities in Bristol ordered that no tapster (a retailer of ale) was to have any ale from the brewers until householders and poor people had been first served. Also, tapsters were to sell their ale in a public place and not in secret chambers, and their product was to be openly advertised with a sign.[561]

Tapsters seemed to face increasing legal antipathy, as mirrored in literature.[562] An ordinance for Bristol in 1505 complained of brewers and tapsters who subtly mixed unwholesome ale with new ale in order to sell it to customers who 'oftentymes taken infeccion and disease'. In a public demonstration of such deceit, any such corrupt ale was to be cast

---

[557] Coss (ed.), *Early Records of Medieval Coventry*, p. 41 (1278); *CLB*, A, p. 216 (1276–8), H, pp. 337 (1388), 373 (1391–2); *Beverley*, p. 42 (1371); *Leicester*, ii, p. 288 (1467), iii, p. 17 (1520); *Northampton*, i, p. 373 (late fifteenth century); *Coventry*, pp. 25 (1421), 678 (1521), 683 (1522); Sillem (ed.), *Records*, pp. 17, 22, 47 (Roll LL), nos. 21, 44, 180 (1373–5). In Norwich, 1290, three pots were expected to contain one gallon. *Norwich*, i, p. 368 (1290).

[558] *Great Red Book*, i, p. 139 (late fifteenth century). See also *Coventry*, p. 25 (1421).

[559] Bennett, *Ale*, p. 101; Courthope and Formoy (eds.), *Lathe Court Rolls*, p. 202 (fifteenth century).

[560] *Coventry*, p. 25 (1421); *Winchester*, p. 140 (1525). This practice was forbidden in London until the late fifteenth century. *CLB*, G, pp. 123–4 (1360), H, pp. 184 (1382), 337 (1388), L, p. 288 (1492); *Memorials*, pp. 347–8 (1371); *Liber Albus*, pp. 312–13 (1335).

[561] *Great Red Book*, i, p. 140 (1452); *Bristol*, ii, p. 30 (1346?). See also Toulmin Smith (ed.), *English Gilds*, pp. 405–6.

[562] See pp. 106–15.

into the street before the door of the alehouse.[563] A fourteenth-century ordinance for Bristol complained that traventers of ale (excluding brewers and innkeepers) caused 'great grievances and injuries' to the commonalty, particularly because of their willingness to allow thieves and evildoers to undertake business in their alehouses which caused 'great injury and scandal' to the town.[564] There were several cases in the Great Tourn of Nottingham where both male and female hostelers were accused of harbouring dicers, thieves and harlots.[565] The by-laws of Coventry went even further in 1492, declaring that no one in the city was to 'fauour eny tapster, or woman of evell name, fame or condicion to whom eny resorte is of synfull disposicioun, hauntyng the synne of lechery'.[566] In civic legislation, alehouses and tapsters were sometimes directly associated with brothels and prostitutes, and alehouses and taverns were to have no customers after curfew had been rung.[567] In Colchester in 1311, Agnes de Ardleye was accused of selling at her tavern to foreigners who arrived at night, who were then both drunken and noisy.[568] The wording and barely concealed vitriol of these ordinances parallels the literary portrayals of alewives that were common by the fifteenth century.

Overall, the assize of ale was intended as a check on quality, supply, measures and price, and those who offended were to be amerced or punished. However, the system in many places seems to have been based upon a notion of fining everyone, in the manner of a licence and, in effect, challenging the brewers to show they had not sold contrary to the assize and should not therefore be liable. An entry from Bury St Edmunds stated: 'And if a brewster can acquit herself single handed that she has in no way sold contrary to the assize, she shall be quit'.[569] Similarly, at Torksey, in 1345: 'The brewsters . . . shall be asked whether or not they brew and sell ale outside the house against the assize. If they say not, they shall have a day at the next court to make their law three-handed, with women neighbours on either side or with others.'[570] These ordinances demonstrate how the judicial procedure of presentment, whereby the onus of proof was passed onto the defendant, made possible an effectual transition of the assize into a licensing scheme. The laws of the assize of ale presented a severe view towards offences

---

[563] Stanford (ed.), *Ordinances of Bristol*, p. 4 (1505).

[564] *Bristol*, ii, pp. 37–8 (fourteenth century).

[565] *Nottingham*, ii, pp. 62–3 (1408).   [566] *Coventry*, p. 545 (1492).

[567] *King's Lynn*, p. 268, no. 325 (1465); Goldberg, 'Women in fifteenth-century town life', p. 118; *CLB*, c, p. 16 (1293); *Memorials*, p. 193 (1334); *Liber Albus*, pp. 240–1 (1272–1307); *Bristol*, ii, p. 225 (late fourteenth century); Alsford, *Towns* (Lynn, early fifteenth century); *Great Red Book*, i, p. 140 (late fifteenth century).

[568] Jeayes (ed.), *Court Rolls*, i, p. 45 (1311).

[569] Goldberg (ed.), *Women in England*, p. 185.   [570] *Ibid.*, p. 185.

and demanded corporal punishments for severe or repeated offences, but as with all trading regulations, enforcement ultimately resided in local hands. In law, malpractices were associated with criminality and deterrence was the prime consideration beyond fiscal levies. However, in practice, the assizes were a franchise upon which a lord expected a return and the practicalities of the assize may have called for more lenience in its actual enforcement.[571] Also, since brewing was not a monopolistic or high profit-making occupation, the ease of brewing often meant there was sufficient competition to guard against the continual fraud of an individual. The assize of ale was basically a consumer-protective device in terms of the legal ideology it espoused, laying down rules that all could understand and adhere to, including the customers. Rules were set for the margins of acceptable trading behaviour, so that flagrant abuses could be prevented by the recognition of minimum standards and moral behaviour.

Wine

Wine was also subject to assize regulation from at least the twelfth century and the reign of Henry II.[572] Wine cannot be considered a staple product in the manner of bread or ale, and its main consumers in the thirteenth century were the upper ranks of society. However, the importance of this particular group in formulating certain regulations might indicate that they had faced problems from price-raising wine merchants and sought a unified, royal response at an early date. Price limits were generally set on retail prices, not wholesale, and attention was again directed at issues of quality and supply.

The articles of the eyre for Edward I included provision to investigate wines sold contrary to the assize in towns and who sold them, while *Judicium Pillorie* ordered inquiries into the price at which vintners sold a gallon and if the wine was corrupt. *Statutum de Pistoribus* set the price of a gallon ('sextertium') of wine at 12d., and ordered that taverners (retailers of wine from a permanent place) who exceeded this should be forbidden to continue trading.[573] By the early fourteenth century,

---

[571] This is discussed further on pp. 297–323.

[572] Britnell, *Commercialisation*, p. 94; *Great Roll of the Pipe*, pp. 126, 184 (1176); Stenton (ed.), *Great Roll of the Pipe, 1 John*, p. 15; Maitland (ed.), *Select Pleas of the Crown*, i, pp. 24 (1202), 98 (1221).

[573] *Statutes*, i, p. 233, Edw I?; i, pp. 201–4, 'Judicium Pillorie' and 'Statutum de Pistoribus'. See also *Fleta*, ii, pp. 121–2, bk. ii, c.12 (late thirteenth century); *Britton*, i, pp. 192–3, ch. 31, c.9 (1291–2).

statutory law noted that the number of taverners was increasing but that, due to a lack of specified punishments, many were selling corrupt wines at any price 'to the great hurt of the people'. Rather than setting a specific rate, the statute of 1330 demanded that wines should be sold at a reasonable price, based on the price at ports and subsequent expenses (presumably transport and storage). An assay of wine should be held at least twice a year, and all corrupt wines should be poured out and their vessels broken.[574] Such a requirement had been anticipated in the 1301 ordinances for York, where any taverners found with bad or putrid wine had their vessels publicly broken up, as well as being fined.[575] In 1381, Parliament sought to set the price for several sorts of wine to be sold gross or retail, as well as preventing the retailing of sweet wines. They did, however, recognise the need for merchants to cover their costs if transporting the wine further into the country and allowed $\frac{1}{2}$d. on a gallon of wine for every fifty miles travelled.[576] Other legislation after the Black Death was mostly directed at ensuring that all wines were gauged by the king's officials, under threats of forfeiture and imprisonment. This was to ensure that tuns and pipes of wine contained the right number of gallons according to the assize and to check for any corrupt wine.[577] The basic principles thus remained unchanged but legislators were concerned to close loopholes and tightened the law. For instance, past statutes failed to delineate between all types of wine and some traders avoided inspection. In 1380, all vessels of imported wine, sweet wine, honey, liquors and oil were to be gauged.[578]

At a local level, authorities generally followed statutory and royal stipulations, though there were also specific regulations relevant to their own concerns. In York (1301), the price was set at 4d. a gallon for 'good old wine' and 5d. a gallon for new wine.[579] Londoners had to wait

---

[574] *Statutes*, i, p. 264, 4 Edw III c.12 (1330). See also *CCR, 1330–3*, p. 410; *Parl. Rolls*, c.8, January 1333; *CPR, 1345–8*, pp. 387–8 (Nottingham, 1347); *Memorials*, pp. 408–9 (1377). Accusations against vintners and taverners were often related to the practice of mixing old dregs with new wine. Gross (ed.), *Select Cases*, p. 62 (St Ives, 1293); *Black Book*, ii, pp. 176–7, c.82 [79] (c.1309); Jeayes (ed.), *Court Rolls*, i, pp. 3, 7 (1310); *Leicester*, ii, pp. 20–1 (1335–6), 58–9 (1343); *CLB*, F, pp. 19 (1337–8), 77 (1342), G, p. 301 (1372). In York, in 1433, the searchers of the vintners found sweet wine in the house of John Asper which was 'unabell to be sald' and as punishment the forfeited wine barrels were broken: 'the hevedes [heads] smyten oute openly in syght of the people'. *York*, iii, p. 157 (1433).

[575] Prestwich (ed.), *York*, p. 12 (1301).

[576] *Statutes*, ii, pp. 18–20, 5 Ric II st.1 c.4 (1381). The following year they lifted the ban on selling sweet wines by retail. *Ibid.*, ii, p. 28, 6 Ric II st.1 c.7 (1382).

[577] *Ibid.*, i, p. 331, 27 Edw III st.1 cc.5–8 (1353), i, p. 350, 31 Edw III st.1 c.5 (1357), ii, p. 313, 18 Hen VI c.17 (1439). *Parl. Rolls*, c.43, May 1432, c.56, November 1439.

[578] *Statutes*, ii, p. 16, 4 Ric II c.1 (1380).   [579] Prestwich (ed.), *York*, p. 12 (1301).

until wine cargoes had been unladen, the casks gauged and the wine assayed before they could make any purchases. In 1311, the best wine sold for 5d., the next best at 4d. and the rest for 3d. Those who sold wine with false measures faced prison and the vessels would be burnt. There were also fourteenth-century regulations that ordered taverners to keep in sight their casks so that customers could see that 'the wine drawn is clean and from what cask his wine be drawn'.[580] The level of disgust shown towards taverners who sold wine that was considered unwholesome 'in deceit of the common people' and 'to the shameful disgrace of the officers of the City' was shown in the penalty inflicted upon John Penrose for this offence. He was made to drink a draught of the same wine, before the remainder was poured over his head and he was made to forswear the calling of vintner for ever.[581] For most vintners who mixed wines or adulterated them, the pillory was the threatened punishment.[582]

Seabourne has noted how the price of wine in some towns was sometimes set with reference to the price elsewhere, demonstrating a regulatory relationship between localities.[583] Wine sold in Oxford was to be inspected to ensure it was not putrid and sold no dearer than $\frac{1}{2}$d. a gallon more than the price in London.[584] By the mid-fifteenth century, taverners were being given strict orders regarding the advertising of prices. Their gallons, pottles, quarts, pints, half-pints and penny pots all had to be checked and sealed, and was each marked with the price of the wine sold in that vessel.[585] In fifteenth-century Coventry, all wine had to be surveyed by the authorities before it could be sold, upon the threat of a 20s. fine. They wanted to ensure that the wine was of good quality, sold in sealed measures, and no dearer than 8d. a gallon for Gascon wine, 6d. a gallon for Rochell white wine and 16d. a gallon for Malmesey and Romeney.[586]

[580] *Memorials*, pp. 81–3 (1311), 181–3 (1331), 213–14 (1342), 341–3 (1370); *CLB*, F, pp. 245–6 (1352); *Liber Albus*, pp. 85–6 (1237–8); Riley (ed.), *Munimenta Gildhallae*, ii, 'Liber Custumarum', pp. 304, 425 (1320–1). See also *CLB*, E, pp. 44 (1315), 72–3 (1316).
[581] *Memorials*, pp. 318–19 (1364).   [582] *Ibid.*, pp. 670–2 (1419).
[583] Seabourne, *Royal Regulation*, p. 85.
[584] Salter (ed.), *Munimenta*, pp. 21–2, no. 24 (1311); Salter (ed.), *Medieval Archives*, i, pp. 118–19, nos. 74–5 (1330–1). See also *York*, i, p. 172; Keene, *Survey*, p. 271.
[585] *Great Red Book*, i, p. 145 (1452). See also *Northampton*, i, p. 375 (late fifteenth century); *Leicester*, ii, pp. 20–1 (1335–6), 84 (1352), 93 (1354), 288 (1467); *Norwich*, ii, pp. 153–4 (1496).
[586] *Coventry*, pp. 24–5 (1421). Similar prices were set out in *CLB*, K, p. 16 (1423–3); *Statutes*, iii, p. 670, 28 Hen VIII c.14 (1536).

Administering the assizes

Robert Ricart, the town clerk for Bristol, wrote his 1479 *Kalendar* to celebrate civic prestige and liberties, and he described various oaths, duties and ceremonies performed by the town's luminaries. The mayor's role included holding courts, supervising the brewers and bakers, and regulating the market. Indeed, Ricart describes how the Mayor of Bristol directly counselled brewers and bakers about their provisioning duty to the town, and provides an insight into the purpose of the assize legislation at an urban level. The mayor was deemed ultimately responsible for overseeing the assizes, as a proxy Clerk of the Market, so an annual display of his authority is not surprising. However, Ricart also suggests that the mayor personally oversaw the weighing of bread during the year, both at his own instigation and in response to complaints, and that he often accompanied the 'alekonner' on Wednesdays and Saturdays 'to walke in the morenynges to the brewers howses, to oversee theym in seruyng of their ale to the pouere commens of the toune, and that they have theire trewe mesure3'.[587] Whether such personal involvement by the mayor was as frequent as Ricart implies is doubtful, but such demonstrations of authority still served to uphold the mayor's image of moral integrity and commercial control.[588]

The mayor was expected to provide just government for the good of all. In 1522, the Mayor of Bristol sought supplies of grain from Worcestershire in response to high prices. This was explained in terms of the mayor's 'gode disposition inclynyng his charitie towardes the comen wele and profite of this towne'.[589] It was important for the successful functioning of a market to present a confident appearance of vigilance and justice for all its users. Officers not only had to enforce the rules but also make sure that everyone else knew them. Written laws were therefore read aloud in the marketplace, probably by officials standing in front of the market cross, to ensure that no one could claim ignorance. The ordinances and charters of Bristol were recited at least every Michaelmas in the fourteenth century so 'that every one may know and hear both these liberties and customs'.[590] The assizes of bread and ale were the commonplace lodestone by which a market's reputation could be judged,

---

[587] Toulmin Smith (ed.), *The Maire*, pp. 82–3 (1479).

[588] In similar rhetoric, Ricart's account of the Bristol mayor-making ceremony stressed the association between the mayor's authority and the virtue of obedience to the king, as a justification of their (increasingly oligarchic) governance. Fleming, 'Telling tales', pp. 180–2.

[589] Stanford (ed.), *Ordinances of Bristol*, p. 49 (1522); Toulmin Smith (ed.), *The Maire*, p. 49.

[590] *Bristol*, i, pp. 39–40 (1344).

and Ricart was keen to portray a mayor who was diligent in upholding such market laws and thus the unity of the commercial community.

In a similar manner, the London authorities held four Hallmotes a year to administer the assize of bread 'by common counsel and prudent foresight of the City'. All bakers were expected to attend, in order to see that the assizes were being upheld according to the statutes and 'to the well-being of the commonwealth'. Similar Hallmotes were held for fishmongers so that 'there may be no doubting, but certainty, as to how the folks of such trade ought to comport themselves'. Such forums remained an important part of the apparatus to protect the provisioning of London, 'to studye the remedyes of all manner thingis preiudiciall to the cytee', and to demonstrate that the mayor and council took seriously their obligation to protect the 'comon wele'.[591] They also served a purpose in educating the market traders as to their obligations and the existing regulations. As Evelyn Welch noted for medieval Italian towns, 'lists of prices provided a visible marker of legality and communal constraints; they allowed participants to decide whether they were part of a commonly instituted and accepted basis for sales, or whether they were operating on the edge of social order'.[592]

Conversely, a threat to the reputation of a town's authorities in the administration of the assizes can be seen in an ordinance for Northampton in 1467. Bakers were ordered not to send any more bread into the countryside because too much had evaded the assizes and was of insufficient quality and weight 'to an vniu[er]sall hurte of the king[es] liege people. Causyng great rumor and noyse to be spoken to the dishonure of the maire for the tyme beyng and oppyn disclaundre of the same town.' All bread was to be duly assayed under the threat of a penalty of 6s. 8d.[593] Social disorder could stem from a perception that municipal authorities were failing in their obligations. During disputes at Coventry in both 1374 and 1387, citizens threw loaves at the mayor and bakers regularly asked for a restatement of the assize of bread.[594]

The assizes, in particular, were the most obvious sign of market control and authorities needed to show that they were working efficiently for the good of all. In Norwich, four assayers of the assize bought grain, ground

---

[591] *Liber Albus*, pp. 310–11 (1272–1307), 327–8 (1279–80); Arnold, *Customs of London*, p. 88 (*c.*1519). See Carrel, 'Food, drink and public order', 184–93.

[592] Welch, *Shopping*, p. 89.

[593] *Northampton*, i, pp. 309–10 (1467). During the long-running dispute between the town and university of Oxford, the townsmen asserted in 1355 that recent problems with the quality and sale of bread were a matter for the university assayers: 'the cause and fault lie with you who have the assize to keep, and with no one else'. Salter (ed.), *Munimenta*, pp. 135–7, no. 140 (1355).

[594] Willcox, *Bakers' Company*, p. 7.

and sieved it, and then baked it into bread, which they then sold openly in the town, 'so that they may see that the people be not deceived but rather that they be served with it rightly and faithfully without fraud'.[595] In London, in 1298–9, Roger de Len was fined two casks of wine for claiming that the mayor and aldermen had been bribed by William de Leyre 'against the common good' to produce an assize of wine at $1\frac{1}{2}$d. for the gallon.[596] Public confidence and assurance in the mechanism of the assizes was paramount for an ordered and well-run marketplace.

Late medieval authorities, at both a national and local level, thus imposed limitations upon traders to prevent speculators from hiking prices in times of shortage and to ensure a level of stability in the market. In other words, the assize price kept prices to a minimum for consumers, but enabled producers and traders to maintain a 'reasonable' livelihood. To drive traders out of business was counter-productive, but they could not countenance any incentives of excessive profit or speculation. Town price policies were thus in harmony with requirements of justice as conceived by the Church and theologians. Traditional social theories provided an important context for price-fixing, for traders were expected to work for the benefit of the community and be content with minimal recompense. As Britnell stated: 'the setting of prices is a culturally embedded phenomenon', and cultural norms had an effect in addition to the economic laws of supply and demand.[597] The authorities were attempting to enforce economic stability, partly for the benefit of employers and lords but also to preserve the social status quo. Controlling food prices helped preserve the governing hierarchy, peace and order.[598] Legislation drew upon the ideology of the social body where each appendage existed to serve the whole and those who followed their calling diligently would receive their due recompense. Traders were expected to serve the public and community in supplying their goods at a reasonable price and not to make excessive profits which would have *de facto* come from high prices.

Middlemen

Local authorities could only control prices and bargaining practices once supplies had reached a town. Irregular or lack of supplies created price fluctuations which officials could only temper rather than reverse.

---

[595] *Norwich*, i, pp. 174–6 (early fourteenth century). There were complaints in London, in 1310–11, that the bread of their assay had been badly baked, making the assize too severe to keep. It was agreed that a new assay would take place. *CLB*, D, p. 243 (1310–11).

[596] Thomas (ed.), *Calendar*, pp. 24–5 (Roll B, 1298–9).

[597] Britnell, 'Price-setting', 15.   [598] Poos, 'Social context'.

Because of this, trading legislation was intimately connected with the mechanisms of supply and demand in medieval England. Many laws were devoted to ensuring that particular goods were supplied in plentiful quantities to specific sites so as to meet essential demand. Other regulations attempted to tie the chains of supply to privileged traders, often where either supply or demand was limited and competition more fierce. The recognition that supply networks were essential to any price regulation was also one of the prime motivations behind the legislation against middlemen that blossomed in the thirteenth and fourteenth centuries, especially those laws dealing with forestallers, engrossers and regraters.

Forestalling was the interception of goods before they reached an open market. It was a concept that was only fully explicated during the thirteenth century through English laws and statutes.[599] *Judicium Pillorie* defined forestalling as buying goods before the accustomed hour, or outside of the market itself, so that traders would sell them again more dearly than otherwise would have been the case, 'against the good state and weal of the town and market'.[600] It was not considered forestalling if the goods were acquired for personal consumption, only if they were to be sold again for profit.[601] Forestallers most often acted in collusion with travelling producers or traders and offered rural prices.[602] The seller profited by not having to pay tolls and the transaction also lowered their transport and time costs. A forestaller made money on the higher urban price and usually did not have to pay tolls in their own town. However, town authorities feared price hikes since they could not control the price of goods outside the town and they understood that supply affected price in retail markets. Middlemen could legally go out to manors to buy up commodities in bulk, as this ensured that the supply to the town was enhanced. However, once the product was actually on its way to market,

[599] Britnell, 'Forstall'. This article traced the evolution of the term 'forestalling' from its original meaning as a forceful appropriation of goods on the highway, to a later notion of collusive or consensual dealing that raised prices. *First Report of the Royal Commission*, i, appx I, p. 33 (Laws of Edward the Confessor, *c*.1042–66); Downer (ed.), *Leges Henrici Primi*, pp. 248–9, c.80,2, c.80,4, c.80,4a. An entry in Northampton's *Liber Custumarum* described forestallers 'lyen in a wayte with oute the town or market'; *Northampton*, i, p. 376 (late fifteenth century). See also Seabourne, *Royal Regulation*, ch. 4.
[600] *Statutes*, i, pp. 201–2, 'Judicium Pillorie'.
[601] Cam (ed.), *Eyre of London*, pp. 310–11, 357–8.
[602] Consensual forestalling was defined in a variety of national statutes and orders. Britnell, 'Forstall', 94–5, 100; Seabourne, *Royal Regulation*, p. 127; *Statutes*, i, pp. 202–4, 'Statutum de Pistoribus'; *CChR, 1257–1300*, p. 98 (1268). Coercion against outside traders did still occur throughout the later Middle Ages, but most forestalling was a consensual activity. Seabourne, *Royal Regulation*, pp. 132–4.

via land or water, authorities usually viewed the forestaller's actions as only conducive to raising prices and avoiding tolls.[603]

Forestallers were often bakers, brewers, cooks or innkeepers who consequently avoided restrictions which allowed personal needs to be met first, and they did this outside of the purview of market officials.[604] The bakers of fifteenth-century Bristol were not only forbidden to forestall corn, under the threat of a fine of half a mark, but were also ordered not to buy corn within seven miles of the city.[605] Forestalling led to suspicion from authorities who put much energy into ensuring publicity and open trade, and such suspicion was transformed into accusations of heightened prices ('to the great hurte of the Comons').[606] Additionally, by intercepting goods a forestaller was effectively using prior information to usurp his fellow townsmen and this contravened privileged notions of shared bargains, profits and dues.

Although forestallers performed a function which aided producers and they still had to sell at a competitive market price, their actions undermined nearly all the official medieval market laws, the principles of a public market, and privileges of supply and price. He was the medieval 'free rider' who was seen as damaging the whole market community. It was perhaps the wide-ranging implications of forestallers for the medieval system of market regulation that meant the term 'forestalling' became a vague, all-encompassing catchword. Often those regraters who bought victuals in the market before the proper hour were deemed to be forestallers, as well as those who went beyond the market to intercept goods or bought in private houses.[607] The customs of Beverley (1360s) stated that forestallers were to be judged according to the laws of the realm 'and that in every inquiry held by the lord's steward as to forestallers, the steward or bailiff shall explain in set terms to the jurors what constitutes a forestaller and what not'.[608] Obviously, the jurors themselves needed reminding as to the definition of offenders.

The commodities that were most consistently forestalled were primary products of agriculture and the sea, which were affected by supply networks and regional price differences. An ordinance for Bristol in 1473

---

[603] *Statutes*, i, p. 315, 25 Edw III st.3 c.3 (1350–1); i, pp. 337–8, 27 Edw III st.2 c.11 (1353); i, pp. 348–9, 28 Edw III c.13 (1354).

[604] *BBC, 1216–1307*, p. 297 (*CPR, 1266–72*, p. 195) (Cambridge, 1268); *CLB*, E, p. 56 (1316); *Memorials*, p. 432 (1379); *Great Red Book*, i, pp. 134–5, 140–1 (late fifteenth century); *Coventry*, p. 197 (1441).

[605] *Great Red Book*, i, p. 138 (late fifteenth century). This restriction was increased to ten miles in 1519–20, Stanford (ed.), *Ordinances of Bristol*, p. 13 (1519–20).

[606] *Ibid.* See also *Nottingham*, i, pp. 318–19, 322–5 (1396).

[607] *Nottingham*, i, pp. 276–9 (1395).   [608] *Beverley*, p. 9 (1360s).

listed wheat, rye, barley, oats, beans, fish, poultry, wildfowl, cheese, butter, eggs, onions, oatmeal and fruit as all commodities that were being
forestalled and regrated.[609] In late fourteenth-century London, forestallers apparently made 'false suggestions' to cheese dealers and then
privately bought the cheese and sold it by retail without it ever entering
the marketplace.[610] Fish offered perhaps the best profit and opportunity,
being irregularly transported along known routes from specific supply
points. It was also a perishable commodity and obtained a significant
price differential caused by transport costs. Great Yarmouth had several regulations that targeted forestallers of fish, particularly herring, and
those who sent 'pikers or other ships to meet ships coming to port'. All
fish was to be unladen openly and exposed for sale by fishermen during
daylight hours with no interference by forestallers or hostelers.[611] The
ordinances of Ipswich stated that no regrater (known or a stranger) was
to go out of the bounds of the town market to either bargain, buy or forestall fish coming to the town to be sold. Those caught doing so forfeited
their fish (for the common use) and had to make 'gre' (compensation) to
the seller for the merchandise.[612]

Most town ordinances included specific and harsh sanctions against
forestallers, often involving the pillory, and these drew upon both legislative norms and moral concerns about 'grete disceyte' or 'hurtyng of
the pore people'.[613] The ordinances for Beverley stated that no burgess
fisherman should be punished for any fault except by amercement and
by the conviction of twelve fellow burgesses. The only exception was
forestalling, 'then he or she convicted may be punished according to
the law of the land [i.e. statute law] and the measure of the offence'.[614]
The widespread examples of laws against forestalling suggest that it was
difficult to suppress.[615]

[609] *Great Red Book*, iii, p. 97 (1473).   [610] *Memorials*, p. 406 (1377).
[611] *Statutes*, i, pp. 353–5, 31 Edw III st.2 cc.1–2 (1357); *CCR, 1354–60*, pp. 231, 423;
CCR, 1360–4, pp. 129–30; *CPR, 1354–8*, pp. 654–5. See also *BBC, 1216–1307*,
pp. 295–6 (Grimsby, 1258); *Liber Albus*, pp. 323–6 (thirteenth century), 328–9 (1279–
80); *Oak Book*, i, pp. 66–7, no. 65 (c.1300); *Black Book*, ii, pp. 158–61, c.68 [66]
(c.1309); *Salisbury*, p. 213, no. 414 (1447); *Great Red Book*, i, pp. 134, 141 (late
fifteenth century); *Northampton*, i, p. 264, c.80 (c.1460); *Leicester*, ii, p. 289 (1467);
Coventry, p. 635 (1512).
[612] *Black Book*, ii, pp. 100–1, c.26 (c.1309). Sellers were generally considered to be innocent parties in these particular dealings, rather like domestic buyers in marketplaces,
though they could be accused of selling outside appointed places. See Seabourne, *Royal
Regulation*, pp. 136–7.
[613] *Northampton*, i, pp. 223–5, cc.25 and 29 (c.1460), 264 (c.1393), 376 (late fifteenth
century).
[614] *Beverley*, p. 9 (1360s).
[615] For municipal forestalling laws, see *BBC, 1216–1307*, pp. 294–5 (Canterbury, 1256;
Great Yarmouth, 1306); Coss (ed.), *Early Records of Medieval Coventry*, p. 42 (1278);

The engrosser represented a further and associated category of middlemen. The act of engrossing involved cornering (or monopolising) a market by buying up large quantities of certain merchandise. In the sumptuary statute of 1363, grocers were accused of collusion and mischief in engrossing a variety of merchandise in order to enhance prices, particularly at times of scarcity.[616] Engrossing was a rarer offence than forestalling, as it was difficult to monopolise a medieval market in basic goods without a great deal of capital, except at times of scarcity when other considerations besides price came into force. In 1375, John de Gaywode was accused of forestalling and engrossing so many eggs that he filled twenty-eight barrels and sent them out of the kingdom, as well as butter and cheese, that there was a great dearness for four years. He was amerced 20s.[617] Sometimes, general foodstuffs or fuels were engrossed, as in late fourteenth-century York, when the retailers of coal, lime, malt, corn, or any victuals were warned against hoarding.[618] The merchants of late thirteenth-century Berwick were not allowed to have more than one buyer of wool and hides, including their wives, and faced a fine of 8s. and forfeiture for engrossing such goods to the detriment of other traders in the town.[619]

However, the main accusation levelled at engrossers concerned the hoarding of corn in secret, thereby avoiding the regulations that such commodities should be made available on the open market.[620] The bakers of Leicester were prohibited from hoarding flour at times of bread shortage and regratresses were to put bread for sale in their windows and not hide it in 'hutches or corners'.[621] There was a particular antipathy

---

Leicester, i, p. 181 (1279), ii, pp. 20–1 (1335–6), 292 (1467); *Liber Albus*, pp. 172–3, 230–1 (1272–1307), 236–7 (1272–1307), 396 (1383–4); Toulmin Smith (ed.), *English Gilds*, pp. 343, 345–6 (Berwick, 1283–4), 396–7 (Worcester, 1467); *Oak Book*, i, pp. 64–5, 68–9, cc.63 and 69 (*c.*1300); Hill, *Medieval Lincoln*, appx VII (*c.*1300); Prestwich (ed.), *York*, pp. 13–14 (1301); *CChR*, iii, pp. 344–5 (Ipswich, 1317); *Norwich*, i, pp. 181–2 (early fourteenth century); *Bristol*, i, pp. 38–9 (1344), 225–6 (late fourteenth century); *CCR, 1354–60*, pp. 231–2; Ingleby (ed.), *Red Register*, ii, p. 216, fol. 146d (1368); *Memorials*, pp. 387–8 (1375), 406 (1377); Alsford, *Towns* (Lynn, early fifteenth century); *Coventry*, pp. 25 (1421), 623 (1508), 646–7 (1515), 666 (1519); Arnold, *Customs of London*, p. 3 (*c.*1519).

[616] *Statutes*, i, p. 379, 37 Edw III c.5 (1363). See also *Parl. Rolls*, c.15, October 1363. In Warwickshire in 1381, several poulterers were fined 18d.–24d. for forming an illegal conventicle. Kimball (ed.), *Rolls*, pp. 114–15 (roll WI), nos. 78–80.

[617] *Norwich*, i, pp. 381–2 (1375).

[618] *York*, i, p. 15 (1371).

[619] Toulmin Smith (ed.), *English Gilds*, pp. 343, 345 (Berwick, 1283–4).

[620] *Coventry*, pp. 26–7 (1421); *BBC, 1042–1216*, p. 212 (Tewkesbury, 1147–83); Alsford, *Towns* (Lynn, early fifteenth century); *Coventry*, p. 272 (1452); *Henley*, p. 71 (1472).

[621] *Leicester*, ii, p. 107 (1357); *Liber Albus*, pp. 232–3 (1272–1307). Hutches were large boxes.

towards any who stored corn secretly from one market until the next in the hope of causing a scarcity and higher prices, reflecting the comments of moralists.[622] Since arbitrage was considered socially unacceptable at times of dearth, there was little storage of grain by speculators in medieval England, despite the notoriously unstable seasonal grain prices. But neither did many towns seem to store corn on a regular basis to guard against times of shortage. Purveyance officials instead tended to resort directly to large demesnes since those storing grain were proto-capitalist farmers. Large towns preferred to ensure that individuals had access to available supplies at all times and looked further afield when crisis ensued. A 1434 covenant in the *Little Red Book* of Bristol recorded the bequest of a merchant, Mark William, of 100 marks, to be kept in a common chest and to be used by the town authorities to buy corn at times of scarcity.[623]

Legislation about engrossing was intricately linked with fears about the scarcity of vital foodstuffs, particularly in the larger towns. In Norwich in 1304, a complaint was made to a judicial commission that rich men and forestallers were colluding to buy up victuals before they reached the town and thus selling them at higher prices in the market.[624] Later, in 1391, five merchants (Simon Ashfield, Hugh Hedenham, John Erlham, Thomas Bloker and William Attewater) were accused of making a confederacy and conspiring together to control the market in wheat and other grains in order to heighten the price, 'whereof great outcry exists'. They were fined 100s.[625] There were a number of cases in municipal courts, hundred courts, King's Bench and Justices of the Peace commissions where offenders were presented for illegal confederacies that raised prices to the impoverishment of the people.[626] The butchers and tanners of late fifteenth-century Coventry were warned against making confederacies 'which myght be hurtfull to ether of þe seid craftes or contrarie to þe comien wele'. In particular, this ordinance was aimed at preventing engrossing and ensuring that these traders did not usurp the burgess and craft privileges of others. The stigma of such behaviour was reflected in the potential 20s. fine.[627]

---

[622] *Norwich*, i, p. 361 (1288); *Oak Book*, i, pp. 50–1, c.39 (c.1300); *Bristol*, ii, p. 225 (late fourteenth century); *CLB*, H, p. 354 (1390); *Salisbury*, p. 171, no. 344 (1438); *Great Red Book*, i, p. 141 (1451–2), iii, p. 97 (1473); *Leicester*, ii, p. 294 (1467); *Northampton*, i, p. 351 (1545).

[623] *Bristol*, i, pp. 174–7 (1434).

[624] *CPR, 1301–7*, p. 294 (1304); Seabourne, *Royal Regulation*, pp. 132–3.

[625] *Norwich*, i, p. 385 (1391); Hudson (ed.), *Leet*, p. 74 (1390–1).

[626] Seabourne, *Royal Regulation*, pp. 138, 153.

[627] *Coventry*, p. 585 (1497). See also Putnam (ed.), *Proceedings*, p. 64, no. 30, concerning Henry Hoxhull who bought and detained grain in Devon in 1351, 'in oppression and impoverishment of the people', cf. Seabourne, *Royal Regulation*, p. 133.

In law, middlemen and engrossers were condemned for many of their activities. The statutes which mention forestalling are vitriolic in their condemnation, with the legislators having clearly drawn upon clerical imagery:

no forestaller be suffered to dwell in any town, which is an open oppressor of poor people and of all the commonalty, and an enemy of the whole shire and country, which for greediness of his private gain doth prevent others in buying grain, fish, herring, or any other thing to be sold coming by land or water, oppressing the poor, and deceiving the rich, which carrieth away such things, intending to sell them more dear; the which come to merchants strangers that bring merchandise, offering them to buy, and informing them that their goods might be dearer sold than they intended to sell; and a whole town or a country is deceived by such craft and subtilty.[628]

A fourteenth-century Norwich ordinance demanded that no one 'encourage such men in their evil-doings or maintain or defend them in any wise, because by such very great scandal arises in the city and may daily arise'.[629] There was evidently widespread anxiety about the possibility of food supplies being cut short or sold above their market value and this was perhaps understandable in communities that had to absorb harvest fluctuations.[630] The lack of national integration in the grain trade also meant that local supplies could not always be offset by supplies from further afield. Thus, the regulation of the grain trade was especially designed to prevent monopolies and the artificial hiking of prices. Merchants had to tread warily under such scrutiny.

Britnell has regarded the late medieval regulation of middlemen as protecting the interests of consumers through price control.[631] The condemnation of middlemen lay in the ideological concept that they were making money without adding value or taking risks, artificially manipulating the just price and harming the common good. By modern economic criteria, forestallers and middlemen are regarded as rationalising elements in a commercial economy, saving the time and expense of the producer in marketing, search and transport costs. However, we should be wary of attempts to press modern economic theories onto medieval commercial circumstances. In medieval England, the economy operated for two basic purposes – for the benefit of the franchise holders and

---

[628] *Statutes*, i, pp. 203–4, 'Statutum de Pistoribus'. This statute was copied into the *Little Red Book* of Bristol and the *Liber Custumarum* of Northampton. *Bristol*, ii, p. 220; *Northampton*, i, pp. 320–1.

[629] *Norwich*, i, p. 183 (early fourteenth century?).

[630] Farmer, 'Prices and wages', pp. 443–5.

[631] Britnell, *Growth and Decline*, pp. 39–40; Britnell, 'Price-setting', 10; Salzman, *English Trade*, pp. 80–1.

for the creation of a stable system of supply, price and profit. These dual notions were based on social theories and an economic environment that had developed in the thirteenth century. Nevertheless, some moralists and legislators were beginning to recognise the utility of middlemen in an increasingly complex English economy. They understood how merchants could move corn to the places of greatest need and that price determined these movements.[632] Those middlemen who served the nation and circulated commodities over longer distances were accepted, including those who bought at the farmgate and delivered supplies to a town. They were even actively encouraged, as long as they obeyed the rules, and were recognised as a means of bringing supplies to where they were needed.[633] This was not so distant from modern ideas, but neither could it be described as free trade.

Medieval market users still feared the apparent potential of middlemen to raise prices, control supplies and speculate for profit to the detriment of the wider community. This might be anathema to promoters of free-market ethics, but in the conditions of medieval England one could regard such paternal legislation as prudent. Checks were placed upon enterprising merchants and tradesmen by authorities who felt that their activities harmed others with the framework of an inelastic market. In particular, the entrepreneurial pursuit of profit when dealing in the necessities of life was considered immoral. Middlemen themselves were not expunged from commercial life, but medieval authorities and consumers were not yet confident of the market's ability to circumscribe opportunists. It was the opportunists, hanging around the edge of town or in the marketplace, who had not expended any formative energies, that were disparaged as leeches on the community.

However, it is unlikely that many forestallers or engrossers had enough capital to create a monopoly or significant price rises, except when supplies became scarce and very irregular. Often, forestalling involved petty traders with little capital searching for minor gain.[634] They themselves were poor, but regulations charged them for oppressing the poor. Whether juries always judged the individual merits of forestalling is difficult to know; the laws themselves focused on the harmful effects of all forestalling and engrossing. Britnell has argued that the laws of forestalling were instrumental in creating their own market ethic.[635] We should be certainly wary of distinguishing starkly between a moral ethic in the literature and sermons and a pragmatic approach in laws.

---

[632] See p. 119.   [633] Gras, *Evolution*, pp. 157–8.   [634] Britnell, 'Price-setting', 13.
[635] Britnell, 'Town life', p. 165; Britnell, 'Urban economic regulation'.

Legislators were just as idealistic in many ways and avidly used moral ideology to justify their edicts.

Like forestallers and engrossers, regraters also lived on the margin of respectability, but their activities of buying up batches of foodstuffs to sell again by retail in the same market were condoned provided they conducted themselves within strict laws. The cooks of Bristol were threatened with fines of 40d. for buying fresh fish simply to sell again, rather than cooking it for 'the vse of the peple'.[636] Regrating of raw meat was prohibited in thirteenth-century Leicester, but cooks were allowed to buy calves, pigs and sheep to sell again as cooked products.[637] As discussed previously, such traders were banned from the market within the first few hours of opening while people purchased goods for their own consumption.[638] The Northampton Custumal stated that regraters should only buy their corn, fish, flesh and poultry after the due hour set by ordinance, so that 'the kynges people schulde bye at the ffyrst hande of them that owith hit'. Otherwise, 'the pore man muste by of them at the secounde honde', which meant unconscionable price rises. Those traders who sent others to buy up goods, deceitfully pretending that they were buying victuals for their own consumption, were similarly condemned as regraters and forestallers. In fifteenth-century York, some cooks were accused of subtly using such partnerships 'in blyndyng and deseyvyng of the market keper' in order to acquire significant stocks of fish before the allowed time. They then retailed the fish 'to the most dere value that tham lykes, in hynderyng of the commun pople'.[639]

The greatest fear of legislators seems to have been that if regraters were allowed to work unrestricted then prices would rise steeply, particularly for victuals. A statute of 1353, reacting to the economic upheaval after the plague but also drawing on age-old concerns, lamented the 'outrageous dearth' caused by regraters of victuals 'to the great damage of the people' and ordered justices be chosen to inquire into their 'deeds and outrages'.[640] Yet, these same traders were also viewed as useful proxy agents for more respectable bakers and regular brewers of a town and they provided a service to travellers and townsfolk in the evening. Also,

---

[636] *Great Red Book*, i, pp. 134–5 (1452).

[637] *Leicester*, i, pp. 180–1 (1279), ii, p. 289 (1467). See also Jeayes (ed.), *Court Rolls*, i, p. 50 (1311); Coss (ed.), *Early Records of Medieval Coventry*, p. 42 (1278); *Oak Book*, i, pp. 70–1, c.70 (c.1300); *Memorials*, pp. 406–7 (1377); *Coventry*, pp. 25 (1421), 29 (1421), 361 (1470), 651–2 (1517).

[638] See above, pp. 182–3.

[639] *York*, i, pp. 222–3 (fifteenth century?). See also Riley (ed.), *Munimenta Gildhallae*, ii, pp. 117–18 (1274–6).

[640] *Statutes*, i, p. 330, 27 Edw III st.1 c.3 (1353). See also *Black Book*, ii, pp. 102–3, c.27 (c.1309).

many country sellers of cheese, poultry, butter and eggs may have found it more convenient to sell such goods to regraters and hucksters rather than have to market the items themselves. Such outside traders might need to return home but still have residual goods when the bell rang to allow reselling.[641] Regrating was thus a means of facilitating exchange for the producer, processor and consumer. Regraters offered more convenient options of scale, such as selling by the mug for ale, or by taking the produce to the source of demand, rather than following the practices of shopkeepers and stallholders who waited for their customers. Their existence in all medieval markets suggests that they were a consistent and useful presence in normal conditions, taking on the risk of disposing of surplus, perishable commodities. They were, nevertheless, regarded as treading a fine line between aiding and hindering the market.[642] In early fourteenth-century Oxford, there were even limits on the number of regraters who were allowed to operate in the market (thirty-two in 1305).[643]

Pedlars and hawkers had a slightly different social and economic role compared to regraters, being more wandering purveyors of trinkets and hardware. They seem to have attracted only animosity in regulations.[644] Borough records presented a continual theme of restriction or even expulsion. Lynn prohibited wandering hawkers, regarding them as nuisances who impeded upon the liberties of the town and stallholders. In particular, they avoided payment of stallage fees.[645] A Beverley court in 1398 warned of foreign pedlars called 'snarlers' and 'hawkers', 'who often buy goods and jewels stolen in the town to the great damage and deceit of the common people'. Wandering traders were banned by the civic authorities and they demanded that all should hire stalls or else face imprisonment and a fine of 6s. 8d.[646] The Colchester ordinances also expressed anxiety that many chapmen were acting as receivers of stolen beads, silver spoons and other small wares, and reiterated that all transactions should take place in the open market to prevent such dishonesty.[647]

The regulations suggest that there was a general perception that market trade and retailers could endanger the social order.[648] It also seems that an offender's social status affected the type of regulation imposed upon them. Merchants were able to have much more entrepreneurial

---

[641] *Liber Albus*, p. 329 (1279–80).   [642] Swanson, *British Towns*, p. 29.

[643] Salter (ed.), *Munimenta*, pp. 8–10, 14–15, nos. 9, 11 and 17 (1305 and 1310).

[644] Davis, 'Men as march with fote packes'.

[645] *King's Lynn*, p. 264, no. 313 (1424). See also *Winchester*, p. 16 (1409); *Red Paper Book*, p. 150 (1455); *Northampton*, i, p. 264, c.79 (1397).

[646] *Beverley*, p. 42 (1398).   [647] *Red Paper Book*, p. 148 (1455).

[648] Hilton, 'Medieval market towns', 22.

leeway than lowly market traders, while poor hucksters and pedlars were treated with more suspicion and vitriol than artisans or sedentary victuallers. 'Huckster' and 'regrater' had pejorative overtones; there were connotations that such people looked to make profit in any possible petty way.[649] The early fifteenth-century oath for the bedels of London included the provision that thieves, prostitutes, hucksters of ale, 'or other women commonly reputed of bad and evil life' should be cast out of their Ward.[650] Popular and legal hostility was exacerbated by fears of such traders causing heightened petty crime, street obstruction, abuses and disorder. It is not unlikely that jurors allowed such impressions to influence their decision-making processes. Most noticeably, strangers were treated cautiously and it is likely that poor unknown outsiders were generally distrusted unless they had some contact or relative in the town. Nevertheless, itinerant retail traders were perhaps both immoveable and unstoppable in the markets of the late Middle Ages.

Punishment

A Cambridge ordinance (1268) against regraters ordered that they 'be amerced according to the quantity and quality of his offence'.[651] The main weapon in the armoury of officials was the amercement, which was set (often by appointed affeerers) in relation to both the severity of the crime and the means of the offender. For flagrant or repeat offenders, corporal punishment could be utilised. A market necessarily included the apparatus of the pillory and tumbrel as these were the corporal punishments specifically prescribed for breaches of the assizes of bread and ale.[652] The pillory was an immoveable, vertical stocks placed in a public area, while the tumbrel simply involved public exposure on a stool mounted high on a cart (sometimes known as the cucking-stool) in the marketplace. A 'tumbrel' was also shameful in that it was a dung-cart.[653] The penalties for brewers or bakers who broke the assize were laid out in a definite scheme. For the first, second and third occasions they were to be amerced 'according to the quantity of their offence'. Beyond that,

---

[649] Kowaleski, 'Women's work', p. 148; Salzman, *English Trade*, pp. 75–80; Hilton, 'Lords, burgesses and hucksters'; Hilton, 'Women traders', p. 208.

[650] *Liber Albus*, p. 272 (early fifteenth century).

[651] *BBC, 1216–1307*, p. 297 (*CPR, 1266–72*, p. 195) (Cambridge, 1268).

[652] These instruments of corporal punishment were appended to the jurisdiction of view of frankpledge and not to the franchise of the market, but the two often overlapped. Masschaele, 'Public space', 400–5; *Britton*, i, p. 191, ch. 31, c.7 (1291–2); *Fleta*, ii, p. 121, bk. II, c.12 (late thirteenth century).

[653] Spargo, *Juridical Folklore*. The 'ducking-stool' was a later development of the cucking-stool, and involved plunging offenders into water in order to purge them of sins.

offenders were to suffer 'judgement of the body', in the form of the pillory for bakers and the tumbrel, trebuchet or 'castigatorie' for brewers.[654] The differentiation of apparatus was seemingly based more on the assumption that bakers would be male and brewers female, rather than any occupationary discrimination. The pillory required an upright stance, while offenders were seated in the tumbrel, but both involved humiliation as a punishment.

The aims of corporal punishment reflected the market conditions of medieval towns and villages. A fifteenth-century assize for beer-brewers specifically stated that for a fourth offence the offender should be placed in the pillory and that this punishment was to last for three market days.[655] This was not necessarily three consecutive days, as many towns had only one market day a week and the scheduling of the castigation emphasises the importance of public humiliation. The punishment was not only uncomfortable and perhaps painful, but it tarnished the individual's reputation and affected future business and credit. It also prevented the trader from working and earning on the most important marketing day of the week. Nevertheless, humiliation could only be really effective if it was accompanied by a public recognition of the shame of an offender's actions. There was thus a dramatic element to many punishments for this publicised the crime and developed a communal symbolic memory of the sinfulness of the offences. In late thirteenth-century Norwich, the pillory was the mandated penalty for forestallers 'so that his punishment may be the terror of others and his fault may be made manifest to the people, and let public proclamation be made in the market concerning the cause of his punishments in this matter'.[656] Publicly burning false goods under the noses of offenders was also commonplace, such as in London in 1319 when William Sperlyng had his 'putrid and poisonous' meat burnt beneath him at the pillory.[657] These secular punishments were endorsed by religious authorities, who added their own canon of spiritual sanctions to the avaricious and fraudulent.[658]

---

[654] *Statutes*, i, pp. 199–200, 'Assisa Panis et Cervisie'; i, pp. 201–2, 'Judicium Pillorie'.

[655] BL, MS Landowne 796, fol. 6r (late fifteenth century).

[656] *Norwich*, i, pp. 182–3 (early fourteenth century?).

[657] *Memorials*, pp. 132–3 (1319). See also *ibid.*, pp. 139–40 (1320), 328 (1365), 336 (1368), 367 (1372), 446 (1380), 448–9 (1381), 464 (1382), 471–2 (1382), 486 (1385); *CLB*, E, pp. 110–11 (1319), also E, pp. 126, 132–3 (1320), F, p. 208 (1350); Bellamy, *Crime and Public Order*, pp. 184–6; Hill, *Medieval Lincoln*, appx VII (*c.*1300); Prestwich (ed.), *York*, p. 16 (1301).

[658] See pp. 122–34. Even non-corporal punishments might involve a performative element. In the Fair Court of St Ives in 1300, the false vessels of the brewster, Agnes Hervy of Ely, were broken in front of the whole court. Goldberg (ed.), *Women in England*, p. 189.

Figure 17: Bakers and corporal punishment

Notes: These illustrations accompanied information on the assize of bread in London's *Liber de Assisa Panis* (late thirteenth to early fourteenth centuries). The first drawing depicts the baker at work, and the second drawing is a baker being drawn on a hurdle with a faulty loaf about his neck.

Source: City of London, London Metropolitan Archives, MS Custumal 4, *Liber de Assisa Panis*, fol. 1r (COL/CS/01/004).

London authorities appear to have been particularly exasperated by offending bakers and gave them no leeway for initial misdemeanours. Instead, they ordered the immediate use of corporal punishment in dramatic fashion:

If any default shall be found in the bread of a baker of the city, the first time, let him be drawn upon a hurdle from the Guildhall to his own house, through the great streets where there may be most people assembled, and through the great streets that are most dirty, with the faulty loaf hanging from his neck. If a second time he shall be found committing the same offence, let him be drawn through the great street of Chepe, in manner aforesaid, to the pillory; and let him be put upon the pillory, and remain there at least one hour in the day. And the third default shall be found, he shall be drawn, and the oven shall be pulled down, and the baker [made to] foreswear the trade within the city for ever.[659]

A pictorial depiction of the punishment that faced fraudulent bakers was placed at the start of London's *Liber de Assisa Panis* (see Figure 17).[660] In 1347, Bristol was granted a royal charter that gave its

[659] *Liber Albus*, p. 232 (1272–1307). For similar regulations for forestallers in York, see Prestwich (ed.), *York*, pp. 13–14 (1301).
[660] John Bretun proclaimed in 1297 that the use of the hurdle to punish bakers should be abolished. *CLB*, B, pp. 243–4 (1297). However, the hurdle was in use again two years later, along with the pillory. Thomas (ed.), *Calendar*, p. 67 (Roll C, 1299–1300); Riley

Figure 18: Baker drawn on a hurdle

Notes: This decorative initial was part of the 1347 charter of Edward III to the city of Bristol. It shows a baker being drawn on a hurdle, with the unequal balance representing his offence and a faulty loaf around his neck.

Source: City of Bristol Record Office, No. 01250(1).

officers similar powers to punish bakers on the hurdle. This was depicted on the illuminated initial of the charter, which shows the unbalanced scales that suggest the baker was accused of selling short-weight bread (see Figure 18).

The most vivid examples of punishments and frauds can be found in London records and these have tended to colour many historians' views of petty traders. A commonly cited example by historians was John Brid, who was prosecuted in 1327 for making a hole in his baking-table, through which a servant drew the dough of customers to their loss and 'to the scandal and disgrace of the whole city'. He and nine other bakers were placed in the pillory with dough hung from their necks.[661] There were other instances of the pillory being used in London, such as when a

---

(ed.), *Chronicles*, p. 251 (1314); *Memorials*, pp. 119–23 (1316); *CLB*, A, pp. 120–1 (1282), B, p. 13 (1282), K, p. 56 (1425); Riley (ed.), *Munimenta Gildhallae*, iii, appx I, pp. 411–29 (1307–27); Seabourne, 'Assize matters', 44–5. Sometimes the punishment of the hurdle was remitted due to the old age of the offender. In 1318, the bakers of London petitioned the king and Parliament to abolish the punishment of the hurdle in the city, but the king refused. *Parl. Rolls*, c.196, October 1318.

[661] *Memorials*, pp. 162–5 (1327).

cook, Henry le Passelewe, sold a putrid and stinking capon in a pastry in 1351; and when John Gylessone, in 1348, sold carrion found in a ditch 'in deceit and to the peril of the lives of persons buying the same', and was placed in the pillory with the meat burnt beneath him.[662]

Other towns went beyond the remit of the statutes in their stipulated punishments for fraudulent victuallers. The customs of Hereford in the early fourteenth century adjudged that any who committed an offence worthy of punishment in the pillory or tumbrel should lose his freedom. Bakers and brewers were to be expelled for one year and not to brew and bake for that time, after which they might redeem their freedom by favour of the commonalty for twice as much as before.[663] Other regulations used the threat of expulsion from the town as a final sanction, if the humiliation of corporal punishment had failed to deter.

An apt moral aspect to the punishment of traders can be seen in several ordinances where goods were forfeited to the poor, sick or prisoners. The forfeited bread of bakers of Bristol, who bought grain before their allotted time, was distributed to the prisoners at Monkenbridge; while the forfeitures of regraters and forestallers in Oxford were given to the poor and infirm at the hospital of St John, 'so that no profit therefrom accrue'.[664] The lepers of York were not so fortunate, for they received the forfeited meat that had been found to be 'measly'.[665] A notable provision was included in the regulations of fifteenth-century Northampton, where butchers were ordered to only sell unwholesome meat from beneath the pillory, or else the meat was forfeited to the sick men of St Leonard's.[666] The instrument of punishment had become a public symbol for those who wished to sell substandard goods. The regulation left the decision of purchase to the consumer in the belief that the open advertisement of rotten meat would deter buyers and perhaps tarnish the reputation of the butcher. Any butcher prepared to offer such products from under the pillory, or a consumer prepared to buy them, did so at their own risk.

A rough comparison can be made of the punishments prescribed in town ordinances for different offences. Most ordinances laid down

---

[662] *Ibid.*, pp. 240–1 (1348), 266–7 (1351); *CLB*, F, pp. 181 (1348), 226–7 (1351). See also *Memorials*, pp. 319 (1364), 498 (1387); *CLB*, G, p. 175 (1364), H, pp. 322–3 (1387).

[663] Johnson (ed.), *Hereford*, p. 31.

[664] *Bristol*, ii, pp. 221–2 (1327); *BBC, 1216–1307*, p. 297 (Oxford, 1284). See also *Memorials*, pp. 38–9 (1298); Toulmin Smith (ed.), *English Gilds*, p. 343 (Berwick, 1283–4). Any forfeited pigs or ducks in Bristol were to go to prisoners. *Great Red Book*, i, p. 144 (1452).

[665] Prestwich (ed.), *York*, pp. 12–13 (1301).

[666] *Northampton*, i, p. 230, c.47 (*c.*1460). See also *Black Book*, ii, pp. 144–7, c.58 [57] (*c.*1309); Davis, 'The cross and the pillory', pp. 258–9.

punishments for offences on a sliding scale, increasing in severity for recidivists. The 1301 ordinances for York were particularly harsh, in an attempt to re-establish trading equilibrium after the arrival of the royal household. Comparatively, cooks of bad food and forestallers faced the most severe penalties of the pillory for the first offence, followed by the hurdle, imprisonment and exile. Bakers who committed extreme abuses were subjected to the pillory immediately and at the third offence, their oven was destroyed and they were expected to abjure their calling forever. Brewers were fined first and then faced the tumbrel at the third and fourth offences.[667] These regulations were enacted in very particular circumstances, but the London penalties throughout the fourteenth and fifteenth centuries followed a similar schema, plus the use of the hurdle for bakers.[668]

The authorities of mid-fourteenth-century Bristol ordered the most severe penalties for cooks and butchers who sold corrupt meat, with a second offence leading to the pillory, followed by imprisonment and then expulsion from the town. Forestallers faced the pillory at their third offence and, thereafter, enforced forswearing of their trade. By contrast, brewers and ale-sellers who sold at excessive prices or in secret, merely faced increasing fines and forfeitures with only an implied threat of corporal punishment at the fourth offence, despite a stated annoyance that they 'will not be chastened, whereof the poor people of the Commonalty make great complaint'.[669]

In central legislation, forestalling punishments were steeper than for other trading offences, such as breaking the assize or regrating, but similar in nature to those for selling corrupted foodstuffs. Amercements and forfeiture were allocated for the first offence, the pillory for the second, imprisonment for the third and, finally, expulsion from the town. A further statute against forestalling was issued by Edward III in 1350–1, which ordered the forfeiture of all forestalled merchandise or their equivalent value, or else the offender would be imprisoned for two years or more. This legislation made clear that it was the forestaller who was deemed to have offended, while the seller was considered an innocent party who was to keep any payment made for goods bought. Encouragement was also offered to third parties to bring suits against forestallers by way of the offer of half of the items forfeited.[670] The stipulated punishments in

---

[667] Prestwich (ed.), *York*, pp. 10–16 (1301).

[668] *Liber Albus*, pp. 232–3 (1272–1307), 307 (1272–1307), 312 (1335), 400 (1383–4).

[669] *Bristol*, i, pp. 34 (1344), 38–9 (1344); ii, pp. 30 (1346?), 36–8 (1346?), 218 (fourteenth century), 221 (fourteenth century).

[670] *Statutes*, i, p. 315, 25 Edw III St.3 c.3 (1350–1); confirmed by *ibid.*, ii, p. 8, 2 Ric II St.1 c.2 (1378).

central law were reflected in local regulations. By the late fifteenth century, forestallers in Bristol were threatened with a 20s. amercement
for the first offence, forty days' imprisonment for the second, and
both imprisonment and expulsion from the town's liberty thereafter.[671]
In early fourteenth-century Norwich, forestallers faced the pillory on
the second offence, and the punishment was not to be redeemed 'for
that thing touches the whole community and the people of the whole
country'.[672]

Thus, punishments outlined in the regulations followed a basic pattern
of increasing severity, from an initial fine and confiscation of offending
goods, to imprisonment, corporal punishment and, finally, expulsion
from their trade or town for a year and a day. The official penalties
thus provided standardised schemes and were, in some cases, especially
harsh and unforgiving. Those who committed blatant fraud, middlemen
offences or crimes against public health were particularly vilified, showing
a similar approach to that of many moralists. However, whether these
schemata were followed in practice is another matter.

Late medieval preachers and moralists were scathing of the authorities'
slackness in enforcing corporal punishments.[673] *Judicium Pillorie* specifically stated that the twelve lawful men who inquired into assizes should
investigate whether any bailiff had been bribed to release an offender
from penal punishment. They also had to check on the maintenance
of the pillory and tumbrel, which had to be of sufficient strength so as
not to imperil offenders and which had to be upkept according to the
franchise requirements of a market.[674] However, 'Clerk of the Market'
estreats and courtly evidence suggest that the remittance of corporal
punishment for fines was widespread and that the upkeep of the penal
apparatus was often insufficient.[675] Legislators claimed that this was not
only due to a blatant disregard for statutory law, but also ignorance.
Fleta stated: 'it does happen that lords are amerced [by the Clerk of the
Market], sometimes because they do not know the technicalities of the
assize and consequently, being ignorant of the law, it is to be assumed

[671] *Great Red Book*, iii, p. 97 (1473). See also *Coventry*, pp. 25–6 (1421), 192 (1439), 277 (1453).
[672] *Norwich*, i, pp. 182–3 (early fourteenth century).   [673] See pp. 129–31.
[674] *Statutes*, i, pp. 201–2, 'Judicium Pillorie'; i, p. 203, 'Statutum de Pistoribus'. See also *Britton*, i, pp. 191–2, ch. 31, c.8 (1291–2). Robert Reynes's version of the assize of bread also states that bakers found with excessively underweight loaves should 'haue iugement of þe pilory and nou3t 3euyn for gold ne syluer'. Louis (ed.), *Commonplace Book*, pp. 136–7.
[675] TNA, e101/256/14, 15, 25; e101/257/1, 11(2), 17; e101/258/1, 2. See also Stapleton (ed.), *De Antiquis Legibus Liber*, pp. 121–2 (London, 1269); *Northampton*, i, p. 373 (late fifteenth century).

that they will be unable to administer it rightly'.[676] By 1389–90, the 'Statute of Victuallers' demanded that no corporal punishments should be remitted if statute law demanded it.[677]

The king could revoke a franchise if it was found that fines were taken when corporal punishment was due.[678] An entry in the *Little Red Book* of Bristol in 1283 suggested anxiety that the king's authority could harm their liberty: 'the Mayor and Commonalty of the town of Bristol fear that they will be severely punished unless the assize in the town aforesaid be strictly observed by the same Mayor and Commonalty'.[679] The royal demand that corporal punishment should not be remitted for any payment suggests, of course, that remittance did take place. In York in 1304 and Lincoln in 1331, the authorities were rebuked for their leniency in not assessing the assizes as often as was necessary and remitting corporal methods when traders deserved them. Indeed, in 1311, Oxford University complained that the townsmen had allowed a convicted baker to climb onto the pillory scaffold and then come down again, without ever being affixed in the pillory for the stipulated hour.[680]

In practice, the use of corporal punishment and even the amercements proffered do not seem to have followed the levels or graduations prescribed in law. Indeed, the idealism of the laws was tempered by a recognition that many officials were prepared to be flexible in their interpretation of legal practices. Perhaps the factors which mattered more than laws themselves were the people who enacted them, who administered them and in whose interests regulations were enforced.[681]

Conclusion

Throughout this chapter, the parallels between moralistic literature and legal statements have been strikingly apparent. Late medieval writers and

---

[676] *Fleta*, ii, p. 121, bk. ii, c.12 (late thirteenth century).

[677] *Statutes*, ii, p. 63, 13 Ric II st.1 c.8 (1389–90); *Parl. Rolls*, c.38, January 1390.

[678] *Fleta*, ii, p. 121, bk. ii, c.12 (late thirteenth century). In 1254, London was briefly taken into the king's hands for non-observance of the assizes of bread and ale. Riley (ed.), *Chronicles*, pp. 22–3, also p. 150 (1271). Seabourne regards these exceptional cases as a means to rectify problematic enforcement of the assizes and as a 'product of a successful exercise in royal supervision of a local jurisdiction'. Seabourne, *Royal Regulation*, pp. 92–5.

[679] *Bristol*, ii, pp. 222–3 (1283).

[680] Prestwich (ed.), *York*, pp. 18–22 (1301); *CIM*, ii (1307–49), pp. 294–5, no. 1201; Salter (ed.), *Munimenta*, pp. 22–3, no. 25 (1311), pp. 29–30, no. 32 (1315). See also *Liber Albus*, p. 232 (1272–1307); *Leicester*, ii, pp. 194–5 (1379); *CChR*, iv, pp. 57–8 (Cambridge, 1327).

[681] Rigby, *English Society*, p. 303.

legislators used similar phrases, made references to communal benefits and the needs of the poor, and conveyed a consistent dislike of middlemen and profiteers. However, there was an additional agenda in many urban regulations whereby justificatory rhetoric hid differing sectional interests. It is this balance of motivations that is so difficult to disentangle. Town authorities appeared to walk a tightrope between the need to address moral, paternal considerations and the privileges of their own burgesses or residents. Consumers needed low prices and assured supply and quality, while those within the liberty wanted law and order, revenue and protection of their trading rights.[682] Some of these aims overlapped, particularly when linked to worries about social cohesion and the advantages of communal consent. Town governors also realised that they could not prosper without attracting the trade of outsiders, allowing victuallers to proliferate and make a livelihood, and providing facilities to encourage the conduct of commercial transactions. Unenfranchised traders desired fewer restrictions while burgesses sought economic privileges, but both wanted the safeguards of trading regulations.[683] Medieval trading law was therefore not elucidated in clear and defined terms, but involved a composite of moral, social, economic and legal ideas, moulded by vested interests.

Medieval writers placed emphasis on social order and the protection of the poor, their ideas embedded in notions of natural justice and divine law. Most clerics and moralists, from the thirteenth to fifteenth centuries, encouraged traders to perform their occupations for the communal good and to be almost philanthropic in their activities. Although such notions have been dismissed by some historians as the abstract concepts of late medieval theologians, social theories did provide a foundation for many local regulations, such as the assizes, and were a comparative tool by which the justice of laws could be examined. At the same time, the laws themselves were generating ethical norms, laying down moral principles relating to the monitoring of prices, profit, quality, middlemen, burgess rights and the open marketplace. Indeed, the clergy provided one means by which to disseminate the legal rules and boundaries of trading activity, demonstrating a mutual reinforcement of market ethics. There were certainly hints of moral rectitude in law regarding the potential sinfulness and sordidness of trade – this was not confined to the purview of the Church.

---

[682] Kowaleski, *Local Markets*, pp. 180–92; Britnell, *Commercialisation*, pp. 90–7.
[683] Rigby, *English Society*, p. 160; Rigby, *Medieval Grimsby*, p. 47.

Legislators thus subscribed to notions of common welfare and justice, but also advanced favouritism and privilege wherever possible. Market regulations could be either socially inclusive or exclusive, depending on the particular commodity, economic context, and social or moral anxieties. Outside or foreign traders were subjected to differing levels of restrictions and levies, while even those resident within a town, but outside elite administrative institutions, were often disadvantaged by town ordinances. 'Common profit' in this context clearly referred to those who contributed to a town's government and coffers, rather than those who worked there but paid only *ad hoc* dues. Historians have often characterised this elitism as restrictive and oppressive and some argue that it encouraged monopolistic oligarchies but squashed commercial enterprise. Yet, towns could not survive without a regular influx of traders and merchandise, and they had to provide conducive market facilities. To create the conditions needed for confidence in trade, medieval authorities recognised the need for constant surveillance and controls over the tools of trade in order to dampen any temptation to commit fraud or extortion. A considerable element of regulation concerned the ability of market officials to ensure sales transactions were undertaken in an acceptable manner. However, the laws themselves hint at a flexibility regarding such issues as profit-making, credit dealings, margins of error, low quality and Sunday trading. Market authorities seemingly understood the realities of everyday trade, but they also possessed only limited administrative resources and had to work within the strictures of fluctuating supply and demand.

There remains a conceptual gap between the regulations themselves and the apparatus of administration; there was a difference between enacting law and enforcing it. It is because of this that ideologies and religious representations were so vital, for they indirectly circumscribed the actions of most traders and consumers in union with actual market mechanisms. For example, guilds demanded a certain standard of morals for their members, as well as exerting informal social pressure. Even local gossip and neighbourly opinion could encourage social and economic conformity, particularly by attacking a trader's reputation. It is perhaps unsurprising that many laws were framed in terms of religiosity and sin. Trust, reputation and social mores lay behind the effective working of the medieval market system and were additional barriers to the 'free rider'. These moral notions were not, however, inconsistent with many traders working beyond or at the margins of the law or officials exercising an element of flexibility in their interpretation of regulations. Indeed, too many historians have lumped together the everyday fines of general trading activities, which were not perceived as particularly objectionable, with the flagrant frauds and offences that so offended medieval sensibilities. It is this complex interplay of medieval morals, laws, informal controls and pragmatism that will be examined in the next chapter. How did commercial regulations and ethical precepts equate with practical experience?

3   The behaviour of market traders

The influences of literary and legal proclamations upon everyday medieval practices were not necessarily direct or straightforward. Indeed, petty traders may have ignored elements of law and moral strictures when possible, while courts and jurors were arguably flexible in their use of regulations, depending on the parties involved and social norms.[1] Legal codifications and moral writings are therefore insufficient evidence for actual trading practices and need to be supplemented by sources of local administration. As Britnell stated, 'behind the verbiage of urban court rolls lies a rich variety of interplay between law and social values'.[2] Were traders really regarded by local officials as generally dishonest and in need of constant monitoring? Were there notable discrepancies between literary and legislative ideals of trade and its actual regulation in a medieval community? This chapter surveys the day-to-day operations of town markets and their traders. In doing so, it is necessary to occasionally step back from the minutiae of regulations and credit transactions and regard the general picture. What were the rationales behind the management of markets and trade? Were there more informal means of regulation that were beneficial to traders, consumers and market efficiency?

In order to look further at the behaviour of market traders, the implementation of commercial regulation and the ethical framework within which markets operated, this chapter will look at court roll evidence from three markets in late medieval Suffolk: the two small market towns of Newmarket and Clare and the larger borough of Ipswich. This can only give us a glimpse into the activities of the medieval market, since the study is concentrated on both one small region of the country and a relatively short time period in the late fourteenth and fifteenth centuries. Nevertheless, such a focused and detailed comparison can perhaps give

---

[1] Britnell, 'England: towns, trade', p. 58; Schofield, 'Peasants and the manor court', 5–7; Poos and Bonfield, 'Law and individualism'.
[2] Britnell, 'England: towns, trade', p. 58.

a better insight into the influence of moral values and regulation upon the behaviour of medieval market traders.

The markets of Suffolk

Suffolk cannot be considered a 'typical' county in medieval England. In a national comparison, Suffolk might be viewed as possessing a weak, fragmented manorial structure by 1300, with many small manors and a significant proportion of freemen and lower-status lords. There were a few, interspersed aristocratic manors with a high number of unfree tenures and villein tenants, held by ecclesiastical institutions such as the abbey of Bury St Edmunds or the convent of Ely, or a great lay lord like the Earl of Norfolk, who dominated the political life of the county. However, most of Suffolk was independent of such strong lordship in terms of everyday manorial administration. Bailey argues that this encouraged care and efficiency from the minor lords, as well as economic freedom, independence and enterprise among their tenants; it appears to have generated complex tenurial relations.[3] The majority engaged in land transactions, sold surpluses in the market, exploited commercial opportunities and were relatively mobile. Large numbers of these peasants were smallholders or landless who needed to make a living through agricultural labour, domestic service and petty trade or craftwork.[4]

Suffolk was a low-lying county consisting of good arable land, but also extensive patches of woodland, grassland, heaths and wetlands.[5] It was well supplied with river valleys and waterways which could be navigated by small boats or barges, leading to the estuaries of the Orwell, Stour and Deben.[6] It was a fairly wealthy county by national standards, especially in the fifteenth century. Schofield's comparative analysis of the tax subsidies of 1334 and 1515 showed that Suffolk rose up in the rankings of counties from eighteenth to seventh in lay wealth per acre.[7] It contained a high density of small market towns and demonstrated signs of relatively advanced commercialisation. In particular, High Suffolk developed a significant leather and dairy industry by the fifteenth

---

[3] Bailey, *Medieval Suffolk*, chs. 2 and 3. This volume provides an excellent summary of the economic and social history of late medieval Suffolk.

[4] *Ibid.*, pp. 36–9. Fragmentation of free holdings was a common theme in thirteenth-century England. It was driven by population and economic pressures, and facilitated by the right to buy and sell at will and by customs of partible inheritance. By *c.*1300, some 75 per cent of holdings in Suffolk were under ten acres, and most under five acres.

[5] Scarfe, *Suffolk Landscape*, pp. 149–91; Bailey, *Medieval Suffolk*, pp. 1–2, ch. 5.

[6] Darby, *Medieval Fenland*; *VCH: Suffolk*, i, p. 1.

[7] Schofield, 'Geographical distribution'.

and sixteenth centuries.[8] The cloth industry was also flourishing in the small towns and villages of Babergh, Cosford and Samford hundreds in the south-west of the county, particularly as internal demand grew and cloth exports increased in the fourteenth and fifteenth centuries.[9] The Poll Tax return for Hadleigh in 1381 showed a significant proportion of cloth-workers, some one-fifth of the recorded adult population.[10] The growing wealth of the Stour Valley in the fifteenth century, on the back of its broadcloth and heavy kersey production, was demonstrated by the magnificent perpendicular churches of Long Melford, Lavenham and Hadleigh, which were mostly funded by successful local clothiers.[11]

Suffolk was notable for its high level of commercial activity, in its market structures, high level of commercialised agriculture and proximity to London and the Continent. The social and economic structure of the county aided the development of the cloth industry and also determined the high density of markets and small towns. Large numbers of wage-earners and smallholders required forums for the exchange of foodstuffs, while the towns themselves generated demand.[12] By 1349 there had been some ninety-six market foundations in Suffolk, though they did not necessarily exist simultaneously and many markets were perhaps never established or were short-lived.[13] Nevertheless, an examination of the official foundation-dates illustrates an extensive period of activity during the mid-thirteenth century (1225–74), when nearly 50 per cent of all the medieval markets were founded.[14] Thereafter there was a slackening of foundations with just six new markets in the two centuries after the Black Death. This accords with the trend found in other counties; nationally, the number of official markets tripled from the twelfth century to the early fourteenth century, totalling some 1,500–2,000 by the latter period, including some 400 new boroughs.[15] A similar thirteenth-century surge can be also discerned for Suffolk fairs, of which 113 had been founded by 1349 and only fourteen thereafter. Small agricultural village fairs were the most numerous in Suffolk, lasting just one to three days, and acting as

---

[8] Clarkson, 'Leather crafts', 30.   [9] Bailey, 'Technology'.
[10] Fenwick (ed.), *Poll Taxes*, ii, pp. 512–14; Powell, *Rising*, p. 111.
[11] Amor, 'Merchant adventurer'; Britnell, 'Woollen textile industry'; Bailey, *Medieval Suffolk*, pp. 269–76. Lavenham became the fourteenth wealthiest English town in the 1524 Lay Subsidy. *VCH: Suffolk*, ii, pp. 253–5; McClenaghan, *Springs of Lavenham*; Betterton and Dymond, *Lavenham*, p. 3.
[12] For a similar situation in Kent, see Mate, 'Rise and fall', 66.
[13] Dymond and Northeast, *A History*, p. 46.
[14] Scarfe, 'Markets and fairs'; Letters, *Gazetteer*; Dymond and Martin (eds.), *Historical Atlas*, pp. 76–7.
[15] Britnell, 'Proliferation'.

outlets for wholesale produce or agricultural supplies (such as livestock), which could not be guaranteed in weekly markets. There were a few larger fairs in Suffolk that lasted for a week or two, such as the fair at Bury St Edmunds in July, which was known to have attracted clothiers from across England and from Flanders, as well as supplying cloth to the king.[16]

The growth in markets and fairs was part of the inexorable increase in market dependency by the hinterland peasantry and a decline in self-sufficiency.[17] Many of the new markets were in rural locations and were serving a growing need for basic provisions. They were also part of seigneurial initiatives to profit from such growing trade. Before the plague, lords continued to look for niches in the marketing network to take advantage of high grain prices and demand, high rents and cheap labour. There was, however, a relative lack of borough foundations in Suffolk, possibly as low as nine, perhaps related to the social structure of the county, with a large number of minor landlords and free tenants.[18] It appears that seigneurial small towns were capable of sustaining and even stimulating commercial endeavour. Suffolk's commercial infrastructure thus resided in a few boroughs and a myriad of small towns and village markets.

This, then, was the marketing structure of medieval Suffolk, particularly for the thirteenth century. The highly decentralised nature of the market network suited the economic conditions at this time, with a large number of peasants selling and buying vast quantities of low-value, perishable goods in small lots. However, this organisation was not set in stone and the influence of various towns changed over time; their primary hinterlands fluctuated in size and some markets disappeared, while others prospered. Indeed, Britnell estimated that some two-thirds of village markets disappeared throughout England between the thirteenth and sixteenth centuries.[19] The demographic plunge after the Black Death meant that the total demand for grain and basic foodstuffs fell significantly, causing market decline and failures. Hilton pointed out that half of the village markets in the West Midlands and 60 per cent in Lincolnshire had disappeared by the sixteenth century.[20] In Suffolk, there were several village markets where the settlement was depopulated or

[16] Lobel, *Borough of Bury St Edmunds*, pp. 65–6; Gottfried, *Bury St Edmunds*, p. 90; Bailey, *Medieval Suffolk*, pp. 119–20. See Moore, *Fairs*; Lee, *Cambridge*, pp. 114–41.

[17] See pp. 9–19.

[18] These were Beccles, Bury St Edmunds, Clare, Dunwich, Eye, Ipswich, Lidgate, Orford and Sudbury. Bailey adds Bungay and Exning to that list. Bailey, *Medieval Suffolk*, pp. 120–2.

[19] Britnell, *Commercialisation*, p. 160.   [20] Hilton, 'Medieval market towns', 10.

deserted by the fifteenth century, Easton Bavents, Flixton and Sotherton among them.[21] It is difficult to trace the exact pattern of market failures due to the problems with the foundation data discussed above, but the process of attrition appears to have increased after the Black Death. By the sixteenth century just thirty-two of the 102 market foundations survived in Suffolk, often older foundations and those situated on the main road and river transport links.[22] These surviving institutions took advantage of business displaced from smaller and lost markets. Overall, there appears to have been a realignment of the market structure of Suffolk, with clusters less tightly packed, but most of the county still well covered. Early demographic and agrarian expansion had required a multiplicity of small centres of exchange, while the economic changes after the Black Death required fewer markets of a more specialised nature.

PART I: THE SMALL TOWN MARKETS OF NEWMARKET AND CLARE

No single small town can adequately represent all the diversities that existed in late medieval England. However, small towns did provide significant sanctums for petty trade. Small town traders regularly produced and exchanged supplies of foodstuffs and cheap manufactured goods, while also depending upon the surrounding countryside for produce and custom.[23] Newmarket and Clare, two small towns from Suffolk, have been chosen for primary study because of their high level of commercial activity and the extent of surviving records from the late fourteenth and fifteenth centuries. The court rolls of Newmarket, in particular, provide a significant body of evidence relating to the regulation of petty trade. Other Suffolk towns, as well as existing historical research, are drawn upon for comparison. As already discussed, it must be borne in mind that East Anglia was a highly commercialised area compared to other parts of England, particularly in the north and west. This means that many of the conclusions are likely to be regionally specific and not necessarily applicable to late medieval England in general. Nonetheless, these case studies provide a useful vantage point from which to assess the behaviour and regulation of petty traders in a small town context.

---

[21] Beresford, *Lost Villages*, pp. 386–7. The market at Easton Bavents had been reconfirmed in a charter of 1336, after it had been struggling to operate, while the fair was moved from December to June. It appears that such encouragement proved unsuccessful. *CChR*, iv, p. 353.

[22] Historians have used Everitt's figures for markets in the sixteenth century as a comparison to medieval foundations. Everitt, 'Marketing'. This, of course, assumes that Everitt did not greatly underestimate the markets that still existed in Tudor times.

[23] Hilton, 'Medieval market towns'; Dyer, 'Consumer', 320.

Newmarket and its marketing hinterland

Newmarket, on the border of Suffolk and Cambridgeshire, exhibited all the characteristics of a small town, with its lack of an agricultural base, its relatively wide-ranging occupational structure, relaxed tenures, formal weekly market and twice-yearly fair.[24] There was little arable land and fifty-five basic tenements which probably supported a population of *c*.400 after the Black Death.[25] However, Newmarket was not an incorporated borough with formal self-government, nor did its tenants enjoy the privileges of full burgess tenure or trade guilds. Newmarket was thus a seigneurial small town at the very lowest end of the urban scale. In the early fifteenth century, most of the town was part of the manor of Sir William Argentein, who was an absentee lord;[26] though the manor of Newmarket had been divided in 1318 when John Argentein's two daughters took one half. This was called Butler's Manor and its lords were also absentees. Nevertheless, the late medieval administration of Newmarket appears to have remain united under one bailiff.[27]

Beresford has regarded Newmarket as a planned town rather than a natural growth alongside the road.[28] However, it is likely that the town was a mixture of both, with an early informal trading function for itinerant traders and consumers abetted by its position on the main London to Norwich road, as well as manorial (Newmarket and Ditton Valens), parish (Exning and Woodditton) and county (Suffolk and Cambridgeshire) boundaries.[29] This market was then formalised, perhaps as a prescriptive foundation (before 1199 and hence there is no extant

---

[24] There is no surviving charter for the market, but there is evidence that it was in operation by the early thirteenth century. Letters, *Gazetteer*; TNA, c60/9, m.6, c133/33/16. There are thirteenth-century charters for the two fairs, dating from 1227 and 1292, but other evidence suggests that there was a Newmarket fair from at least as early as 1223. *RLC*, ii, pp. 106, 175; *CChR*, i, p. 11, ii, p. 429. For an excellent local study of Newmarket, see May, *Newmarket: Medieval and Tudor*; May, 'Newmarket and its market court'.

[25] The lack of arable or pastoral output is shown by the lack of agricultural entries in the Newmarket account rolls for 1428–40 and 1472–82. There was only one arable area of 180 acres, which was all leased out; SRO(B), Acc.1476/12, 1476/13, 359/3. The manor of Newmarket was approximately 250 acres in total size. TNA, c133/33/16. Some tenements would have been subdivided, and it is likely that further tenements existed on the other side of the High Street which were consequently located in the manor of Ditton Valens and thus not entered in the account rolls. The court rolls did, however, combine both parts of the town.

[26] The lord seems to have visited Newmarket for the fair, when the rolls record quite high expenses for his hospitality and horses. BL, Additional Charters 25867. When John Argentein died in 1413, his two sisters married two brothers, William and Robert Alington. May, *Newmarket: Medieval and Tudor*, p. 17.

[27] *Ibid.*, p. 18. [28] Beresford, *New Towns*, pp. 490–1.

[29] The dual administrative existence of Newmarket meant that it was not recorded as a separate taxation entity until 1524.

market charter), with additional fair foundations and an elaboration of the topographical layout in the thirteenth century. The fourteenth-century marketplace was a planned later addition to the earlier road-side market, while the tenement layout was fairly uniform in size and distribution.[30] These commercial facilities were spurred on by the Argen-tein family, who perhaps saw the potential of this site during a time of general proliferation for marketing establishments.

Newmarket's marketplace formed the heart of the town. It provided stalls every Tuesday, arranged in rows by commodity: le Draperie, le Bocherye, le Merserie, le Lyndraperie, le Barkersrowe, le Cordewen-errowe and le Spyserye, as well as rows for ironmongers, ropers and cheese-sellers. These market rows indicate that there were retail trades in meat, leather, clothes, shoes, metal goods and a few luxuries, though many traders also seemed to acquire vacant stalls with little regard to their location or their designated trade. For instance, Robert Gateward had stalls in le Merserye, le Lyndraperye, le Barkersrowe, le Spyserye and le Cordwenerrowe.[31] In the 1472 account rolls, some thirty-six stalls and seventy-two shops can be identified, as well as a tollhouse that prob-ably served as the administrative focus of the town.[32] Court and account rolls draw a clear distinction between shops and stalls. The latter were generally cheaper, usually 4d.–6d. a year, though larger or prominent stalls were rented at over 2s. per annum.[33] They were presumably tem-porary awnings in the marketplace, covering a space of some forty to fifty square feet. Inevitably, many stalls became more permanent over time and, along with shops, encroached onto the market area. Shops were actual lodgings, slightly larger than stalls, with a frontage onto the mar-ket or main street. They were sometimes built on the long and narrow tenements, for which tenants paid a fixed rent and were relatively free to choose how they sold or sublet. This arrangement was similar to burgage tenure, but the residents still had to pay a customary entry fee to the lord, which ranged from 2s. to 24s. Any tenant who avoided this fee was considered to have sold their tenement or shop without licence and the property could be seized into the lord's hands.[34]

Occupational profiles of late medieval towns provide further indication of urban status. In Newmarket and other towns, this profile is sometimes difficult to determine. Surnames can be used as a rough guide to a person's trade, but by the late fourteenth and early fifteenth centuries surnames were often hereditary, rather than personal, and can therefore

[30] May, 'Site of the medieval market'.   [31] SRO (B), Acc.1476/1/26, 30, 32, 39.
[32] SRO (B), Acc.359/3.   [33] SRO (B), Acc.1476/1/30, 43.
[34] E.g. SRO (B), Acc.1476/1/19, 22.

be misleading. After 1350, many traders did not have the occupations that their surnames denoted, or else they only referred to an incidental trade.[35] Nevertheless, in early fifteenth-century Newmarket, there is evidence that John Chaundeler partly worked according to his surname, dealing in tar, oil, bitumen and wax, as well as engaging in brewing and baking. Similarly, Nicholas Sadlere was a saddler, but also indulged in supplementary brewing and regrating. Overall, the occupational profile of Newmarket was fluid and it is often impossible to designate a primary trade to residents. Many of Newmarket's traders were involved in more than one occupation, or their wives brewed and regrated foodstuffs for additional income. In total, some twenty-two different, non-agricultural occupations can be identified by direct references in court rolls and a further eleven if occupational surnames are used.[36] These figures are comparable to the small town of Romford, in Essex, where thirty non-agrarian occupations were mentioned in the early fifteenth century.[37] The residents of Newmarket were mostly freemen who retailed goods in the market, or ran small inns, shops and alehouses in the High Street. Indeed, Newmarket's prime importance lay in its location upon two main roads, including the Icknield Way, and its positioning some twelve miles from the main centres of Cambridge and Bury St Edmunds.[38] Much trade came by way of provisioning travellers who used Newmarket as a stopping point to and from Cambridge, Bury, Norwich, Ely and London. Retailing and victualling were thus dominant professions in this small Suffolk town.

Debt pleas from Newmarket's market court give a general idea of the scope of the town's marketing hinterland. Manorial court records and debt cases were mostly restricted to local transactions and do not necessarily reflect extensive merchant bargains. However, the early fifteenth-century records can show us the extent and range of retail trade contacts, particularly in foodstuffs.[39] Often the clerk actually stated the home town of an outside trader, such as Walter Tennison of Newport Pagnell.

[35] Fransson, 'Middle English surnames'.
[36] The directly referenced occupations were: victualler (baker, brewer, butcher, cook, fisher, maltseller and poulterer); leather and cloth workers (barker, cordwainer, currier, draper, glover and tanner); and miscellaneous occupations (chandler, ironmonger, mercer, pedlar, roper, saddler, smith, spicer and turner). Occupational surnames additionally give: barber, brasier, carter, clerk, drawer, drover, fletcher, fuller, skinner, tailor, weaver.
[37] McIntosh, *Autonomy and Community*, p. 152. See also Hilton, 'Lords, burgesses and hucksters'; Miller and Hatcher, *Medieval England: Towns*, pp. 128–9.
[38] Communications played a vital role in the development of trading settlements. O'Donnell, 'Market centres', 186, 189.
[39] For a study of Newmarket's hinterland, see May, *Newmarket: Medieval and Tudor*, pp. 48–9.

Another, less accurate, indication of traders' places of origin occurred in locational surnames, such as Robert Peterborough, but these are mainly useful where the trader is specifically identified as an outsider. By collating these place references, an idea of the marketing and social links for Newmarket can be formed.

The Newmarket court rolls mention some sixty-one different places which had contacts with the town in the early fifteenth century, the majority of which (forty-one) were within twelve miles and surrounded the town in a fairly even pattern (see Figure 19). Only a handful of places provided more than two visitors in the court roll references: Exning, Bottisham, Fordham, Wilbraham, Haverhill, Soham, Swaffham, Stetchworth, Mildenhall, Burwell, Chippenham and Bury St Edmunds. Unsurprisingly, these are mostly the neighbouring villages and towns for Newmarket, though the economic reach of Bury St Edmunds and Haverhill (both twelve miles away) is notable. There were also some twenty places beyond twelve miles, mostly lying on the main roads that bisected Newmarket. Dyer's study of market towns and their hinterlands showed that the majority of commercial contacts were within a radius of eight miles, though the shape of the hinterland was additionally influenced by geographic and economic factors.[40] Only a few small-town folk had a social and economic reach beyond the immediate sphere of influence around their town. Immigrants to towns most likely came from the immediate hinterland, and they presumably kept contacts with family and friends which fed into commercial links.[41] Nevertheless, some traders also moved from Newmarket into larger centres, reflecting the wider networks that did exist. For instance, in 1404–5, Adam Chapman transferred his rights in a holding and a croft at Newmarket to his brother, Nicholas, who was a burgess merchant of Lynn.[42] In broad terms, the pattern of debt cases in Newmarket reveals a prominent inner ring of contacts with the immediate hinterland, but also wider, more sporadic links further afield.[43]

There is further evidence of outside producers coming to Newmarket to sell grain and agricultural goods. In particular, bakers, butchers and other traders came from the immediate hinterland and set up stalls in the marketplace. Stallholders from Ashley, Stetchworth, Swaffham, Fordham, Chippenham, Soham and Bury St Edmunds are all recorded

---

[40] Dyer, 'Market towns'.
[41] For immigration, see McClure, 'Patterns of migration'; Carus-Wilson, 'First half-century', p. 53; Hilton, 'Lords, burgesses and hucksters', 10–13.
[42] BL, MS Additional 5823, fols. 239r–240r.
[43] For instance, there was a Newmarket merchant trading in Hockham (Norfolk) in 1358. Bailey, *A Marginal Economy*, pp. 146, 149.

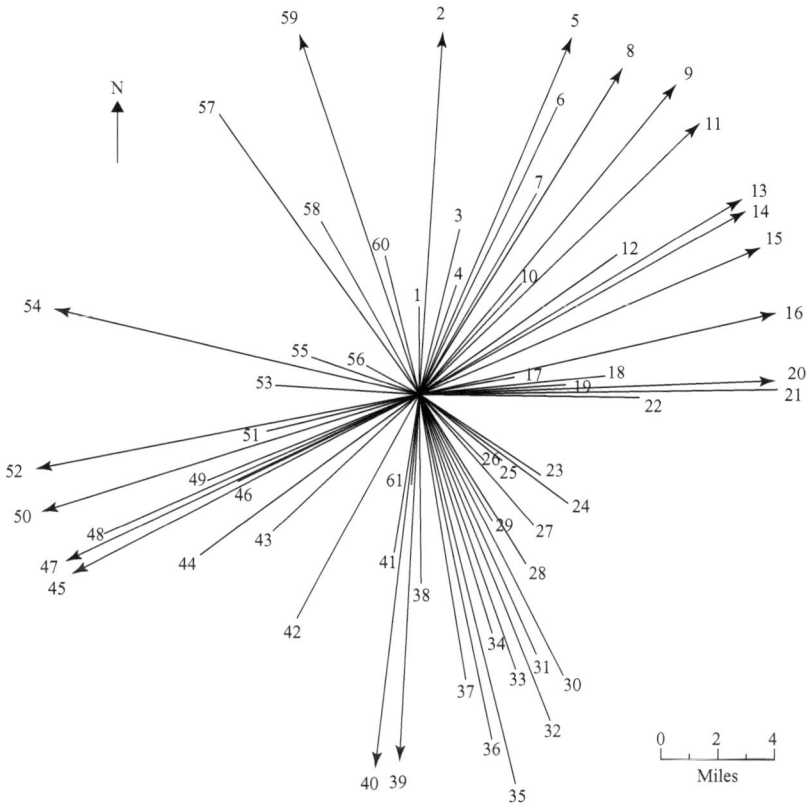

Figure 19: Marketing hinterland of Newmarket, 1399–1413.

Notes: 1. Snailwell (3 miles away, in a direct line); 2. Lynn (38); 3. Freckenham (6); 4. Chippenham (4); 5. Feltwell (20); 6. Eriswell (11); 7. Mildenhall (8); 8. Brandon (18); 9. East Dereham (40); 10. Kennett (5); 11. Thetford (19); 12. Cavenham (8); 13. Diss (31); 14. Botesdale (26); 15. Hoxne (35); 16. Halesworth (47); 17. Moulton (3); 18. Higham (7); 19. Gazeley (5); 20. Mendlesham (29); 21. Bury St Edmunds (12); 22. Barrow (8); 23. Dalham (5); 24. Ousden (6); 25. Ashley (4); 26. Cheveley (3); 27. Lidgate (6); 28. Cowlinge (7); 29. Kirtling (5); 30. Hundon (11); 31. Barnardiston (10); 32. Kedington (12); 33. Great Wratting (10); 34. Thurlow (8); 35. Bumstead (14); 36. Haverhill (12); 37. Withersfield (10); 38. Carlton (7); 39. Thaxted (20); 40. Dunmow (26); 41. Brinkley (5); 42. Balsham (9); 43. Wilbraham (7); 44. Teversham (10); 45. Banbury (76); 46. Bottisham (7); 47. Newport Pagnell (49); 48. Cambridge (12); 49. Quy (8); 50. Bedford (38); 51. Swaffham (5); 52. St Neots (28); 53. Reach (5); 54. Willingham (15); 55. Burwell (4); 56. Exning (2); 57. Ely (13); 58. Soham (7); 59. Peterborough (24); 60. Fordham (5); 61. Stetchworth (3).

Sources: SRO (B), Acc.1476/1/1–48; May, *Newmarket: Medieval and Tudor*, pp. 48–9.

as coming weekly to Newmarket.[44] In 1439–40, William Claydon of Haverhill made a bequest in his will that his son should take over his Newmarket stall.[45] These were perhaps peripatetic traders who moved from market to market in order to meet periodic demand for specialised goods.[46] Indeed, the infiltration of small towns by outside producers appears to have gained momentum throughout England by the fifteenth century, having previously been primarily a rural phenomenon.[47] Newmarket thus represented an important locus on the market-circuit for traders. Bury St Edmunds, Cambridge and Ely were the main provincial centres of trade in the region, but local merchants also travelled in search of agricultural goods between the local markets at Newmarket, Moulton, Barrow, Ousden, Mildenhall, Brinkley, Chippenham and Reach.[48] Of these, Newmarket was the only local market held on a Tuesday and seems to have dominated the local hinterland on this day, due in part to its convenient road-junction location. Also, the surrounding markets of Worlington, Moulton, Exning, Ousden, Barrow, Great Thurlow, Wicken, Chippenham and Swaffham all fell by the wayside during the fifteenth century, suggesting that they were more localised in their trading activities. Only Newmarket and Reach survived into the sixteenth century to compete for the distributive and service trades of this particular area.

Clare and its marketing hinterland

While Newmarket was on the very lowest rung of small towns in terms of both size and function, Clare was a slightly more 'secure' small town, with basic borough status and a part in the local cloth industry. Clare, located in the Stour Valley of south-west Suffolk, in Risbridge hundred, was at a crossing point of a rivulet of the Stour river where the main road led to London.[49] The town thus lay at the heart of the developing cloth industry of fifteenth-century Suffolk. Wool from the surrounding Clare manors was sold both locally and regionally, with some going to the capital. There are references to spinners, dyers, weavers and fullers

---

[44] John Coupere and William Howesson of Stetchworth, Thomas Eustas of Swaffham, Thomas Predynton of Fordham, Thomas Spenser of Chippenham, Thomas Warner and John Wilkyn of Saham, and John Wynde of Bury St Edmunds all owned stalls in Newmarket. SRO (B), Acc.1476/1. The account rolls for 1472–3 also listed stallholders such as Thomas Todde of Bury, John Simond of Barrow and John Webb of Bottisham. SRO (B), Acc.359/3.

[45] Northeast (ed.), *Wills*, p. 21, no. 50.   [46] Smith, 'A periodic market', p. 478.

[47] Postles, 'An English small town', 29.

[48] Dymond and Martin (eds.), *Historical Atlas*, pp. 62–3. For Cambridgeshire markets, see Masschaele, *Peasants*, p. 185.

[49] For a study of Clare, see Thornton, *A History of Clare*.

in the borough court rolls and debt pleas, and from the late fourteenth century, a fulling mill on the river was mentioned.[50] Clare clothiers also began to appear in a range of sources by the mid-fifteenth century and were prosperous enough to contribute to the building of the Church of St Peter and St Paul.[51] Yet, it should be noted that fifteenth-century Clare did not reach the prosperous heights of nearby Sudbury, Lavenham or Long Melford.[52]

The weekly market of Clare had existed and thrived since before the Norman Conquest and thus no formal market charter was created. The *Domesday Book* entry for the town included forty-three burgesses, while the court rolls regarded the town as a 'Burgus' separate from the manor of Clare.[53] The town had a planned market square, laid out before the castle mound and surrounded by burgage tenements. Although Clare was designated as a borough and had early origins, the town nevertheless remained relatively small, with perhaps a population of some 700–800 in the late fourteenth century.[54] Like Newmarket, Clare did not gain extensive autonomous privileges and remained in seigneurial hands. By the mid-fourteenth century, Clare's lord was Elizabeth de Burgh and she (and her officials) spent considerable time *in situ* administering the extensive holdings in the Honor of Clare, which included lands in Suffolk, Norfolk and Essex.[55] Elizabeth de Burgh died in 1360 and was followed by Lionel of Clarence, Earl of Ulster (d.1369) and then the Mortimers,[56] before the lands finally fell into the hands of the young Richard, Duke of York, from 1425. Although the lords resided less in the town after the 1360s, there was still a permanent steward who constituted executive authority and kept a close hold on seigneurial affairs and revenue. Clare was therefore an example of a medieval seigneurial or 'mesne' borough, slightly above Newmarket in the urban hierarchy, complete with burgage

---

[50] E.g. TNA, sc2/203/48, 50, 54, 57, 63; Cromarty stated that in March 1416, John Berymelle de Clare, a dyer, was in debt to Thomas Hykedon of Walden, a dyer. Cromarty, 'Chepyng Walden', 122.

[51] Thornton, *A History of Clare*, pp. 144–92.   [52] See pp. 275–6.   [53] *DB*, 389b.

[54] There were some eighty free tenants recorded in 1307, though this does not necessarily mean there were eighty tenements since several could have been subdivided. Thornton, *A History of Clare*, p. 36. The population of Clare in the late fourteenth century was probably in the region of 700–800, since the 1377 Poll Tax lists 425 taxpayers. Fenwick (ed.), *Poll Taxes*, ii, p. 500. In order to convert the Poll Tax number into a plausible population figure, Rigby argues for an estimated multiplier of 1.9. Rigby, 'Urban population', 398–9.

[55] She inherited from her brother, Gilbert de Clare, in 1314, after he was killed at the Battle of Bannockburn. See Underhill, *For Her Good Estate*.

[56] Edmund Mortimer, 3rd Earl of March (d.1381–2), Roger Mortimer, 4th Earl of March (d.1398), Edmund Mortimer, 5th Earl of March (d.1425). Thornton, *A History of Clare*, pp. 11–13.

tenements and a borough court. However, it never established the size
or status of independent larger boroughs such as Ipswich or Cambridge,
and there is no evidence of a borough charter or fully constituted self-
government.

However, Clare did provide some privileges for its residents, including
burgage tenure, exemptions from tolls and stallage, a borough court, the
election of borough officials and an element of freedom in marketing
activities.[57] In return, the chief pledges collected a common fine of 10s.
from their tithingmen, which was then paid to the lord on behalf of
the borough.[58] Individuals also paid a once-only fine of 2s. to the lord
in return for liberties of the town, recumbent upon burgess status.[59]
Burgess status was thus not automatic for all of Clare's inhabitants, but
a large number of free tenants appear to have paid the fine during the
late fourteenth century, as well as a few individuals from outside the
town. For instance, in 1359, a smith from Hintlesham paid a fine of 3s.
4d. in return for liberties; others from the neighbouring towns of Stoke
and Hundon paid from 12d. to $\frac{1}{2}$ mark (usually 2s.) throughout the late
fourteenth century.[60]

In addition, Clare's Friday market was farmed to its burgesses for £6
a year, officially noted in the records from 1425 but probably in their
hands since at least 1370.[61] The farm combined miscellaneous dues,
including the rents of market stalls and tolls, into a lump sum. This
probably meant that the trade of the town was increasingly regulated for
the benefit of burgesses rather than the lord. Indeed, there is evidence
that the burgesses were prepared to promulgate their own by-laws. In
October 1453, the bailiffs proclaimed in the market that no one was
to sell victuals in winter until after the hour of eight nor in autumn
until after the hour of seven, and that no fishmongers were to sell their
produce at night.[62] The marketplace itself lay in the centre of the town,
between the church and castle, and included a moothall (first mentioned
in 1481),[63] pillory and woolhall.[64] The stalls were of a similar size to those
in Newmarket (eight feet by six feet) and there were also more permanent
shops. The rents for stalls were relatively inexpensive, just 2d.–6d. per

---

[57] For similar liberties, see Hilton, 'Small town society', pp. 59–64.

[58] Thornton, *A History of Clare*, pp. 32–3. Thornton argues that this fine was originally
intended to cover the expenses of the leet court.

[59] TNA, sc2/203/46–7, 57, 62.

[60] TNA, sc2/203/55, 62; Thornton, *A History of Clare*, p. 37.

[61] TNA, DL29/992/15, DL29/993/7, DL29/994/10; Thornton, 'A study', 100–2. In a similar
way, Sudbury market was farmed to the burgesses for £10 a year. Thornton, *A History
of Clare*, pp. 41–2.

[62] TNA, sc2/203/70.   [63] TNA, sc2/203/72.

[64] In 1357, the bailiffs were also ordered to repair 'le Cuckyngstol'. TNA, sc2/203/53.

annum.[65] Like Newmarket, there is evidence of foreign traders hiring stalls in Clare, such as John Boxted of Sudbury, whose will in 1440 showed that he held four stalls in Clare as well as two in Lavenham and one in Sudbury.[66] Clare also had an annual fair, held in nearby Wentford, which was first granted in 1231 and was used for exchanging agricultural goods, wool and cloth.[67]

From 1377 to 1425, fifteen non-agricultural occupations were directly mentioned in the Clare court rolls and a further thirty-seven were indicated by surnames, though these are not necessarily a reliable guide to a person's occupation.[68] There were the usual urban victuallers and leather workers, but the variety of references suggest a slightly wider occupational diversity than in Newmarket as well as a greater manufacturing base. In particular, the cloth and building trades were well represented, the latter perhaps due to the significant administrative and consumption demands of the castle (with some 250 in its household) and the substantial house of Augustinian friars.[69] Unsurprisingly, a significant victualling sector developed in Clare at an early date.

Like Newmarket, we can determine the trading hinterland of Clare by reference to the town's debt pleas in 1377–1422 and the stated origins of traders, when such information was provided by the clerk (see Figure 20). These references give forty-seven different, identifiable destinations. Of these, only nine places are mentioned more than twice: Stoke by Clare, Sudbury, Gosfield, Long Melford, Haverhill, Belchamp, Hundon, Chilton and Cavendish. Perhaps unsurprisingly, all of these were within ten miles of Clare, while Stoke, Chilton, Cavendish, Hundon and Belchamp were neighbouring communities. Indeed, the majority of places in Figure 20 were within twelve miles of Clare, again highlighting the importance of the immediate hinterland to the trading networks of small towns. However, given the expanding English cloth industry one might have expected more extensive links beyond the town's nearby hinterland. The pattern of connections also shows a lack of contacts to the north-east, south-east and west, along the Stour Valley, demonstrating a skewing of Clare's hinterland due to the influence of the growing

[65] TNA, sc2/203/67.   [66] Northeast (ed.), *Wills*, p. 25, no. 62.
[67] TNA, sc2/203/58.
[68] These were: baker, barber, barker, brewer, butcher, cook, dyer, fisher, fuller, maderer, merchant, miller, tailor, tanner, weaver; and brasier, card-maker, carter, chapman, chandler, clerk, coal-maker, cordwainer, cornmonger, cooper, currier, draper, fletcher, gardener, glover, goldsmith, lawyer, maltster, mason, midwife, mustarder, quilt-maker, pedlar, porter, roper, saddler, spicer, skinner, smith, sewster, taverner, thatcher, tiler, turner, vintner, woolman, wheelwright.
[69] The Augustinian priory was founded by Richard de Clare in 1248. Stokes, 'Clare priory', 108–9.

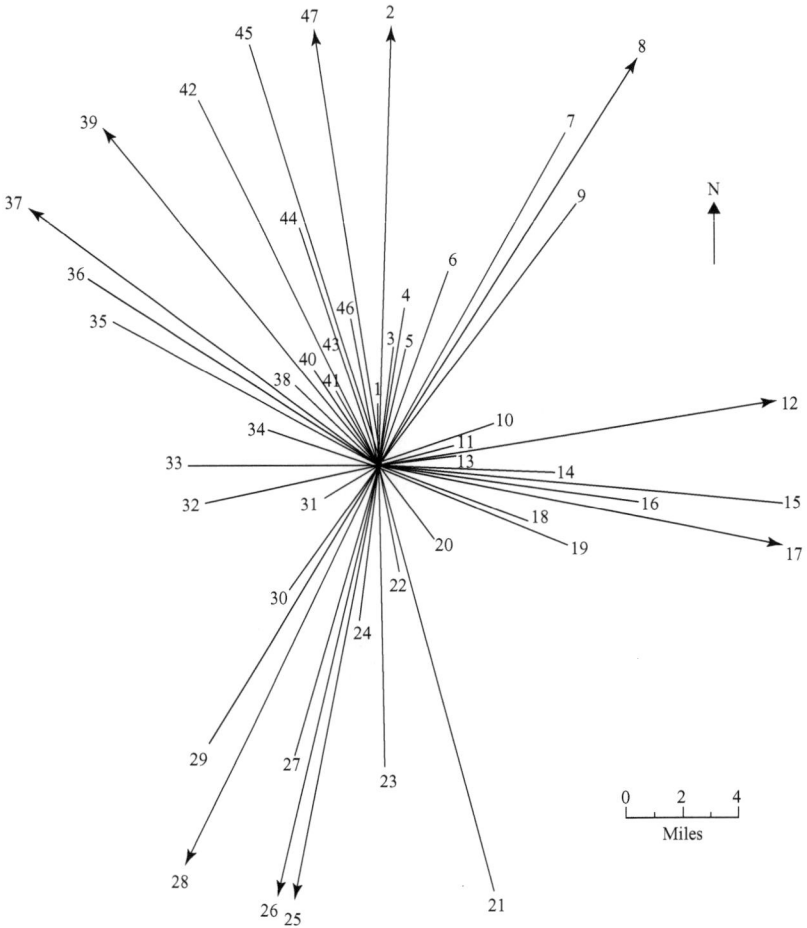

Figure 20: Marketing hinterland of Clare, 1377–1422.

Notes: 1. Poslingford (2 miles away, in a direct line); 2. Weeting (27); 3. Denston (4); 4. Clopton (6); 5. Stansfield (4); 6. Rede (7); 7. Bury St Edmunds (13); 8. Honington (20); 9. Welnetham (11); 10. Glemsford (4); 11. Cavendish (3); 12. Darsham (45); 13. Pentlow (3); 14. Long Melford (6); 15. Kersey (14); 16. Waldingfield (9); 17. Hadleigh (16); 18. Borley (6); 19. Sudbury (7); 20. Belchamp (3); 21. Coggeshall (15); 22. Yeldham (4); 23. Gosfield (10); 24. Toppesfield (5); 25. Chelmsford (25); 26. Tilbury (44); 27. Wethersfield (10); 28. Great Dunmow (18); 29. Bardfield (11); 30. Stambourne (5); 31. Stoke by Clare (2); 32. Bumstead (6); 33. Haverhill (7); 34. Kedington (4); 35. Brinkley (11); 36. West Wratting (12); 37. Colne (31); 38. Thurlow (4); 39. Burwell (17); 40. Barnardiston (4); 41. Hundon (3); 42. Newmarket (14); 43. Chilton (1); 44. Lidgate (9); 45. Kennett (15); 46. Stradishall (5); 47. Mildenhall (19).

Source: TNA, sc2/203/62–7.

cloth towns of Haverhill, Sudbury and Long Melford. All of these towns lay within seven miles of Clare and most likely drew potential traders away. Clare traders themselves may have travelled there, such as Robert Brynkele, who was involved in a debt plea in Sudbury in 1409–10 with a miller, John Grey.[70]

As in Newmarket, the scope of activities for Clare's traders was heavily influenced by the surrounding markets and the commercial opportunities they provided. Both Newmarket and Clare were especially dependent upon the custom and produce of their hinterlands. Each also had a significant retailing sector, which needed to be regulated but also required efficient marketing facilities to prosper. The remainder of this study will examine the activities of the retailers in these towns and attempt to discern the motivations behind their regulation.

Sources, courts and officials

Our primary sources for trading activity in Newmarket and Clare are the surviving manorial court rolls. Manor courts had three main functions in the late Middle Ages: the control of seigneurial rights and revenue; handling inter-personal pleas and disputes; and maintaining peace and order.[71] Additionally, leet courts adjudged minor criminal offences and their jurisdiction extended to all tenants. Manorial court rolls are a problematic type of source because their primary purpose was the recording of jurisdictional amercements for the lord, rather than providing a detailed log of proceedings and offences. This could result in selective coverage and few detailed entries.[72] It must also be remembered that significant sectors of society were omitted from the legal record or made only fleeting appearances, such as women, subtenants, servants and the poor. In the case of women, their primary appearances in court rolls were limited to commercial matters, particularly brewing and regrating. A further difficulty associated with the context of court rolls was the way in which the clerk was influenced by formalised precedents in compiling courts rolls; any variations in the nature and frequency of litigation may reflect changing clerical processes as much as real economic or social changes.[73] Indeed, the standardised style of reporting in court rolls may have created a number of legal fictions. In a commercial context, court rolls often seem to exaggerate the contentious side of medieval trading and give the impression that bad trading practices were the order of the

---

[70] TNA, SC2/204/13 (1409–10).   [71] McIntosh, *Controlling*, p. 35.
[72] See Bennett, *Women*, appx, pp. 199–231.
[73] Beckerman, 'Customary law', pp. 112–16; Briggs, 'Manor court procedures', 520–1.

day. We therefore need to keep in mind the mass of uncontentious deal-ings that have gone unrecorded when assessing the nature of day-to-day trade, particularly in relation to late medieval moral ideas and legislation. Despite the partial nature of the sources, court rolls nevertheless provide the best available picture of life in a medieval small town and, with care-ful examination, they can reveal much about trading administration and enforcement. Beyond the sometimes turgid reiteration of regular busi-ness, we can glimpse elements of self-administration, court rituals, dra-matic interludes and communal consensus. Indeed, these manor courts were assemblies for the whole community, and it appears that coercion was the exception since most had internalised conceptions about the ordering of their society and market.

Newmarket has an outstanding series of rolls for 1399 to 1413 covering four different types of court.[74] Although they only span fourteen years, and a few are missing (see Table 1, below), they are still exceptional in the trading evidence they provide for such a small town. The biannual general court (held around Easter and late October or early November) was concerned with seigneurial rights which, in Newmarket, meant that the court's main work revolved around the assizes of bread and ale and the administration of retail trade, as well as trespass and encroachment. The leet court was held annually in August and regulated the minor rights of the king, with issues ranging from public nuisances to street brawls. It was also here that the lord exercised his right to view of frankpledge. The market court, held every two to three weeks on market day (Tuesday), was unusual for a small town and reflected the large number of inter-personal pleas (especially debts) in Newmarket. Finally, the fair court was mainly concerned with the renting and upkeep of stalls and shops, though there were also some debt pleas from the two fairs, which ran on 9–16 June (around St Barnabas's Day) and 27–9 October (three days around the feast of St Simon and St Jude). Overall, the quantity of trade offences recorded in the court rolls was unusual for a small town. The number of presentments could be interpreted as a sign of over-regulation and a strict adherence to the moral and legal notions of vigilance. However, such a level of official oversight was not necessarily incompatible with a practical encouragement of trade, while the recording of infringements does not necessarily mean that the laws were strictly applied. Newmarket's role as a local distribution centre and provisioning stop for travellers also accounts for the high level of entries, which involved a large proportion of the town's community.

[74] SRO (B), Acc.1476/1/1–48.

Despite being a larger settlement, Clare's court business was not subdivided to the same extent as Newmarket's. Clare's borough court was held every three weeks and there were also two leet courts a year, held around Easter and Michaelmas. Most assizes and trading activities were administered at the leet court and it was also here that the view of frankpledge was regulated by capital pledges. The borough court was primarily responsible for handling transfers of land and inter-personal pleas of debt and trespass. The extant rolls for the borough court start in 1312 and continue into the sixteenth century, but with some gaps.[75] From 1377 to 1425, the main missing rolls are from 1392–6, 1402, 1408–10 and 1415. For the leet courts, there are forty-four surviving rolls and fifty-two missing rolls from November 1377 to April 1425 (see Table 2), the period chosen for comparison with Newmarket.

The courts of Newmarket and Clare were serviced by jurors and officials who were seemingly elected from leading members of the community. There were also capital pledges, who were the mouthpieces of their tithings in the leet court and presented the offences of their members. These men were also considered part of the local office-holding elite, traditionally associated with the obligations of tenants holding suit-owing land and certainly those considered to be responsible, upright members of the community.[76] No women served as jurors or were elected as bailiffs, constables, capital pledges, aletasters or affeerers in either Clare or Newmarket.[77] Their influence was mostly informal or via their husbands, but ultimately this was a patriarchal society that limited women's legal capacity and public role. Nevertheless, as will be discussed below, we do see women acting in occasional legal roles, such as court plaintiffs and defendants.

An analysis of the Newmarket court rolls reveals that twenty-nine of thirty-seven capital pledges, and most of the jurors, were definitely involved in trade or retailing. Over half of those who appeared on the juries of the general court had also been on lists for breaches of the assize. Regular jurors, such as John Waleys, John Schelleye, Peter Fydelere, John Ballone, John Barbor, John Smyth and William Ray, were all heavily involved in victual trades. It is likely that they were aware of the pragmatic needs of a commercial community and perhaps sought a lenient stance in trading regulation. However, as we shall see below, moral and

---

[75] TNA, sc2/203/38–72.

[76] Schofield, 'Late medieval view of frankpledge', pp. 426–39.

[77] There was a widespread exclusion of women from these positions in medieval English towns and villages. Jewell, *Women*, pp. 74–6, 104–8.

legal considerations were not totally bypassed and some supervision was regarded as beneficial.

In a similar manner, the bailiffs, constables, capital pledges and jurors of Clare, all of whom were heavily involved in the administration of the market and the enforcement of court decisions, were also usually traders. This is again unsurprising in a small town where the market and trade were the main impetus for the inhabitants. A statute of 1382 had declared that no victualler was to exercise urban judicial power, except where there were no sufficient replacements.[78] However, in Clare, a designated borough, there were either no possible replacements or the statute was ignored. Of the thirty-five bailiffs in Clare between 1377 and 1425, only ten cannot be identified as having a household connection to trade, particularly brewing, fishing, tanning and butchery. From the constables that can be identified in the same period, half of them (six of twelve) or their wives were amerced at some stage for a trading infringement in brewing, baking, fish-selling, butchery, regrating or tanning. This does not mean that the other bailiffs and constables were not involved in trade or crafts, merely that their activities were not relevant to the proceedings of the court. The upper echelons of this local society were thus extensively involved in market activities, both in production and vending, and this must have influenced the way they approached their participation as officials and in the courts.

Mark Bailey has posited that 'the manorial system clearly imposed minimal burdens on the residents of Newmarket, yet provided an effective legal framework to encourage their trading activities'.[79] In a small town, officials had considerable room for manoeuvre in order to establish a suitable trading atmosphere, while the decisions of capital pledges and jurors represented the concerns of the leading town residents. This was especially so in Newmarket, which had continually absent lords whose interest in the manor seemingly extended little beyond the assurance of a regular income from rents, tolls and fines. Argentein's representative in the early fifteenth century was the steward, William Chevele, who was primarily interested in upholding the lord's rights, as can be seen in the hefty amercements imposed upon those who evaded tolls or traded in the market without licence. As long as pecuniary benefits were channelled in the lord's direction, the men who dominated the courts were relatively free to decide which trading offences to prosecute and which to ignore, as well as the degree of punishment to impose upon malefactors.

---

[78] *Statutes*, ii, p. 28, 6 Ric.II st.1 c.9. See above, p. 167.
[79] Personal communication. See also Bailey, 'Trade and towns', 204–5; Bailey, *Medieval Suffolk*, pp. 142–4.

McIntosh noted a similar situation in Havering, Essex, where jurors had great discretion in handling misbehaviour without undue lordly exploitation. Additionally, the independence of the steward was curtailed, for he could act only upon information provided by local people and the communication of such knowledge was controlled by capital pledges and jurors.[80] Britnell similarly recognised the striking freedom of local courts in their enforcement of economic regulations, but noted that this could differ from town to town.[81] For instance, in his study of Buntingford, Bailey portrayed a small town managed by an independent community, which had minimal feudal demands and demonstrated relative efficiency as a market centre. By comparison, the town of Standon, which had a powerful lord, became subdued and restricted in its commercial activity.[82] Clare similarly had powerful lordship. Even though the lords were absent more regularly from the 1360s, after the death of Elizabeth de Burgh, Clare still remained the centre of the Honor with a permanent steward based at the castle. However, it must not be assumed that lordly interference was inimical to market development, or that a lord's desire for income usually led to a more restrictive atmosphere.[83] There was still seemingly room for commercial enterprise within the existing feudal structure, though the most successful small towns appear often to have been those that were less directly controlled by their lord. The lord of Newmarket, particularly, appears to have acquiesced in allowing his manorial courts to be adapted to the needs of traders.

There were several official posts in small towns, from bailiffs to ale-tasters, constables and affeerers. They were answerable to the court juries, particularly in the absence of the lord's steward. Bailiffs were the executive officers of the court, ensuring compliance and attendance; constables were responsible for keeping the peace and enforcing order; and affeerers assessed the penalties for offences. All these officers were theoretically elected by the jurors in Newmarket and the burgesses in Clare, though it seems that the capital pledges actually undertook this elective role. In a similar manner to 'lot and scot' in chartered boroughs, office-holding was intertwined with property. Ownership of tenements imposed an obligation to serve when required. Failure to do so might lead to social as well as pecuniary penalties.

Such officials also had to avoid being seen pursuing vendettas or favouritism. One Newmarket bailiff was amerced in 1411 for bringing

---

[80] McIntosh, *Autonomy and Community*, pp. 89, 181–6, 201–4.
[81] Britnell, 'Morals', p. 29. See also Smith, 'A periodic market', pp. 480–1.
[82] Bailey, 'A tale of two towns'.
[83] Even in Halesowen, where the lord had close control, a clique of jurors and officials dominated administration. Hilton, 'Small town society'; Razi, *Life, Marriage and Death*.

a false presentment against Richard Tornor regarding the occupation of a piece of land; this demonstrates that the power of the bailiffs was not unlimited. Additionally, the power of officials was, to an extent, curtailed by their part-time status and by the administrative machinery available to them. There were no references in the Newmarket sources to corporal punishment or to a gaol, though the tollhouse may have served this purpose. Conversely in Clare, there are some sporadic references to a pillory and the castle could have served as a gaol when necessary. However, an official's main tools of enforcement were the fines and amercements that increased with the seriousness of the offence. An offender could also be distrained and their goods taken as surety, particularly when attendance at court needed to be guaranteed.

The tasks of the bailiff were widespread, stretching from enforcing the decisions of the courts to distraining, attaching, pledging, collecting dues and supervising the marketplace. Indeed, the bailiff was the most important official for ensuring the efficient, day-to-day running of the market. Only two are recorded in both Newmarket and Clare during any one year, so they must have found their tasks particularly onerous, time-consuming and probably detrimental to their own livelihoods. Bailiffs did, however, receive recompense, in the form of expenses and a 'fealty'.[84] Also, at least two Newmarket bailiffs, William Godard and Peter Fedelere, were prepared to serve more than one term in office. Most of the Newmarket bailiffs were from the town itself (though one was from the neighbouring village of Exning) and many can be identified as involved in some sort of commercial activity. Half of the fourteen recorded bailiffs were actively involved in retail trade and they (and their wives) infringed retailing regulations with persistent regularity. In Clare, John Wynchester, John Broun, Thomas Cumbwell, William Norfolk, Peter Barker, John Fadirless, William Wardrobe and Simon Derby all served more than one term as bailiff between 1377 and 1425, though many more did not. Fewer bailiffs in Clare, compared to Newmarket, can be explicitly identified in the court rolls as actively involved in trade, though some of their households were involved in brewing. However, given that most acted as either plaintiffs or defendants in debt cases, it is very possible that they were active in the market. Thus, bailiffs must not be seen in isolation from the marketplace and the traders whom they administered. They were probably chosen for their positions because they were knowledgeable about the problems and needs of the town, as well as being prosperous members of the community.

---

[84] BL, Additional Charters 25867.

Aletasters were responsible for checking batches of ale once they were brewed, to ensure they were of sufficient quality and were being sold for the right price in standard measures. It is also possible that aletasters were responsible for inspecting the output of bakers and other victualling trades and presenting their findings at court. Few other surveying officials are mentioned in the records of these small towns, except in Newmarket where Stephen Gille, Robert Doushole, John Barkere were named as tasters of leather and John Farewell as taster of meat. However, in 1357, it was the aletasters of Clare who presented badly tanned leather in court.[85] The role of aletaster was seemingly perceived as a respectable duty. In Clare, there were several occasions when a certain pair worked well together and remained in the job for a number of years.[86] After the Black Death, the office of aletaster also served as a stepping-stone to the position of bailiff for men like Walter Bory, Thomas Luccessen, William Shepherd, Peter Colyrob, John Cardemaker, Imbert Brus, William Skynnere and William Worlyth, though this progression was by no means certain.

There is no doubt that there was an element of self-interest in being involved in the governance of a town and not only because an orderly administration was conducive to thriving businesses. Certain advantages could probably be gained in pleas and regulation through official positions. However, self-interest and competitive values were not necessarily incompatible with communal organisation. Although we must be cautious of the term 'communalty',[87] the administrative structures of Clare and Newmarket were highly dependent upon cooperation. As McIntosh has stated, the 'pairing of individual economic assertiveness with group political activity was characteristic of many medieval communities, especially towns'.[88] In market-oriented towns like Newmarket and Clare, the issues of administrative competence went beyond individual commercial success and asked questions of community aspirations. If the town had a good, reputable market, the local elite in the town had everything to gain economically and socially.

Thus, questions of who provided trading administration, and for what purpose, are as important as the market mechanisms themselves. Unfortunately, it is difficult to identify the wealth and status of the men of

---

[85] TNA, sc2/203/54, also 59. In Henley-on-Thames, 'tastatores victualium' are first mentioned in the early fifteenth century. *Henley*, pp. 48, 56, 70, 80.

[86] Thomas Baron and Stephen Wyndont (1377 to 1379); John Webbe and Robert Barker (1388–90); William Warderobe and Richard Sare (1403–5); John Lamb and John Porter (1406–13); and Thomas Couling and Thomas Broun (1419, 1421–2).

[87] Hilton, 'Medieval market towns', 21; Rubin, 'Small groups'.

[88] McIntosh, *Autonomy and Community*, pp. 181–6.

Newmarket and Clare beyond inferences from their roles as officers, jurymen, creditors, debtors and capital pledges. There were also occasional references to stall and shop transfers, but not enough to construct a complete profile of the tenancies and property ownership in the town. Nor are there surviving tax returns listing the Newmarket and Clare residents for this period. Thus, any attempts to analyse the retailers according to their socio-economic status is inevitably circumscribed by the paucity of the records. We are, instead, left identifying the elite through their roles in office-holding and administration. DeWindt has argued that such offices were usually given to prominent and wealthier members of a community.[89] But Razi rightly pointed to the problem of any assumed association between office and wealth as well as the factor of social mobility over time, both of which could skew the significance of office-holding as a stratifying indicator.[90] Nevertheless, even if office-holding should not be considered a direct reflection of economic differentiation, it does tend to indicate the social hierarchy within a small town. As such, records of office-holding remain the best socio-economic indicator we have for Newmarket and Clare households.

Some sixty-nine men were involved in different aspects of the administration process in Newmarket over fourteen years, implying a less exclusive elite than might be supposed. Jurymen, although often drawn from Newmarket, could, in the fair and market courts, include men from outside the town, reducing the exclusivity of these bodies and illustrating the importance of the town's hinterland. In categorising the socio-economic status of the traders, they have been divided them into four main groups: those with primary status, for bailiffs, capital pledges and constables; secondary status, for affeerers, tasters and jurors; and the remainder as either outsiders or of low socio-economic status. The detail of the Newmarket court rolls allows us to compare these categories to known occupations. Thirty-two traders had primary status, their main trades being:[91] innkeeper (eight), brewer (six), cook (four), baker (three), butcher (two), malterer (one), smith (one), draper (one) and spicer (one). There were thirty-seven with secondary status, with their known trades being: butcher (seven), tanner or leather dealer (four), spicer (four), innkeeper (three), brewer (three), cook (two), mercer (two), draper (two), cordwainer (one), roper (one), ironmonger (one) and malterer (one). Additionally, there were 189 other identified traders, which

---

[89] DeWindt, *Land and People*, pp. 207–20; Bennett, *Ale*, p. 213.
[90] Razi, 'Toronto School's reconstitution', 147–8.
[91] These are their main, identifiable trades, and it is possible that they were involved in other trades as well.

included both Newmarket residents and those of unknown origin, as well as another thirty-eight known outsiders. It is striking how many of the town's elite were innkeepers and butchers, but generally, a wide range of trades were represented within the offices of Newmarket.[92] In Clare, some seventy-two different men can be identified serving as bailiffs, constables or aletasters from 1377 to 1425, again suggesting that the officials of the town were drawn from an extensive number of families. The composition of officials and jurors had a demonstrable impact on how market laws were interpreted. The regulations could not be enforced to such a stringent level as to antagonise a major portion of the community, especially when the enforcers themselves had a vested interest in the prosperity of retail trade.

The assizes of bread and ale

The court rolls of Newmarket and Clare both list a number of different trading offences, but the vast majority of commercial entries concern traders who breached the assizes of bread and ale. The authorities of Newmarket and Clare were expected to stabilise supplies and prices based on national assize legislation, and their court roll entries often stated that the assizes were regulated according to statute law. However, the presentments rarely provide additional details of the specific offences perpetrated by named bakers and brewers. Rather, they list offenders beneath the bland statements of 'pistores panis et vendunt contra assisam' and 'brasiatores cervisie et vendunt contra assisam'. Despite this lack of direct information, it is still viable to compare the national guidelines with local patterns of presentment and amercement levels. Although the reasons behind amercement levels are difficult to interpret, it is possible that the highest penalties were related to offences that carried some moral stigma, particularly if the wording of the presentment went beyond the norm.[93] A close analysis of the offenders and court roll entries in Clare and Newmarket may shed some light on how regulations were interpreted and enforced by small-town officials.

Several studies of assize enforcement in late medieval England have noted the repeat offenders and continual small fines in court rolls, which went against the stipulations for escalating punishments outlined in *Assisa Panis et Cervisie*. Historians have traditionally argued that the

[92] Butchers would have benefited from the increasing demand for meat in the fifteenth century, as well as supplying subsidiary trades with hides, horn, fat, and other by-products of animal slaughter.
[93] Britnell, 'Urban economic regulation', p. 2; Britnell, 'England: towns, trade', p. 58.

local enforcement of the assizes was 'largely illusory' and that authorities overlooked continual minor offences in return for a steady income.[94] Most brewers and bakers thus broke the assize, either deliberately or in simply trying to keep their cost and waste margins to a minimum. Indeed, some leet court rolls simply stated that 'all brewers' were guilty of infringements.[95] Brewers may have regarded any penalty for such offences as aptly offset by the gains made.[96] It has thus been asserted that the assizes were no deterrent to traders offending with impunity. Frederic Maitland suggested that 'the assize seems to have been broken with as much regularity as the most orthodox of political economists could possibly demand'.[97] However, this emphasis on the laxity of assize enforcement and the criminality of traders perhaps misunderstands the way in which the law was interpreted and enforced.

More recent historians agree that the lists of those 'breaking the assize' were a legal fiction and they included everyone involved in the ale and bread trades, not just those who had actually cheated.[98] Judith Bennett has argued that all brewers, good and bad, usually faced nominal amercements as a type of *de facto* licensing system. In effect, the lords or corporations were exacting a percentage of the traders' profits.[99] They perhaps regarded this as a customary right. The 'Seneschaucy' (thirteenth century) advised that 'without warrant from the lord no baking or brewing ought to take place on any manor', and in many places, particularly in the thirteenth and fourteenth centuries, lords explicitly gave actual licences or imposed tolls for brewing.[100] The brewers of thirteenth-century Sevenhampton (Wiltshire) paid a flat toll of 1d. as well as being amerced between 2d.–6d. for breaking the assize.[101] Seabourne argues that in some places there was a conflation of the toll system and the assize of

---

[94] Lipson, *Economic History*, i, p. 296; Hudson (ed.), *Leet*, pp. xxxviii–xxxix; *Norwich*, i, pp. cxxxviii–cxxxix; *Beverley*, p. liv.

[95] Pugh (ed.), *Court Rolls*, pp. 6–7.

[96] Post, 'Manorial amercements', 305, 308.

[97] Maitland (ed.), *Select Pleas in Manorial*, p. xxxviii; Ratcliff (ed.), *Elton*, p. lxii; Powell and Malden (eds.), *Court Rolls*, pp. xiii–xiv; Pugh (ed.), *Court Rolls*, p. 6; Wood, *Medieval Economic Thought*, p. 98; Rosenthal, 'Assizes'.

[98] Bennett, *Ale*, pp. 4–5; Britnell, *Growth and Decline*, pp. 89, 195–7, 269–71; Britnell, *Commercialisation*, p. 94; Dyer, *Lords and Peasants*, p. 346; Hilton, *English Peasantry*, p. 45; Cam, *The Hundred*, p. 211. The by-laws of Petworth (Sussex) stated that every brewer, tapster and baker would be amerced at the fair, which suggests that they would pay whether they were guilty of an offence or not. West Sussex Record Office (Chichester), 6/1/18 HVI.

[99] Bennett, *Ale*, p. 163; Williamson, 'Dispute settlement', 137.

[100] Oschinsky (ed.), *Walter of Henley*, pp. 270–1, c.22; Landor (ed.), 'Alrewas court rolls', pp. 87–137; Barley (ed.), *Documents*, pp. 18–19, 33 (Newark, 1225–31); Ratcliff (ed.), *Elton*, pp. xxi–xxii, lxiii, 7, 394.

[101] Pugh (ed.), *Court Rolls*, pp. 6–7.

ale, while elsewhere they remained separate.[102] However, generally, the assizes represented another means to impose an effective licence fee upon all. In addition, the system of assize regulation also meant that brewers could be presented more than once, for brewing, measures and regrating.

Variations upon a basic *de facto* licensing system can be seen across Suffolk by the late fourteenth and fifteenth centuries. In Walsham le Willows, amercements for the assize of ale ranged from 3d. to 12d. throughout the fourteenth century, with the same two to four people being regularly amerced year after year.[103] Bennett provided an example from the small village of Earl Soham in which Walter and Agnes Bele were presented at every court from 1356 to 1376 for breaking the assize and brewing. Other couples were presented in the village throughout the period 1378–99, such as Ralph and Agnes Coluyll, John and Isabell Couyn and John and Alice Nene, who were usually amerced either 12d. or 24d.[104] These high amercement levels either suggest that trade was brisk or else the lord, Margaret Mareschall, Countess of Norfolk, was prepared to extract a high fine from her tenants in order to supplement her income. A similarly high level of amercements for brewers can be found at her larger Suffolk manors of Walton and Trimley, where penalties were normally in the range 12d.–24d. for 1381–99. Notably, amercement levels had fallen significantly on both manors by the 1410s, when the average penalty for brewing families in Earl Soham was 3d.–12d. and in Walton, 6d.–12d., even though the number of brewing amercements had remained fairly constant. The evidence suggests that they were linked to production and the manorial courts of Walton, Trimley and Earl Soham imposed a standard 3d. amercement for every brewing batch. This 'licence fee' had fallen to 2d. sometime during the reign of Henry IV. Indeed, in late fourteenth-century Walton and Trimley, the court justified the assize lists by stating that the offenders had brewed and baked without licence of the lord.[105] In other towns and villages in Suffolk, those who had specifically brewed once ('semel') were usually amerced 1d.–3d. and 6d.–12d. for brewing twice ('bis') or on several occasions.[106]

---

[102] Seabourne, *Royal Regulation*, pp. 109–10. In thirteenth-century Exeter, brewgavel, baking-gavel and chepgavel were paid by brewers, bakers and retailers respectively as essentially licences to trade; while in thirteenth-century Lincoln, brewers paid ale-toll twice a year, though there were also subject to separate amercements for selling ale. Schopp and Easterling (eds.), *Anglo-Norman Custumal*, pp. 30–1, no. 34 (1237–57); Wilkinson, *Women*, pp. 100–3.

[103] Lock (ed.), *Walsham le Willows 1303–1350*; Lock (ed.), *Walsham le Willows 1351–99*.

[104] Bennett, *Ale*, p. 162; SRO (I), v5/18/1.2–1.4.

[105] SRO (I), HA119:50/3/17–19 (1381–1413).

[106] SRO (I), HA68:484/135 (Aldham, 1347–71); SRO (I), HA119:50/3/142 (Bacton, 1413–23); SRO (I), HB8/1/663 (Bramford, 1354-); SRO (I), HA91/1 (Bradfield, 1318–77);

In effect, the assizes became a local seigneurial tax on brewing and baking profits, and it appears that amercements were related, roughly, to the level of production.[107] However, the relationship between amercement level, production, social status, seigneurial power and the degree of offence is not always clear-cut. Practices do seem to have differed between courts and over time. For instance, some courts allied the regular amercements to individual production levels, while others cut the administrative burden and set a standardised amercement for all. Nevertheless, this whole system may be related to the increasing dominance of the presentment jury from the late thirteenth century, to which offenders could not answer. This system had replaced the initiation of numerous cumbersome lawsuits brought by individual manorial officers and thus speeded up business and reduced costs.[108] However, this does not mean that the assizes were ineffectual as an enforcement tool. Notable cases could still be raised by officials when the need arose, leading to harsher penalties. Indeed, this specific, more rigorous application of the assizes of ale and bread appears to have been the procedure in most leet courts, and implied a more directed means of moral censure.[109]

Clare's court rolls recorded an average of twenty-seven brewers and just under six bakers in each listing of assize presentments (see Table 2, below), though an average of four bakers was more common after 1397. Similarly, Hilton found that Halesowen, a town of about 600, had about twenty-five brewers and four to five bakers amerced annually in the court rolls.[110] The bakers and brewers of Clare, for the period 1377–1425, were dispersed around thirty-three baking households and 198 brewing households (see Table 4). In Newmarket, an average of nineteen brewers and twelve bakers were presented at each court, though this included both regular and sporadic producers. Overall, seventy-seven brewing households and sixty-one baking households can be identified in Newmarket over fourteen years (see Tables 1 and 3). This was a large number, perhaps incorporating nearly all the identifiable households in Newmarket. There were almost twice the number of households engaged in baking, at varying levels of intensity, compared to Clare, whose figures are taken from a much longer period.

SRO (I), HA246/A1/1 (Higham, 1344–66); SRO (I), s1/10/9.1–9.11 (Holbrook, 1378-); SRO (I), HB8/1/778–89 (Tattingstone, 1335–). See also Powell and Malden (eds.), *Carshalton*, esp. p. 23, where brewers were fined 2d. for each brewing and one man was fined 5s. 6d. for thirty-three brewings.

[107] Britnell, *Growth and Decline*, p. 89; Postles, 'An English small town', 13; Hilton, *A Medieval Society*, p. 155; Hilton, *English Peasantry*, pp. 45–6.

[108] Beckerman, 'Procedural innovation', 226–50; Briggs, 'Manor court procedures', 541.

[109] Bennett, *Ale*, pp. 3, 100–1.   [110] Hilton, 'Small town society', p. 60.

Table 1. *Bakers and brewers amerced for breaking the assize, Newmarket, 1400–1413*

Date of court[a]	Number of brewers amerced[b]	Total amercement[d]	Average amercement per brewer	Number of bakers amerced[c]	Total amercement[d]	Average amercement per baker
26 Apr 1400	12	4s. 8d.*	4.7d.	9	3s. 9d.*	5.0d.
9 Oct 1400	17	5s. 2d.*	3.6d.	10	4s. 2d.*	5.0d.
5 Apr 1402	16	4s. 9d.	3.6d.	13	3s. 1d.	2.8d.
6 Oct 1402	19	6s. 11d.	4.4d.	14	4s. 11d.	4.2d.
13 Oct 1403	18	7s. 1d.*	5.0d.	14	5s. 5d.*	4.6d.
16 Apr 1404	21	7s. 9d.	4.4d.	10	2s. 11d.	3.5d.
6 Oct 1404	19	9s. 10d.	6.2d.	13	3s. 6d.	3.2d.
9 Nov 1405	19	8s. 2d.*	5.2d.	8	3s. 5d.	5.1d.
28 Apr 1406	16	7s. 2d.	5.4d.	9	3s. 10d.	5.1d.
6 Oct 1407	17	6s. 3d.	4.5d.	11	4s. 3d.	4.6d.
16 Jun 1408	20	5s. 8d.	4.5d.	13	3s. 8d.	4.4d.
3 Nov 1408	19	6s. 3d.	3.9d.	9	3s. 2d.	4.2d.
11 Apr 1409	15	7s. 4d.	5.9d.	9	2s. 10d.	3.8d.
25 Nov 1409	15	5s. 1d.	4.1d.	11	3s. 10d.	4.2d.
16 May 1410	18	6s. 2d.	4.1d.	15	4s. 9d.	3.8d.
8 Nov 1410	29	15s. 2d.	6.3d.	9	4s. 1d.	5.4d.
23 Apr 1411	19	8s. 6d.	5.4d.	16	5s. 8d.	4.3d.
2 Nov 1411	19	6s. 6d.	4.3d.	13	5s. 3d.	4.8d.
16 May 1412	26	9s. 9d.*	4.5d.	16	4s. 8d.*	3.5d.
4 Nov 1412	26	6s. 8d.	3.8d.	9	2s. 10d.	3.8d.
16 Jun 1413	16	7s. 5d.	5.9d.	12	4s. 2d.	4.2d.
Total	396	£7 12s. 3d.	4.8d.	243	£4 4s. 2d.	4.2d.

Notes: a – the records of six courts are missing (out of twenty-seven) in the period April 1400 to June 1413; b – brewers who broke the assize; c – bakers who broke the assize; d – the totals noted by the clerk in the Newmarket rolls were not always equivalent to the sum of the individual amercements as written above the names of individuals. This was probably due to incorrect calculations by the scribe or later additions and the differences were usually only 1d.–2d. The individual amercements have been used and * signifies a discrepancy between this total and the clerk's. Certain amercements were either illegible or not given (thirteen for the brewers and three for the bakers) and these were not included in the calculations for the amercement averages, but were included in the number of offences.

Source: SRO (B), Acc.1476/1/1–48.

The market traders of Newmarket were obviously catering for more than just local demand, attesting to the widespread nature of commodity production, as well as the importance of the victualling trade in this small town. However, many of the brewers and bakers may have specifically processed foodstuffs to meet the increased biannual demand at fairs or simply disposed of their surplus domestic produce. Fifty-four of the seventy-seven brewing households and forty-four of the sixty-one baking households in Newmarket were presented four or fewer times over twenty-one general courts (see Table 3). In Clare, nineteen of thirty-three

Table 2. *Bakers and brewers amerced for breaking the assize, Clare, 1377–1425*

Date of court[a]	Number of brewers amerced[b]	Total amercement[d]	Average amercement per brewer	Number of bakers amerced[c]	Total amercement[d]	Average amercement per baker
13 Nov 1377	30	17s. 9d.	7.1d.	8	3s. 10d.	5.8d.
5 Oct 1378	42 (1)	26s. 1d.	7.8d.	7	3s. 0d.	6.0d.
12 Apr 1379	35	16s. 19d.	7.2d.	10	4s. 4d.	6.5d.
18 Oct 1379	37	19s. 2d.	6.2d.	8	4s. 6d.	6.8d.
3 Apr 1380	43	24s. 7d.	6.9d.	10	6s. 3d.	6.3d.
29 Apr 1382	33	8s. 7d.	3.2d.	8	2s. 8d.	4.0d.
6 Oct 1383	28	7s. 10d.	3.4d.	9	2s. 9d.	3.7d.
12 Apr 1384	29 (1)	15s. 11d.	6.6d.	8	3s. 9d.	5.6d.
10 Oct 1385	26 (1)	9s. 1d.	4.2d.	5	1s. 9d.	4.2d.
7 May 1386	41 (2)	16s. 6d.	4.8d.	7	2s. 3d.	3.9d.
14 Oct 1387	28	12s. 4d.	5.3d.	8	2s. 11d.	4.4d.
21 Apr 1388	38 (2)#	23s. 7d.#	7.4d.#	9	3s. 2d.	4.2d.
6 Oct 1388	37	15s. 10d.	5.1d.	7*	2s. 8d.	4.6d.
4 May 1389	35 (1)	19s. 1d.	7.2d.	7	2s. 8d.	4.6d.
21 Oct 1389	36	15s. 5d.	5.1d.	7 (1)	2s. 2d.	3.7d.
26 Apr 1390	42 (3)	19s. 4d.	5.5d.	7	2s. 6d.	4.3d.
8 Oct 1397	26 (1)	9s. 0d.	4.2d.	5	1s. 6d.	3.6d.
? Apr 1398				3	2s. 0d.	8.0d.
8 Oct 1398	24 (1)	11s. 1d.	5.5d.	4	2s. 8d.	8.0d.
15 Apr 1399	25 (2)	9s. 9d.	4.7d.	5	1s. 9d.	4.2d.
? Oct 1399	29	10s. 2d.	4.2d.	3	9d.	3.0d.
27 Apr 1400	40 (1)	12s. 4d.	3.7d.	5	1s. 6d.	3.6d.
13 Oct 1400	31 (1)	10s. 10d.	4.2d.	4	1s. 8d.	5.0d.
20 Apr 1401	31 (1)	9s. 8d.	3.7d.	4	1s. 1d.	3.3d.
9 Oct 1403	23	6s. 6d.	3.5d.	4	1s. 4d.	4.0d.
22 Apr 1404	25	7s. 1d.	3.4d.	6	1s. 6d.	3.0d.
7 Oct 1404	26	8s. 2d.	3.8d.	6	1s. 10d.	3.7d.
5 May 1405	27	8s. 3d.	3.7d.	4	1s.. 6d.	4.5d.
10 Oct 1406	29 (1)	8s. 4d.	3.4d.	5	1s. 8d.	4.0d.
22 Apr 1407	30	9s. 5d.	3.8d.	5	3s. 2d.	7.6d.
20 Oct 1411	24	7s. 10d.	3.9d.	4	1s. 6d.	4.5d.
19 Apr 1412	23	6s. 4d.	3.5d.	4	1s. 5d.	4.3d.
6 Oct 1412	20	6s. 3d.	3.8d.	4	1s. 6d.	4.5d.
2 May 1413	21	7s. 1d.	4.0d.	4	2s. 0d.	6.0d.
14 Oct 1416	19	6s. 2d.	3.9d.	4	1s. 3d.	3.8d.
21 Apr 1417	19	6s. 0d.	3.8d.	4	1s. 4d.	4.0d.
10 Oct 1419	17	5s. 2d.	3.6d.	4	1s. 4d.	4.0d.
? Apr 1420	16	5s. 0d.	3.8d.	5	1s. 8d.	4.0d.
14 Oct 1421	21	7s. 0d.	4.0d.	4	1s. 5d.	4.3d.
20 Apr 1422	20	7s. 2d.	4.3d.	3	1s. 0d.	4.0d.
6 Oct 1422	17	5s. 4d.	3.8d.	4	1s. 0d.	3.0d.
21 Apr 1423	14	3s. 11d.	3.4d.	6	1s. 4d.	2.7d.
17 Oct 1424	13	3s. 4d.	3.3d.	2	7d.	3.5d.
18 Apr 1425	13	2s. 11d.	2.7d.	3	8d.	2.7d.
Total	1183 (19)	£23 8s. 9d.	4.5d.	243 (1)	£4 13s. 1d.	4.5d.

Notes: a – the records of fifty-two courts are missing (out of ninety-six) in the period November 1377 to April 1425. The brewers amercements for April 1398 are illegible; b – common brewers who brewed and sold ale against the assize; c – bakers who broke the assize and used false weights; # – brewers were also specifically amerced in this court for not bringing their measures to court; * includes two bakers of horsebread. Figures in parentheses are the number of pardons for that court (included in the total). Certain amercements were either illegible or not given (fifteen for brewers, three for bakers) and these were not included in the calculations for the amercement averages, but were included in the number of offences.
Source: TNA, sc2/203/61–7.

Table 3. *Baking, brewing and regrating offences in Newmarket, 1400–1413*

Number of offences	Baking households	Brewing households	Regrating households
1	29	26	24
2	7	12	7
3	6	11	4
4	2	5	3
5		3	1
6	4	2	
7	3	1	1
8	2	2	
9	1		1
10	2	2	1
11			
12		1	
13	1	1	1
14		2	1
15			
16	2	2	1
17		1	1
18		1	1
19	1	2	
20	1	1	
21		2	
Total	61	77	47

Source: SRO (B), Acc.1476/1/1–48.

baking households and 109 of 198 brewing households can be deemed irregular (see Table 4). There were significant numbers of sporadic producers in both Newmarket and Clare, reflecting how easy it could be to enter a victualling trade on an irregular basis.

Ale was the most widely commercialised product in medieval England and even village courts had presentments of ale-brewers. Much ale was brewed domestically because little equipment was needed for small-batch production, and most women and men were capable of brewing. The process of brewing only required a large pot, a vat, ladles and straining cloths. In addition, the brewer needed a supply of water and fuel, as well as the barley itself.[111] The barley was soaked for several days,

---

[111] The 1454 will of John Newman, a baker of Sudbury, described how his wife should be allowed access 'to the bakehouse of the messuage for baking and brewing, and to the well there for drawing water as necessary, and also to the yard of the messuage for putting her firewood in'. Northeast (ed.), *Wills*, p. 295, no. 818.

Table 4. *Baking, brewing and regrating offences in Clare, 1377–1425*

Number of offences	Baking households	Brewing households	Regrating households
1	9	55	19
2	5	21	4
3	4	21	1
4	1	12	2
5	2	16	2
6	1	13	
7	2	10	2
8	1	9	1
9		5	2
10		4	
11		1	
12		4	1
13	2	2	1
14		6	
15	1	3	
16	1	5	
17		2	
18		2	
19	1		
20		1	
>20	3	6	
Total	33	198	35

Source: TNA, sc2/203/62–7.

then the excess water was drained away, resulting in germination. The resulting malt was dried either in the sun or in a kiln, and many small brewers may have purchased ready-made, kiln-dried malt. The malt was then ground, hot water added for fermentation ('mashing'), and the wort drained off. Finally, herbs were added and sometimes additional yeast beaten in. A bushel of barley was expected to produce about seven to eight gallons of good ale and twice as much weaker liquor.[112] Although the process was widely practised, it was also time-consuming. For many, it was doubtless more convenient to buy ale from commercial outlets, particularly when disposable incomes increased after the Black Death. Additionally, weak ale soured within days and transported badly, so continual brewing may not have been cost-effective without a substantial capital outlay and reliable demand in the immediate locality of a town.

[112] Bennett, *Women*, p. 121; Bennett, *Ale*, pp. 17–18, 23–4.

Nevertheless, commercial ale-brewing was a useful ancillary occupation, often undertaken on an irregular and modest scale. Indeed, many women simply brewed for their families, but tried to sell any surplus ale in order to prevent wastage and augment their domestic incomes. The prominence of women in brewing and selling ale has received considerable comment from historians such as Judith Bennett, Helena Graham and Helen Jewell.[113] It was the most common cause for the entry of women's names into manorial court rolls, as numerous wives and single women sought to earn extra income. In general, women engaged in marginal, low-capital, low-skilled processing and retailing, while men apparently dominated the more capital-intensive and specialised butchering and baking trades. Bakers, for instance, required their own special oven in a structure that reduced the risk of fire, as well as troughs, moulding boards, sieves, a brake (to mix the dough), measuring equipment, tubs, pans and storage space. They also needed a plentiful supply of water and fuel. Comparatively, baking was a much costlier enterprise than brewing.

Because of the recording practices of clerks, there are certain methodological problems involved in identifying an actual brewer or household group in court rolls. Often, a husband was named in lieu of his wife because he was legal head of the household. In common law, a wife was subordinate to her husband, even if she took primary responsibility for brewing.[114] Males were consequently named even when it was their wives who undertook the trade. In Newmarket and Clare, both husbands and wives were recorded in the assize presentments, though rarely at the same session. Usually, the clerk named a man, or an unidentified 'wife of A' or 'B, wife of C', and only occasionally in these lists was a woman directly recorded by herself. It is likely that such sole references referred to a widow or single woman. The method of entry in Newmarket varied from year to year, with the most popular style following the pattern 'wife of A'. In Clare it is noticeable that women were consistently recorded by name in the courts from October 1352 to April 1384 and mostly between October 1406 to May 1413. Before 1352 they tended to be named in conjunction with their husband, though the practice was not consistent, and again after 1384 recording practices were more sporadic though it was again more common for women to be identified directly or indirectly through their husband, unless they were single or widows. Whether these

---

[113] Bennett, *Ale*; Bennett, 'Village ale-wife'; Kowaleski, 'Women's work'; Graham, 'A woman's work'; Jewell, 'Women', 60–3; Hilton, 'Women traders'.
[114] Jewell, 'Women', 61–4; Bennett, *Women*, pp. 66, 176; Bennett, *Ale*, pp. 158–86; Jewell, *Women*, pp. 72–3.

trends were due to a change in clerk or something more fundamental in the aftermath of the Black Death is difficult to know.

Given the difficulties in interpreting the presentment lists, the various alternatives are that the husband was the brewer, it was a joint household work, or the wife undertook all the brewing and her husband was merely her legal representative in court.[115] It is possible that the urban brewing trade was not always monopolised by women to the same extent it was in rural villages. In Newmarket, for example, members of households, including the male heads, seemed to be all involved in a wide range of victualling activities. This was because victual production constituted a primary occupation in the town as opposed to the *ad hoc* and supplementary brewing of rural women married to agricultural workers. However, any attempt to delineate the separate tasks of particular urban household members is difficult, given the paucity of evidence. Certainly, Newmarket was dominated by male innkeepers, cooks and butchers, and the primary occupation of many men was victualling. Nevertheless, specific references to brewing sales did refer to women, such as John Redere's wife who illegally sold thirty-six gallons of ale.[116] Additionally, regraters of ale were almost exclusively women, even in those years when their husbands were named in assize presentments.[117] Similarly, in Clare, women were regularly named in both brewing and ale-selling presentments, either under their own name or as a wife, but so were many of their husbands and it is difficult to know for certain the exact division of labour.

Nevertheless, the regular and irregular brewers of Newmarket and Clare can be analysed, based upon the household unit, in order to reveal aspects of the brewing trade in these small towns. The household, for the purpose of this study, is deemed to be the primary unit of husband and wife. Sons or daughters constitute another household unit. Regular brewing households in Newmarket have been defined as those which were amerced in eleven or more of the twenty-one courts (that is, over 50 per cent), semi-regular brewing households were those who appeared in between five and ten sessions, while irregular brewers appeared in less than five sessions (see Table 5). It is possible that some regular brewers had reached the end or beginning of their regular production life-cycle at the extremes of our data collection. However, these practitioners do not appear to be significant in number, judging by those who only brewed during the first three or last three courts of this data set. Additionally, it is possible that a few traders moved from the town or to another trade,

---

[115] McIntosh, *Working Women*, p. 143.   [116] SRO (B), Acc.1476/1/14.
[117] See below, p. 324.

Table 5. *Newmarket households and their socio-economic status, 1400–1413*

	Regular				Semi-regular				Irregular				Tot.
	Pri	Sec	Other	Outsider	Pri	Sec	Other	Outsider	Pri	Sec	Other	Outsider	
Bakers	4	1			4		3	5	7	2	30	5	61
Brewers	13				5	1	4		9	7	32	6	77
Regraters		3	2		1		2	1	6	3	23	6	47
Innkeepers/ Cooks	3	1						1	10	3	9	1	28

Notes: Pri: Primary office-holder (bailiff, constable, capital pledge); Sec: Secondary office-holder (ale-taster, affeerer, juror). Regular brewers, bakers, regraters and cooks/innkeepers: amerced in 11–21 courts; Semi-regular traders: amerced in 5–10 courts; Irregular traders: amerced in 1–4 courts.
Source: SRO (B), Acc.1476/1/1–48.

Table 6. *Clare households and their socio-economic status, 1377–1425*

	Regular			Semi-regular			Irregular			Tot.
	Pri	Sec	Other	Pri	Sec	Other	Pri	Sec	Other	
Bakers	4		4	3		3	2	1	16	33
Brewers	21	2	9	24	1	32	18	6	85	198
Regraters	2		5	3		2	8		15	35

Notes: Pri: Primary office-holder (bailiff, constable, capital pledge); Sec: Secondary office-holder (aletaster, affeerer, juror). Given the long time period involved, and the missing court rolls, many bakers and brewers may have died or given up their trade within the period. The same criteria have thus been used as for Newmarket, though the figures are not directly comparable. Bakers and brewers: 1–4 appearances – irregular; 5–10 appearances – semi-regular; 11 or more – regular. Regraters: 1–2 appearances – irregular; 3–5 – semi-regular; 6 or more – regular.
Source: TNA, sc2/203/62–7.

thus slightly affecting the validity of the figures. A similar criterion is used for Clare, where forty-four extant leet courts cover forty-nine years. This is a significant period of time and the occupations of most bakers and brewers could be considered 'regular' if they appeared in more than a quarter of these courts. Consequently, as with Newmarket, regular brewing and baking households in Clare are deemed to be those that were amerced in eleven or more of the courts, the semi-regular were those appearing in five to ten, and the irregular between one and four (see Table 6). Regraters were amerced infrequently in the Clare court so regular regraters are defined as those appearing in six or more courts and semi-regular in three to five.

Thirteen regular brewing households can be identified in Newmarket's court rolls, all of which had male heads with primary office-holding status (see Table 5).[118] This constituted over two-thirds of the average number of brewers presented at each session. There were ten semi-regular brewers, of whom five were primary office-holders and one was secondary. Two others, namely Agnes Schoppe and Johanna Tapstere, were probably single women and were not identified with men in any of their presentments. Of the remaining fifty-four irregular brewers, nine were primary office-holders, seven were secondary and five were outsiders (from nearby Sutton, Eriswell, Ashley and Exning). In Clare, there are also a significant number of regular brewing households (thirty-two (16 per cent) of all brewing households), the majority of which had a primary office-holder, while 44 per cent of semi-regular brewers were from the upper echelons of the local community (see Table 6). For instance, John and Johanna Broun were regular brewers, with some twenty-eight offences at an average amercement of 4.5d., and he served as bailiff in 1378–9. John Babir was similarly bailiff (1404–5), and he and Margaret Babir offended against the assize of ale twenty-nine times at 5.8d. Even amongst the 109 irregular brewing households there was a significant presence of such men, but the vast majority (78 per cent) were not connected and had only minimal impact on the court rolls outside their brewing offences.

Thus, brewers came from a wide socio-economic background. However, most of the regular and semi-regular brewing households came from leading families of the town. This was probably because they needed capital and equipment to brew commercially on a large scale, as opposed to *ad hoc* production. There was apparently no inherent stigma attached to brewing if such high-status members of the town's community were included in the assize presentments.[119] Those who brewed occasionally, in contrast, probably either used only a small amount of grain or bought on credit.[120] It is also likely that infrequent brewers were women brewing for a supplementary income to support a household which was primarily based in another trade, or else they were single women or at the start of their life-cycle of court appearances.[121]

[118] These were the households of John Ballone Smyth, John Barbor, Thomas Cook, Peter Fedelere, William Fyschere, Thomas Pere, John Pere, William Ray, John Redere, Robert Skynnere, Roger Smyth, Thomas Sowcere and John Waleys.
[119] Britnell, *Growth and Decline*, pp. 89–90; Laughton, 'Alewives', p. 197; Britnell, 'Town life', p. 164.
[120] Bennett, *Ale*, pp. 30–2; Postles, 'Brewing', 140.
[121] Smith (ed.), *Land, Kinship*, pp. 27–30.

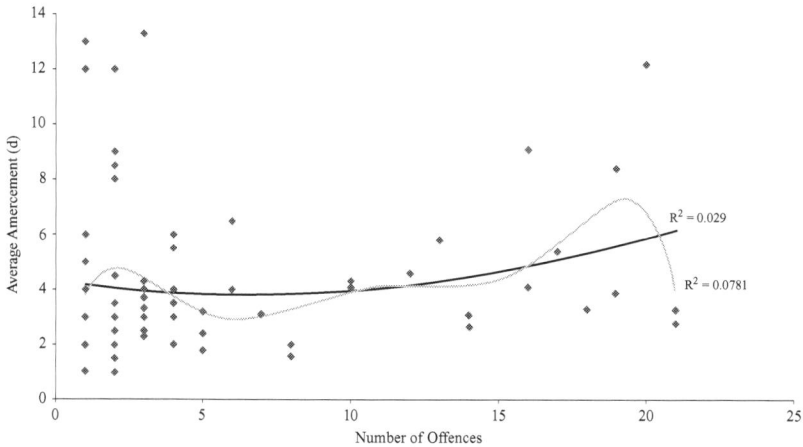

Figure 21: Scatter graph of amercements and brewing offences in New-market, 1400–1413.

Notes: Each point on this graph represents a single household's number of brewing offences, 1400–13, and the average amercement for those offences. For these calculations, a household is considered to consist of a husband and wife; daughters or sons are considered to be separate working units. Two polynomial trendlines are presented: Order 2 (black) and Order 6 (grey).
Source: SRO (B), Acc.1476/1/1–48.

The differences between regular and irregular brewers is partly seen in the amercement levels paid by each group. Figure 21 suggests that the level of amercement in Newmarket was more likely to be high if the brewer regularly appeared at court. However, in general, there is no statistical relationship between the level of amercement and the number of offences. Although some occasional brewers were fined above-average amounts, the majority were clustered around 2d.–4d. The overall average amercement was 4.8d., but just ten of sixty-eight amercements over 7d. were given to irregular brewers. A few regular brewers, such as John Redere, Thomas Cook and John Waleys, received amercements of up to 14d. In line with an effective licensing scheme, it is likely that the level of amercement in these cases was related to production output, rather than that regular brewers committed greater offences against the assize. However, the frequency and quantity of brewing was unspecified in the Newmarket court rolls.

In Clare, from 1377 to 1425, the majority of brewing amercements were for 3d., 4d., or 6d., no matter how often you brewed

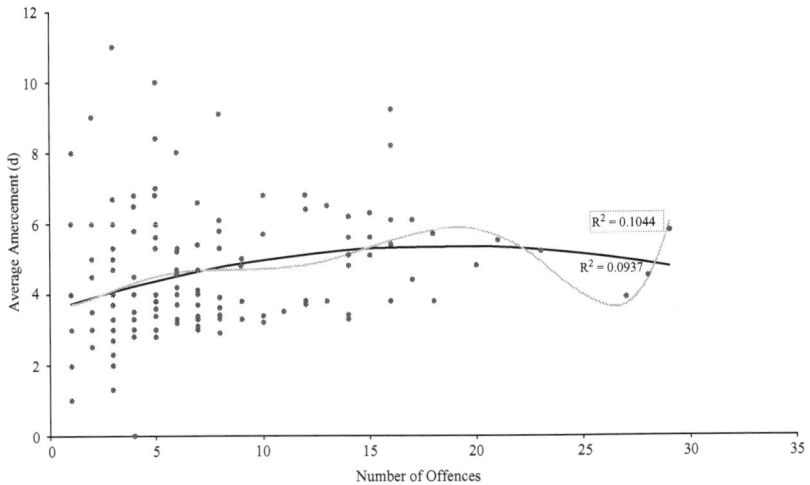

Figure 22: Scatter graph of amercements and brewing offences in Clare, 1377–1425.

Notes: Each point on this graph represents a single household's number of brewing offences, 1377–1425, and the average amercement for those offences. For these calculations, a household is considered to consist of a husband and wife; daughters or sons are considered to be separate working units. Two polynomial trendlines are presented: Order 2 (black) and Order 6 (grey).

Source: TNA, SC2/203/62–7.

(see Figure 22). Unlike Newmarket, the regular brewers of Clare and their wives generally faced average amercements of 3d.–6d., which perhaps contradicts any suggestion of a correlation with the level of production. If one considers that the average wage for an unskilled labourer was 4d.–5d. a day in the early fifteenth century, then the amercement levels were equivalent to one or two days' wages. Only Thomas and Katherine Danoun (8.2d.) and Adam and Johanna Stonhard (9.2d.), with sixteen offences for each couple, had both regular levels of production and a high average amercement. Why they were picked out for special attention is uncertain. Other than them, it is a few irregular brewers who face high average amercements over 8d.: the wife of William Brokhole, the wife of Roger Barker, Agnes Markaunt, Matilda Goolde, Margaret Northerne and Margery Robelard. One possibility is that they were deemed recalcitrant users of false weights and measures. In 1377, Agnes and Matilda had been amerced 12d. and Margery 6d., while Johanna Stonhard and Thomas Danoun had been amerced 6d. in 1377 and 1388 respectively, for failing to bring their measures to court. This offence sometimes generated a higher than normal amercement, but others saw their amercements subsequently fall back. It is possible that this was a repeated accusation against these particular individuals and the affeerers imposed a heavier penalty in an attempt to bring them into line, though this implies a new effort to enforce such standards.[122]

Bennett, McIntosh and Mate have all argued that there was a gradual disappearance of casual and irregular ale-brewers in fifteenth-century small towns, despite buoyant demand for their product. Instead, there were more commercial brewers, operating on a larger scale and often male.[123] Bailey has noted how the number of brewers in both Sudbury and Lakenheath declined significantly over the course of the fourteenth and fifteenth centuries, while brewing in Brandon became concentrated in the hands of a few leading residents, many of whom ran inns.[124] It is possible that the same trends were also discernible in the baking trade, allowing bakers to travel to markets to sell their bread. The trend in Newmarket is difficult to decipher over such a short evidential period, though brewing was certainly dominated by a number of individual households, usually headed by a male innkeeper. In Clare, there was a notable drop in the number of both brewers and bakers from the 1370s to 1420s, both groups effectively halving in number (see Table 2).

Individual Newmarket bakers faced a similar regularity of amercements over time as brewers, apparently based on their level of output rather than any overt breach of the regulations. For instance, John Redere faced amercements of 8d.–14d. every year from 1400 to 1412, except for three sessions in which he only faced a 4d. amercement. By defining the bakers in a similar way to that adopted for brewers, regular and irregular producers of Newmarket can be compared (see Table 5). Only five baking households were regular: John and Mariot Choun; Thomas Cook and his wife; John Redere and his wife; Roger Smyth and his wife; and John Waleys and his wife. All but John Choun were primary office-holders and he faced comparatively low fines of only 1d.–2d. compared with the other regular bakers, who were given average fines of 3.8d., 5.7d., 6.8d. and 10.3d. Of the twelve semi-regular baking households, four contained primary office-holders, while a further five were from outside Newmarket. The semi-regular bakers included householders like John Barbor, Nicholas Chapman, Robert Cheyne, William Fyschere, Peter Fedelere and John Smyth, all of whom were active in a myriad of victualling fields.

---

[122] TNA, sc2/203/55. In 1359, the amercement for this offence was increased to 3d. for each brewer.

[123] Bennett, *Ale*; McIntosh, *A Community Transformed*, pp. 281–91; Mate, *Daughters, Wives and Widows*, pp. 59–68; Mate, *Trade and Economic Developments*, pp. 60–80. See also DeWindt and DeWindt, *Ramsey*, pp. 164, 227.

[124] Bailey, *Medieval Suffolk*, p. 267.

Of the remaining forty-four irregular bakers, seven were primary office-holders, two were secondary and four were outsiders, so the majority (70 per cent) lacked such indicators of status. Overall, it was unusual for those of a lower socio-economic status to be involved as regular or even semi-regular bakers, reflecting the high levels of capital needed to maintain a professional baking business.

Despite the fair number of irregular bakers, the five regular bakers and twelve semi-regular bakers of Newmarket must have dominated production, considering that the number of offenders year to year ranged only from eight to sixteen and the total amercements at a court session from 34d. to 68d. (see Table 1). In terms of the conditions of the assize of bread, whereby 111 loaves were expected to be produced for 4d. profit, the five regular bakers of Newmarket between them would have needed to produce at least 555 loaves in total if they were to earn that amount every day.[125] Given that an individual might have eaten one, possibly two, loaves a day, the figures either suggest that the bakers supplied a considerable number of the residents of Newmarket (plus travellers), or that this profit was spread over more than one day. Nevertheless, the socio-economic distribution of bakers in itself implies that regular baking was worthwhile.

Similar conclusions are evident from looking at the regular bakers in Clare. There were nine regular baking households in all, four of which contained a primary office-holder. John Baker Litil (or 'paruus') first appears in the court rolls in 1374 and died in 1404/5. He was amerced for breaking the assize of bread twenty-five times at an average amercement of 6.7d. During this time he served as capital pledge, juror and aletaster (1385–6), as well as being the plaintiff in six debt pleas and the defendant seven times. There are also hints of his activities beyond baking. He was amerced 10d. in April 1384 for allowing his pigs to trespass on the castle's outer bailey, while he and his wife, Johanna, were amerced twelve times (at an average of 6.4d.) for brewing. Two of these amercements occurred after John's death, indicating that Johanna continued this by-occupation as a widow. John Priour was amerced some nineteen times from 1390 to 1420. Like John Baker Litil, he also served as capital pledge and aletaster (1416) and was involved in six debt pleas as plaintiff or defendant, including one claim against Hugh de Godiston for 5s. 6d. Also, like most regular baking households in Clare, his wife, Isabella, was an active brewer, being amerced nine times. William Baker was elected to the office of bailiff in 1421, having baked regularly since 1404, while his wife brewed semi-regularly. Lastly, John Cook and

---

[125] See above, pp. 235–6.

his wife, Katherine, faced twenty-two baking amercements and eighteen brewing amercements (all at an average of 3.8d.) from about 1397. He was bailiff in 1411, capital pledge and aletaster. It appears that he took over the business from his mother and father, Sarra and John Cook, sometime between 1390 and 1399. It may well have been as early as May 1390 when he was convicted of forestalling grain and named as the son of Sarra Cook. His parents had been regular bakers and brewers, though John senior did not apparently rise to the same status and offices as his son. It also seems that both mother and daughter-in-law were heavily involved in the baking business since they were named as offenders against the assize of bread on numerous occasions. Baking was truly a family affair.

Two other regular bakers were possibly from outside the town as indicated by their surnames, John Baker atte Barres and John Lydgate, and thus would not have been officer-holders. In a similar manner, there was a significant contingent of outside producers who came to Newmarket to sell bread regularly. These outsiders were Gilbert Bakere of Bottisham, Henry Baxtere of Bottisham, Robert Cheyne of Bottisham, Mariot Deke of Eriswell and Richard Prat of Ashley, plus five irregular bakers from Fordham, Burwell, Kentford and Ely. Bakers commonly carried wares into other villages and smaller towns, particularly by the early fifteenth century, perhaps to sell directly at retail or in small-bulk to regraters. In Earl Soham, four different foreign bakers were amerced for selling bread against the assize and appeared in the court rolls for the first time from 1413 to 1421. In the records of Saxted and Framlingham for 1402–3, Robert Baxstere, Robert Foul and Thomas Brame were recorded as having delivered bread from outside. Lastly, in Walton, Augustus Baxter came from Ipswich regularly during the period 1398 to 1412 in order to sell bread. He was joined at various times by five other bakers from Ipswich and John Spyser from Hemley and Richard Bakere of Woodbridge.[126] They appear to have usurped the local bakers and the lord of the manor took the opportunity to impose heavy amercements of 8d.–20d. on their activities 'against the assize'. Generally, in towns and villages, there were many more outsiders among bakers than brewers. This was partly because ale was difficult to transport, but also reflected the more professional and capital-intensive nature of baking in comparison with ale-brewing.

[126] SRO (I), v5/18/1.3–1.4; Cambridge, Pembroke College, Framlingham Court Rolls c, D1, D2; SRO (I), HA119:50/3/17–19. See also SRO (I), HA119:50/3/142; Bailey (ed.), *Bailiffs' Minute Book*, pp. 19–20; Sear, 'Trade and commerce', p. 42.

Nevertheless, there were those who only baked irregularly, presumably cooking in small makeshift ovens or pans or in shared ovens, and selling small amounts of their domestic surplus for supplementary income. These producers included women. For instance, in Newmarket, Agnes Lexham, Margaret Lexham, Rose Grant and Johanna Tapstere were all named as producing bread on one or two occasions. Females were also sometimes cited as regular bakers, apparently aiding their husbands and being cited with or instead of them in the court rolls. Baking in Newmarket could be as much of a household affair as brewing. The most significant women bakers for whom no husband was mentioned were Mariot Deke of Eriswell and Agnes Schoppe. Mariot Deke faced prosecution six times for an average fine of 5d., while Agnes Schoppe was presented seven times for an average fine of 4.1d. It is very likely that they were either single women or widows and they usefully illustrate the point that a few women accumulated enough capital to bake on a reasonably commercial scale. In Clare, only one women baker is mentioned without reference to a husband, Petronilla Turnour. She was amerced at a relatively low average of 3.7d. for each presentment and she brewed for just three years. It is likely that she was producing very low-quality and cheap bread on a sporadic basis. Most other irregular bakers in Clare were men and only dabbled in the trade just once or twice.

A scatter graph of the number of offences against average fines for individual bakers in Newmarket shows a trend of steadily increasing amercements, much more clearly than for brewers (see Figure 23). Regular bakers faced, on average, 6d. fines. If they were making 4d. a day, six days a week, than the yearly amercement of 12d. constituted a 'tax' of just 1 per cent. However, this theory assumes they sold the required amount of bread and does not account for other losses. The semi-regular and irregular bakers were given, on average, 3d.–4d. fines, and it is difficult to know whether this was proportional to their output or a higher percentage tax on their overall turnover. In general, of thirty-six amercements of 8d. or over, only five were not given to regular or semi-regular bakers and only one above 8d. was not given to a regular baker (see Table 3). Regular bakers apparently produced more and were amerced in relation to their output. However, this was not the case in Clare where, like the brewers, the amercements were fairly standard without reference to the regularity of production (see Figure 24). Indeed, the few higher-than-average penalties were for irregular bakers, though one of these was a William Baker who died in 1379/80 and had been a regular baker in the previous decade.

An effectual licensing system appeared to be in operation in both Newmarket and Clare, but was there any concern about a rigid enforcement

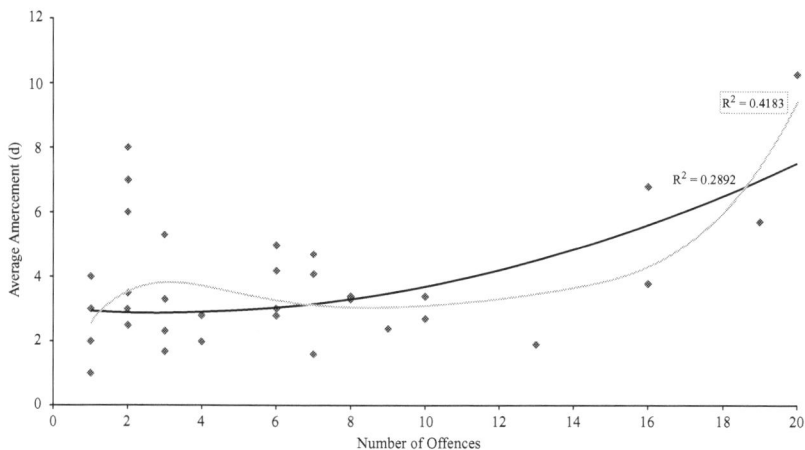

Figure 23: Scatter graph of amercements and baking offences in New-market, 1400–1413.

Notes: Each point on this graph represents a single household's number of baking offences, 1400–13, and the average amercement for those offences. For these calculations, a household is considered to consist of a husband and wife; daughters or sons are considered to be separate working units. Two polynomial trendlines are presented: Order 2 (black) and Order 6 (grey).
Source: SRO (B), Acc.1476/1/1–48.

of the statutes? In 1389–90, Parliament ordered that bodily punishment should be enforced when required by statutory law.[127] However, the officials in Newmarket and Clare appear to have ignored this, despite persistent offenders, and adopted their own standards of enforcement. There were no cases of corporal punishment in Newmarket and only two in Clare, both in 1360. In April 1360, John Bakere was not amerced because he had undergone the judgement of the pillory for his baking offences. The court rolls show that he was amerced 8d.–12d. in five previous sessions, but, despite corporal punishment, he continued to be amerced a comparatively high 24d. for the next two sessions, before this was reduced to 6d.–8d. thereafter.[128] In the same year, Alice Slyman was sent to the 'colliari' (probably a type of thewe, an upright post with a neck-ring) for a brewing offence. She had not previously been entered in the rolls for any offence and was only to appear once more the following year for the unusually high fine of 18d.[129] The physical punishments and

[127] *Statutes*, ii, p. 63, 13 Ric.II st.1 c.8 (1389–90). See pp. 269–70.
[128] TNA, sc2/203/54–8.   [129] TNA, sc2/203/56–7.

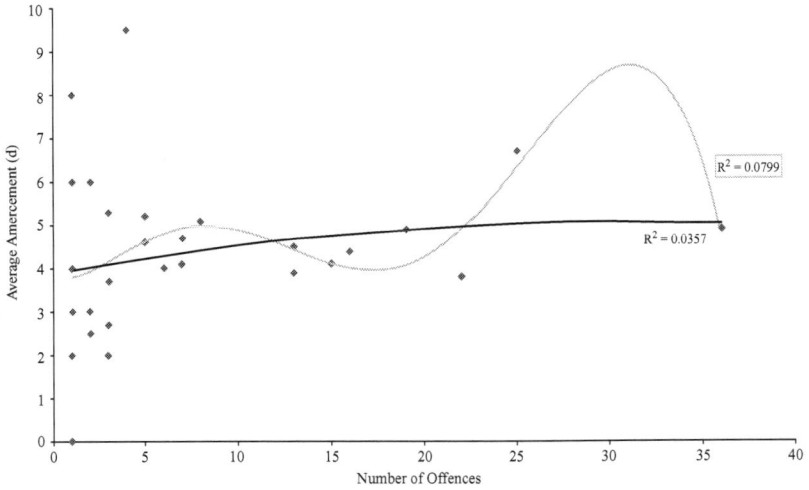

Figure 24: Scatter graph of amercements and baking offences in Clare, 1377–1425.

Notes: Each point on this graph represents a single household's number of baking offences, 1377–1425, and the average amercement for those offences. For these calculations, a household is considered to consist of a husband and wife; daughters or sons are considered to be separate working units. Two polynomial trendlines are presented: Order 2 (black) and Order 6 (grey).
Source: TNA, sc2/203/62–7.

high fines, which were well above average, even for regular offenders, imply that both John Bakere and Alice Slyman were flagrant offenders. Such cases suggest that the use of corporal punishment was regarded as exceptional rather than customary, reserved for those who had incurred the community's strongest disapproval.[130] Seabourne has also noted that there were few signs of corporal punishment being used for offenders against price regulation at any level of jurisdiction, from the royal courts to the Wakefield tourn rolls and Sutton court rolls.[131] In late thirteenth-century Tamworth, Bennett found only one case of corporal punishment amongst over 500 assize cases.[132]

---

[130] Britnell, 'Urban economic regulation', pp. 2–3. In Tottenham (Middlesex) in 1377, William Bakere was found deficient in the weight of half-penny loaves of white bread by 23s. 4d. and Robert Bakere was deficient by 13s. 4d., and both were sent to the pillory as well as being fined 16s. 8d. between them. This was a significant departure in wording and from the usual fines of 3d.–12d. for breaking the assize in that same year. Oram (ed.), *Court Rolls*, pp. 179–80.

[131] Seabourne, *Royal Regulation*, pp. 102–4.

[132] Bennett, *Ale*, pp. 104–5. Bennett has posited that corporal punishments may have been under-recorded because it brought no pecuniary benefits to the court, corporation or

The best interests of the town were not usually served by using pillories and tumbrels. Instead, money fines were more attractive and could provide a regular income for a town's lord. Also, officials probably did not want to temper a baker or brewer's productivity since they contributed to the prosperity and stability of the market. Market traders generally worked within much smaller margins of error than merchants of luxury products and could not afford to allow their transaction costs to fluctuate greatly. Rather, market traders needed to spread their risks and keep costs low. The authorities in Newmarket and Clare seemed to recognise this and gave market traders a greater margin for error by interpreting the assizes as a licensing system. This conceit provided traders with a convenient legal and moral cover for both potential minor misdemeanours, while reducing the administrative burden on the court officials and providing revenue for the lord.[133]

Presentment for breaches of the assize was so commonplace that it was not considered a stigma in itself, and many leading residents and local officials were included in the lists. Indeed, it should not be assumed that all who were presented broke the stipulations of the assizes and there are examples where aletasters noted those who sold honestly.[134] Even if they did commit offences, it was seen as within margins that were regarded as acceptable by the community, especially given the difficulties of the everyday working environment that all had to face. However, for this system to work, everyone had to accept that there were moral limits to these margins. This was not a *carte blanche* for breaking the assizes.[135] It was deliberate, as opposed to unavoidable or technical, transgressions that were frowned upon and the officials were discriminate in identifying those offences that the community considered flagrant. Thus, alongside the main lists for 'offenders' against the assize we also see occasional cases where particularly notable offences were separately presented.

Bennett has argued that offences involving fraudulent quality and false measures were usually punished more heavily than other trading malpractices, mostly with substantial monetary fines.[136] Similarly, in Clare and Newmarket, there were a handful of ale and bread offences which

---

lord. However, offenders were not usually both pilloried and amerced, and most courts would have noted why no amercement was being levied.

[133] Seabourne is probably right to downgrade the suggestion that the prime purpose of the assizes was to raise revenue. The varying annual income, as well as the relative lesser importance of such revenue compared to rents and fines for land transactions, suggests that other motives were equally influential. Seabourne, *Royal Regulation*, pp. 108 (n. 297), 110–11.

[134] Bennett, *Ale*, p. 3; Hudson (ed.), *Leet*, p. 30.

[135] Bennett, *Ale*, pp. 162–3; Seabourne, *Royal Regulation*, p. 110.

[136] Bennett, *Women*, p. 120.

were recorded outside the assize listings and that did incur heavy censure. In Clare, in December 1379, three bakers faced distraint and extra fines because they had baked loaves well below assize stipulations: Robert Bultel made cocket bread deficient in weight by 10s., John Baker by 6s. 8d. and Sarra Cook by 6s. 8d.[137] In 1370, four regular bakers were identified in December, outside the leet court, for selling bread with false weights. Cristina Sygor (18d.), John Lydgate (12d.), William Baker (18d.) and John Baker (18d.) all paid amercements some 6d.–10d. higher than they normally did during the 1360s and 1370s, which suggests that this was an extraordinary punishment.[138] Similarly, in Newmarket on 5 April 1402, Thomas Cook was fined 3s. 4d. and John Waleys 12d. for bread weighing 'below how it ought for 8s.'.[139]

In Clare, certain brewing offences were presented separately within the leet court, such as a failure to submit to aletasters or selling ale at a particularly high price. In July 1371, four brewers were distrained for selling ale at 3d. a gallon. A further brewer, Cristina Pacher, had been selling her ale at 4d. and she was distrained and amerced twice during that year in addition to the usual assize of ale payments.[140] Three times between 1372 and 1374, a large group of Clare brewers were named and specifically fined for selling ale at an excessive price. In Newmarket, John Redere's wife was ordered to pay 4s. 6d. for holding back thirty-six gallons of ale from local men so that she could sell it at a higher price to strangers, in a similar manner to Langland's character 'Rose the Regrater'.[141] Refusing to sell ale that had been made in bulk was considered as much an offence as not calling for the aletasters.[142] The case against John Redere's wife was presented at court because of the vehement complaints of her disaffected customers.

Beyond the basic assize presentments, courts apparently relied heavily upon consumer pressure. This highlights the importance of an accepted moral environment within the marketplace. In addition, competitive forces were increasingly significant as the number of permanent alehouses and inns grew in number in the fifteenth century, providing ale and bread on a continuous basis.[143] Part-time officials would have found it difficult to keep a track of all victualling traders in such a commercial environment. Authorities thus relied greatly upon consumer vigilance to guard against exceptionally fraudulent activities, as well as using competitive forces to ensure self-regulation. The large number of brewers and

---

[137] TNA, sc2/203/62.
[138] TNA, sc2/203/60. A fifth irregular baker, Simon Skynnere, was amerced 6d.
[139] SRO (B), Acc. 1476/1/8.   [140] TNA, sc2/203/60.   [141] SRO (B), Acc. 1476/1/14.
[142] TNA, sc2/203/59.   [143] See below, pp. 335–40.

bakers in a town like Newmarket or Clare in itself ensured that there was less opportunity for producers to collude in monopoly practices.[144]

Nevertheless, local courts asserted legal as well as popular pressure on their traders. Market towns or franchise holders were required to appoint inspectors annually to uphold the assizes and brewers were supposed to summon these 'aletasters' whenever they produced a batch.[145] There were cases where brewers failed to send for the aletaster as required by law. In Clare, William Brokhole and the wife of Peter le Smyth were attached by 40d. and 80d. worth of ale (at 2d. a gallon) respectively in order to answer this charge.[146] Such rare cases, noted separately in the court rolls, perhaps indicate that the supervisory mechanisms of the assizes were taken very seriously and that the community had a collective interest in ensuring that the authority of the officials was upheld and respected.[147] In Newmarket, only eleven different men served as ale-tasters from 1400 to 1413 and all were fined 3d. each year they served for 'non fecerunt officium'. The same regular amercement was imposed upon the aletasters of Clare for failing to undertake their office suffi-ciently. Nevertheless, a number of aletasters were consistently elected to serve more than once, and in Newmarket all but two served as a bailiff or capital pledge.

It is likely that aletasting was an onerous duty in towns with so many brewing households and it is perhaps hardly surprising that many ale-tasters were amerced for failing to properly fulfil their office. Indeed, this was a common entry in many medieval court rolls, commonly related to aletasters failing to maintain the requirements of their oath of office.[148] In Earl Soham and Walton, the aletasters, none of whom were brewers

[144] Britnell, *Growth and Decline*, p. 90.
[145] Brewers could be amerced for selling before the aletasters were summoned. Ratcliff (ed.), *Elton*, pp. 194, 236–8; Pugh (ed.), *Court Rolls*, pp. 6–7; Ault (ed.), *Ramsey*, pp. 183, 188, 191, 195–6, 199.
[146] TNA, sc2/203/49.
[147] Seabourne notes that 'failures to present or to comply with the tasters do not seem to have been common'. Seabourne, *Royal Regulation*, p. 113, nn. 329–30.
[148] SRO (I), HD:68/314 and 484/76 (Horham, 1393–1408); Cambridge, Pembroke Col-lege, Framlingham Court Rolls c, D1, D2 (Framlingham and Saxtede, 1400–21); SRO (I), HA68:484/135 (Aldham, 1347–71); SRO (I), HA119:50/3/142 (Bacton, 1413–23); SRO (I), HA91/1 (Bradfield, 1318–77); SRO (I), HA6:51/4/4.7 (East Bergholt, 1382–); SRO (I), HB9:50/13/2.1–2.11 (Hacheston, 1347–); SRO (I), HA246/A1/1 (Higham, 1344–66); SRO (I), s1/10/9.1–9.11 (Holbrook, 1378–); SRO (I), HB8/1/778–89 (Tat-tingstone, 1335–); Ratcliff (ed.), *Elton*, pp. 7, 34, 39, 92, 261, 303, 311, 391, 393; Powell and Malden (eds.), *Carshalton*, pp. 22–3; Ault (ed.), *Ramsey*, p. 178; Lock (ed.), *Walsham le Willows 1303–1350*; Lock (ed.), *Walsham le Willows 1351–99*. Only in occasional jurisdictions do we find aletasters who are not amerced and are considered to have 'presented well and truly and have concealed nothing'. Oram (ed.), *Court Rolls*, pp. 241, 251, 282 (Tottenham); Amphlett and Hamilton (eds.), *Court Rolls*, i, p. xxxvi.

or bakers themselves, were amerced up to 6d. every year for not keeping their office.[149] The office could also be occasionally unpopular and raise tensions between the aletaster and his neighbours. For instance, in Clare in 1338, Catherine Pentelowe was amerced 12d. for hindering the aletasters in their office and abusing them.[150] In 1352, Edmund le Taillour was insulted by Thomas le Mason while undertaking his ale-tasting and he sought damages as recompense.[151] Several other brewers in the 1360s and 1370s were also amerced for showing contempt to the aletaster while he was attempting to do his office.[152] Similar disrespect for the aletaster can be seen in other Suffolk markets, such as in late fourteenth-century Walsham le Willows, where John Lester, a regular brewer, twice obstructed the aletasters as they tried to taste his ale, insulting them, threatening them and even tearing their clothes.[153]

It is possible that the purpose of the amercements upon aletasters was to punish them for neglect in their office, which might be expected in the face of such obstacles. It must have been easy to miss a brewing, forget a case, or misjudge the quality of a batch. However, the regularity of the amercement of aletasters in court rolls raises speculation as to the nature of these annual fines. It could be argued that the standardised amercement was an accepted financial arrangement to allow aletasters a margin of liability in their duties.[154] They could not hope to inspect all brewings, especially when they had their own trades to administer, and thus minor amercements gave them some leeway for error. It was perhaps comparable to the fixed and regular 'beaupleder' fines imposed upon jurors in thirteenth-century sheriffs' tourns as a means of excusing them from a myriad of minor oversights.[155] The regularity of fines did not therefore mean that aletasters were negligent or took bribes. Indeed, aletasters were occasionally upbraided separately for specific corruption.[156] In early fourteenth-century Elton (Huntingdonshire), aletasters were frequently amerced for generally failing to perform their office, but there were also specific, separate accusations of concealment or neglecting to confiscate inferior ale.[157] Most aletasters appear to have performed their role satisfactorily.[158] The more regular amercements of aletasters were therefore legal fictions, rather like assize amercements, imposed both as a

---

[149] SRO (I), v5/18/1.3–1.4 (1378–99, 1413–22); SRO (I), HA119:50/3/17–19 (1381–1413).
[150] TNA, sc2/203/43.   [151] TNA, sc2/203/49.   [152] TNA, sc2/203/59–60.
[153] Lock (ed.), *Walsham le Willows 1351–99*, pp. 108 (1370), 149 (1385).
[154] Bennett, *Ale*, p. 161.   [155] Brand, *Kings, Barons and Justices*, pp. 87–90.
[156] Britton, *Community*, p. 100.   [157] Ratcliff (ed.), *Elton*, pp. 34, 92.
[158] Seabourne, *Royal Regulation*, pp. 113–14; Britnell, *Commercialisation*, p. 96; Bennett, *Ale*, pp. 112, 163.

revenue raiser and for jurisdictional security. Paradoxically, the amercement can even be seen as a means of ensuring that all brewers accepted
the testimony of the aletasters, because the fines suggested that an aletaster's minor misdemeanours had already been censured in advance, or
at least in retrospect.

Interestingly, the Newmarket aletasters, Peter Brabon, Peter Fedelere,
William Fyschere, John Pepyr, John Pere and John Ray, all presented their
spouses for breaking the assize of ale.[159] Similarly, being an aletaster in
Clare did not preclude their wives from brewing and being amerced.
John Ascelote's wife was amerced in 1344 (though she was not amerced
for the next two years while her husband was in office), John Stoke's
wife in 1350–1, Robert Turnour's wife in 1382–3, William Warderobe's
wife in 1397 and John Priour's wife in 1415–16, all while their husbands
were serving as aletaster. However, equally, John Porter appears to have
stopped brewing a few years before he served a long stint as aletaster
from 1406, and neither John Costyn or John Ponney and their wives
brewed while they were aletasters in 1416–17 and 1419–20 respectively.
Nevertheless, it has been argued that familial relations might have actually
encouraged cooperation with the court and confidence in the assize of
ale.[160] It appears that aletasters were prepared to present all brewers and
that there was no real social stigma attached to being included on the
assize lists.

Overall, the assizes of ale and bread should best be seen in the context that producers were given the opportunity to operate without cumbersome and perpetual interference. The rarity of heavy amercements
implies that most acted within the margins of acceptability and breaches
of the assize were regarded as minor offences, with only slight detrimental effects upon the community. However, certain offences were regarded
as outrages against moral propriety and social justice. If it were deemed
necessary, town authorities were prepared to stamp down on flagrant
lawbreakers within the remit of assize legislation.

Britnell has suggested that the lenient punishments of trading offenders, in conjunction with the regularity of breaches of the assize, mean that
it is inconceivable to think that there was any close connection between
legal and moral precepts in the late Middle Ages. The way that the assizes
were enforced in such a technical manner, with little regard for the detrimental effects of traders' actions, demonstrated a sceptical attitude that

---

[159] SRO (B), Acc.1476/1/4, 8, 12, 14, 23, 24, 26, 39, 44, 48. Bennett found the same in
        Brigstock; Bennett, *Women*, pp. 122–3. In Clare, Robert Barker presented his wife for
        breaches of the assize of ale. TNA, sc2/203/63–4.
[160] DeWindt and DeWindt, *Ramsey*, pp. 225–6.

was in contrast to the demands of law and moral writings.[161] Indeed, many medieval moralists warned that the law was not upheld strictly enough and market traders were negligent of their own spiritual welfare. If all assize presentments were effectively regarded as taxes by the public and officials, then moral considerations and criminal associations were perhaps being negated under such generalised accusations of malpractice. The assizes had become another means of assuaging collective guilt about not upholding the strictest moral standards in the face of the reality of everyday life.

However, we should not totally dismiss morals as irrelevant to the actual conduct and regulation of traders. When there were infringements considered harmful to the general community, or instances of excessive profit-making beyond the margins allowed by local officials, the court rolls of Newmarket and Clare show that offenders were punished quite severely. This was a demonstration of law degenerating into a form of local custom, which was flexibly interpreted according to parochial standards and interests.[162] Some social ideals remained influential in such local interpretations of the law, even if many late medieval writers lamented at the way in which local practice deviated from Church doctrine. Indeed, the perception of moral boundaries still continued to be prevalent in towns, especially when trading actions were considered to be excessively harmful to communal prosperity and 'reasonable prices'.

Linked to concepts of morality, assize amercements were sometimes set according to a person's ability to pay and many were pardoned because of their poverty ('quia pauper'). In other words, a fine for a minor offence was not expected to affect a person's means to live; pardons were an institutional means to show mercy and charity.[163] In Clare, there were several pardons on the grounds of poverty, but most occurred before the Black Death when perhaps economic conditions were harsher for the average townsman. Similarly, in Sudbury, the cases of pardons from brewing amercements due to poverty all occurred before the Black Death.[164]

---

[161] Britnell, 'Morals', pp. 27–9.   [162] *Ibid.*, p. 29.

[163] May, 'An index'; Casson, 'A comparative study', pp. 206–7, 431–2. A medieval treatise on court procedures stated that everyone should be fined according to his trepass 'saving to a gentleman the contenement of his house, to a merchant his merchandise, to a land-tenant his plough and cart'. Maitland and Baildon (eds.), *Court Baron*, p. 101.

[164] TNA, sc2/203/112–115, sc2/204/3–20. For other pardons due to poverty, see Baildon (ed.), *Court Rolls*, i, p. 121; Pugh (ed.), *Court Rolls*, pp. 6–7; Lister (ed.), *Court Rolls*, pp. 123–4; Marcham (ed.), *Court Rolls*, pp. 3, 9, 19, 35; Ratcliff (ed.), *Elton*, pp. 91, 195, 237–8.

Several brewers also had their amercements remitted by Clare's court as a type of occupational perk because they were in office as bailiffs or constables, or because they had provided hospitality and victuals for guests at the castle.[165] For instance, Thomas Cumbwell's wife was a regular brewer and twice, in 1388–9, she was pardoned because her husband was serving as bailiff. Similarly, the wives of John Warde, John Chaundeler, John Wynchester and Nicholas Parsey were pardoned from brewing amercements while their husbands held the office of bailiff.[166] Whether this was because they had abstained from brewing as stipulated by the 1389–90 statute, or this was a benefit of the job, is difficult to ascertain. However, Thomas Cumbwell's wife, Sara, did pay 3d. in October 1388 which suggests that she was still brewing while he held office during 1388, as were Adam Stonhard's wife, Johanna, and John Broun's wife, Johanna, during 1378–9 while they were bailiffs. Such pardons were also less frequent by the fifteenth century.[167] It is thus possible that some assize amercements were assessed to fit the ability of the offender to pay them or as a type of fealty, but this does not detract from the likelihood that most amercements were part of a more standardised licensing system.

Regrating and forestalling

Brewing and baking were spread across the social spectrum, but those in the upper strata of the town community dominated regular production. By contrast, we might expect regrating, as a low-capital venture, to be concentrated in the hands of poorer sectors of the community, including single women. Regraters usually distributed the produce of regular brewers and bakers, either hawking victuals in the streets or selling ale by the mugful in temporary or permanent alehouses. An apt definition of regrating is found in the Newmarket court rolls: 'John Brunne and John Ostler are regraters of horsebread, that is they bought three loaves for a penny and sold two loaves for a penny'.[168] However, regraters of bread were rare in Newmarket and these two men were only fined 1d. and 2d. respectively for selling at an excessive profit. Regraters of ale were more

---

[165] See also Coleman (ed.), *Court Roll*, p. 99.

[166] These pardons extended beyond brewing: William Darnel for fishmonger offences, Thomas Bory as butcher, William Paycock as tanner. The same pardons for amercements due to office-holding, or service to the steward, occurred in Sudbury after the Black Death (1354–5, 1357–8, 1380, 1385, 1388–9, 1391–2, 1396, 1405, 1430). TNA, sc2/203/112–115, sc2/204/1–20.

[167] Similarly, in Ramsey from the 1380s, there are no mentions of special considerations or excused fines. DeWindt and DeWindt, *Ramsey*, p. 226.

[168] SRO (B), Acc.1476/1/38.

common than those of food, perhaps because of their social connection with alehouses. Alehouses were usually a regrater's or brewer's own home, from which they not only sold ale to be taken away in customers' own vessels, but also vended drink in cups and pots to be consumed on the premises at rough benches and tables. This is why so many were amerced for using illegal cup measures. Not all regraters had a sufficient turnover or home to operate an alehouse from and the more irregular were probably hucksters who wandered through the streets and market.

Forty-seven Newmarket households were amerced for regrating ale, with an average of ten presentments per court (see Tables 3 and 7). Only six regular regraters of ale can be identified, of whom three were from households of secondary status. Of all the other regraters, six were from households of primary rank and four were from those of secondary rank (see Table 5). The presented offenders were mostly wives or single women, with only three men ever presented for ale-regrating in Newmarket (Simon Baldewyne, Nicholas Hurton and John Odye). In particular, there were two identifiable single women, Matilda Rokelond and Johanna Tapstere, as well as the daughters of Robert Barkere, Robert Doushole and Robert Gateward. The regrating of ale was therefore primarily a female occupation and generally a more lowly socio-economic trade than regular brewing; though it may have been merely an initial stage of the work life-cycle for single women. Overall, ale-regraters in Newmarket received a higher average amercement than brewers of 7d., with seven to thirteen offenders presented per session (see Table 7). However, this average amercement figure was skewed by the fines given to half a dozen regraters, who faced particularly high average amercements, like the wives of Robert Doushole, John Greyne, John Odye and Richard Wryte, who were fined an average of 12.6d., 12.9d., 11.5d. and 6.3d. respectively, and who may have been working from inns. Figure 25, where most regraters are clustered in the bottom-left corner of the graph, highlights the point that most irregular regraters were given relatively low amercements of 2d.–3d.

Comparatively, in Clare, most regraters were amerced 2d.–3d., whether they were regular malefactors or not (see Figure 26). There were many more regraters of bread in Clare, perhaps reflecting the concentration of baking in fewer hands and the sale of bread from inns and cookhouses. Also, a greater percentage of regraters in Clare were of primary or secondary socio-economic status. For instance, Thomas Coupere was both capital pledge and briefly an aletaster (1383–4) and Adam Glouere was a capital pledge. Households like that of John and Johanna Stonham were brewing regularly at the same time as they were regrating bread. However, there were also a significant number of regraters who

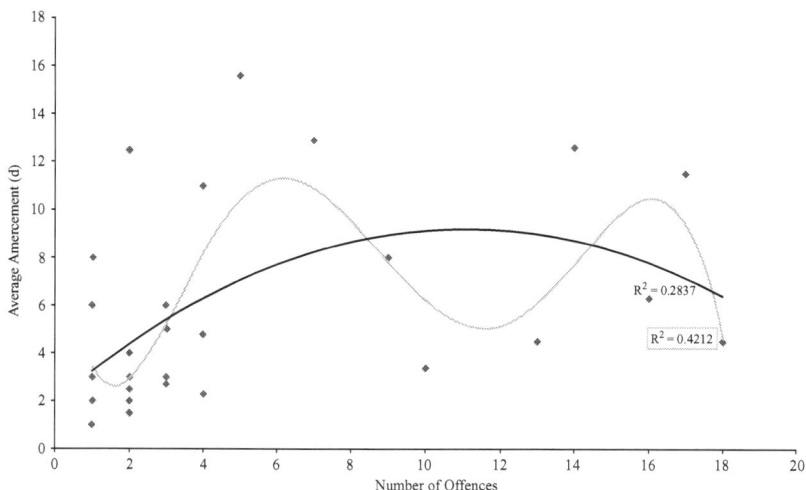

Figure 25: Scatter graph of amercements and ale-regrating offences in Newmarket, 1400–1413.

Notes: Each point on this graph represents a single household's number of regrating offences, 1400–13, and the average amercement for those offences. For these calculations, a household is considered to consist of a husband and wife; daughters or sons are considered to be separate working units. Two polynomial trendlines are presented: Order 2 (black) and Order 6 (grey).

Source: SRO (B), Acc.1476/1/1–48.

are less visible in the records, such as Robert and Margaret Cornmonger, William and Johanna Hunte, and John and Margaret Exale. Looking further back in the records, certain individuals who had been regraters in the early 1360s, seemingly moved forward in their business, such as Peter Colyrob, who went on to become bailiff in 1366 and 1370-1.

Whether the level of amercements was related to the amount of regrating activity (as with the assizes in Newmarket) or actual offences is uncertain. The different amercement practices relating to regraters in Newmarket and Clare are notable, with much more variation and higher average penalties in the former. It is possible that regraters of ale and bread in Newmarket were regarded with more suspicion than producers. The margins of flexibility provided for regular regraters may therefore have been depressed, even though the potential to make reasonable profit within the confines of the regulations was low. On the other hand, many regraters perhaps operated out of alehouses, which may have made supervision by officials difficult and possibly encouraged the use of an assessed

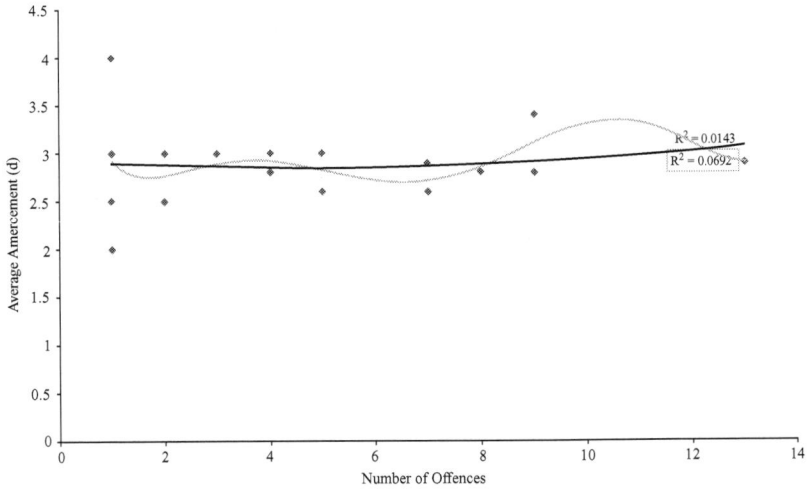

Figure 26: Scatter graph of amercements and regrating offences in Clare, 1377–1425.

Notes: Each point on this graph represents a single household's number of regrating offences, 1377–1425, and the average amercement for those offences. For these calculations, a household is considered to consist of a husband and wife; daughters or sons are considered to be separate working units. Two polynomial trendlines are presented: Order 2 (black) and Order 6 (grey).

Source: TNA, SC2/203/62–7.

fine based on perceived activity. Certainly, many regular regraters of ale continued to practise their trade and were seemingly able to cover their costs, despite being amerced repeatedly in the Newmarket court rolls. Regraters in Clare were amerced at a much more consistent and lower rate, redolent of a licensing style but demonstrating little distinction between different levels of activity. The level of official supervision in Clare may have been much lower than in Newmarket, thus leading to standardised amercements. Alternatively, regrating was simply a lesser activity, as suggested by the lower numbers presented in the Clare court rolls, and perhaps often combined with other trade and production activities.

The main anxiety regarding regraters was that they raised prices through the reselling of commodities. Newmarket was a small town that relied extensively on the provisioning of travellers, and may have therefore ostensibly displayed greater concern about those who made excessive profits or sold goods at 'unreasonable' prices, ranging from ale and bread, to meat, fish, tar and candles. Richard Tornor, for example, was amerced 2s. for selling tar at 8d. a gallon, which he had bought in the same market for 4d. a gallon.[169] However, there is little indication that officials were actively seeking to stamp out regrating or forestalling through court punishments. Given the disdainful attitude towards forestallers in the regulations and literature, one imagines that officials would take a harsh line against such activities. This does not seem to be borne out by the court roll evidence.

Numerous goods were forestalled by market traders, but fish was the commodity most associated with forestalling, with over 80 per cent of cases in our small towns involving this foodstuff. Fish was an important part of the medieval diet, not only during Lent but for the whole of the year and large amounts were transported inland from Yarmouth and other fishing towns of East Anglia. Saul has noted that the Clare households regularly sent fish carts to Yarmouth from Bardfield (Essex) and Bury St Edmunds.[170] Sea-fish was either preserved in salt or brine, or smoked or dried, while fresh fish was stored in wet reeds and transported as quickly as possible because of its perishable nature. Consequently, freshwater fish was often expensive and stocks were jealously guarded. A late fifteenth-century assize specifically stated that no fish should be regrated or forestalled and should only be sold in the 'playne market'. Fishers (meaning those who sold fish, either fishermen themselves or fishmongers) were to take only a penny out of a shilling of fish as profit and were not to sell any fish that had gone bad.[171] In Clare, there were several fishers (or fishmongers) who were regularly amerced for selling either corrupt fish or at excessive prices in the late fourteenth century, such as William Norfolk, who was amerced eight times (average of 6d.). These trading malpractices did not prevent him from officiating as a capital pledge, constable and bailiff (1391–2 and 1403). His wife, Johanna, was fined 12d. in 1399 for 'contemptuously selling ale outside her home', while more generally they were amerced twenty-three times between them for brewing (average 5.2d.). In a similar manner, William Darnel sold corrupt fish four times between 1384 and 1388, but was only amerced 2d. on three occasions and on the fourth was excused the fine because he was serving as bailiff.

In enforcing the forestalling laws, the court officials of Newmarket and Clare appear to have been similarly ambivalent. In early fifteenth-century Newmarket, Thomas Cook, John Greyne and John Pepyr all forestalled fish and meat before the cross to the nuisance of all in the

---

[169] Tar was used as a sheep-salve.   [170] Saul, 'Herring', 37.
[171] BL, MS Lansdowne 796, fol. 5r.

town.[172] John Bogeys of Wilbraham was accused of forestalling sheep and chickens 'ad finem ville' (at the end of town), so that neither the town nor the neighbourhood were served.[173] Overall, only twelve traders were named as forestallers in Newmarket, but their fines of 1d.–6d. probably did not cover the value of the goods forestalled, as prescribed by statute. This was despite a coda following the offences, which stated that they were 'ad commune nocumentum contra statutum'. This picture of leniency is enhanced by a particular sequence of persistent forestalling conducted by four traders, Thomas Cook, John Leyseter, John Lane and John Redere. The court finally asserted that things were getting out of hand when they warned them in April 1411 that they should no longer offend under threat of a penalty of 40d. each. Yet, by May 1412, three of them were again amerced for the same offences at only 1d. each.[174] It can only be surmised that the court initially feared a monopolistic coalition of four such prominent traders, but that these fears had receded a year later. Fears of scarcity were thus simmering beneath the surface of town regulation, yet the court usually reverted to a more lenient path than statutory requirements demanded. Overall, those who forestalled or sold meat and fish at excessive prices in Newmarket never faced penalties above 6d. Most forestallers at Clare also faced relatively minor amercements of 2d.–6d. for forestalling diverse victuals on the roads outside the town.[175] William Darnel was amerced just 2d. for forestalling victuals and fish in 1386. Three years later, John Serle from Honington (north Suffolk) was amerced 6d. for forestalling victuals. In 1390, 3d. amercements were placed upon Richard Pety as the seller and John son of Sarra Cook as buyer of the same corn before it came to the market.

It appears that greater opprobrium was attached to forestalling before and just after the Black Death in comparison to later years. In the 1340s and 1350s, suspected forestallers in Clare were often distrained to respond to the lord and community and judged by an inquisition jury, rather than simply presented and amerced. Some were found not guilty and those convicted were generally only amerced 6d., but the fact that such offences went through these procedures suggests that offenders were concerned about damage to their reputation if they were convicted in court of forestalling.[176] The language of the courts stressed that such

[172] SRO (B), Acc.1476/1/12. If this refers to the market cross, then it might suggest that forestalling and regrating were sometimes used as interchangeable terms, but it may refer to markers placed at the edge of the town.
[173] SRO (B), Acc.1476/1/14.   [174] SRO (B), Acc.1476/1/39, 44.
[175] TNA, sc2/203/63–5.   [176] TNA, sc2/203/45–9.

activities were to the damage of the community.[177] In 1351, the Clare jury presented that Peter le Smyth and Johanna le Pulter bought corn in 'le Cornhel' before the set time and all their neighbours had been unable to have their market share.[178] Other notable cases included Robert Bory and Peter Colyrob, who were both fined 12d. for contempt in forestalling victuals in 1360, while Alex de Newtone, a cook, faced consistently high penalties of 12d.–18d. for forestalling various victuals in the early 1370s.[179] However, after the 1370s, forestalling appears infrequently in Clare's court, with amercement levels consistently below 6d. A similar pattern can be seen in the small town of Sudbury. For most years in the 1350s, significant numbers were amerced in Sudbury for forestalling victuals to the prejudice of the market or community. However, there were no such amercements just before the Black Death and few after 1370.[180]

Forestalling was increasingly considered a minor practical problem in the markets of Clare and Newmarket, causing only moderate price increases, though it was still considered essentially immoral. Indeed, an element of the moral stigma attached to forestalling can be seen in the Clare court rolls in 1360, which recorded a feud between Richard Punge, an aletaster, and Robert Bory. In July, Richard claimed that Robert had assaulted him so badly that he had lost his hearing and asserted that Robert had also called him false and untrustworthy for having presented Robert for forestalling. Richard claimed that such slander had lost him credence in the neighbourhood to damages of 20s. The subsequent inquiry in August found that Robert, along with Peter Colyrob, had been guilty of forestalling and amerced them both 12d., but Richard Punge was amerced 6d. for a false plea of trespass.[181] Richard would not let the matter lie and pursued his plea again at the leet court in October. An inquiry in November agreed that Robert had committed trespass against Richard, but the plaintiff received only minimal recompense of 6d. damages. Nevertheless, this incident does highlight the importance of reputation in the market for both traders and officials. The accusation of forestalling had aroused Robert Bory's violent indignation and Richard Punge was determined to defend his own standing in the community.

---

[177] TNA, sc2/203/50.   [178] TNA, sc2/203/49.
[179] TNA, sc2/203/57.
[180] TNA, sc2/203/112–115, sc2/204/1–20. In Colchester, the amercement of 'common forestallers' was abandoned from 1412. Britnell, *Growth and Decline*, p. 132; Britnell, *Britain and Ireland*, p. 360. DeWindt and DeWindt noted a similar disappearance of forestalling cases in the court of Ramsey after 1412. DeWindt and DeWindt, *Ramsey*, p. 165, n. 56.
[181] TNA, sc2/203/56–7.

Table 7. *Regraters, cooks and forestallers in Newmarket, 1400–1413*

Date of court	Number of regraters of ale	Average amercement per regrater of ale	Number of regraters of bread	Average amercement per regrater of bread	Number of cooks[a] amerced	Average amercement per cook	Number of forestallers[b]	Average amercement per forestaller
26 Apr 1400	13	5.8d.			2	2.5d.	2	2.0d.
9 Oct 1400	8	6.8d.			1	2.0d.	1	
5 Apr 1402	13	4.5d.			7	2.6d.		
6 Oct 1402	8	6.8d.	1	2.0d.	11	3.5d.		
13 Oct 1403	11	8.5d.			9	2.6d.	2	6.0d.
16 Apr 1404	9	6.1d.			3	4.7d.	2	3.0d.
6 Oct 1404	10	7.2d.					4[e]	4.5d.
9 Nov 1405	10	7.2d.			7	3.4d.	3	3.0d.
28 Apr 1406	9	5.4d.			2	4.5d.	1	4.0d.
6 Oct 1407	9	9.0d.			3	6.3d.		
16 Jun 1408	7	6.1d.						
3 Nov 1408	8	6.4d.			2	2.5d.		
11 Apr 1409	10	7.9d.					1	4.0d.
25 Nov 1409	11	4.2d.			2	2.5d.		
16 May 1410	12	9.8d.	2	1.5d.	10	2.6d.		
8 Nov 1410	-[c]		7	2.7d.	5	4.2d.	3	2.7d.
23 Apr 1411	9	10.0d.			5	4.0d.	4	3.5d.
2 Nov 1411	7	9.0d.			5	3.6d.		
16 May 1412	-[c]		16[d]	3.5d.	5	2.2d.	4	1.0d.
4 Nov 1412	-[c]				5	3.0d.		
16 Jun 1413	8	5.6d.			3	2.0d.	1	-[f]
Total	172	7.0d.	26	2.4d.	87	3.2d.	28	3.2d.

Notes: a – Cooks sold corrupt foodstuffs (such as fish, meat and other victuals) or at excessive price; b – Forestallers dealt in a variety of goods, some of which were included under the generic phrase 'diversorum victualium', and others which were specifically stated as fish, oysters, meat, sheep and chickens; c – these cases were perhaps included with the breakers of the assize; d – these regraters were included with bakers selling contrary to the assize; e – John Pepyr was fined twice, presumably for two different offences; f – no amercement was noted.

Source: SRO (B), Acc.1476/1/1–48.

In a small town, forestalling and regrating were still seen as disreputable and potentially problematic, but, in reality, few traders had the capital to hoard enough goods to raise general prices to an excessively harmful level. Those traders with sufficient capital would deal directly with producers and buy in bulk, and this was not considered illegal. Forestalling was more of a survival strategy for poorer market traders.[182] The authorities realised the functionality of certain middlemen and used the legislation to raise revenue for the lord, while equally recognising that such transgressions were mostly small-scale affairs intended to turn a quick profit on the margins of the market. The court was consequently more lenient than statutory requirements and imposed amercements that seemed worthy of the offence.

Weights and measures

All petty traders of Newmarket and Clare were subject to regulations concerning the weights and measures they employed. National legislation promoted the use of standard weights and measures throughout the country. All vessels and weights were expected to be checked regularly by local authorities and marked by a seal, with any improper weights or measures supposedly destroyed.[183] However, this practice was rarely recorded in Newmarket, with the only instance being when Thomas Brasyer used false measures that were subsequently seized into the lord's hands.[184] In most cases, traders were simply fined for failing to bring their measures to court for inspection. This happened so regularly with brewers and regraters of ale that sometimes, in both Newmarket and Clare, the offence was merely combined with breaches of the assize. At some sessions, the offence was not mentioned at all. When it was listed separately, there was no consistency about whether traders were fined 1d., 2d. or 3d., even though there were many repeat offenders.

Presumably, if there was a general feeling that the use of improper measures was getting out of hand, there would have been tougher measures in court. There were regular instances of the use of improper, unsealed measures in Newmarket by William Cleydon, William Spyser (from Haverhill), Thomas Predyngton (from Fordham) and Thomas Tornor, who all traded in oil and tar. At almost every court they were fined 2d.–3d. for selling by the wrong measures, or for failing to bring

---

[182] Britnell, *Growth and Decline*, p. 40; Rigby, *English Society*, p. 273.

[183] E.g. *Statutes*, i, pp. 201–2, 'Judicium Pillorie'; i, p. 117, 25 Edw I, *Magna Carta* c.25 (1297); i, p. 285, 14 Edw.III st.1 c.12 (1340); ii, pp. 63–4, 13 Ric.II c.9 (1389–90). See pp. 189–96.

[184] SRO (B), Acc.1476/1/45.

Table 8. *Regraters, butchers, fishmongers and tanners in Clare, 1377–1425*

Date of court	Number of regraters of bread[a]	Average amercement per regrater	Number of butchers[b]	Average amercement per butcher	Number of fishmongers[c]	Average amercement per fishmonger	Number of tanners[d]	Average amercement per tanner
13 Nov 1377								
5 Oct 1378								
12 Apr 1379								
18 Oct 1379	3	3.0d.						
3 Apr 1380	3	3.0d.	10	9.2d.	1	6.0d.	5	8.0d.
29 Apr 1382	2	2.0d.	14	3.3d.	1	3.0d.	5	3.2d.
6 Oct 1383	3	2.0d.	1	3.0d.				
12 Apr 1384	3	2.0d.	14	3.4d.	12	2.6d.	4	5.0d.
10 Oct 1385								
7 May 1386	3	3.0d.	19	2.9d.	12	2.7d.	6	3.5d.
14 Oct 1387			4	3.5d.				
21 Apr 1388	4	2.8d.	16	4.1d.	7	5.1d.	5	6.0d.
6 Oct 1388	2	3.0d.						
4 May 1389	2	3.0d.	16	4.9d.	8	4.9d.	5	6.0d.
21 Oct 1389	2	3.0d.						
26 Apr 1390	3	3.3d.	20	3.1d.	20	2.7d.	6	3.4d.
8 Oct 1397								
? Apr 1398								
8 Oct 1398	4	3.0d.						
15 Apr 1399	4	3.0d.						
? Oct 1399	4	3.0d.	1	4.0d.				

Date	(a) No.	(a) Av.	(b) No.	(b) Av.	(c) No.	(c) Av.	(d) No.	(d) Av.
27 Apr 1400	7	3.0d.			5	3.6d.		
13 Oct 1400	4	3.0d.						
20 Apr 1401	7	2.1d.						
9 Oct 1403	5	3.0d.						
22 Apr 1404	6	2.5d.						
7 Oct 1404	4	4.0d.						
5 May 1405	8	3.0d.						
10 Oct 1406	6	3.0d.						
22 Apr 1407	3	3.0d.						
20 Oct 1411	2	3.0d.						
19 Apr 1412								
6 Oct 1412	3	3.0d.						
2 May 1413	2	4.5d.	3	12.0d.	1	12.0d.		
14 Oct 1416	2	3.0d.	1	3.0d.	2	4.5d.		
21 Apr 1417								
10 Oct 1419			2	6.0d.				
? Apr 1420	1	3.0d.						
14 Oct 1421	4	3.0d.	2	9.0d.	2	5.0d.		
20 Apr 1422			1	3.0d.	2	3.0d.		
6 Oct 1422	3	3.0d.	2	3.0d.	4	3.0d.		
21 Apr 1423	1	3.0d.			1	3.0d.		
17 Oct 1424	2	3.0d.						
18 Apr 1425	2	2.0d.						
Total	**114**	**2.9d.**	**126**	**4.7d.**	**78**	**3.5d.**	**36**	**5.0d.**

Notes: a – Regraters mostly sold bread and horsebread against the assize, though some also sold ale from 1404; b – Butchers were accused of selling corrupt meat and meat at an excessive price; c – Fishmongers sold corrupt fish and fish at an excessive price; d – Tanners sold leather at an excessive price and badly tanned their leather.

Source: TNA, sc2/203/62–7.

them to court to be checked. John Smyth of Exning, William Spyser and John Spicer of Haverhill did not even use a measure to sell oil.[185] In Clare in the 1350s, there were several entries in the court rolls where brewers were specifically accused of using unsealed measures, such as cups and bowls, and were each amerced 1d.–2d.[186] For some ten years after 1367, the butchers and chandlers of Clare were fined 1d.–3d. at least six times for selling by false measures. On the last recorded occasion in 1377, the penalty for six offenders was increased to 12d. and this seemingly served as a deterrent for there were no further references to this offence in the court rolls. It appears that, in cases of false weights and measures, the authorities were prepared to overlook some persistent offences and show flexibility in standards, leaving an element of choice in the hands of the consumer, especially for commodities like ale and tar. Selling ale by the mugful, or tar in unstandard barrels, meant that an exact correlation of prices could be difficult for the public. But, equally, customers could obtain a bargain or a deal of convenience if they were willing to take a risk in balancing the market indicators of volume, quality and price for themselves. As already discussed, Newmarket's officials intervened only when individual traders overstepped the flexible margins of acceptable practice. Otherwise, the town courts seemed content to allow irregular measuring practices to continue, in return for a small fee.

However, an illustration of what the courts considered to be unacceptable practices can be seen in their condemnation of users of the 'auncel'. The auncel had been banned by statute law in 1351–2 because it depended very much on the integrity of the trader whose hand did the balancing.[187] At Wentford fair, Clare, in 1362, a 'false' auncel and twenty woollen cloaks were forfeited by Peter Risby.[188] By 1390, Clare's court issued a by-law, reinforcing statute law, that no one was to use the auncel or else they would face a penalty of half a mark.[189] In Newmarket in 1410, John Byrd of Qwye was fined 12d. because he was accused of having used hand-measures in selling flour in order to 'fraudulently deceive the neighbourhood'.[190] Thomas Predyton, John Felyp and William Ropere were similarly fined for not selling ropes and canvas by the balance.[191]

The courts also kept a watchful eye on bushel measures of grain, indicating a desire to control both the price and marketing of this particular commodity. John Baker Litil was amerced 6d. in Clare in February 1380 for a substandard bushel. The courts and officials may have been fairly

[185] SRO (B), Acc.1476/1/3.
[186] TNA, sc2/203/49–50. See also SRO (I), HD:68/314 and 484/76 (Horham, 1393–4).
[187] *Statutes*, i, pp. 321–2, 25 Edw.III St.5 c.9 (1352). See pp. 195–6.
[188] TNA, sc2/203/58.   [189] TNA, sc2/203/64.
[190] SRO (B), Acc.1476/1/38.   [191] SRO (B), Acc.1476/1/3, 7, 8, 14, 26, 43.

lenient about the margins of ale and bread production, but the initial cost of the grain presumably needed to be protected and less open to fraudulence, if confidence in the market was to remain stable. Thus, in Newmarket in 1403, twenty-four men, probably middlemen from the surrounding area, were fined either 3d. or 8d. each for using heaped measures when selling malt, 'contrary to statute'.[192] In Newmarket, it was the regular victuallers and innkeepers, such as John Redere, William Fyschere, John Smyth, Thomas Cook, Peter Fedelere, John Waleys, John Barbor and John Greyne (see Table 9), who were continually warned about bringing their grain and fodder measures to court. However, despite the persistence of their neglect, they were only amerced 1d.–3d. each time.[193]

Innkeepers and cooks

Innkeepers and cooks were some of the most prominent and influential traders in the small towns of Newmarket and Clare. By 1472, we find thirteen inns or larger alehouses recorded in the Newmarket account rolls, but evidence of at least half a dozen can also be found in the early fifteenth-century court rolls, owned by men like John Redere, Thomas Cook and John Waleys.[194] These were not all merely drinking- or victualling-houses, and a number did offer accommodation to travellers, as shown by Thomas Playter, whose expenses for a journey to London in 1459–60 indicated that he paid 6d. 'for my dyner and horsmete' at a Newmarket inn.[195] In Clare, there are also occasional references to inns, such as 'le Swan' or 'Quilters', which was mentioned in the 1361 court roll.[196] Similar inn names were seen in the late fifteenth-century account rolls of Newmarket.[197]

The main medieval drinking establishments were the inn, alehouse and tavern, each of which provided a particular service. The alehouse was a drinking house, often temporary, though becoming a more permanent fixture in many towns and villages by the fourteenth and fifteenth centuries. The tavern offered wine and some food, usually to a higher class of clientele. Such places were not common in small towns and there are

---

[192] SRO (B), Acc.1476/1/14.   [193] SRO (B), Acc.1476/1/8, 23, 24, 26, 38, 39.
[194] SRO (B), Acc.359/3.
[195] Richmond, 'Expenses', 46. See also Edelen (ed.), *Description*, p. 399.
[196] TNA, sc2/203/57.
[197] SRO (B), Acc.359/3. Each was given a name: Angel, Bear, Bell, Bull, Christopher, Hart, Griffin, Ram, Swan, Sword, Saracen's Head, Ship, and Fanfair. Other towns saw a proliferation of inns and alehouses in the late fourteenth and fifteenth centuries, see Searle, *Lordship and Community*, p. 409; Keene, *Survey*, i, pp. 166–7; Rosser, *Medieval Westminster*. John Lee notes the activities of Cambridge inns in selling firewood, hiring out horses and buying saffron. Lee, *Cambridge*, pp. 109, 148, 161.

only a couple of references in Clare to William Gosenol, Mabilia Boterie and Isabel Howy selling wine against the assize in 1363–6.[198] The inn provided a variety of drinks, food and accommodation to travellers. However, any demarcations should not be overemphasised in the Middle Ages when even alehouses may have provided rudimentary accommodation or food, while inns in small towns may have been poor cousins to their borough counterparts. Nevertheless, it seems that all these institutions grew in number, size and function after the Black Death, with their licensing first codified in the sixteenth century.[199] Britnell noted a growth in the number of inns, shops and taverns in Colchester after the Black Death.[200] Inns also proliferated in late medieval Southwark and Winchester, though this may have been partly a documentary aberration due to the naming of these establishments which highlighted them in the records.[201] Shops and inns had long existed in English towns, but the fifteenth century was perhaps an important period for the development of the 'public house' and the village shop.[202]

Inns were important focal points for social activities in England. This has been attributed to a decline in private and charitable hospitality after the Black Death, but perhaps partially reflected increasing standards of living, the proliferation of petty consumption and the mobile nature of society. All social groups were increasingly dependent upon public accommodation and hospitality, while popular activities moved from the churchyard to the alehouse.[203] In his study of the small town of Brandon, Bailey identified a large number of inns which existed in 1471, many of which were associated with suspicious clientele, prostitution, games and gambling.[204] The condemnation of morally illicit activities in inns was common in regulations and the keeping of a brothel was considered more heinous than selling at an excessive price. In York, Colchester and Lynn there was specific legislation to forbid brothels being established and to prevent common tapsters from frequenting inns.[205] There was also a suspicion of strangers lodged at inns, inferring a connection between inns and criminality. Beverley innkeepers were expected to harbour only 'honest folk' and no one was to stay for an excessive time

[198] TNA, sc2/203/58–9.
[199] Clark, *Alehouse*, pp. 6–14; Hunter, 'Legislation, royal proclamations', pp. 1–28.
[200] Britnell, *Growth and Decline*, p. 131.
[201] Keene, *Survey*, i, pp. 167, 274; Carlin, *Medieval Southwark*, pp. 191–200.
[202] Dyer, *Lords and Peasants*, p. 349.
[203] Heal, *Hospitality*, pp. 55–6, 201–4, 229, 238–9, 300, 365; Clark, *Alehouse*, pp. 23–34.
[204] Bailey, *A Marginal Economy*, p. 169.
[205] Prestwich (ed.), *York*, pp. 16–17; *King's Lynn*, p. 268, no. 325; *Red Paper Book*, p. 19; BL, MS Lansdowne 796, fol. 5v.

unless registered.[206] A curfew was often imposed on drinking establishments, and innkeepers were answerable for the deeds of anyone who lodged there for more than a day and a night.[207] Indeed, McIntosh has argued that the increasing local anxieties about disorder and immorality in late fifteenth-century alehouses and inns was a contributory factor in the decline of female proprietresses.[208] The fifteenth-century court rolls of Clare certainly provide references to disturbances of the peace taking place in alehouses.[209] However, other direct references to immoral activities within drinking establishments were not conspicuous in the court records of either Clare or Newmarket.

Innkeepers of late medieval England were often involved in a variety of trading activities. A concern of one late fifteenth-century assize was to ensure that innkeepers did not abuse their occupation by selling goods at excessive prices. This assize fixed the gain innkeepers could make on 'provandre' as a penny on every bushel bought at the market price. They were to offer a 'botell' of hay weighing 7lb. at $\frac{1}{2}$d. and charge nothing for the litter from which a horse could feed. A pot of three pints of ale was to cost 1d., but if they brewed, they were to sell according to the assize of ale. Even the dimensions of a faggot of wood were strictly defined and priced by length and girth. Additionally, the assize stated that no innkeeper was to bake bread to sell: this was a common prohibition in town ordinances and drew upon central legislation.[210] However, this prohibition was seemingly not applied to the innkeepers of Newmarket or Clare, as the offence does not appear in the court rolls of either town and many of the innkeepers appear to have both baked and brewed. Indeed, this multiplicity of activity is one indicator of a general trader or innkeeper, and although the potential innkeepers of Clare are not as clearly identifiable as in Newmarket, it is possible that John Wode, Elias Wheler and John Stoke all ran such establishments (see Table 12).

We certainly find several innkeepers in the Newmarket court rolls, as well as cooks, though where the differentiation between these occupations lay is often difficult to tell. Twenty-eight households were presented for reheating victuals, selling victuals at an excessive price or being 'common cooks', usually of fish or meat. Whether they were regular offenders or irregular cooks, their amercements were mostly between 2d.

---

[206] *Beverley*, p. 15. See also *Liber Albus*, pp. 234, 409.

[207] Ratcliff (ed.), *Elton*, p. 66. See also *Liber Albus*, pp. 240–1.

[208] McIntosh, *Working Women*, pp. 178–81.

[209] TNA, sc2/203/72; Thornton, *A History of Clare*, p. 104.

[210] BL, MS Lansdowne 796, fol. 5v. This was influenced by the 'Statute of Victuallers and Hostelers and other Sellers of Victuals', in *Statutes*, ii, p. 63, 13 Ric II st.1 c.8 (1389–90).

and 4d., at an overall average of 3.2d. (see Table 7). Only John Redere had a slightly higher individual average amercement at 5.3d. Three of the regular offenders were of primary office-holding status, and even among the irregular offenders, ten were primary, three secondary and two were outsiders (see Table 5). It appears that the professional and regular provisioners of Newmarket can be found among these presentments, either running inns, cookhouses or market stalls for victuals.[211] It also seems that these establishments were household concerns and attempting to differentiate between the general roles of husband and wife is perhaps disingenuous. We can thus examine the 'prominent victuallers' and households of Newmarket, defined here as those who appeared in at least three of the five main listings of offences (see Table 9).

Only five 'prominent victuallers' were not from households with primary or secondary office-holding status. Two of these, Matilda Rokelond and Johanna Tapstere, were apparently unmarried women (whether single or widowed). Their irregular forays into varying aspects of victualling suggest a huckstering or alehouse lifestyle, as does Johanna's surname. Conversely, most of the prominent victualling households in Newmarket constituted a significant element of the governing class of the town. Sixteen held primary offices and two secondary. Several of these households baked and brewed regularly or semi-regularly and also cooked and regrated. Some were certainly innkeepers, and figures such as Thomas Cook and John Redere were ubiquitous traders in Newmarket who (together with their wives) paid small fines for myriad offences. These could total some 2s.–3s. a year.

Peter May has identified John Redere as the landlord of the 'Hart' inn,[212] while Thomas Cook seems to have rented his tenement from another resident, as seen in a claim by John Prat for his rent in November 1407.[213] It appears that both men ran inns or permanent cookshops in Newmarket and, consequently, dealt in a variety of victuals. Redere and Cook also served as capital pledges, while John Redere was bailiff in 1406. Additionally, they were involved in credit dealings and the procedures of debt recovery, acting as pledges for the plaintiffs, as well as being holders of attachments for the defendants. Their role in community and commercial administration suggests that they were trusted and prominent members of Newmarket. Nevertheless, they apparently tried many ruses to make money and were presented for numerous trading offences,

---

[211] A similar trend, towards more general victuallers who sold a variety of foods and goods, can be tracked in both Durham and the small town of Ramsey in the fifteenth century. Bonney, *Lordship*, pp. 149–50; DeWindt and DeWindt, *Ramsey*, pp. 165, 167–8.

[212] May, 'Newmarket and its market court', 35.

[213] SRO (B), Acc.1476/1/28.

Table 9. *The prominent victuallers of Newmarket, 1400–1413*

	Status	Baker	Brewer	Regrater	Cook	Forestaller
Simon Baldewyne and wife	Pri		I	*	*	
John and Amicia Barbor	Pri	S-R	R	*	*	
Thomas Bette and wife		I	S-R	*	*	
Thomas Bolehed and wife		I	I		*	
John Chaundeler and wife	Pri	I	I		*	*
Robert Cheyne and wife	Pri	S-R	S-R	*	*	
John and Mariot Choun	Sec	R	I	*	*	
Thomas Cook and wife	Pri	R	R	*	*	*
Richard and Mariot Deke		I	I	*	*	
Peter Fedelere and wife	Pri	S-R	R	*	*	
William Fyschere and wife	Pri	S-R	R			
John and Beatrix Greyne	Sec	I	I	*	*	*
Thomas Maynard and wife	Pri	I	I		*	
John and Matilda Pepyr	Pri		I	*	*	*
John Ray and wife	Pri	I	S-R	*		
John Redere and wife	Pri	R	I	*	*	*
Matilda Rokelond			I	*	*	*
Robert Skynnere and wife	Pri		R	*	*	
John Smyth and wife	Pri	S-R	S-R	*	*	
Roger Smyth and wife	Pri	R	R	*		
Thomas Sowcere and wife	Pri	I	R	*		
Johanna Tapstere		I	S-R	*	*	
John Waleys and wife	Pri	R	R	*	*	

Notes: Pri: Primary office-holder; Sec: Secondary office-holder; R: Regular offender; S-R: Semi-regular offender; I: Irregular offender. Where both husband and wife are named in presentments, they are entered jointly here. The petty traders entered in this table were listed in at least three of the five stated categories of offences in the Newmarket court rolls. *Source:* SRO (B), Acc.1476/1/1–48.

which, presumably, were minor enough to be constantly overlooked by customers. Indeed, in Newmarket, Redere, Cook and other innkeepers opened their tenement doors onto the market or fair without the licence of the lord and were fined 3d.–24d. for doing so.[214] The court rolls recorded the reasoning behind such amercements by stating that Robert Cartere, by opening his door onto the market, had avoided tolls of the lord to the value of 40d.[215] However, licences were made available to those

---

[214] SRO (B), Acc.1476/1/21, 23, 34, 38, 39, 42, 44, 45, 48.
[215] SRO (B), Acc.1476/1/32. Similarly, any Leicester resident who opened their doors onto the marketplace during the market day, faced fines and even imprisonment. *Leicester*, ii, p. 292 (1467).

who applied for permission to open their doors, such as that obtained by John Ray in 1413. Enterprising activity can therefore be seen in the formalisation of inns and cookhouses. These establishments opened on a daily basis, provisioned both travellers and locals, and gradually their owners became more diversified in their sales and commercial activities. Overall, everyday demand was apparently significant enough to sustain quite a number of inns, alehouses and cooks.

Whereas innkeepers were sedentary traders based in permanent premises, cooks were more likely to hawk their pasties, pies and roasted meats in the marketplace, or from market stalls, like medieval 'fast-food' vendors. For instance, John and Beatrix Greyne and Richard and Mariot Deke travelled into Newmarket from Exning and Eriswell respectively to sell their cooked foodstuffs: roasted meat, pies, pastries and stews. However, in late medieval England, suspicions surrounded cooks concerning the wholesomeness of their food and practices. National and local regulations, as well as much literature, depicted a continual fear of unhealthy or badly cooked food.[216] Bailey and McIntosh have suggested that the proliferation of victual traders did not reduce any suspicions towards them, but instead, led to more claims of immoral excess and aberrant behaviour.[217] However, the court rolls of Newmarket and Clare do not show an excessive number of vehement accusations. In Clare, several cooks were accused of selling unwholesome meat and fish, and even corrupt candles, oil and butter.[218] However, they were only amerced between 2d. and 6d. each, which does not correspond to the opprobrium expressed in late medieval laws and literature.

There was perhaps a practical acceptance in local trading communities of the problems involved with perishability, storage and quality differences. Several butchers in Clare were accused of selling corrupt meat, but were fined just 4.7d. on average (see Table 8). William Auncel was presented nine times in the surviving court rolls for selling corrupt meat or at an excessive price, but he faced average amercements of just 4d. Outside butchers from Stanesfield and Stoke-by-Clare also faced average amercements of less than 4d. In July 1352, John Bory was amerced 3d. for selling an unbaited bull 'to the damage of all the community'.[219]

---

[216] See above, pp. 115–16 and 221–2.

[217] Bailey, *A Marginal Economy*, pp. 169–70; McIntosh, *Autonomy and Community*, pp. 255–9.

[218] TNA, sc2/203/62–7. There are also earlier cases of cooks selling reheated meat. TNA, sc2/203/49–59.

[219] TNA, sc2/203/49. Increasingly, by the fifteenth century, there were town ordinances that demanded that butchers should not kill any unbaited bulls; baiting usually involved dogs and was thought to make the meat tender. Coss (ed.), *Early Records of Medieval Coventry*, p. 42 (1278); Jeayes (ed.), *Court Rolls*, i, pp. 96–8 (1330); *CLB*, κ, p. 10 (1423); West Sussex Record Office (Chichester), 6/1/18 HVI Petworth (1440); *Great*

Several Clare butchers who were amerced regularly for excessive price and putrid meat were also capital pledges and jurors in the town, such as William Auncel, John Bory and William Gapold, while Thomas Skot and Thomas Bory even served as bailiffs. These were prosperous tradesmen, in the local context, and their influence may have been significant in tempering the level of punishment. However, it is also possible that a certain margin was accepted in the dealing of perishable foodstuffs, as long as it was not considered to be deliberate fraud. Similarly, in Framlingham, in the first few years of the fifteenth century, there were a few instances where butchers were accused of selling unwholesome and stale meat 'in abomination and prejudice' but were only amerced 3d.–6d.[220]

In Newmarket, there was a distinct lack of such presentments for corrupt meat. The election of a meat-taster, Richard Farwell, suggests that butchering had become an ample trade in Newmarket by the early fifteenth century, but there were no regular presentments on the scale of the assizes of bread and ale.[221] Occasionally, there were harsher fines, like the case recorded in 1421, when William Humfrey of Clare faced an amercement of 12d. for selling reheated horse meat in the market.[222] However, the general level of amercements for commercial offences was quite low. Figure 27 illustrates that the majority of amercements for Newmarket brewers, bakers, regraters, cooks and forestallers lay between 2d. and 4d. (60 per cent) or 2d. and 6d. (73 per cent), with an additional few at 8d. and 12d., presumably the more regular traders or innkeepers. Beyond that it was mostly individual regraters of ale who faced the highest amercements, rather than cooks or forestallers. In Clare, it is even more noticeable that there were just a handful of baking and butchering offences that faced 12d. amercements, along with some brewers, but that the majority of offences (60 per cent) were grouped in the 2d.–4d. range or even the 2d.–6d. range (81 per cent) (see Figure 28). There was perhaps a generally low level of actual commercial malpractice and fraud, which has been obscured behind the fiscal nature of the numerous small-town presentments for trading offences.

Quality and the consumer

There were few other instances of trading infringements in the Newmarket and Clare court rolls, beyond the statutory requirements for

---

Red Book, i, p. 144 (1452); Leicester, ii, pp. 133 (1363), 289 (1467), 321–2 (1489?); BL, MS Lansdowne 796, fol. 5r (late fifteenth century); Beverley, p. 129 (1510).
[220] Cambridge, Pembroke College, Framlingham Court Rolls C, D1, D2.
[221] SRO (B), Acc.1476/1/31.   [222] TNA, sc2/203/66.

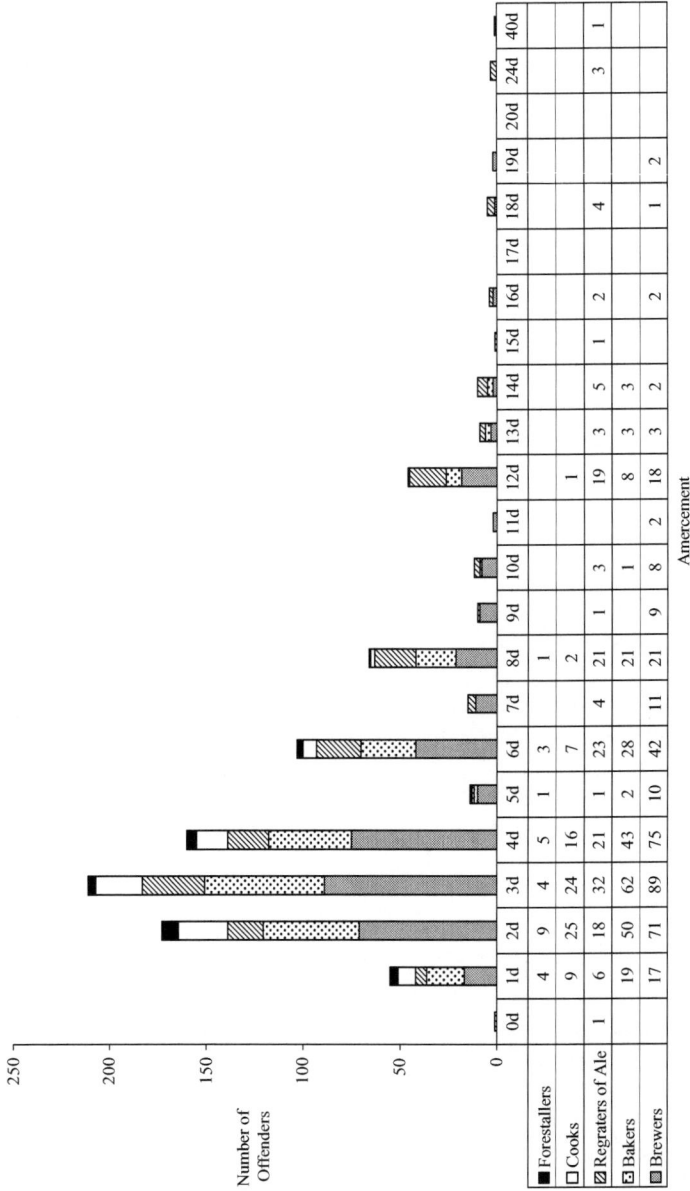

Figure 27: Frequency of amercements for trading offences in Newmarket, 1400–1413.

Notes: The total number of offences: brewers (383), bakers (240) regraters of ale (169), forestallers (27), cooks (84). A number of amercements were illegible or not given and they are not included here.
Source: SRO (B), Acc.1476/1/1–48.

	0d	1d	2d	3d	4d	5d	6d	7d	8d	9d	10d	11d	12d	13d	14d	15d	16d	17d	18d	19d	20d	24d	40d
Forestallers		4	9	4	5	1	3		1														
Cooks		9	25	24	16		7		2				1										
Regraters of Ale	1	6	18	32	21	1	23	4	21	1	3		19	3	5	1	2		4			3	1
Bakers		19	50	62	43	2	28		21		1		8	3	3								
Brewers		17	71	89	75	10	42	11	21	9	8	2	18	3	2		2		1	2			

Amercement

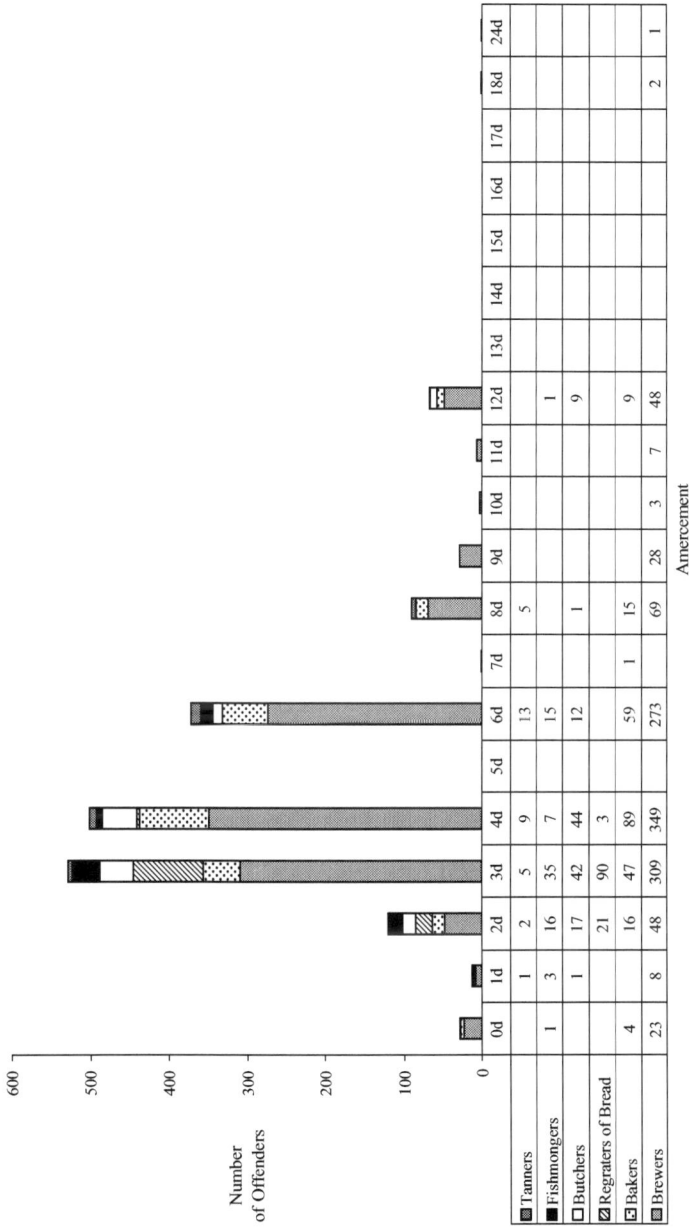

	0d	1d	2d	3d	4d	5d	6d	7d	8d	9d	10d	11d	12d	13d	14d	15d	16d	17d	18d	24d
Tanners		1	2	5	9		13		5											
Fishmongers	1	3	16	35	7		15	1												
Butchers		1	17	42	44		12		1				9							
Regraters of Bread			21	90	3															
Bakers	4		16	47	89		59	1	15				9							
Brewers	23	8	48	309	349		273		69	28	3	7	48						2	1

Amercement

Number
of Offenders

Figure 28: Frequency of amercements for trading offences in Clare, 1377–1425.

Notes: The total number of offences: brewers (1168), bakers (240), regraters (114), butchers (126), fishmongers (78), tanners (35). One amercement for a tanner was not given and is not included here.
Source: TNA, sc2/203/62–7.

assizes, weights and measures, reasonable price, regrating and fore-stalling. Indeed, there were hardly any indications of the flagrant decep-tions so vividly described by medieval moralists, and only a handful of court entries concerning susceptible quality. It is possible that some of the greater frauds were referred to the royal courts and thus escape mano-rial court rolls. Nevertheless, within local courts, there were sporadic instances where offences were evidently considered to be more signifi-cant, and perhaps more iniquitous, than breaches of the assize. They were often also brought to the attention of the court by individual consumers, rather than by court officials, suggesting that more controversial matters were not always captured by the system of presentment. In the court rolls for Newmarket, in 1407, Richard Derlyng claimed that Thomas atte Heel had fraudulently sold him a horse 'knowing it to be unsound in wind and limb' ('tubiis et membris') and yet warranting otherwise. Derlyng was awarded damages, including and above the 10s. value of the horse.[223] This was the type of offence that was directly condemned by works like *Ayenbite of Inwyt*.[224] Another case of quality and deception occurred in 1413, when William Parmenter was fined 20d. for selling insufficiently tanned leather to Robert Reeshin. This was the highest amercement for a tanning offence in Newmarket (most were fined just 3d.), suggesting that the offence was perhaps more flagrant or deliberate than usual.[225] The only other specific example of fraud listed in Newmarket's court rolls took place in 1408, when Laurence Horn sued John Baxtere, a stranger, for damages of 3s. 4d., claiming that he had been sold a brass pot that was actually made of lead. In fact, the jury decided that it was made of brass but had been badly cast ('insipida') and they only awarded damages of 4d.[226]

In Clare, there were similarly few cases of blatant deceit and most were initiated by individual pleas, which allowed a controversial case to be dealt with by a specially empanelled jury of inquisition. For instance, in 1357 John Onyton brought a plea of trespass against Richard Munde for selling him incompetently tanned leather; they reached a final agree-ment privately.[227] Otherwise, the tanners' amercements for badly tanned leather and excessive price appear to have become mere licence fees of between 3d. and 6d. This had long been the case, with Richard Munde's penalties of 12d.–24d. in the 1350s being the exception rather than the rule. In 1358, William Herde brought a suit against John Jay of Cavendish concerning fifteen pounds of woollen yarn he had given him for weaving.

[223] SRO (B), Acc.1476/1/28.   [224] *Ayenbite of Inwyt*, p. 44. See also above, p. 76.
[225] SRO (B), Acc.1476/1/47.   [226] SRO (B), Acc.1476/1/20.
[227] TNA, sc2/203/54.

When Jay produced the finished cloth for William it weighed less than eight pounds, though Jay denied the accusation.[228] In 1365, William Coupere sold and warranted to John Cardemaker a barrel containing twenty-four gallons of ale, but the ale proved to be defective and John claimed damages of 13s. 4d.[229] Beyond these cases, it seems that the extent of deceitful trading was either much lower than many moralists espoused or else traders were exceptionally good at escaping detection.

The above instances also demonstrate that quality was monitored as much by consumers as by officials, through personal pleas and juries of inquisition.[230] The actions of buyers were very important to the practices of trade. Dyer has argued that the decisions of consumers largely conformed to the geographical theories of purchasing, based on choice, quality and convenience, as well as their own purchasing power and transport.[231] But there were occasional idiosyncrasies in trading patterns based on personal links, preferences or inadequate information. Consumer awareness and choice were therefore important ingredients in the mix of trading behaviour. Modern anthropologist, Clifford Geertz, suggested that the reputed links between petty traders and deceitful activities arose mainly from asymmetry of information in a periodic market economy, rather than from the uninhibited 'acquisitive impulse' of men.[232] He argued that when a poor labourer or peasant, with little intensive knowledge of commercial conditions, bought from a retailer with business skills and information, the transaction could arouse suspicions and accusations based upon ignorance by the customer. This explains why, in medieval England, there was a widespread need for assizes and official intervention in the exchange of staple products. The system of the assizes standardised information that might otherwise be lacking and provided a basis upon which consumers could assess trading practices and prices. Equally, the assizes allowed bakers and brewers some flexibility and protected them from possibly inaccurate accusations of infringements.

Besides official regulatory tools, trading competition and personal reputation were the two main elements of 'informal' enforcement and cost minimisation, and both relied on consumer awareness. Where goods were widely available in the marketplace, consumer choice could help keep prices at the level demanded by law. This process of competition required a market in which the production of commodities was not restricted to a few. Indeed, a consumer's role in setting the conditions of a bargain was

---

[228] TNA, sc2/203/54.   [229] TNA, sc2/203/59.
[230] See also p. 318 for customer complaints against the wife of John Redere, and pp. 79–83 for moralists' views of customers.
[231] Dyer, 'Consumer'; Dyer, 'Trade, towns and the church', pp. 66–7.
[232] Geertz, Peddlers, p. 34.

heightened when there was abundance in vendors and commodities and reduced when there was scarcity. In times of abundance, traders who did not conform to expected basic levels of quality and fair price could suffer, for consumers simply took their business elsewhere. But when there were shortages in either staples or goods with growing demand (such as meat and wine), officials probably felt obliged to take action as the circumstances dictated.[233]

Conversely, for products of elastic demand, like cloth and spices, sellers and buyers were better placed to conduct a process of haggling. In his studies of the modern towns of Modjokuto (Indonesia) and Sefrou (Morocco), Geertz observed that haggling was a skilled process that allowed buyers and sellers to explore their respective market positions and needs in order to achieve a reasonable, agreed price. Bargaining itself was not merely utilitarian but could be hedged by mutually accepted moral and social etiquettes.[234] This rendered the process more transparent, for it enabled buyers to assess the risks and level of trust involved in the deal. Some moralists, such as John Gower, complained of lies and exaggeration during the bargaining process and an element of this naturally took place,[235] but excessive lies and failure to evoke trust could temper the possibility of concluding a deal.

In theory, long-term and reciprocal economic relationships ('clientelisation') reduced the costs of transacting by imposing their own social restraints, and would have been actively cultivated by both sellers and buyers.[236] The risks attached to making a bad purchase from an unknown trader were larger (if also potentially more profitable) than from a known trader where previous deals had been satisfactory. Reciprocal dealing would have existed at a high level in the petty trade of towns like Newmarket and Clare, unlike the impersonalised, short-run, maximising deals between strangers that epitomised classical economic theory and much modern marketing.[237] Few traders would have been actively involved in flagrant fraud if they thought they would be discovered or if it ultimately lost them business. An illustrative case occurred in West Halton (Lincolnshire) in 1315, when Cecily Ode called William the Clerk false for selling unsound ale. The court found that her slander had cost William

---

[233] Britnell, 'Forstall', 102.   [234] Geertz, *Peddlers*, pp. 32–6; Geertz, 'Suq', pp. 221–9.
[235] See pp. 71–2.
[236] Plattner, 'Economic behavior'; Geertz, 'Suq', pp. 204–8, 217–21. Douglass North stated that repeat dealings and personal knowledge of participants lowered transaction costs. North, 'Transaction costs', 560; North, *Institutions*, p. 51.
[237] Modern businesses recognise the worth of reciprocal relationships. They invest in the advertising of brand-names and quality-assurance as part of the attempt to encourage customers to engage in repeated dealings.

some 40d. in sales due to lost reputation.[238] The 1435 regulations for
wiredrawers, smiths and girdlers in Coventry extolled the importance
of not using 'gyle or disseyte' in their work 'lest he lost his custemers'.
An imaginary conversation between a wiredrawer and smith outlined
the consequences for those selling deceitful wares: 'Sir, I hadde of you
late badde wire. Sire, amend your honde, or, in feithe, I wille no more
bye of you.'[239] A mixture of rational self-interest and moral integrity
was needed to maintain an economic relationship. According to Geertz,
knowledge of a trader's personality, family and past became intrinsic to
the exchange and the level of risk, as well as criteria of the law.[240] In a
similar vein, Dyer also remarked on the importance of mutual trust and
working for the common good within medieval communities. Traders
who were defamed or 'lost credit' through failing to meet their debts
could damage their own precarious livelihoods.[241]

Medieval consumers were probably, as today, looking for the right
price, choice and quantity, and the flexible conditions of a small town
market might offer potential bargains for those prepared to accept the old
maxim of *caveat emptor*. But transactors also had the added protection of
a formal court system and of bailiffs watching day-to-day practices in case
flagrant abuses took place. The legal mechanisms of most late medieval
courts were undoubtedly influenced by cultural mentalities of the time.
The language of Clare and Newmarket's court rolls, for example, reflects
the borrowing of ideas or phrases from Church sermons, moral tracts and
other forms of literature. The clerks of Clare and Newmarket repeatedly
used expressions like 'for the common good' and 'excessive price' in justifying the prosecutions of offending traders, even if there was no definite
notion of their meanings or applicability.[242] The tag 'common' was frequently attached to brewers in the court roll presentments, advancing the
notion that they produced for the common profit or that they were more
regular and professional. Deveson has suggested that the epithet 'common' applied to traders presented for multiple offences, perhaps those
running more permanent establishments as hostelers.[243] However, the
term 'common' was used generically in Clare and Newmarket for a variety of bakers and brewers, regular and irregular, and seems to be more
a reminder of their duty to the public and the common good. Overall,
trading offences were recorded in court rolls in a very formulaic way and
generally referred to communal profits or peace. Nevertheless, elements

---

[238] Goldberg (ed.), *Women in England*, p. 174.   [239] *Coventry*, pp. 180–4 (1435).
[240] Geertz, 'Suq', pp. 221–9.   [241] Dyer, 'Urbanizing of Staffordshire', 26–7.
[242] Geertz, 'Suq', pp. 207–10.   [243] Deveson, 'Medieval Whitchurch', 105.

of legal flexibility and personal reputations also came into play beyond the mere reiteration of substantive law.[244]

In terms of the presentation of market traders, there was some variance between the information contained in Clare's and Newmarket's court rolls and the moralistic writings and sermons of churchmen. According to what the court rolls tell us, traders committed fewer major offences or deceits than medieval writers implied. The number of exceptional presentments or controversial pleas every year in Newmarket and Clare was meagre compared to the mass of trading transactions reflected in the volume of debt pleas. It is likely that local courts were highly pragmatic in choosing which infringements they considered to be more important (for example, those involving grain) and were willing to deal leniently with minor offences, or leave buyers and sellers to establish their trading relationships. In the prevailing economic circumstances of the fifteenth century, small town authorities like those of Newmarket and Clare preferred a lightly regulated, but efficient and competitive, marketplace, to the heavily controlled one which medieval writers like Langland and Gower demanded.

Credit and debt

Credit was vitally important in maintaining regular trade and its vitality hinged upon the good reputation of its participants and, most importantly, the ability of the court to handle speedily disputes and small debts. An examination of the debt pleas in both Newmarket and Clare reveals the effectiveness of the towns' market regulations as well as the informal mechanisms that existed in credit relationships.

A market court was held every two to three weeks in Newmarket and this institution handled the practical business of the market, particularly the settlement of debt disputes in personal pleas. These debt cases illustrate the diversity of commercial exchange within Newmarket.[245] Nevertheless, litigation itself only shows a small percentage of the transactions that actually occurred, since most were uncontentious. In addition, the amount of debt litigation is not necessarily a direct indication of the levels of credit at any given time, but rather the number of debtors unable to make repayments. It is likely that social pressure was often brought to bear before a dispute became intractable and a debt plea begun.[246]

---

[244] McIntosh, *Controlling*, pp. 38–40; Schofield, 'Peasants and the manor court'.

[245] For a discussion of the pleas of the market court, see May, 'Newmarket and its market court'.

[246] Briggs, 'Manor court procedures', 524. For a full discussion of the intricacies involved in interpreting the evidence of debt cases, see Briggs, *Credit and Village Society*.

However, an intricate network of credit is still revealed by the debt pleas, demonstrating vigorous economic activity and a capital market that oiled the wheels of trade.[247]

In the market court, a plea was initiated by the plaintiff either for debt, trespass, contract, or detention of chattels. Debt pleas accounted for 85 per cent of known pleas in Newmarket's courts, some 292 over 174 extant court roll sessions (across fifteen years) being a testimony to the availability of credit. However, any study of debt records, particularly in small towns, is hampered by the lack of detail provided by the rolls and the formulaic nature of the entries. Also, credit in late medieval small towns rarely involved written financial instruments and most remained oral and undocumented. In Newmarket, John Farewell and Thomas Stonham were both ordered to pay their debts when a written 'recognition' was produced, but there were no other instances.[248] Of the debts themselves, seventy-nine pleas gave details, but forty-one of these merely stated monetary values and it is difficult to know whether these were sales or money loans. A further twenty-nine concerned deferred payment for goods or advance payment for goods promised.[249] The goods mentioned in such debt cases included cloth, pots, utensils, sheep, horses, barley, malt, skins, leather, wool, pepper, onions, oats and a saddle. The remaining nine pleas involved rents, services, amercements or arrears. It appears that only a minority of pleas were initiated by non-traders since a significant majority of claimants were designated as 'mercator'. Although in some cases this was clearly a secondary occupation, the label confirmed the trading context of the plea.

The commercial nature of many of the pleas in the Newmarket records is also suggested by the value of the claims, as represented by either the stated amount or the value of detained goods. In either case, the majority of pleas were over 2s. and a very significant number were over 10s., amounts that indicated exchanges much larger than those merely for personal consumption (see Table 10).[250] Additionally, two deals involving sheep for £3 and 50s. respectively, and another for wool for £6 2s. 6d., show that the nominal upper limit of 40s. for local debt cases in

---

[247] Clark, 'Debt'; Schofield, 'L'endettement'; Postan, 'Credit'.

[248] In theory, a manorial court did not have the competence to test the validity of written instruments except tallies. Schofield, 'L'endettement', p. 81.

[249] Newmarket appears to have been more commercialised than Whittle, where Clark identified 50 per cent of all debts as involving credit sales. Clark, 'Debt', p. 254.

[250] Postles found that 47 per cent of loans at Loughborough involved debts over 5s., while in the villages of Kibworth Harcourt and Kibworth Beauchamp only 30 per cent were over 5s., and in the village of Barkby only 3 per cent. Postles, 'An English small town', 17–18.

Table 10. *Value of debt pleas in Newmarket courts, 1399–1413*

	<1s.	1s. 1d.–2s.	2s. 1d.–5s.	5s. 1d.–10s.	>10s.
Stated values	3	8	14	22	22
Attachments	15	17	36	40	53

Notes: The actual value of the debt claim, whether for money or goods, is known in sixty-nine cases, and these are shown as 'Stated Values'. An approximate value of the debt plea can also be ascertained by reference to the value of the attachment, which varied according to the particular case and often mirrored the debt claim where both values are specified (but could also be merely the items that were available to be attached at the time). These are listed under 'Attachments'.
Source: SRO (B), Acc.1476/1/1–48.

Table 11. *Value of debt pleas in Clare courts, 1377–1422*

	<1s.	1s. 1d.–2s.	2s. 1d.–5s.	5s. 1d.–10s.	>10s.
Stated values	14	15	15	17	26

Notes: The value of the debt plea is known in seventy-seven cases.
Source: TNA, sc2/203/62–7.

manorial courts was not always adhered to.[251] Nevertheless, most debts over 40s. (mostly long-distance trade) were probably handled in central or large borough courts, while the majority of cases in Newmarket were transactions of petty trade.[252] For instance, there were several credit-based exchanges of animal by-products, from butchers to tanners or chandlers.[253] Similarly, small grain transactions are documented within debt pleas: John Coupere, a brewer, was a defendant in a debt case with a dealer in barley, Ralph Parker; and Robert Cheyne, a cook, was twice in debt within a year and a half to John Bakere, a maltster, probably from Cambridge.[254]

The borough court of Clare handled debt cases in a similar fashion to Newmarket and, again, a significant number of claims were over 10s. in value (see Table 11). 517 debt pleas can be discerned from the

---

[251] SRO (B), Acc.1476/1/16, 43; Beckerman, 'Forty-shilling', pp. 110–17.
[252] For instance, in 1390, John atte Mere of Newmarket owed John Hadde, citizen and draper of London, £8 6s. 8d., either registered in Chancery or sealed under a recognisance of the Staple of Lynn, and Chancery issued a writ for the recovery of the debt and imprisonment of Mere. TNA, c131/208/3, 14.
[253] SRO (B), Acc.1476/1/1, 16, 29.   [254] SRO (B), Acc.1476/1/35, 36, 40.

surviving Clare courts for the years 1377 to 1422. Taking into account
the missing court rolls for both towns, this is comparable to the number
of debt cases per year presented in Newmarket. Nominally, there were
19.5 debt cases per year in Newmarket, but to this figure can be added
pleas of contract and the majority of the unknown pleas, so the final
average is closer to twenty-six, which is just above the average number of
debt cases per year in Clare (around sixteen to twenty). This is perhaps
surprising given the larger size of Clare, but it is perhaps an indication
of just how commercialised and organised Newmarket and its courts
had become. The Clare pleas are generally less informative than those
in Newmarket, but some useful material can be gleaned. There were
some 264 different plaintiffs and 267 different defendants in the Clare
debt pleas, demonstrating the wide use of the court. Of these, some forty
were plaintiffs in three or more cases and thirty-seven were defendants
in three or more cases. Some notable individuals can be identified from
those who appear most in debt pleas (five or more as either a plaintiff or
defendant).

Table 12 almost reads like a *Who's Who* of Clare's society and the
men who dominated the local community. William Orgon, a prominent
butcher who was often amerced for selling meat against the assize, seemingly had ongoing transactions with skinners, tanners, cooks and other
butchers in the town, some of which led to debt cases. One debt plea for
John Chapman in 1407 sought to gain payments of 7s. 6d. and 5s. for
meat and herring sold to John Grey some five years previously. In 1411,
he also recognised a debt of 18s. 9d. owed to John Caketon.[255] It was this
group of creditors and debtors who were involved in many of the pleas for
large sums: Thomas Coulyng faced claims for debts of 42s. and 12s., one
of which at least was for woollen cloth, while Giles Strut had a debt of
42s. 8d. As plaintiff, Hugh Frаuceys was owed some 23s. by a butcher
of Clare. However, it is noticeable that, apart from Hugh Frauceys,
John Burgeys, Agnes Imberd and William Orgon, those who pursued
debt pleas most often were men who had served as officers within the
town.

A number of the Clare debt pleas identify the commodities of transaction, such as woollen cloth, spun wool, barley, malt, straw, bark, pigs,
calves, meat and herrings. One credit exchange for 8s. worth of calves
even stipulated that they were bought on 2 May 1420 and would be paid
for on 26 May. The claim for an unpaid debt was sent to inquisition
on 17 June.[256] Additionally, Clare had several pleas which were judged
according to *lex mercatoria*. Merchant Law was used in five cases, from

[255] TNA, sc2/203/65.   [256] TNA, sc2/203/66.

Table 12. *Regular debtors and creditors in Clare, 1377–1422*

	Plaintiff (no.)	Defendant (no.)	Offices[a]	Occupation
John Baker Litil	6	7	CP, J, A	Baker
William Baker	9	2	B, CP	Baker
John Barker	3	6		Tanner?
William Brokhole	7	1	B	
Imbert Brus	5	0	B, CP, A	
John Burgeys	11	3		Butcher
John Chapman	7	5	CP, J	Merchant
Thomas Coulyng	2	6	A	Cloth-merchant
Alex Eustace	7	0	C, CP, J	
John Fadirless	5	2	B, C, CP, J, A	
Hugh Fraunceys	8	0		Merchant?
John Fuller	5	1	CP, J	Thatcher
Agnes Imberd	5	0		Brewer
William Orgon	7	5		Butcher
William Praty	5	1	CP, J, A	Cloth-merchant
John Robat	4	8		Fishmonger
Thomas Scot	5	7	B, CP	Butcher
William Smyth	6	0	C, CP	
John Stoke	5	1	B, CP, A	Innkeeper?
Adam Stonhard	5	1	B, CP	
Giles Strut	1	5	CP, J	
Elias Wheler	0	5		Brewer/Innkeeper?
John Wode	2	5	B, C, CP, J	Brewer/Innkeeper?
William Wryghte	1	9		Butcher?

Notes: This table includes all individuals who appeared at least five times either as a plaintiff or a defendant. Offices are listed if they served at least once: a – bailiff (B), constable (C), capital pledge (CP), juror (J), aletaster (A). It is not possible to assign occupations to all these individuals. Those which have been designated are taken from references in the court rolls and assize amercements. It is possible that they undertook more than one trade or changed trades during this period.
Source: TNA, sc2/203/62–7.

1377 to 1422, all for fairly substantial amounts (3s., 5s., 5s. 8d., 7s. and 21s. 6d.).[257] Thornton has argued that these pleas emanated from a separate market court held by burgesses for the speedy settlement of trading disputes in the market or fair; there are just a couple of references to such a court in the 1340s but it may have continued in the hands of the burgesses.[258] Instead of viewing it as separate court with different

[257] TNA, sc2/203/40, 62, 64.   [258] Thornton, *A History of Clare*, pp. 37–8, 177.

officials or court rolls, it is more likely it was an exceptional subsidiary of the borough court that allowed Merchant Law and piepowder procedures to be utilised at short notice. It was held infrequently and the results were collated at the borough court. Clare either did not have the level of business or little inclination to constitute a market court more formally in the manner of Newmarket.

Overall, the commercial bias of debt pleas in Newmarket and Clare is perhaps unsurprising, given their dominant market profiles. The following summary of the local commercial credit system is based mostly around Newmarket, but relevant comparisons are drawn with Clare. In all, there were 204 different plaintiffs and 195 defendants in Newmarket debt cases, including thirty-nine plaintiffs and thirty-four defendants who resided outside the town. In addition, fifty-four plaintiffs made two or more pleas, of whom eight were of primary status and twelve of secondary. Similarly, of fifty multiple defendants, there were only four of primary status and six of secondary. This tentatively suggests that wealthier Newmarket residents were more likely to be creditors, but not exclusively. Indeed, a number of higher-status individuals were involved in debt cases as both plaintiffs and defendants.

Women were also not excluded from pleading, but only a handful of debt cases in Newmarket show women as sole plaintiffs or defendants. It is possible that most of these women were widows or single women, and that husbands generally acted as legal representatives for their wives in debt pleas.[259] Beatrix Skynnere was certainly a widow when she appeared as a defendant in 1406, while Matilda Rokelond, Cristina Croxton, Mariot Fokes, Elisabeth Brunne and Amicia Leeff can also be identified as single women at the time of their debt cases. Conversely, Dionisia Petrych was actually named with her husband when she appeared as a debtor in 1403, as was Agnes Tapstere (and her husband) in a plea of broken contract in 1409. The evidence of the rolls, however, suggests that men were considered to be the primary suitors in court and this makes it very difficult to estimate the true extent of female credit participation. There were no provisions for *femme sole* and independent agency in Newmarket. This does not mean that wives were not involved in debt and credit relations, merely that their husband had legal responsibility. Married women would have had the support of their husband's capital and credit networks, as well as his representation

---

[259] Bennett found that no married women appeared as parties to pleas of debt or broken contract in Brigstock. Mostly it was single or widowed women. Bennett, *Women*, pp. 110–11.

in court.[260] However, conversely, this might have affected assessments of risk and marginalised women's ability to obtain credit on their own.[261]

On many manors, it appears that few women were involved directly in credit relations, usually less than 10–15 per cent of all litigants if the evidence of debt records is a valid indicator.[262] This situation appears to pertain in Clare, where thirty-three different women appear across twenty-four debt cases as plaintiff and twenty-two as defendant, which together constitute some 9 per cent of all cases and 5 per cent of participants. The most notable female individuals in Clare were Matilda Hale, Margaret Coulyng and Agnes Imberd, who all appear in debt pleas more than once, with Matilda and Margaret acting as both plaintiff and defendant in separate pleas. Matilda Hale's debts were sometimes fairly substantial, ranging from 1s. to 12s., while in one case she was owed 4s., though this was well below the level of many debts incurred by male suitors. Margaret Coulyng was certainly married, but it is uncertain whether the other two were; all were amerced several times for brewing and selling ale. It is possible that their debt pleas were related to the ale trade, both in purchases of malt and in sales credit. However, this is only a supposition because the cases rarely provide details of the reasons behind the debt. Nevertheless, there is another example of a common female by-occupation when Margaret Praty claimed 3s. from Thomas Haner in 1379 for spun wool.[263] In all forty-six cases the woman is solely named; there are only five additional cases where the husband and wife appear together, which appears to be an exceptional arrangement. This does not mean that all these other women were single or widows and, indeed, some can be identified as married, which suggests that in certain commercial pleas they could act alone, effectively operating as *femme sole* even if this privilege was not formally enrolled. It is also notable that women acted as executors of their husband's wills, such as Avelena Imberd who defended a significant debt claim from John Seler in 1401 for £4 10s. of woollen cloth.[264] The courts were certainly not closed to

---

[260] McIntosh, *Working Women*, pp. 96–7.

[261] Briggs, 'Empowered or marginalized?', 23–5. Briggs argues that the role of women in credit relations may have been greater during the sixteenth century. See also Muldrew, *Economy of Obligation*. Bennett and Mate have both suggested that the popular depiction of alewives as corrupt and deceitful may have affected the credit-worthiness of women. Bennett, 'Misogyny'; Mate, *Daughters, Wives and Widows*, pp. 66–7.

[262] Briggs, 'Empowered or marginalized?', 13–15; Clark, 'Debt', p. 252; McIntosh, *Autonomy and Community*, p. 219; Postles, 'An English small town', 28.

[263] TNA, sc2/203/64.   [264] TNA, sc2/203/65.

female suitors in Clare and some took advantage of this to engage in credit dealings.

The use of credit did involve a wide range of people and traders from various backgrounds. Some historians have noted that in rural courts, vertical ties of dependence were common because loans were mainly for consumption and were made repeatedly from wealthier to poorer villagers. However, Chris Briggs has challenged this traditional view and has highlighted the extent of horizontal borrowing in the medieval villages of Cambridgeshire, often for investment as much as consumption.[265] In market centres we would similarly expect to find a broad pattern of horizontal indebtedness where parties acted as both debtors and creditors.[266] In Newmarket, thirty-four people were both creditors and debtors. This included five of primary status, ten of secondary status and three outsiders. Nearly all of them were involved in capital-intensive trades, as can be identified by cross-referencing the information within the court rolls. These trades were: six barley, malt or grain dealers; eight butchers, leather or livestock dealers; seven 'prominent victuallers' or innkeepers; four cloth traders; two spicers; a saddler; and a timber trader. Capital flow was dependent upon complicated commercial relationships and the welfare of creditors and debtors was interlinked.[267] Like clientelisation in exchange, the use of credit in a town like Newmarket involved a level of trust, which could be diminished by the failure of one party to keep to an agreed schedule. Additionally, in petty trade, it is unlikely that a creditor wanted individual debts to mount up, since debtors would then control too much of his capital and the risk of default was also too great for the creditor to bear the financial burden.[268] Reciprocity was one means to temper this liability, with repeated credits and debts effectively cancelling each other out. Unless there was a reciprocal movement of money and commerce, which kept the overall debt small, most traders probably preferred to recoup their debts at regular intervals.[269] In the Clare court rolls, for instance, many of the named commodity debts were brought to court around Easter, when accounts were traditionally settled.[270]

---

[265] Briggs, *Credit and Village Society*.

[266] Clark noted a high level of horizontal and reciprocal debt at Writtle, reflecting a relatively significant amount of commercial activity. Clark, 'Debt', pp. 264–71. See also Britnell, *Growth and Decline*, p. 104. Kowaleski noted otherwise in Exeter. Kowaleski, *Local Markets*, p. 108.

[267] Clark, 'Debt', pp. 269–70; Geertz, *Peddlers*, p. 37.

[268] Dyer, *Standards*, pp. 179–80; Schofield, 'L'endettement', p. 77.

[269] Geertz, *Peddlers*, p. 37.   [270] TNA, sc2/203/66.

Personal plaints began by an oral approach to the court officers and then the defendant was summoned. They were allowed five essoins (excuses), one at each consecutive court, before they had to appear before the court and answer the plea. John Skynnere and Richard Gardyner, for example, both lost cases because they failed to appear at one of five consecutive Newmarket court sessions.[271] During this time distraint could be taken and personal pledges found for their attached goods. Pledges might be required at other points during the plea for both the plaintiff and defendant. There were then several ways by which a debt plea proceeded in court: the defendant defaulted by failing to appear; the plaintiff withdrew his plea; the defendant recognised the debt; both parties agreed to a private settlement away from the court ('licentia concordandi'); or, if the defendant denied any liability, the case was decided by a jury or the 'waging of one's law' (compurgation). In Table 13, a large percentage of the known cases for Newmarket (35.6 per cent for debt pleas) led to a request for a licence of concord, whereby the defendant paid 3d. and the parties were allowed to reach a private settlement outside the court. In these cases, both parties would have weighed up the costs and benefits of ending a plea early compared to pursuing the more fulsome mechanisms of the court for dispute settlement. In a further 23.8 per cent of debt pleas, the defendant appeared at court ('ponit se'), but no further decision was recorded, perhaps implying that an agreement was reached privately without using any further mechanisms of the court, or that the defendant had recognised the debt and agreed to pay.[272] This could also be the reason for the 13.8 per cent of cases where a plaintiff did not prosecute after initially bringing the plea. Alternatively, the plaintiff may have realised the futility of continuing the plea to a successful conclusion. In these instances, the plaintiff was liable to pay an amercement to the lord's coffers. Generally, the figures for 'debt pleas only' are similar to those for all pleas, as can be seen in Table 13. Interestingly, if a decision was taken by the court, as in 22.7 per cent of 'all pleas', it was four times more likely to go in favour of the plaintiff. In debt cases this ratio increased slightly to 5:1, with 26.8 per cent of debt pleas being decided within the court.

It is possible that many plaintiffs merely tried to spur defendants into agreeing to a licence of concord by initiating a plea. The conclusive bias of court decisions in favour of plaintiffs may have left most defendants with

---

[271] SRO (B), Acc.1476/1/16.

[272] May argued that 'ponit se', entered above a defendant's name, meant that the court agreed that the case could be settled privately; May, 'Newmarket and its market court', 37. However, if there are no further mentions of the case, it can only be surmised that the defendant either admitted liability or else a private settlement was reached.

Table 13. *Debt plea decisions in Newmarket, 1399–1413*

	Debt pleas		All pleas	
	No	%	No.	%
Defendant to settle privately[a]	72	35.6%	127	39.4%
Defendant presents himself at court[b]	48	23.8%	78	24.2%
Plaintiff does not proceed	28	13.9%	44	13.7%
Decision in favour of plaintiff	45	22.3%	58	18.0%
Decision in favour of defendant	9	4.5%	15	4.7%
Sub-total	202		322	
Unknown outcome[c]	90		140	
Total	292		462	

Notes: a – this generally referred to a licence of concord; b – a defendant appeared before the court ('ponit se') but no further action was taken or noted; c – several cases were initiated by the plaintiff but there was no further mention or detail in the court records; 'All pleas' includes 118 pleas of unknown type, twenty-one trespass, fourteen contract, eight detention of chattels and nine miscellaneous.

Source: SRO (B), Acc.1476/1/1–48.

little choice. If a defendant did deny liability, they had two basic options. The first course was waging law, or compurgation, which involved the testimony of a certain number of 'sufficient' men as to the good character and honesty of the defendant. They were, in effect, character witnesses and could be used when no firmer written or oral proof was available. If a defendant met the requirements of the court for a certain number of wagers, then he was quit of all charges. In Newmarket, eleven debt cases were concluded by a defendant waging their law, while in Clare, there were four (between 1377 and 1422), with each case requiring a different number of pledges (from three to six).[273] The weakness of compurgation was that it might favour residents against outsiders, as well as those of higher socio-economic status. For instance, in Newmarket, when a servant pleaded against John Beck for 5s. worth of unpaid services, the latter man had sufficient social status to be able to successfully wage his law with six hands. However, this system did not necessarily prejudice outsiders, provided they had local connections; in Clare, in 1377, John Sadeler of Newmarket successfully waged his law with three hands that he did not owe 18d. to Reginald Colemaker.[274]

[273] TNA, sc2/203/62, 65.   [274] TNA, sc2/203/62.

The other alternative for defendants was a trial by an 'inquisition' jury of twelve men. This occurred in Newmarket on thirty-eight occasions in debt pleas and the jury could either uphold the plaintiff's plea or decide that they had brought an unjust plea. It could be argued that the formalisation of the jury system encouraged plaintiffs to litigate in the expectation of more predictable results.[275] Certainly, Newmarket's court rolls give no indication of dissension against the decisions of juries and the vast majority of decisions went in favour of the plaintiff. There were, however, occasional problems in gathering twelve jurors to judge the case, with groups of them defaulting at the allocated time. The fines for shirking jury-duty were low at first, indicating that the authorities of a town were sympathetic to the problems of time-management. However, the bailiffs who organised these juries were also anxious to uphold the integrity of the market court and protect the court's ability to conclude cases. Thus, continual delays could lead to severe penalties of 2s.–3s. being threatened and sometimes enforced on persistently defaulting jurors.[276]

Judging by the evidence, market court officials attempted to deal with cases as swiftly as possible. Most cases in Newmarket were initiated at one court session and a decision about the procedure to be adopted, including licences of concord, was heard at the next court a fortnight or so later. From the initial plea to a final conclusion, the time span varied from six to twenty-one weeks, depending partly upon the number of sessions during that period. However, the majority, even those partly delayed, were completed within three months.[277] A further facility was available to some plaintiffs to call the defendant five times during one session. There were fifteen instances of this procedure in the Newmarket court rolls, including some in the fair court, such as between Thomas Tenersham and Peter Wanton on 29 October 1408. Similarly, on 3 July 1408, Walter Truyt failed to appear after being called five times in a plea brought by John Grase.[278] Although the term was not used in the rolls, this procedure was the equivalent of a 'piepowder court', which allowed a speedy decision for plaintiffs who might have business elsewhere.[279] Outside of the fair, plaintiffs presumably had to show good reason to

---

[275] Beckerman argued that there was an increasing use of trial juries in manorial courts from the late thirteenth century, replacing the hitherto dominant role of the whole body of suitors and encouraging more litigation; Beckerman, 'Procedural innovation'.

[276] SRO (B), Acc.1476/1/1, 6, 7, 13, 15, 16, 19, 20, 25, 28, 35, 36, 43, 46, 47.

[277] In the manorial court of Oakington, Briggs found that most pleas, in the period 1351 to 1380, took under six months to complete. Briggs, 'Manor court procedures', 541.

[278] SRO (B), Acc.1476/1/29.   [279] See p. 208.

demand such a piepowder court, which was potentially disadvantageous for defendants.

The court rolls of Clare are much less informative than those of Newmarket regarding debt cases and seemingly less intensive in their enforcement mechanisms. Nevertheless, the following observations can be made. Plaintiffs could initiate pleas upon payment of 1d.–3d.[280] Further amercements were required at the second (3d.–4d.), third (3d.–6d.) and fourth (6d.–12d.) summons, but it is not clear whether this was payable by the defendant or plaintiff. Plaintiffs were, however, charged an additional 2d.–4d. if that plea was found to be false or if they failed to pursue the prosecution. Defendants faced amercements of 2d.–6d. if the inquisition found against them, in addition to payment of the debt and damages. Defendants could be distrained to encourage attendance, and the court rolls suggest that they could be summoned up to five times before they forfeited any attachment. Giles Strut was exceptionally called five times before he recognised a debt of 42s. 8d. to Nicholas Andrew, but he also had to pay 12d. damages on 15 December 1416. John Casse was called four times between 8 October and 24 December 1397 to answer Thomas Gerold in a plea of debt, before they decided to pursue a private agreement through a licence of concord on 28 January 1398. John Belcham and William Vynt took four summons and nearly six months (2 August 1412 to 14 January 1413) before they too accepted a private settlement.

Licences of concord were the most dominant form of debt settlement in Clare, with some 66 per cent of pleas being settled privately (see Table 14) after a payment of 2d.–3d., probably by the defendant. In addition, there were forty-two recognitions by the defendant that they were liable for the debt and the cases are no longer pursued after a payment of 2d.–3d. by the debtor and an order that payment be levied. It may be that in these cases the level of proof was strong enough to ensure that the defendant did not dispute the claim. Yet, equally, in a large number of cases (14 per cent) the plaintiff failed to proceed with the prosecution by not appearing in court to pursue their plea. In another sixty-nine cases, the debt was disputed and several options were used. In fifty-six cases the plea was considered through an inquisition by jury, while six followed the procedures of law merchant, and five were resolved by compurgation. On two further occasions the defendant defaulted by failing to appear. As in Newmarket, there does appear to have been some difficulty in getting

---

[280] By comparison, Briggs found in his village case studies that, unless the case was lost, plaintiffs were not charged by the lord for initiating debt litigation. Briggs, *Credit and Village Society*, p. 13.

Table 14. *Debt plea decisions in Clare, 1377–1422*

	Debt pleas	
	No.	%
Defendant to settle privately[a]	334	66.1%
Defendant recognises debt[b]	42	8.3%
Plaintiff does not proceed	72	14.3%
Decision in favour of plaintiff	29	5.7%
Decision in favour of defendant	28	5.5%
Sub-total	505	
Unknown outcome[c]	12	
Total	517	

Notes: a – this generally refers to a licence of concord; b – a defendant appeared before the court and recognised that he/she was liable for the debt, which the court ordered should be paid; c – several cases went to inquisition but there was no further mention or detail in the court records.

Source: TNA, sc2/203/62–7.

the juries to assemble to inquire into debt cases and there are several cases of non-appearance by jurors, leading to individual amercements of 2d.–4d. However, there are forty-five inquisition cases where a decision can be discerned or is implied. In eleven cases the outcome is not known. In nine cases the jury assessed the amount of debt and damages, which suggests that a decision was made in favour of the plaintiff. In inquisition cases, plaintiffs and defendants are almost equally balanced in achieving favourable outcomes. However, when law merchant was employed in six cases, to quicken the proceedings, then plaintiffs invariably proved successful (in five out of six), while the opposite was true for the five occasions when compurgation was used (four for the defendant and one unknown).

Newmarket and Clare officials enforced the decisions of the court through powers of distraint and attachment. To ensure the defendant's compliance upon the initiation of a plea, the bailiff retained property from the defendant as security. Any defaulting defendant forfeited their attached goods. These attachments mirrored the value of the debt being pleaded, though they also reflected what was available to be attached at the time. This accounted for the prevalence of horses (52 per cent) as attached items in Newmarket, which were a vital tool for the itinerant trader (see Figure 29). Other prominent attachments, such as meat, leather and grain, illustrate the commercial property of the debtors. There

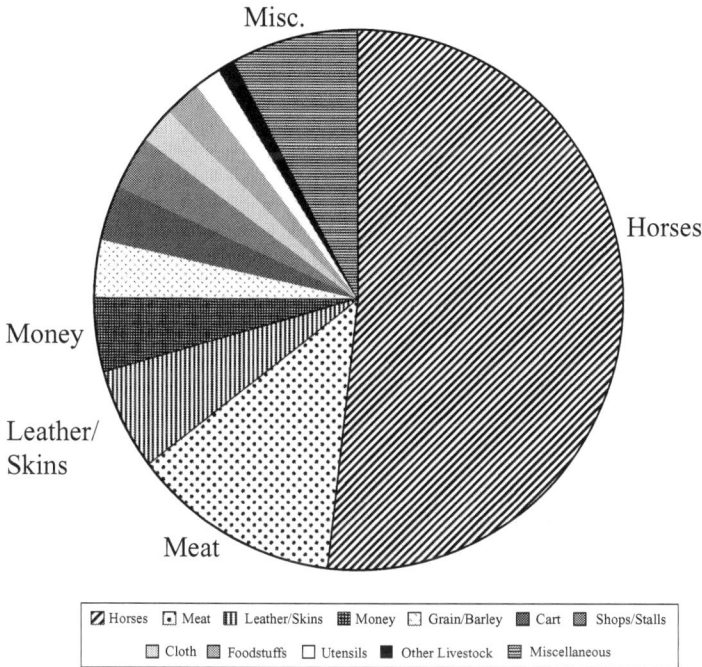

Figure 29: Attachments in Newmarket debt cases.
Source: SRO (B), Acc.1476/1/1–48

were even attachments of market stalls.[281] Similarly, in Clare, the items distrained in debt cases, from 1377 to 1422, included horses, woollen cloth, skins, pots, bowls, clothes, boots, cards, a pair of shears, a cart, pigs, money and a lead vessel. All attachments were valued by fellow traders. In Newmarket, there was a pound for horses and animals, while other commodities were put into the hands of trusted members of the community, usually bailiffs or ex-bailiffs. The system of distraint and attachment in these towns appears to have been organised and fairly effective.

One of the most important elements of the plea procedure was the system of pledging. Although there is no evidence that this system was used in Clare, pledges were seemingly a vital aspect of the Newmarket debt-case procedures. Pledges were needed in Newmarket at various stages of

[281] SRO (B), Acc.1476/1/33.

a case, to allow the plaintiff to proceed with a suit, to ensure a defendant's appearance and to guarantee payments. Plaintiffs often required a pledge to initiate a plea so that an amercement could be guaranteed if they lost the case, or if they were judged to have brought an unjust plea.[282] Theoretically, the pledge was responsible for the defaults of those they had pledged for, but there are no recorded cases of this happening in Newmarket. Pledges had to be acceptable to the court and were either the bailiff or regular, respectable stallholders, who were probably chosen via their relationship with the claimant as a friend, relative or business associate. The most consistent pledges in Newmarket were Thomas Sowcere, William Godard, Thomas Pere, Adam Foster, Peter Fedelere and John Chaundeler. These bailiffs and ex-bailiffs constituted 59 per cent (130 of 211 prosecution pledgings; 12 of 30 defence pledgings) of all pledges in debt pleas. It is likely that they were pledges as part of their official duties. Additionally, those of a higher socio-economic status (including bailiffs) undertook 81 per cent of pledgings (169 of 211 prosecution pledgings; 26 of 30 defence pledgings) and consequently dominated the court mechanisms of security.

Edwin DeWindt and Ambrose Raftis argued that reciprocal pledging emphasised the solidarity of community and that a decline in pledging demonstrated a weakening of community spirit. However, Martin Pimsler suggested that most pledges were paid and non-reciprocal; while Dave Postles maintained that pledging was an institutional relationship and did not always reflect friendship or kinship, merely the social control of the elite. Similarly, Richard Smith highlighted socio-economic divisions and status as significant in pledging. Consequently, the pledging system worked against outsiders and much pledging took place within a small nucleus of principal men. A core elite was distinguished by reciprocal pledging from the majority who relied upon official pledges.[283] For some, therefore, pledging was intended as a reciprocal arrangement and encouraged cooperation and mutual support. If traders could call upon someone they trusted, this encouraged the initial use of credit and ensured lower negotiation and enforcement costs. Those who regularly visited Newmarket from the surrounding region were perhaps also able to call upon trusted pledges. However, those from further afield may have been at more of a disadvantage and probably had to rely upon the bailiff to support their claim.

---

[282] May, 'Newmarket and its market court', 35
[283] DeWindt, *Land and People*, pp. 242–63; Raftis, *Tenure and Mobility*, pp. 101–4, 263–75; Pimsler, 'Solidarity'; Postles, 'Personal pledging'; Smith, 'Kin and neighbours'; Olson, 'Jurors of the village court', 245–7.

Kowaleski has found that the courts of Exeter had a clear bias in favour of burgesses, with outsiders and the unenfranchised being less successful in obtaining guilty verdicts and more often declared to have false claims.[284] Was such a bias evident in the small town of Newmarket, which did not have the apparatus of a borough charter? Outsiders can sometimes be identified in the records because they were documented as a stranger or their home town was listed, perhaps as an aide to the bailiff's duties of distraint. A cautious comparison of all pleas involving outsiders and Newmarket residents can be made, given the data available. An examination of cases where a defendant failed to turn up shows that outsiders were much more recalcitrant than Newmarket residents, though this may have been more logistical than deliberate. In comparing the cases won by the plaintiff to those won by the defendant, outside plaintiffs had only a $2\frac{1}{2}$ to 1 ratio of finding a decision went in their favour, whereas Newmarket plaintiffs had a success ratio of 6 to 1. This implies an element of bias or advantage for locals. Conversely, a Newmarket defendant was more likely to lose his case, at 8 to 1, while an outside defendant faced only a 3 to 1 ratio of having to pay (see Table 15). Residents of Newmarket were probably more readily attached and impelled to come to court and this was reflected in a high percentage of Newmarket defendants proceeding to jury or oath.

The figures, based on Newmarket's court rolls, are very difficult to interpret, especially since so many did not record the final outcome. Also, the generally low number of decisions in favour of the defendant (only nine in debt cases and fifteen in all) means that the ratios are not necessarily significant as statistical evidence. The additional difficulty of identifying the home town for all outsiders means that a comparison between those from the immediate hinterland and those from further afield is impractical. The general impression given is that there was some bias in decision-making, but much of this may have been due to practical and logistical concerns, rather than a deliberate prejudice. For instance, outside defendants did not significantly suffer in decisions compared to Newmarket defendants, and there was also representation by outsiders from the immediate hinterland on market court juries and as pledges. It is likely that outsiders who appeared frequently in the local market increased their creditworthiness. An interesting case in 1405 involved two outsiders who appear to have chosen the Newmarket court as neutral ground in order to settle their dispute. John Maliard of East Dereham brought a plea of debt against John Wynde of Bury St Edmunds concerning arrears in his accounts of ten marks, the latter being Maliard's

[284] Kowaleski, *Local Markets*, pp. 215–21.

Table 15. *Plea decisions for resident and outside litigants in Newmarket, 1399–1413*

	Defendants from Newmarket[a]		Defendants from elsewhere[b]		Plaintiffs from Newmarket[a]		Plaintiffs from elsewhere[b]	
	No.	%	No.	%	No.	%	No.	%
Defendant to settle privately	28	40.6%	37	39.4%	38	45.2%	38	8.1%
Defendant presents himself at court	14	20.3%	25	26.6%	18	21.4%	19	24.1%
Plaintiff does not proceed	8	11.6%	8	8.5%	8	9.5%	8	10.1%
Decision in favour of plaintiff	17	24.6%	18	19.1%	17	20.2%	10	12.7%
Decision in favour of defendant	2	2.9%	6	6.4%	3	3.6%	4	5.1%
Sub-total	69		94		84		79	
Unknown outcome	47		36		41		29	
Total	116		130		125		108	

Notes: a – residents who are named as being from Newmarket or are known to be so from other references; b – the court rolls often specifically identified the home town of plaintiffs and defendants. The data are taken from all pleas, a large number of which may have been debts but are not specifically identified as such (see Table 13). Unfortunately, there are not enough data and identifications of origin to be able to compare conclusively known debt pleas.

Source: SRO (B), Acc.1476/1/1–48.

bailiff.[285] The men perhaps had links to the market or residents of the town, while the lord would not have discouraged additional jurisdictional revenue. Ultimately, this was an example of two men who probably trusted the efficiency and procedures of the Newmarket court, as well as appreciating how the procedures of the court had developed to suit the needs of litigants.

Overall, the procedures in Newmarket's market court were standardised and seemingly efficient, which would have bred confidence in creditors even when debtors defaulted. The costs of pleading were also not

[285] SRO (B), Acc.1476/1/25; May, 'Newmarket and its market court', 32.

excessive, especially when one considers that most debt claims were over 2s. The main amercement of 3d.–6d. for the plaintiff was apparently for the initiation of the plea. The defendant was then amerced for failures to appear and for licences of concord. The main burden of expense thus fell upon those defendants who continually delayed proceedings. In 18 per cent of cases plaintiffs had to pay extra costs when they decided not to continue the prosecution or if they lost their case, and this small risk had to be balanced against the sum they could possibly recover and any damages they might receive. Presumably the plaintiff had previously resorted (unsuccessfully) to more informal means of recovery. Considerations of cost and time were then taken into account before proceeding to litigation. Some plaintiffs returned several times to enforce varied debts in the courts. The number of presentments and the recording of attachments in a significant number of cases seem to indicate that decisions were successfully implemented. There were certainly instances of attachments being yielded to the plaintiff when the defendant defaulted. With the majority of cases being decided, often by licence, within one to three months, the process of litigation appeared to be relatively efficient. Overall, compared to central courts where delays and deliberate stalling were common, the cases at Newmarket were speedy and plaintiffs had a good chance of recovering their debt. Indeed, Elaine Clark argued that plaintiffs considered it worthwhile to pursue a case if the result was either an agreement to settle privately, a defendant presenting themselves at court, or a decision in favour of the plaintiff.[286] Some 82 per cent of known outcomes ended in one of these scenarios for plaintiffs in Newmarket. Similarly in Clare, 80 per cent of cases were decided this way, though many more went to licence of concord in Clare than in Newmarket.

It should not be assumed that interest was charged on credit deals, which were often reliant on intangible personal and social rewards. However, there must have been occasions when supplementary incentives to extend credit were required. Usury was illegal and condemned as immoral by the Church and thus any interest charges were hidden.[287] There are few overt cases in Newmarket or Clare. In an unusual entry for Clare in 1347, John le Parker was fined 40d. as a 'common usurer of divers things in his merchandise', perhaps reflecting an exceptionally flagrant offence.[288] In the normal run of cases, interest was possibly

---

[286] Clark, 'Debt', p. 253.

[287] It has been argued that by the fourteenth century only extortionate usury was forbidden by the Church, though this might have applied more to consumption loans than trading deals. Most might have preferred to conceal interest rates to avoid accusations. See above, pp. 213–15.

[288] TNA, sc2/203/46.

Table 16. *Damages claimed and awarded in Clare and Newmarket courts*

		% of principal	
	No. of cases	Inter-quartile range	Mean
Newmarket			
Original Claim	20	25–50%	36.3%
Adjusted by Jury	15	2.8–15.4%	12.2%
Clare			
Original Claim	8	33.3–66.7%	64.9%
Adjusted by Jury	34	4.5–11.1%	9.3%

Notes: The Newmarket figures are from 1399–1413; Clare from 1377–1422.
Source: SRO (B), Acc.1476/1/1–48; TNA, sc2/203/62–7.

concealed in 'purchase price advances', where cash was paid immediately but the delivery of goods came at a later date when the market price of those goods had changed.[289] Alternatively, did the awards of 'damages' represent a way of charging licit interest payments? Plaintiffs could claim damages and, in response, jurymen decided what they considered reasonable. This decision was perhaps dependent on the type and value of the deal, the costs of initiating the plea, or else related to whether the creditor had lost money due to the delay in repayment. There was a fine theoretical margin between damages as recompense for loss and as an interest charge.[290] Briggs found that there was no systematic guarantee of damages in rural debt pleas, nor did creditors regularly claim them.[291] In addition, payment of damages was reliant on default by the debtor, so they did not provide a guaranteed profit upon loans, unless there was some form of collusion between the creditor and debtor. Damages were perhaps not directly analogous to interest charges, but rather represented a penalty on overdue debts.

Newmarket's court certainly accepted damages as routine in debt pleas. On average, in twenty cases, the plaintiffs requested damages of 36.3 per cent of the principal, with the majority distributed around this figure.[292] Rarely did they receive such amounts and the juries lowered the rate to an average of about 12 per cent (see Table 16). Even this

---

[289] Briggs, *Credit and Village Society*, pp. 38–9, 74–7.
[290] Schofield, 'L'endettement', pp. 92–3; See also Bailey, 'Peasant welfare', 243.
[291] Briggs, *Credit and Village Society*, pp. 77–9.
[292] This should not be confused with an annual interest rate, the calculation of which would require (unavailable) information on the duration of loans.

percentage was skewed by three of fifteen cases where unusually high damages claims of 50, 33 and 33 per cent were accepted rather than lowered; if these are removed the average figure drops from 12 per cent to 5 per cent.

The figures for Clare debt cases show an even higher disparity, with original claims averaging 64.9 per cent of the principal and those awarded by the jurors just 9.3 per cent (see Table 16). Interestingly, two of the three cases in Newmarket where the jury awarded high damages involved large transactions in wool and skins valued at £6 2s. 6d. (damages of 40s.) and 13s. 4d. (damages of 6s. 8d.), perhaps because the jury recognised the harm caused to plaintiffs by the absence of a large amount of capital.[293] In effect, the decisions of the jury set the bounds of damages, striking a balance between borrower equity, attracting capital and encouraging mercantile enterprise.[294] The jury's general tendency to reduce claims to much lower levels might also imply a notion of reasonable and non-usurious limits for damages.

Overall, informal means and the moral pressures of client relationships may have been the primary method of compulsion in pursuing trade debts. Litigation in court was a formalised and more aggressive action for traders to protect their interests, but even in this forum a high percentage of cases resorted to 'licences of concord' and more amicable settlements. However, there was apparently a willingness to use full court procedures if needed. Debt recovery was an important influence on whether outsiders used a market. Traders desired courts that could compel defendants to appear, were limited in their financial costs, and were efficient in their expedition of pleas. In Newmarket, litigation was relatively cheap and efficient and the procedures of the court were rarely questioned, especially since many of the constituents of the court were themselves regular users of its mechanisms. In Clare, there was a greater resort to licences of concord, no ostensible use of pledges, and some problems in empanelling juries of inquisition (though this also occurred in Newmarket). One suspects that Newmarket's market court had a formidable reputation for a small town, whereas Clare's legal structure was more ordinary in its debt-recovery facilities. This may, in turn, have influenced the use of their markets by foreign traders. The fact that so many outsiders chose to settle their trading disputes in Newmarket's court points towards a local repute for efficient and effective justice.

---

[293] SRO (B), Acc.1476/1/43, 35, 36.
[294] Searle, *Lordship and Community*, pp. 401–3. In Battle, juries generally awarded damages of 15–30 per cent of the principal. In the late fourteenth-century Suffolk village of Earl Soham, across a sample of just nine cases, the court awarded damages of just 3–10 per cent at a mean of 5.5 per cent. SRO (I), v5/18/1.3.

It is likely that credit enforcement needed to be more secure as trade expanded and impersonalised credit relationships were formed, often stretching beyond local confines and informal means of control. Generally, confidence in efficient credit relationships was highly important for petty trade, and those of Newmarket and Clare were established upon a complex foundation of legal and moral assumptions.

Administering the marketplace

Small-town authorities had to administer the physical marketplace itself to ensure a conducive and safe environment for trade and to make sure that the rights of the lord were upheld. The basic offences and procedures highlighted in the court rolls appear to conform closely to those outlined in the regulations of major towns. For instance, in 1453, the bailiffs of Clare proclaimed that no one should sell victuals, or trade on Sundays, which was a straightforward repetition of the statute enacted by Henry VI.[295]

Within the marketplace, officials kept a close eye on the renting of shops and stalls, with particular attention to their maintenance. In Newmarket's fair court there were several instances of ruined stalls and deteriorating shops leading to threats of severe penalties, including forfeiture, if they were not repaired. It is not entirely evident that such threats were always effective, since traders like Richard Farwel consistently appeared in the records for such offences, being amerced 3d.–6d. on each occasion. But the threats were not entirely without teeth, as both Robert Gateward and John Coupere had their stalls seized for neglect or failure to comply with the court's orders. Indeed, Robert Gateward's persistent negligence in upkeeping his holdings led to increasing penalties being held over his head: 2s., half a mark, 20s. and, finally, a second threat of forfeiture.[296] It is not known whether any of these sanctions were carried out.

Formal markets also carried the implied right for the lord to levy stallage and tolls.[297] Consequently, a major duty of bailiffs was the collection of tolls in the weekly market, though it is possible that others were hired to carry out the practical rounds. The burgesses of Clare were actually freed from payment of tolls as part of their acquired liberty, whereas the residents of Newmarket did not have such privileges and were often accused of avoiding tolls and stallage. For instance, Ralph Brabon, a Newmarket

---

[295] TNA, sc2/203/70.
[296] SRO (B), Acc.1476/1/3, 5, 9, 21, 22, 26, 30, 32, 38, 39.
[297] Mate, 'Rise and fall', 66–7; Kowaleski, *Local Markets*, pp. 192–202.

resident, apparently sold forty-nine 'mattys' in the market and fair without paying the lord's toll and in 1403, John Fabyan of Exning was fined 6d. for striking the bailiff and refusing to pay a tax of a farthing on four bushels of barley.[298] Fabyan's reaction appears to be out of proportion to such a small tax. Excessive tolls were not only condemned by central government, but discouraged visiting traders. Consequently, most tolls only totalled $\frac{1}{4}$d. to $\frac{1}{2}$d., perhaps accounting for 1 per cent of the value of goods exchanged.[299] Did the traders really consider these charges to be burdensome enough to risk larger fines for evasion? It seems likely that instances of toll evasion were not commonplace, though we cannot of course know how many people successfully avoided tolls and escaped detection. However, it is noticeable that three of the Newmarket cases were taken to trial because the defendants denied having avoided tolls in the first place.

Other prime considerations for town officials included keeping urban spaces safe, orderly, hygienic and accessible. At every leet court of Newmarket the bailiffs presented a few individuals for obstructing the roads or water-courses of the town.[300] Those who obstructed it with timber may have been attempting to draw off water more efficiently for their own use in brewing or tanning processes.[301] Other residents dug gutters and banks in the road to prevent floods entering their houses but, in turn, obstructed street traffic.[302] Commonly, offenders discarded waste in the roads: dung, intestines or the corrupted remains of an animal were probably unwanted by-products of the livestock industry. For instance, William Bocher was presented for placing intestines in the king's road to the public nuisance.[303] The widespread problem of dung being dumped around the common land became serious enough for the court of Newmarket to enact a by-law that this was to happen no more under the threat of a penalty of 40d. to the lord and 40d. to the chapel of Blessed Mary.[304] A similar set of offences were listed in the Clare court rolls. According to the records, residents commonly obstructed the road, ditches and river with timber, dung and gutters, as well as various kinds of domestic and commercial rubbish. In the 1360s, the butcher John Bory was accused of leaving blood and offal by the door of John, servant of Robert Marchal, so that there was a bad smell and no one would come to his house, while William Slaughtere had left his waste next to the church.[305] The

[298] SRO (B), Acc.1476/1/7, 14, 27, 32, 42.
[299] Masschaele, *Peasants*, p. 68; Kowaleski, *Local Markets*, p. 194.
[300] SRO (B), Acc.1476/1/2, 10, 17, 18, 26, 37.   [301] SRO (B), Acc.1476/1/2, 10, 17.
[302] SRO (B), Acc.1476/1/10, 18.   [303] SRO (B), Acc.1476/1/18.
[304] SRO (B), Acc.1476/1/18.   [305] TNA, sc2/203/58, 60.

repetition of cases suggests that pollution and waste was a continual problem in even small marketplaces.

Many of the waste products that littered towns stemmed from animal husbandry. Breeding pigs and other animals provided useful supplementary foodstuffs or income for a variety of townsfolk, even though only a small amount of pasture was available and was tightly controlled.[306] In Newmarket, Walter Clak and John Manston regularly let their pigs trespass on the cornfield, while Robert Bocher, John Redere and Nicholas Chapman allowed their cows and horses onto the lord's meadow without permission.[307] The number of trespassing animals, as well as complaints of dung and offal in the streets, suggests attempts by townsfolk to take advantage of an increasing demand for pork and bacon. In Clare, in 1384, John Gardener and Cristina Brokhole were both upbraided for placing pigsties in the main road to the nuisance of others.[308] However, in both cases the offenders only paid amercements of a few pence, which appeared to be *de facto* licences in a similar way to assize presentments.

Although the communities of small towns like Newmarket and Clare exerted personal influences and social pressures upon local traders, we must be careful not simply to characterise small towns as harmonious and self-regulating environments. Individual acts of waste disposal, trespass and negligence were sometimes committed in the face of communal opinion or the best interests of the public. The act of bargaining could also inflame spirits and a certain level of 'communal policing' was required, especially on market day. The record of assaults and quarrels in the court rolls unfortunately does not include any details of the origins of spats. Only occasionally can we infer that a trade dispute was involved, such as when Richard Bocher scuffled with a 'foreign' butcher in 1402–3.[309]

Searle has suggested that the locals of Hastings (East Sussex) received more lenient treatment than foreigners in the leet court and that the more unusual criminal or assault cases involved foreigners.[310] A similar comparison can be made in Newmarket and Clare. About 28 per cent of the cases before the Newmarket leet court involved a foreigner as either the offender or the victim, but unfortunately the lack of detail means that we cannot always establish the context of these fights. The most interesting cases involved bailiffs and constables who were assaulted while employed

[306] SRO (B), Acc.1476/1/4, 8, 12, 14, 23, 31.
[307] SRO (B), Acc.1476/1/10, 17, 38, 39.
[308] TNA, sc2/203/62. The trespass of pigs and encroachment of pigsties had been a long-term problem in Clare. TNA, sc2/203/45. Similarly, in Earl Soham several brewing and baking families had pigs, which they allowed to trespass on the lord's land. SRO (I), v5/18/1.3–1.4.
[309] SRO (B), Acc.1476/1/10.   [310] Searle, *Lordship and Community*, pp. 392–3.

in the tasks of their office.[311] There were seven cases of men illegally recovering attached goods from bailiffs or constables and, in the process, assaulting them. Presumably these were usually minor scuffles, reflected in the low 3d.–12d. fines on men like Walter Skynnere, Richard Farewell, John Walter and William Denys. These were also local men who may have been subjected to more informal means of sanction. By contrast, when John Landwade, John Godard and Simon Tanherde attacked the constable, John Ballone, they were given fines of 40d. each. The high fines may have been given because the act was a group assault, but additionally, the attackers seem to have been outsiders. John Landwade, for example, was from Reach, while the other two men are not mentioned in any town context. Similarly, Depyng Taylour, probably a foreigner, was fined 40d. for striking the constable and drawing blood.

However, townsfolk also faced heavy sanctions when their actions were deemed excessive, such as when John Odye and John Heyham, both of Newmarket, separately prevented the bailiff from carrying out the duties of his office. They had their tenements seized as the ultimate penalty. Disrespect towards officials was not countenanced. The court rolls of Clare also recorded assaults upon officials while they attempted to undertake their duties: a servant of Robert Cook of Lavenham was amerced 2s. for attacking the bailiff John Babir; John Pedder of Colne was fined 6d. for assaulting Robert Barker the aletaster; and a servant of the Lord of Clopton was fined 10s. for assaulting Thomas Cumbwell the bailiff and beating him.[312] All these cases, it should be noted, involved outsiders. However, as seen in Newmarket, even local men were rebuked heavily if they violently contravened local official controls. In 1388, another stranger attacked and badly hurt the Clare bailiff while he was trying to collect toll. The stranger took shelter with a local man, William Mylde (who went on to serve as bailiff the following year), and then they both fled the town. In response, an inquisition ordered that all of William's goods and animals were distrained in lieu of a severe 40s. penalty.[313] For the administrative apparatus of a town to operate efficiently, the authority of those who supervised the market had to be upheld and seen to be upheld, especially when the supposed elite of the town spurned the mechanisms of justice.

Enterprise and efficiency

The institution of the market itself represented a means of lowering the transaction costs of search, negotiation and enforcement.[314] These

---

[311] SRO (B), Acc.1476/1/2, 10, 17, 18, 26, 37.   [312] TNA, sc2/203/64, 65.
[313] TNA, sc2/203/64.   [314] Kowaleski, *Local Markets*, pp. 179–80.

could be regarded as the primary aims of any market administration, but these elements had to be balanced against the needs and wants of the local community, its leaders and the traders themselves. The elite might seek extra revenues and privileges that counteracted attempts to keep costs low. Additionally, a trader's costs could be adversely affected by inefficient and incompetent administration. Thus, the administrative tools of town officials, and especially how these tools were used, were highly influential factors in gauging the intentions and efficiency of a small town market.

Britnell felt that late medieval entrepreneurial ambition was deterred by increasing government intervention and extensive regulations in larger boroughs, where the burgesses had become more protectionist and distrustful of outsiders during the fifteenth century. Profit-making became easier in smaller, less-regulated communities.[315] In her work on fifteenth-century Romford and Havering, McIntosh identified a lack of regulation, a broad dispersal of capital and an absence of concentrated financial power. These conditions created an environment in which personal efforts had maximum scope for enterprising action and reward. She suggested that there was no 'moral economy' and that individual behaviour was heightened by the commercial environment.[316]

The market traders of Newmarket and Clare were not wealthy individuals and many lived on marginal profits. However, this does not mean that they lacked the spirit of entrepreneurs. In Newmarket, enterprising activities can be discerned in various court roll entries signifying an extensive use of credit, the accumulation of property and stalls, and the expansion of shops and businesses. Even some of the offences, such as forestalling, regrating and opening windows onto the marketplace, can perhaps (though not always) be regarded as indicative of initiative and flexibility. For these traders to be truly entrepreneurial, in the strict sense of the term, they would have had to change long-established patterns of commercial activity. This was often not the case, but what we can sometimes observe are traders with enterprise and business acumen.

A few individuals had two or three servants, which could imply that they had larger-scale enterprises than their neighbours.[317] Servants, journeymen and apprentices are, however, rarely mentioned in the court rolls except in incidental references. In Newmarket, John Ballone Smyth, Walter Bocher, Thomas Cook, John Kyrkeby, John Langham, Thomas Pere, John Smyth and John Waleys apparently had two or three servants, and

[315] Britnell, *Commercialisation*, pp. 177–8.
[316] McIntosh, *Autonomy and Community*, pp. 176–8.
[317] Hilton, *English Peasantry*, p. 80.

these men were all heavily involved in all different aspects of victualling and provisioning trades, with most probably running inns or large cook-houses (see Table 9). John Kyrkeby was also regularly amerced 6d. for displaying a signpost by the door to his house or inn, perhaps because it was too large or low and therefore caused an obstruction.[318] His persistent offending suggests that the advertisement for his inn was more than worth the minor inconvenience of a 6d. amercement every year. Such infringements upon the margins of the law were perhaps the consequence of entrepreneurial activity. Similarly, John Ballone Smyth was fined 6s. 8d. for making a window in his tenement and having a stall annexed to the same window, thus encroaching on the lord's land.[319] Although the trader faced a large fine, it is probable that its payment meant the extension became a permanent fixture. Similarly, in 1472, Thomas Pyngyll paid 4d. a year for an empty plot in front of the window of his shop to display his merchandise on a board.[320]

There are other occurrences in property transactions which illustrate the accumulation, consolidation and expansion of shops by some New-market individuals. John Odye sublet three shops to William Sygo, Robert Doushole and Robert Gateward, and went to court in 1409 to obtain the rents due to him.[321] He was also sued by Thomas Clerk and had to pay damages of 10s. for taking the rent for a shop but failing to hand it over.[322] Thomas Tornor had to pay a 40d. fine for enlarging his two shops, while Richard Farewell, Robert Gateward and Alexander Barkere all owned several stalls in different areas of the market, which probably indicates the widening scale of their interests.[323] The administrative bodies of towns had to adapt their regulations in order to reconcile existing legislation with the issues created by new trading conditions, while also finding ways of keeping up revenues to the lord. Flexible, but firm, regulation allowed a range of personal initiatives, though at a small cost to the trader. There was no real interference in the running of inns and shops, provided they did not encroach upon the lord's rights and kept within the margins of acceptable trading behaviour. There was little pro-active encouragement of entrepreneurial behaviour, but neither was entrepreneurial behaviour necessarily opposed to communal effort and moral influences, as was suggested by McIntosh. The court systems in Newmarket and Clare, at least, seem to have operated fairly successfully and were based on cooperation, trust and a fairly wide inclusion of local

[318] SRO (B), Acc.1476/1/2, 10, 17, 18, 26.   [319] SRO (B), Acc.1476/1/32.
[320] SRO (B), Acc.359/3.   [321] SRO (B), Acc.1476/1/21.
[322] SRO (B), Acc.1476/1/36.
[323] SRO (B), Acc.1476/1/3, 5, 9, 21, 22, 26, 27, 30, 32, 38, 39.

tradesmen. Many disputes were solved amicably, while regulations were sometimes lenient and conducive to trade.

The courts were pragmatic in choosing which infringements were punished severely or leniently and when to leave the buyers and sellers to their own devices. Many poorer retailers may have transgressed trading regulations as a necessary survival strategy, as much as for extra profit.[324] Regraters often operated on very fine economic margins and this was problematic when selling foodstuffs that were usually highly perishable. For bakers and brewers it was probably difficult to process the right quantity of goods for sale without ending up with unsold produce, especially when the assizes ostensibly provided little room for error and losses. Hucksters and regraters filtered some of the risks for producers by taking on the sale of excess output, but regraters themselves had no such insurance and needed to sell all their goods to make any profit according to the law. Some poorer traders may thus have pushed the margins of the law in order to make a reasonable living. Additionally, the variable quality of goods was perhaps unavoidable for medieval producers, compared to the standardised products we take for granted today. There was a considerable difference between deliberate fraud and slack quality production, even if medieval legislation could not frame such subtleties without providing unwanted ambiguities and loopholes. The officials of the small towns like Newmarket and Clare appear to have understood this dilemma and allowed some flexibility in their application of the law, especially since a level of competition and consumer-awareness guarded against greater infringements. For instance, the assizes became effectively a means of licensing, but their presence also ensured that traders did not take too many liabilities in pushing the acceptable margins of price and quality.

Admittedly, the development of the assizes into a licensing system was also linked to the inability of part-time officials to inspect an increasingly professional and full-time victualling sector. However, when the courts and officials were challenged to uphold their authority, they could stamp down hard on traders. Equally the financial rights of the lord were consistently upheld, perhaps to ensure a steady income was maintained so that the lord had little reason to interfere directly. Nevertheless, as long as the market was flourishing, there seemed little need for excessively restrictive law-keeping in small towns. The Newmarket administration did not seem to act too jealously to maintain the interests of its own residents; this was partly because the people of Newmarket did not possess privileges that

---

[324]   Britnell, *Growth and Decline*, pp. 39–41.

needed protecting, which meant they operated a more open and accessible market than perhaps found in large boroughs. Inevitably, Newmarket traders had the advantage of first-hand knowledge of the market and officials, but equally, they were more easily attached and distrained when needed. Administrative and legal mechanisms had their limitations, and some persistent problems did continue to affect the efficiency of the marketplace, but generally regulations ensured that the costs of enforcement, negotiation and search remained competitively low.

The commercial regulations and operations of Newmarket can be further understood in the context of wider changes in the economy and market networks in the later Middle Ages. From the thirteenth century, English society was becoming increasingly market-oriented and institutional commercial growth was widespread, including the emergence of small towns and village markets to meet the demand for basic foodstuffs.[325] After the Black Death, as Mark Bailey has pointed out, many urban centres suffered from decline in the face of new competitive realities, with the contracting trade in foodstuffs biting into their prosperity. Nevertheless, there was generally a leaner marketing structure, with economic resilience demonstrated by the surviving small towns.[326] Newmarket may have been one of the towns that prospered in this new competitive environment, just as Buntingford did in Hertfordshire, with its roadside location and lack of lordly control.[327] Both Bailey and Epstein have suggested that there was a weakening of seigneurial and urban authority and jurisdiction after the fourteenth century, which may have aided the development of trade in these difficult economic conditions.[328] There was certainly a relaxation of seigneurial pressures in many small towns and a reversion to controls by traders themselves, via the manorial courts.

The administrative structure of places like Newmarket was highly advantageous and leading men seemed to recognise the need to provide a flexible, lenient, but potentially strong, marketing structure. Newmarket not only survived but prospered in the fifteenth century, when its market stall and shop rents increased almost continuously from £1 16s. 10d. in 1402–3 to £6 15s. 7d. in 1472–3. The town was also able to build a new 'Tolbooth' and add further stalls by 1472. Income from the courts also remained fairly buoyant over the early fifteenth century, despite some

---

[325] Britnell, 'Proliferation'.
[326] Britnell, *Commercialisation*, p. 166; Bailey, 'Historiographical'.
[327] Bailey, 'A tale of two towns', 358, 362–6, 370. Romford market was also prospering commercially due to its lightly regulated and politically autonomous state. McIntosh, *Autonomy and Community*, pp. 51, 89, 129–37, 176–8.
[328] Bailey, 'A tale of two towns', 355–6; Epstein, 'Regional fairs'.

fluctuations, though the perquisites of the market court did fall notably in the 1470s.[329] Interestingly, the profits of the town's fair fell significantly over the same period and its June fair appears to have ceased operation in the late 1430s, perhaps due to the increasing attractions of Stourbridge Fair at nearby Cambridge. Newmarket found it difficult to compete in the luxury and wholesale trades of Stourbridge Fair, but its local market and everyday provisioning was thriving. Newmarket provided a relatively attractive site to traders, with fairly secure surroundings, relaxed regulation, quick adjudications and steady customers.

Conversely, Clare did not prosper significantly from its cloth trade in the fifteenth century, unlike nearby Hadleigh or Lavenham. Instead, it appears that the town was staving off a general economic downturn. Clare was one of the thirty-two surviving markets in fifteenth-century Suffolk, though it was ranked only twenty-third in assessed wealth compared to other markets in the 1525 lay subsidy.[330] In 1425, the bailiffs sought a reduction in the amount of rent to be collected. A jury also reported that eleven stalls could not be let and that Wentford Fair had not been held since 1421 because nobody went there.[331] Additionally, there are no references in Clare's court rolls to burgess rights by the fifteenth century and the practice may have lapsed or been recorded in a now lost document.[332] Despite its early borough privileges, and the control of trading matters by the burgesses through their farm or market income, Clare did not gain additional chartered liberties nor did it develop any occupational guild structures. It could be argued that Clare's burgesses squandered any potential advantages they had in the fourteenth century, such as in the local cloth industry. Thornton has suggested that Clare failed to develop significantly because of strong lordship and local competition.[333] The relationship between Clare's inhabitants and its lord (and lord's officials) was certainly much closer than was the case for Newmarket. Clare remained the centre of administration for the Honor, even when the lands became royal possessions, and the Honor court was held by the steward on the same day as the borough court. However, there is still evidence that the burgesses had gained greater *de facto* control of Clare's market and its regulation by the fifteenth century, as amercement levels fell and enforcement was relaxed.[334] This may well have propped

[329] SRO (B), Acc.1476/12–13, Acc.359/3; May, 'Newmarket 500 Years Ago', 263.
[330] Sheail, *Regional Distribution*, ii, pp. 321–36.
[331] TNA, sc2/203/67; Britnell, *Growth and Decline*, pp. 190, 208.
[332] Thornton, 'A study', 96; Thornton, *A History of Clare*, p. 37.
[333] Thornton, *A History of Clare*, pp. 42–6.
[334] For a discussion of the long-term developments in the retail trade of Clare, throughout the fourteenth and fifteenth centuries, see J. Davis, 'Selling food and drink in the

up the weekly market and aided the business of the town's remaining retailers and innkeepers.

Piety and morality

The preceding examination of the marketplaces of Newmarket and Clare has demonstrated the complex relationship between medieval morals, laws and behaviour. It is hard to know the extent to which traders broke the law or infringed upon perceived levels of moral behaviour, especially since many offences listed in the court rolls were often *de facto* licences, while informal sanctions may have operated undocumented. However, evidence from a number of wills does suggest that traders experienced contrition as well as an understanding of general moral concerns.

A handful of wills survive from fifteenth-century Newmarket, all dated after 1438, and these can be compared more generally with wills of traders from fifteenth-century Suffolk.[335] Two of these wills were left by men who were prominent in the extant court rolls of Newmarket: John Grene (will dated to 1452) and John Ray (1459). Generally, the only wills we have are those of the more affluent and influential men of the town. Other testators included John Joos (1449) who owned the 'Bear' inn, Arthur Greysson (1479) who owned four inns in Newmarket, and William Baron (1439) who owned the 'Gryffyn' inn as well as significant lands worth over £20 in Ditton Valens, Saxton and Cheveley. The trading bias of the testators of Newmarket was shown not only in the properties they owned, but also the bequests they made. John Ray gave 6s. 8d. for the repair of Saxton Lane and another 6s. 8d. for Dermundeslane. He also gave his daughter his best cauldron, reflecting his household's interest in the brewing trade. Similarly, Adam Colakyr (1477) bequeathed barley to several people and a brass pot to Matilda Grene.

Like John Ray, numerous Suffolk traders made bequests to maintain roads, ways and bridges, the maintenance of which served traders' best interests.[336] In 1453, William Curby of Lavenham donated 20s. to repairing the highways between Lavenham and Sudbury, while John Holm of Barrow in 1443 made a significant bequest of 100s. for 'the emendation of the muddy and faulty ways in the town of Barrow, starting at the entrance of my house, towards the town of Bury'.[337] Most bequests were

---

aftermath of the Black Death', in M. Bailey and S. Rigby (eds.), *England in the Age of the Black Death* (forthcoming, 2011).

[335] The surviving wills were collated in May (ed.), *Twenty Newmarket Wills*. For a wider set of Suffolk wills, see Northeast (ed.), *Wills*.

[336] Northeast (ed.), *Wills*, pp. 67–8, 353, 359, nos. 180, 1009, 1035.

[337] *Ibid.*, pp. 106–7, 277, nos. 290, 768.

more modest, but traders' interests remained predominantly local, such as Thomas Wodesey's gifts of 3s. 4d. and 20d. for mending the roads around his home of Stoke by Nayland.[338] Occasionally, bequests were more obscure in terms of their motivation. In 1441, Thomas Dobbys of Sudbury left 6s. 8d. 'to the repairing of a cross' at Wiggen End, which may have been inspired by piety, nostalgia, civic pride or self-esteem.[339]

Testamentary evidence is notoriously difficult to examine, given the mixture of idiosyncratic individual statements and conventional formulae. Many were written by clerks who possibly exaggerated the orthodoxy of a testator's statements since the wills were often formulaic in content and form. Additionally, most wills from the fifteenth century were those of relatively wealthy men, rather than the poorer retailers.[340] Despite these problems, preambles of wills illustrate basic beliefs that resonated within communities, particularly highlighting the testators' beliefs in the power of intercessionary acts and the worth of the parish church as a focus of lay piety. There are even occasional glimpses into personal circumstances and attitudes, expressed through the prism of the clerk's text. We cannot quantify the level of piety among these traders from wills (or, indeed, from any other form of evidence), but they can reveal individualistic pangs of conscience from certain traders.

Most of the surviving wills from Newmarket made basic provision for wives and children. However, additional connections outside the town were also mentioned, with executors and beneficiaries from Soham, Kirtling, Bury St Edmunds, Fordham, Saxham Parva, Thetford and Cambridge. Some testators gave money to churches and institutions, as well as individuals, within and outside Newmarket. John Bonde (1476) gave money to Snailwell Church and Saham Church, while Arthur Greysson (1479) bequeathed money to the Cathedral Church of Norwich. However, most bequests were made to Newmarket All Saints' Church and the chapel of Blessed Mary Within. Such donations to churches were common and expected, while many Suffolk testators also gave readily to prisoners and the poor as acts of charity.[341] The desire to make legacies to the poor and needy was intimately related to notions of mercy and social justice that were constantly invoked from the pulpit.

The usual formulaic concern for the health of one's soul was commonplace in wills, with bequests of cash to the Church to be used for the provision of prayers, Masses and torches. In 1440–1, John Place of Lavenham wanted a significant amount of his goods sold after his death

[338] *Ibid.*, p. 331, no. 930.   [339] *Ibid.*, p. 71, no. 188.
[340] Heath, 'Urban piety', p. 212.
[341] Northeast (ed.), *Wills*, pp. 51–2, 67–8, 93–4, 106–7, 195, 277, 311, 353, nos. 130, 180, 254, 290, 511, 768, 865, 1009.

and then for his executors 'to sell and dispose the money for my soul and the souls for whom I am bound'.[342] More specifically, some traders picked up on the idea of restitution and asked for any outstanding debts to be paid in full. William Palgrave of Newmarket (1451) stated: 'I will that, for the health of my soul, if there be any man or woman who by reliable witnesses and by true and legal evidence can well and justly prove that I the aforesaid William have taken anything unjustly from them, restitution should be made by my executors for what has been taken unjustly'.[343] He also made several contributions to the Church and friars, including 10s. for a chaplain to say a trental. John Joos, an innkeeper, similarly asked for his debts to be paid and charitable works to be performed, including the distribution of 40s. among the poor and eight marks for a chaplain to celebrate his soul. The insertion of such clauses, though partly conventional, might suggest that traders experienced anxiety about the fraudulent potential of exchange. These fears were perhaps influenced by ideologies transmitted by the clerics, friars and guilds.

Other East Anglian wills show traders were fearful about their wealth and guilty about possible cheating and unpaid bills.[344] Thomas Gatle of Great Livermere (1440) asked for 'the true payment of my just debts', while John Bownde of Lavenham (1452) required that his executors were 'firstly to pay debts which are proved genuine as quickly as possible'.[345] John Derby, a mercer of Sudbury, also asked in his will of 1453–4 that his 'debts for which I am bound in any way to be paid first'.[346] Wills do display a certain concern that debts were paid, undoubtedly linked to spiritual messages about restitution communicated from the pulpit. Thomas Sheperde of Botesdale (1460–1) was prepared to leave his shop to his son, John, but only on the condition that he paid all his father's outstanding debts; otherwise his wife would receive the shop.[347] It was commonplace to see the residue of goods explicitly left to executors to pay for debts, particularly tithes, whether the testator was a trader or not. However, the image of repaying debts suggests that commercial language was readily combined with religious ideas of restitution.[348]

---

[342] *Ibid.*, pp. 48–9, no. 126. See also *ibid.*, pp. 50, 72–3, 195, nos. 127, 193, 511.

[343] May (ed.), *Twenty Newmarket Wills*, p. 21.

[344] McMurray Gibson, *Theater of Devotion*, pp. 27–8; Tanner, *Church*, p. 106; Dyer, *An Age*, p. 122.

[345] Northeast (ed.), *Wills*, pp. 67–8, 195, nos. 180, 511.

[346] *Ibid.*, p. 289, no. 803. See also *ibid.*, pp. 268, 295, 296, 311, 312, 370, nos. 740, 818, 820, 865, 868, 1068.

[347] *Ibid.*, p. 465, no. 1341. See also Tymms (ed.), *Wills*, pp. 81–3; *York*, iii, pp. 45–7.

[348] For other wills asking for debts to be repaid: Northeast (ed.), *Wills*, pp. 35, 46, 58, 59, 63, 69, 75, 77, 78–9, 92, 94, 98, 157, 163, 188, 193, 200, 201, 224, 234, 268, 271, 273–4, 291, 334, 363, 387, 470, 473.

In his will, Adam Colakyr made mention of a Guild of St Thomas in Newmarket. Although the institution is not mentioned elsewhere, the reference shows that a parish guild did exist in this town for mutual religious and social support. Robert Percyvale had attachments to guilds outside Newmarket and gave 20d. to those of St Peter in Stetchworth and Holy Trinity in Ditton. Many other towns in Suffolk had similar socio-religious guilds, as seen in the returns to the king for 1389.[349] For instance, Clare had the guilds of St Mary, St Peter, Corpus Christi and St John the Baptist. Augustinian friars were also a daily presence in Clare, both as preachers and customers. John Barkere and John Watlok of Clare both bequeathed money in 1440 to Austin friars in their town.[350] The presence of such friars within Newmarket is illustrated by the testament of John Upryght (1445), who was the guardian of the chapel of Blessed Mary. He gave a pocket breviary to Nicholas Laycestre and five marks to John Avys, an Augustinian friar.

Ultimately, the wills of traders followed testamentary conventions for burials, purgatory and donations, but these were sometimes also prefaced by particular commercial concerns in both practical and spiritual matters. There is no indication that the statements of deathbed conscience were not sincere, but, equally, whether these were reflective of their views during the majority of their lifetime is difficult to know. The perils of purgatory could be a great impulsion to last-minute repentance. Nicholas Amor also found that the clothiers of Suffolk were prepared to invest heavily in spiritual insurance through Masses for their soul and bequests to the friars.[351] A more pertinent question is not whether late medieval clerks expressed profound piety in drafting these wills, but whether they took on board popular criticisms of the trading classes. It appears that some traders had and tried to meet the requirements of 'social justice' in their wills, and the language of debt and credit had become increasingly pervasive.

Conclusion

This chapter has demonstrated that there was a crucial difference between passing legislation and enforcing it in the medieval marketplace. In the small towns of Newmarket and Clare, the penalties for traders were relatively low and much more was tolerated than medieval literary

[349] Redstone, 'Chapels'; Westlake, *Parish Gilds*, pp. 225–30.
[350] Northeast (ed.), *Wills*, pp. 17, 43, nos. 43, 112. See also *ibid.*, pp. 151–2, 195, 295, nos. 130, 511, 818; Thornton, *A Short History*, p. 14.
[351] Amor, 'Merchant adventurer', 424, 428–9.

depictions or legislation might suggest. Consequently, petty trade was not exceptionally encumbered by legal tenets and decrees of the Church. Indeed, the fact that large numbers of bakers, brewers, innkeepers, cooks and butchers could thrive in small towns suggests in itself that the application of laws was not overly restrictive. It seems that the local interpretation of law evolved to accommodate social and economic changes and support the efficiency of the market. In essence, local market authorities and users were manipulating the proclamations of the state to suit their own commercial circumstances. Regular amercements were collected, but they were not so heavy as to jeopardise a trader's productivity and livelihood.[352] There was seemingly an implicit, basic understanding of the market economy and the best means to maintain institutional efficiency within the economic, legal, administrative and social realities of the time. Royal and parliamentary legislation, as well as the admonitions of the pulpit, were sticks to wave at erring traders, but they were employed sparingly and judiciously.

Newmarket's courts, in particular, were run by local traders for the benefit of commercial interaction. The regulatory structure of this small market town offered an effective and flexible framework within which traders could make a living and yet also feel protected against deceit. The system worked because it kept transaction costs down for both traders and purchasers through openly acquiescing with the medieval concepts of fairness and justice. Market traders were allowed by officials to work within acceptable margins of the law on payment of an annual amercement. This provided a flexibility that was vital given contemporary commercial circumstances and productive constraints. However, traders were not given a free hand and all knew that officials and neighbours would stamp down on flagrant breaches. There was therefore a selective element in how morality and laws were interpreted in order to facilitate everyday life. As Mark Bailey has noted, market and court officials 'consciously sought to maintain a pragmatic balance between minimal interference in the dealings of market traders and preventing persistent or serious misconduct'.[353] This was a fairly effective and flexible means of facilitating market trade within the constraints and moral environment of late medieval England, drawing actively upon common conceptions of morality, trust and cooperation.

This was not an entirely harmonious or successful environment: debts were not always recovered, market deceits occurred, and officials had to

---

[352] Raftis argues that a similar arrangement can be seen in late medieval Ramsey. Raftis, *Peasant Economic Development*, p. 119.
[353] Bailey, *Medieval Suffolk*, p. 143.

act strictly against those who challenged their authority. Also, whether local officials constrained growth and entrepreneurship through some aspects of law-enforcement, such as against middlemen, is more than possible. Marketing growth was fairly haphazard in the fifteenth century, as illustrated by the long-term fortunes of Newmarket and Clare. Additionally, developments in rural industries and informal trade suggest other attempts were made to circumvent existing trade regulations, which perhaps lagged too far behind the needs of many enterprising traders and manufacturers. Although the practice of trade and interpretation of law in small towns was adaptable and flexible, officials still worked within the broad conceptual boundaries and constraints defined by legislation and moral preconceptions, rather than constructing a new commercial infrastructure. The trading behaviour of local petty traders still remained bound by traditional moral and legal considerations. However, the regulatory framework generally worked and small towns like Newmarket may have provided a more accessible and open trading environment than most boroughs by the fifteenth century, showing that market traders could flourish without formal burgess status.[354] These small Suffolk towns, while still espousing the veneer of traditional medieval ethics, were thus in the process of accepting the values of commercialisation.

PART II: THE BOROUGH MARKET OF IPSWICH

It remains to place the market trade of small towns into a broader context by briefly considering the conduct of commerce in larger towns and boroughs. The evidence from the small towns of Newmarket and Clare suggests that strict regulation of equitable participation and price control was becoming less appropriate in the fifteenth century. Traders needed more room for entrepreneurial manoeuvre in an increasingly competitive environment. Many offences merely became revenue raisers for towns in need of cash and the authorities were often prepared to overlook minor trading infringements. By comparison, borough corporations and craft guilds seemingly became highly protective and stringent in the face of expanding commercial and manufacturing competition. The emergence of the craft and trade guilds as regulatory bodies with extensive powers led to stricter controls on quality and supplies, at least within their own jurisdictions.[355]

   Can we therefore surmise that there was more room for petty enterprise in small market towns than large boroughs?[356] Certainly, many large

[354] *Ibid.*, pp. 144–5.   [355] See pp. 169–75.
[356] Hilton, 'Medieval market towns', 21–2.

towns had suburbs where petty retailers tried to escape the authority of the town corporation and could proliferate unmolested.[357] Compared to small towns, there was also a greater gap between the ruling merchant elite and the mass of petty traders. The vested interests of the whole-saling mercantile elite therefore took precedence over those of retailers. However, it is possible that the extent to which retailers faced height-ened controls in larger towns has been tainted by our knowledge of the mercantile and manufacturing sectors. There are many important issues raised by a comparison between small and large towns, which cannot all be addressed within the scope of this book. The following analysis will thus look only briefly at these questions, in order to highlight further areas of investigation for the study of market ethics. In keeping with the focus of these case studies on Suffolk, the following survey will look at retail trade in the large borough of Ipswich.

Ipswich ('Gippeswych') was the prime town of Suffolk, in both its administrative and marketing role. It had developed its self-governing administration since the charter of 25 May 1200 and been a borough since before the *Domesday Book* of 1086.[358] It was not in the very top rank of medieval English towns but, along with the Suffolk towns of Bury St Edmunds and Sudbury, Ipswich was ranked among the fifty wealthiest in England in 1334.[359] The late fourteenth-century population of Ipswich can be estimated at 3,000–3,500, based upon the 1377 Poll Tax, which gives 1,507 over the age of fourteen, though this did not include the very poor and inevitable evasions.[360] Stephen Alsford estimates that there were some 150–350 freemen in Ipswich, a fairly small number of men who held privileges and dominated executive offices within the town.[361]

Lying on the rivers Orwell and Gipping, Ipswich served as a sheltered port for its prosperous agricultural hinterland. The town also probably placed an extensive demand for foodstuffs and raw materials upon the hinterland, which stretched up to fifteen miles in radius.[362] Several local manorial lords purchased exemptions from tolls for the produce they

---

[357] Keene, 'Suburban growth'.

[358] *DB*, 290a–b; *RCh*, i, p. 65. See also Martin, 'The governance of Ipswich', pp. xvii–xxix.

[359] Ipswich was ranked nineteenth, while Bury St Edmunds was twenty-sixth. Both had improved to ninth and fourteenth respectively by 1524. Bailey, *Medieval Suffolk*, pp. 128–30; Britnell, 'Economy of British towns', p. 329; Kermode, 'Greater towns', pp. 441–65.

[360] Fenwick (ed.), *Poll Taxes*, ii, pp. 496–536; *VCH: Suffolk*, i, p. 647. In 1381, 963 were assessed.

[361] Alsford, *Towns*, 'The Men Behind the Masque: Office-Holding in East Anglian Bor-oughs, 1272–1460', ch. 3.

[362] As a comparison, Lee argued that the local hinterland for Cambridge extended between ten and fifteen miles in radius around the town, though goods like stone and fuel had to be brought from further afield. Lee, 'Feeding the colleges', 243–64.

brought to Ipswich market.[363] It had few nearby rivals for its commercial dominance, the nearest large towns being Yarmouth and Norwich to the north, Colchester and Maldon to the south and Cambridge and Bury St Edmunds to the west. Dunwich had long been in decline by the late fourteenth century. Ipswich's burgesses had quickly asserted their authority over Woodbridge in 1233 and obtained half of their tolls, as well as the right to trade in Woodbridge's market without paying toll.[364] Its main rival had been Harwich, which was situated at the mouth of the Orwell and had the powerful patronage of the Earl of Norfolk in the late thirteenth century.[365] However, legal action in 1340 later confirmed Ipswich's jurisdiction over the port.

The Orwell estuary was the principal commercial artery, making Ipswich into a safe haven and an international port. Its merchants traded with the Low Countries, the Baltic and the Rhineland, importing wine, spices, fruits, dyes, oil, salt, iron, timber and many other wares, and exporting wool and the cloth from the small towns of the Stour Valley.[366] The enrolled customs accounts suggest that a fair amount of raw wool was exported by Ipswich's citizens throughout the fifteenth century, though the figures fluctuate between a few hundred and a couple of thousand sacks each year.[367] The customs accounts show that the peak of cloth exports occurred in the late 1430s and 1440s, after the signing of a treaty between England and the Hanseatic League in 1437.[368] This resurgence for both local and German merchants was followed by a relative slump in the 1470s and 1480s. Nevertheless, Ipswich benefited from the general growth of the East Anglian cloth trade in the fifteenth century, but more as a centre of distribution than as an industrial centre. The hub of this export trade was at the Quay and the small wharves on the Orwell, which handled both overseas and coastal traffic.

Retail markets were mostly located in the north of the town, particularly on Cornhill. These markets exchanged both imported goods and those of hinterland producers who bought their commodities through the North and West Gates. Cornhill lay at the heart of the town and comprised the centre of the retail market infrastructure, with the market cross and also a moothall or 'Tolhous' on its south side, abetting commercial administration. Many commodities were retailed here but, like

---

[363] Alsford, *Towns*, 'History of Medieval Ipswich – Economy'.
[364] *Curia Regis Rolls*, xiv, pp. 353–4.   [365] Bailey, *Medieval Suffolk*, p. 124.
[366] Redstone, *Ipswich*, pp. 27–33, 37; Wodderspoon, *Memorials*, pp. 131, 165; Martin, 'Borough and the merchant community of Ipswich', p. 171; Power and Postan (eds.), *Studies*, pp. 330, 339.
[367] Carus-Wilson and Coleman, *England's Export Trade*, pp. 134–5.
[368] *Ibid.*, pp. 102, 152–3; Britnell, *Growth and Decline*, pp. 170–1. However, Britnell also notes that the enrolled customs records combined Ipswich, Harwich, Colchester and Maldon for administrative purposes.

many large boroughs, market activity spread into the sprawling streets. A shambles was situated on its south side, while more markets for cattle, dairy, poultry, cloth, wine, timber, wooden wares and fish lay further afield. Inns, taverns, alehouses and cookshops were scattered throughout the town, though there was a specific Cook's Row. Trade also took place at the Quay in the south-east of the town, particularly wholesale bargains for wine, grain and fish as they arrived on ships. As the dominant urban settlement for the region it is likely that the markets were open daily, except Sundays. From the mid-fourteenth century, the revenue sources for many of the different retail markets and other customs were farmed out to individual burgesses for lump sums, but this was discontinued by 1400.

A huge variety of products were bought and sold, as illustrated by toll lists.[369] Thirty-seven occupations are mentioned specifically in the leet rolls,[370] and a further seventeen might be implied from surnames, but this is an unreliable source of occupational data by the fifteenth century. One would, of course, expect a wider range of trades and occupations in a large borough compared to the occupational profile of Clare or Newmarket. Overall, Ipswich had a fairly stable and prosperous economy by the early fifteenth century, based on a wide number of economic functions and its role as a cloth and wool distributor. There are only a few indicators that it was suffering from the widespread urban malaise seen elsewhere in English towns.[371] There were several wealthy merchants in Ipswich who were heavily involved in the import–export trades and who also comprised a significant element of the town's governing and propertied class.[372] Ipswich was primarily a centre of trade and its burgesses tried to protect their privileged position against the incursion of outsiders. The royal charter of 1200 formally gave burgesses the right to choose their

---

[369] *Black Book*, ii, pp. 178–207 (*c*.1309).

[370] These were baker, barber, beerbrewer, bowyer, brewer, butcher, butler, card-maker, carpenter, carter, clerk, cook, cooper, cordwainer, ditcher, drover, dyer, fishmonger, fletcher, fuller, furbisher, hunter, innkeeper, mariner, mason, merchant, ploughman, roper, shepherd, skinner, smith, tailor, tanner, vintner, weaver, woad dealer and wright. The additional occupational surnames were chandler, chapman, cobbler, cork-maker, draper, glover, goldsmith, haberdasher, net-maker, patten-maker, porter, potter, saddler, spicer, taverner, tiler and turner.

[371] In 1447 the chamberlains were ordered to repair decaying houses. Richardson (ed.), *Annalls of Ipswche*, p. 104. A charter of 1463 did complain about problems raising money due to a burdensome fee farm and royal tallages, losses in shipping, and the emigration of wealthier burgesses. Allen, *Ipswich Borough Archives*, p. 6; *CChR*, vi, pp. 197–9. However, it is not easy to interpret how these complaints relate to the general and per capita prosperity of Ipswich in light of the post-Black Death population decline and administrative difficulties. See Dobson, 'Urban decline' and above, pp. 13–14.

[372] Nicholas Amor has identified some thirty-six Ipswich burgesses in the 1390s who were involved in overseas trade, especially the export of cloth and import of wine (personal communication). See also Bailey, *Medieval Suffolk*, p. 281.

own officers, collect and pay a farm of £40 to the royal Exchequer, control their own jurisdiction, and be impleaded in the borough courts regarding their tenements and debts contracted within the town.[373] Those who were at 'lot and scot' also had freedom of tolls and stallage throughout the town and country.

The government and courts of Ipswich

Ipswich had the greatest powers of self-government of any borough in Suffolk, and throughout the later medieval period the borough continued to receive numerous confirming or amending charters, usually expanding their liberties.[374] In the early fourteenth century (1328), all freedom-holders had to own a house in the borough within a year and a day of being made a burgess, partly to help the enforcements of distraint in court but also to ensure they had a stake in town affairs.[375] The community of Ipswich was keen to outline who did and did not have access to rights and liberties. The charters and burgess status emphasised unity and loyalty, the delineation of certain privileges and the obligations of residents. By the fourteenth century, the main governing body of the borough was to consist of two bailiffs, four coroners (reduced to two in 1317) and twelve chief portmen, as well as officers such as sergeants, chamberlains and clerks.[376] The twelve portmen of Ipswich were the representatives of the parishes and were supposedly elected by 'common assent'. However, all the candidates were drawn from a narrow selection of the 'better, more discreet' men of the borough and so urban authority was concentrated in the hands of a small elite.[377] Only freemen of the town were eligible for office, and the early bailiffs also served as coroners and all coroners as chief portmen. There were thus, each year, four men who were dominant in Ipswich's governance.

The charter for Ipswich also formalised a guild merchant, which effectively established the commercial hierarchy. The merchant guild may

---

[373] *RCh*, i, p. 65; Gross, *Gild Merchant*, ii, pp. 116–23.

[374] See Martin, 'The governance of Ipswich', pp. xix–xxv.

[375] Alsford, *Towns*, 'History of Medieval Ipswich – Development of Local Government'; Martin, 'Ipswich', pp. 91–2; *Black Book*, pp. 154–7, c.63 [61] (*c.*1309).

[376] The town government remained largely in this form until the mid-fifteenth century. The office of mayor never developed in medieval Ipswich. In a charter of 1446, Ipswich was formally incorporated and gave the borough the formal right to a common seal and to acquire corporate lands and rents, both of which had long been in use. Royal officials were excluded from the liberties, and the powers of Justices of the Peace were vested in the two bailiffs and four of the chief portmen. *CChR*, vi, pp. 54–5; Alsford, *Towns*, 'History of Medieval Ipswich – Development of Local Government'; Martin, 'The governance of Ipswich', p. xxvii.

[377] Bailey, *Medieval Suffolk*, p. 136.

well have existed informally before then, even acting as a *de facto* town council.[378] In thirteenth- and early fourteenth-century Ipswich, there was a close connection between the merchant guild and town government. The town hall was called the guild hall and the officials of the guild, such as the aldermen, were originally elected by parish representatives of the town. However, the merchant guild was reconstituted as the Corpus Christi Guild by 1325 and had a more ceremonial purpose, organising the annual pageant and feast in order to reinforce the solidarity of the town community. The pageant also asserted the comparative status and prestige of the individual trade groups. It is possible that the guild still played a lesser governmental role in the later period, particularly in regulating certain artisans. Aldermen were still elected, all burgesses were members of the guild, and no formal trade or craft guilds (with ordinances) were established in Ipswich. However, it does appear that much of the trading regulation became based around the borough officials and courts.

The charter of 1200 formally granted the townsmen a degree of autonomy and surely bolstered their communal self-confidence. The town courts and officers now upheld the customs of the borough and the privileges of the burgesses. The main judicial institution at this time was the Portmanmote, which handled admissions of burgesses, pleas initiated by royal writ and pleas relating to burgage tenements. By the fourteenth century, the business of petty pleas had been devolved to the petty court, while the Portmanmote often became known as the great court, responsible for great pleas. However, while the great court was ostensibly the main judicial assembly, by the late fourteenth century its administrative business had been seemingly hived off to a general court.[379] In addition, the administration of land transactions was supported by the more regular recognisance court (or Petty Court of Recognizances). The Portmanmote lost its pre-eminence completely after the Black Death and lay in abeyance for long periods due to lack of business. Indeed, the Petty Court was probably the most active court in Ipswich, dealing not only with personal pleas but also with matters of public policy.[380] Sometime during the early fifteenth century, the structure was formalised and the Portmanmote was responsible only for infrequent real actions, while the general court (which now itself came to be called the Great Court) was

---

[378] *Ibid.*, pp. 139–40.

[379] Martin, 'The governance of Ipswich', p. xxvi; Allen, *Ipswich Borough Archives*, pp. 42–4.

[380] The Petty Court rolls provide a wealth of detail regarding the broader dimensions of trade in Ipswich, particularly debts and contracts. An extensive study is being undertaken by N. R. Amor for his forthcoming book, *Late Medieval Ipswich*.

the assembly of free burgesses, issuing ordinances, admitting burgesses and electing officers.[381]

There was also the leet court, an ancient institution which annually dealt with policing matters of the four wards of the borough. The jurisdiction of the leet and the system of frankpledge was a franchise delegated by the Crown.[382] The bailiffs had oversight in Ipswich, but the sub-bailiffs (or sergeants) were the chief regulatory and enforcement officers for the decisions of the courts and councillors. They were easily recognisable, dressed in the borough's livery, and they were expected to uphold the assizes and regulation of victuals and other trading regulation, as well as deal with nuisances and minor assaults.[383] Most retail trading offences were thus recorded at the yearly leet court, held on Tuesday in Whitsun week, to which all males over the age of twelve were compelled to attend. A separate court was held for the four wards (North, South, East and West) and was presided over by the two bailiffs and three capital pledges (or 'headboroughs') for each ward, who constituted the jury. Affeerers decided on the level of amercement for offences. With no craft guilds and the declining influence of the merchant guild, a small group of officials and merchants thus controlled the government of Ipswich and regulated trade. There are a number of sources from Ipswich with which to recover evidence of the daily regulation and activity of retail trade, such as the debt litigation in the Petty Court rolls. However, the main sources used for this case study are fifteen surviving borough leet court rolls up to 1468 (those from 1359, 1415, 1416, 1419, 1421, 1423, 1424, 1434, 1436–8 and 1465–8).[384] These in turn only cover forty-two of the sixty courts held in the four different wards.[385] This makes it difficult to analyse the data in any systematic way and this brief survey will only highlight some of the main impressions that these leet courts provide. The prosecutions and presentments can also be compared to Ipswich's trading ordinances.

As already seen, the trading regulations of boroughs were partly based upon national laws and partly upon their own codification of privileges and customs. In Ipswich, these customs were compiled into a text called

---

[381] After Edward IV's charter of 1463, the Portmanmote's judicial role contracted even further. Martin has discussed the administrative changes that took place in Ipswich in the fourteenth and fifteenth centuries; Martin, 'The governance of Ipswich'. See also Allen, *Ipswich Borough Archives*, pp. 42–4.

[382] See above, pp. 147–9.   [383] Bailey, *Medieval Suffolk*, p. 135.

[384] A single leet court roll also survives for the 1440s/50s, but the ward is not identifiable and it has not been used for this study. SRO (I), c/2/8/1/12. This study only looks at the years up to 1468, but further leet court rolls are available from 1471 onwards.

[385] SRO (I), c/2/8/1/1–11, c2/10/1/2–6 (with sincere thanks also to Nicholas Amor for allowing me to view his own data from these courts).

'le Domesday', one of the earliest custumals in England. After the original custumal was stolen in 1272 by a former common clerk, John le Blake, a new set of ordinances was compiled from memory (and with amendments) in 1291 by twenty-four of the burgesses. There was a concerted attempt to preserve ancient usages but, as Martin states, it is likely that the burgesses were 'dignifying some current practices with the stamp of antiquity'.[386] This new Domesday roll does not survive, but several rescensions were made thereafter until the late fifteenth century, with the earliest dated to around 1309.[387] There were few notable additions regarding specific market regulations through to the fifteenth century, and the longevity of many trade ordinances emphasises consistent concerns about the medieval marketplace.

However, one notable development was the emphasis on forestalling in the 1320 reforms, following a royal charter acquired in 1317 and earlier petitions to the Crown by 'poor men' of Ipswich in 1304.[388] The document also emphasised that it was a common right, by reason of the franchise, that every burgess paying scot and lot and contributing to aids of the town had equal entitlement to a share in any merchandise being sold in the town (a principle that forestalling undermined). However, certain burgesses had contravened this, particularly by becoming hosts of outsider merchants and selling their goods for them in private places, sometimes even without consent of the visiting merchants, and claiming a quarter of the merchandise as their hostage fee. Consequently, the following ordinances (which went far beyond correction of the problem identified in the preamble) were enacted. Goods brought into Ipswich by outside merchants were to be sold only in official marketplaces, without any interference from hosts or forestallers. Anyone convicted of forestalling was to forfeit the merchandise involved and be disenfranchised. Contracts of sale, including the dates of payment and the names of sureties, were to be confirmed in the presence of the bailiffs, which ensured that possessions could be attached if payment was not made. These 1320 ordinances also decreed that all merchandise should be freely offered for sale in the town, and that strangers who kept to the good usages of the town deserved protection.[389]

---

[386] Martin, 'The governance of Ipswich', p. xxii.

[387] Martin, *Early Court Rolls*, pp. 7–9. The versions in *Black Book*, ii, pp. 16–207, are an early fourteenth-century (*c*.1309) French edition (BL, MS Additional 25012) and a fifteenth-century English edition (BL, MS Additional 25011). There are other thirteenth-century copies, such as the Black Domesday (SRO (I), c/4/1/1) and the White Domesday (SRO (I), c/4/1/2). Allen, *Ipswich Borough Archives*, pp. 412–21.

[388] *CChR*, iii, pp. 344–5; Allen, *Ipswich Borough Archives*, pp. xxiii–xxiv; Alsford, *Towns*, 'History of Medieval Ipswich – Development of Local Government'.

[389] Martin, 'The governance of Ipswich', p. xxiii.

The earliest extant 'Little Domesday' of Ipswich was thus an early fourteenth-century modification of the town's ordinances. It exemplified the controls of the corporation over commercial matters. In the eighty-three chapters of this custumal, most covered rights of property and laws of inheritance, ten concerned the conduct of officials, and a further fifteen covered aspects of marketing. There was a particular concern with the devices of credit, debt and contract, which were the lubricants for a successful market community. The custumal ordered that wardens be assigned to the market to ensure that the regulations were upheld 'for the common profit of the town and surrounding region', and that ordinances were announced publicly in the market. All goods coming to Ipswich were to be freely and openly offered for sale. Bargains were to be acknowledged before the bailiffs and goods brought to appointed places of sale and not forestalled.[390] Traders and pedlars from outside the town were not to sell before the hour of prime and only in open market.[391] These ordinances were mainly to allow all burgesses the right to share in bargains. However, the suspicion remained that many merchants hosted foreign traders and privately bargained for their goods.

Another basic condition of the custumal was that all measures of the town were approved and sealed with the town seal. Anyone caught using unsealed weights and measures was to be heavily amerced. As in Clare and Newmarket, Ipswich's authorities specifically watched out for those who sold by the auncel, 'contrary to statute', and several wool merchants were upbraided for this offence in 1415.[392] Bailiffs had the power to test weights and measures at any time, to prevent fraud 'in the forseyd toun of Gippeswich among such maner of mesurys in esclaundre of the toun, ne of damage to the pepele'.[393] A few cases appear in the leet court which highlighted this need for standardisation in weights and measures. For instance, in 1466, Remkyn Taylour was fined 40d. for having a weigh-beam within his inn, when he should have been using the common weigh-beam of the town. He was ordered to desist under pain of a further 40s. penalty. The rhetoric of communal benefit and a fear of harming the town's reputation were thus constant themes in the custumal and, as seen below, were repeated in court roll entries. The interests of resident merchants and manufacturers were protected, but the customs also drew upon broader principles of trade conduct and ethics.

---

[390] *Black Book*, ii, pp. 100–1, c.26 (*c.*1309).   [391] *Ibid.*, ii, pp. 102–3, c.28 (*c.*1309).
[392] SRO (I), c/2/8/1/2.   [393] *Black Book*, ii, pp. 176–7, c.83 [80] (*c.*1309).

The assizes of bread and ale

The bulk of leet court trading prosecutions in Ipswich were for breaches of the assizes of bread and ale. The Ipswich Custumal concerning the assize of bread drew upon statute law, in that bakers were to be amerced according to the enormity of their trespass, with a fourth offence leading to the pillory. Additionally, as in many larger boroughs, a fifth offence was deemed significant enough for a baker to give up his business. Bakers were also expected to specialise in particular breads: either wastel, cocket and trayt; simnel and trayt; or wholewheat and corn breads.[394] In another local specification, the Ipswich Custumal included an extra entry on equipment. Any bakers who made wastel, simnel or first cocket, were to use a fine bolter from Rennes, or else their bolter would be burned beside the pillory. Similarly, in the leet court itself, bakers were warned for not bringing their bolters to be checked, to the 'grave damage of the community', and there was concern about the fineness of flour. However, there are no indications of any bakers facing the pillory or being expelled, and they appear to have been amerced according to the size of their output.

There were relatively few bakers presented in any of the wards.[395] It seems that baking in Ipswich was concentrated in the hands of a few, large-scale commercial operations, with poorer, irregular bakers either pushed out or to the fringes. Overall, an average of one to two bakers are presented in each of the North, South and East Wards per session, and just over three in the West Ward. This constitutes an average of just eight bakers each year for the whole of Ipswich. All were men except for a single reference to Gundre Joye, the widow of the baker Richard Joye, who was amerced 40d. in 1421, again implying that large-scale baking was a household affair.[396] The individuals listed in the leet court were often termed 'common bakers' of bread and could be fined quite large amounts. The amercements for each ward averaged between 23.8d. and 33.2d. per baker, though individual amercements could reach as high as 4s.-10s.

There were a number of individuals who dominated production in the 1420s and 1430s. Three bakers were prominent in the West Ward: Gilbert Bobat (average amercement of 35d.) and the two John Turnours (averaging 36d. and 29d.). Thomas Bast, in the North Ward, was fined

---

[394] *Ibid.*, ii, pp. 172–5, c.80 [77] (*c.*1309).   [395] SRO (I), c/2/8/1/1–11, c2/10/1/2–6.

[396] The male domination of urban baking is attested in other studies. Goldberg, *Women, Work, and Life Cycle*, pp. 88–92; Kowaleski, *Local Markets*, p. 139; McIntosh, *Working Women*, pp. 182–6.

extensive sums for baking against the assize, an average of nearly 60d. across six courts between 1423 and 1438. John Wode (East Ward) was another central figure in the baking trade, as well as many other trading activities in Ipswich, for which he received the second-highest average amercement at 44d. By the 1460s it was men like Robert Doye (West Ward, average 32d.), Ralph Laurence (North, average 22d.) and Thomas Medewe (North, average 24d.) who were predominant in the baking trade, though their average amercements were slightly less than those working some thirty to forty years earlier. Despite the high amercements in several cases, and the promulgation of stringent borough regulations, it appears that the fifteenth-century assize of bread was as much an effectual licensing scheme in Ipswich as in Newmarket and Clare. There were recurrent offenders, listed year after year, and little indication that the employment of corporal punishment was even considered. Amercements levels varied year to year, but did not necessarily rise annually as stipulated by both statute and municipal laws. Instead, the high levels of amercements seemingly reflect the output and prosperity of certain bakers, and such a 'production tax' certainly generated a useful income stream for the corporation (an average of nearly £1 per year for all four wards).

There is evidence that not all large towns operated the assize of bread in this manner. In early fourteenth-century Oxford, the wide variation in amercements and regular use of the pillory appear to suggest that actual offences, as well as production levels, were being monitored in a carefully regulated market, though again there are cases of bakers being amerced consistent amounts over long periods.[397] Similarly, in late fifteenth-century Southampton, where there was an intensive regulatory system that made assize checks every two to four weeks, there are numerous occasions where bakers are noted as having produced bread of 'good weight and satisfactory' and they are not amerced. It appears that in some larger towns, at times when the sale of bread was contentious and under strain, assize regulations were enforced more strictly.[398]

The bailiffs of Ipswich announced the assize of ale every Michaelmas and any brewing contrary to the assize was to be judged according to the statutes of the realm.[399] In the leet court rolls, the standard formula for offences against the assize of ale increasingly included the statement that the amercements were also for brewers who were using cups and dishes

[397] Salter (ed.), *Medieval Archives*, ii, pp. 143–82.
[398] Anderson (ed.), *Assize of Bread Book*, pp. 2–9.
[399] *Black Book*, ii, pp. 174–5, c.81 [78] (c.1309).

instead of lawful measures. In contrast to the bakers, ale-brewers faced consistently low amercements, averaging 6.7d.–7.1d. per offence across the four wards. Many of the individual brewers were amerced every year, such as Thomas Hawe who faced 6d.–8d. penalties every recorded year between 1421 and 1438. Only occasional individuals faced an amercement higher than 12d. This included John Wode, a regular brewer as well as baker, who was amerced 12d.–24d. throughout the 1410s to 1430s. In South Ward, the number of brewers averaged fourteen per year, in the North, sixteen, in the West, twenty-three, and in the East, eighteen. This meant an average of seventy-one brewers for the whole of Ipswich per year, and perhaps some 270 separate brewing households appearing in the surviving court rolls from 1415 to 1468. If we assume that most were part of a larger household, many of whom would have partaken in the brewing process, then the brewers of Ipswich constituted about a tenth of the urban households in any one year. From 1415 to 1468, we can identify thirty-eight brewers who were amerced 10d. and above and it is likely that they were the more regular and substantial producers. This included fifteen men who were owners of 'common inns' and thus needed a regular supply of ale and bread (see Table 17). Again, the regularised nature of the presentments and continual amercements at a standard level, without any indication of corporal punishment, are suggestive of a licensing system allied to production levels.

It was mostly men who were presented for brewing offences in the Ipswich leet, possibly in lieu of their wives. Indeed, many men named as brewers or sellers of ale can be identified as pursuing a more notable primary occupation, whether as a tanner, dyer, baker, butcher, fishmonger or even mason. However, there were also a handful of women presented each year. In all, there are sixty-eight appearances by sole women in the 723 surviving offences for the assize of ale, which constitutes nearly 10 per cent of the cases. These included women who appear four times in the surviving court rolls, such as Agnes Davy (1419–24), Beatrice Toly (1434–8) and Joan Gigoo (1465–8). Given the predominance of men in the lists, it appears that the privileges of *femme sole* did not extend to presenting married women in these lists. It seems more likely that such presented women were unmarried or widows, such as Margery Thorp who was listed as the widow of William in 1421 and amerced the hefty amount of 24d. for brewing against the assize. It is difficult to determine what role married women played in the brewing trade and it is too easy to assume that their husbands were simply presented at court in their place. Bennett, McIntosh and Mate all argue that urban brewing was becoming more professionalised and concentrated in male hands during the fifteenth century, particularly the larger urban operations.[400] Many of the men presented for brewing in Ipswich were also on the lists as bakers, butchers, innkeepers or fishmongers, and it is very possible that the production and sale of victuals was a joint household activity, especially for the more regularly presented, who were perhaps selling from permanent shops or inns.[401] The more irregular traders might be concealing a supplementary brewing by an alewife. Untangling the actual division of labour within a household is problematic given the available court records and the complications of patriarchal presentment.

Several 'Duchemen', perhaps part of the immigrant community for the cloth industry, were also fined in the leet court for illicit brewing of beer.[402] Beer became increasingly popular in England during the fifteenth century, drawing on continental expertise in its early manifestations.[403] The addition of hops meant that it lasted longer and was more easily transported, making a more viable and profitable commodity. However, it was also more capital and labour intensive in its production. It appears that in the 1410s and 1420s, beer-brewers like Geoffrey Pape and Dirrik van Graven required a licence from the borough authorities in order to brew and sell this new product. They faced fines of up to between 4s. and 13s. By the 1430s, however, they too were subject to an assize and were accused of both excessive prices and selling with unlawful measures. This could incur heavy penalties of between 1s. and 10s. for this early generation of beer-brewers in England.[404] It is difficult to know exactly why amercements were so much higher for beer-brewing than ale-brewing. It might be a case of discrimination against aliens or against this new product, or possibly beer had already developed into a high-profit business. Many of the lesser fines for beer-brewing occur between 1423 and 1434, either side of which the amercements are significant across the board. One could suggest that the early years were an attempt to bring beer-brewing fully within the auspices of the town authorities; once achieved, for a short period they treated the beer-brewers much like the ale-brewers. Indeed, in 1437, Pape was amerced 6d. as an ale-brewer, even though he was surely making beer as he was in the years both before and after, including 160d., 120d. and 6d. as beer-brewer in 1419, 1421

---

[400] Bennett, *Ale*; McIntosh, *A Community Transformed*, pp. 281–91; Mate, *Daughters, Wives and Widows*, pp. 53–71.

[401] See also Newman, *Late Medieval Northallerton*, pp. 94–8.

[402] 'Duchemen' could refer more generally to northern, continental Europeans.

[403] For a discussion about the emergence of beer-brewing in England, see Mate, *Trade and Economic Developments*, ch. 5; Bennett, *Ale*, ch. 5; Britnell, *Growth and Decline*, pp. 195–7; McIntosh, *Working Women*, pp. 163–6.

[404] SRO (I), c/2/8/1/3, 4, 5, 6, 7.

and 1434 respectively. However, by the 1460s the Ipswich authorities were making a firm distinction between ale and beer and attempting to draw maximum revenue from these brewing immigrants who might be less able to complain.

There are other indications in the leet court that these 'Duchemen' were discriminated against while undertaking their trades in beer, leather and cloth. In 1421, Geoffrey Pape was amerced a hefty 80d. for depositing filth, excrement and the malt dregs of beer in the water gates, from which a very bad smell arose to the nuisance of the people, as well as the destruction and raising of the gates. He was ordered not to do so in the future under penalty of 40d. When Matthew Duchman assaulted Richard Duchman and John Duchman in 1424 he was amerced 6s., a significantly higher amount than for similar assaults. It is possible that it was an especially brutal assault, or else it was an indication that officials wished to keep these outsiders in order. Similarly, in 1437, Joice Duchman was fined 2s. for assaulting Isabell Duchewoman. Cornelius Duchman and Gerard Duchman also faced significant fines of 44d. and 40d. for their leather-making in 1468. Alien residents were seemingly subject to rigorous penalties if they transgressed.

Regraters

The Ipswich Custumal expressed a continual dislike of middlemen, based upon principles of the common good and the maintenance of public order. No non-burgess or regrater was to make a bargain outside of the market or town, or else they faced forfeiture and then imprisonment. Any forestallers of fish or poultry were to face forfeiture and imprisonment for the first offence, the pillory for the second, and abstaining from his occupation for a year and a day.[405] No regrater in the market was to buy from another regrater, since this pushed prices up. Again the stipulated punishments for repeat offences were confiscation, imprisonment, pillory and finally giving up their occupation for a year and a day.[406]

However, in the actual leet court, there is little indication of moral opprobrium and regraters of bread and ale were nearly all amerced 3d.– 4d. over a number of sessions.[407] Compared to brewing or baking, the average amercement levels for regrating were much lower, indicative of a more humble activity that generated very low profits. In the East Ward, in 1424, regraters were accused of selling cupfuls of ale at $\frac{1}{2}$d. each

---

[405] *Black Book*, ii, pp. 100–1, c.26 (c.1309).   [406] *Ibid.*, ii, pp. 102–3, c.27 (c.1309).
[407] SRO (I), c/2/8/1/1–11, c2/10/1/2–6.

where ten of these cups made a gallon in volume. Consequently, these regraters were effectively selling a gallon of ale for 5d., well above the assize rate which was normally not more than $1\frac{1}{2}$d.–2d. a gallon, yet they were generally amerced only 4d. each. As with brewing, significant numbers of regraters were amerced a standard amount at each court session. For instance, either Edmund Bercok or his wife, Katherine, were amerced 4d. for gannoking ale at eight separate leet courts in the 1420s and 1430s. These consistently low amercement levels again indicate a type of licensing system, without any appreciable attempt at deterrence. There was no real indication of greater penalties, besides occasional fines of 8d.–12d., despite warnings against using cups and dishes instead of sealed measures.

In Exeter, Kowaleski found that large numbers were fined small amounts (3d.–6d.) for retailing without membership of the freedom or for forestalling and regrating. She suggested that this was a clear sign that the ruling elite found it impossible to restrict retailing and middlemen activities to the franchised members of the town. The authorities thus used regulations as a means of licensing, control and raising revenue, rather than as a true deterrent. Nevertheless, higher fines were used when certain retailers challenged trading monopolies or price controls.[408] Regraters perhaps served a recognisably useful purpose in larger towns, where there were fewer bakers and brewers per head. There were specific ordinances which limited regraters to later times of the day, but they served as redistributors of produce, aiding producers and consumers.

There was an average of twenty-two regraters of bread presented each year, dispersed fairly evenly across all four wards, and sixty-three 'gannokers' (ale-sellers). Over the span of the court rolls, there are hints of an occupational cycle, with certain individual households rising up the business tree. Edmund Lamb was recorded as a gannoker from 1421–4 but as a brewer in 1434–8, and similarly Alexander and Margery Fordham rose from gannokers to brewers during the 1420s. Just eighteen (8 per cent) of the 198 cases for regrating bread were specifically named as women, while just 6 per cent (38 from 679 cases) of the gannokers were named as women. This is a surprisingly small number, but may simply reflect the same tendency seen in the assize of ale for husbands to be named in leet courts instead of their wives. The named females were probably single women or widows, perhaps selling ale and bread from temporary alehouses, alongside their husbands in inns or shops, or by cupfuls in the street.[409] Dozens of petty retailers sold both bread

[408] Kowaleski, *Local Markets*, p. 186.
[409] Mate, *Trade and Economic Developments*, p. 74.

and ale and a handful of them also forestalled a variety of victuals. It is possible that this all points to the existence of more general shops in Ipswich, where households sold ale, bread, meat, poultry, eggs, fish and even candles.

Innkeepers

Fifty-five different Ipswich households were recorded as running guest-houses or inns ('hospicium') across the surviving leet courts for 1415 to 1468. On average, there were apparently some eighteen inns in operation at any one time across the city, if the recorded offences cover all the establishments. The main innkeeping offences were to bake white bread and horsebread against the assize, and to sell victuals, bread, fish, meat, hay and oats for excessive profit, to the 'grave damage of the town'. These baking offences were not included under the standard baking assize list and were considered to be particular to innkeeping. In the 1410s to 1430s, John Wode (of the North then East Ward) faced heavy amercements of between 32d. and 160d. (average of 90.5d.), for baking in his inn. In comparison to the amercements handed out to others he paid significantly heavier fines, perhaps indicating flagrant breaches of the law or a larger operation than most.[410] He was indeed a very active man from 1415 to 1437 in both brewing and baking, and his exceptionally heavy amercements slightly skew the figures for innkeepers in the East. Indeed, the high overall average amercement of 14.2d. for Ipswich innkeepers is determined by the activities of a few prominent individuals with average amercements of 18d. or more, notably John Wode, Robert Blomfeld, Walter Colk, John Denys, John Joye and John Sudbury (see Table 17). In the 1430s, Walter Colk's fines averaged over 40d. for his excessive profits in his North Ward inn. He was also regularly amerced 6d.–12d. for brewing and selling ale and 4d. for selling bread. In effect, Colk and Wode were amerced three or four times at every court, including increasingly large amounts for brewing and innkeeping. We cannot be certain whether these fines were indicative of growing, profitable businesses or of a court trying to rein in illegal, belligerent activities.

Most other innkeepers were fined 4d.–12d. for selling at an exces-sive price, either 'two pennies for that worth 1d.', or 'three pennies for the value of two pennies'.[411] In 1424, John Robard baked white and horsebread forty times in his inn and did not keep the assize, but he only paid a 6d. amercement.[412] They were probably taking advantage of the private nature of their transactions, as well as using a variety of

[410] SRO (I), c/2/8/1/2, 3, 6, 7.   [411] SRO (I), c/2/8/1/6, 7.   [412] SRO (I), c/2/8/1/7.

unsealed measures. Like John Wode and Walter Colk, many of the identifiable innkeepers or their wives appeared in the leet court for other
trading offences, demonstrating a range of activities that could be tied
into the services offered by inns (see Table 17). It was quite common
that innkeeping households also brewed; indeed, some forty-one of the
fifty-five households (75 per cent) were amerced at some stage for brewing against the assize of ale, while twenty-four households gannoked ale
(44 per cent). The function and size of these inns appears to have been
diverse, catering not just to travellers but also operating as victualling
houses in providing food and drink to local people. It is difficult to determine who within the household actually ran the inn on a day-to-day
basis. Most of the named proprietors were male but, like brewing, the
presentment procedures might hide the actual division of labour. There
are only a few recorded instances that suggest that women did run inns,
such as Katherine Aldham who was amerced just 4d. in 1465 and 1466
for innkeeping offences. John Hardyng's wife appears to have taken over
the inn in 1468 upon the death of her husband, while Anna Watkyn
was also recorded as a widow in 1465–7. A similar scenario is found in
Exeter, where a small number of widows ran inns, perhaps suggesting
that they were also primarily responsible when their husbands were alive,
or at least contributed to the inn's upkeep, perhaps by brewing.[413]

Some of the more notable innkeepers, Robert Blomfeld, John Depyng,
Richard Maiet, John Myddlylton and John Wode, were also involved in
the wine trade. This was easily the most valuable of all Ipswich's import
trades, perhaps accounting for nearly 90 per cent of the value of all
imports in the late fourteenth century, when wine imports were reaching a
peak across England.[414] The Ipswich Custumal outlined that the taverns
and cellars of the town should be searched and the wine tasted each year
by the bailiffs and some honest vintners. Any wine that was unfit to drink
or be mixed ('ony wyn that be corrupt and perlous to drynkyn for mannys
body, or for to medelyn with newe wyn') was to be seized. The ordinance
decreed a public and humiliating ritual for the disposal of corrupt wine. It
would be poured into the high street while the bailiff publicly condemned
it: 'there in comoun sight of men dampnyn the tunne of the pipe'.[415] In
1424, John Wode was amerced 20s. as a 'vintner' for selling 600 gallons
of red wine in his tavern (or inn) at 8d. a gallon when statute law stated
the price should be 6d.[416] This was obviously considered a flagrant and

[413] Kowaleski, *Local Markets*, p. 144; Mate, *Women*, p. 45; McIntosh, *Working Women*, pp. 202–9.
[414] Personal communication with Nicholas Amor.
[415] *Black Book*, ii, pp. 176–7, c.82 [79] (*c*.1309).   [416] SRO (I), c/2/8/1/7.

Table 17. *The innkeepers of Ipswich, 1415–1468*

| | | | Regrater | | | | | |
Innkeepers	Average amercement	Brewer	Baker	Ale	Bread	Fish[a]	Meat	Vintner	Office
Katherine Aldham	4d.								
John Asselot	12d.	*				*			
Henry Barbour	12d.	*		*					
Robert Blomfeld	23d.							*	CP, A
John Bunt	3d.	*							
Alexander Bush	15.3d.			*					
Thomas and Isabel Cadon #	6.8d.	*		*					CP
John Caldewell	12d.	*							B
John Campyon	6d.	*							A
William Chambre	–	*							
Walter Colk	28.9d.	*		*	*				
Anthony Denys	12d.	*							
John Denys #	18d.			*					
John Depyng	13d.	*	*		*		*		
John Deve	4d.	*		*		*			CP
Robert Deye	10.5d.		*						
Richard Disse (and wife)	9d.	*		*					
Thomas Dobill	5d.	*		*					
John Dust	6d.	*			*				
Robert Fynche	3d.	*		*					
Reginald Gardyner	12d.			*					
Richard Godfrey[b]	6d.			*		*			
John Hardyng (and widow)	5d.	*							
John Hecham	7d.	*		*					
Robert Heryng[c]	4d.				*	*			
John Joye	18d.	*							B, C
Robert Kyrkehous	5d.			*		*			
John Kyrre	5d.	*	*						
Nicholas Lamb	4d.	*		*					
William Langlonde	8d.	*				*			
Richard Maiet	10d.	*		*		*		*	
Robert Martyn	5d.	*							

(cont.)

Table 17. (*cont.*)

| Innkeepers | Average amercement | Brewer | Baker | Regrater | | | | | |
				Ale	Bread	Fish[a]	Meat	Vintner	Office
Adam Mey	4d.	*							
John Myddylton	17.3d.		*					*	
Peter Parker	4d.	*							
John and Katherine Peyton	5d.	*							
Thomas Prat	8d.	*		*		*			
John Priour	4d.	*							
John Robard	6d.	*							
John Smyth (at the quay)	6d.	*			*				
John Smyth (dutchman) #	12d.	*		*					
Thomas Smyth	4d.	*		*					
William Smyth	4d.	*		*					
William Snow	11.3d.	*		*					
William Sparhauk[d]	8d.	*		*	*				
Matthew Stabeler	4d.	*				*			
John Sudbury	24d.	*		*			*		
Remkyn Taylour	6.7d.			*					
John Turnour (dyer)	4d.	*	*						
Anna Watkyn (widow)	12d.								
William Whethereld	10d.	*							B, C
Robert/ Walter/ Margaret Whytlok	5.3d.	*							
John Wode	90.5d.	*	*					?	C
Robert Wulcy #	3.5d.	*					*		
Thomas Wynter	6d.	*							CP, A

Notes: a – includes forestalling fish; b – sold candles for excessive profit; c – forestalled wheat; d – sold badly tanned leather; B – bailiff; C – coroner; CP – capital pledge; A – affeerer; # – allowed fornication and prostitutes within their houses.

Source: SRO (I), c/2/8/1/1–11, c2/10/1/2–6.

significant offence. By comparison, John Tonge, a taverner, was fined only 12d. in the same session for selling 100 gallons of red wine at 8d. a gallon, and William Debenham and John Kneppyng, both formerly bailiffs, were fined 2s. each for selling eighty gallons at 8d. There were several cases in the 1460s of wine sold at an excessive price and most were amerced only 4d.–6d., such as William Wattys who was both a capital pledge and affeerer when presented. The exception was Godfrey Makynham who was amerced 10s. in this decade for dealing 'contrary to the ordinances of the town and the proclamation of the bailiffs, selling wine for 8d. a gallon'. This severe penalty again suggests a flagrant breach of the laws that the authorities wanted to punish effectively.

It is likely that certain innkeepers, particularly those involved in the wine trade, ran substantial establishments, while lesser innkeepers ran places that were more akin to alehouses but with a couple of guest rooms. Overall, however, many Ipswich innkeepers appear to have been fairly prosperous and influential men. There were a number who served as bailiff at some point during their careers: John Joye (1420–2, 1425–6), William Whethereld (1428–9), John Caldewell (1425–6, 1436–7); while John Joye (1419–20, 1424–5), John Wode (1419–21) and William Whethereld (1421–3, 1425–6, 1436–8) were elected as coroners. This was despite the statutory legislation of 1382 against victuallers holding urban office,[417] and the fact that, by 1429, the Ipswich Custumal specifically stated that no bailiff was to sell ale or victuals, nor own a hostelry, during his term of office, or else face a heavy fine of £10.[418] This ordinance was perhaps intended to prevent abuse of the office for personal profit, though it also had implications for the dignity of such retailing professions. Both John Wode and William Whethereld certainly faced amercements for innkeeping offences while they were serving in office as coroners, but it is not known whether they did so while serving as bailiff.[419] Other individuals also appear in the assize amercement lists while acting as bailiffs, such as John Joye in 1421, Edmund Wynter in 1467 and William Style in 1468. Style was amerced the hefty amount of 40d., perhaps because he was contravening the prohibition on retailing while in office.[420] Ultimately, however, innkeepers in Ipswich rose to the top of the official tree and it seems likely that they would continue to do so. Kowaleski similarly found that Exeter innkeepers, taverners

[417] See pp. 167–8.   [418] Alsford, *Towns* (Ipswich, Appx 2, c.86).
[419] SRO (I), c/2/8/1/5, 6.
[420] Britnell likewise found that most bailiffs in late fourteenth-century Colchester were involved in commerce, either wholesaling or retailing. Britnell, *Growth and Decline*, p. 111. See also Holt, 'Gloucester', p. 150.

and hostelers were relatively wealthy, involved in occupations outside hostelling, and found among the upper ranks of citizens and officials.[421]

The reputations of innkeepers must have been fairly resilient. McIntosh argued that smaller inns were often viewed by authorities as potential hotbeds of disorder, attracting vagabonds, whores, thieves and the unruly.[422] Whether the inns of Ipswich were readily associated with disreputable activities is not certain.[423] In 1434, John Asselot was amerced 12d. for bypassing the public market (where fish should be sold) and selling instead from his private inn. He was threatened with an 80d. fine if he continued to undermine the basic precept of the 'public market'. He was also fined for a lean-to that encroached into the road, presumably an attempt to expand his inn's area for customers. Another activity that might have brought innkeepers into disrepute was the harbouring of prostitutes and thieves. There were five cases from 1415 to 1422, but these concerned men who are not identifiable innkeepers. The entries specifically state that it was their home or a common brothel, rather than an inn or hostel, including the home of Robert Lucas, who was to become bailiff the following year. However, these places may have been operating as alehouses. Thomas Barbour was a common gannoker and also convicted in 1416 of harbouring prostitutes and thieves in his house, while in 1419 Adam March (a brewer and seller of bread and ale) secretly entertained strangers and nightwalkers in the middle of the night. However, many more cases occurred in the 1460s, especially in 1468 when it appears that there was an extensive clamp-down on brothels, both in alehouses and inns. Fourteen individuals in 1468 were amerced between 1s. and 8s. (average 30d.) for encouraging fornication, adultery and prostitutes within their houses. Some, like Roger Bour, Peter Deye and John Heynes, were common gannokers and it is likely that they too were running alehouses. At least four others (Thomas Cadon, John Denys, John Smyth dutchman and Robert Wulcy) ran inns, which hints at how these establishments too might overstep common standards of moral behaviour.

Butchers, cooks and fishmongers

The other increasingly dominant victuallers, in terms of wealth and position, were the butchers. Britnell argued that the economic problems of the fifteenth century, and the competitive environment, encouraged town

---

[421] Kowaleski, *Local Markets*, pp. 143–7. See also Swanson, *Medieval Artisans*, p. 23.
[422] McIntosh, *Working Women*, pp. 204–5.
[423] Keene suggested that running an inn was seen as dishonourable. Keene, *Survey*, i, pp. 274–6.

authorities to pursue wider commercial regulation. For instance, by the 1420s, they began to punish more regularly butchers and innkeepers who sold their goods at an 'excessive' price.[424] Certainly, there were more cases of innkeepers and butchers being presented for trading infringements, but this might have reflected their increased numbers and heightened demand due to rising standards of living, as much as greater enforcement.

The hygiene problems of a large-scale butchering industry put increased pressure on many large towns. Several Ipswich butchers were prosecuted for leaving entrails and bones in the road and by their stalls, and for slaughtering animals in unauthorised places and streets.[425] In the 1430s and 1460s, there was a significant number of prosecutions for butchers who failed to bait bulls in Cornhill before slaughter; the penalty for this varied widely between 3d. and 12d. There were also butchers condemned for selling corrupt and putrid meat, with average amercements of 9.9d. (from thirteen cases) compared to 10.9d. for selling at excessive price. Some care has to be taken with these figures because of the terminology employed by the court clerk. For two separate leet courts in the West Ward, in 1421 and 1423, the same butchers were amerced similar amounts for corrupt meat in 1421 and excessive price in 1423 and no other butchery offences are recorded in those years, while in 1468 these offences were specifically delineated in the same court.[426] Nevertheless, there are hints that the selling of corrupt foodstuffs carried a certain stigma. The customs of Ipswich apparently allowed butchers to sell unwholesome meat from beneath the pillory, the market symbol of communal disapproval, ensuring that any sub-quality meat was advertised.[427] There is no evidence to tell us if butchers were actually prepared to risk their reputation in this way.

The customs of Ipswich also tried to halt the selling of meat from stolen animals ('wher off oftyn tyme gret slaundre is in the cuntre to gret dishonour to the toun') by demanding that any carcasses brought into the town should be accompanied by their skins and hides, which bore the owners' marks. Otherwise it was deemed suspicious and the meat was thus confiscated. No skins or hides were to be removed from public view before the hour of prime.[428] Some seventeen cases survive with butchers being amerced (average 5d.) for failing to bring the hides of their animals

---

[424] Britnell, *Growth and Decline*, pp. 236–8.   [425] SRO (I), c/2/8/1/5,6,7.
[426] SRO (I), c/2/8/1/5,6,7.
[427] *Black Book*, ii, pp. 144–7, c.58 [57] (*c.*1309). Davis, 'The cross and the pillory', pp. 258–9.
[428] *Black Book*, ii, pp. 142–5, c.57 [56] (*c.*1309).

into Ipswich market. This law not only provided protection against stolen goods, but also ensured a regular supply of skins into the town.

The customs of Ipswich also condemned cooks and poulterers who sold foodstuffs past their reasonable storage time, or any that were rotten and unsuitable for consumption.[429] Cooks faced confiscation of their chattels, then the pillory, and then expulsion from their occupation for a year and a day. A fourth time and they were ordered to give up the occupation for ever. If the cook had no chattels to forfeit he was to suffer the pillory the first time, implying that there were many cooks who were poor retailers with few assets.[430] However, there are no specific recorded instances of cooks selling unfit food in the extant leet court rolls, though this may be because they were amalgamated with fish and meat offences. There were certainly cooks plying their trade; men like John Cok and his wife, who were amerced for selling ale and bread, and William Cok, who was amerced for gannoking ale and leaving entrails and waste in the road and river. There was also John Aleyn, who was convicted of selling bread and corrupt fish, and forestalling eggs, fowl and butter in 1416 and 1419.

Much more common in the court rolls were prosecutions for those selling putrid fish. According to the custumal, any regrater who displayed any spoiled or out-of-date fish was to have their fish confiscated and given to the poor. On the second occasion, they faced the pillory, and on the third, they had to give up their occupation for a year and a day.[431] All fish (such as 'purpays, samoun, cungger and turbut') brought to Ipswich were to be cut up only 'in the comoun place of the market', and no fish were to be stored privately and overnight without being shown to the keeper of the fish market.[432] Those who brought mussels, oysters and other shellfish to Ipswich quay were to be sold by the same men who carried them, without the meddling interference of middlemen, upon pain of confiscation and a 40d. amercement, 'as wel for the comoun profit of poure men as of ryche'.[433] The regulations for the fish trade were thus dominated by concerns for the price and edibility of this most perishable commodity, as well as its supply. Leet court prosecutions reflect the same concerns for health and price, especially fresh fish that was too old and had become fetid. Several fishmongers were amerced 4d.–24d. for displaying over-aged, poorly stored, corrupt and stinking fish in the common market 'to the grave damage of all the community'.

---

[429] *Ibid.*, ii, pp. 104–5, c.32 (*c.*1309).   [430] *Ibid.*, ii, pp. 146–7, c.59 [58] (*c.*1309).
[431] *Ibid.*, ii, pp. 104–5, c.30 (*c.*1309).   [432] *Ibid.*, ii, pp. 102–3, c.29 (*c.*1309).
[433] *Ibid.*, ii, pp. 160–1, c.69 [67] (*c.*1309). Alsford suggested that the term 'medele' (i.e. to meddle) has etymological associations here with middlemen; Alsford, *Towns* (Ipswich, App. 2, c.69).

This rhetoric was repeated constantly and victuallers were left with no doubt as to the expectation of their common responsibility.

Why the affeerers decided on different amercements for similarly described offences is difficult to discern. Some like Robert Kyrkehous and John Stabeler were amerced escalating amounts (4d., 6d. or 8d., 24d.) in 1465–8 for selling corrupt fish, while John Depyng faced consec-utive fines of 8d., 12d. and 8d. for the same offences. However, generally, amercements for selling corrupt fish were greater than those for selling at an excessive price. Fishwives like Agnes Skylly, Anne Reed, Isabel Stepyng, Joan Thompson, Alice Brookmane and Mrs John Roberd were simply amerced 2d.–4d. every year for selling at excessive profit over 1466–8.[434] In 1467–8, the main fish-selling offences were recorded sepa-rately in the same East Ward leet court. Fourteen were accused of selling fish for excessive profit and were amerced on average 3.6d., while the thirteen traders presented for selling unwholesome fish were amerced an average of 9.8d. This gives an indication of the relative stigma of these practices. There appears to have been a case-by-case assessment based on the perceived severity of the offence.

Forestallers

In terms of the number of presentments and the level of amercements, one of the greatest concerns for officials was the tendency of fishmongers to forestall fish at the Quay. For example, in 1424, John Parmenter forestalled 200 mackerel outside Ipswich, priced 6s. 8d. (i.e. five mackerel for 2d.), and John Catfield forestalled twenty baskets of mackerel and mullet, valued at 40s.[435] Across ninety-four cases for forestalling, the average amercement was nearly 12d. Forestallers, on average, thus faced a much heavier penalty than for most other trading infringements, except certain bakers and innkeepers. Yet, some forestallers of fish, like Robert Smith, Alice Gateward, John Sherrene, Alice Maykyn, Alice Kendale, Alice Sygor and Alice Kertelyng, were only amerced 4d.[436] They were not mentioned as fishmongers in other contexts and it is likely that they were low-capital regraters, buying fish from ships at the Quay to sell on. This was termed forestalling by the clerk because it took place before the fish had been officially landed, but the term 'forestalling' was used for a wide number of offences by the fifteenth century. Although fish was the most common item specifically mentioned as forestalled 'to the grave

[434] Female fish-sellers were found in major towns across England. E.g. Kowaleski, *Local Markets*, p. 139; McIntosh, *Working Women*, pp. 194–6.
[435] SRO (I), c/2/8/1/7.   [436] SRO (I), c/2/1/8/3, 5,6,7.

damage of the community', other victuals were also named in the court rolls: wheat, eggs, butter, cheese, bulls, pheasants, pigeons and small birds. Many of the accused went out of Ipswich both by land and water to intercept goods, and places like Stoke (a suburb south of the river) and Caldewell (probably Cauldwell, a suburb about one mile east) were specifically named as places where wares were forestalled

It is difficult to discern precisely why some offenders faced amercements of only 4d. while others were given heavier penalties of up to 24d., unless it was related to the severity of the offence. The main fear of enhanced prices is sometimes noted in the court rolls, but there is no pattern in the amercements related to the, admittedly formulaic, descriptions. Robert Kyrkehous and Geoffrey Gerard were amerced 6d. in 1465 for forestalling fish coming to the market and were ordered not to do so again under pain of a further penalty of 40d. They both offended again the next year and were specifically reprimanded for not heeding the warning of the last leet. However, they were then only amerced 12d. each, a higher penalty but not as great as threatened. There were some consistent offenders, like the fishmonger William Burstall who appeared five times for forestalling fish and other victuals, between 1419 and 1424, and received fines that increased from 4d. to 12d. to 24d., which might indicate escalating punishment aimed at deterrence. Joan Fadinor, on the other hand, received amercements of 24d. in 1434 and just 6d. in both 1436 and 1437 for the same forestalling offence, while her husband, Robert, was convicted five times between 1416 and 1423 for fluctuating amercements. John Marcavit, Alice Rolf and Beatrice Leme were amerced just 4d. for their offences between 1436 and 1438. In 1416, John Smyth forestalled 200 quarters of grain, thereby greatly enhancing the price, but he only faced a 6d. fine. There was no real consistency in such amercements, despite the demands of statute law. Each case appears to have been judged on its individual merits, and when previous offences were taken into account the penalties were not always as harsh as threatened.

Britnell identified a great deal of consternation over individual cases of forestalling in Colchester, especially in the fish trade through Hythe, but generally less concern over petty forestallers.[437] A similar situation can be discerned in Ipswich. For instance, both Robert Fadinor and his wife, Joan, forestalled various victuals, alongside selling corrupt fish and ale by improper measures. From 1416 to 1437, Robert Fadinor or his wife were amerced between 4d. and 24d. (average 11.5d.) for their forestalling

---

[437] Britnell, *Growth and Decline*, pp. 131–4.

activities.[438] Their daughter, Joanna, continued in both selling ale and forestalling in the late 1430s. In the mid-1410s, the family had been selling from their home in St Stephen's Lane, where they were accused of leaving dung and household sweepings in the street, as well as erecting a post, perhaps for a building extension or to hold up an awning for an unofficial stall. They also entertained various prostitutes within their home. The Fadinor family were small-scale retailers, involved in a variety of petty trades and drawing the occasional attention of the court, as well as reasonably high, but variable, amercements. Conversely, John Breklys was heavily amerced at 20s. for forestalling twenty quarters of wheat at the Quay. This was a forestalling offence that obviously involved a great deal of capital by a more significant merchant, and it might have had more significant and wider consequences for the 'common price'.[439] He was also bypassing the privileges of the burgesses and this could not be condoned by the authorities.

The market environment

As well as petty trading offences in Ipswich, there was the usual mishmash of encroachments, obstructions and waste disposal. The ditch surrounding the town was often used as a refuse pit for animal, craft or household waste, which should have been carried to the town's dunghill on Col-hill. Dung, timber and carcasses were also just left or dumped in the road. Both tanners and butchers were accused of throwing 'skepfuls' of waste (entrails and dung) in the river at Friar's Bridge, thereby impeding the mill's dam. This bridge provided access to communal pasturage so was frequently used by butchers. Waste from the fish market was often discarded by the walls of St Stephen's Lane or into the marketplace. John Sewale and John Parmonter were both amerced 4d. in 1423 for depositing fish entrails and straw in the fish market.

Industrial waste was generally a nuisance. Tanners often dug pits in the streets and allowed their waste to seep into the common watercourses that ran down the centre of Brook Street; while water tainted with dyes (woad and madder) flooded streets and seeped into the common waterwells and rivers, thereby polluting drinking water and damaging fish stocks. Brewing waste from the holding of Simon Bierbrewere so raised the channel that the district was flooded. Brewers who did not maintain their drains appear to have been a consistent irritant. Innkeepers were also warned about drains that were causing a nuisance and posts, perhaps for awnings or signs, which had to be removed. In 1438, Nicholas Lamb

[438] SRO (I), c/2/8/1/3, 4, 5, 6, 7.   [439] SRO (I), c/2/8/1/4.

was specifically upbraided for putting cooking filth in the common way. A consistent problem for innkeepers appears to have been the disposal of horse dung, accumulating from their guests' animals. For instance, Walter Colk was presented for depositing forty loads in the ditch by the north gates, as well as by the churchyard of St Laurence. Many in Ipswich also had pig-sties in the street, which caused a nuisance. The owners of pigs included innkeepers, presumably for provisioning their customers and meeting the growing demand for meat. Pigs often escaped and were found wandering in the streets. Indeed, pigs, sheep, horses, geese and cows were all discovered illegally grazing on the embankments, ditches and common ways within the town. These everyday hazards were all part of the problems that came with developing market trade.

Conclusion

This brief examination of the retail marketing environment of Ipswich has raised aspects of both similarities and differences to the small towns of Suffolk. There were certainly instances of leniency in larger communities, with a complex interplay of forces at work to discourage repressive action by the authorities. The assumption that the larger towns were stricter may have been expressed in the tighter and more detailed ordinances and moral rhetoric, but in practice retailers apparently faced very similar controls to those exercised in smaller towns. The basic premise of the regulations remained the same mixture of morals, practicality and vested interests: to safeguard privileges, to keep prices low, and to protect the health of the general consumer. An increase in written regulations did not necessarily mean that the authorities became stricter. The main differences between small and large towns were largely due to pressure on resources and space, leading to a greater number of presentments for waste and hygiene issues. There were also more retailers and victuallers in Ipswich than Newmarket or Clare, and some were relatively prosperous. This may have led to higher average amercements for certain bakers and innkeepers, based as much on output as offences. Fishmongers, butchers and innkeepers certainly faced greater direct control than before, but this was partly due to their increasing numbers and heightened consumer demand.

However, it must be noted that Ipswich was on the smaller side of the larger corporate boroughs. The civic authorities may not have overtly raised the level of retail regulation, except for forestalling, flagrant offenders and aliens, but whether this was also the case in other provincial centres is debatable. For instance, the lack of craft guilds in Ipswich may have allowed retailers to enjoy a wider scope of action than in, say, Norwich,

York or London. Attitudes and levels of enforcement may have differed between borough markets, depending on vested interests and those who controlled the courts. There also remained a strong ethos of localism, as well as paternal concern, in the way traders and consumers viewed their marketplace and how outsiders were regarded.

Nevertheless, all borough authorities had to achieve a pragmatic amalgam of overarching supervision and facilities that bred trust and lowered transaction costs, alongside an understanding of the vagaries inherent in certain medieval trades and the flexibilities required to allow tradesmen to prosper. Market users recognised the basic laws and moral principles, but they also identified those offences which were worthy of the community's censure and those which could pass for a minor amercement without further comment. These petty fines assuaged the trader's conscience, lined the corporation's or lord's pockets, and reminded all of the legal oversight and constraints of assizes and other market regulation. Effective law did not require zero-tolerance enforcement in order to facilitate an efficient market. Cultural and religious views permeated everyday trade, but this does not mean that they were incompatible with a regard for the opportunities of the market, the needs of traders, and how a prosperous market could benefit all. Even the idealism of literature and law demonstrated recognition (sometimes grudgingly) that honest commerce needed its way smoothed. This was a paternalistic economy, but not in the restrictive, unbending way that this phrase has been made to suggest.

4   An evolving market morality?

In 1971, E. P. Thompson wrote a seminal article entitled 'The moral economy of the English crowd in the eighteenth century', which has spurred historical debate ever since.[1] What made this topic so intriguing was that an 'old moral economy of provision', based on the needs of the consumers and control of the market, was juxtaposed against a developing eighteenth-century 'new political economy of the free market', which sought to diminish interference and controls.[2] For Thompson, this moral economy was a selective reconstruction of paternalist legislation stretching back to medieval and sixteenth-century England; a holistic moral economy hostile to a Smithian free-market, *laissez-faire* model. This book has already addressed the complexities involved in unravelling medieval conceptions of a 'moral economy'. If eighteenth-century attitudes of the 'crowd' were embedded in long-held notions of market morality and behaviour, then it is worth reconsidering why they had survived for so long in the face of economic change.

The attitudes of English market users were gradually formed during centuries of commercial and market development. However, attempting to track a definitive chronology of transition from subsistence-based, collective ethics to individualistic, profit-based motivations is not only elusive but problematic in its basic premise. Changes in commercial ethics and market culture were slow and piecemeal, and traditional mores remained important even while new economic attitudes were shaped. The marketplace was an intense and complex arena of cultural negotiation between a variety of forces – ideology, laws, economics, vested interests and social needs. Indeed, we should not create too stark a dichotomy between concepts of a traditional 'moral economy' and an emerging

---

[1] Thompson, 'Moral economy'; Thompson, *Making*, pp. 66–78; Thompson, 'Moral economy reviewed'. Numerous historians have been influenced by Thompson's work and concept of the 'moral economy'. E.g. Williams, 'Morals'; Stevenson, 'Moral economy'; Bohstedt, 'Moral economy'; Randall and Charlesworth (eds.), *Moral Economy*.

[2] Bohstedt, 'Moral economy', 266; Thompson, *Making*, pp. 67–73.

'market economy' as though they are diametrically opposed and incompatible. Recourse to moral justifications does not necessarily exclude motivations of self-preservation or profit, while market relations were interpreted in the way they impacted on notions of communal justice. A moral language permeated commercial regulation.[3] As John Stevenson has suggested, 'if anything like a *moral economy* can ever be said to have existed, it was remarkably flexible and adaptive to change'.[4]

As we have seen, historians stress that medieval concepts of the economy were not necessarily incompatible with market values. The works of Hilton, Britnell, Dyer, Campbell and other medieval historians have shown that England was already highly commercialised in the thirteenth century and that society was becoming increasingly market-oriented. The growth of medieval marketing institutions and opportunities served to awaken market values, such as competitive bargaining and an acquisitive, monetarised impulse. There is no doubt that the Church was dubious of the market and such money-making impulses, and that scholars and moralists did not support gain for its own sake. However, a closer examination of the imagery and representation of medieval traders presents a more nuanced picture than simply straightforward suspicions and outmoded notions of a natural economy or an anti-market ethos. Ultimately, moral norms and accepted behaviour were adapting to the changing medieval market conditions and there was perhaps a greater flexibility in ethics, law and enforcement than many historians once thought.

However, it is the early modern period that is viewed by some historians as the significant period of economic transition and tension, leading to a new questioning of economic attitudes and culminating in Adam Smith's *Wealth of Nations*.[5] For instance, Keith Wrightson has argued that medieval economic culture was antagonistic to individual economic freedom and the pursuit of gain, as well as lacking the concept of a self-regulating market order. Medieval people assessed the legitimacy of economic activity 'in terms of moral imperatives and their attitudes were both enshrined in their economic institutions and expressed in practice'.[6] Wrightson argued that they recognised the utility of the market but were anxious about the potential abuses and ambivalent about market practices. There remained a desire for close regulation and the subordination of the market to ethical considerations. However, in many ways, this argument depends upon how medieval contemporaries constructed the notion of a 'moral economy' and how they interpreted their actual

[3] Muldrew, 'Interpreting', 176–8.   [4] Stevenson, 'Moral economy', p. 238.
[5] Muldrew, 'Interpreting', 180–1.   [6] Wrightson, *Earthly Necessities*, pp. 29, 110.

relationship to the market. There is an assumption that a moral economy and an efficient market system are somehow incompatible.

Some historians of early modern England have tended to define the moral economy within the context and certainties of classical theories of political economy, rather than always understanding the complex preconceptions of the communities that adhered to this value system. Smithian notions that the free and unfettered market was the only true and inevitable market culture still have a strong hold over opinion, as do Polanyi's and Tawney's views that market institutions and participants needed to break away from the hindrances of the medieval Church, society and culture in order to achieve their potential.[7] In this paradigm, the 'moral economy' of medieval and sixteenth-century England is regarded as an anti-market ideology that subordinates all trading activity to the protective needs of society and to the detriment of commercial advancement. Consequently, some have asserted that any early modern vestiges of a 'moral economy' that drew upon the concepts of medieval and sixteenth-century England were, by their very nature, antagonistic to market efficiency. A traditional moral economy was based on unrealistic ideas of a 'natural' economy, which stressed subsistence living and direct links between farmer and consumer.

As a counter to such assumptions regarding marketing in late medieval England, Craig Muldrew posited that a clearer understanding of the importance of regulation and morals in medieval markets is needed as a comparative basis when studying early modern markets.[8] In this vein, this chapter seeks to take forward the discussion and findings of the previous chapters in order to make some comparative observations with the prominent commercial concerns of early modern England. Historians should not only consider the nuances of late medieval market morality, and its confluence with pragmatic economic anxieties, but also the longevity of basic social concerns. This perhaps accords with Thompson's classic thesis on the 'moral economy' of the eighteenth-century crowd, whom, he argued, sought to reassert traditional moral norms and regulations in the face of dearth.[9] However, the extent to which such ethical assertions were anti-market or anachronistic can be further elucidated through a clearer understanding of the medieval principles that underlay such market morality. This chapter is intended only as an initial sketch of the potential questions that could be raised when considering the development of market morals and mercantile ethics over the last millennium. There has been extensive historical discussion about the

[7] Polanyi, *Great Transformation*; Polanyi, 'Our obsolete market mentality'; Tawney, *Religion*.
[8] Muldrew, 'Interpreting', 174, n. 61.   [9] Thompson, 'Moral economy'.

development of early modern commercial ethics and I will only touch upon some of these debates by considering retail traders, the assizes and middlemen, particularly as regards the trade in vital foodstuffs.

Profit and the commonweal in the early modern economy

There were undoubtedly developments in the early modern economy that meant that market relations grew in scale, pervasiveness and power. In the sixteenth to eighteenth centuries we see the expansion of a consumer society, new crops and industries, inflation, a renewal of demographic growth and growing overseas markets. A growing social polarisation has been highlighted, contrasting a wealthy 'middling sort' with increasing general poverty.[10] Urbanisation also continued apace in England, though the country was still dominated by small towns before the late eighteenth century. London's growth and demands continued to outstrip other urban centres, and agriculture and supply networks were increasingly organised for the capital's needs, though how quickly England became an integrated commercial system is debatable. Nevertheless, the development and increasing scale of internal trade from 1500 to 1750 was significant, with regional markets linked by improving transport routes.[11] Agricultural surpluses and specialisation increased in response to commercial pressures, and it could be argued that large-scale middlemen, badgers (middlemen in grain) and pedlars came into their own in distributing both the commodities of the countryside and those imported from overseas.[12] Below the national nexus of trade, there remained the flow of daily and weekly transactions in the local marketplaces and a hierarchy of market centres that served regions and hinterlands. The market remained the principal institution in pre-industrial England for the exchange of rural produce and urban goods or services.[13] These structural changes, and continuities, were accompanied by notable periods of crisis, particularly during 1580–1630 when population growth was at its height, with price inflation and disastrous harvests.[14] Dearth brought food riots, social disorder and a strain upon the government's ability to maintain grain supplies.[15] After a time of relative stability in the late seventeenth century, England again faced intermittent harvest crises during the eighteenth century.

[10] Wrightson, *English Society*, pp. 140–2.   [11] Chartres, 'Marketing', pp. 220–46.
[12] For a detailed discussion of middlemen and their activities in early modern England, see Everitt, 'Marketing'; Chartres, 'Marketing'; Spufford, *Great Reclothing*, pp. 5–12.
[13] Dyer, 'Market towns', 123–34.   [14] Wrightson, *English Society*, pp. 142–59.
[15] Sharp, 'Popular protest', pp. 285–7; Walter, 'Grain riots', pp. 71–7.

There were thus some important economic and commercial changes, as well as social upheavals, during the early modern period. But how far were these accompanied by shifts in attitudes towards commerce and the marketplace? Much ink has been used in discussing the Protestant work ethic, the growing mercantile class, mercantilism and individualism – the supposed creeds of 'capitalism'. It is a frequent assertion by historians that merchants and their thrifty, hard-working ways were becoming newly lauded by the late sixteenth century,[16] and that during the seventeenth century there was a transition from government policies that favoured consumers and good order to one that favoured producers and merchants, giving them more freedom in their commercial activities. Margo Todd has argued that medieval theologians denigrated any notion of profit, even that used for the commonweal, while merchants were left out of the 'hierarchy of callings'. The humanists and puritans, by contrast, venerated industry, secular vocation and discipline, and also justified a certain profit, provided it was used for the common good.[17] Men like Richard Baxter espoused the virtues of work and supposedly encouraged economic individualism: 'Every one that is able, must be statedly and ordinarily imployed in such work as is serviceable to God, and the common good' (1673).[18] However, there is not a word in Baxter's writings that urges the pursuit of private profit as a way of earning favour from God.[19]

Paul Seaver has posited that puritan economic attitudes were essentially conservative and traditional, seeking less a sanctification of entrepreneurialism and profits than an assurance that good intention was enough.[20] For instance, Francis Bacon, in 1625, saw that trading profits could be honest, provided they were achieved through diligence and fair dealing. This was little different from the medieval definition of reasonable gains. Bacon also disparaged those traders who sought to profit from the necessities of others, used cunning in their bargains, and indulged in the practice of regrating.[21] Similarly, Thomas Dekker (1606) was wary of merchants with their apparent credit-worthiness, thrift and humility, which might be an artifice to grow rich and then forgo on larger credit deals.[22] Chaucer's merchant was perhaps mocked for a similar

---

[16] Stevenson, *Praise and Paradox*; McVeagh, *Tradefull Merchants*, pp. 1–30.

[17] Todd, *Christian Humanism*, pp. 127, 147–9, 156–7, 174.

[18] Baxter, *A Christian Directory*, p. 133.   [19] MacKinnon, 'Longevity of the thesis'.

[20] Seaver, 'Puritan work ethic revised'; Seaver, *Wallington's World*, ch. 5.

[21] Richard Bacon, *The Essayes or Counsels, Ciuill and Morall, of Francis Lord Verulam, Viscount St Alban* (London, 1625), cf. Fisher and Jurica (eds.), *Documents*, p. 510.

[22] Thomas Dekker, *The Seven Deadly Sinnes of London* (London, 1606), in Collier (ed.), *Illustrations*, ii, pp. 17–18.

façade. George Gascoigne in *The Steele Glas* (1576), in a very conservative vein, saw that the merchant's role was to enrich the whole country by his toil, but that they were often led astray by avarice and vanity.[23]

There may have been a slightly different emphasis on personal profit in the writings of early modern moralists, but ultimately the trader's role was service to the commonweal, which should be undertaken without sin and with concern for social justice. This was essentially a reiteration of medieval social and divine models, which declared that the diligent pursuit of individual callings was beneficial to society as a whole and thus to the individual's own prosperity and ultimate salvation. Although poverty was no longer an ascetic virtue, excessive luxury was still despised and merchants were expected to be stewards of wealth for the greater good. Medieval attitudes were not easily displaced and were recycled with new Renaissance emphases on work, material prosperity and the proper use of wealth.[24] Profit was still to be used for the common good, while excessive gain and an appetite for money was regarded as a temptation to sin and avarice.

As in medieval teachings, traders were warned about the sins of deceit and greed, while moderation was exhorted as part of godly living. Surplus profits, beyond the needs of the household, were to be distributed as charity to serve the Church, state and poor.[25] Although work and wealth could be a sign of election, early modern traders were expected to remain subordinate to godly living, including closing shops on Sundays. Such attitudes were encapsulated in the diary of Nehemiah Wallington (d. 1658):

> My conscience tells me I have been very remiss and unwise in some kind both in getting and in spending. But I hope and trust the Lord hath forgiven me this and all other of my sins . . . It is the desire of my heart that in everything I either buy or sell that I take God with me in lifting up of my heart to God saying shall I buy or shall I sell that, or thus, Lord give me wisdom in my buying and selling.[26]

If there was a development of a distinct entrepreneurial ethic among the mercantile and middling classes of England, it was a very long drawn-out process that perhaps did not see dramatic shifts in general attitudes until the late eighteenth century.[27] Praise for material accumulation as a sign of God's favour was still couched with traditional caveats regarding the temptations of avarice and the need for charitable giving. As Stevenson noted: 'In times of social change, tradition has greater psychological

---

[23] Wallace (ed.), *George Gascoigne's 'The Steele Glas'*, pp. 121–2, ll. 750–7. See also Grosart (ed.), *Life and Complete Works*, xi, p. 230; Stevenson, *Praise and Paradox*, pp. 133–6.
[24] Stevenson, *Praise and Paradox*, pp. 136–7.   [25] Todd, *Christian Humanism*, pp. 152–3.
[26] *Ibid.*, pp. 154–5 (cf. BL, MS Additional 40883, fol. 15v).
[27] Stevenson, *Praise and Paradox*, pp. 156–8.

appeal than innovation'.[28] Traditional denunciations of trading sins thus remained prominent in early modern literature. William Perkins declared in 1612:

In the calling of the merchant and tradesman, there is false weights, and false measures, divers weights and divers measures; ingrossing, mingling, changing, setting a glosse on wares by powdering, startching, blowing, darke shops, glozing, smoothing, lying, swearing, and all manner of bad dealing.[29]

Perkins was even more disparaging of the producers and middlemen who took advantage of dearths, in lines that appear to reiterate the sentiments of medieval moralists:

In the husbandman and cornemonger, there is exceeding injustice, in hording up graine till the time of further advantage: and in taking whatsoever they can get for their own, though it be to the shedding of the blood of the poore.[30]

Was the medieval model of ideal marketing practice essentially different from depictions we find in the early modern period? One of the most evocative principles underlying medieval mentalities was the moral duty of traders towards the common good. Similarly, in his sermons of 1550, Thomas Lever recognised the veracity of mercantile endeavours and those who laboured 'with faithful diligence to provide for the common wealth'.[31] The concept of vocation, 'so every man travail in his degree', remained a predominant theory. William Perkins in 1612 stated that there was 'a certain kind of life ordained and imposed on man by God for the common good' and 'there be sundry parts and members and every one hath his several use and office, which it performeth not for it self but for the good of the whole body; as the office of the eye is to see, of the ear to hear, and the foot to go'.[32] John Cook too, in *Unum Necessarium* (1648), was forthright about the moral context of economic activities. Men should cooperate and accept their responsibilities because of their natural needs. Those who profited from the scarcity of corn to the risk of other men's lives were no better than criminals. Instead, he argued: 'if the magistrate inforce him to sell at a reasonable rate, it is but just by the law of God . . . that one man's superfluity should give place to another man's conveniency, his conveniency to another's necessity . . . every man to live according to the rule of nature and right

[28] *Ibid.*, p. 6.
[29] William Perkins, *A Treatise of the Vocations or Callings of Men* (London, 1612), in Breward (ed.), *Work*, pp. 467–8.
[30] Perkins, *A Treatise*, i, p. 771.
[31] Williams (ed.), *English Historical Documents*, pp. 360–1.
[32] Perkins, *A Treatise*, in Breward (ed.), *Work*, pp. 446–7, 449. See also Waddell, 'Economic immorality', 170–1.

reason'.[33] These have been viewed as intellectual creations of Protestant reformers – a concept of divinely ordained vocation.[34] However, although there was a slight change in its secular emphasis, the continuity of these thoughts with medieval ideas is striking. The acquisition of wealth should not be achieved to the detriment of the common good and the traders' own salvation. Everyone had a responsibility to the commonweal.[35]

A petition to the Justices of the Peace in 1629 from the inhabitants of Blackburn demonstrated this general attitude of common responsibility. They complained that badgers were causing shortages of meal in the marketplace and several, particularly one Lawrence Hargreaves, were transporting grain elsewhere in order to make a better profit outside the open market and 'doth unjustlie enrich himselfe against all equitie and good conscience . . . to the overthrowe and impoverishment of your petitioners and many more who cannot buy one halfe pecke of meale or lesse'.[36] The petitioners argued that such a situation needed to be redressed for the good of the commonwealth and that it was also contrary to statute law. The marketing of food and foodstuffs remained subject to traditional, moral scrutiny. Joyce Appleby argued that in seventeenth-century England, 'social purposes and religious doctrines were so clearly defined that deviations could not escape notice'.

The prime factor that drove all these interpretations of the economy was that, in matters affecting the feeding of the people, individual actions based purely on considerations of private gain were sufficiently detrimental to the commonweal to be named crimes.[37] Indeed, in an early seventeenth-century court account, a corn merchant of Burnham Deepdale (Norfolk) was described as:

a man of very covetous mind and desire, and hunting exceedingly after gain and bargains, and engrossing of corn . . . thirsting and greatly desiring to enrich himself thereby; . . . many poor people . . . endure want and fare much the worse.[38]

The rhetoric of the moral economy had entered the vocabulary of everyday marketing. A maltster of Marlborough was similarly accused of 'little respecting the necessity of the commonwealth . . . but wholly seeking his own gain and the extremest advantage of his bargain'.[39] Alan Everitt noted that appeals to social justice did sometimes fall on deaf ears. A maltster of Over (Cambridgeshire), accused of covetousness and hard dealing, replied that the complainant had endangered his credit and

---

[33] Cook, *Unum Necessarium*, p. 13; Appleby, *Economic Thought*, p. 56.
[34] Hill, *Society and Puritanism*, ch. 4.   [35] Cox and Dannehl, *Perceptions*, pp. 21–2.
[36] Richardson and James (eds.), *Urban Experience*, pp. 52–3, no. 46.
[37] Appleby, *Economic Thought*.   [38] Everitt, 'Marketing', pp. 568–9.
[39] *Ibid.*, p. 570.

weakened his estate with his indiscreet bargains.[40] We thus see grain sellers defend themselves by emphasising the legality of contracts made in the market rather than countering the accusations of sin. Everitt argued that the notions of social duty were no longer of practical interest to the merchants and middlemen of early modern England. However, the examples he provided are not necessarily an example of capitalist values overcoming social idealism and Christian morals. They could be interpreted as a way of fighting one piece of moral rhetoric with another, rather than an explication of personal convictions. In general, moral ideals and appeals to social obligation were still a prominent part of the commercial language of dispute.

Similarly, the just price remained an important consideration for the pre-industrial market economy. In the late seventeenth century, John Locke's conception of the just price was the market price, free from cheating, extortion or oppression.[41] The market price was determined by forces of labour, supply and demand rather than the natural inherent properties of the grain or product. Similar to medieval scholastic writers, there was no absolute just price, rather it was the absence of fraudulent intent and the need for transparency that were the prime preconditions. Taking advantage of anyone's ignorance, necessity or distress was deceitful and against justice. Indeed, according to Locke, strict justice ensured that all traders sold at the market price equally to all consumers, so that sellers could make a livelihood, middlemen would be discouraged, and the poor would be served. A trader had to make a reasonable profit or else he would have no livelihood, but such profit was difficult to predetermine and was better left to market mechanisms. If deals were undertaken scrupulously and honestly, then the trader's profits would be reasonable and not excessive. Perhaps drawing on Aquinas, Locke also recognised that prices of corn increased during famine, though he appealed to the virtues of charity that traders should recognise others' necessities at times of desperation and try not to leave them without the means for subsistence. This was an offence both against the commonweal and also against the merchant's own soul.

The basic moral principles had not altered much since medieval times. A just price was one based on a common market estimation, partly taking into account original cost, but more so scarcity and utility in the place where a commodity was sold. Locke was also no more accommodating than many medieval moralists concerning the bargaining mechanisms that were involved in reaching a just market price: 'The measure that is common to buyer and seller is just that if one should buy as cheap

---

[40] *Ibid.*, pp. 570–1.   [41] Kelly (ed.), *John Locke*, ii, pp. 496–500.

as he could in the market the other should sell as dear as he could there, every one runing venture and takeing his chance, which by the mutual and perpetualy changing wants of mony and commodities in buyer and seller comes to a pretty equal and fair account'. Similarly, Samuel Ward of Ipswich stated in 1612: 'Let the mutual profit of buyer and seller be the rule of buying and selling, and not the gain of one of them alone'.[42] In essence, this was a reiteration of standard scholastic arguments regarding commutative justice, mutual benefit, bargaining and the equilibrium of exchange. Indeed, many early modern writers, such as Thomas Hobbes, Thomas Wilson, Richard Baxter and William Scott, viewed bargaining in the marketplace as a means towards achieving justice and equity in exchanges through common estimation.[43] Richard Baxter warned against taking advantage of another's need (lyther bargaining) and emphasised that traders should take due account of their duty to aid the poor.[44] They were drawing directly on the theories of medieval scholars. There were even examples, at times of dearth, where corn merchants actually sold grain to the needy below the market rate, simply as an act of charity.[45] Profit should not be made through deceit, usury and other harmful means, but only earned through honest labour and sale. Little had really changed. The problem of allying moral concerns to economic pragmatism was not one that disappeared after the medieval period.

Early modern retailers

The petty trader who neglected both his social duty and spiritual salvation remained a commonplace character in sixteenth- and seventeenth-century literature. Like the late medieval commentator, John Gower, late sixteenth-century ballads appealed to a golden past, one of them asserting that 'trew dealyng now is fled and gone' and that most traders flattered and deceived.[46] Gascoigne despaired of the frauds and deceits of shoe-makers, tailors, tanners, tinkers, weavers, pewterers and cutlers in their crafts and selling.[47] Other early modern moralists repeated medieval accusations that a draper might use dark shops to 'shadow

[42] Todd, *Christian Humanism*, p. 149.   [43] Muldrew, *Economy of Obligation*, pp. 44–6.
[44] Richard Baxter, *Chapters from a Christian Directory*, cf. Muldrew, *Economy of Obligation*, pp. 45–6.
[45] Walter, 'Social economy', pp. 103–4, 106–7, 114.
[46] Wright and Halliwell (eds.), *A Collection*, pp. 134–8.
[47] Wallace (ed.), *George Gascoigne's 'The Steele Glas'*, pp. 134–5, ll. 1066–1109.

the dye and wooll of his cloth' to fool their customers, while crafts-men worked deceitfully at night.[48] Indeed, the actual cloth-sellers of early seventeenth-century Norwich were disparaged for their 'corrupt desires' that led some to sell false clothes, untruly measured and dyed. They regarded such activities as 'to the great dishonour of this king-dome and the slander and discreditt of this great comoditie, and the hindrance and losse of the buyer'.[49] In *The Defence of Conny-Catching* (1592), Robert Greene accused numerous traders, through their 'coose-nage' and 'knaueries', of taking advantage of simple men and their lack of trading knowledge, caring only for private gains. Through their subtleties they would 'beguile the poore communalty' with infe-rior goods, poor craftsmanship, forestalling, excessive price and lyther bargaining.[50]

Thomas Dekker (1606) believed that the art of lying and forswear-ing permeated every trade, alongside false weights and measures. In his view, any buyers and sellers 'abused by such hell hounds' of lying and fraud gained but a little silver since these sins would ultimately destroy their souls.[51] The imperilment of traders' souls through false swearing and deceit remained a consistent theme. The early seventeenth-century poem, *Times' Whistle* (c.1614–16), despaired that dealers were interested only in gain and took no account that they would 'sell their soules vnto eternall paine'.[52] It also lamented that tradesmen allowed the Sabbath to 'reeke with sweat of their vngodly labour, when they should repaire to church with other men'.[53] Such condemnations were mirrored in laws against trading on Sundays or during divine service, which continued to be enacted and were joined by new edicts against selling meat and other victuals during Lent.[54]

The deceitful, avaricious and unrepentant retailer thus remained a stock figure for moral commentators.[55] Nancy Cox has remarked how the 'intellectual and regulatory environment' for retail tradesmen remained fairly hostile through the sixteenth and much of the seven-teenth centuries.[56] Hugh Alley, in the 1590s, spoke of a 'Greedie kinde of

---

[48] Grosart (ed.), *Life and Complete Works*, xi, p. 69; Dekker, *Seven Deadly Sinnes*, in Collier (ed.), *Illustrations*, ii, pp. 31, 34–5. See also Camp, *The Artisan*, pp. 87–91.

[49] *Norwich*, ii, pp. 259–66 (1613 and 1638).

[50] Grosart (ed.), *Life and Complete Works*, xi, pp. 260–87.

[51] Dekker, *Seven Deadly Sinnes*, in Collier (ed.), *Illustrations*, ii, pp. 27–8.

[52] Cowper (ed.), *Times' Whistle*, pp. 43, 54.   [53] *Ibid.*, pp. 16–17.

[54] *Beverley*, p. 130 (1554); *Northampton*, ii, pp. 281–2 (1558), 305 (1624); *TRP*, iii, pp. 204–9 (1600); *SRP*, i, pp. 413–16, 450–4 (1619).

[55] Cox, 'Beggary of the nation', pp. 36–43.

[56] *Ibid.*, p. 43. Cox concentrated on ideas about luxury, balance of payments, the open market and credit.

people, inhabitinge in and aboute the citty, and suburbs of the same, called haglers, hawkers, huxters, and wanderers, uppe and downe the streets, in buyenge into their owne handes, to rayse the prices, for their owne luker, and private gayne'.[57] Accusations against market traders regarding the selling of unwholesome victuals, excessive price, false weights and measures and outright deceit remained prominent. John Powell's treatise in 1601 included fears that butchers sold meat from diseased animals, sold unbaited bulls, 'or geld the kidneys of their muttons, veales, or lambes, taking away the fatte thereof, nor deceitfully raise the same kidneyes, with any stopping or underputting them, to deceiue the ignorant buyers therof'.[58] Robert Greene asserted that butchers would prick and 'puffe vp his meate to please the eye' and wash old meat with new blood 'in deceiuing the poore'.[59] Many of Greene's other rhetorical, entertaining complaints similarly reflected medieval concerns: millers were still accused of having a 'golden thumbe', bakers for falsifying the weight of their loaves, brewers for adulterating their ale and beer, horse-corsers for beguiling their customers and vintners for mixing water with wine.[60] His cooks sold 'filthy meat . . . when it is bad enough for dogs', badly cooked or reheated, poisoning 'some honest poore men'.[61]

As in medieval texts, early modern bakers were regarded as inherently dishonest, greedy and potentially harmful to the common good. Andrew Boorde, in the 1540s, exhorted bakers to make good bread that would 'comforte, confyrme, and doth stablysshe a mannes hert', but he despaired of them in a later edition of the same treatise, saying: 'And evyll bakers the whyche doth nat make good breade of whete, but wyl myngle other corne with whete, or do not order and seson hit, gyvinge good weight, I wolde they myght play bopepe thorowe a pyllery'.[62] Robert Greene's view in the late sixteenth century was even more disparaging, declaring how the baker loved to be seen in the pillory. He argued that the baker:

craue but one deare yeare to make your daughter a Gentlewoman, you buy your corne at the best hand, and yet wil not be content to make your bread weight by many ounces, you put in yeast and salt to make it heuie, and yet al your policy

---

[57] Archer, Burrow and Harding (eds.), *Hugh Alley's Caveat*, pp. 15–29, 35–6; Muldrew, *Economy of Obligation*, p. 49.
[58] Powell, *Assise of Bread*, F2v.
[59] Grosart (ed.), *Life and Complete Works*, xi, pp. 69, 273–4. See also Taylor, *Works*, 'The Trauels of Twelve-Pence', p. 70.
[60] Wallace (ed.), *George Gascoigne's 'The Steele Glas'*, pp. 134–5, ll. 1066–1109.
[61] Grosart (ed.), *Life and Complete Works*, xi, pp. 281–2.
[62] *Ibid.*, p. 261 and p. 260, n. 5 (edition of 1547).

cannot make it but fine for the pillory: the poore crie out, the rich find fault, and the lord maior and the sheriffs like honorable and worshipful maiestrats, euery day walke abroad and weigh your bread, and yet al will not serue to make you honest men.[63]

Similarly, brewers and tipplers were still being upbraided for brewing unwholesome or weak ale and beer, using unsealed measures, and generally failing to heed the assize.[64] Boorde's diatribe against brewers and alewives continued the growing antagonism towards these particular vendors:

euyl ale-brewers and ale-wyues, for theyr euyl brewyng and euyl measure, shuld clacke and ryng theyr tankardes...standynge in the Temmes [Thames] vp to the harde chynne, and iii ynches aboue, that whan you do come out of the water you myght shake your eares as a spanyell that veryly commeth out of the water.[65]

Brewers were accused of adulterated ale that poisoned their customers, or making weak brews of 'smale beare' in order to make more profit.[66] In a poem by John Taylor in 1630, tapsters were characterised as small thieves because they 'nick' their pots, thus cheating men of full measures. Tapsters also allegedly took advantage of their customer's drunken state, though Taylor saw this as almost sweet justice.[67] Taylor drew on earlier depictions, such as by Robert Greene (1592), and accused alewives of raising the bottom of their ale-pots or using smaller cups ('petty cannes') than standard for their weak beer, half-filled with froth; though he also suggested that they did such deceits in order to scratch a living.[68] Indeed, some fairly positive images of alewives and alehouses were disseminated, such as Donald Lupton's early seventeenth-century image: 'if her ale bee strong, her reckoning right, her house cleane, her fire good, her face faire, and the towne great or rich, shee shall seldome or neuersit without chirping birds to beare her company, and at the next churching or christning, shee is sure to be ridd of two of three dozen of cakes and ale by gossiping neighbours'.[69] Similarly, a seventeenth-century ballad recited:

[63] Grosart (ed.), Life and Complete Works, xi, p. 275.
[64] Strype (ed.), Survey, ii, pp. 201–4; Powell, Assise of Bread, E3v–E4v.
[65] Furnivall (ed.), Compendyous Regyment, pp. 260–1.
[66] Wright and Halliwell (eds.), A Collection, p. 63; Grosart (ed.), Life and Complete Works, xi, pp. 274–5.
[67] Taylor, Works, 'The Trauels of Twelve-Pence', p. 70, and 'A Thiefe', p. 118.
[68] Grosart (ed.), Life and Complete Works, xi, pp. 68, 275–6.
[69] Lupton, London and the Countrey, pp. 130–1; Thirsk and Cooper (eds.), Seventeenth-Century Economic Documents, p. 348.

A man that hath a signe at his doore,
and keeps good ale to sell,
A comely wife to please his guests,
may thrive exceeding well.[70]

These were more endearing portrayals than Skelton's Elynour Rummyng, even if the gossiping woman using her feminine wiles to attract customers was still predominant.

In a similar manner, Greene complained of vintners who were an easy friend to both customers and their money.[71] His innkeepers were able to sell 'a crab for a pipping' [crab apple for a pippin] to simple men,[72] while Taylor's innkeepers were thieves who deliberately underfed the horses and thus deceived their customers.[73] Dekker exclaimed: 'shoote but your eye through the iron grates into the cellers of the vintners, there you shall see him hold his necke in a jin made of a clift hoope-sticke, to throttle him from telling tales, whilest they most abhominably jumble together all the papisticall drinkes that are brought from beyond the sea'.[74] Such admonitions against the adulteration of wine were repeated in the edicts of law, where vintners were warned not to 'mix or alter the verdure and proper nature of their wines'.[75]

These condemnations of literature and moralists were reflected in the rhetorical anxieties of early modern market laws.[76] For example, sixteenth-century Oxford brewers were ordered to sell ale or beer at the set price-rate and in sealed measures, and not to hold back or refuse to sell any available drink to those that demanded it.[77] In the early seventeenth century, common brewers were ordered to desist from making their ale and beer too strong and thus out of the price range of the 'poorer sort'.[78] Bakers and innkeepers were still upbraided for short-weight, wine-sellers for breaking the assize, butchers for disreputable slaughtering practices,

---

[70] Chappell (ed.), *Roxburghe Ballads*, i, 'Choice of Inuentions', p. 109, ll. 113–16.
[71] Grosart (ed.), *Life and Complete Works*, xi, pp. 68–9, 278–9.
[72] *Ibid.*, xi, pp. 68–9.   [73] Taylor, *Works*, 'A Thiefe', pp. 118–19.
[74] Dekker, *Seven Deadly Sinnes*, in Collier (ed.), *Illustrations*, ii, pp. 34–5.
[75] Powell, *Assise of Bread*, F2r–v.
[76] Chartres, 'Marketing', p. 247; e.g. *Statutes*, v, pp. 421–2, 14 Car II c.26 (1662); vi, p. 98, 1 Gul&Mar c.33 (1688); viii, p. 49, 1 Anne c.9 (1702); ix, pp. 248–51, 8 Anne c.19 (1709).
[77] Stanford (ed.), *Ordinances of Bristol*, pp. 24–5 (1555–6). A hefty penalty was proposed, consisting of disenfranchisement until a fine of £40 was paid for readmission. See also *Coventry*, p. 713 (1532); Morgan (ed.), *Hereford*, pp. 2–3, 12 (1554–76); Tawney and Power (eds.), *Tudor Economic Documents*, i, pp. 127–8 (Norwich, 1564); Turner (ed.), *Selections*, pp. 400–2 (Oxford, 1579); Stanford (ed.), *Ordinances of Bristol*, pp. 72–3 (1581); *Northampton*, ii, p. 303 (1606).
[78] *SRP*, i, p. 201 (1608), also p. 455 (1619).

424 Medieval market morality

and fishmongers for corrupt fish.[79] There was little that was starkly new in the principles underlying market supervision, and much drew directly upon medieval laws.

The assizes of bread and ale remained a mainstay of commercial law and were frequently reinforced and revived during times of dearth. However, it has been argued by historians that the assize of bread was generally ignored by bakers in the late sixteenth and early seventeenth centuries, with punishments rarely invoked even when traders continually broke the assize's stipulations.[80] As we have seen, the assize of bread was often not fully invoked in the medieval period, except as a means to prevent flagrant abuses. A lenient enforcement of regulations was not incompatible with a strong moral desire for such legislation to remain in place in order to be implemented when necessary. Indeed, the stark protests of early modern bakers do suggest that the assize of bread was still taken seriously, and we need to be careful in interpreting lists of infringements against the assize. There is other evidence that the continued enforcement of the assize of bread was an important, real presence, rather than a lapsed one by the start of the eighteenth century as suggested by the Webbs and by Petersen.[81] There are numerous offences noted throughout eighteenth-century court leets: lists of assize prices, justices setting the assize, and local identification of short-weight bread. Wendy Thwaites finds little evidence of disobedience by bakers in eighteenth-century Oxford and the inhabitants appeared committed to the legislation.[82] It was still set according to the market price of wheat and bakers were accorded an allowance for their livelihood and expenses.

The assize of bread epitomises the debates about the moral economy and the market and how the two could potentially co-exist. The medieval assize of bread was meant to react to market conditions and the fluctuating price of wheat, and thus provide a fair compromise for both consumer and producer. It was also intended to give bakers the opportunity to make a profit within the consensus of the 'moral economy'. It was not a fixed allowance, as Thompson has implied by arguing that bakers could only enhance their profit beyond the allowance by the illegal methods of short weight and adulteration. In fact, they could legitimately increase their profits by enlarging their consumer base.

[79] Tawney and Power (eds.), *Tudor Economic Documents*, i, pp. 127–8 (Norwich, 1564); Powell, *Assise of Bread*, F1r– F2v.
[80] Benbow, 'Court of aldermen', 109–11; Boulton, 'London's "dark ages"?', 489; Boulton, *Neighbourhood and Society*, p. 76; Thrupp, *Company of Bakers*, pp. 25–30.
[81] Webb and Webb, 'Assize', 198–9; Petersen, *Bread*, p. 99.
[82] Thwaites, 'Assize of bread', 174–6.

However, Thwaites notes that bakers were seemingly able to sell bread more cheaply than the assize indicated, except at times of dearth when it caused them hardship, especially if they failed to obtain grain at the price set by assize officials.[83] Early modern bakers often complained that the stipulated allowance was insufficient. There was, unfortunately, an error in the early modern calculation of the assize compared to the medieval system. The former assumed that the level of consumption was constant rather than the amount available to spend on bread.[84] Thus, as the price of grain increased an early modern baker needed to sell more loaves in order to make a profit, which contradicted the entire premise of the medieval assize. Complaints about the inadequacy of the allowance led to it being increased over the centuries to account for inflation in the cost of living; but this did not take into account the generally increasing grain prices. This is possibly why there were downward revisions in the amount of bread that it was considered could be made from each quarter of wheat, from 418lb. in the seventeenth century to 365lb. in 1758, in order to compensate the bakers.[85] The early modern reconstitutions of the assize of bread also failed to solve its integral mathematical flaw that had mistakenly left bakers unable to supply brown bread to the poor at an adequate allowance.[86] In 1795 there was an attempt by London aldermen to revise the assize tables for wholemeal bread so as to provide a better allowance to the bakers. However, this ended in failure when they declared that they could not fathom the principles upon which the assize was founded.[87] Lastly, fluctuating flour prices no longer matched wheat prices. In 1735 the Bakers' Company complained to Parliament that the assize needed to be set according to the price of flour and meal.[88] The integral flaws in the early modern assize undoubtedly undermined its efficacy.

Nevertheless, the authorities, bakers and consumers all seemed to feel that the assize of bread remained of value well into the eighteenth century. Most importantly, the regulatory apparatus of the assizes added a sense of security and helped maintain social order. Thompson argued that the assize of bread was the visible paraphernalia of paternalism and protected

---

[83] *Ibid.*, 179.

[84] The baker's allowance was now added directly to the price of wheat from which the assize weight was determined (e.g. if price of wheat was 5s. 3d. and the allowance 1s. 3d., the assize was set in relation to 6s. 6d. on the table). This distorted calculations compared to the medieval assize, for the amount a baker earned was no longer directly proportional to the number of loaves they sold but rather the weight of bread they sold. See Davis, 'Baking', 488, 493–4.

[85] Thwaites, 'Assize of bread', 171–81.   [86] Davis, 'Baking', 493–4.

[87] Brown, 'A just and profitable commerce', 315.

[88] Nicholas, 'Assize of bread', 336; Thrupp, *Company of Bakers*, pp. 23–4.

bakers from the worst excesses of popular wrath.[89] Thwaites has found evidence that the assize of ale was still being set in Oxford as late as 1701, while the assize of bread continued for much longer.[90] In 1756 at Leicester, in order to undermine potential collusion among native bakers and maintain supplies, several country bakers were allowed to freely enter the borough and sell their bread, as long as they kept to the assize of bread.[91] Charles Smith commented in 1764 that 'in large towns and cities it will be always necessary to set the assize, in order to satisfy the people that the price which the bakers demand is no more than is thought reasonable by the magistrates'.[92] The assize of bread thus remained in the same essential form from the thirteenth to eighteenth centuries.[93]

In a similar manner, problems and frauds involving the use of unlawful weights and measures were ongoing throughout the early modern period. William Harrison pronounced that every market town employed a different bushel measure, while many 'unconscionable dealers' used one measure to sell by and another to buy with.[94] An Elizabethan proclamation of 1587 lamented that 'the greatest part of her loving subjects of this realm of England and Wales be ignorant of contents, differences, and true knowledge and uses of the weights of the same realm, and that the weights commonly used within the realm be uncertain and varying one from another to the great slander of the same and the deceiving of many, both buyers and sellers'.[95] Many boroughs continued to demand that all equipment be sealed and enforced the use of a common beam for bulk deals.[96] All weights, Troy and Avoirdupois, were expected to conform to the standards found at the Westminster Exchequer. Elizabeth I ordered the mayors and bailiffs of every borough and town to send men to the Exchequer to receive and pay for standards to then be kept and used for the commonalty in each town in sealing local weights and measures. Regular inspections were expected to take place and false items destroyed. However, some fifteen years later, there were again complaints that the

---

[89] Thompson, 'Moral economy', 105–7; Thwaites, 'Assize of bread', 179; Walter and Wrightson, 'Dearth', 37–40.

[90] Thwaites, 'Oxford food riots', pp. 142–3.

[91] Fisher and Jurica (eds.), Documents, p. 271.

[92] Cf. Thompson, 'Moral economy', 106.

[93] The assize of bread was repealed in London in 1822 and all over England in 1836. Statutes of the United Kingdom, xxii, p. 1036, 3 Geo IV c.106 (1822), xxviii, p. 108, 6&7 Will IV c.37 (1836).

[94] Edelen (ed.), Description, pp. 251–2. See also Grosart (ed.), Life and Complete Works, xi, pp. 68, 259.

[95] TRP, ii, pp. 543–8 (1587).

[96] Richardson and James (eds.), Urban Experience, p. 48, no. 41 (Devizes, 1617); Stanford (ed.), Ordinances of Bristol, p. 56 (1574); Roberts (ed.), Evesham, p. 1, no. 1; Turner (ed.), Selections, pp. 400–2 (Oxford, 1579); Strype (ed.), Survey, ii, pp. 257–8.

standards had been neglected or abused and variations in weights and measures were still rife.[97] In 1670, a statute of Charles II complained about the great variety of measures and ordered that there should be 'one measure of brasse provided and chained in the market-place'.[98]

A royal proclamation in 1619, concerning and extending the jurisdiction of the royal Clerk of the Market, lamented the 'frauds and abuses now generally used in buying and selling (especially by Inne-keepers and Victuallers)'.[99] The Clerk of the Market was still expected to inquire into the weights, measures and deceit of victuallers and retailers, ensuring that their products were wholesome or of good quality, as well as sold at a reasonable price.[100] The just price remained an important consideration and the notions of 'reasonable gains' and 'excessive prices' were increasingly exemplified, as seen in regulations for the price of victuals, meat and tallow. For instance, several royal proclamations were issued regarding the retail price of meat, particularly in London, though they had to be continually adjusted upon petition from butchers to account for seasonal variations. The butchers of sixteenth-century England were to be allowed reasonable gains 'as they might honestly live withal according to their behaviors'; several ordinances were adapted to take into account gross and retail margins. However, they would face (undefined) 'uttermost perils' if they were deemed to have sold at excessive prices.[101] Similarly, a statute in 1548 decried conspiracies to sell victuals at unreasonable prices and threatened severe penalties for transgressors: 'for the first offence £10 to the king's highness, or twenty days imprisonment on bread and water, and for the second offence £20, or the pillory, and for the third offence £40 and the pillory with the loss of one of his ears'.[102] Orders to local justices enjoined them to make lists of victuallers and inquire into those selling their wares at excessive prices.[103] They were increasingly given the power to set reasonable prices for victuals when required 'for relief'. A proclamation of 1587 declared that unreasonable prices needed to be redressed because of the queen's 'princely care and love towards her people, utterly condemneth and earnestly desireth to remedy for the relief of the poorer sort'. Elizabeth I was quite prepared to intervene and impose price controls if the 'poorer sort' were seen to

---

[97] *TRP*, iii, pp. 241–5 (1602). See also *SRP*, i, pp. 416–17 (1619).
[98] *Statutes*, v, pp. 622–3, 22 Car II c.8 (1670).
[99] *SRP*, i, p. 417 (1619).   [100] *Ibid.*, i, p. 418 (1619).
[101] *TRP*, i, pp. 208–9 (1533), 212–15 (1534), 218–19 (1534), 226–7 (1535), 233–4 (1535), 237–8 (1536), 240–1 (1536), 287–8 (1540), 291–3 (1540), 331–5 (1544), 464–9 (1549); *SRP*, i, pp. 86–7 (1604), 297–9 (1613).
[102] *Statutes*, iv (i), pp. 58–9, 2&3 Edw VI c.15 (1548). See also *ibid.*, iii, pp. 436–8, 25 Hen VIII cc.1–2 (1533); *TRP*, i, pp. 464–9 (1549).
[103] Tawney and Power (eds.), *Tudor Economic Documents*, i, pp. 148–50.

be suffering or supplies were being held back from the market. At a time of international crisis, and to protect the provisioning of her army, a list of maximum prices for a wide range of corns and victuals was issued in 1588.[104]

Linked intimately to issues of just price was a concern that supplies of victuals should be maintained. For instance, a Winchester brewer, Robert Bagger, was accused in 1550 of refusing to brew an 'abundance of malte redye in his howse to have byn brewed' at a time of dearth and scarcity. The injunction described him as neglectful of the townspeople and the poor 'to thevill example of the rest of victuallers'; his actions were 'ungentill and unnaturall' and he was henceforth prohibited from brewing again.[105] The bakers of sixteenth-century Northampton were accused of buying up large quantities of grain and conveying it out of the town at times of crisis 'to their own great lucre and advantage and to the raysyng of the price' against the commonwealth. Restrictions were thus placed on the amount of grain that could be carried into the country so as to protect the borough's own supply.[106] A Southampton tallower, Mr Barwycke, was accused of dominating the trade and taking advantage of a time of scarcity in 1587: he 'does presently refuse to serve the inhabitants at any reasonable price'. The presentment emphasised that he was neglecting his duty to serve the community, particularly 'the poorer sort of people [who] are most of all pinched', and was instead more interested in his own gain.[107]

The substance and rhetoric of medieval marketing laws had thus endured and even become more virulent in its tone. The early modern marketplace itself was also subject to similar controls to those seen in the medieval period. The need to keep the marketplace clean and free from obstructions or filth required increasingly detailed municipal proclamations.[108] Ordinances still complained about corrupt and unwholesome meat, and the unsanitary practices of butchers, particularly regarding the disposal of blood and entrails.[109] The butchers of Northampton, Winchester and London were warned about selling

---

[104] *Statutes*, iii, p. 438, 25 Hen VIII c.2 (1534); iv (i), p. 120, 3&4 Edw VI c.21 (1550); *TRP*, ii, pp. 532–4 (1587); iii, pp. 19–22 (1588).

[105] *Winchester*, pp. 181–2 (1550). For similar concerns, see Turner (ed.), *Selections*, p. 10 (1512–13).

[106] *Northampton*, ii, p. 278 (1553?).

[107] Williams (ed.), *English Historical Documents*, p. 985 (Southampton, 1549); Fisher and Jurica (eds.), *Documents*, p. 251 (Southampton, 1587).

[108] Strype (ed.), *Survey*, ii, pp. 306–7 (1562).

[109] Turner (ed.), *Selections*, p. 144 (Oxford, 1536); Morgan (ed.), *Hereford*, pp. 3, 5, 12 (1554–76); Strype (ed.), *Survey*, ii, p. 307 (1562).

diseased or out-of-date meat, as well as for undertaking dubious slaugh-tering practices.[110] The market day also continued to be delineated by ringing of a market bell, with householders allowed to buy provisions for their own use first, followed by retailers who would be condemned as forestallers or regraters if they bought before the appointed time.[111] For instance, the temporal division of the market day was reiterated in Beverley in 1555, where no bakers could buy any grain at the market before 1pm nor store any grain in their houses on market day, except for their own use.[112] All grain and victuals entering the market had to be brought to the open forum for sale and badgers were not allowed to transact business until the second ringing of the bell. Consumption needs had to be met before middleman practices were allowed.[113] If anything, sixteenth-century market regulations became more precise, detailed and comprehensive.[114]

The open marketplace, especially for victual transactions, continued to be a mainstay against forestallers and regraters, and certain traders, particularly outsiders, were compelled to deal in assigned places.[115] Foreign bakers entering the sixteenth-century market of Coventry were only allowed to come on Wednesdays and Fridays and sell only in 'Fleete-streite and Jordan'well', while the fishmongers and sellers of tanned leather has to stand beneath the Cheeping Conduit.[116] The London authorities wanted hucksters and country sellers of victuals to stand in certain areas of the market 'to the intent they may be perfectly known'. They were also to deal only on assigned market days. In the seventeenth-century suburbs, itinerant hawkers, pedlars, fishwives and other petty hucksters were expected to keep on the move and not lay their goods on the ground, causing obstructions, or remain standing without paying stallage fees.[117] Those who owned fixed shops were particularly hostile to itinerant traders and Parliament legislated in favour of shopkeepers.[118]

The retail market trader of the sixteenth and seventeenth centuries was just as unpopular in common culture as retailers of the medieval period.

---

[110] *Northampton*, ii, pp. 280–2 (1558); Atkinson, *Elizabethan Winchester*, pp. 195–6; Strype (ed.), *Survey*, ii, p. 307 (1562).

[111] Strype (ed.), *Survey*, ii, pp. 309–10 (1697).   [112] *Beverley*, pp. 39–40 (1555).

[113] Morgan (ed.), *Hereford*, pp. 5–6, 13 (1554–76); *Northampton*, ii, p. 303 (1586).

[114] E.g. *Northampton*, ii, pp. 280–3 (1558); Turner (ed.), *Selections*, pp. 333–4 (1570–1).

[115] *TRP*, i, p. 527 (1551); *Statutes*, iv (i), p. 119, 3&4 Edw VI c.19 (1549).

[116] *Coventry*, pp. 798–9 (1551). See also Turner (ed.), *Selections*, pp. 106–9 (Oxford, 1531–2); *Northampton*, ii, p. 283 (1568).

[117] Strype (ed.), *Survey*, ii, pp. 308 (1562), 309 (1697); Boulton, *Neighbourhood and Society*, pp. 74–5.

[118] Cox and Dannehl, *Perceptions*, ch. 3.

This is demonstrated starkly by legal and literary attitudes towards pedlars and hawkers. For instance, they were still restricted in their movements around the streets of Bristol and threatened with forty days imprisonment.[119] Regraters or hucksters of victuals were banned from the city for two years, 1566 to 1568, before an order in 1570 limited the numbers of hucksters in Bristol selling fruit to five and those selling oatmeal to two. These wandering traders were bound by two sureties of £5 each towards their good behaviour, in particular that they would not regrate and forestall commodities. Consumers were given an incentive of 5s. to report any hucksters that broke these prohibitions.[120] If anything, the moral opprobrium towards petty traders, as reflected in the literature, ordinances and prescribed penalties, was increasingly stringent throughout the sixteenth and seventeenth centuries. William Cupper preached in 1592 that 'vserers, also brokers, badgers and hucksters, and such like locusts that eat vp the poore and cause the markets to be inhaunced should bee bridled to the ende the poore may haue things better cheape'.[121]

By the late sixteenth century, itinerant pedlars and petty chapmen were deemed to be rogues and vagabonds.[122] Since Edward VI's reign, and well into the eighteenth century, pedlars and traders had to be licensed by designated officers and sureties collected.[123] In 1618, there was recognition that certain 'industrious, honest' chapmen were useful to the trade of the realm, particularly in supplying remote areas, but associations with 'rogues and idle wandering persons' was still prominent. The dislike of the pedlar was allied to his itinerant activities, which meant that much of his trade circumvented official markets and their regulations. They were deemed both damaging to local, settled tradesmen and socially disruptive due to begging, larceny and drunkenness.[124] In both literature and regulation, pedlars were socially marginalised.[125] Greene described the pedlar and tinker as 'both cozin germaines to the deuil'. His tinker was a bawdy, drunken thief who made more holes than he mended and had no fear of God; while his pedlar was a worse villain, wandering the

---

[119] Stanford (ed.), *Ordinances of Bristol*, p. 25 (1555–6).

[120] *Ibid.*, pp. 34 (1566), 38 (1568), 42 (1570). By 1585, fifteen hucksters were allowed in the city (presumably dealing in a variety of goods). *Ibid.*, p. 84 (1585).

[121] Cupper, *Certaine Sermons*, p. 343; Archer, *Pursuit of Stability*, p. 53.

[122] *Statutes*, iv (i), pp. 590–2, 14 Eliz c.5 (1572); iv (ii), p. 899, 39 Eliz c.4 (1597).

[123] *Ibid.*, iv (i), p. 155, 5&6 Edw VI c.21 (1552); *SRP*, i, pp. 393–5 (1618); Spufford, *Great Reclothing*, pp. 7–10; Willan, *Inland Trade*, pp. 54–5.

[124] Beier, *Masterless Men*, pp. 89–91; Blondé, Stabel, Stobart and Van Damme (eds.), *Buyers and Sellers*, introduction, pp. 7–30.

[125] Woodbridge, 'The peddler'.

country with his mistresses ('docksey') and being placed in the stocks for drunkenness and lechery.[126]

In reality, the potential competition of pedlars, hawkers and tinkers was resented and resisted by the town authorities and shopkeepers. In 1691, a petition was offered to Parliament arguing that the activities of pedlars, hawkers and petty chapmen were damaging the trade of more worthy traders 'to the great inconvenience and danger of the whole nation'. Although Parliament rejected this petition as only benefiting shopkeepers and inconvenient to customers, highlighting the utility of pedlars in certain aspects of commerce, an act was passed in 1696–7 to reinforce the licensing of hawkers and pedlars.[127] It could be argued that the ongoing attempts to license pedlars and petty chapmen actually legitimised their activities, giving them some respectability and even encouraging retailers to cooperate with them. Alternatively, it is also possible that licensing disrupted supply as much as aided it, by reinforcing suspicions of itinerant traders and by making ambiguous the position of many itinerant wholesalers through all-embracing definitions.[128] More importantly, those outside the system were disparaged and castigated as vagrants and rogues by both Parliament and fixed-shop retailers. However, whether consumers viewed them the same way is questionable, especially given the success of such traders even as they operated on the margins of acceptability.

Many other traders had to be formally licensed to operate.[129] During the early sixteenth century in Winchester, only twenty-four appointed tipplers could receive and sell ale from the brewers.[130] These twenty-four, and all other regraters, were prohibited from selling eggs, butter or poultry, except by consent of the mayor.[131] Badgers of corn (and victuals) and drovers of cattle were declared unlawful engrossers and forestallers unless they were licensed by the Justices of the Peace.[132] Licences for running alehouses first became mandatory in 1552, when keepers had to post bonds to maintain good order. By July 1577, the Privy Council

---

[126] Grosart (ed.), *Life and Complete Works*, xi, pp. 282–3. The reputation of tinkers and pedlars as flirtatious and lecherous was reinforced in several ballads, e.g. Chappell (ed.), *Roxburghe Ballads*, iii, 'Room for a Jovial Tinker: Old Brass to Mend', p. 230.

[127] Thirsk and Cooper (eds.), *Seventeenth-Century Economic Documents*, pp. 417–21 (1691–3), 423–6 (1696–7). See also *ibid.*, pp. 428–9 (John Houghton, *A Collection for the Improvement of Husbandry and Trade* (1727)); Spufford, *Great Reclothing*, pp. 12–14.

[128] Cox and Dannehl, *Perceptions*, pp. 50–2.

[129] Stanford (ed.), *Ordinances of Bristol*, pp. 72–3 (1581).

[130] *Winchester*, pp. 140 (1525), 147 (1531), 157 (1535), 167 (1540); Atkinson, *Elizabethan Winchester*, pp. 186–7. See also Greaves (ed.), *First Ledger Book*, pp. 72–3, 85, nos. 88 and 107 (Wycombe, 1527 and 1559).

[131] *Winchester*, pp. 179 (1549), 182 (1550).

[132] *Statutes*, iv (i), pp. 439–41, 5 Eliz c.12 (1563).

ordered full returns of the names of those licensed as keepers of taverns, inns and alehouses.[133] Owners of inns and alehouses in sixteenth-century Coventry had to be given permission by the mayor and Justices of the Peace in order to operate.[134] Throughout Tudor and Stuart England, such places were considered havens for the undesirables of society ('evyll dysposed personns' or 'certeyne lewde persons') who got drunk and gambled.[135] They were seen to contribute nothing to social harmony or order, only idleness, immorality and ungodliness.

Peter Clark argues that, in reality, 'criminal activity centred on alehouses was amateur, small-scale, and sporadic', though there does appear to have been an increasing tendency towards drunkenness.[136] Alehouses were also important centres for the local community, but they still remained susceptible to accusations of marketing misdemeanours, such as regrating and engrossing, as well as the traditional short-measures and adulterated drink.[137] The borough of Evesham sought to establish common brewhouses from 1611 as a means to suppress 'meane typplinge and blind alehouses' that brewed contrary to the law and failed to supply the needs of the poor at reasonable prices.[138] A royal proclamation of 1600 declared that there was a surfeit of alehouses and victualling houses in England, which were a haven of 'waste, riot, and expenses' as well as 'infinite idleness, thefts, and other inconveniences and disorders'.[139] Justices of the Peace were ordered to keep down the number of such establishments and only allow respectable persons to run them, who were then bound by financial sureties to maintain good order. It was important that action was seen to be taken. Licences and recognisances issued to alehouse-keepers in 1619 outlined their duty to prevent unlawful games within their premises, close on Sundays, during divine service and after curfew, keep the assizes of bread, ale and beer, and report to the constable any strangers who stayed longer than a day and a night.[140] Ultimately, the authorities did not want any vagabonds, rogues or thieves resorting

---

[133] *Ibid.*, iv (i), pp. 157–8, 5&6 Edw VI c.25 (1552), pp. 168–70, 7 Edw VI c.5 (1553). See also *SRP*, i, pp. 409–13 (1619).

[134] *Coventry*, p. 781 (1546).

[135] *Ibid.*, p. 808 (1553); *Northampton*, ii, p. 301 (1570); Dyer, *City of Worcester*, p. 144; Clark, 'The alehouse'; Wrightson, 'Alehouses', pp. 11–13, 17–18; Mayhew, *Tudor Rye*, pp. 225–8; Yates, *Town and Countryside*, p. 100.

[136] Clark, 'The alehouse', pp. 57–9.

[137] *Ibid.*, p. 68; Wrightson, 'Alehouses'; Slack, 'Books of Orders', 16–17.

[138] Roberts (ed.), *Evesham*, p. 10, no. 40.

[139] *TRP*, iii, pp. 205–6 (1600); *Statutes*, iv (i), p. 422, 5 Eliz I c.5 (1563).

[140] *SRP*, i, pp. 409–13 (1619). See also *Statutes*, iv(ii), pp. 1026–7, 1 Jac. I c.9 (1603); iv(ii), pp. 1141–3, 4 Jac. I cc.4–5 (1606); iv(ii), p. 1167, 7 Jac. I c.10 (1609); iv(ii), pp. 1216–17, 21 Jac. I c.7 (1624); v, p. 3, 1 Car. I c.4 (1625); v, pp. 26–7, 3 Car. I c.4 (1628).

to these establishments and local men of 'the better sort' were expressing their social anxieties through such legislation.[141] However, the actual leet court records suggest that not all illegal alehouses were suppressed, particularly in the seventeenth century, as officials sought to profit from their existence or did not wish to overburden poor families.[142] As in medieval England, the strict letter of the law was not always enforced and local officials exercised flexible, but effective, discretion in identifying what they saw as the true moral dangers from the popular, local operations that provided regular fines.

As Susan Amussen has stated, regulations were often advanced by local notables 'to get rid of undesirables, but not harm the worthy'.[143] She provided the example of an Anne Bassham, in Castle Rising in 1657, who had been serving small beer to the disadvantage of the poor, but when she withdrew this service it was recognised that this was equally harmful as her brewing was 'necessary and for the good of the greatest part of the town'. Regulations that overly inhibited the flow of trade and prevented traders from earning a livelihood suited no one. Nevertheless, there was a stark paternalism behind early modern regulations, whereby market traders were expected to operate to the benefit of the commonwealth and the poor.[144] Notions of the just price and mutual communal responsibility were still prominent.

Middlemen and dearth

Maintaining the supply of corn, at reasonable prices, remained a mantra of early modern authorities, who were especially fearful about dearth at a time of population renewal.[145] Regulation and intervention in the marketing of grain was thus common at times of harvest failures, largely to maintain social order.[146] Indeed, well into the eighteenth century, 'traditional paternalistic moral notions about the entitlement of the poor to locally produced grain resulted in legislation which gave magistrates the power to intervene in local markets' if there was a likelihood of potential food shortages and disorder.[147]

---

[141] Wrightson, *English Society*, pp. 159, 166–70, 227; Wrightson, 'Alehouses'.
[142] King, 'Regulation of alehouses'; Clark, 'The alehouse', pp. 49, 70; Roberts, 'Alehouses', 54.
[143] Amussen, *An Ordered Society*, p. 155.   [144] *Ibid.*, pp. 155–6.
[145] Everitt, 'Marketing', pp. 562–71, 576–86.
[146] Walter and Wrightson, 'Dearth'; Walter, 'Social economy'; Outhwaite, 'Dearth'; Renton, 'Moral economy', pp. 116–17, 133; Brown, 'A just and profitable commerce', 330.
[147] Muldrew, *Economy of Obligation*, p. 47.

Corn-dealers who moved corn from place to place had long been regarded as legitimate, as long as they were not denuding the former location of necessary supplies and were meeting important demand elsewhere. A statute of 1552 allowed badgers, who were licensed by three Justices of the Peace, to buy grain, cattle, fish, butter or cheese where they wished and resell or transport them.[148] In 1627, traders were able to sell grain both inside and outside pitched markets and transport it where they wished, but only when corn was below a certain price.[149] Outside of times of dearth, middlemen had a fairly free scope of action. However, middlemen who merely intervened to turn a quick profit, with little extra labour, were disparaged, particularly forestallers, engrossers and regraters.[150] Statutes and royal proclamations were issued regularly against these activities, which were seen as causing scarcity to the detriment of the commonweal. If anything, these laws became more vehement in their condemnation, perhaps reflecting the more pressurised economic circumstances of the sixteenth century. In 1534, a royal proclamation declared: 'there is no just ground or cause why such grain should be so high enhanced in price as it is', blaming it on 'the subtle invention and craft of divers covetous persons'.[151] In 1551, another proclamation stated that excessive prices were mostly caused by 'the greedy and insatiable covetous desires and appetites of the breeders, broggers, engrossers, graziers, victuallers and forestallers (minding only their own lucre without respect of the commonwealth, to the great damage, impoverishing, and disquieting of his majesty's subjects)'.[152] This ordinance was effectively an abridged version of *Statutum de Pistoribus*, though it sought to punish price-enhancers by means 'more sharp and penal than any former law or proclamation heretofore made or ordained hath been'.

Elizabethan and Jacobean proclamations also asserted that covetousness, engrossing, forestalling and false rumours were causing dearth and high prices in the country. The *Book of Orders*, first promulgated in 1587

[148] *Statutes*, iv(i), p. 148, 5&6 Edw VI c.14 (1552); Everitt, 'Marketing', pp. 579–81. See also *Statutes*, iv(i), p. 439, 5 Eliz c.12 (1563), p. 562, 13 Eliz c.25 §7 (1571).

[149] *Statutes*, v, p. 30, 3 Car I c.5 §5 (1627). See also *ibid.*, v, p. 449, 15 Car II c.7 (1663).

[150] Sacks, 'The greed of Judas'.

[151] *Statutes*, iii, p. 422, 24 Hen VIII c.6 (1532); iii, p. 440, 25 Hen VIII c.4 (1533); *TRP*, i, pp. 172–4 (1527), 180–1 (1528), 188, 190–1 (1529), 221–2 (1534). The export of grain, victuals and other goods was also repeatedly forbidden or controlled due to fears that such activities raised prices. *Ibid.*, i, pp. 201–3 (1531), 419–20 (1548), 423–4 (1548), 429–30 (1548), 490–1 (1550); iii, pp. 61–2 (1590); iv (i), pp. 243–4, 1&2 Philip & Mary c.5 (1555); *SRP*, i, pp. 187–8 (1608), 285–6 (1613), 521–2 (1621); ii, pp. 271–3 (1630), 312–14 (1631); Gras, *Evolution*, pp. 138–43, 221–32; Sharp, 'Popular protest', pp. 279–80; Outhwaite, 'Dearth', 389–92. After 1670, controls on export of corn were relaxed.

[152] *TRP*, i, pp. 526–7 (1551); ii, p. 182 (1562).

but effectively a codification of past practices, attempted to keep the grain trade out of the hands of such speculators.[153] It allowed Justices of the Peace and local juries to regulate stores of corn, licences of badgers and sales of surpluses, and to ensure the priority of poor consumers. Just as in medieval laws, wholesale purchasers were not permitted to deal during the first part of the market day, which was reserved for the poor and other consumers, while grain was meant to be transacted in the open, public market.[154] The regulations also controlled the use of grain for non-essential purposes, such as in unlicensed alehouses, distilling and starch-making.[155] Most notably, however, the royal council appealed to the justices to suppress profiteering middlemen, engrossers and regraters.[156] In 1598, royal orders stated that: 'the wicked and unsatiable greediness of sundry bad-disposed persons, who, preferring their own private gain above the public good... forestall, regrate, and engross all manner of grains and so raise high prices thereby, to the great oppression of the poorer sort'. It was proclaimed that both corporal punishment and fines should be used by local justices and magistrates for the chastisement of offenders.[157] In the reign of James I, the Privy Council could find no other reason for the high prices of corn and victuals than the practices of engrossing and withholding supplies from the marketplace.[158] The Books of Orders were a clear effort by the government to show they were on the side of the poor consumer against the profiteering middlemen and farmers, with the ultimate aim of defusing potential discontent and disorder.[159]

The *Book of Orders* was reissued several times (1587, 1594, 1608, 1622, 1630) and its effect was felt widely in the community. For example, in 1608 in Leicester, husbandmen, tradesmen and others were held back from the market for barley so 'that the poor and others which buy for provision of bread may be first served'.[160] In 1630–1, in Lutterworth,

---

[153] Slack, 'Books of Orders'; Sharp, *In Contempt of All Authority*, pp. 50–80.

[154] Dyer, *City of Worcester*, pp. 140–1.

[155] Slack, 'Books of Orders'; Gras, *Evolution*, pp. 236–42; Roberts, 'Alehouses', 47.

[156] Appleby, *Famine*, pp. 142–4.

[157] *TRP*, ii, pp. 276–8 (1566), 532–4 (1587); iii, pp. 165–6 (1596), 193–5 (1598); *Orders Deuised by the Especiall Commandement of the Queenes Maiestie, for the Reliefe and Stay of the Present Dearth of Graine within the Realme* (STC 9194, London, 1586); *A New Charge Giuen by the Queenes Commandement* (STC 9202, London, 1595).

[158] *SRP*, i, pp. 186–8 (1608); *Orders Appointed by his Maiestie to be Straightly Obserued for the Preuenting and Remedying of the Dearth of Graine and other Victuall* (STC 9217, London, 1608). The *Book of Orders* was reissued in 1630 (STC 9253); *SRP*, i, pp. 563–5 (1622); *SRP*, ii, pp. 298–304 (1630).

[159] Clay, *Economic Expansion*, p. 228.

[160] Goodacre, *Transformation of a Peasant Economy*, pp. 182–3.

as arrangements were made to help the poor of Leicester after a disastrous harvest, John Price was accused of being 'a forestaller of our market which maketh out corn very dear that we cannot get corn to relieve our poor but at excessive rates and scarce to relieve our own families'.[161] It seems likely that he was purchasing corn to resell outside the area, something that was increasingly common when prices were high. However, John Goodacre argues that his actions were defended by others in the town who had wide commercial connections and wanted to trade freely, and there was perhaps a 'direct conflict of interests between people at opposite ends of the economic scale'.[162] The poor were competing with the cornmongers, maltsters, bakers and innkeepers for the weekly breadcorn. In 1662, William Petty accused corn traders of 'being onely a kind of Gamesters, that play with one another for the labours of the poor; yielding of themselves no fruit at all, otherwise then as veins and arteries, to distribute forth and back the blood and nutritive juyces of the Body Politick'.[163] In this manner, more and more of the grain supply was being withdrawn from the open market and entering wider (more integrated) networks, and consequently the authorities were struggling to cope at times of grain shortage. The common people looked to traditional regulations of the 'moral economy' to be upheld in order to protect supplies, but the realities of commerce were not so easy to counteract.

Demand for grain was fairly inelastic and supplies were still subject to notable fluctuations. Despite its increasing complexity, the corn market remained susceptible to speculation and middlemen. This was exacerbated by the fact that much of the trade was operating beyond the open market and within the 'private' sector, such as at the farmgate or inn.[164] 'Private marketing' was certainly not new, but it does appear that inns and private houses were increasingly used in the early modern period for a myriad of wholesale exchanges, storage and credit functions. Everitt described inns as 'the hotel, the bank, the warehouse, the exchange, the scrivener's office, and the market-place of many a private trader'.[165] The improper receiving of corn into private houses, rather than being placed in the open marketplace, was a recurrent concern.[166] In Warminster (Wiltshire), in 1576, no foreigner was to buy any corn in the market before 11am and all corn was to be displayed in open market and not hoarded, so that 'the poorer sort of the town and country shall first be

[161] *Ibid.*, pp. 184–5, 231.   [162] *Ibid.*
[163] Gras, *Evolution*, pp. 203–4; Petty, *A Treatise*, p. 11.
[164] Baker, 'Marketing of corn', 139.
[165] Everitt, 'Marketing', p. 559; Palliser, *Tudor York*, p. 184; Boulton, *Neighbourhood and Society*, pp. 76–7.
[166] *Winchester*, p. 149 (1531); Wells, *Wretched Faces*, p. 81.

suffered to buy before badgers and other strangers'.[167] A letter from the overseers of the market at Middlewich, in 1648, complained about corn being sold privately to bakers rather than openly in the market, 'so the poor are forced to have it upon their terms or else starve'.[168]

Paternalist language and pejorative moral overtones were widely reflected in local petitions and laws. Sixteenth-century York ordinances argued that grain was hoarded due to 'insatiable greediness against all charity' and beyond any household needs, and that such engrossers cared not who perished in their search for gain. It was argued that engrossing, forestalling and regrating of grain caused unreasonable prices, dearth and destruction to the people. A judgement in Star Chamber in 1631 remarked that the engrossing of corn by Archer of Southchurch (Essex) was an offence 'of high nature and evil consequence, to the undoing of the poor'. He was fined 100 marks to the king and £10 to the poor, and was also made to stand in the pillories of Newgate, Leadenhall and Chelmsford markets for an hour each, with a paper detailing his crime of enhancing the price of corn.[169] However, it should be noted that the regulations also highlighted the utility of badgers and stated that they should not be molested in carrying grain from market to market, as long as they did so without fraud and greed.[170]

Statutes and laws regarding forestalling, regrating and other trading activities were expected to be proclaimed publicly in the markets and fairs of England, while town officials were enjoined to enforce such edicts with all due diligence.[171] Similarly, in the early seventeenth century, it was ordered that the duties of the Clerk of the Market and his deputies should be announced in every market town and displayed 'where it may continue to be seene and read by any that will'. The proclamation was also to be read by the minister in every parish church on the Sunday before the feast of All Saints, and twice more in the year, as well as displayed in the church permanently.[172] The early modern punishment for middleman offences was even more stark than those envisaged by medieval statute law: two-months' imprisonment for the first offence; six-months' imprisonment and forfeiture of double the value of the goods for the second; pillory, forfeiture and imprisonment for the third.[173] In

---

[167] Fisher and Jurica (eds.), *Documents*, pp. 250–1 (1576).
[168] *Ibid.*, pp. 518–19 (1648).
[169] Bland, Brown and Tawney (eds.), *English Economic History*, pp. 391–6 (1631).
[170] Williams (ed.), *English Historical Documents*, pp. 992–3 (York, 1549); Thirsk and Cooper (eds.), *Seventeenth-Century Economic Documents*, p. 36 (Nottinghamshire, 1630–1).
[171] *TRP*, i, p. 527 (1551).   [172] *SRP*, i, pp. 420–1 (1619).
[173] *Statutes*, iv (i), p. 148, 5&6 Edw VI c.14 §.4, 5, 6, 9, 14 (1552).

1697, the common council of London printed and reissued sections from past statutes, such as *Judicium Pillorie* and *Statutum de Pistoribus*, in order to reiterate their moral disgust about forestalling and the need for strict punishment.[174] The moral stigma attached to the offences of forestalling and engrossing had, if anything, become stronger since medieval times though the rhetoric was noticeably similar.

Literary references to middlemen throughout the sixteenth and seventeenth centuries also appealed to the same sentiments as medieval literature, though they concentrated more consistently on the specific iniquities of forestallers and engrossers. It is possible that the increasing frequency of dearth in the early modern period served to intensify condemnation of these middlemen. In the mid-sixteenth century, Robert Crowley told forestallers to repent for manipulating needful foodstuffs or else the Clerk of the Market would punish them all.[175] Thomas Lever (1550) was utterly disparaging of middlemen and regraters, whom he characterised as 'merchants of mischief coming betwixt the bark, and the tree' and 'idle vagabonds, living upon other men's labours'. They merely raised prices unnecessarily, created artificial dearths, and took advantage of the needy, all to serve their own greed.[176] In the late sixteenth century, William Harrison complained that middlemen held back their corn from the market and waited until the price had increased before gradually releasing supplies. In other words, although the activities of middlemen served to dampen the volatilities of the national market for grain, the practice withheld grain from the market when the poor could afford it most (just after the harvest) and also meant that a greater proportion of the final price of grain lined the pockets of badgers and cornmongers.[177] Harrison alleged that middlemen travelled secretly to various markets buying up all the corn, thus preventing the poor from obtaining necessary provisions at a reasonable price. 'I wish that God would once open their eyes that deal thus to see their own errors, for as yet some of them little care how many poor men suffer extremity, so that they may fill their purses and carry away the grain'.[178] In a similar vein during the mid-seventeenth century, Robert Powell argued that forestalling and engrossing was 'a privie stealer (though a publike enemy) of the birth of the wombe', and those who hoarded and forestalled prevented people from performing their livelihoods for the good of the realm.[179]

---

[174] Strype (ed.), *Survey*, ii, pp. 308–9 (1697).
[175] Cowper (ed.), *Select Works*, 'One and Thirty Epigrammes', p. 33.
[176] Williams (ed.), *English Historical Documents*, pp. 360–1.
[177] Chartres, 'Marketing'; Muldrew, *Economy of Obligation*, p. 50.
[178] Edelen (ed.), *Description*, pp. 246–53 (1587).
[179] Powell, *Depopulation Arraigned*, pp. 4–5.

Adherents to the ideals of the moral economy thus interpreted such middlemen practices as unscrupulous and exploitative, as well as against the traders' social responsibility. An eighteenth-century essayist even wrote a piece entitled *An essay to prove that regraters, engrossers, forestallers, hawkers and jobbers of corn, cattle, other marketable goods, provisions and merchandizes, are destructive of trade, oppressors to the poor, and a common nuisance to the kingdom in general* (1718).[180] Many clergymen reiterated such anger towards merchants and cornmongers. Their sermons reached out to a broad audience who were exhorted to help bring market sinners to account and to reinforce the traditional order. As Brodie Waddell has argued, 'it is hardly surprising to find villagers quoting scripture in their protests against perceived injustice'.[181]

Despite this litany of opprobrium heaped upon middlemen, they remained important cogs in the commercial system. Many of them became wealthy in the economic conditions and their utility was increasingly appreciated. Indeed, during the eighteenth century, there were significant advocates of the new political economics that sought to free up trade and detach middlemen from paternal oversight. The belief that the 'market' could act as a beneficent hand for the common good if it was allowed to be self-regulated, and if all paternalist intervention was expunged, was becoming an orthodoxy among powerful groups in the eighteenth century. The *Gentleman's Magazine* of 1757 argued that the laws against forestalling, engrossing and regrating were 'so antiquated and the circumstances and manner of living of all ranks of people so altered, that a rigorous execution of them would rather contribute to famish than feed in many places great numbers of the poorer sort'.[182] In a well-known passage from *Wealth of Nations* in 1776, Adam Smith declared: 'The popular fear of engrossing and forestalling may be compared to the popular terrors and suspicions of witchcraft'.[183] In this sentence, Smith dismissed the utility of such traditional regulations while also recognising their continuing popular appeal. Nevertheless, he wished to see market trade liberalised and he provided a justification of the middleman in all his guises: 'The interest of the inland dealer, and that of the great body of the people, how opposite soever they may at first sight appear, are, even in years of greatest scarcity, exactly the same'.[184] In Smithian economic theory, the middlemen rationed out supply so that corn would be available at even the times of the greatest scarcity. The

---

[180] Cf. Thompson, 'Moral economy', 95.   [181] Waddell, 'Economic immorality', 177.
[182] *Gentleman's Magazine*, vol. 27 (1757), p. 430, cf. Stevenson, 'Moral economy', p. 229.
[183] Smith, *An Inquiry*, i, p. 534; Britnell, 'La commercializzazione', 652.
[184] Smith, *An Inquiry*, bk iv, ch. v.

common man might not have viewed it this way, particularly since the burden of harvest failures usually fell inordinately upon the poor.[185] Nevertheless, under pressure from powerful vested interests, Edward VI's statute against forestalling and regrating was finally repealed in 1772, though they remained offences under common law.[186] Indeed, forestalling and regrating were still prosecuted in Oxford well into the 1780s, while in 1800 the Birmingham Gazette stated that the 'high price of provisions having manifestly been occasioned by forestalling and regrating, more than by any real scarcity'.[187] It could be argued that the views of the political and intellectual elite did not necessarily match those of the majority, who still clung tenaciously to their traditional view of market morality.

Thompson's moral economy

E. P. Thompson argued that not all food riots during the dearths of the late eighteenth century were compulsive, irate attacks lacking any thought or direction, but were rather guided and moderated by custom, culture and reason.[188] In particular, he suggested that the crowd were informed by the belief that they were defending traditional rights of justice in the grain trade, which were supported by the wider consensus of the community.[189] Riots were triggered by times of dearth and hunger, but grievances were aimed at what were considered to be illegitimate and dishonest practices in marketing, milling and baking, which raised the price of grain and bread above the 'just price'. This, in turn, was grounded upon a consistent traditional view of the obligations of traders within the concept of the commonweal, in particular the maintenance of a supply of foodstuffs for all, the maintenance of an open market for grain and the prevention of manipulative profiteering. At times of dearth, in particular, prices should be regulated, corn ought to be brought to the local pitching market, poorer consumers given the first opportunity to buy grain and profiteers condemned. Transparency

---

[185] Overton, *Agricultural Revolution*, pp. 143–5.

[186] *Statutes at Large*, vii, p. 207, 12 Geo III c.71 (1772). Chartres, 'Marketing', p. 247; Hay, 'Moral economy', pp. 96–8; Overton, *Agricultural Revolution*, pp. 143–5; Rose, 'Eighteenth century price riots', 290; Brown, 'A just and profitable commerce', 309, 313.

[187] Thwaites, 'Oxford food riots', p. 150; *Aris's Birmingham Gazette*, 4 August 1800, cf. Toulmin Smith (ed.), *English Gilds*, p. 369.

[188] Rudé posited a similar theory about social purpose and customary rights as dimensions shaping crowd activity. Rudé, *The Crowd*. See also Holton, 'The crowd in history', 223–4, 228–9.

[189] Thompson, 'Moral economy', 78; Charlesworth and Randall, 'Morals', 200.

in market transactions remained the lodestone of local commerce. Those who engaged in suspicious market activities like forestalling, regrating, engrossing and selling by sample were to be restricted. Thompson termed this traditional paternalistic model the 'moral economy' of the poor.[190]

The poor would effectively take over a grain market and exercise authority in a manner they perceived to be legal and just; selling grain at a 'fair price' and often even returning the profits to grain merchants. In the mid-eighteenth century, John Wesley remarked on the actions of a mob in James' Town (Ireland): 'their business was only with the forestallers of the market, who had bought up all the corn far and near, to starve the poor, and load a Dutch ship, which lay at the quay; but the mob brought it all out into the market, and sold it for the owners at the common price. And this they did with all the calmness and composure imaginable, and without striking or hurting anyone.'[191] Often people feared that exports of grain would leave them to starve and consequently grain-ships and the transportation of grain were targeted.[192] At other times, crowds directed their ire at middlemen, millers or farmers. However, despite occasional thefts and violence, the general level of restraint was notable. Money was returned to dealers after their produce had been sold at a 'just price' and thieves within the rioters' ranks had been decried.[193] In general, there was an apparent moral, just and self-disciplined dimension to the crowd's actions; a belief that they were enforcing laws which the authorities had been neglecting. Accusations were levelled at officials that they were failing in upholding social justice and the law. Officials were expected to restrain profiteers and prevent exploitation of the needy and the rioters perceived their own actions as reinforcing established authority and law, not subverting it.[194]

---

[190] Thompson, 'Moral economy', 79, 83–4, 112.   [191] Cf. Thompson, *Making*, p. 69.

[192] Sharp, 'Popular protest', pp. 280–3; Sharp, *In Contempt of All Authority*, pp. 13, 19, 22; Walter and Wrightson, 'Dearth', 27; Wrightson, *English Society*, p. 176.

[193] Stevenson, *Popular Disturbances*, pp. 105–6; Charlesworth and Randall, 'Morals', 209–11; Rose, 'Price riots', 282, 286–7.

[194] Sharp, 'Popular protest', pp. 271–2, 279, 288–9; Walter and Wrightson, 'Dearth', 32–4; Slack, 'Books of Orders', 17; Walter, 'Grain riots', pp. 51, 81. Late sixteenth-century London rioters similarly appropriated market authority in response to crises, demanding that foodstuffs be sold in the open market for a just price and that forestallers and regraters should be strictly regulated. Archer, *Pursuit of Stability*, pp. 6, 200–2. See also Clark, 'Popular protest'; Walter and Wrightson, 'Dearth'; Walter, 'Grain riots', pp. 60, 64; Wrightson, *English Society*, pp. 174–5. Sharp points to the precedent of riots in 1347 in Boston, Lynn and Bristol, where crowds boarded grain ships, as examples of the continuity in behaviour, attitudes and expressed aims. Sharp, 'Popular protest', pp. 280–1, 286; Sharp, 'Food riots of 1347'.

According to Thompson, the legitimacy of the crowd's actions was based on a 'selective reconstruction' of traditional, paternalistic regulations which favoured the poor.[195] He stated: 'the paternalist model had an ideal existence, and also a fragmentary real existence. In years of good harvest and moderate prices, the authorities lapsed into forgetfulness. But if prices rose and the poor became turbulent, it was revived, as least for symbolic effect.'[196] The scale of these actions prompted Thompson to argue that they 'indicate an extraordinarily deep-rooted pattern of behaviour and belief', underwritten by old market customs and culture.[197] As already seen, an acceptance of such traditional market morality was noticeable throughout English society. In another example, in 1758, the old *Book of Orders* was reprinted and presented to William Pitt, Secretary of State, and Henry Legge, Chancellor, as a potential remedy against the recent dearth, though it was not adopted.[198] Nevertheless, Thompson recognised that angst about middlemen 'endured with undiminished vigour, both in popular tradition and in the minds of some Tory paternalists, including no less a person than the Lord Chief Justice (Kenyon), who made it known his view, in 1795, that forestalling and engrossing remained offences at common law'.[199] The view that middlemen activities were incompatible with commercial justice thus remained prominent in the eighteenth century. Condemnation of profiteering, adulteration and deception, plus the need for regulation at times of crisis and dearth, were embedded in the views of not only common market users but also the authorities, clergy and press.[200]

However, Thompson also suggested that the 'paternalist model was breaking down' when confronted with commercial reality and the development of classical economics during the eighteenth century.[201] The assize of bread could not control the price of corn, middlemen were needed to supply the urban markets, and many deals were made at the farmgate and not in the marketplace. In addition, attempts to free up mercantile trade and reduce restrictions threatened local customary systems of bargaining and protecting vulnerable customers. The crowd were

---

[195] Thompson, 'Moral economy', 98.   [196] *Ibid.*, 88.
[197] Thompson, *Making*, p. 71; Randall and Charlesworth (eds.), *Markets*, p. 24.
[198] Gras, *Evolution*, p. 207.
[199] Thompson, *Making*, p. 72; Thompson, 'Moral economy', 88; Brown, 'A just and profitable commerce', 310; Wells, *Wretched Faces*, pp. 86–7; Hay, 'Moral economy', pp. 98–112.
[200] Randall and Charlesworth (eds.), *Markets*, pp. 12–15; Sharp, 'Popular protest', p. 272; Walter, 'Grain riots', pp. 50–1; Slack, 'Books of Orders', 16; Wells, *Wretched Faces*, pp. 82–3.
[201] Thompson, 'Moral economy', 87.

reacting against these economic developments and changes in marketing practice. However, in contrast, Williams, Stevenson and Bohstedt have argued that most of the eighteenth-century rioters were willing participants in a modernising market economy. Williams noted how many of the rioters, rather than being poor and rural, were urban retailers and manufacturers who were therefore 'informed by the imperatives of the marketplace' rather than a moral economy.[202] Similarly, Stevenson has pointed to how many rioters were prepared to accept fluctuating prices based on market forces, rather than preconsidered 'just prices' from a supposed golden age. Stevenson and John Bohstedt have even questioned whether the moral economy was a truly held value system of the crowd rather than merely a tactical, pragmatic device employed in circumstances of dearth.[203] Bohstedt has argued that eighteenth-century rioters acted in terms of a 'pragmatic economy' rather than due to 'hoary traditions'. He dismissed rioters' occasional references to forestallers and engrossers as mere generic condemnations stretching from biblical times, thus implying that longevity reduces the power of such tropes rather than reinforcing moral assumptions.[204] Bohstedt suggested that rioters were merely looking for food and the punishment of hoarders came a distant second, largely because people accepted market forces and knew they could not buck the imperatives of supply and demand.[205]

However, this all perhaps creates too stark a division between a 'moral economy' and a 'market economy', even suggesting that they were diametrically opposed.[206] Indeed, when reconsidered, much of Bohstedt's evidence actually supports the specification of customary targets, against middlemen, engrossers, millers and exports, rather than random attacks on all holders of grain and food. Hunger was undoubtedly a primary force and some riots did escalate, but it is interesting that many rioters preferred to scatter corn in the streets as a protest rather than collect it. The authorities similarly fell back on traditional regulations and values in restoring social order. Admittedly, food riots were not about defending traditional moral values *per se* and were very much a reaction to need, dearth and hunger. However, such primal motivations could co-exist with and were legitimised by traditional moral values and ideas concerning legitimate market practices. Elsewhere, Bohstedt has stated: 'The moral economy was not a wholesale condemnation of capitalist trade and profit. What rioters seemed to object to were cheating, false weights

---

[202] Williams, 'Morals', 58–9, 70, 73.
[203] Bohstedt, 'Moral economy'; Stevenson, 'Moral economy'.
[204] Bohstedt, 'Pragmatic economy', p. 55.   [205] *Ibid.*, pp. 75–8.
[206] Thompson, 'Moral economy reviewed', pp. 266–7.

444 Medieval market morality

and measures, extortionate prices, not just high prices.'[207] Indeed, as we
have seen, the moral economy was not incompatible with an acceptance
of market forces in setting prices; the rioters would have argued that it
was not them but greedy middlemen who were trying to buck artificially
the natural forces of supply and demand.

There is a tendency to misunderstand how medieval markets worked
and for how long the market had been part of people's lives. Market practices were certainly expected to accord with moral principles, but these
were forged in a long and complex cultural process that did partly take
into account the needs of commerce, while many regulations were set
in place to facilitate market activity. Thompson rightly warned against
'equating regulated markets with a moral economy'.[208] Equally, a practical, moral basis is important for any economic system. As Susan Brown
stated, 'religious reinforcement should be distinguished from an evangeli-
cal crusade against commercial transgressions'.[209] Medieval market users
and moralists accepted that prices were formed by supply and demand,
but wanted an open, competitive marketplace; they were more market
savvy than has sometimes been assumed. It was a pragmatic moral economy and this remained the crux of the food riots in the late eighteenth
century.

It was in times of dearth that conflict arose because ordinary consumers
realised that nothing substantial had replaced the paternalist legislation
that was being eroded in the name of free markets. Parliament repealed
old statutes concerning forestalling in 1772 and failed to lift the export
bounty on grain in 1766, even though stocks were low.[210] This meant
that merchants were effectively encouraged by the government to maximise their profits from the export of grain even while there was dearth at
home. The realities of the early modern corn trade and the inelasticity of
demand meant that the idealism of classical economics was not conducive
to the welfare of the commonalty. This was not the open, competitive
market of Smithian economics, but a seller's market ripe for speculation. Many contemporaries argued that the abstract theories espoused
by Adam Smith, and leading men like Pitt, were detached from the realities of the marketplace where individual speculators could artificially
distort supplies and raise prices and where there were extensive uncertainties and asymmetries in information.[211] Paradoxically, the protesters

---

[207] Bohstedt, 'Moral economy', 267.
[208] Thompson, 'Moral economy reviewed', p. 288.
[209] Brown, 'A just and profitable commerce', 325.
[210] *Statutes at Large*, xi, p. 630, 12 Geo III c.71 (1772); Williams, 'Morals', 64; Rose,
'Price riots', 289–90.
[211] Brown, 'A just and profitable commerce', 319–21.

argued that they were looking to protect the forces of supply and demand by preventing monopolies and encouraging competition.

The 'crowd' did not view the moral economy as diametrically opposed to the free market, but they were anxious about the implications of Smith's *laissez-faire* theories in an actual market system that was not fully integrated or matured, despite improvements in communications and regional linkages. The reality could not match the ideals of Smith's philosophy.[212] In the eyes of poorer consumers, who had a substantive knowledge about how markets worked day-to-day, there was now little to protect them from the embedded fear of manipulative, exploitative middlemen. Indeed, they probably viewed legislative changes as the product of pressure by powerful, vested trade interests, which took their local grain away to distant towns and ports for individual benefit. The old certainties of the pragmatic moral economy were being replaced with little substantive to assuage the anxieties of the crowd. Popular complaints were not about opposing the development of the market and drowning it under moral imperatives. It was rather a debate about how social justice could be served in the new economic environment and a fear that *laissez-faire* policies led to the neglect of ethical principles and the commonweal.

How far rioters' fears were based on reality is not something that can be discussed at length within the bounds of this chapter. Alfred Coats contended that the scope for manipulation of the market was limited, while Brian Outhwaite suggested it was severe grain dearth that fed criticisms of badgers and cornmongers through the early modern period.[213] Similarly, Norman Gras and John Chartres argued that people throughout the pre-industrial age failed to recognise the value of cornmongers in making the supply of bulk goods more regular and predictable, but rather turned on them at times of scarcity, perhaps damaging the development of the economy.[214] However, Thwaites and Roger Wells have posited that dealers were well capable of market manipulation, and were prepared to withhold stocks from markets and forestall grain supplies in times of scarcity.[215] Indeed, Thwaites argued that those with capital had the economic power and few qualms in holding the consumer to ransom. It is possible that traders were detaching themselves from the moral economy and adhering more to notions of the political economy regardless of the consequences for the needy. Grain traders and bakers

---

[212] Thompson, 'Moral economy reviewed', pp. 272, 275.

[213] Coats, 'Contrary moralities', 130–3; Outhwaite, 'Dearth', 396; Chartres, 'Marketing', pp. 225–9.

[214] Gras, *Evolution*, p. 206; Chartres, 'Marketing', pp. 247–52; Chartres, *Internal Trade*, p. 63.

[215] Thwaites, 'Dearth'; Wells, *Wretched Faces*, pp. 84–7.

may well have believed that the economy had moved on and that free markets were ultimately beneficial for all. However, equally, the growth in entrepreneurial and capital-laden traders made manipulation of the market easier than it had been in previous generations.

Long-term economic trends had made many more vulnerable to the pressures of the market.[216] It was perhaps the action of the crowd and the fears of the authorities that provided the main check to market manipulation. Thwaites has noted how the extraordinary persistence of carefully regulated marketing practices in Oxford through to the early nineteenth century, such as the assize of bread, owed everything to interests of the town's elite and a concern to maintain steady supplies and domestic tranquillity – in opposition to government pressure and market imperatives.[217] Government paternalist regulations were also reintroduced in response to dearth and riots in the late eighteenth century, probably in an attempt to placate the rioters and keep social order. Local authorities had to be seen taking action in the face of the worst effects of harvest failures and trading abuses, even if that action was either old-fashioned or relatively ineffectual.[218] Despite the rhetoric of the authorities, in referring to the protests as 'tumults' and 'mutinies', it was notable how often they tried to satisfy the rioters' demands rather than punish them. Some uprisings were deemed serious enough to require severe reprisals, but others led officials to establish relief measures or prosecute forestallers and engrossers. There was seemingly a common consensus regarding notions of the moral economy and social justice, particularly at times of scarcity.[219]

In general, market rules drew substantially upon traditional religious teaching and highlighted the vices of avarice, fraud, injustice and selfishness, as against the virtues of generosity, honesty, justice, moderation and providence. For all the historical arguments that a new market morality was being gradually created in England in parallel with economic development – a type of inevitable evolution from a paternalist moral economy to an acquisitive political economy – the reality was that traditional concerns of social justice and morality were belligerent. They were not easily usurped by a new market ethos of self-interested 'homo economicus'. Adam Smith may have argued that a true market economy could be both selfish and self-regulating, achieving benevolence through the 'invisible

---

[216] Everitt, 'Marketing', p. 578.   [217] Thwaites, 'Oxford food riots'.
[218] Everitt, 'Marketing', pp. 585–6. Everitt argued that the intervention of the state in basic factor markets may have mitigated the worst effects of harvest failures in the short term, but in the long term it was myopic, disruptive to the vital activities of middlemen, and detrimental to the welfare of consumers.
[219] Wrightson, *English Society*, pp. 177–80; Walter, 'Grain riots', pp. 74, 81.

hand', but this was as ideal and unrealistic a model as a truly autarkic medieval economy. Smith's model assumed perfect knowledge of supply and demand within a homogeneous system of economically rational individuals intent on maximising their material self-interest, but the reality was much more blurred and imperfect. Irrationality, imperfect competition and social conditioning were major obstacles, but so too was the issue of long-held morals and rights. Ultimately, the market required a balance between acquisitiveness and probity for its success and stability. This had existed in the food markets since the thirteenth century and the views established then changed only in emphasis rather than substance by the late eighteenth century.

Trying to track the influence of a medieval ideology across 500 years is, of course, exceptionally problematic. I do not wish to suggest that the views held in the seventeenth and eighteenth centuries were entirely consistent with those of the medieval period, but there are striking similarities that should lead us to question how ordinary people viewed the concepts of just price, fair profits, the utility of middlemen and social responsibility, which lay at the heart of Thompson's 'moral economy'. If eighteenth-century attitudes of the 'crowd' were embedded in long-held notions of market behaviour, as many historians suggest, it is worth reconsidering what these long-held notions might have been and why they might have survived for so long in the face of economic change. Understanding both the perception and pragmatic use of medieval market morality can perhaps help us to understand more clearly why the rioters of the late eighteenth century found solace in the precepts of the traditional and pragmatic moral economy.

Conclusion

It appears, in this brief survey, that many medieval ideas continued to permeate the market culture of early modern England. Although there were changes in emphasis, the basic principles remained remarkably consistent. Thus, the moral economy of E. P. Thompson was embedded in a system of mutual social responsibility, where everyone performed their own vocation for the good of all. Middlemen were distrusted and price-raising tactics deplored. This was not, however, a frontal attack upon the market system or even a call for customary fixed prices of grain, but rather a suspicion that traders were inclined to manipulate the market and create 'artificial price rises' for their own gain. Gain at the expense of the poor remained a crime in the eyes of the moral economy – marketing as an economic mechanism was not.

Ironically, the moral economy may have actually gained in strength among consumers in the face of growing capitalist instincts. Relatively stable harvests in the late seventeenth century may have delayed a revision of attitudes, but when dearth returned middlemen were subject to even more opprobrium and their social responsibility emphasised. Traditional customs held a strong hold over the people of England. Their moral rights, however, were not expressed in anti-market terms. The precepts of the moral economy accepted that just prices were those determined by supply and demand and middlemen and bakers had a right to profit. What they did not have a right to do was undertake practices that caused harm to their fellows in the search for the best profits. This was the traditional, consistent moral economy that Thompson referred to in his discussion of rioters in late eighteenth-century England. It was not an ideology that was in conflict with the market, but it was a belligerent popular ethic that could not adapt to the new *laissez-faire* policies of the late eighteenth century that sought to erode traditional paternal notions.

There are many other aspects of early modern market culture that are worthy of discussion, such as changes in public attitudes towards usury and, in turn, the influence of Protestantism upon economic ideology and the mercantile ethic. One could also consider contemporary concerns about national wealth, credit and debt, enclosure, attitudes to work and poverty and consumerism. This chapter has only touched the surface of a complex and important subject. Nevertheless, by examining the concepts of the medieval moral economy, a picture seems to have emerged that suggests early modern market users were entrenched in many of their views. The similarity in constructs of the moral economy between the thirteenth and eighteenth centuries may have been because few alternatives were presented. There was perhaps an inadequacy of cultural and social tools to cope with the complexity of a transitional and expanding economy. Whereas the medieval Church and ideology had adapted and even compromised by drawing market development within its moral framework, the moral economy of the early modern period was stagnant and conservative and increasingly detached from economic change and new mercantile ethics. There was a general belief that the marketplace remained a forum for unprincipled greed and fraud, from which the commonwealth needed constant protection. Indeed, as the market grew and economic tensions heightened, with increasing anxieties about social order, vagrancy and food supplies, a reversion to traditional moral ethics, embedded within the legal system, perhaps became ever more important.

Admittedly, there are often lags between practical developments and revised ideological statements, especially during periods of rapid change. Hence the difficulties faced by theorists such as Pierre Bourdieu when trying to explain how new realities are introduced into a set of inherited values.[220] The similarities between the medieval and eighteenth-century moral economy are suggestive of a broader ideology that had become entrenched and almost mythic in its appeal. Market attitudes were slow to change and were long embedded with social assumptions, traditional values and moral norms. However, the secular virtues and needs of commerce were sometimes appropriated in the creation of a hybrid and pragmatic market morality. By the end of the eighteenth century, we still do not see the victorious emergence of selfish, competitive individualism, as eulogised by classical economists, but rather the persistence and subtle assimilation of traditional notions of social and communal justice in the face of economic upheaval.

[220] Bourdieu, *Outline*.

Conclusion

It has been a recurrent theme of the historiography of the Middle Ages to encapsulate the conduct of market trade within the terms 'paternal' and 'moral economy'. Some historians following this approach have contended that there existed an antipathy between prevailing Christian ideology that denigrated commercial activity and the actual needs of the marketplace. Medieval market prosperity was thus subordinated to upholding the welfare of the poor, the privileges of the elite and issues of salvation. In the resulting clash between various interest groups, economic efficiency suffered and growth was inhibited. However, the reality of medieval trade and its control was far more complex. Market morals, law and practice were not necessarily incompatible and, indeed, could be mutually supportive.

Amongst the myriad of market regulations and institutions can be discerned a set of shared values that informed medieval people about the boundaries for acceptable behaviour. Anxieties were rehearsed in clerical exhortations and literature, which also acted as warnings for participants in the marketplace. A common theme of preachers was a sense of obligation to the poor and neighbours, linked to an acceptance of mutual responsibilities. Traders were recognised as important for the sustenance of society, but there was a continuing suspicion about their motives and the potential for abuses and damage to the community. Medieval literature presented an image of persistent fraud, trickery and greed. There were fears that ill-regulated petty retailers left the poor unserved, led to moral decay and caused social disorder, while the traders' own souls would rot in hell. However, even as they clung tenaciously to conventional convictions and tropes, many late medieval writers were well aware of the complex social and economic realities of their time. They discussed the just price in terms of the market price, recognised the utility of middlemen, and chronicled the growing pervasiveness of market activity.

A close examination of court records suggests that the disreputable figures of moral writings were not so common in the actual marketplace, but such images were perhaps influential in the way the medieval market was perceived and run. Legislators were often as idealistic as moralists in their portrayal of economic practices and acquiesced with the rhetoric of communal equity. Indeed, both law and literature recognised that markets could foment self-interest, profit-making, greed, aggression and mistrust, and there were real anxieties about the insecurities and temptations. Law reflected moral anxieties and also laid down ethical boundaries for market users. However, this did not preclude a practicality as to how law was employed and interpreted in everyday affairs.[1] Christopher Dyer goes further and suggests that 'the general lesson that can be learned is not that regulation was harmful and stunted economic growth, but that it did not make a great deal of difference. The flow of commerce was more powerful than the efforts of government to control behaviour.'[2] In other words, medieval officials did not always have the apparatus or resources to ensure strict adherence to regulations in the face of potent commercial forces. Effective policing in medieval England was difficult and costly, with few authorities powerful enough to ensure social behaviour matched the ideals of either law or church. In practical terms, the medieval market suffered from problems of information transmission, a lack of integration and the high costs of policing and enforcement. However, we should not underestimate the importance of commercial laws, even if not strictly enforced, in generating confidence in the marketplace and acting as a bulwark against flagrant abuse.

Strict ideas and rules of right behaviour were not the same as exerting a rigid, anti-commercial, moral high ground. Indeed, it could be argued that a veneer of paternal concern, fed by a diet of sermons, confessionals, murals and legal diatribes, was necessary to the way a market operated. Given the problems faced by medieval officials, formal regulations could only be effective within the context of a broadly accepted, embedded market morality.[3] Market users had an incentive to abide by laws when there was a consensus as to their moral worth and utility. Many medieval market functions were self-regulating, reliant on consumer denunciations or delineated by informal constraints. Everyday commercial and legal experience may have inured people to the ways of the world, and people did often trade in a rational, economic and acquisitive manner, but their decisions and actions cannot be disappropriated from their social, cultural and moral environment.[4] As Richard Wilk has suggested, 'moral issues are never far from economic life'.[5]

---

[1] Britnell, *Britain and Ireland*, p. 34.
[2] Dyer, *Making*, p. 320.   [3] See also Welch, *Shopping*, pp. 93–4.
[4] Britnell, *Britain and Ireland*, pp. 32–4.   [5] Wilk, *Economies and Cultures*, p. 106.

The workings of the medieval market can be compared to the models of economists, particularly those relating to institutions. Douglass North stated that 'institutions are the rules of the game in a society or, more formally, are the humanly devised constraints that shape human interaction'.[6] Institutions thus influence individual decision-making. Such institutions include the formal apparatus of laws, regulations and contracts, which require both structured measurement and enforcement. Other institutions are informal and embrace accepted social norms, customs and inward moral values. They are more difficult to discern and describe, but are informed by both outward, observable considerations of credit, reputation, repeated interactions and acceptable behaviour, and by more internally enforced religious beliefs and moral values.[7] Together, this complex, elaborate amalgam of formal and informal constraints, varying in particular situations and times, shapes choices within the market and determines the costs of transacting in individual bargains.[8]

It should not be assumed that everyone acts in a classical economic mode of self-interest, utility and maximisation of profit, though this motivation is certainly important and many moral concerns might have a wealth-maximising outcome. However, market behaviour is a lot more complex than a simple classical economic model might imply, and other cultural imperatives also shape individual market choices. Informal constraints or 'self-imposed codes of behaviour', which are specific to the prevailing ideological and cultural context, might reduce the enforcement costs implicit in formal constraints, by encouraging cooperation, engendering confidence in transactions and introducing extra religious sanctions. To paraphrase Avner Grief, cultural beliefs inform how individuals expect each other to act in various circumstances.[9] We internalise morals and social ideology, which helps regulate our behaviour and encourages social cooperation.

However, in reality, society does not always work so harmoniously and requires regulation and other means of control. Formal institutions are needed in order to provide information as to when potential punishment by a third-party is required against a free rider or flagrant offender, and also to enact that punishment. Formal rules might also gradually replace, modify or reinforce numerous informal constraints. Indeed, the law itself, or at least its enforcement, often reflects shared moral values

---

[6] North, *Institutions*, pp. 3–4.
[7] *Ibid.*, p. 61; Aoki, *Toward a Comparative Institutional Analysis*, pp. 1–10; Ogilvie, '"Whatever is, is right"?'.
[8] North, *Institutions*, pp. 66–8.   [9] Grief, 'Cultural beliefs', 943.

and behaviour, and we should not draw too harsh a divide between formal and informal constraints. This complicated mix of the formal and informal can potentially provide a pragmatic balance between a stable, secure structure for exchange and the need to keep enforcement costs low. North thus argued that the 'institutional framework plays a major role in the performance of an economy'.[10]

However, it is not axiomatic that all institutional constraints raise or maximise economic efficiency. The costs of exchange are necessarily above the ideal neoclassical level, and creating conditions for effective enforcement and relevant moral constraints is a slow and arduous process. In addition, economic developments, such as a notable increase in impersonal dealings, or even changes in the political, social, cultural or natural conditions, might mean that existing institutional constraints are no longer the best means to facilitate the majority of market transactions. At this point the institutions can adapt or be replaced. In England throughout most of the medieval and early modern period, the main model appears to be an incremental adaptation in the formal rules and informal constraints rather than a wholesale revision of the institutional structures. However, a crisis point came in the mid to late eighteenth century. At this time, the existing commercial institutions came to be regarded as overly inhibiting for some individuals, while many others continued to regard them as efficacious for their needs and even survival.[11] The tension that ensued came to a head when those in power were able to alter the formal rules and began to institute a major change in the formal institutional framework. However, the process was fraught and inconsistent, and accepted moral values and concerns were much slower to change. Even though men like Adam Smith saw old market institutions as a hindrance to economic growth, the 'traditional' moral economy could not be easily discarded and, indeed, continued to be adapted well into the nineteenth century.[12] As North suggested: 'informal constraints that are culturally derived will not change immediately in reaction to changes in the formal rules. As a result the tension between altered formal rules and the persisting informal constraints produces outcomes that have important implications for the way economies change.'[13]

This book has sought to demonstrate how daily market behaviour and choices in medieval England were shaped by numerous institutions and constraints, both formal and informal. Without a proper understanding of the morality and social conventions of the marketplace, the historian

[10] North, *Institutions*, p. 69, also pp. 43, 55–8.
[11] Ogilvie, '"Whatever is, is right"?', 656.
[12] Searle, *Morality*.   [13] North, *Institutions*, p. 45.

cannot understand the influence of formal institutions. We see in late medieval England, from the twelfth century onwards, a growth in formal rules and institutions for governing market behaviour. Old customs regarding the open market, just exchange, warranty and the social order are all developed in a more sophisticated, but gradual, manner to suit the growing market economy. However, even as formal rules are elaborated, informal constraints remained pervasive. A commercial ethic or 'market morality' was formed and moulded between 1200 and 1500 that reflected a variety of economic, social and cultural changes: commercialisation, urbanisation, borough autonomy, expanding royal government, changing standards of living and social upheaval. The church and government solidified informal social norms through their own formal proclamations. Transaction costs were not only lowered by regulation, law and order, but also by a conducive moral environment that facilitated security and trust and encouraged an equilibrium that was seen as beneficial to the majority and the common good.[14] The morality of the pulpit was therefore not necessarily antithetical to the efficient running of markets. Indeed, morals might act as a lubricant, since all were expected to conform and thus benefit from reduced costs. Morality and law could be thus mutually reinforcing and self-enforcing. This does not mean that all conformed, and medieval people recognised that this would never happen, but at a time of relatively low-level official policing and asymmetrical information, shared moral expectations were beneficial in facilitating exchanges. The growth of medieval marketing was thus aided by a variety of informal institutions, including the publicising of accepted trade behaviour and disreputable practices.

The very morality that some historians have identified as a rigid constraint on commercial development and market liberalisation thus helped medieval marketplaces to function effectively. Behavioural norms aided in modifying the degree to which participants engaged in unfair exchange and thus lowered the risks involved. Collective moral assumptions were transmitted in law, pulpit, peer groups and community 'performance' or punishment, and this reinforced the stability of marketing institutions. Together, these formal and informal institutional arrangements informed individual market decisions and acted as a guard against cheating, opportunism and the free rider.

In medieval England, it is possible that the market system was workable for the aggregate outcomes demanded and facilitated local commerce, even if it did not necessarily engender maximum economic growth and commercial efficiency. However, judging the effect of laws and morality

---

[14] Hatcher and Bailey, *Modelling*, pp. 131, 138.

on market efficiency is a problematic task. In a sense, they were workable within the conditions of the time and not as ineffectual or obstructive as has been suggested, but whether they were the most efficient means to ensure market prosperity, rather than simply maintaining the status quo, is another question. The institutions of the pragmatic moral economy were seemingly flexible, accepting market forces to a certain extent, but they also served vested interests as much as consumer needs. The rhetoric of morality and the 'common good' did often conceal the private ambitions of the wealthier, ruling classes. There were contradictions between assumed moral values and enacted laws, particularly when it came to protecting burgess privileges, state authority and the social order. Similarly, institutional rules were interpreted at a local level in a sometimes contradictory fashion, which suggests that other rules might have been more efficient even though they did not meet social ideals. This was not a simple, efficient alignment of institutions and cultural beliefs, but rather a heady and complex mixture of vested interests, pragmatism and idealism that varied according to the prevailing circumstances.

Medieval market authorities faced a precarious balancing act to maintain confidence, flexibility and regulation, attempting to combine effectively the existing formal institutions and vested interests with more informal constraints and a moral framework that provided a conducive environment for buyers and sellers. People might have internalised norms of behaviour and had a disposition to obey such norms, but no society could rely exclusively on such a disposition. There remained an important role for enforcement and punishment, particularly in markets where there were more impersonal dealings. Officials were often anxious about outsiders, whose reputation could not be so easily tarnished and upon whom informal constraints might not be so effective as formal constraints. Similarly, marginal participants within the market, such as hucksters, tapsters and humble pedlars, male or female, were also seen as potentially beyond moral constraints and disruptive to the social order. Market users needed reassurance that everybody was following the rules and that there were effective sanctions against free riders who transgressed the margins of acceptable behaviour. Ultimately, God oversaw the marketplace. The perils of damnation were an extra incentive for market users. However, in addition, people themselves could denounce their fellows, sometimes for a reward or by paying to bring them to court in a private plea. In addition, an effective market required respect towards officials and authority. People needed to be convinced about the validity and justice of the law in order to facilitate enforcement. Thus, the rhetoric of the communal good remained prevalent in law, including moral indignation at belligerent offenders, who would be stigmatised through public punishment. This was applied sparingly, for excess deployment of corporal punishment or performative humiliation might have lost its social impact. Reputation and trust played an important part in medieval society, particularly for groups of people who engaged in regular reciprocal exchanges.

Market morality was complex and disputable and not compelling in itself, despite providing another layer that encouraged cooperation. Court rolls are evidence that many were prepared to work beyond both moral norms, as regards the strict ideas of the church and even the more pragmatic social norms of their community, if they thought they could see advantages. Many individuals only obeyed norms because of a fear of sanction, physical or spiritual, and they judged the cost-benefit of continuing to do so. Medieval people, like today, found ways to reconcile their own moral values with everyday reality and to interpret the limits of law with the same approach. The basic ethics extolled by law and morality could reinforce behavioural norms, but they needed reinforcement from local enforcement. Through these frameworks and practical functions, a consensus developed regarding what was perceived as lawful, ethical action by market users themselves. This, in turn, enabled the pursuit of common interests. This might differ, from powerful lords who were concerned about control, provision or revenue and were able to impose their views upon their tenants, to burgesses seeking to protect their hard-won privileges against outsiders. In small market towns like Newmarket and Clare, it led to the development of fairly functional, secure markets and credit structures for the prevailing economic conditions.

The evidence from Newmarket and Clare suggests that traders needed more room for manoeuvre in an increasingly competitive environment, and many offences merely became revenue raisers for authorities often prepared to overlook minor trading infringements. To an extent, small town authorities colluded in allowing retailers a certain scope of flexibility, such as shaping the assizes into an effective licensing system. Traders were regularly presented and paid amercements to assuage their conscience and line the lord's purse. Consumers were content that the spirit of the law was upheld, competition was alive and bargains could still be found. However, those that abused this system and acted beyond accepted moral margins faced stricter punishments from the court and the censure of the community. This was a practical amalgam of close supervision, which bred trust and lowered transaction costs, together with an understanding of the vagaries inherent in medieval markets, particularly fluctuating harvests and political interests. Rivalry, conflict, ambition, profiteering and overbearing lordship were all grit in the system, but might also demonstrate a lack of trust in the respective market and have an adverse effect on its success. Similarly, intrusive laws, applied to the letter, were constraining and untenable. Instead, sellers and buyers were aided by a certain level of flexibility that gave a market every chance to work effectively. But this flexibility was still informed and limited by a consensual, mutual market ethic that built up trust and confidence in the market transactions. For petty traders, laws, morals and market forces were all constraining factors that constantly framed their business and behaviour.

By comparison, many larger borough corporations and craft guilds seemingly protected their own interests and the measures they took were stringent in the face of expanding competition. The vested interests of the wholesaling mercantile elite took precedence over those of retailers. However, the actual enforcement of retail market laws in medieval Ipswich bore many comparisons with that undertaken in smaller markets, even though the amounts involved were greater. The assizes were largely enforced as an effective licensing system, with fines allied to levels of production, and there were only occasional cases, such as forestalling and corrupt foodstuffs, where traders were deemed to have stepped beyond the bounds of acceptable practice.

Developments in the post-medieval world suggest the persistence of a similar pragmatic compromise between the forces of economics, laws and morals – what might be termed a 'pragmatic moral economy'. The Elizabethan era saw a small shift in attitudes which resurrected the 'virtues' of accumulation, which had previously been denigrated by the medieval Church. However, many sixteenth-century commercial attitudes had a long provenance.[15] Indeed, by the eighteenth and nineteenth centuries, there continued to be worries about the spiritual implications of trade and the possible exploitation of the poor. Adam Smith's *laissez-faire* theory suggested that, in the long term, the free, unrestrained operation of market forces would achieve a natural harmony. He saw no limit to acquisitivism, but expected the participants would put wealth towards the general good of the community as part of a self-interest rationale. However, Smith's theory was not generally accepted by his contemporaries and even nineteenth-century 'utilitarians' feared the consequences of unrestrained capitalist forces upon ethics and morality. They instead sought spiritual and legislative incentives or deterrents to create a balance of forces that would control trading behaviour and prevent a decline into immorality.[16] The problem of allying moral concerns to economic pragmatism was not one that disappeared after the Middle Ages.

---

[15] Stevenson, *Praise and Paradox*.
[16] Searle, *Morality*; Thomas, 'Cases of conscience', pp. 30–1.

The question of how forces of supply and demand can be reconciled with the needs of economic prosperity and contemporary 'moral ethics' has thus remained a consistent theme of commercial history. The accumulative trader and the vulnerable consumer are both stock figures that are evident even in the twentieth century. The pragmatic moral economy lingers on in new guises. We have entered an era of moral and commercial debates that presents us with similar paradoxes. Multinationals, banks, globalisation, genetically modified crops and even the familiar supermarkets, arouse indignation, moral rhetoric, laws and everyday complaints. Christian business associations in the US encourage their members to follow biblical morality in their affairs.[17] There is a growing demand for ethically responsible and environmentally friendly products. Despite suggestions that modern market ethics lack scruples and morality, it is clear that such issues cause hand-wringing and consternation. Trade, law and ideology still remain inseparable and yet contradictory bedfellows. There continue to be ethical debates about the boundaries between selfish, profit-making individualism and the equitable rights of the community. The influences of the pragmatic moral economy endure.

[17] Wilk, *Economies and Cultures*, p. 106.

Bibliography

MANUSCRIPT SOURCES

BRITISH LIBRARY

MS Additional 5823, 11284, 18852, 27695, 28162, 29253, 37677, 42130, 47682
MS Additional Charters 25867
MS Cotton Vespasian E.ix
MS Harleian 45, 149, 367, 463, 913, 2252, 2255, 2398, 4894, 6563
MS Lansdowne 796
MS Royal 8.C.i, 10.E.iv, 17.B.xlvii, 18.B.xxiii, 19.B.iv
MS Sloane 2593, 3160

CAMBRIDGE, GONVILLE AND CAIUS COLLEGE

MS 261

CAMBRIDGE, PEMBROKE COLLEGE

A2, B, D1–2, E1–2, F–G Framlingham and Saxtead Court Rolls

CAMBRIDGE, ST JOHN'S COLLEGE

MS 37 / B.15

CAMBRIDGE, TRINITY COLLEGE

VI.18.3 Jacobus de Cessolis, *De Ludo Scachorum* (trans. W. Caxton, Westminster, 1483)

CAMBRIDGE UNIVERSITY LIBRARY

MS Additional 3584
MS Ii.vi.17

CITY OF BRISTOL RECORD OFFICE

No. 01250(1)

CITY OF LONDON, LONDON METROPOLITAN ARCHIVES

MS Custumal 4 *Liber de Assisa Panis* (Image ref. COL/CS/01/004)

THE NATIONAL ARCHIVES

c60/9	Fine Rolls
c131/208/3, 14	Chancery: Extents for Debts
c133/33/16	Inquisitions Post-Mortem
DL29/992/15	Ministers' Accounts
DL29/993/7	Ministers' Accounts
DL29/994/1–13	Ministers' Accounts
DL29/1006/9–28	Ministers' Accounts
E101/256	Clerk of the Market Accounts
E101/257	Clerk of the Market Accounts
E101/258	Clerk of the Market Accounts
sc2/203/23–34	Chilton Court Rolls
sc2/203/38–72	Clare 'Burgess' Court Rolls
sc2/203/112–15	Sudbury Court Rolls
sc2/204/1–20	Sudbury Court Rolls

NOTTINGHAM UNIVERSITY LIBRARY

MS 50 (previously A.6.2, Lincoln Cathedral Chapter Library)

OXFORD, BODLEIAN LIBRARY

MS Bodley 95, 283, 649
MS Douce 5, 104
MS Laudian Misc. 77, 511

SAN MARINO, CALIFORNIA, HUNTINGTON LIBRARY

EL 29 C 9 Ellesmere manuscript

SUFFOLK RECORD OFFICE (BURY ST EDMUNDS)

Acc. 359/3	Account Roll, Manor of Newmarket
Acc. 1476/1/1–48	Court Rolls, Manor of Newmarket
Acc. 1476/12	Account Rolls, Manor of Newmarket
Acc. 1476/13	Account Rolls, Manor of Newmarket

SUFFOLK RECORD OFFICE (IPSWICH)

c/2/8/1/1–12	Ipswich Leet Rolls
c/2/10/1/2–6	Ipswich Composite Enrolments
HA6:51/4/4.7	Manor of Old Hall (East Bergholt) Court Rolls
HA68: 484/135	Manor of Aldham Court Rolls
HA91/1	Manor of Bradfield Court Rolls

HA119:50/3/17–19	Manor of Walton with Trimley Court Rolls
HA119:50/3/142	Manor of Bacton Court Rolls
HA246/A1/1	Manor of Higham (Hall) Leet Roll
HB8/1/663	Manor of Bramford (Hall) Court Rolls
HB8/1/778–89	Manor of Tattingstone Court Rolls
HB9:50/13/2.1–2.11	Manor of Hacheston Court Rolls
HD68: 314 and 484/76	Manor of Horham Court Rolls
s1/10/9.1–9.11	Manor of Holbrook Court Rolls
v5/18/1.2–1.4	Manor of Earl Soham Court Rolls

WEST SUSSEX RECORD OFFICE (CHICHESTER)

6/1/18 HVI Petworth   Transcript of Petworth House Archives 6766

PRINTED PRIMARY SOURCES

Adams, J. Q. (ed.), *Chief Pre-Shakespearean Dramas* (London, n.d.)

Amphlett, J. and Hamilton, S. G. (eds.), *Court Rolls of the Manor of Hales, 1272–1307*, 2 vols. (Worcestershire Historical Society, Oxford, 1910–12)

Anderson, R. C. (ed.), *The Assize of Bread Book, 1477–1517* (Southampton Record Society, Southampton, 1923)

A New Charge Giuen by the Queenes Commandement (STC 9202, London, 1595)

Anstey, H. (ed.), *Munimenta Academica, or Documents Illustrative of Academical Life and Studies at Oxford. Part I: Libri Cancellarii et Procuratorum* (Rolls Series, 50, London, 1868)

Archer, I., Burrow, C. and Harding, V. (eds.), *Hugh Alley's Caveat: The Markets of London in 1598* (London, 1988)

Arnold, M. S. (ed.), *Year Books of Richard II: 2 Richard II, 1378–1379* (The Ames Foundation, vol. 1, London, 1975)

Arnold, R., *The Customs of London otherwise called Arnold's Chronicle* (2nd edn, 1520–1, repr. London, 1811)

Arnold, T. (ed.), *Select English Works of John Wyclif*, 3 vols. (Oxford, 1871)

Ashbee, E. W. (ed.), *Occasional Facsimile Reprints*, 2 vols. (London, 1868–71)

Attenborough, F. L. (ed.), *The Laws of the Earliest English Kings* (Cambridge, 1922)

Ault, W. O. (ed.), *Court Rolls of the Abbey of Ramsey and of the Honor of Clare* (New Haven, Conn., 1928)

Ayto, J. and Barratt, A. (eds.), *Aelred of Rievaulx's De Institutione Inclusarum* (Early English Text Society, n.s. 287, London, 1984)

Baildon, H. B. (ed.), *The Poems of William Dunbar* (Cambridge, 1907)

Baildon, W. P. (ed.), *Court Rolls of the Manor of Wakefield, Volume 1: 1274 to 1297* (Yorkshire Archaeological Society Record Series, 29, 1901)

Court Rolls of the Manor of Wakefield, Volume II: 1297 to 1309 (Yorkshire Archaeological Society Record Series, 36, 1906)

Bailey, C. (ed.), *Transcripts from the Municipal Archives of Winchester* (Winchester, 1856)

Bailey, M. (ed.), *The Bailiffs' Minute Book of Dunwich, 1404–1430* (Woodbridge, 1992)

Baker, D. C., Murphy, J. L. and Hall Jr, L. B. (eds.), *The Late Medieval Religious Plays of Bodleian MSS Digby 133 and E Museo 160* (Early English Text Society, n.s. 283, Oxford, 1982)

Ballard, A. (ed.), *British Borough Charters 1042–1216* (Cambridge, 1913)

Ballard, A. and Tait, J. (eds.), *British Borough Charters 1216–1307* (Cambridge, 1923)

Banks, M. M. (ed.), *An Alphabet of Tales: An English Fifteenth Century Translation of the Alphabetum narrationum of Etienne de Besançon* (Early English Text Society, o.s. 126, London, 1904)

Barley, M. W. (ed.), *Documents relating to the Manor and Soke of Newark-on-Trent* (Thoroton Society Record Series, 16, Nottingham, 1956)

Barnum, P. H. (ed.), *Dives and Pauper* (Early English Text Society, n.s. 275, 280, Oxford, 1976–80)

Bateson, M. (ed.), *Records of the Borough of Leicester*, 3 vols. (London, 1899–1901)
Borough Customs, 2 vols. (Selden Society, 18 and 21, London, 1904–6)

Baxter, Richard, *A Christian Directory, or, A Summ of Practical Theologie and Cases of Conscience* (London, 1673)

Benham, W. G. (ed.), *The Red Paper Book of Colchester* (Colchester, 1902)

Benson, L. D. (ed.), *The Riverside Chaucer* (Boston, Mass., 1987)

Bevington, D. (ed.), *Medieval Drama* (Boston, Mass., 1975)

Bickley, F. B. (ed.), *The Little Red Book of Bristol*, 2 vols. (Bristol, 1900)

Bird, W. H. B. (ed.), *The Black Book of Winchester* (Winchester, 1925)

Blake, N. F. (ed.), *Quattuor Sermons printed by William Caxton* (Middle English Texts, 2, Heidelberg, 1975)

Bland, A. E., Brown, P. A. and Tawney, R. H. (eds.), *English Economic History: Select Documents* (London, 1914)

Borgström, E., 'The Complaint of God to Sinful Man and the Answer of Man. By William Lichfield', *Anglia*, 34 (1911), 498–525

Bornstein, D. (ed.), *The Middle English Translation of Christine de Pisan's 'Livre du Corps de Policie'* (Middle English Texts, 7, Heidelberg, 1977)

Bowers, R. H., 'A Middle English mnemonic poem on usury', *Mediaeval Studies*, 17 (1955), 226–32

Bozire, J. and Colledge, E. (eds.), *The Chastising of God's Children and the Treatise of Perfection of the Sons of God* (Oxford, 1957)

Bradley, H. (ed.), *Dialogues in French and English, by William Caxton* (Early English Text Society, extra ser. 79, London, 1900)

Brandeis, A. (ed.), *Jacob's Well: An English Treatise on the Cleansing of Man's Conscience* (Early English Text Society, o.s. 115, London, 1900)

Breward, I. (ed.), *The Work of William Perkins* (Cambridge, 1970)

Brewer, J. S. (ed.), *Registrum Malmesburiensie*, 2 vols. (Rolls Series, 72, London, 1879)

Briers, P. M. (ed.), *Henley Borough Records: Assembly Books i–iv, 1395–1543* (Oxfordshire Record Society, 41, Oxford, 1960)

Briggs, H. M. (ed.), *'Here may a young man see how he should speak subtly in Court': Translated from a Thirteenth or Fourteenth Century Manuscript* (London, 1936)

Brodie, D. M. (ed.), *The Tree of Commonwealth: A Treatise written by Edmund Dudley* (Cambridge, 1948)

Bromyard, John de, *Summa Predicantium* (Nuremburg, 1518)

Broomfield, F. (ed.), *Thomae de Chobham, Summa Confessorum* (Analecta Mediaevalia Namurcensia, 25, Louvain, 1968)

Burke, R. B. (ed.), *Treatise on the Power and Utility of Money* (London, 1930)

Butler, H. E. (ed.), *The Chronicle of Jocelin of Brakelond* (London, 1949)

Calendar of Charter Rolls, 6 vols. (London, 1903–27)

Calendar of Close Rolls, 46 vols. (London, 1892–1963)

Calendar of Inquisitions Miscellaneous, 7 vols. (London, 1916–68)

Calendar of Patent Rolls, 54 vols. (London, 1891–1916)

Cam, H. M. (ed.), *The Eyre of London, 14 Edward II, AD1321*, 2 vols. (Selden Society, 85–6, Year Book Series 26–7, London, 1968–9)

Carr, D. R. (ed.), *The First General Entry Book of the City of Salisbury 1387–1452* (Wiltshire Record Society, 54, Trowbridge, 2001)

Cessolis, Jacobus de, *De Ludo Scachorum [The Play of Chess]* (trans. William Caxton, Westminster, 1483)

Chambers, E. K. and Sidgwick, F. (eds.), *Early English Lyrics: Amorous, Divine, Moral and Trivial* (London, 1907)

Chappell, W. (ed.), *The Roxburghe Ballads*, 3 vols. (London, 1869–71)

Childs, W. R. and Taylor, J. (eds.), *Anonimalle Chronicle 1307 to 1334* (Yorkshire Archaeological Society Record Series, 147, Leeds, 1991)

Cigman, G. (ed.), *Lollard Sermons* (Early English Text Society, n.s. 294, London, 1989)

Collier, J. P. (ed.), *Illustrations of Old English Literature*, 2 vols. (New York, 1866, repr. 1966)

Coleman, M. C. (ed.), *Court Roll of the Manor of Downham 1310–1327* (Cambridge, 1996)

Conlee, J. W. (ed.), *Middle English Debate Poetry: A Critical Anthology* (East Lansing, Mich., 1991)

Cook, John, *Unum Necessarium, or, The Poore Mans Case* (London, 1648)

Coss, P. R. (ed.), *The Early Records of Medieval Coventry* (Records of Social and Economic History, new ser. 11, London, 1986)

Courthope, E. J. and Formoy, B. E. R. (eds.), *Lathe Court Rolls and Views of Frankpledge in the Rape of Hastings AD1387 to 1474* (Sussex Record Society, 37, Lewes, 1934)

Cowper, J. M. (ed.), *The Times' Whistle: or A Newe Daunce of Seven Satires, and other Poems* (Early English Text Society, o.s. 48, London, 1871)

Select Works of Robert Crowley (Early English Text Society, extra ser. 15, London, 1872)

Crane, T. F. (ed.), *The Exempla of Jacques de Vitry* (London, 1890)

Crotch, W. J. B. (ed.), *The Prologues and Epilogues of William Caxton* (Early English Text Society, o.s. 176, London, 1928)

Cupper, William, *Certaine Sermons Concerning Gods Late Visitation in the Citie of London* (London, 1592)

Curia Regis Rolls, 15 vols. (London, 1922–72)

Davies, R. T. (ed.), *Medieval English Lyrics* (London, 1963)

Davis, N. (ed.), *Non-Cycle Plays and Fragments* (Early English Text Society, suppl. text 1, Oxford, 1970)

Denholm-Young, N. (ed.), *The Life of Edward the Second by the so-called Monk of Malmesbury (Vita Edwardi Secundi)* (Edinburgh, 1957)

Devlin, M. A. (ed.), *The Sermons of Thomas Brinton, Bishop of Rochester (1373–1389)*, 2 vols. (Camden Society, 3rd ser., 85 and 86, London, 1954)

Dickinson, J. (ed.), *Policraticus* (New York, 1927)

Dilks, T. B. (ed.), *Bridgwater Borough Archives, 1200–1485* (Somerset Record Society, 48, 53, 58, 60 and 70, 1933–71)

Downer, L. J. (ed.), *Leges Henrici Primi* (Oxford, 1972)

Edelen, G. (ed.), *The Description of England by William Harrison* (New York, 1968)

Eichmann, R. and DuVal, J. (eds.), *Cuckolds, Clerics and Countrymen: Medieval French Fabliaux* (Fayetteville, Ark., 1982)

Ellis, H. (ed.), *The New Chronicles of England and France by Robert Fabyan* (London, 1811)

Embree, D. and Urquhart, E. (eds.), *The Simonie: A Parallel-Text Edition* (Middle English Texts, 24, Heidelberg, 1991)

Erbe, T. (ed.), *Mirk's Festial: A Collection of Homilies, by Johannes Mirkus (John Mirk)* (Early English Text Society, extra ser. 96, London, 1905)

Evelyn, C. d' (ed.), *Peter Idley's Instructions to his Son* (London, 1935)

Fenwick, C. C. (ed.), *The Poll Taxes of 1377, 1379, and 1381*, 3 vols. (Oxford, 1998–2005)

Fisher, H. E. S. and Juřica, A. R. J. (eds.), *Documents in English Economic History: England from 1000 to 1760* (London, 1977)

Flenley, R. (ed.), *Six Town Chronicles of England* (Oxford, 1911)

Fowler, D. C., Briggs, C. F. and Remley, P. G. (eds.), *The Governance of Kings and Princes: John Trevisa's Middle English Translation of the De Regimine Principum of Aegidius Romanus* (New York and London, 1997)

Fox, D. (ed.), *Robert Henryson: The Poems* (Oxford, 1987)

Francis, W. N. (ed.), *The Book of Vices and Virtues* (Early English Text Society, n.s. 217, London, 1942)

Friedberg, A. (ed.), *Corpus Iuris Canonici*, 2 vols. (Leipzig, 1881)

Furley, J. S. (ed.), *The Ancient Usages of the City of Winchester* (Oxford, 1927)

Furnivall, F. J. (ed.), *Early English Poems and Lives of Saints* (Berlin, 1862)
  Political, Religious, and Love Poems (Early English Text Society, o.s. 15, London, 1866)
  The Babees Book (Early English Text Society, o.s. 32, London, 1868)
  The Fyrst Boke of the Introduction of Knowledge made by Andrew Borde // A Compendyous Regyment or A Dyetary of Helth by Andrewe Boorde (Early English Text Society, extra ser. 10, London, 1870)
  Jyl of Breyntford's Testament, by Robert Copland, Boke-Prynter . . . And Other Short Pieces (London, 1871)
  The Pilgrimage of the Life of Man, by John Lydgate AD1426, from the French of Guillaume de Deguileville AD1330, 1355 (Early English Text Society, extra ser. 77, 83, 92, London, 1899–1904)

Robert of Brunne's 'Handlyng Synne', AD1303 (Early English Text Society, o.s. 119, London, 1901)

The Minor Poems of the Vernon MS, Part 2 (Early English Text Society, o.s. 117, London, 1901)

Furnivall, F. J. and Stone, W. G. (eds.), *The Tale of Beryn* (Early English Text Society, extra ser. 105, London, 1909)

Gallagher, J. (ed.), *The Doctrinal of Sapience* (Middle English Texts, 26, Heidelberg, 1993)

Gardner, H. (ed.), *The New Oxford Book of English Verse, 1250–1950* (Oxford, 1972)

Gem, S. H. (ed.), *An Anglo-Saxon Abbot, Ælfric of Eynsham* (Edinburgh, 1912)

Given-Wilson, C., Brand, P., Curry, A., Horrox, R., Martin, G., Philips, S. and Ormrod, W. M. (eds.), *The Parliament Rolls of Medieval England, 1275–1504 (PROME)* (Scholarly Digital Editions, Leicester, 2005)

Goldberg, P. J. P. (ed.), *Women in England c.1275–1525: Documentary Sources* (Manchester, 1995)

Gray, D. (ed.), *The Oxford Book of Late Medieval Verse and Prose* (Oxford, 1985)

Great Roll of the Pipe for the Twenty-Second Year of the Reign of King Henry II, AD1175–1176 (Pipe Rolls Society, 25, London, 1904)

Greaves, R. W. (ed.), *The First Ledger Book of High Wycombe* (Buckinghamshire Record Society, 2, Welwyn Garden City, 1947)

Green, R. B., 'Virtues and vices in the chapter house vestibule in Salisbury', *Journal of the Warburg and Courtauld Institutes*, 31 (1968), 148–58

Greene, R. L. (ed.), *The Early English Carols* (Oxford, 1935)

Grisdale, D. M. (ed.), *Three Middle English Sermons from the Worcester Chapter Manuscript f.10* (Leeds School of English Language Texts and Monographs, 5, Leeds, 1939)

Grosart, A. B. (ed.), *The Life and Complete Works in Prose and Verse of Robert Greene*, 15 vols. (New York, 1881–6)

Gross, C. (ed.), *Select Cases Concerning the Law Merchant, AD1270–1638, Volume 1. Local Courts* (Selden Society, 23, London, 1908)

Hall, G. D. G. (ed.), *The Treatise on the Laws and Customs of the Realm of England commonly called Glanvill* (London, 1965)

Hall, H. (ed.), *Red Book of the Exchequer*, 3 vols. (London, 1896)

The Pipe Roll of the Bishopric of Winchester, 1208–9 (London, 1903)

Hall, H. and Nicholas, F. J. (eds.), *Select Tracts and Table Books Relating to English Weights and Measures (1100–1742)* (Camden Miscellany, xv, Camden Society, 3rd ser. 41, London, 1929)

Hardy, T. D. (ed.), *Rotuli Litterarum Clausarum*, 2 vols. (London, 1833–44)

Rotuli Chartarum (London, 1837)

Harris, M. D. (ed.), *The Coventry Leet Book* (Early English Text Society, o.s. 134, 135, 138, 146, London, 1907–13)

Harrison, A. (ed.), *Examples of San Bernardino* (London, 1926)

Hassall, W. O. (ed.), *The Holkham Bible Picture Book* (London, 1954)

Hellman, R. and O'Gorman, R. (eds.), *Fabliaux: Ribald Tales from the Old French* (London, 1965)

Heyworth, P. L. (ed.), *Jack Upland, Friar Daw's Reply and Upland's Rejoinder* (Oxford, 1968)

Hilton, R. H. (ed.), *The Stoneleigh Leger Book* (Dugdale Society, 24, Oxford, 1960)

Hitchcock, E. V. (ed.), *The Donet, by Reginald Pecock* (Early English Text Society, o.s. 156, London, 1921)

Holland, M. J. (ed.), *Year Books of Richard II: 7 Richard II, 1383–1384* (The Ames Foundation, vol. iii, Ann Arbor, Mich., 1989)

Holt, J. C., *Magna Carta* (Cambridge, 1965)

Hopper, C. (ed.), *The Childe of Bristow: A Poem by John Lydgate* (Camden Miscellany, iv, Camden Society, 1859)

Horstmann, C. (ed.), *The Minor Poems of the Vernon MS, Part 1* (Early English Text Society, o.s. 98, London, 1892)

Hudson, W. (ed.), *Leet Jurisdiction in the City of Norwich during the XIIIth and XIVth Centuries* (Selden Society, 5, London, 1891)

Hudson, W. and Tingey, J. C. (eds.), *The Records of the City of Norwich*, 2 vols. (Norwich, 1906)

Hughes, P. L. and Larkin, J. F. (eds.), *Tudor Royal Proclamations*, 3 vols. (New Haven, Conn., 1964–9)

Hull, F. (ed.), *A Calendar of the White and Black Books of the Cinque Ports 1432–1955* (Kent Archaeological Society Record Series, 19, London, 1966)

Ingleby, H. (ed.), *The Red Register of King's Lynn*, 2 vols. (King's Lynn, 1919)

James, M. R., Brooke, C. N. L. and Mynors, R. A. B. (eds.), *Walter Map, De Nugis Curialium: Courtiers' Trifles* (Oxford, 1983)

Jamieson, T. H. (ed.), *The Ship of Fools translated by Alexander Barclay*, 2 vols. (London, 1874)

Jeayes, I. H. (ed.), *Court Rolls of the Borough of Colchester*, 4 vols. (Colchester, 1921–41)

Jewell, H. M. (ed.), *The Court Rolls of the Manor of Wakefield, from September 1348 to September 1350* (Yorkshire Archaeological Society, Leeds, 1982)

Johnson, R., *The Ancient Customs of the City of Hereford* (London and Hereford, 1868)

Kail, J. (ed.), *Twenty-Six Political and Other Poems* (Early English Text Society, 124, London, 1904)

Kane, G., 'The Middle English verse in MS Wellcome 1493', *London Mediaeval Studies*, 2 (1951), 50–67

Kane, G. (ed.), *Piers Plowman: The A Version – Will's Visions of Piers Plowman and Do-Well* (Berkeley, Calif., 1988)

Kane, G. and Donaldson, E. T. (eds.), *Piers Plowman: The B Version – Will's Visions of Piers Plowman, Do-Well, Do-Better and Do-Best* (Berkeley, Calif., 1988)

Kelly, P. H. (ed.), *John Locke: Locke on Money*, 2 vols. (Oxford, 1991)

Kengen, J. H. L. (ed.), *Memoriale Credencium* (Nijmegen, 1979)

Kimball, E. G. (ed.), *Rolls of the Warwickshire and Coventry Sessions of the Peace 1377–1397* (Publications of the Dugdale Society, 16, London, 1939)

King, M. H. (ed.), *The Life of Marie D'Oignies by Jacques de Vitry* (Toronto, 1993)

Kristol, A. M. (ed.), *Manières de Langage (1396, 1399, 1415)* (Anglo-Norman Texts, 53, London, 1995)

Landor, W. N. (ed.), 'Alrewas court rolls, 1259–61', in *Collections for a History of Staffordshire* (William Salt Archaeological Society, London, 1907), pp. 87–137

Larkin, J. F. and Hughes, P. L. (eds.), *Stuart Royal Proclamations. Volume I: Royal Proclamations of King James I, 1603–1625* (Oxford, 1973)

Larkin, J. F. (ed.), *Stuart Royal Proclamations, Volume II: Royal Proclamations of King Charles I, 1625–1646* (Oxford, 1983)

Larson, L. M. (ed.), *The King's Mirror* (New York, 1917)

Leach, A. F. (ed.), *Beverley Town Documents* (Selden Society, 14, London, 1900)

Lefébure, M. (ed.), *St Thomas Aquinas: Summa Theologiæ* (London, 1975)

Lenaghan, R. T. (ed.), *Caxton's Aesop* (Cambridge, Mass., 1967)

Lister, J. (ed.), *Court Rolls of the Manor of Wakefield, Volume III: 1313 to 1316 and 1286* (Yorkshire Archaeological Society, Record Series, 57, 1917)
   Court Rolls of the Manor of Wakefield, Volume IV: 1315 to 1317 (Yorkshire Archaeological Society, Record Series, 78, 1930)

Little, A. G. (ed.), *Liber Exemplorum ad Usum Praedicantium* (Aberdeen, 1908)

Lock, R. (ed.), *The Court Rolls of Walsham le Willows 1303–1350* (Suffolk Records Society, 41, Woodbridge, 1998)
   The Court Rolls of Walsham le Willows 1351–99 (Suffolk Records Society, 45, Woodbridge, 2002)

Lorris, Guillaume de, and Meun, Jean de, *The Romance of the Rose* (trans. H. W. Robbins and C. W. Dunn, New York, 1962)

Louis, C. (ed.), *The Commonplace Book of Robert Reynes of Acle* (London, 1980)

Lumiansky, R. M. and Mills, D. (eds.), *The Chester Mystery Cycle*, 2 vols. (Early English Text Society, suppl. ser. 3, Oxford, 1974)

Lupton, Donald, *London and the Countrey Carbonadoed and Quartred into Seuerall Characters* (London, 1632)

Macaulay, G. C. (ed.), *The Complete Works of John Gower*, 4 vols. (Oxford, 1899)

MacCracken, H. N. (ed.), *The Minor Poems of John Lydgate, Part II: Secular Poems* (Early English Text Society, o.s. 192, London, 1934)

Maitland, F. W. (ed.), *Select Pleas of the Crown, vol I: AD 1200–1225* (Selden Society, 1, London, 1888)
   Select Pleas in Manorial and Other Seignorial Courts (Selden Society, 2, London, 1889)

Maitland, F. W. and Baildon, W. P. (eds.), *The Court Baron* (Selden Society, 4, London, 1891)

Maitland, F. W. and Bateson, M. (eds.), *The Charters of the Borough of Cambridge* (Cambridge, 1901)

Marcham, W. M. (ed.), *Court Rolls of the Manor of Tottenham, Middlesex, 1318–1377* (Manor of Tottenham Series, 1, London, 1950)

Markham, C. A. (ed.), *The Liber Custumarum: The Book of the Ancient Usages and Customs of the Town of Northampton* (Northampton, 1895)

Markham, C. A. and Cox, J. C. (eds.), *The Records of the Borough of Northampton*, 2 vols. (Northampton, 1898)

Massingberd, W. O. (ed.), *Court Rolls of the Manor of Ingoldmells in the County of Lincoln* (London, 1902)

Matthew, F. D. (ed.), *The English Works of Wyclif hitherto unprinted* (Early English Text Society, o.s. 74, London, 1880)

May, P. (ed.), *The Court Rolls of Newmarket in Suffolk 1408–10* (Newmarket, 1973)

   Twenty Newmarket Wills, 1439–1497: A Glimpse of Fifteenth Century Newmarket (Suffolk, 1974)

Méril, E. du (ed.), *Poésies Populaires Latines du Moyen Age* (Paris, 1847)

Millar, E. G. (ed.), *The Luttrell Psalter* (London, 1932)

Millett, B. and Wogan-Browne, J. (eds.), *Medieval English Prose for Women* (Oxford, 1990)

Mills, D. (ed.), *The Chester Mystery Cycle: A New Edition* (East Lansing, Mich., 1992)

Moffat, D. M. (ed.), *The Complaint of Nature, by Alain de Lille* (New York, 1908)

Morgan, F. C. (ed.), *The Regulations of the City of Hereford* (Hereford, 1945)

Morris, R. (ed.), *Dan Michel's Ayenbite of Inwyt, or, Remorse of Conscience. In the Kentish Dialect, 1340 AD* (Early English Text Society, o.s. 23, London, 1866)

   Old English Homilies and Homiletic Treatises of the Twelfth and Thirteenth Centuries (Early English Text Society, o.s. 34, London, 1868)

   An Old English Miscellany containing a Bestiary, Kentish Sermons, Proverbs of Alfred, Religious Poems of the Thirteenth Century (Early English Text Society, o.s. 49, London, 1872)

   Old English Homilies of the Twelfth Century (Early English Text Society, o.s. 53, London, 1873)

Mozley, J. H. and Raymo, R. R. (eds.), *Nigel de Longchamps: Speculum Stultorum* (Berkeley, Calif., 1960)

Myers, A. R. (ed.), *English Historical Documents 1327–1485, Volume IV* (London, 1969)

Nelson, V. (ed.), *A Myrour to Lewde Men and Wymmen* (Middle English Texts, 14, Heidelberg, 1981)

Nelson, W. (ed.), *A Fifteenth Century School Book* (Oxford, 1956)

Nichols, F. M. (ed.), *Britton*, 2 vols. (Oxford, 1865)

Northeast, P. (ed.), *Wills of the Archdeaconry of Sudbury, 1439–1474: Wills from the Register 'Baldwyne', Part 1: 1439–1461* (Suffolk Records Society, 44, Woodbridge, 2001)

Oram, R. (ed.), *Court Rolls of the Manors of Bruces, Dawbeneys, Pembrokes (Tottenham), 1377–1399* (Manor of Tottenham Series, 2, London, 1961)

Orders Appointed by his Maiestie to be Straightly Obserued for the Preuenting and Remedying of the Dearth of Graine and other Victuall (STC 9217, London, 1608)

Orders Deuised by the Especiall Commandement of the Queenes Maiestie, for the Reliefe and Stay of the Present Dearth of Graine within the Realme (STC 9194, London, 1586)

Oschinsky, D., *Walter of Henley and other Treatises on Estate Management and Accounting* (Oxford, 1971)

Owen, D. M. (ed.), *The Making of King's Lynn: A Documentary Survey* (Records of Social and Economic History, new ser. 9, London, 1984)

Owen, N. H., 'Thomas Wimbledon's sermon: "Redde racionem villicacionis tue"', *Mediaeval Studies*, 28 (1966), 176–97

Peacock, E. (ed.), *Instructions for Parish Priests. By John Myrc* (Early English Text Society, o.s. 31, London, 1868)

Pearsall, D. and Scott, K. (eds.), *Piers Plowman: A Facsimile of Bodleian Library, Oxford, MS Douce 104* (Cambridge, 1992)

Pearsall, D. (ed.), *William Langland, Piers Plowman: The C-Text* (Exeter, 1994)

Percy, J. W. (ed), *York Memorandum Book, volume III* (Surtees Society, 186, Durham, 1973)

Perkins, William, *The Workes of that Famous and Worthy Minister of Christ in the Universitie of Cambridge*, 3 vols. (London, 1617–26)

Petty, William, *A Treatise of Taxes and Contributions* (London, 1662)

Poos, L. R. (ed.), *Lower Ecclesiastical Jurisdiction in Late-Medieval England: The Courts of the Dean and Chapter of Lincoln, 1336–1349, and the Deanery of Wisbech, 1458–1484* (Records of Social and Economic History, new ser. 32, Oxford, 2001)

Powell, D. L. and Malden, H. E. (eds.), *Court Rolls of the Manor of Carshalton from the Reign of Edward the Third to that of Henry the Seventh* (Surrey Record Society, 2, London, 1916)

Powell, John, *The Assise of Bread* (London, 1601)

Powell, Robert, *Depopulation Arraigned, Convicted and Condemned* (London, 1636)

Power, E. (ed.), *The Goodman of Paris (Le Ménagier de Paris): A Treatise on Moral and Domestic Economy by a Citizen of Paris (c.1393)* (London, 1928)

Powicke, F. M. and Cheney, C. R. (eds.), *Councils and Synods with other Documents relating to the English Church*, 10 vols. (Oxford, 1964)

Prestwich, M. (ed.), *York Civic Ordinances, 1301* (Borthwick Papers, 49, York, 1976)

Pugh, R. B. (ed.), *Court Rolls of the Wiltshire Manors of Adam de Stratton* (Devizes, 1970)

Putnam, B. H. (ed.), *Proceedings before the Justices of the Peace in the Fourteenth and Fifteenth Centuries, Edward III to Richard III* (London, 1938)

Ratcliff, S. C. (ed.), *Elton Manorial Records 1279–1351* (Cambridge, 1946)

Remnant, G. L., *A Catalogue of Misericords in Great Britain* (Oxford, 1969)

Rendell, A. W. (ed.), *Physiologus: A Metrical Bestiary of Twelve Chapters by Bishop Theobald* (London, 1928)

Richardson, H. G. and Sayles, G. O. (eds.), *Fleta* (Selden Society, 72, London, 1953)

Richardson, R. C. and James, T. B. (eds.), *The Urban Experience: A Sourcebook. English, Scottish and Welsh Towns, 1450–1700* (Manchester, 1983)

Richardson, W. H. (ed.), *The Annalls of Ipswche. The Lawes, Customs and Government of the Same Collected out of ye Records, Bookes and Writings of that Towne, By N. Bacon... 1654* (Ipswich, 1884)

Riley, H. T. (ed.), *Munimenta Gildhallae Londoniensis; Liber Albus, Liber Custumarum, et Liber Horn*, 3 vols. (Rolls Series, 12, London, 1859)

Liber Albus: The White Book of the City of London (London, 1861)

Chronicles of the Mayors and Sheriffs of London, 1188 to 1274, and the French Chronicle of London, 1259 to 1343 (London, 1863)

Memorials of London and London Life in the XIIIth, XIVth, and XVth Centuries . . . AD1276–1419 (London, 1868)

Roberts, S. K. (ed.), *Evesham Borough Records of the Seventeenth Century, 1605–1687* (Worcestershire Historical Society, new ser. 14, 1994)

Robbins, R. H. (ed.), *Secular Lyrics of the XIVth and XVth Centuries* (2nd edn, Oxford, 1955)

Historical Poems of the XIVth and XVth Centuries (New York, 1959)

Ross, W. O. (ed.), *Middle English Sermons* (Early English Text Society, n.s. 209, London, 1940)

Rotuli Parliamentorum, 6 vols. (London, 1783)

Royster, J. F., 'A middle English treatise on the ten commandments', *Studies in Philology*, 6 (1910), 1–39

Rumble, A. (ed.), *Domesday Book, 34: Suffolk*, 2 parts (Chichester, 1986)

Russell, G. and Kane, G. (eds.), *Piers Plowman: The C Version – Will's Visions of Piers Plowman, Do-Well, Do-Better and Do-Best* (Berkeley, Calif., 1997)

Salter, H. E. (ed.), *Medieval Archives of the University of Oxford*, 2 vols. (Oxford, 1920)

Munimenta Civitatis Oxonie (Oxford Historical Society, 71, Devizes, 1920)

Sands, D. B. (ed.), *The History of Reynard the Fox, Translated and Printed by William Caxton in 1481* (London, 1960)

Scattergood, J. (ed.), *John Skelton: The Complete English Poems* (New Haven, Conn., 1983)

Schopp, J. W. and Easterling, R. C. (eds.), *The Anglo-Norman Custumal of Exeter* (Oxford, 1925)

Scott, H. von E. and Swinton Bland, C. C. (eds.), *The Dialogue on Miracles by Caesarius of Heisterbach, c.1220–1235*, 2 vols. (London, 1929)

Sellers, M. (ed.), *York Memorandum Book* (Surtees Society, 120 and 125, Durham, 1912–15)

Seymour, M. C. (ed.), *Selections from Hoccleve* (Oxford, 1981)

Sharpe, R. R. (ed.), *Calendar of Letter-Books of the City of London*, 12 vols. (London, 1899–1912)

Shepherd, G. (ed.), *Ancrene Wisse: Parts Six and Seven* (London, 1959)

Sigmund, P. E. (ed.), *St Thomas Aquinas on Politics and Ethics* (London, 1988)

Sillem, R. (ed.), *Records of Some Sessions of the Peace in Lincolnshire 1360–1375* (Lincoln Record Society, 30, Hereford, 1936)

Silverstein, T. (ed.), *Medieval English Lyrics* (London, 1971)

Simmons, T. F. and Nolloth, H. E. (eds.), *The Lay Folks' Catechism* (Early English Text Society, o.s. 118, London, 1901)

Sinclair, J. D. (ed.), *The Divine Comedy of Dante Alighieri*, 3 vols. (rev. edn, London, 1948)

Sisam, C. and Sisam, K. (eds.), *The Oxford Book of Medieval English Verse* (Oxford, 1970)

Skeat, W. W. (ed.), *The Lay of Havelok the Dane* (Oxford, 1902)

Smithers, G. V. (ed.), *Havelok* (Oxford, 1987)

Spearing, A. C. and Spearing, J. E. (eds.), *Poetry of the Age of Chaucer* (London, 1974)

Stanford, M. (ed.), *The Ordinances of Bristol, 1506–1598* (Bristol Record Society Publications, 41, Gloucester, 1990)

Stapleton, T. (ed.), *De Antiquis Legibus Liber* (Camden Society, 34, London, 1846)

Statutes at Large of England and of Great Britain, 10 vols. (ed. J. Raithby, London, 1811)

Statutes of the Realm (1101–1713), 11 vols. (ed. A. Luders, T. Edlyn Tomlins, J. France, W. E. Tauton and J. Raithby, London, 1810–28, repr. 1963)

Statutes of the United Kingdom of Great Britain and Ireland (1807–1868/69), 63 vols. (ed. G. K. Rickards, London, 1807–69)

Stenton, D. M. (ed.), *The Great Roll of the Pipe, 1 John, 1199* (London, 1933)

Stevens, M. and Cawley, A. C. (eds.), *The Towneley Plays*, 2 vols. (Early English Text Society, suppl. ser. 13, Oxford, 1994)

Stevenson, J. (ed.), *De Vita et Miraculis S. Godrici, Heremitae de Finchale* (Surtees Society, 20, London, 1847)

Stevenson, W. H. (ed.), *Records of the Borough of Nottingham, 1155–1485*, 2 vols. (London, 1882–3)

Stockton, E. W. (ed.), *The Major Latin Works of John Gower* (Seattle, Wash., 1962)

Strype, J. (ed.), *A Survey of the Cities of London and Westminster, John Stow (1633)*, 2 vols. (London, 1720)

Stubbs, W. (ed.), *Chronicles of the Reigns of Edward I and Edward II*, 2 vols. (Rolls Series, 76, London, 1883)

  Chronica: Magistri Rogeri de Houedene, 4 vols. (Rolls Series, 51, London, rev. 1964)

Studer, P. (ed.), *The Oak Book of Southampton*, 2 vols. (Southampton Record Society, 10–11, Southampton, 1910)

Sutherland, D. W. (ed.), *The Eyre of Northamptonshire 1329–30* (Selden Society, 97, London, 1983)

Swan, C. (ed.), *Gesta Romanorum* (London, 1905)

Swanton, M. (ed.), *Anglo-Saxon Prose* (London, 1975)

Swinburn, L. M. (ed.), *The Lanterne of Li3t* (Early English Text Society, o.s. 151, London, 1917)

Tawney, R. H. and Power, E. (eds.), *Tudor Economic Documents*, 3 vols. (London, 1951)

Taylor, John, *The Works of John Taylor the Water-Poet* (London, 1630)

Thirsk, J. and Cooper, J. P. (eds.), *Seventeenth-Century Economic Documents* (Oxford, 1972)

Thomas, A. H. (ed.), *Calendar of Early Mayor's Court Rolls preserved among the Archives of the Corporation of the City of London at the Guildhall* AD. *1298–1307* (Cambridge, 1924)

Thomas, A. H. and Jones, P. E. (eds.), *Calendar of Plea and Memorandum Rolls*, 6 vols. (Cambridge, 1924–61)

Thomas, A. H. and Thornley, I. D. (eds.), *The Great Chronicle of London* (London, 1938)

Thomson, I. and Perraud, L. (eds.), *Ten Latin Schooltexts of the Later Middle Ages: Translated Selections* (Mediaeval Studies, 6, Lampeter, 1990)

Thornley, I. D. (ed.), *Year Book of Richard II: 11 Richard II, 1387–1388* (The Ames Foundation, vol. v, London, 1937)

Toulmin Smith, L. (ed.), *English Gilds* (Early English Text Society, o.s. 40, London, 1870)

The Maire of Bristowe is Kalendar, by Robert Ricart (Camden Society, new ser. 5, London, 1872)

York Plays (New York, 1885)

Trigg, S. (ed.), *Wynnere and Wastoure* (Early English Text Society, n.s. 297, Oxford, 1990)

Tubach, F. C., *Index Exemplorum: A Handbook of Medieval Religious Tales* (Helsinki, 1969)

Turner, W. H. (ed.), *Selections from the Records of the City of Oxford, 1509–1583* (Oxford, 1880)

Twiss, T. (ed.), *The Black Book of the Admiralty or Monumenta Juridica*, 2 vols. (Rolls Series, 55, London, 1871–3)

Tymms, S. (ed.), *Wills and Inventories from the Registers of the Commissary of Bury St Edmunds and the Archdeacon of Sudbury* (Camden Society, 49, London, 1850)

Vaughan, R. (ed.), *Chronicles of Matthew Paris* (Gloucester, 1984)

Veale, E. W. W. (ed.), *The Great Red Book of Bristol* (Bristol Record Society, 2, 4, 8 and 16, 1931–51)

Walker, J. W. (ed.), *Court Rolls of the Manor of Wakefield, Volume V: 1322–1331* (Yorkshire Archaeological Society Record Series, 109, 1945)

Walker, S. S. (ed.), *The Court Rolls of the Manor of Wakefield from October 1331 to September 1333* (Yorkshire Archaeological Society, Leeds, 1983)

Wallace, W. L. (ed.), *George Gascoigne's 'The Steele Glas' and 'The Complainte of Phylomene': A Critical Edition with an Introduction* (Salzburg Studies in English Literature, Elizabethan and Renaissance Studies, 24, Salzburg, 1975)

Warner, G. (ed.), *The Libelle of Englyshe Polycye: A Poem on the Use of Sea-Power, 1436* (Oxford, 1926)

Warren, F. (ed.), *The Dance of Death* (Early English Text Society, o.s. 181, London, 1931)

Weinbaum, M. (ed.), *British Borough Charters 1307–1660* (Cambridge, 1943)

Wenzel, S. (ed.), *Fasciculus Morum: A Fourteenth-Century Preacher's Handbook* (London, 1989)

Wheatley, H. B. (ed.), *Stow's Survey of London* (London, 1912)

Wilkins, D. (ed.), *Concilia Magnae Britanniae et Hiberniae*, 4 vols. (London, 1737)

Williams, C. H. (ed.), *English Historical Documents, 1485–1558* (London, 1971)

Wilson, R. M. (ed.), *The English Text of the Ancrene Riwle* (Early English Text Society, n.s. 229, London, 1954)

Wilson, W. B. (ed.), *John Gower, Mirour de l'Omme (The Mirror of Mankind)* (East Lansing, Mich., 1992)

Windeatt, B. A. (ed.), *The Book of Margery Kempe* (London, 1994)

Wright, T. (ed.), *Political Poems and Songs relating to English History*, 2 vols. (Rolls Series, 14, London, rev. 1965)

Wright, T. and Halliwell, J. O. (eds.), *Reliquiae Antiquae*, 2 vols. (London, 1841–3)

A Collection of Seventy-Nine Black-Letter Ballads and Broadsides, Printed in the Reign of Queen Elizabeth between the years 1559 and 1597 (London, 1867)

Wyer, Robert, *The Assyse of Breade* (c.1540), in E. W. Ashbee (ed.), *Occasional Facsimile Reprints*, 2 vols. (London, 1868–71), VII.

Zeydel, E. H. (ed.), *The Ship of Fools, by Sebastian Brant* (New York, 1944)

Zutphen, J. P. W. M. van (ed.), *A Litil Tretys on the Seven Deadly Sins by Richard Lavynham* (Rome, 1956)

SECONDARY SOURCES

Abraham, D. H., 'Cosyn and cosynage: pun and structure in The Shipman's Tale', *Chaucer Review*, 11 (1976–7), 319–27

Abrams, P. and Wrigley, E. A. (eds.), *Towns in Societies: Essays in Economic History and Historical Sociology* (Cambridge, 1978)

Adams, R., 'The concept of debt in The Shipman's Tale', *Studies in the Age of Chaucer*, 6 (1984), 85–102

Aers, D., *Chaucer, Langland and the Creative Imagination* (London, 1980)

Community, Gender, and Individual Identity: English Writing 1360–1430 (London, 1988)

Faith, Ethics and Church: Writing in England, 1360–1409 (Cambridge, 2000)

'Justice and wage-labor after the Black Death: some perplexities for William Langland', in D. Aers, *Faith, Ethics and Church: Writing in England, 1360–1409* (Cambridge, 2000), pp. 56–75

Aers, D. (ed.), *Medieval Literature: Criticism, Ideology and History* (Brighton, 1986)

Alford, J. A. (ed.), *A Companion to Piers Plowman* (Berkeley, Calif., 1988)

Allen, D., *Ipswich Borough Archives 1255–1835* (Suffolk Records Society, 43, Woodbridge, 2000)

Allen, M., 'The volume of the English currency, 1158–1470', *Economic History Review*, 54 (2001), 595–611

Alsford, S., *Medieval English Towns*, at: www.trytel.com/~tristan/towns/towns.html (accessed 11 October 2009)

Amor, N. R., 'Merchant adventurer or Jack of all trades? The Suffolk clothier in the 1460s', *Proceedings of the Suffolk Institute of Archaeology and History*, 40 (2004), 414–36

Amsler, M., 'The Wife of Bath and women's power', *Assays: Critical Approaches to Medieval and Renaissance Texts*, 4 (1987), 67–83

Amussen, S. D., *An Ordered Society: Gender and Class in Early Modern England* (Oxford, 1988)

Anderson, B. L. and Latham, A. J. H. (eds.), *The Market in History* (London, 1986)

Anderson, M. D., *The Imagery of British Churches* (London, 1955)

Drama and Imagery in English Medieval Churches (Cambridge, 1963)

History and Imagery in British Churches (Edinburgh, 1971)

Aoki, M., *Toward a Comparative Institutional Analysis* (Cambridge, Mass., 2001)

Appleby, A. B., *Famine in Tudor and Stuart England* (Liverpool, 1978)

Appleby, J. O., *Economic Thought and Ideology in Seventeenth-Century England* (Princeton, NJ, 1978)

Archer, I. W., *The Pursuit of Stability: Social Relations in Elizabethan London* (Cambridge, 1991)

Archer, R. E. (ed.), *Crown, Government and People in the Fifteenth Century* (Stroud, 1995)

Ashby, J. E., 'English medieval murals of the Doom: a descriptive catalogue and introduction' (MPhil, University of York, 1980)

Ashley, K., 'Historicizing Margery: *The Book of Margery Kempe* as social text', *Journal of Medieval and Early Modern Studies*, 28, 2 (1998), 371–88

Ashley, W. J., *An Introduction to English Economic History and Theory*, 2 vols. (New York, 1888)

Astill, G. G., 'Archaeology and the smaller medieval town', *Urban History Yearbook* (1985), 46–53

Astill. G. G. and Grant, A. (eds.), *The Countryside of Medieval England* (Oxford, 1988)

Aston, T. H. and Philipin, C. H. E. (eds.), *The Brenner Debate: Agrarian Class Structure and Economic Development in Pre-Industrial Europe* (Cambridge, 1985)

Atkinson, C. W., *Mystic and Pilgrim: The Book and the World of Margery Kempe* (Ithaca, NY, 1983)

Atkinson, T., *Elizabethan Winchester* (London, 1963)

Axton, R., *European Drama of the Early Middle Ages* (London, 1974)

Bailey, M., 'The rabbit and the medieval East Anglian economy', *Agricultural History Review*, 36 (1988), 1–20

  A Marginal Economy? East Anglian Breckland in the Later Middle Ages (Cambridge, 1989)

  'A tale of two towns: Buntingford and Standon in the later Middle Ages', *Journal of Medieval History*, 19 (1993), 351–71

  'Historiographical essay: the commercialisation of the English economy, 1086–1500', *Journal of Medieval History*, 24 (1998), 297–311

  'Peasant welfare in England, 1290–1348', *Economic History Review*, 2nd ser., 51 (1998), 223–51

  'Trade and towns in medieval England: new insights from familiar sources', *Local Historian*, 29 (1999), 194–211

  Medieval Suffolk: An Economic and Social History, 1200–1500 (Woodbridge, 2007)

  'Technology and the growth of textile manufacture in medieval Suffolk', *Proceedings of the Suffolk Institute of Archaeology and History*, 42 (2009), 13–20

Bainbridge, V. R., *Gilds in the Medieval Countryside: Social and Religious Change in Cambridgeshire c.1350–1558* (Woodbridge, 1996)

Baker, D., 'The marketing of corn in the first half of the eighteenth century: north-east Kent', *Agricultural History Review*, 18 (1970), 126–50

Baldwin, A. P., *The Theme of Government in Piers Plowman* (Cambridge, 1981)

Baldwin, J. W., 'The medieval theories of the just price: Romanists, canonists, and theologians in the twelfth and thirteenth centuries', *Transactions of the American Philosophical Society*, 49 (1959), 1–92

    Masters, Princes and Merchants: The Social Views of Peter the Chanter and his Circle, 2 vols. (Princeton, NJ, 1970)

Barath, D., 'The just price and the costs of production according to St Thomas Aquinas', *New Scholasticism*, 34 (1960), 413–30

Barnicle, M. E., 'The exemplum of the penitent usurer', *Publications of the Modern Language Association of America*, 33 (1918), 409–28

Barron, C. M., 'The "golden age" of women in medieval London', *Reading Medieval Studies*, 15 (1989), 35–58

    London in the Middle Ages: A Government and People, 1200–1500 (Oxford, 2004)

Basing, P., *Trades and Crafts in Medieval Manuscripts* (London, 1990)

Bearman, R. (ed.), *The History of an English Borough: Stratford-upon-Avon, 1196–1996* (Stroud, 1997)

Beckerman, J. S., 'Customary law in English manorial courts in the thirteenth and fourteenth centuries' (Ph.D., University of London, 1972)

    'The articles of presentment of a court leet and court baron, in English, c.1400', *Bulletin of the Institute of Historical Research*, 47 (1974), 230–4

    'The forty-shilling jurisdictional limit in medieval English personal actions', in D. Jenkins (ed.), *Legal History Studies 1972* (Cardiff, 1975), pp. 110–17

    'Procedural innovation and institutional change in medieval English manorial courts', *Law and History Review*, 10 (1992), 197–252

Beier, A. L., *Masterless Men: the Vagrancy Problem in England, 1560–1640* (London, 1985)

Bellamy, J. G., *Crime and Public Order in England in the Later Middle Ages* (London, 1973)

Benbow, R. M., 'The court of aldermen and the assizes: the policy of price control in Elizabethan London', *Guildhall Studies in London History*, 4 (1980), 93–118

Bennett, J. M., 'The village ale-wife: women and brewing in fourteenth-century England', in B. A. Hanawalt (ed.), *Women and Work in Preindustrial Europe* (Bloomington, Ind., 1986), pp. 20–36

    Women in the Medieval English Countryside: Gender and Household in Brigstock Before the Plague (Oxford, 1987)

    'Misogyny, popular culture, and women's work', *History Workshop*, 31 (1991), 166–88

    Ale, Beer, and Brewsters in England: Women's Work in a Changing World, 1300–1600 (Oxford, 1996)

Benson, J. and Ugolini, L. (eds.), *A Nation of Shopkeepers: Five Centuries of British Retailing* (London, 2003)

Benton, G. M., 'Archaeological notes: irregular markets held at Fingringhoe, etc., temp. Henry VI', *Transactions of the Essex Archaeological Society*, 21 (1934), 137–9

Beresford, M. W., *The Lost Villages of England* (Gloucester, 1954)

    New Towns of the Middle Ages: Town Plantation in England, Wales and Gascony (London, 1967)

Beresford, M. W. and Finberg, H. P. R., *English Medieval Boroughs: A Hand-List* (Newton Abbot, 1973)

Berthe, M. (ed.), *Endettement Paysan et Crédit Rural dans l'Europe médiévale et moderne* (Toulouse, 1997)

Bestul, T. H., *Satire and Allegory in 'Wynnere and Wastoure'* (Lincoln, Nebr., 1974)

Betterton, A. and Dymond, D., *Lavenham: Industrial Town* (Woodbridge, 1989)

Beveridge, W. H., 'A statistical crime of the seventeenth century', *Journal of Economic and Business History*, 1 (1928), 503–33

Biddick, K., 'Medieval English peasants and market involvement', *Journal of Economic History*, 45 (1985), 823–31

'Missing links: taxable wealth, markets and stratification among the medieval peasantry', *Journal of Interdisciplinary History*, 18 (1987), 277–98

Bisson, L. M., *Chaucer and the Late Medieval World* (London, 1998)

Blake, N. F., 'Reynard the Fox in England', in E. Rombauts and A. Welkenhuysen (eds.), *Aspects of the Medieval Animal Epic* (Louvain, 1975), pp. 53–65

Blanch, R. J. (ed.), *Style and Symbolism in Piers Plowman: A Modern Critical Anthology* (Knoxville, Tenn., 1969)

Blondé, B., Stabel, P., Stobart, J. and Van Damme, I. (eds.), *Buyers and Sellers: Retail Circuits and Practices in Medieval and Early Modern Europe* (Turnhout, 2006)

Bloomfield, M. W., *The Seven Deadly Sins* (Lansing, Mich., 1952)

Bohstedt, J., 'The moral economy and the discipline of historical context', *Journal of Social History*, 26, 2 (1992), 265–84

'The pragmatic economy, the politics of provisions and the "invention" of the food riot tradition in 1740', in A. Randall and A. Charlesworth (eds.), *Moral Economy and Popular Protest: Crowds, Conflict and Authority* (Basingstoke, 2000), pp. 55–92

Boitani, P. and Mann, J. (eds.), *The Cambridge Chaucer Companion* (Cambridge, 1986)

Bolton, J. L., *The Medieval English Economy 1150–1500* (London, 1980)

Bonney, M., *Lordship and the Urban Community: Durham and its Overlords 1250–1540* (Cambridge, 1990)

Bothwell, J., Goldberg, P. J. P. and Ormrod, W. M. (eds.), *The Problem of Labour in Fourteenth-Century England* (Woodbridge, 2000)

Boulton, J., *Neighbourhood and Society: A London Suburb in the Seventeenth Century* (Cambridge, 1987)

'London's "dark ages"? Food prices and the standard of living in London in the "century of revolution"', *Economic History Review*, 2nd ser., 53 (2000), 479–513

Bourdieu, P., *Outline of a Theory of Practice* (Cambridge, 1977)

The Logic of Practice (trans. R. Nice, Cambridge, 1990)

Bowden, M., *A Commentary on the General Prologue to the Canterbury Tales* (London, 1973)

Brand, P., *Kings, Barons and Justices: The Making and Enforcement of Legislation in Thirteenth-Century England* (Cambridge, 2003)

Bras, G. le, 'Conceptions of economy and society', in M. M. Postan, E. E. Rich and E. Miller (eds.), *Cambridge Economic History of Europe, Volume III: Economic Organisation and Policies in the Middle Ages* (Cambridge, 1963), pp. 554–75

Brewer, J. and Styles, J. (eds.), *An Ungovernable People: The English and their Law in the Seventeenth and Eighteenth Centuries* (London, 1980)

Bridbury, A. R., *Economic Growth: England in the Later Middle Ages* (London, 1962)

'Markets and freedom in the Middle Ages', in B. L. Anderson and A. J. H. Latham (eds.), *The Market in History* (London, 1986), pp. 79–119

Briggs, C., 'Empowered or marginalized? Rural women and credit in later thirteenth- and fourteenth-century England', *Continuity and Change*, 19, 1 (2004), 13–43

'Manor court procedures, debt litigation levels, and rural credit provision in England, *c.*1290–*c.*1380', *Law and History Review*, 24, 3 (2006), 519–58

Credit and Village Society in Fourteenth-Century England (Oxford, 2009)

Britnell, R. H., 'English markets and royal administration before 1200', *Economic History Review*, 2nd ser., 31 (1978), 183–96

'King John's early grants of markets and fairs', *English Historical Review*, 94 (1979), 90–6

'*Advantagium Mercatoris*: a custom in medieval English trade', *Nottingham Medieval Studies*, 24 (1980), 37–50

'Burghal characteristics of market towns in medieval England', *Durham University Journal*, 42 (1981), 147–51

'The proliferation of markets in England, 1200–1349', *Economic History Review*, 2nd ser., 34 (1981), 209–21

Growth and Decline in Colchester, 1300–1525 (Cambridge, 1986)

'Forstall, forestalling and the Statute of Forestallers', *English Historical Review*, 102 (1987), 89–102

'Commerce and capitalism in late medieval England: problems of description and theory', *Journal of Historical Sociology*, 6 (1993), 359–76

'Morals, laws and ale in medieval England', in U. Müller, F. Hundsnurcher and C. Sommer (eds.), *Le droit et sa perception dans la littérature et les mentalités médiévales* (Göppingen, 1993), pp. 21–9

'Commercialisation and economic development in England, 1000–1300', in R. H. Britnell and B. M. S. Campbell (eds.), *A Commercialising Economy: England 1086–1300* (Manchester, 1995), pp. 7–26

'Price-setting in English borough markets, 1349–1500', *Canadian Journal of History*, 31 (1996), 1–15

The Commercialisation of English Society 1000–1500 (2nd edn, Manchester, 1996)

'La commercializzazione dei cereali in Inghilterra (1250–1350)', *Quaderni Storici*, 96 (1997), 631–61

'The economy of British towns 1300–1540', in D. M. Palliser (ed.), *Cambridge Urban History of Britain, Volume 1: 600–1540* (Cambridge, 2000), pp. 313–34

'Specialization of work in England, 1100–1300', *Economic History Review*, 2nd ser., 54 (2001), 1–16

'England: towns, trade and industry', in S. H. Rigby (ed.), *A Companion to Britain in the Later Middle Ages* (Oxford, 2003), pp. 47–64

'The woollen textile industry of Suffolk in the later Middle Ages', *The Ricardian: Journal of the Richard III Society*, 13 (2003), 86–99

Britain and Ireland 1050–1530: Economy and Society (Oxford, 2004)

'Town life', in R. Horrox and W. M. Ormrod (eds.), *A Social History of England, 1200–1500* (Cambridge, 2006), pp. 134–78

'Markets, shops, inns, taverns and private houses in medieval English trade', in B. Blondé, P. Stabel, J. Stobart and I. Van Damme (eds.), *Buyers and Sellers: Retail Circuits and Practices in Medieval and Early Modern Europe* (Turnhout, 2006), pp. 109–24

'Urban economic regulation and economic morality in medieval England', in R. H. Britnell, *Markets, Trade and Economic Development in England and Europe, 1050–1550* (Farnham, 2009), ch. xix

Britnell, R. H. and Campbell, B. M. S. (eds.), *A Commercialising Economy: England 1086–1300* (Manchester, 1995)

Britnell, R. H. and Hatcher, J. (eds.), *Progress and Problems in Medieval England: Essays in Honour of Edward Miller* (Cambridge, 1996)

Britton, E., *The Community of the Vill* (Toronto, 1977)

Brown Jr, E., 'Chaucer, the merchant, and their tale: getting beyond old controversies', *Chaucer Review*, 13 (1978–9), 141–56, 247–62

Brown, P. (ed.), *A Companion to Medieval English Literature and Culture c.1350–c.1500* (Chichester, 2009)

Brown, S. E., '"A just and profitable commerce": moral economy and the middle classes in eighteenth-century London', *Journal of British Studies*, 32 (1993), 305–32

Bulst, N. and Genet, J.-P. (eds.), *La Ville, La Bourgeoisie et La Genèse de L'État Moderne (XIIe–XVIIIe siècles)* (Paris, 1988)

Cahn, K. S., 'Chaucer's merchants and the foreign exchange: an introduction to medieval finance', *Studies in the Age of Chaucer*, 2 (1980), 81–119

Cam, H. M., *The Hundred and the Hundred Rolls: An Outline of Local Government in Medieval England* (London, 1930)

Camille, M., *The Gothic Idol: Ideology and Image-Making in Medieval Art* (Cambridge, 1989)

Camp, C. W., *The Artisan in Elizabethan Literature* (New York, 1923)

Campbell, B. M. S., 'A fair field once full of folk: agrarian change in an era of population decline 1348–1500', *Agricultural History Review*, 41 (1993), 60–70

English Seigniorial Agriculture, 1250–1450 (Cambridge, 2000)

Campbell, B. M. S., Galloway, J. A., Keene, D. and Murphy, M., *A Medieval Capital and its Grain Supply: Agrarian Production and Distribution in the London Region c.1300* (Historical Geography Research Series, 30, London, 1993)

Carlin, M., 'Provisions for the poor: fast food in medieval London', *Franco-British Studies: Journal of the British Institute in Paris*, 20 (1995), 35–48.

Medieval Southwark (London, 1996)

'Fast food and urban living standards in medieval England', in M. Carlin and J. T. Rosenthal (eds.), *Food and Eating in Medieval Europe* (London, 1998), pp. 27–51

Carlin, M. and Rosenthal, J. T. (eds.), *Food and Eating in Medieval Europe* (London, 1998)

Carpenter, C., 'Town and "country": the Stratford guild and political networks of fifteenth-century Warwickshire', in R. Bearman (ed.), *The History of an English Borough: Stratford-upon-Avon, 1196–1996* (Stroud, 1997), pp. 62–79

Carr, D. R., 'From pollution to prostitution: supervising the citizens of fifteenth-century Salisbury', *Southern History*, 19 (1997), 24–41

'Controlling the butchers in late medieval English towns', *The Historian*, 70 (2008), 450–61

Carrel, H., 'Food, drink and public order in the London *Liber Albus*', *Urban History*, 33 (2006), 176–94

Carus-Wilson, E. M., 'Evidences of industrial growth on some fifteenth-century manors', *Economic History Review*, 2nd ser., 12 (1959–60), 190–205

'The first half-century of the borough of Stratford-upon-Avon', in R. Holt and G. Rosser (eds.), *The Medieval Town: A Reader in English Urban History 1200–1540* (London, 1990), pp. 49–70

Carus-Wilson, E. M. and Coleman, O., *England's Export Trade 1275–1547* (Oxford, 1963)

Casson, C., 'A comparative study of prosecutions for forgery in trade and manufacturing in six English towns, 1250 to 1400' (Ph.D., University of York, 2009)

Cate, J. L., 'The English mission of Eustace of Flay (1200–1201)', in *Études D'Histoire Dédiées à la Mémoire de Henri Pirenne* (Brussels, 1937), pp. 67–89

'The church and market reform in England during the reign of Henry III', in J. L. Cate and E. N. Anderson (eds.), *Medieval and Historiographical Essays in Honor of James Westfall Thompson* (Chicago, Ill., 1938), pp. 27–65

Cate, J. L. and Anderson, E. N. (eds.), *Medieval and Historiographical Essays in Honor of James Westfall Thompson* (Chicago, Ill., 1938)

Charles, L. and Duffin, L. (eds.), *Women and Work in Pre-Industrial England* (Beckenham, 1985)

Charlesworth, A. and Randall A. J., 'Morals, markets and the English crowd in 1766', *Past and Present*, 114 (1987), 200–13

Chartier, R., *Cultural History: Between Practices and Representations* (trans. L. G. Cochrane, Cambridge, 1988)

Chartres, J. A., *Internal Trade in England 1500–1700* (London, 1977)

'The marketing of agricultural produce, 1640–1750', in J. A. Chartres (ed.), *Agricultural Markets and Trade, 1500–1700* (Cambridge, 1990), pp. 157–255

Chartres, J. A. (ed.), *Agricultural Markets and Trade, 1500–1700* (Cambridge, 1990)

Clark, E., 'Debt litigation in a late medieval English vill', in J. A. Raftis (ed.), *Pathways to Medieval Peasants* (Pontifical Institute of Mediaeval Studies, Toronto, 1981), pp. 247–79

Clark, P., 'Popular protest and disturbance in Kent, 1558–1640', *Economic History Review*, 2nd ser., 29 (1976), 365–82

'The alehouse and the alternative society', in D. Pennington and K. Thomas (eds.), *Puritans and Revolutionaries: Essays in Seventeenth-Century History Presented to Christopher Hill* (Oxford, 1978), pp. 47–72

The English Alehouse: A Social History (London, 1983)

Clark, W. W., Eisler, C., Heckscher, W. S. and Lane, B. G. (eds.), *Tribute to Lotte Brand Philip: Art Historian and Detective* (New York, 1985)

Clarkson, L. A., 'The leather crafts in Tudor and Stuart England', *Agricultural History Review*, 14 (1966), 25–39

Clay, C. G. A., *Economic Expansion and Social Change: England 1500–1700, Volume 1: People, Land and Towns* (Cambridge, 1984)

Clayton, D. J., Davies, R. G. and McNiven, P. (eds.), *Trade, Devotion and Governance: Papers in Later Medieval History* (Stroud, 1994)

Clough, C. H. (ed.), *Profession, Vocation, and Culture in Later Medieval England* (Liverpool, 1982)

Coates, B. E., 'The origin and distribution of markets and fairs in medieval Derbyshire', *Derbyshire Archaeological Journal*, 85 (1965), 92–111

Coats, A. W., 'Contrary moralities: plebs, paternalists and political economists', *Past and Present*, 54 (1972), 130–3

Coleman, J., *English Literature in History, 1350–1400: Medieval Readers and Writers* (London, 1981)

'Lay readers and hard Latin; how Gower may have intended the *Confessio Amantis* to be read', *Studies in the Age of Chaucer*, 24 (2002), 209–34

Connor, R. D., *The Weights and Measures of England* (London, 1987)

Copland, M., 'The Shipman's Tale: Chaucer and Boccaccio', *Medium Aevum*, 35 (1966), 11–28

Coss, P. R. and Lloyd, S. D. (eds.), *Thirteenth Century England IV: Proceedings of the Newcastle Upon Tyne Conference 1991* (Woodbridge, 1992)

Cox, N., '"Beggary of the nation": moral, economic and political attitudes to the retail sector in the early modern period', in J. Benson and L. Ugolini (eds.), *A Nation of Shopkeepers: Five Centuries of British Retailing* (London, 2003), pp. 6–51

Cox, N. and Dannehl, K., *Perceptions of Retailing in Early Modern England* (Aldershot, 2007)

Crane, J. K., 'An honest debtor? A note on Chaucer's merchant, line A276', *English Language Notes*, 4 (1966–7), 81–5

Cromarty, D., 'Chepying Walden 1381–1420, a study from the court rolls', *Essex Journal*, 2 (1967), 104–13, 122–39, 181–6

Cunningham, W., *The Growth of English Industry and Commerce during the Early and Middle Ages* (4th edn, Cambridge, 1905)

Dalton, G. (ed.), *Primitive, Archaic and Modern Economies. Essays of Karl Polanyi* (New York, 1968)

Darby, H. C., *The Medieval Fenland* (Newton Abbot, 1974)

Davis, J., 'Baking for the common good: a reassessment of the assize of bread in medieval England', *Economic History Review*, 2nd ser., 57 (2004), 465–502

'"Men as march with fote packes": pedlars and freedom of mobility in late-medieval England', in P. Horden (ed.), *Freedom of Movement in the Middle*

Ages: Proceedings of the Twentieth Harlaxton Symposium (Harlaxton Medieval Studies, 15, Donington, 2007), pp. 137–56

'The cross and the pillory: symbolic structures of commercial space in medieval English towns', in S. Ehrich and J. Oberste (eds.), *Städtische Räume im Mittelalter* (Forum Mittelalter, Studien Band 5, Regensburg, 2009), pp. 241–59

'Marketing secondhand goods in late medieval England', *Journal of Historical Research in Marketing*, 2 (2010), 270–86

Davis, N. Z., *Fiction in the Archives: Pardon Tales and their Tellers in Sixteenth-Century France* (Stanford, Calif., 1987)

Demant, V. A. (ed.), *The Just Price* (London, 1930)

Deveson, A. M., 'Medieval Whitchurch: the development of a new town', *Proceedings of the Hampshire Field Club and Archaeological Society*, 54 (1999), 102–14

DeWindt, A. R., 'Local government in a small town: a medieval leet jury and its constituents', *Albion*, 23 (1991), 627–54

DeWindt, A. R. and DeWindt, E. B., *Ramsey: The Lives of an English Fenland Town, 1200–1600* (Washington, DC, 2006)

DeWindt, E. B., *Land and People in Holywell-cum-Needingworth: Structures of Tenure and Patterns of Social Organisation in an East Midlands Village 1252–1457* (Pontifical Institute of Mediaeval Studies, 22, Toronto, 1972)

Dilley, R. (ed.), *Contesting Markets: Analyses of Ideology, Discourses and Practice* (Edinburgh, 1992)

Dimmock, S., 'English small towns and the emergence of capitalist relations, *c.*1450–1550', *Urban History*, 28 (2001), 5–24

Dionne, C. and Mentz, S. (eds.), *Rogues and Early Modern English Culture* (Ann Arbor, Mich., 2004)

Dobson, R. B., 'Admissions to the freedom of the City of York in the later Middle Ages', *Economic History Review*, 2nd ser., 26 (1973), 1–22

'Urban decline in late medieval England', *Transactions of the Royal Historical Society*, 5th ser., 27 (1977), 1–22

Dobson, R. B. (ed.), *The Church, Politics and Patronage in the Fifteenth Century* (Gloucester, 1984)

Dodds, B. and Britnell, R. H. (eds.), *Agriculture and Rural Society after the Black Death: Common Themes and Regional Variations* (Hatfield, 2008)

Du Boulay, F. R. H., *An Age of Ambition* (London, 1970)

Duby, G., *The Three Orders: Feudal Society Imagined* (Chicago, Ill., 1980)

Duffy, E., *The Stripping of the Altars: Traditional Religion in England c.1400–c.1580* (New Haven, Conn., and London, 1992)

Duvosquel, J.-M. and Thoen, E. (eds.), *Peasants and Townsmen in Medieval Europe: Studia in Honorem Adriaan Verhulst* (Ghent, 1995)

Dyer, A. D., *The City of Worcester in the Sixteenth Century* (Leicester, 1973)

'The market towns of southern England, 1500–1700', *Southern History*, 1 (1979), 123–34

Decline and Growth in English Towns, 1400–1640 (Cambridge, 1991)

'Urban decline in England, 1377–1525', in T. R. Slater (ed.), *Towns in Decline AD100–1600* (Aldershot, 2000), pp. 266–88

Dyer, C., 'A small landowner in the fifteenth century', *Midland History*, 1 (1972), 1–14

    Lords and Peasants in a Changing Society: The Estates of the Bishopric of Worcester, 680–1540 (Cambridge, 1980)

    'Changes in diet in the late Middle Ages: the case of harvest workers', *Agricultural History Review*, 36 (1988), 21–37

    Standards of Living in the Later Middle Ages: Social Change in England c.1200–1520 (Cambridge, 1989)

    'The consumer and the market in the later Middle Ages', *Economic History Review*, 2nd ser., 42 (1989), 305–27

    'Were there any capitalists in fifteenth-century England?', in J. Kermode (ed.), *Enterprise and Individuals in Fifteenth-Century England* (Stroud, 1991), pp. 1–24

    'Small-town conflict in the later Middle Ages: events at Shipston-on-Stour', *Urban History*, 19 (1992), 183–210

    'The hidden trade of the Middle Ages: evidence from the west midlands of England', *Journal of Historical Geography*, 18 (1992), 141–57

    'How urbanized was medieval England?', in J.-M. Duvosquel and E. Thoen (eds.), *Peasants and Townsmen in Medieval Europe: Studia in Honorem Adriaan Verhulst* (Ghent, 1995), pp. 169–83

    'Market towns and the countryside in late medieval England', *Canadian Journal of History*, 31 (1996), 17–35

    'Taxation and communities in late medieval England', in R. H. Britnell and J. Hatcher (eds.), *Progress and Problems in Medieval England: Essays in Honour of Edward Miller* (Cambridge, 1996), pp. 168–90

    'Medieval Stratford: a successful small town', in R. Bearman (ed.), *The History of an English Borough: Stratford-upon-Avon, 1196–1996* (Stroud, 1997), pp. 43–61

    'Trade, towns and the church: ecclesiastical consumers and the urban economy of the West Midlands, 1290–1540', in T. R. Slater and G. Rosser (eds.), *The Church in the Medieval Town* (Aldershot, 1998), pp. 55–75

    Bromsgrove: A Small Town in Worcestershire in the Middle Ages (Worcestershire Historical Society, 9, Worcester, 2000)

    'Small towns 1270–1540', in D. M. Palliser (ed.), *Cambridge Urban History of Britain, Volume 1: 600–1540* (Cambridge, 2000), pp. 505–37

    'Work ethics in the fourteenth century', in J. Bothwell, P. J. P. Goldberg and W. M. Ormrod (eds.), *The Problem of Labour in Fourteenth-Century England* (Woodbridge, 2000), pp. 21–41

    'Small places with large consequences: the importance of small towns in England, 1000–1540', *Historical Research*, 75 (2002), 1–24

    'The urbanizing of Staffordshire: the first phases', *Staffordshire Studies*, 14 (2002), 1–31

    Making a Living in the Middle Ages: The People of Britain 850–1520 (New Haven, Conn., 2002)

    An Age of Transition? Economy and Society in England in the Later Middle Ages (Oxford, 2005)

Dymond, D. and Martin, E. (eds.), *An Historical Atlas of Suffolk* (2nd edn, Bury St Edmunds, 1989)

Dymond, D. and Northeast, P., *A History of Suffolk* (Chichester, 1985, rev. 1995)

Eaglen, R. J., 'The evolution of coinage in thirteenth-century England', in P. R. Coss and S. D. Lloyd (eds.), *Thirteenth Century England IV: Proceedings of the Newcastle Upon Tyne Conference 1991* (Woodbridge, 1992), pp. 15–24

Eberle, P. J., 'Commercial language and the commercial outlook in the General Prologue', *Chaucer Review*, 18 (1983), 161–74

Edwards, A. S. G. and Pearsall, D., 'The manuscripts of the major English poetic texts', in J. Griffiths and D. Pearsall (eds.), *Book Production and Publishing in Britain 1375–1475* (Cambridge, 1989), pp. 257–78

Edwards, A. S. G., 'Manuscripts and readers', in P. Brown (ed.), *A Companion to Medieval English Literature and Culture c.1350–c.1500* (Chichester, 2009), pp. 93–106.

Ehrich, S. and Oberste, J. (eds.), *Städtische Räume im Mittelalter* (Forum Mittelalter, Studien Band 5, Regensburg, 2009)

Ellis, D. S., 'The merchant's wife's tale: language, sex, and commerce in Margery Kempe and in Chaucer', *Exemplaria: A Journal of Theory in Medieval and Renaissance Studies*, 2 (1990), 595–626

Epstein, S. A., *An Economic and Social History of Later Medieval Europe, 1000–1500* (Cambridge, 2009)

Epstein, S. R., 'Business cycles and the sense of time in medieval Genoa', *Business History Review*, 62, 2 (1988), 238–60

'Regional fairs, institutional innovation, and economic growth in late medieval England', *Economic History Review*, 2nd ser. 47 (1994), 459–82

'Craft guilds, apprenticeships, and technological change in pre-industrial Europe', *Journal of Economic History*, 58 (1998), 684–713

Everitt, A., 'The marketing of agricultural produce', in J. Thirsk (ed.), *The Agrarian History of England and Wales, Volume IV: 1500–1640* (Cambridge, 1967), pp. 466–592

Farber, L., *An Anatomy of Trade in Medieval Writing: Value, Consent, and Community* (Ithaca, NY, 2006)

Farmer, D. L., 'Two Wiltshire manors and their markets', *Agricultural History Review*, 37 (1989), 1–11

'Marketing the produce of the countryside 1200–1500', in E. Miller (ed.), *The Agrarian History of England and Wales, Volume III: 1348–1500* (Cambridge, 1991), pp. 324–430

'Prices and wages, 1350–1500', in E. Miller (ed.), *The Agrarian History of England and Wales, Volume III: 1348–1500* (Cambridge, 1991), pp. 431–525

Fichte, J. O. (ed.), *Chaucer's Frame Tales: The Physical and the Metaphysical* (Cambridge, 1987)

'Chaucer's "Shipman's Tale" within the context of the French fabliaux tradition', in J. O. Fichte (ed.), *Chaucer's Frame Tales: The Physical and the Metaphysical* (Cambridge, 1987), pp. 51–66

Fienberg, N., 'Thematics of value in the book of Margery Kempe', *Modern Philology*, 87 (1989), 132–41

Finlayson, J., 'Chaucer's *Shipman's Tale*, Boccaccio, and the "civilizing" of fabliau', *Chaucer Review*, 36 (2002), 336–51

First Report of the Royal Commission on Market Rights and Tolls (London, 1889)

Fleming, J. V., 'Historians and the evidence of literature', *Journal of Interdisciplinary History*, 4 (1973), 95–105

Fleming, P., 'Telling tales of oligarchy in the late medieval town', in M. Hicks (ed.), *Revolution and Consumption in Late Medieval England* (Woodbridge, 2001), pp. 177–93

Fletcher, A. and Stevenson, J. (eds.), *Order and Disorder in Early Modern England* (Cambridge, 1985)

Fransson, G., 'Middle English surnames of occupation 1100–1350', *Lund Studies in English*, 3 (1935), 1–217

Fraser, C. M., 'Medieval trading restrictions in the North East', *Archaeologia Aeliana*, 4th ser., 39 (1961), 135–50

Fulton, H., 'Mercantile ideology in Chaucer's *Shipman's Tale*', *Chaucer Review*, 36 (2002), 311–28

Futamura, H., Akishino, K. and Ebi, H. (eds.), *A Pilgrimage through Medieval English Literature* (Tokyo, 1993)

Gardner, A., *Minor English Wood Sculpture 1400–1550* (London, 1958)

Geertz, C., *Peddlers and Princes: Social Change and Economic Modernization in Two Indonesian Towns* (Chicago, Ill., 1963)

'Suq: the bazaar economy in Sefrou', in C. Geertz, H. Geertz and L. Rosen (eds.), *Meaning and Order in Moroccan Society: Three Essays in Cultural Analysis* (Cambridge, 1979), pp. 123–313

Geertz, C., Geertz, H. and Rosen, L. (eds.), *Meaning and Order in Moroccan Society: Three Essays in Cultural Analysis* (Cambridge, 1979)

Gemmill, E., 'Town and region: the corn market in Aberdeen, *c*.1398–*c*.1468', in B. Dodds and R. H. Britnell (eds.), *Agriculture and Rural Society after the Black Death: Common Themes and Regional Variations* (Hatfield, 2008), pp. 56–69

Gemmill, E. and Mayhew, N., *Changing Values in Medieval Scotland: A Study of Prices, Money, and Weights and Measures* (Cambridge, 1995)

Gilchrist, J., *The Church and Economic Activity in the Middle Ages* (London, 1969)

Gillett, E. and MacMahon, K. A., *A History of Hull* (Oxford, 1980)

Glennie, P. D., 'A commercialising agrarian region: late medieval and early modern Hertfordshire' (Ph.D., University of Cambridge, 1983)

Goddard, R., *Lordship and Medieval Urbanisation: Coventry, 1043–1355* (Woodbridge, 2004)

Godden, M., *The Making of Piers Plowman* (London, 1990)

Goff, J. le, *Time, Work and Culture in the Middle Ages* (trans. A. Goldhammer, Chicago, Ill., 1980)

Your Money or Your Life: Economy and Religion in the Middle Ages (New York, 1988)

Goff, J. le (ed.), *The Medieval World* (trans. L. G. Cochrane, London, 1990)

Goldberg, P. J. P., 'Women in fifteenth-century town life', in J. A. F. Thomson (ed.), *Towns and Townspeople in the Fifteenth Century* (Gloucester, 1988), pp. 107–28

Women, Work, and Life Cycle in a Medieval Economy: Women in York and Yorkshire c.1300–1520 (Oxford, 1992)

'Craft guilds, the Corpus Christi play and civic government', in S. Rees Jones (ed.), *The Government of Medieval York: Essays in Commemoration of the 1396 Royal Charter* (Borthwick Studies in History, 3, York, 1997), pp. 141–63

Goldberg, P. J. P. (ed.), *Woman is a Worthy Wight: Women in English Society c.1200–1500* (Stroud, 1992)

Goodacre, J., *The Transformation of a Peasant Economy: Townspeople and Villagers in the Lutterworth Area 1500–1700* (Aldershot, 1994)

Gottfried, R. S., *Bury St Edmunds and the Urban Crisis: 1290–1539* (Princeton, NJ, 1982)

Gould, J., 'The medieval burgesses of Tamworth: their liberties, courts, and markets', *Transactions of the South Staffordshire Archaeological and Historical Society*, 13 (1971–2), 17–42

Graham, H., '"A woman's work . . . ": labour and gender in the late medieval countryside', in P. J. P. Goldberg (ed.), *Woman is a Worthy Wight: Women in English Society c.1200–1500* (Stroud, 1992), pp. 126–48

Grant, L. (ed.), *Medieval Art, Architecture and Archaeology in London* (British Archaeological Association, Leeds, 1990)

Gras, N. S. B., *The Evolution of the English Corn Market from the Twelfth to the Eighteenth Century* (Cambridge, 1915)

Gray, N. J., 'The clemency of cobblers: a reading of "Glutton's Confession" in Piers Plowman', *Leeds Studies in English*, 17 (1986), 61–75

Green, A. S., *Town Life in the Fifteenth Century*, 2 vols. (London, 1894)

Green, R. B., 'Virtues and vices in the chapter house vestibule in Salisbury', *Journal of the Warburg and Courtauld Institutes*, 31 (1968), 148–58.

Green, R. F., 'John Ball's letters: literary history and historical literature', in B. A. Hanawalt (ed.), *Chaucer's England: Literature in Historical Context* (Minneapolis, Minn., 1992), pp. 176–200

Grief, A., 'Cultural beliefs and the organization of society: a historical and theoretical reflection on collectivist societies', *Journal of Political Economy*, 102, 5 (1994), 912–50

Institutions and the Path to the Modern Economy: Lessons from Medieval Trade (New York, 2006)

Griffiths, J. and Pearsall, D. (eds.), *Book Production and Publishing in Britain 1375–1475* (Cambridge, 1989)

Griffiths, L., *Personification in Piers Plowman* (Woodbridge, 1985)

Gross, C., *The Gild Merchant: A Contribution to British Municipal History*, 2 vols. (Oxford, 1890)

Grössinger, C., *The World Upside-Down: English Misericords* (London, 1997)

Gurevich, A. J., *Categories of Medieval Culture* (trans. G. L. Campbell, London, 1985)

Medieval Popular Culture: Problems of Belief and Perception (trans. J. M. Bak and P. A. Hollingsworth, Cambridge, 1988)

'The merchant', in J. le Goff (ed.), *The Medieval World* (trans. L. G. Cochrane, London, 1990), pp. 243–83

Hahn, T., 'Money, sexuality, wordplay and context in the *Shipman's Tale*', in J. N. Wasserman and R. J. Blanch (eds.), *Chaucer in the Eighties* (Syracuse, NY, 1986), pp. 235–49

Hamaguchi, K., '"Debt" and the wife as a verbal exchanger in *The Shipman's Tale*', in H. Futamura, K. Akishino and H. Ebi (eds.), *A Pilgrimage through Medieval English Literature* (Tokyo, 1993), pp. 123–44

Hammond, P. W., *Food and Feast in Medieval England* (Stroud, 1993)

Hanawalt, B. A., 'Introduction', in B. A. Hanawalt (ed.), *Chaucer's England: Literature in Historical Context* (Minneapolis, Minn., 1992), pp. ix–xxii

Hanawalt, B. A. (ed.), *Women and Work in Preindustrial Europe* (Bloomington, Ind., 1986)

Chaucer's England: Literature in Historical Context (Minneapolis, Minn., 1992)

Hanawalt, B. A. and Wallace, D. (eds.), *Bodies and Disciplines: Intersections of Literature and History in Fifteenth-Century England* (Minneapolis, Minn., 1996)

Hanham, A., *The Celys and their World: An English Merchant Family of the Fifteenth Century* (Cambridge, 1985)

Hanna III, R., 'Brewing trouble: on literature and history – and alewives', in B. A. Hanawalt and D. Wallace (eds.), *Bodies and Disciplines: Intersections of Literature and History in Fifteenth-Century England* (Minneapolis, Minn., 1996), pp. 1–17

Haren, M., *Sin and Society in Fourteenth-Century England: A Study of the Memoriale Presbiterorum* (Oxford, 2000)

Hatcher, J., *Plague, Population and the English Economy 1348–1530* (London, 1977)

'English serfdom and villeinage: towards a reassessment', *Past and Present*, 90 (1981), 3–39

'England in the aftermath of the Black Death', *Past and Present*, 144 (1994), 3–35

'The great slump of the mid-fifteenth century', in R. H. Britnell and J. Hatcher (eds.), *Progress and Problems in Medieval England: Essays in Honour of Edward Miller* (Cambridge, 1996), pp. 237–72

'Labour, leisure and economic thought before the nineteenth century', *Past and Present*, 160 (1998), 64–115

Hatcher, J. and Bailey, M., *Modelling the Middle Ages: The History and Theory of England's Economic Development* (Oxford, 2001)

Hay, D., 'Moral economy, political economy and law', in A. Randall and A. Charlesworth (eds.), *Moral Economy and Popular Protest: Crowds, Conflict and Authority* (Basingstoke, 2000), pp. 93–122

Heal, F., *Hospitality in Early Modern England* (Oxford, 1990)

Hearnshaw, F. J. C., *Leet Jurisdiction in England* (Southampton, 1908)

Heath, P., 'Urban piety in the later Middle Ages: the evidence of Hull wills', in R. B. Dobson (ed.), *The Church, Politics and Patronage in the Fifteenth Century* (Gloucester, 1984), pp. 208–34

Helmholz, R. H., *Canon Law and the Law of England* (London, 1987)

'Usury and the medieval English church courts', in R. H. Helmholz, *Canon Law and the Law of England* (London, 1987), pp. 323–39

Hibbert, A. B., 'The economic policies of towns', in M. M. Postan, E. E. Rich and E. Miller (eds.), *Cambridge Economic History of Europe, Volume III: Economic Organisation and Policies in the Middle Ages* (Cambridge, 1963), pp. 157–229

Hicks, M. (ed.), *Revolution and Consumption in Late Medieval England* (Woodbridge, 2001)

Hieatt, C. B., 'A cook they had with hem for the nones', in L. C. Lambdin and R. T. Lambdin (eds.), *Chaucer's Pilgrims: An Historical Guide to the Pilgrims in the Canterbury Tales* (London, 1996), pp. 199–209

Hill, C., *Puritanism and Revolution* (New York, 1958)

Society and Puritanism in Pre-Revolutionary England (2nd edn, London, 1967)

Hill, J. W. F., *Medieval Lincoln* (Cambridge, 1948)

Hilton, R. H., *The English Peasantry in the Later Middle Ages* (Oxford, 1975)

'Introduction', in R. H. Hilton (ed.), *The Transition from Feudalism to Capitalism* (London, 1976), pp. 9–30

'Lords, burgesses and hucksters', *Past and Present*, 97 (1982), 3–15

'Capitalism – what's in a name?', in R. H. Hilton, *Class Conflict and the Crisis of Feudalism* (London, 1985), pp. 268–77

Class Conflict and the Crisis of Feudalism (London, 1985)

'Medieval market towns and simple commodity production', *Past and Present*, 109 (1985), 3–23

'The small town and urbanization – Evesham in the Middle Ages', in R. H. Hilton, *Class Conflict and the Crisis of Feudalism* (London, 1985), pp. 1–8

'Women traders in medieval England', in R. H. Hilton, *Class Conflict and the Crisis of Feudalism* (London, 1985), pp. 205–15

'Small town society in England before the Black Death', in R. Holt and G. Rosser (eds.), *The Medieval Town: A Reader in English Urban History 1200–1540* (London, 1990), pp. 71–96

'Towns in English medieval society', in R. Holt and G. Rosser (eds.), *The Medieval Town: A Reader in English Urban History 1200–1540* (London, 1990), pp. 19–28

English and French Towns in Feudal Society: A Comparative Study (Cambridge, 1992)

'Low-level urbanization: the seigneurial borough of Thornbury in the Middle Ages', in Z. Razi and R. Smith (eds.), *Medieval Society and the Manor Court* (Oxford, 1996), pp. 482–517

'Status and class in the medieval town', in T. R. Slater and G. Rosser (eds.), *The Church in the Medieval Town* (Aldershot, 1998), pp. 9–19

Hilton, R. H. (ed.), *The Transition from Feudalism to Capitalism* (London, 1976)

Hirshler, E. E., 'Medieval economic competition', *Journal of Economic History*, 14 (1954), 52–8

Historical Manuscripts Commission, *Report on Manuscripts in Various Collections, Volume iv* (London, 1907)

Hodges, L. F., *Chaucer and Costume: The Secular Pilgrims in the General Prologue* (Cambridge, 2000)

Holt, R. A., *The Early History of the Town of Birmingham 1166–1600* (Dugdale Society Occasional Papers, 30, Oxford, 1985)

'Gloucester in the century after the Black Death', in R. A. Holt and G. Rosser (eds.), *The English Medieval Town: A Reader in English Urban History 1200–1540* (London, 1990), pp. 141–59

Holt, R. A. and Rosser, G., 'Introduction', in R. A. Holt and G. Rosser (eds.), *The Medieval Town: A Reader in English Urban History 1200–1540* (London, 1990), pp. 1–18

Holt, R. A. and Rosser, G. (eds.), *The Medieval Town: A Reader in English Urban History 1200–1540* (London, 1990)

Horrox, R., 'Urban gentry', in J. A. F. Thomson (ed.), *Towns and Townspeople in the Fifteenth Century* (Gloucester, 1988), pp. 22–44

Horrox, R. (ed.), *Fifteenth-Century Attitudes: Perceptions of Society in Late Medieval England* (Cambridge, 1994)

Horrox, R. and Ormrod, W. M. (eds.), *A Social History of England, 1200–1500* (Cambridge, 2006)

Hunt, E. S. and Murray, J. M., *A History of Business in Medieval Europe 1200–1500* (Cambridge, 1999)

Hunter, J., 'Legislation, royal proclamations and other national directives affecting inns, taverns, alehouses, brandy shops and punch houses 1552–1757' (Ph.D., University of Reading, 1994)

Ibbetson, D., 'From property to contract: the transformation of sale in the Middle Ages', *Journal of Legal History*, 13 (1992), 1–22

Jacobs, N., 'The typology of debate and the interpretation of "Wynnere and Wastoure"', *Review of English Studies*, 36 (1985), 481–500

James, M. K., *Studies in the Medieval Wine Trade* (ed. E. M. Veale, Oxford, 1971)

James, M., 'Ritual, drama and social body in the late medieval English town', *Past and Present*, 98 (1983), 3–29

Janson, H. W., *Apes and Ape Lore in the Middle Ages and the Renaissance* (London, 1952)

Jarrett, B., *Social Theories of the Middle Ages, 1200–1500* (2nd edn, London, 1968)

Jenkins, D. (ed.), *Legal History Studies 1972* (Cardiff, 1975)

Jewell, H. M., 'Women at the courts of the manor of Wakefield, 1348–1350', *Northern History*, 26 (1990), 59–81
  Women in Medieval England (Manchester, 1996)

Johnson, O. E., 'Was Chaucer's merchant in debt? A study in Chaucerian syntax and rhetoric', *Journal of English and Germanic Philology*, 52 (1953), 50–7

Jones, G. F., 'Chaucer and the medieval miller', *Modern Language Quarterly*, 16 (1955), 3–15

Jordan, W. C., *The Great Famine: Northern Europe in the Early Fourteenth Century* (Princeton, NJ, 1996)

Joseph, G., 'Chaucer's coinage: foreign exchange and the puns of the Shipman's Tale', *Chaucer Review*, 17 (1982–3), 341–57

Justice, A. D., 'Trade symbolism in the York cycle', *Theatre Journal*, 31 (1979), 47–58

Justice, S., *Writing and Rebellion: England in 1381* (Berkeley and Los Angeles, Calif., 1994)

Karras, R. M., *Common Women: Prostitution and Sexuality in Medieval England* (Oxford, 1996)

Katzenellenbogen, A., *Allegories of the Virtues and Vices in Mediaeval Art* (London, 1939)

Kaulla, R., *Theory of the Just Price* (London, 1940)

Kaye, J., *Economy and Nature in the Fourteenth Century: Money, Market Exchange, and the Emergence of Scientific Thought* (Cambridge, 1998)

Keen, M., *English Society in the Later Middle Ages 1348–1500* (London, 1990)

Keene, D, *Survey of Medieval Winchester*, 2 vols. (Oxford, 1985)

    'Suburban growth', in R. Holt and G. Rosser (eds.), *The Medieval Town: A Reader in English Urban History 1200–1540* (London, 1990), pp. 97–119

    'Shops and shopping in medieval London', in L. Grant (ed.), *Medieval Art, Architecture and Archaeology in London* (British Archaeological Association, Leeds, 1990), pp. 29–46

Kermode, J. I., 'The merchants of three northern English towns', in C. H. Clough (ed.), *Profession, Vocation, and Culture in Later Medieval England* (Liverpool, 1982), pp. 7–48

    'Introduction', in J. I. Kermode (ed.), *Enterprise and Individuals in Fifteenth-Century England* (Stroud, 1991), pp. ix–xiii

    Medieval Merchants: York, Beverley and Hull in the Later Middle Ages (Cambridge, 1998)

    'The greater towns 1300–1540', in D. M. Palliser (ed.), *Cambridge Urban History of Britain, Volume 1: 600–1540* (Cambridge, 2000), pp. 441–65

Kermode, J. I. (ed.), *Enterprise and Individuals in Fifteenth-Century England* (Stroud, 1991)

King, S., 'A shipman ther was, wonynge fer by weste', in L. C. Lambdin and R. T. Lambdin (eds.), *Chaucer's Pilgrims: An Historical Guide to the Pilgrims in the Canterbury Tales* (London, 1996), pp. 210–19

King, W. J., 'Regulation of alehouses in Stuart Lancashire: an example of discretionary administration of the law', *Transactions of the Historic Society of Lancashire and Cheshire*, 129 (1980), 31–46

Kinney, T. L., 'The temper of fourteenth-century English verse of complaint', *Annuale Mediaevale*, 7 (1966), 74–89

Kiralfy, A., 'Custom in mediaeval English law', *Journal of Legal History*, 9 (1988), 26–39

Knight, S., *Geoffrey Chaucer* (Oxford, 1986)

Knott, T. A., 'Chaucer's anonymous merchant', *Philological Quarterly*, 1 (1922), 1–16

Kowaleski, M., 'Women's work in a market town: Exeter in the late fourteenth century', in B. A. Hanawalt (ed.), *Women and Work in Preindustrial Europe* (Bloomington, Ind., 1986), pp. 145–64

    'The commercial dominance of a medieval provincial oligarchy: Exeter in the late fourteenth century', in R. A. Holt and G. Rosser (eds.), *The Medieval Town: A Reader in English Urban History 1200–1540* (London, 1990), pp. 184–215

    Local Markets and Regional Trade in Medieval Exeter (Cambridge, 1995)

    'A consumer economy', in R. Horrox and W. M. Ormrod (eds.), *A Social History of England, 1200–1500* (Cambridge, 2006), pp. 238–59

Lacey, K. E., 'Women and work in fourteenth- and fifteenth-century London', in L. Charles and L. Duffin (eds.), *Women and Work in Pre-Industrial England* (Beckenham, 1985), pp. 24–82

Ladd, R. A., 'The mercantile mis(reader) in *The Canterbury Tales*', *Studies in Philology*, 99 (2002), 17–32

Lambdin, L. C. and Lambdin, R. T. (eds.), *Chaucer's Pilgrims: An Historical Guide to the Pilgrims in the Canterbury Tales* (London, 1996)

Langholm, O., *Economics in the Medieval Schools: Wealth, Exchange, Value, Money and Usury according to the Paris Theological Tradition 1200–1350* (Leiden, 1992)

   The Legacy of Scholasticism in Economic Thought (Cambridge, 1998)

   The Merchant in the Confessional: Trade and Price in the Pre-Reformation Penitential Handbooks (Leiden, 2003)

Laslett, P, 'The wrong way through the telescope: a note on literary evidence in sociology and in historical sociology', *British Journal of Sociology*, 27 (1976), 319–42

Laughton, J., 'Aspects of the social and economic history of late medieval Chester, 1350–c.1500' (Ph.D., University of Cambridge, 1994)

   'The alewives of later medieval Chester', in R. E. Archer (ed.), *Crown, Government and People in the Fifteenth Century* (Stroud, 1995), pp. 191–208

Laughton, J. and Dyer, C., 'Small towns in the East and West Midlands in the later Middle Ages: a comparison', *Midland History*, 24 (1999), 24–52

Lawton, D. (ed.), *Middle English Alliterative Poetry and its Literary Background* (Bury St Edmunds, 1982)

Lee, J. S., 'Feeding the colleges: Cambridge's food and fuel supplies, 1450–1560', *Economic History Review*, 56 (2003), 243–64

   Cambridge and its Economic Region 1450–1560 (Hatfield, 2005)

   'The functions and fortunes of English small towns at the close of the Middle Ages: evidence from John Leland's *Itinerary*', *Urban History*, 37 (2010), 3–25

Lehmann, H. and Roth, G. (eds.), *Weber's Protestant Ethic: Origins, Evidence, Contexts* (Cambridge, 1993)

Letters, S., *Online Gazetteer of Markets and Fairs in England Wales to 1516*, at: www.history.ac.uk/cmh/gaz/gazweb2.html [Suffolk] (accessed 23 July 2009)

Lilley, A. L., 'The moral and spiritual factors in the Middle Ages', in V. A. Demant (ed.), *The Just Price* (London, 1930), pp. 46–59

Lilley, K. D., *Urban Life in the Middle Ages 1000–1450* (Basingstoke, 2002)

Lipson, E., *The Economic History of England, Volume 1: The Middle Ages* (12th edn, London, 1959)

Lisca, P., 'Chaucer's guildsmen and their cook', *Modern Language Notes*, 70 (1955), 321–4

Little, L. K., 'Pride goes before Avarice: social change and the vices in Latin Christendom', *American Historical Review*, 76 (1971), 16–49

   Religious Poverty and the Profit Economy in Medieval Europe (London, 1978)

Lobel, M. D., *The Borough of Bury St Edmunds: A Study in the Government and Development of a Monastic Town* (Oxford, 1935)

Lopez, R. S., *The Commercial Revolution of the Middle Ages 950–1350* (Englewood Cliffs, NJ, 1971)

Lumiansky, R. M., 'Comedy and theme in the Chester *Harrowing of Hell*', *Tulane Studies in English*, 10 (1960), 5–12

Macfarlane, A., *The Origins of English Individualism* (Oxford, 1978)

MacKinnon, M. H., 'The longevity of the thesis: a critique of the critics', in H. Lehmann and G. Roth (eds.), *Weber's Protestant Ethic: Origins, Evidence, Contexts* (Cambridge, 1993), pp. 211–43

Maddicott, J. R., 'Poems of social protest in early fourteenth-century England', in W. M. Ormrod (ed.), *England in the Fourteenth Century: Proceedings of the 1985 Harlaxton Symposium* (Woodbridge, 1986), pp. 130–44

Maguire, S., 'The significance of Haukyn, Activa Vita, in Piers Plowman', *Review of English Studies*, 25 (1949), 97–109

Mair, O., 'Merchants and mercantile culture in late medieval Italian and English literature' (Ph.D., University of Western Australia, 2005)

Manly, J. M., *Some New Light on Chaucer* (London, 1926)

Mann, J., *Chaucer and Medieval Estates Satire: The Literature of Social Classes and the General Prologue to the Canterbury Tales* (Cambridge, 1973)

Martin, G. H., *The Early Court Rolls of the Borough of Ipswich* (Department of English Local History, University College of Leicester, Occasional Papers, 5, 1954)

   'The borough and the merchant community of Ipswich, 1317–1422' (D.Phil., Oxford University, 1955)

   'The governance of Ipswich from its origins to *c*.1550', in D. Allen, *Ipswich Borough Archives 1255–1835* (Suffolk Records Society, 43, Woodbridge, 2000), pp. xvii–xxix

Martindale Jr, W., 'Chaucer's merchants: a trade-based speculation on their activities', *Chaucer Review*, 26 (1992), 309–16

Masschaele, J., 'Market rights in thirteenth-century England', *English Historical Review*, 107 (1992), 78–89

   'Urban trade in medieval England: the evidence of foreign gild membership lists', in P. R. Coss and S. D. Lloyd (eds.), *Thirteenth Century England V* (Woodbridge, 1995), pp. 115–28

   Peasants, Merchants, and Markets: Inland Trade in Medieval England, 1150–1350 (London, 1997)

   'The public space of the marketplace in medieval England', *Speculum*, 77 (2002), 383–421

Mastoris, S. N., 'Regulating the Nottingham markets: new evidence from a mid-thirteenth century manuscript', *Transactions of the Thoroton Society of Nottinghamshire*, 90 (1986), 79–83

Mate, M., 'The rise and fall of markets in southeast England', *Canadian Journal of History*, 31 (1996), 59–86

   Daughters, Wives and Widows after the Black Death: Women in Sussex, 1350–1535 (Woodbridge, 1998)

   Women in Medieval English Society (Cambridge, 1999)

   Trade and Economic Developments 1450–1550: The Experience of Kent, Surrey, and Sussex (Woodbridge, 2006)

May, A. N., 'An index of thirteenth-century peasant impoverishment? Manor court fines', *Economic History Review*, 2nd ser., 26 (1973), 389–402

May, P., 'Newmarket 500 years ago', *Proceedings of the Suffolk Institute of Archaeology and History*, 33 (1975), 253–74

'The site of the medieval market at Newmarket', *Suffolk Review*, 4 (1975–6), 191–4

'Newmarket and its market court, 1399–1413', *Proceedings of the Suffolk Institute of Archaeology and History*, 35 (1981), 31–9

Newmarket: Medieval and Tudor (Norfolk, 1982)

Mayhew, G., *Tudor Rye* (Falmer, 1987)

Mayhew, N. J., 'Money and prices in England from Henry II to Edward III', *Agricultural History Review*, 35 (1987), 121–32

McClenaghan, B., *The Springs of Lavenham and the Suffolk Cloth Trade in the XV and XVI Centuries* (Ipswich, 1924)

McClure, P., 'Patterns of migration in the late Middle Ages: the evidence of English place-name surnames', *Economic History Review*, 2nd ser., 32 (1979), 167–82

McGalliard, J., 'Characterization in Chaucer's *Shipman's Tale*', *Philogical Quarterly*, 54 (1975), 1–18

McIntosh, M. K., *Autonomy and Community: The Royal Manor of Havering, 1200–1500* (Cambridge, 1986)

'Local change and community control in England, 1465–1500', *Huntington Library Quarterly*, 49 (1986), 219–42

A Community Transformed: The Manor and Liberty of Havering, 1500–1620 (Cambridge, 1991)

Controlling Misbehaviour in England, 1370–1600 (Cambridge, 1998)

Working Women in English Society, 1300–1620 (Cambridge, 2005)

'The benefits and drawbacks of *femme sole* status in England, 1300–1630', *Journal of British Studies*, 44 (2005), 410–38

McLaughlin, T. P., 'The teaching of the Canonists on usury', *Mediaeval Studies*, 1 (1939), 81–147, and 2 (1940), 1–22

McMurray Gibson, G., *The Theater of Devotion: East Anglian Drama and Society in the Late Middle Ages* (Chicago, Ill., 1989)

McRee, B. R., 'Religious gilds and regulation of behavior in late medieval towns', in J. Rosenthal and C. Richmond (eds.), *People, Politics and Community in the Later Middle Ages* (New York, 1987), pp. 108–22

McVeagh, J., *Tradefull Merchants: The Portrayal of the Capitalist in Literature* (London, 1981)

Melitz, J. and Winch, D. (eds.), *Religious Thought and Economic Society: Four Chapters of an Unfinished Work by Jacob Viner* (Durham, NC, 1978)

Merrington, J., 'Town and country in the transition to capitalism', in R. H. Hilton (ed.), *The Transition from Feudalism to Capitalism* (London, 1976), pp. 170–95

Middleton, A., 'The audience and public of *Piers Plowman*', in D. Lawton (ed.), *Middle English Alliterative Poetry and its Literary Background* (Bury St Edmunds, 1982), pp. 101–23

Miller, E. and Hatcher, J., *Medieval England: Rural Society and Economic Change 1086–1348* (London and New York, 1978)

Medieval England: Towns, Commerce and Crafts, 1086–1348 (London and New York, 1995)

Miller, E. (ed.), *The Agrarian History of England and Wales, Volume III: 1348–1500* (Cambridge, 1991)

Mitchell, A. G., 'Lady Meed and the art of Piers Plowman', in R. J. Blanch (ed.), *Style and Symbolism in Piers Plowman: A Modern Critical Anthology* (Knoxville, Tenn., 1969), pp. 174–93

Mitchell, W., *An Essay on the Early History of the Law Merchant* (Cambridge, 1904)

Mohl, R., *The Three Estates in Medieval and Renaissance Literature* (New York, 1933)

Moore, E. W., *The Fairs of Medieval England: An Introductory Study* (Pontifical Institute of Mediaeval Studies, 72, Toronto, 1985)

Morrill, J., Slack, P. and Woolf, D. (eds.), *Public Duty and Private Conscience in Seventeenth-Century England* (Oxford, 1993)

Morrison, K. A., *English Shops and Shopping: An Architectural History* (New Haven, Conn., 2003)

Moss, D., 'The economic development of a Middlesex village', *Agricultural History Review*, 28 (1980), 104–14

Muldrew, C., 'Interpreting the market: the ethics of credit and community relations in early modern England', *Social History*, 18 (1993), 163–83

  The Economy of Obligation: The Culture of Credit and Social Relations in Early Modern England (London, 1998)

  'From a "light cloak" to an "iron cage": historical changes in the relation between community and individualism', in A. Shepard and P. Withington (eds.), *Communities in Early Modern England: Networks, Place, Rhetoric* (Manchester, 2000), pp. 156–77

Mullaney, S., 'Fashion and morality in BL MS Add. 37049', in J. Scattergood and J. Boffy (eds.), *Texts and their Contexts: Papers from the Early Book Society* (Dublin, 1997), pp. 71–86

Müller, U., Hundsnurcher, F. and Sommer, C. (eds.), *Le droit et sa perception dans la littérature et les mentalités médiévales* (Göppingen, 1993)

Murray, A., 'Religion among the poor in thirteenth-century France: the testimony of Humbert de Romans', *Traditio*, 30 (1974), 285–324

  Reason and Society in the Middle Ages (Oxford, 1985)

Musson, A., 'New labour laws, new remedies? Legal reaction to the Black Death "crisis"', in N. Saul (ed.), *Fourteenth Century England I* (Woodbridge, 2000), pp. 73–88

Musson, A. (ed.), *Expectations of the Law in the Middle Ages* (Woodbridge, 2001)

Nederman, C. J., 'The monarch and the marketplace: economic policy and royal finance in William of Pagula's *Speculum regis Edwardi III*', *History of Political Economy*, 33 (2001), 51–69

  'The virtues of necessity: labor, money, and corruption in John of Salisbury's thought', *Viator: Medieval and Renaissance Studies*, 33 (2002), 54–68

Nevo, R., 'Chaucer: motive and mask in the "General Prologue"', *Modern Language Review*, 58 (1963), 1–9

Newhauser, R., *The Early History of Greed: The Sin of Avarice in Early Medieval Thought and Literature* (Cambridge, 2000)

Newman, C. M., *Late Medieval Northallerton: A Small Market Town and its Hinterland, 1470–1540* (Stamford, 1998)

Newhauser, R., *The Treatise on Vices and Virtues in Latin and the Vernacular* (Turnhout, 1993)

Nicholas, F., 'The assize of bread in London during the sixteenth century', *Economic History*, 2 (1930–3), 323–47

Nightingale, P., *A Medieval Mercantile Community: The Grocers' Company and the Politics and Trade of London, 1000–1485* (New Haven, Conn., and London, 1995)

'Money and credit in the economy of late medieval England', in D. Wood (ed.), *Medieval Money Matters* (Oxford, 2004), pp. 51–71

Noonan, J. T., *The Scholastic Analysis of Usury* (Cambridge, Mass., 1957)

North, D. C., *Structure and Change in Economic History* (New York and London, 1981)

'Transaction costs in history', *Journal of European Economic History*, 14 (1985), 557–76

Institutions, Institutional Change, and Economic Performance (Cambridge, 1990)

North, D. C. and Thomas, R. P., *The Rise of the Western World: A New Economic History* (Cambridge, 1973)

O'Brien, G., *An Essay on Medieval Economic Teaching* (London, 1920)

O'Connor, S., 'Adam Fraunceys and John Pyel: perceptions of status among merchants in fourteenth-century London', in D. J. Clayton, R. G. Davies and P. McNiven (eds.), *Trade, Devotion and Governance: Papers in Later Medieval History* (Stroud, 1994), pp. 17–35

O'Donnell, J., 'Market centres in Herefordshire 1200–1400', *Transactions of the Woolhope Naturalists' Field Club*, 40 (1971), 186–94

Ogilvie, S., '"Whatever is, is right"? Economic institutions in pre-industrial Europe', *Economic History Review*, 60 (2007), 649–84

Olson, P. A., *The Canterbury Tales and the Good Society* (Princeton, NJ, 1986)

Olson, S., 'Jurors of the village court: local leadership before and after the plague in Ellington, Huntingdonshire', *Journal of British Studies*, 30 (1991), 237–56

Origo, I., *The Merchant of Prato* (Harmondsworth, 1957)

Ormrod, W. M. (ed.), *England in the Fourteenth Century: Proceedings of the 1985 Harlaxton Symposium* (Woodbridge, 1986)

Outhwaite, R. B., 'Dearth and government intervention in English grain markets, 1510–1700', *Economic History Review*, 2nd ser., 34 (1981), 389–406

Overton, M., *Agricultural Revolution in England: The Transformation of the Agrarian Economy 1500–1850* (Cambridge, 1996)

Owst, G. R., *Literature and Pulpit in Medieval England: A Neglected Chapter in the History of English Letters and of the English People* (Oxford, 1961)

Page, B., 'Concerning the host', *Chaucer Review*, 4 (1970), 1–13

Palliser, D. M., *Tudor York* (Oxford, 1979)

'Urban decay revisited', in J. A. F. Thomson (ed.), *Towns and Townspeople in the Fifteenth Century* (Gloucester, 1988), pp. 1–21

'Urban society', in R. Horrox (ed.), *Fifteenth-Century Attitudes: Perceptions of Society in Late Medieval England* (Cambridge, 1994), pp. 132–49

Palliser, D. M. (ed.), *Cambridge Urban History of Britain, Volume 1: 600–1540* (Cambridge, 2000)

Palmer, R. C., *English Law in the Age of the Black Death, 1348–1381* (London, 1993)

Park, B. A., 'The character of Chaucer's merchant', *English Language Notes*, 1 (1963–4), 167–75

Parry, J., 'On the moral perils of exchange', in J. Parry and M. Bloch (eds.), *Money and the Morality of Exchange* (Cambridge, 1989), pp. 64–93

Parry, J. and Bloch, M., 'Introduction', in J. Parry and M. Bloch (eds.), *Money and the Morality of Exchange* (Cambridge, 1989), pp. 1–32

Parry, J. and Bloch, M. (eds.), *Money and the Morality of Exchange* (Cambridge, 1989)

Patterson, L., *Negotiating the Past: The Historical Understanding of Medieval Literature* (Madison, Wisc., 1987)

'Critical historicism and medieval studies', in L. Patterson (ed.), *Literary Practice and Social Change in Britain, 1380–1530* (Berkeley and Los Angeles, Calif., 1990), pp. 1–14

'"No man his reson herde": Peasant consciousness, Chaucer's miller, and the structure of the "Canterbury Tales"', in L. Patterson (ed.), *Literary Practice and Social Change in Britain, 1380–1530* (Berkeley and Los Angeles, Calif., 1990), pp. 113–55

Chaucer and the Subject of History (London, 1991)

Patterson, L. (ed.), *Literary Practice and Social Change in Britain, 1380–1530* (Berkeley and Los Angeles, Calif., 1990)

Penn, S. A. C., 'A fourteenth-century Bristol merchant', *Transactions of the Bristol and Gloucestershire Archaeological Society*, 104 (1986), 183–6

Pennington, D. and Thomas, K. (eds.), *Puritans and Revolutionaries: Essays in Seventeenth-Century History Presented to Christopher Hill* (Oxford, 1978)

Persson, K. G., *Pre-Industrial Economic Growth: Social Organisation and Technological Progress in Europe* (Oxford, 1988)

Petersen, C., *Bread and the British Economy, c.1770–1870* (Aldershot, 1995)

Pfander, H. G., *The Popular Sermon of the Medieval Friar in England* (New York, 1937)

Phythian-Adams, C., 'Urban decay in late medieval England', in P. Abrams and E. A. Wrigley (eds.), *Towns in Societies: Essays in Economic History and Historical Sociology* (Cambridge, 1978), pp. 159–85

Desolation of a City: Coventry and the Urban Crisis of the Later Middle Ages (Cambridge, 1979)

'Ceremony and the citizen: the communal year at Coventry, 1450–1550', in R. A. Holt and G. Rosser (eds.), *The Medieval Town: A Reader in English Urban History 1200–1540* (London, 1990), pp. 238–64

Pimsler, M., 'Solidarity in the medieval village? The evidence of personal pledging at Elton, Huntingdonshire', *Journal of British Studies*, 17 (1977), 1–11

Pirenne, H., *Economic and Social History of Medieval Europe* (London, 1937)

Medieval Cities: Their Origins and the Revival of Trade (Princeton, NJ, 1925, trans. 1952)

Plattner, S., 'Economic behavior in markets', in S. Plattner (ed.), *Economic Anthropology* (Stanford, Calif., 1989), pp. 209–21

'Markets and marketplaces', in S. Plattner (ed.), *Economic Anthropology* (Stanford, Calif., 1989), pp. 171–208

Plattner, S (ed.), *Economic Anthropology* (Stanford, Calif., 1989)

Platts, G., 'South Lincolnshire at the beginning of the fourteenth century: The social, economic and cultural environment of Robert Mannyng's *Handlyng Synne*' (Ph.D., Birmingham University, 1978)

Land and People in Medieval Lincolnshire (Lincoln, 1985)

Polanyi, K., *The Great Transformation* (Boston, 1957)

'Our obsolete market mentality', in G. Dalton (ed.), *Primitive, Archaic and Modern Economies. Essays of Karl Polanyi* (New York, 1968), pp. 59–77

Pollard, A. W. and Redgrave, G. R., *A Short-Title Catalogue of Books Printed in England, Scotland and Ireland and of English Books Printed Abroad, 1475–1640*, 3 vols. (rev. edn. W. A. Jackson, F. S. Ferguson and K. F. Pantzer, London, 1986)

Poos, L. R., 'The social context of Statute of Labourers enforcement', *Law and History Review*, 1 (1983), 27–52

A Rural Society after the Black Death: Essex, 1350–1525 (Cambridge, 1991)

Poos, L. R. and Bonfield, L., 'Law and individualism in medieval England', *Social History*, 11 (1986), 287–301

Post, J. B., 'Manorial amercements and peasant poverty', *Economic History Review*, 2nd ser., 28 (1975), 304–11

Postan, M. M., *The Medieval Economy and Society* (London, 1972)

Medieval Trade and Finance (Cambridge, 1973)

'Credit in medieval trade', in M. M. Postan, *Medieval Trade and Finance* (Cambridge, 1973), pp. 1–27

Essays on Medieval Agriculture and General Problems of the Medieval Economy (Cambridge, 1973)

'The fifteenth century', in M. M. Postan, *Essays on Medieval Agriculture and General Problems of the Medieval Economy* (Cambridge, 1973), pp. 41–8

Postan, M. M., Rich, E. E. and Miller, E. (eds.), *Cambridge Economic History of Europe, Volume III: Economic Organisation and Policies in the Middle Ages* (Cambridge, 1963)

Postles, D., 'Brewing and the peasant economy: some manors in late medieval Devon', *Rural History*, 3 (1992), 133–44

'An English small town in the later Middle Ages: Loughborough', *Urban History*, 20 (1993), 7–29

'Personal pledging: medieval "reciprocity" or "symbolic capital"?', *Journal of Interdisciplinary History*, 26 (1996), 419–35

Powell, E., *The Rising in East Anglia in 1381* (Cambridge, 1896)

Power, E. E., *Medieval People* (London, 1924)

The Wool Trade in English Medieval History (Oxford, 1941)

Power, E. E. and Postan, M. M. (eds.), *Studies in English Trade in the Fifteenth Century* (London, 1933)

Raftis, J. A., *Tenure and Mobility: Studies in the Social History of the Mediaeval English Village* (Toronto, 1964)

Peasant Economic Development within the English Manorial System (Montreal, 1996)

Raftis, J. A. (ed.), *Pathways to Medieval Peasants* (Pontifical Institute of Mediaeval Studies, Toronto, 1981)

Randall, A. and Charlesworth, A. (eds.), *Markets, Market Culture and Popular Protest in Eighteenth-Century Britain and Ireland* (Liverpool, 1996)
  Moral Economy and Popular Protest: Crowds, Conflict and Authority (Basingstoke, 2000)
Randall, L. M. C., *Images in the Margins of Gothic Manuscripts* (Berkeley and Los Angeles, Calif., 1966)
Razi, Z., 'The Toronto School's reconstitution of medieval peasant society: a critical view', *Past and Present*, 85 (1979), 141–57
  Life, Marriage and Death in a Medieval Parish: Economy, Society and Demography in Halesowen 1270–1400 (Cambridge, 1980)
Razi, Z. and Smith, R. M. (eds.), *Medieval Society and the Manor Court* (Oxford, 1996)
Reale, N. M., 'A marchant was ther with a forked berd', in L. C. Lambdin and R. T. Lambdin (eds.), *Chaucer's Pilgrims: An Historical Guide to the Pilgrims in the Canterbury Tales* (London, 1996), pp. 93–107
Reay, B. (ed.), *Popular Culture in Seventeenth-Century England* (London and Sydney, 1985)
Redstone, L. J., *Ipswich Through the Ages* (Ipswich, 1948)
Redstone, V. B., 'Chapels, chantries and gilds in Suffolk', *Proceedings of the Suffolk Institute of Archaeology and Natural History*, 12 (1906), 1–87
Rees Jones, S., 'York's civic administration, 1354–1464', in S. Rees Jones (ed.), *The Government of Medieval York: Essays in Commemoration of the 1396 Royal Charter* (Borthwick Studies in History, 3, York, 1997), pp. 108–40
Rees Jones, S. (ed.), *The Government of Medieval York: Essays in Commemoration of the 1396 Royal Charter* (Borthwick Studies in History, 3, York, 1997)
Renton, S., 'The moral economy of the English middling sort in the eighteenth century: the case of Norwich in 1766 and 1767', in A. Randall and A. Charlesworth (eds.), *Markets, Market Culture and Popular Protest in Eighteenth-Century Britain and Ireland* (Liverpool, 1996), pp. 115–36
Report of the Royal Commission on Market Rights and Tolls (London, 1889)
Reynolds, S., *An Introduction to the History of English Medieval Towns* (Oxford, 1977)
  'Decline and decay in late medieval towns', *Urban History Yearbook* (1980), 76–8
Richardson, G., 'Guilds, laws, and markets for manufactured merchandise in late-medieval England', *Explorations in Economic History*, 41 (2004), 1–25
  'Craft guilds and Christianity in late-medieval England: a rational-choice analysis', *Rationality and Society*, 17 (2005), 139–89
Richardson, J., 'The façade of bawdry: image patterns in Chaucer's *Shipman's Tale*', *ELH: Journal of English Literary History*, 32 (1965), 303–13
Richmond, C., 'The expenses of Thomas Playter of Sotterley, 1459–60', *Proceedings of the Suffolk Institute of Archaeology and History*, 35 (1981), 41–52
Rickert, E., 'Extracts from a fourteenth-century account book', *Modern Philology*, 24 (1926–7), 111–19, 249–56
Rigby, S. H., 'Urban decline in the later Middle Ages: some problems in interpreting the statistical data', *Urban History Yearbook* (1979), 46–59

'"Sore decay" and "fair dwellings": Boston and urban decline in the later Middle Ages', *Midland History*, 10 (1985), 47–61

'Late medieval urban prosperity: the evidence of the lay subsidies', *Economic History Review*, 2nd ser., 39 (1986), 411–16

'Urban "oligarchy" in late medieval England', in J. A. F. Thomson (ed.), *Towns and Townspeople in the Fifteenth Century* (Gloucester, 1988), pp. 62–86

Medieval Grimsby: Growth and Decline (Monographs in Regional and Local History, 3, Hull, 1993)

English Society in the Later Middle Ages (London, 1995)

Chaucer in Context: Society, Allegory and Gender (Manchester, 1996)

'England: literature and society', in S. H. Rigby (ed.), *A Companion to Britain in the Later Middle Ages* (Oxford, 2003), pp. 497–520

'English society in the later Middle Ages: deference, ambition and conflict', in P. Brown (ed.), *A Companion to Medieval English Literature and Culture c.1350–c.1500* (Chichester, 2009), pp. 25–39

'Urban population in late medieval England: the evidence of the lay subsidies', *Economic History Review*, 63 (2010), 393–417

Rigby, S. H. (ed.), *A Companion to Britain in the Later Middle Ages* (Oxford, 2003)

Roberts, S. K., 'Alehouses, brewing, and government under the early Stuarts', *Southern History*, 2 (1980), 45–71

Roberts, P. B., *Studies in the Sermons of Stephen Langton* (Pontifical Institute of Mediaeval Studies, Studies and Texts, 16, Toronto, 1968)

Rombauts, E. and Welkenhuysen, A. (eds.), *Aspects of the Medieval Animal Epic* (Louvain, 1975)

Roney, L., '*Winner and Waster's* "wyse wordes": teaching economics and nationalism in fourteenth-century England', *Speculum*, 69 (1994), 1070–1100

Roover, R. de, 'Scholastic economics: survival and lasting influence from the sixteenth century to Adam Smith', *Quarterly Journal of Economics*, 69 (1955), 161–90

'The concept of the just price: theory and economic policy', *Journal of Economic History*, 18 (1958), 418–34

Rose, M. and Hedgecoe, J., *Stories in Stone: The Medieval Roof Carvings of Norwich Cathedral* (London, 1997)

Rose, R. B., 'Eighteenth century price riots and public policy in England', *International Review of Social History*, 6 (1961), 277–92

Rosenthal, J. T., 'The assizes of weights and measures in medieval England', *Western Political Quarterly*, 17 (1964), 409–22

Rosenthal, J. and Richmond, C. (eds.), *People, Politics and Community in the Later Middle Ages* (New York, 1987)

Ross, A. S. C., 'The assize of bread', *Economic History Review*, 2nd ser., 9 (1956–7), 332–42

Rosser, G., 'The essence of medieval urban communities: the vill of Westminster, 1200–1540', *Transactions of the Royal Historical Society*, 5th ser., 34 (1984), 91–112

Medieval Westminster 1200–1540 (Oxford, 1989)

'Crafts, guilds and the negotiation of work in the medieval town', *Past and Present*, 154 (1997), 3–31

Rubin, M., *Corpus Christi: The Eucharist in Late Medieval Culture* (Cambridge, 1991)

'Small groups: identity and solidarity in the late Middle Ages', in J. I. Kermode (ed.), *Enterprise and Individuals in Fifteenth-Century England* (Stroud, 1991), pp. 132–50

Ruddock, A. A., 'Alien hosting in Southampton in the fifteenth century', *Economic History Review*, 1st ser., 16 (1946), 30–7

Rudé, G., *The Crowd in History, 1730–1848* (New York, 1964)

Sabine, E. L., 'Butchering in medieval London', *Speculum*, 8 (1933), 335–53

Sacks, D. H., 'The greed of Judas: avarice, monopoly, and the moral economy in England, ca.1350–ca.1600', *Journal of Medieval and Early Modern Studies*, 28 (1998), 263–307

Salzman, L. F., *English Life in the Middle Ages* (Oxford, 1926)

'The legal status of markets', *Cambridge Historical Journal*, 2 (1928), 205–12

English Trade in the Middle Ages (London, 1964)

Saul, A. R., 'The herring industry at Great Yarmouth *c*.1280–*c*.1400', *Norfolk Archaeology*, 38 (1981), 33–43

'English towns in the late Middle Ages: the case of Great Yarmouth', *Journal of Medieval History*, 8 (1982), 75–88

Saul, N. (ed.), *Fourteenth Century England I* (Woodbridge, 2000)

Scarfe, N., 'Markets and fairs in medieval Suffolk', *Suffolk Review*, 3 (1965), 4–11

The Suffolk Landscape (Bury St Edmunds, 1987)

Scattergood, J., 'Fashion and morality in the late Middle Ages', in D. Williams (ed.), *England in the Fifteenth Century: Proceedings of the 1986 Harlaxton Symposium* (Woodbridge, 1987), pp. 255–72

Scattergood, J. and Boffy, J. (eds.), *Texts and their Contexts: Papers from the Early Book Society* (Dublin, 1997)

Scattergood, V. J., 'The originality of the Shipman's Tale', *Chaucer Review*, 11 (1977), 210–31

Schneider, P. S., '"Taillynge Ynough": the function of money in the *Shipman's Tale*', *Chaucer Review*, 11 (1976–7), 201–9

Schofield, P. R., 'The late medieval view of frankpledge and the tithing system: an Essex case study', in Z. Razi and R. M. Smith (eds.), *Medieval Society and the Manor Court* (Oxford, 1996), pp. 408–49

'L'endettement et le crédit dans la campagne Anglaise au Moyen Âge', in M. Berthe (ed.), *Endettement Paysan et Crédit Rural dans l'Europe médiévale et moderne* (Toulouse, 1997), pp. 69–97

'Peasants and the manor court: gossip and litigation in a Suffolk village at the close of the thirteenth century', *Past and Present*, 159 (1998), 3–42

Peasant and Community in Medieval England, 1200–1500 (Basingstoke, 2003)

Schofield, R. S., 'The geographical distribution of wealth in England, 1334–1649', *Economic History Review*, 2nd ser., 18 (1965), 483–510

Scott, K. L., 'The illustrations of *Piers Plowman* in Bodleian Library MS. Douce 104', *Yearbook of Langland Studies*, 4 (1990), 1–86

Seabourne, G., 'Controlling commercial morality in late medieval London: the usury trials of 1421', *Journal of Legal History*, 19 (1998), 116–42

'Law, morals and money: royal regulation of the substance of subjects' sales and loans in England, 1272–1399', in A. Musson (ed.), *Expectations of the Law in the Middle Ages* (Woodbridge, 2001), pp. 117–34

Royal Regulation of Loans and Sales in Medieval England: 'Monkish Superstition and Civil Tyranny' (Woodbridge, 2003)

'Assize matters: regulation of the price of bread in medieval London', *Journal of Legal History*, 27 (2006), 29–52

Sear, J., 'Trade and commerce in Mildenhall, c.1350–c.1500' (MSt., University of Cambridge, 2007)

Searle, E., *Lordship and Community: Battle Abbey and its Banlieu 1066–1538* (Pontifical Institute of Mediaeval Studies, Studies and Texts, 26, Toronto, 1974)

Searle, G. R., *Morality and the Market in Victorian Britain* (Oxford, 1998)

Seaver, P., 'The Puritan work ethic revisited', *Journal of British Studies*, 19 (1980), 35–53

Wallington's World: A Puritan Artisan in Seventeenth-Century London (London, 1985)

Sharp, B., *In Contempt of All Authority: Rural Artisans and Riot in the West of England, 1586–1660* (London, 1980)

'Popular protest in seventeenth-century England', in B. Reay (ed.), *Popular Culture in Seventeenth-Century England* (London and Sydney, 1985), pp. 271–308

'The food riots of 1347 and the medieval moral economy', in A. Randall and A. Charlesworth (eds.), *Moral Economy and Popular Protest: Crowds, Conflict and Authority* (Basingstoke, 2000), pp. 33–54

Sheail, J., *The Regional Distribution of Wealth in England as Indicated in the 1524/5 Lay Subsidy Returns* (List and Index Society, 28, London, 1998)

Shepard, A. and Withington, P. (eds.), *Communities in Early Modern England: Networks, Place, Rhetoric* (Manchester, 2000)

Shoaf, R. A., *Dante, Chaucer, and the Currency of the Word: Money, Images, and Reference in Late Medieval Poetry* (Norman, Okla., 1983)

Silverman, A. H., 'Sex and money in Chaucer's Shipman's Tale', *Philological Quarterly*, 32 (1953), 329–36

Simons, J. (ed.), *From Medieval to Medievalism* (London, 1992)

Simpson, D., 'Literary criticism and the return to "history"', *Critical Inquiry*, 14 (1988), 721–47

Slack, P., 'Books of Orders: the making of English social policy, 1577–1631', *Transactions of the Royal Historical Society*, 5th ser., 30 (1980), 1–22

Slater, T. R. (ed.), *Towns in Decline AD100–1600* (Aldershot, 2000)

Slater, T. R. and Rosser, G. (eds.), *The Church in the Medieval Town* (Aldershot, 1998)

Smalley, B., *English Friars and Antiquity in the Early Fourteenth Century* (Oxford, 1960)

Smith, A., *An Inquiry into the Nature and Causes of the Wealth of Nations (1776)*, ed. R. H. Campbell and A. S. Skinner, 2 vols. (Oxford, 1976)

Smith, R. M., 'Kin and neighbours in a thirteenth-century Suffolk community', *Journal of Family History*, 4 (1979), 219–56

'Human resources', in G. Astill and A. Grant (eds.), *The Countryside of Medieval England* (Oxford, 1988), pp. 188–212

'A periodic market and its impact upon a manorial community: Botesdale, Suffolk, and the manor of Redgrave, 1280–1300', in Z. Razi and R. M. Smith (eds.), *Medieval Society and the Manor Court* (Oxford, 1996), pp. 450–81

Smith, R. M. and Razi, Z., 'The origins of the English manorial court rolls as a written record: a puzzle', in Z. Razi and R. M. Smith (eds.), *Medieval Society and the Manor Court* (Oxford, 1996), pp. 36–68

Smith, R. M. (ed.), *Land, Kinship and Life-Cycle* (Cambridge, 1984)

Sombart, W., *The Quintessence of Capitalism: A Study of the History and Psychology of the Modern Business Man* (trans. M. Epstein, New York, 1967).

Spargo, J. W., *Juridical Folklore in England: Illustrated by the Cucking-Stool* (Durham, NC, 1944)

Spencer, H. L., *English Preaching in the Late Middle Ages* (Oxford, 1993)

Spiegel, G. M., 'History, historicism, and the social logic of the text in the Middle Ages', *Speculum*, 65 (1990), 59–86

Sponsler, C. B., 'Society's image: estates literature in fifteenth-century England', *Semiotica*, 63 (1987), 229–38

Spufford, M., *The Great Reclothing of Rural England: Petty Chapmen and their Wares in the Seventeenth Century* (London, 1984)

Spufford, P., *Power and Profit: The Merchant in Medieval Europe* (London, 2002)

Stephenson, C., *Borough and Town: A Study of Urban Origins in England* (Cambridge, Mass., 1933)

Stevenson, J., *Popular Disturbances in England 1700–1870* (London, 1979)

'The moral economy of the English crowd: myth and reality', in A. Fletcher and J. Stevenson (eds.), *Order and Disorder in Early Modern England* (Cambridge, 1985), pp. 218–38

Stevenson, L. C., *Praise and Paradox: Merchants and Craftsmen in Elizabethan Popular Literature* (Cambridge, 1984)

Stillwell, G., 'Chaucer's "sad" merchant', *Review of English Studies*, 20 (1944), 1–18

'Chaucer's merchant: no debts?', *Journal of English and Germanic Philology*, 57 (1958), 192–6

Stokes, E., 'Clare priory', *Proceedings of the Suffolk Institute of Archaeology and Natural History*, 14 (1912), 108–9

Stokes, M., *Justice and Mercy in Piers Plowman: A Reading of the B Text Visio* (London and Canberra, 1984)

Stone, D., *Decision-Making in Medieval Agriculture* (Oxford, 2005)

Strohm, P., 'The social and literary scene in England', in P. Boitani and J. Mann (eds.), *The Cambridge Chaucer Companion* (Cambridge, 1986), pp. 1–18

Social Chaucer (London, 1989)

Sutherland, D. W., *Quo Warranto Proceedings in the Reign of Edward I, 1278–1294* (Oxford, 1963)

Swanson, H., 'The illusion of economic structure: craft guilds in late medieval English towns', *Past and Present*, 121 (1988), 29–48

Medieval Artisans: An Urban Class in Late Medieval England (Oxford, 1989)

Medieval British Towns (London, 1999)

Swanson, R. N. (ed.), *The Use and Abuse of Time in Christian History* (Studies in Church History, 37, Woodbridge, 2002)

Sweezy, P., 'A critique', in R. H. Hilton (ed.), *The Transition from Feudalism to Capitalism* (London, 1976), pp. 33–56

Tait, J., *The Medieval English Borough: Studies on its Origin and Constitutional History* (Manchester, 1936)

Tanner, N. P., *The Church in Late Medieval Norwich 1370–1532* (Toronto, 1984)

Tawney, R. H., *Religion and the Rise of Capitalism* (London, 1926)

Thirsk, J. (ed.), *The Agrarian History of England and Wales, Volume IV: 1500–1640* (Cambridge, 1967)

Thomas, K., *History and Literature* (Swansea, 1988)

'Cases of conscience in seventeenth-century England', in J. Morrill, P. Slack and D. Woolf (eds.), *Public Duty and Private Conscience in Seventeenth-Century England* (Oxford, 1993), pp. 29–56

Thompson, E. P., *The Making of the English Working Class* (New York, 1963)

'The moral economy of the English crowd in the eighteenth century', *Past and Present*, 50 (1971), 76–136

'The moral economy reviewed', in E. P. Thompson, *Customs in Common* (London, 1991), pp. 259–351

Thompson, J. J., 'Popular reading tastes in middle English religious and didactic literature', in J. Simons (ed.), *From Medieval to Medievalism* (London, 1992), pp. 82–100

Thomson, J. A. F., 'Wealth, poverty and mercantile ethics in late medieval London', in N. Bulst and J.-P. Genet (eds.), *La Ville, La Bourgeoisie et La Genèse de L'État Moderne (XIIe–XVIIIe siècles)* (Paris, 1988), pp. 265–78

Thomson, J. A. F. (ed.), *Towns and Townspeople in the Fifteenth Century* (Gloucester, 1988)

Thornton, G. A., 'A study in the history of Clare, Suffolk, with special reference to its development as a borough', *Transactions of the Royal Historical Society*, 4th ser., 11 (1928), 83–115

A History of Clare, Suffolk (Cambridge, 1928)

A Short History of Clare, Suffolk (Brentwood, 1963)

Threlfall-Holmes, M., *Monks and Markets: Durham Cathedral Priory 1460–1520* (Oxford, 2005)

Thrupp, S. L., *A Short History of the Worshipful Company of Bakers of London* (London, 1933)

The Merchant Class of Medieval London, 1300–1500 (Chicago, Ill., 1948)

'The gilds', in M. M. Postan, E. E. Rich and E. Miller (eds.), *Cambridge Economic History of Europe. Volume III: Economic Organization and Policies in the Middle Ages* (Cambridge, 1963), pp. 230–80

Thwaites, W., 'Dearth and the marketing of agricultural produce: Oxfordshire c.1750–1800', *Agricultural History Review*, 33 (1985), 119–31

'The assize of bread in 18th-century Oxford', *Oxoniensia*, 51 (1986), 171–81

'Oxford food riots: a community and its markets', in A. Randall and A. Charlesworth (eds.), *Markets, Market Culture and Popular Protest in Eighteenth-Century Britain and Ireland* (Liverpool, 1996), pp. 137–62

Todd, M., *Christian Humanism and the Puritan Social Order* (Cambridge, 1987)

Underhill, F. A., *For Her Good Estate: The Life of Elizabeth de Burgh* (Basingstoke, 1999)

Unwin, G., *The Gilds and Companies of London* (4th edn, London, 1963)

Varty, K., 'Reynard the Fox and the Smithfield Decretals', *Journal of the Warburg and Courtauld Institutes*, 36 (1963), 347–54

    Reynard the Fox: A Study of the Fox in Medieval English Art (Leicester, 1967)

Veale, E. M., *The English Fur Trade in the Later Middle Ages* (Oxford, 1966)

Victoria County History: Chester (London, 1987)

Victoria County History: Suffolk, 2 vols. (London, 1911)

Waddell, B., 'Economic immorality and social reformation in English popular preaching, 1585–1625', *Cultural and Social History*, 5 (2008), 165–82

Walter, J., 'Grain riots and popular attitudes to the law: Maldon and the crisis of 1629', in J. Brewer and J. Styles (eds.), *An Ungovernable People: The English and their Law in the Seventeenth and Eighteenth Centuries* (London, 1980), pp. 47–84

    'The social economy of dearth in early modern England', in J. Walter and R. Schofield (eds.), *Famine, Disease and the Social Order in Early Modern England* (Cambridge, 1989), pp. 75–128

Walter, J. and Schofield, R. (eds.), *Famine, Disease and the Social Order in Early Modern England* (Cambridge, 1989)

Walter, J. and Wrightson, K., 'Dearth and the social order in early modern England', *Past and Present*, 71 (1976), 22–42

Wasserman, J. N. and Blanch, R. J. (eds.), *Chaucer in the Eighties* (New York, 1986)

Webb, S. and Webb, B., 'The assize of bread', *Economic Journal*, 14 (1904), 196–218

Weber, M., *The Protestant Ethic and the Spirit of Capitalism* (trans. T. Parsons, intro. R. H. Tawney, London, 1930)

Welch, E., *Shopping in the Renaissance: Consumer Cultures in Italy, 1400–1600* (New Haven, Conn., and London, 2005)

Wells, R., *Wretched Faces: Famine in Wartime England 1793–1801* (Gloucester, 1988)

Wenzel, S., *Preachers, Poets, and the Early English Lyric* (Princeton, NJ, 1986)

    Latin Sermon Collections from Later Medieval England: Orthodox Preaching in the Age of Wyclif (Cambridge, 2005)

White, H., *The Content of the Form: Narrative Discourse and Historical Representation* (Baltimore, Md., 1987)

Wilk, R. R., *Economies and Cultures: Foundations of Economic Anthropology* (Boulder, Colo., 1996)

Wilkinson, L. J., *Women in Thirteenth-Century Lincolnshire* (Woodbridge, 2007)

Willan, T. S., *The Inland Trade: Studies in English Internal Trade in the Sixteenth and Seventeenth Centuries* (Manchester, 1976)

Willard, J. F., 'Inland transportation in England during the fourteenth century', *Speculum*, 1 (1926), 361–74

Willard, J. F. and Morris, W. A. (eds.), *The English Government at Work, 1327–1336, Volume 1: Central and Prerogative Administration* (Cambridge, Mass., 1940)

Willcox, P., *The Bakers' Company of Coventry* (Coventry and Warwickshire Historical Association Pamphlet, no. 18, Coventry, 1992)

Williams, D. (ed.), *England in the Fifteenth Century: Proceedings of the 1986 Harlaxton Symposium* (Woodbridge, 1987)

Williams, D. E., 'Morals, markets and the English crowd in 1766', *Past and Present*, 104 (1984), 56–73

Williams, N., 'Sessions of the Clerk of the Market of the Household in Middlesex', *Transactions of the London and Middlesex Archaeological Society*, 19 (1958), 76–89

Williamson, J., 'Dispute settlement in the manorial court: early fourteenth-century Lakenheath', *Reading Medieval Studies*, 11 (1985), 133–41

Winchester, A. J. L., *Landscape and Society in Medieval Cumbria* (Edinburgh, 1987)

Withington, R., 'Braggart, devil, and vice', *Speculum*, 11 (1936), 124–9

Wodderspoon, J., *Memorials of the Ancient Town of Ipswich* (Ipswich, 1850)

Wolfthal, D., 'The wandering Jew: some medieval and Renaissance depictions', in W. W. Clark, C. Eisler, W. S. Heckscher and B. G. Lane (eds.), *Tribute to Lotte Brand Philip: Art Historian and Detective* (New York, 1985), pp. 217–27

Wood, D., '"Lesyng of tyme": perceptions of idleness and usury in late medieval England', in R. N. Swanson (ed.), *The Use and Abuse of Time in Christian History* (Studies in Church History, 37, Woodbridge, 2002), pp. 107–16
  Medieval Economic Thought (Cambridge, 2002)

Wood, D. (ed.), *Medieval Money Matters* (Oxford, 2004)

Wood, H., *Medieval Tamworth* (Tamworth, 1972)

Woodbridge, L., 'The peddler and the pawn: Why did Tudor England consider peddlers to be rogues?', in C. Dionne and S. Mentz (eds.), *Rogues and Early Modern English Culture* (Ann Arbor, Mich., 2004), pp. 143–70

Woods, W. F., 'A professional thyng: the wife as merchant's apprentice in the *Shipman's Tale*', *Chaucer Review*, 24 (1989), 139–49

Woolf, R., 'Chaucer as a satirist in the General Prologue to the Canterbury Tales', *Critical Quarterly*, 1 (1959), 150–7

Wrightson, K., 'Alehouses, order and reformation in rural England, 1590–1660', in E. Yeo and S. Yeo (eds.), *Popular Culture and Class Conflict, 1590–1914: Explorations in the History of Labour and Leisure* (Brighton, 1981), pp. 1–27
  English Society 1580–1680 (London, 1982)
  Earthly Necessities: Economic Lives in Early Modern Britain, 1470–1750 (London, 2002)

Wyrick, D. B., 'Withinne that develes temple: an examination of Skelton's *The Tunnyng of Elynour Rummyng*', *Journal of Medieval and Renaissance Studies*, 10 (1980), 239–54

Yates, M., *Town and Countryside in Western Berkshire, c.1327–c.1600* (Woodbridge, 2007)

Yeager, R. F., 'Gower's French audience: the *Mirour de l'Omme*', *Chaucer Review*, 41 (2006), 111–37

Yeo, E. and Yeo, S. (eds.), *Popular Culture and Class Conflict, 1590–1914: Explorations in the History of Labour and Leisure* (Brighton, 1981)

Yunck, J. A., 'Medieval French money satire', *Modern Language Quarterly*, 21 (1960), 73–82

The Lineage of Lady Meed (Notre Dame, Ind., 1963)

'Satire', in J. A. Alford (ed.), *A Companion to Piers Plowman* (Berkeley, Calif., 1988), pp. 135–54

Zupko, R. E., *British Weights and Measures: A History from Antiquity to the Seventeenth Century* (Madison, Wisc., 1977)

Index

Aberdeen, 229
Acle (Norf.), 151
advertising, 73, 74, 186, 246, 250
Aelfric, Abbot of Eynsham, 91, 96
Aers, David, 38, 135
Aethelstan, King of England, 178, 197
affeerers, 263, 293, 296, 311, 388, 401, 405
afterlife, 40, 105, 107, 127, *see also* Last Judgement
Alain de Lille, 63
Albertus Magnus, 57
ale, 8, 15, 71, 105, 115, 168, 231, 241–8, 295, 303–5, 323, 324, 334, 345, 346, 395, 406, 422, 423, *see also* alewives, ale-sellers, assize of ale, brewers
alehouses, 7, 15, 16, 18, 69, 112–13, 247, 323, 324, 325, 335, 337, 396, 401, 402, 422, 431–3, 435
ale-sellers, 185, 244, 263, 268, 396, *see also* alewives, tapsters
aletasters, 167, 244–6, 251, 295, 297, 321
alewives, 16, 38, 43, 106–12, 114, 125, 130, 243, 247, 422
Alexander of Hales, 59, 60
Alfred, King of Wessex, 196
alien traders, 142, 395
Alley, Hugh, 420
Alverthorpe (Yorks.), 205
Anglo-Saxon laws, 177–8
Aquinas, Thomas, 57, 58–9, 64, 78, 81, 418
Argentein, William, 279, 292
Aristotle, 57, 92
assaults, 150, 166, 186, 329, 370, 371, 395
assize, 231–3, 251–3, 297, 321–2, 345, 374, 394, 397, 423, 432, 456
of ale, 107, 146, 241–8, 263, 297–303, 321, 337, 392–4, 398, 426

of bread, 146, 149, 233–41, 252, 263, 297–303, 312, 391–2, 424–6, 442
of cloth, 218
of measures, 190
of wine, 248, 253
attachments, 208, 209, 360–1, 365
Augustine of Hippo, 57
auncel, 79, 195–6, 334, 390
avarice, 2, 23, 28, 49–55, 75, 83, 92, 119, 127, 415, 437, 438
Ayenbite of Inwyt, 42, 344

Babir, John, 308, 371
Bacon, Francis, 414
badgers, 417, 429, 431, 434, 435, 438, 445, *see also* cornmongers
Bailey, Mark, 275, 292, 293, 311, 336, 340, 375, 381
bailiffs, 159, 162, 166, 186, 202, 211, 269, 292, 293, 294, 297, 323, 358, 362, 370, 386, 388, 401, 426
Baker Litil, John, 312, 334
Baker, William, 312, 314, 318
bakers, 1, 7, 51, 80, 96, 103, 104, 105, 109, 113, 117, 125, 130, 148, 149, 157, 179, 206, 221, 233–41, 251, 252, 255, 257, 265, 267, 268, 282, 300, 301, 303, 305, 311–14, 374, 391–2, 397, 421–2, 423, 428, 429, 437
Bakewell (Derb.), 161
Ballone, John, 291, 371
Barbor, John, 291, 311, 335
bargaining, 61, 69–72, 156, 178, 198–202, 205, 230, 346, 390, 418, 419, *see also* lyther bargaining, lot and scot
Baxter, Richard, 414, 419
beer, 15, 264, 394–5, 422, 423, 433
Bennett, Judith, 4, 15, 38, 113, 298, 311, 317
Berwick, 156, 157, 203, 204, 227, 243, 257

18083624R00294

Printed in Great Britain
by Amazon